A Bibliographical Guide to Midwestern Literature

A BIBLIOGRAPHICAL
GUIDE TO MIDWESTERN
LITERATURE

Gerald Nemanic, General Editor

UNIVERSITY OF IOWA PRESS   IOWA CITY

Library of Congress Cataloging in Publication Data
Main entry under title:

A Bibliographical guide to midwestern literature.

1. American literature—Middle West—Bibliography.
2. Middle West—Bibliography. I. Nemanic, Gerald,
1941–   .
Z1251.W5B52 [PS273]   016.81'08'0977   81–4087
ISBN 0–87745–079–X   AACR2

University of Iowa Press, Iowa City 52242

For David Anderson,
who helped invent the Midwest

CONTENTS

INTRODUCTION

THIS BOOK IS an attempt to provide, in a single volume, a reference guide to the study of midwestern literature and culture. In these pages will be found nine topical bibliographies on the region's culture, basic bibliographical data on 120 midwestern authors, and appendices covering additional authors and works of fiction. The volume includes materials published to 1976.

While most of this compilation is devoted to literature, we also recognize that the literary work is at least partly the result of complex cultural forces which help determine the artist's temperament, style, tone, and ostensible subject. Both for that reason, and because no bibliographical guide to midwestern culture has yet been produced, we have supplied, in Part One, fundamental bibliographies on nine significant topics: Literature and Language; History and Society; Folklore; Personal Narratives; Architecture and Graphics; Chicago; Black Literature; Indians; and Periodical Literature.

The nature of so broadly based a guidebook has dictated the presentation of checklists which are selective rather than exhaustive. Of the uncounted thousands of books, pamphlets, and articles available to the student of midwestern culture, only a fraction could be listed here. To make feasible a one-volume work, it was necessary for the editor and contributors to agree upon a number of ground rules, first to enable selection of the topics and authors to be included, and second as instruction for the nearly one hundred scholars who compiled author bibliographies. Herewith is provided a rationale for the limitations we have imposed:

1. For the purpose of the *Guide*, the "Midwest" is defined geographically to include all of eight states (Illinois, Indiana, Iowa, Michigan, Minnesota, Missouri, Ohio, and Wisconsin) and those parts of four others (Kansas, Nebraska, North Dakota, and South Dakota) which lie east of the 100th meridian of longitude. That line roughly demarcates the long grass prairies from the short grass plains, the farm culture from the grazing culture, and the Midwest from the West. It might be argued that certain of the areas we have included, such as the "Egypt" triangle of southern Illinois, or the Missouri Ozarks, are more southern than midwestern, or that northern Minnesota, Wisconsin, and Michigan are part of the vast, forested "Northland" which covers much of eastern Canada and represents a distinct cultural unit divorced from the mid-

western belt of cities and farms. These may be defensible positions, but we felt that to err on the side of inclusiveness would be preferable to the risk of creating important lacunae in the checklists.

2. In Part Two (author bibliographies) we have defined "midwestern author" not by accident of birth, nor even place of residence. Our criteria for inclusion focus on the nature of the author's work. First, it must be literary (thus are excluded such productive authors as historian Frederick Jackson Turner, economist Thorstein Veblen, editor William Marion Reedy, and other important philosophers, social scientists, biographers, etc., although even here we have managed to include some of these writers in Appendix A.) Second, an author's literary work should, in some demonstrable way, reflect the cultural life of the region (thus are excluded writers of exotic romance like Charles Major or Lew Wallace, and many another capable craftsman who has shown minimal interest in exploring the textures of regional thought or place, e.g., John Gardner, Kurt Vonnegut, Eunice Tietjens, Emerson Hough, and Archibald MacLeish). It would be foolish, of course, to assume that we have found any precise yardstick for making these distinctions. Just where does the "regional" quality of a work lie—in its physical setting, in the cast of mind of its characters, in its style or tone? In the face of this complexity, we have opted for simple, if rather prosaic guidance: midwestern provenance as directly indicated by the author. Considered reflection on the larger question must await another volume of its own. Third, important consideration has been given to the quality of the author's work. Of the thousands of midwestern authors who qualify in the first two instances, less than 150 could be singled out for inclusion in the author bibliographies, and another 100 assigned to an appendix. The editor takes full responsibility for this selection process and resigns himself to the inevitable criticisms which, perhaps with justice, will issue from it.

It will be noted that the secondary checklists in Part Two vary in length, from 100 items for major figures down to fifteen or less for many lesser known and contemporary figures. The editor is also responsible for these assigned quotas and would like to indicate that they constitute not solely a qualitative judgment on the authors, but often involve a recognition of the vastly different amounts of secondary material available in the cases of authors established or obscure, long dead, or still in the early stages of promising careers. We have not shied away from including mature contemporary writers like William Gass or James Wright. The importance of such writers seems indisputable. Many younger contemporaries have been assigned to Appendix A, as have a number of older writers of merit who could not be fitted into the limited space provided for the more extensive bibliographies.

3. In Part One the annotated topical bibliographies have been limited, for the most part, to book-length studies, although we have included pamphlets and articles of unusual value. Conversely, longer studies which are dated or ephemeral will not be found.

4. Technical subjects and studies have largely been excluded. One might wish for guidance to midwestern flora and fauna, for books on business, mining, railroading, lumbering, farming, steel making, governance, physical anthropology, and so forth. To include all these would have made a one-volume guide impossible. Indeed, where such subjects have been handled with an eye to cultural history (as in Stewart Holbrook's history of American lumbering, *Old Holy Mackinaw*, or Paul de Kruif's narrative of the development of iron mining in northern Minnesota, *Seven Iron Men*) the titles have been included. By the same token, books of natural history, when written with grace and style, have found a place (e.g., Audubon's narratives, or John Muir's *Story of My Boyhood and Youth*).

5. Omitted finally are books aimed primarily at a juvenile audience.

A NOTE ON THE CONTRIBUTORS

During 1974 the editor was able to bring together a staff of nearly 100 contributors without whom this volume would have been impossible. Most of these scholars had previously published significant work on the authors they agreed to cover. In all cases they have responded promptly with thorough and exacting contributions so that whatever value accrues to this volume can be traced to their generosity and effort. I am deeply in their debt. In a few instances bibliographers handling major authors were allowed to organize the materials in a manner they saw fit. The great majority of entries follow a specific format: short bibliographical essay; checklist of major primary works; selective checklist of secondary sources ranging from fifteen to 100 items depending on the category limits assigned by the editor. (Note that oft-used biographical and composite book sources have been abbreviated and placed at the beginning of the Short References list.)

SHORT REFERENCES
AND ABBREVIATIONS

Blanck — Blanck, Jacob, comp. *Bibliography of American Literature*. New Haven, 1955– .

Burke — Burke, William J. and Will D. Howe. *American Authors and Books: 1640 to the Present Day*. 3d rev. ed. New York, 1972.

CA — *Contemporary Authors: The International Bio-Bibliographical Guide to Current Authors and Their Works*. Detroit, 1962– .

CAA — Millett, Fred B. *Contemporary American Authors: A Critical Survey and 219 Bio-Bibliographies*. New York, 1940.

CB — *Current Biography Yearbook*. New York, 1940– .

CHAL — Trent, William P., et al., eds. *Cambridge History of American Literature*. New York, 1917–21.

DAB — Johnson, Allen and Dumas Malone, eds. *Dictionary of American Biography*. New York, 1928–37. Three supplements, 1944–47.

Duyckinck — Duyckinck, Evert A. and George L., eds. *Cyclopaedia of American Literature*. Rev. ed. Philadelphia, 1875.

Herzberg — Herzberg, Max J., et al. *The Reader's Encyclopedia of American Literature*. New York, 1962. [Revisions in later printings.]

LHUS — Spiller, Robert E., et al., eds. *Literary History of the United States*. 3d rev. ed. New York, 1963.

BDAL — Kunitz, Stanley and Howard Haycraft, eds. *American Authors, 1600–1900: A Biographical Dictionary of American Literature*. New York, 1938.

OCAL — Hart, James D., ed. *Oxford Companion to American Literature*. 4th ed. New York, 1965.

TCA (Supp) — Kunitz, Stanley, ed. *Twentieth Century Authors*. New York, 1942. First Supplement. New York, 1955.

Warfel — Warfel, Harry R. *American Novelists of Today*. New York, 1951.

AA — Akron Alumnus

AAA — Annals of American Academy of Political and Social Science

ABC — American Book Collector

AdS — Advertising and Selling

AH — American Heritage

AHQ — Arkansas Historical Quarterly

AHR — American Historical Review

AI — American Image
AL — American Literature
ALet — Aspetti Letterari
AmCrit — American Criticism
AmJSoc — American Journal of Sociology
ALibB — American Libraries Bulletin of the American Library Association
AmLitR — American Literary Realism
AmM — American Magazine
AmMerc — American Mercury
AmN&Q — American Notes and Queries
AmPref — American Prefaces
AmS — American Speech
AnIowa — Annals of Iowa
AQ — American Quarterly
AR — Antioch Review
ArQ — Arizona Quarterly
ArtsS — Arts in Society
AS — American Speech
ASch — American Scholar
ASR — American-Scandinavian Review
Atl — Atlantic Monthly

BaratR — Barat Review
BayB — Baylor Bulletin
BB — Bulletin of Bibliography
BBAAS — Bulletin of the British Association for American Studies
BBr — Books at Brown
BCMVASA — Bulletin of the Central Mississippi Valley American Studies
     Association
BIowa — Books at Iowa
BlS — Black Scholar
BMMLA — Bulletin of the Midwest Modern Language Association
BNM — Book News Monthly
BNYPL — Bulletin of New York Public Libraries
BSA — Bibliographical Society of America
BSM — Ball State Monograph
BSUF — Ball State University Forum
BulMoHistSoc — Bulletin of the Missouri Historical Society
BuR — Bucknell Review
BW — Black World

CAN — Contemporary American Novelist
CanF — Canadian Forum
CanRevAmerStud — Canadian Review of American Studies

CarletonMisc — Carleton Miscellany
CathW — Catholic World
CE — College English
CEA — CEA Critic
ChiL — Chicago Land
ChiR — Chicago Review
ChriCent — Christian Century
Chron — Chronicle
CIM — Californian Illustrated Magazine
CL — Comparative Literature
CLAJ — College Language Association Journal
CLC — Columbia Library Columns
CLQ — Colby Library Quarterly
CM — Century Magazine
CMHS — Collections of the Minnesota Historical Society
CO — Current Opinion
ColL — College Literature
CollsMinnHistSoc — Collections of the Minnesota Historical Society
Colo — Colophon
ColM — Colorado Magazine
ColQ — Colorado Quarterly
ConcP — Concerning Poetry
ConL — Contemporary Literature (formerly *Wisconsin Studies in Contemporary Literature*)
CosmopMag — Cosmopolitan Magazine
CR — Centennial Review
CRAS — Canadian Review of American Studies
Crit — Critique
CritQ — Critical Quarterly
CSE — Carnegie Studies in English
CUF — Columbia University Forum
CurLit — Current Literature

DAI — Dissertation Abstracts (International)
DartColLibBul — Dartmouth College Library Bulletin
DD — Double Dealer
DilR — Diliman Review
DLR — Delaware Literary Review
DM — Dublin Magazine
DMWR — Denver Westerners Monthly Roundup
DNS — Die Neuren Sprachen
DR — Dalhousie Review

EAM — Early American Literature

EJ — English Journal
ELH — English Literary History
ELT — English Literature in Transition
ES — English Studies
ESQ — Emerson Society Quarterly
Esq — Esquire
EST — English Studies Today
EUQ — Emery University Quarterly
EvR — Evergreen Review
Expl — Explicator

FarP — Far Point
FHA — Fitzgerald-Hemingway Annual
FLe — Fiera Letteraria
FM — Frontier and Midland
FQ — Four Quarters

GaR — Georgia Review
GLR — Great Lakes Review
GoodH — Good Housekeeping

HAB — Humanities Association Bulletin
Harper — Harper's
HarvM — Harvard Month
HB — Historical Bulletin
HC — Hollins Critic
HK — Heritage of Kansas
HN — Hemingway Notes
HudR — Hudson Review
Hum — Humanities
HUSSR — (in McNally entry in Fitzgerald)

IEB — Illinois English Bulletin
IEJ — Indiana English Journal
IEY — Iowa English Yearbook
IHB — Indiana History Bulletin
IJH — Iowa Journal of History and Politics
IL — International Literature (USSR)
IM — Interview Magazine
IMH — Indiana Magazine of History
IQ — Illinois Quarterly
IR — Iowa Review
IS — Inland Seas
ISHSJ — Illinois State Historical Society Journal
ISUJ — Illinois State University Journal
IUB — Indiana University Bookman

JA — Jahrbuch für Amerikastudien
JAAC — Journal of Aesthetics and Art Criticism
JAF — Journal of American Folklore
JAH — Journal of American History
JAmS — Journal of American Studies
JAPA — Journal of the American Psychoanalytic Association
JCMVASA — Journal of the Central Mississippi Valley American Studies
    Association
JEGP — Journal of English and German Philology
JISHS — Journal of the Illinois State Historical Society
JML — Journal of Modern Literature
JNH — Journal of Negro History
JPC — Journal of Popular Culture
JQ — Journalism Quarterly

KFLQ — Kentucky Foreign Language Quarterly
KFR — Kentucky Folklore Record
KHQ — Kansas Historical Quarterly
KHSR — Kentucky Historical Society Register
KM — Kansas Magazine
KQ — Kansas Quarterly
KR — Kenyon Review
KS — Kirjallisyydentutkijain Seuran
KSHSC — Kansas State Historical Society Collections

LA — Living Age
LadiesHJ — Ladies' Home Journal
LCUP — Library Chronicle, University of Pennsylvania
LD — Literary Digest
LH — Lincoln Herald
LHR — Lock Haven Review
LittleR — Little Review
LJ — Library Journal
LM — London Magazine
LQ — Latin Quarterly
LR — Literary Review
LUB — Lincoln University Bulletin

M-A — Mid-America
MAQR — Michigan Alumnus Quarterly Review
MarkR — Markham Review
MASJ — Midcontinent American Studies Journal
MassR — Massachusetts Review
MB — More Books
MD — Modern Drama

ME — Museum Echoes
MenJ — Menorah Journal
MF — Midwest Folklore
MFS — Modern Fiction Studies
MH — Minnesota History
MHC — Michigan History Collections
MHM — Michigan History Magazine
MHR — Missouri Historical Review
MinnLR — Minneapolis Labor Review
MinnR — Minneapolis Review
MJ — Midwest Journal
MD — Modern Drama
MLN — Modern Language Notes
MLQ — Modern Language Quarterly
MLR — Modern Language Review
MM — Midland Monthly
MP — Modern Philology
MPS — Modern Poetry Studies
MQ — Midwest Quarterly
MissQ — Mississippi Quarterly
ModQ — Modern Quarterly
MQR — Michigan Quarterly Review
MinnR — Minnesota Review
MR — Monthly Review
MS — Midland Schools
MTJ — Mark Twain Journal
MVHR — Mississippi Valley Historical Review

NA — Nation and Athenaeum
NALF — Negro American Literature Forum
NAR — North American Review
NASR — Norwegian American Studies and Records
NCF — Nineteenth Century Fiction
NCL — Notes on Contemporary Literature
ND — Negro Digest
NDH — North Dakota History
NDQ — North Dakota Quarterly
NEM — New England Magazine
NEQ — New England Quarterly
NewL — New Leader
NH — Nebraska History
NHB — Negro History Bulletin
NL — New Letters
NLB — Newberry Library Bulletin

NLit — Nouvelles Littéraires
NM — New Masses
NMQ — New Mexico Quarterly
NOQ — Northwest Ohio Quarterly
NOR — New Orleans Review
N&Q — Notes & Queries
NWR — Northwest Review
NR — New Republic
NS — New Statesman
NSN — New Statesman and Nation
N&T — Now & Then
NUTQ — Northwestern University Tri-Quarterly
NWW — New World Writing
NY — New Yorker
NYCTR — New York Critic's Theatre Review
NYFQ — New York Folklore Quarterly
NYHSQ — New York Historical Society Quarterly
NYHTBR — New York Herald Tribune Book Review
NYRB — New York Review of Books
NYTBR — New York Times Book Review
NYTMS — New York Times Magazine Section

OAHSP — Ohio Archaeological and Historical Society Publications
OH — Ohio History
OhioHQ — Ohio Historical Quarterly
OI — Outlook and Independent
OM — Overland Monthly
ON — Old Northwest
OR — Ohio Review
OUR — Ohio University Review
OxR — Oxford Review

PADS — Publications of the American Dialect Society
PAGQ — Phi Alpha Gamma Quarterly
ParisR — Paris Review
PBSA — Papers of the Bibliographical Society of America
PCP — Pacific Coast Philology
PELL — Papers on English Language and Literature
PL — Poet Lore
PLL — Papers on Language and Literature
PM — Putnam's Magazine
PMASAL — Papers of the Michigan Academy of Science, Arts and Letters
PMLA — Publications of the Modern Language Association of America

PoetryR — Poetry Review
P&P — Poetry and the Play
PQ — Philological Quarterly
PR — Partisan Review
PrS — Prairie Schooner
PsyR — Psychoanalytic Review
PULC — Princeton University Library Chronicle
PUSA — Perspectives USA
PW — Publishers Weekly

QJS — Quarterly Journal of Speech
QQ — Queen's Quarterly
QR — Quarterly Review

RAA — Revue Anglo-Américaine
RALS — Resources for American Literary Study
RD — Reader's Digest
REL — Review of English Literature
RevN — La Revue Nouvelle
RJ — Reformed Journal
RLC — Revue de Littérature Comparée
RSWSU — Research Studies of Washington State University
RUS — Rice University Studies
RW — Readers and Writers

SA — Studi Americani
SAB — South Atlantic Bulletin
SAF — Studies in American Fiction
SAH — Studies in American Humor
SAQ — South Atlantic Quarterly
SatR — Saturday Review
SB — Studies in Bibliography
SBL — Studies in Black Literature
SCB — South Central Bulletin
SDHC — South Dakota Historical Collections
SDR — South Dakota Review
SE — Study of English (Japan)
SEL — Studies in English Literature
SEPost — Saturday Evening Post
SFQ — Southern Folklore Quarterly
SHR — Southern Humanities Review
SLJ — Southern Literary Journal
SLN — Sinclair Lewis Newsletter
SM — Scribner's Monthly
SNL — Satire Newsletter

SNNTS — Studies in the Novel (Denton, Texas)
SouR — Southern Review
Sp — Spectator
SP — Studies in Philology
SpM — Speech Monograph
SQ — Southern Quarterly
SR — Sewanee Review
SRom — Studies in Romanticism
SS — Smart Set
SSF — Studies in Short Fiction
SSJ — Southern Speech Journal
SSMLN — Society for the Study of Midwestern Literature Newsletter
SSN — Scandinavian Studies and Notes
StLouisR — St. Louis Review
SUS — Susquehanna University Studies
SW — Southern Workman
SwB — Southwestern Bulletin
SwR — Southwest Review

TA — Theatre Arts
T&C — Travel & Camera
TCL — Twentieth Century Literature
TCW — Twentieth Century Verse
TexSE — Texas Studies in English
TH — Today's Health
ThR — Theatre Research
TISHS — Transactions of the Illinois State Historical Society
TLS — [London] Times Literary Supplement
TPJ — Tennessee Poetry Journal
TQ — Texas Quarterly
TR — Texas Review
TSE — Tulane Studies in English
TSL — Tennessee Studies in Literature
TSLL — Texas Studies in Literature and Language
TT — Time and Tide
TUSAS — Twayne United States Authors Series
TWASAL — Transactions of the Wisconsin Academy of Sciences, Arts and
    Letters

UCQ — University College Quarterly
UCR — University of Chicago Record
UCSLL — University of Colorado Studies in Literature and Language
UKCR — University of Kansas City Review
UKR — University of Kansas Review

UPLL — Utah Papers in Language and Literature
UR — University Review
UTSE — University of Texas Studies in English
UWR — University of Windsor Review

VF — Vanity Fair
VQR — Virginia Quarterly Review

WA — Wisconsin Archaeologist
WAL — Western American Literature
WD — Writer's Digest
WF — Western Folklore
WHR — Western Humanities Review
WLB — Wilson Library Bulletin
WMH — Wisconsin Magazine of History
WR — Western Review
WS — Western Speech
WSCL — Wisconsin Studies in Contemporary Literature
WSL — Wisconsin Studies in Literature
WT — World Today
WW — World's Work

XUS — Xavier University Studies

YLM — Yale Literary Magazine
YR — Yale Review

PART 1

SUBJECT BIBLIOGRAPHIES

LITERATURE AND LANGUAGE

A COMPREHENSIVE HISTORY of midwestern literature has not yet been attempted. There exist thorough and scholarly studies of literature in the periods of exploration and settlement, *viz.* Dorothy Dondore, *The Prairie and the Making of Middle America* (1926), and Ralph Rusk, *The Literature of the Middle Western Frontier* (1925). A few earlier works, still valuable, examine the beginnings and early development of literature in areas at least partially in the Midwest. Most notable of these are: Alexander De Menil, *The Literature of the Louisiana Territory* (1904); William H. Venable, *Beginnings of Literary Culture in the Ohio Valley* (1891); and Mary M. Atkeson, *A Study of the Local Literature of the Upper Ohio Valley* (1921).

At least one genre study has been completed: *The Middle Western Farm Novel in the Twentieth Century* (1965) by Roy W. Meyer. Books dealing with the culture of the Midwest often contain a good deal of information about literature. Two particularly valuable studies in this vein are Lewis E. Atherton, *Main Street on the Middle Border* (1954), and Graham Hutton, *Midwest at Noon* (1946). A number of uncollected articles by John T. Flanagan provide research into the midwestern farm novel and historical novel and into the chronically overlooked area of European influence on midwestern literature.

Much of the information we have about literary accomplishment in the Midwest comes from studies of various trends and movements in American literature, and from histories of American literature. Midwestern writers, and groups of writers, have often played prominent roles in shaping a distinctive American literary heritage. Brief mention may be made here of a few exceptional titles: Van Wyck Brooks, *The Confident Years: 1885–1915* (1952); Oscar Cargill, *Intellectual America* (1941); Alexander Cowie, *The Rise of the American Novel* (1948); Maxwell Geismar, *The Last of the Provincials: The American Novel, 1915–1925* (1947); Vernon L. Parrington, *Main Currents in American Thought: An Interpretation of American Literature from the Beginnings to 1920* (1927–30); Henry Nash Smith, *The Virgin Land* (1950); Charles C. Walcutt, *American Literary Naturalism: A Divided Stream* (1956). A more complete and annotated list appears below.

Every midwestern state has had its chroniclers of native literature. Most of these efforts have been in the nature of biographical dictionaries, or checklists of a state's authors and titles. Articles within state histories, the WPA guides, and occasional critical essays in state and regional periodicals can be valuable resources. Anthologies of state literatures are numerous. The main problem with so many of the above mentioned sources is that they are frequently uncritical, popular, and chauvinistic. And yet among the volumes on state literatures one finds some valuable nuggets, *e.g.,* Meredith Nicholson, *The Hoosiers* (1900); Arthur W. Shumaker, *A History of Indiana Literature* (1962); Clarence Andrews, *A Literary History of Iowa* (1972); James Gray, *Pine, Stream and Prairie: Wisconsin and Minnesota in Profile* (1945). A number of uncollected articles by Flanagan (on Minnesota literature) and by John T. Frederick (on Iowa fiction) are exceptionally good.

1.   MIDWEST: GENERAL

Information on literary history is sometimes contained within general histories of the states or region. For guidance to the appropriate sections of these volumes, see "History and Society."

Atherton, Lewis E. *Main Street on the Middle Border.* Bloomington: Indiana U., 1954.
   Though not primarily a literary history, it provides a gold mine of information on popular culture in the Midwest from frontier times to the present. Chapter four examines midwestern attitudes toward the arts. Although there is no systematic appraisal of midwestern literature, allusions to literary works occur throughout.
Flanagan, John T. "A Bibliography of Middle Western Farm Novels." *MH*, 23 (1942), 156–58.
_____. "European Elements in Mid-Western Literature." *KFLQ*, 2 (1955), 59–66.
_____. "Literary Protest in the Midwest." *SwR*, 34 (1948), 148–57.
_____. "The Middle Western Farm Novel." *MH*, 23 (1942), 113–25.
_____. "The Middle Western Historical Novel." *JISHS*, 37 (1944), 7–47.
_____. "Middlewestern Regional Literature." In *Research Opportunities in American Cultural History.* Ed. by John F. McDermott. Lexington: U. Kentucky, 1961. Pp. 124–39.
_____. "Some Projects in Midwest Cultural History." *IMH*, 47 (1951), 241–50.
Hutton, Graham. *Midwest at Noon.* Chicago: U. Chicago, 1946.
   Englishman's perceptive look at Midwest culture gained from many years residence in the region; contains numerous references to literature.
Inglehart, Babette, and Anthony Mangione. *The Image of Pluralism in American Literature: An Annotated Bibliography on the American Experience of European Ethnic Groups.* New York: Institute of Pluralism and Group Identity, 1974.
Knopfle, John. "Crossing the Midwest." *ALibB*, 3 (1972), 595–610.
   Gauges the current state of the arts, especially literature, in the region; includes bibliography. This essay was reprinted in the American Library Association's collection of *Regional Perspectives* (1973), edited by John G. Burke.
Meyer, Roy W. *The Middle Western Farm Novel in the Twentieth Century.* Lincoln: U. Nebraska, 1965.
   Solid genre study. Includes annotated lists of novels and other bibliography.
Reigelman, Milton M. *The Midland: A Venture in Literary Regionalism.* Iowa City: U. Iowa, 1975.
   History of the pioneering regional periodical published by John T. Frederick between 1915 and 1933.
Waitley, Douglas. *Portrait of the Midwest.* New York: Abelard, 1963. An informal history of the Midwest "from the ice age to the industrial era"; includes several chapters on midwestern literature.
Ziegler, Joseph. *Regional Theatre: The Revolutionary Stage.* Minneapolis: U. Minnesota, 1973.

Anthologies

Becker, May L., ed. *Golden Tales of the Prairie States.* New York: Dodd, Mead, 1932.
   Prairie life in the late nineteenth century; stories by Tarkington, Anderson, Quick, Garland, and others.

Brockway, Wallace and B. K. Winer, eds. *Homespun America*. New York: Simon & Schuster, 1958.

A good part of this anthology is devoted to Midwest writers (about 20 of them represented, ranging from Cartwright to Sandburg).

Conroy, Jack, ed. *Midland Humor: A Harvest of Fun and Folklore*. New York: Wyn, 1947.

Humorous prose and poetry since the Civil War; includes biographical sketches.

Engle, Paul et al., eds. *Midland: 25 Years of Fiction and Poetry Selected from the Writing Workshops of the State University of Iowa*. New York: Random, 1961.

More than 80 pieces by students and teachers.

Finch, Robert, ed. *Plays of the American West*. New York: Greenberg, 1947. Fifteen plays.

Flanagan, John T., ed. *America is West: An Anthology of Middlewestern Life and Literature*. Minneapolis: U. Minnesota, 1945.

The most extensive anthology of midwestern literature to date; includes valuable introductions to the selections.

———. *Folk Plays for Contests*. Chicago: Denison, 1940. Seven plays.

Frederick, John T., ed. *Out of the Midwest: A Collection of Present Day Writing*. New York: McGraw-Hill, 1944.

———. *Stories From the Midland*. New York: Knopf, 1924.

Frederick was the long time editor of the *Midland*, an important periodical which encouraged Midwest writers.

Havighurst, Walter, ed. *Land of the Long Horizons*. New York: Coward-McCann, 1960.

American Vista Series; includes extensive notes.

———. *The Great Lakes Reader*. New York: Macmillan, 1966.

Literature of the Lakes region from Allouez to Hatcher and deKruif.

Inge, Thomas M., ed. *Agrarianism in American Literature*. New York: Odyssey, 1969.

Light on Midwest materials but does include selections reflecting agrarian theory from Garland, Veblen, Bromfield, and Sherwood Anderson.

Johnson, Mary T., ed. *Rural Community Plays*. Dayton, Ohio: Paine, 1925.

Ten plays.

Jones, L. N., ed. *Midwest Prize Plays*. Chicago: Dramatic Publishers, 1938.

Seven plays.

Lee, Charles, ed. *North, East, South, West: A Regional Anthology of American Writing*. New York: Howell, Soskin, 1945.

Midwest Federation of Chaparral Poets Book Association. *From the Valleys to the Mountain: Midwest Poetry*. Minneapolis: Federation, 1945.

Morris, Wright, ed. *Mississippi River Reader*. Garden City, N.Y.: Anchor, 1962.

Rockwell, Ethel T., ed. *American Life as Represented in Native One Act Plays*. Madison: U. Wisconsin, 1931.

Sanford, Anne P. and Robert H. Schauffler, eds. *Pageants of Our Nation*. 2 vols. New York: Dodd, Mead, 1929.

Volume 2 includes nine pageants from midwestern states.

Simpson, Claude M., ed. *The Local Colorists: America in Short Stories, 1857–1900*. New York: Harper, 1960.

Stryck, Lucien, ed. *Heartland: Poets of the Midwest*. DeKalb: U. Northern Illinois, 1967.

Best anthology of contemporary Midwest poetry.

———, ed. *Heartland II: Poets of the Midwest*. DeKalb: Northern Illinois U., 1975.

Supplements *Heartland*.

Warfel, Harry R. and G. H. Orians, eds. *American Local-Color Stories*. New York: American, 1941.

Includes stories by Woolson, Catherwood, Garland, Gale, and others.

Weber, Brom, ed. *An Anthology of American Humor*. New York: Weber, 1962.

Wimberly, Lowry C., ed. *Mid-Country: Writings from the Heart of America*. Lincoln: U. Nebraska, 1945.

Mainly twentieth century; includes biographical sketches.

Bibliography

Coan, Otis W. and Richard G. Lillard. *America in Fiction: An Annotated List of Novels that*

Interpret Aspects of Life in the United States, Canada, and Mexico. 5th ed. Palo Alto: Pacific, 1967.

Dickinson, A. T. *American Historical Fiction.* 3d ed. Metuchen, N.J.: Scarecrow, 1971.
   Annotated lists of historical novels; sections on the "Midwest Frontier" and "Plains States Frontier."

Dougherty, Charles T. "Novels of the Middle Border: A Critical Bibliography for Historians." *HB*, 25 (May 1947), 77–78, 85–88.

Eichelberger, Clayton L. *A Guide to Critical Reviews of United States Fiction, 1870–1910.* Metuchen, N.J.: Scarecrow, 1971.
   Important because of the number of Midwest fiction writers active during the period.

Etulain, Richard W. *Western American Literature: A Bibliography of Interpretive Books and Articles.* Vermillion: Dakota Press, 1973.
   Covers many Midwest writers and books.

Flanagan, John T. "A Bibliography of Middle Western Farm Novels." *MH*, 23 (1942), 156–58.

Gohdes, Clarence. *Bibliographical Guide to the Study of the Literature of the U.S.A.* 3d ed. Durham: Duke U., 1970.
   Sections on regional literature and folklore; a good general work.

———. *Literature and Theatre of the States and Regions of the U.S.A.: An Historical Bibliography.* Durham: Duke U., 1967.
   Includes a good beginning checklist on each state.

Haywood, Charles. *A Bibliography of North American Folklore and Folksong.* 2 vols. Rev. ed. New York: Dover, 1961.
   Includes many literary titles; arranged by state.

Leisy, Ernest. *The American Historical Novel.* Norman: U. Oklahoma, 1950. Sections on "The Northwest Territory," "The Louisiana Purchase," and "The Midwest Frontier," plus an appendix listing more novels.

VanDerhoof, Jack. *A Bibliography of Novels Related to American Frontier and Colonial History.* Troy, N.Y.: Whitston, 1971.

2. PRE-FRONTIER AND FRONTIER PERIODS

Atkeson, Mary M. *A Study of the Local Literature of the Upper Ohio Valley, with Especial Reference to the Early Pioneer and Indian Tales, 1820–1840.* Columbus: Ohio State U., 1921.
   Valuable research on the oft overlooked era and genre.

DeMenil, Alexander N. *The Literature of the Louisiana Territory.* St. Louis: St. Louis News, 1904.
   Thorough collection of short bio-critical sketches of individual authors; includes a short supplementary treatment of additional early authors by state.

Dondore, Dorothy. *The Prairie and the Making of Middle America.* Cedar Rapids: Torch Press, 1926.
   Solid scholarly contribution; our most complete compendium of information about the literature of the pre-frontier and frontier periods.

Grinnell, George B. *Trails of the Pathfinder.* New York: Scribner, 1911.
   Discusses early travel narrative writers of the frontier.

Hounchell, Saul. *The Principal Literary Magazines of the Ohio Valley to 1840.* Nashville: George Peabody, 1934.
   Descriptive analysis of the contents of nine literary magazines.

Rusk, Ralph. *The Literature of the Middle Western Frontier.* 2 vols. New York: Columbia U., 1925.
   Scholarly. Particularly valuable for its extensive bibliographies through 1840.

Venable, William H. *Beginnings of Literary Culture in the Ohio Valley: Historical and Biographical Sketches.* Cincinnati: Clarke, 1891.
   Valuable pioneering work; includes chapters on Flint, Hall, "Some Early Travelers and Annalists," the pioneer book trade, early periodical literature, and the like.

Anthologies

Babcock, C. Merton, ed. *The American Frontier: A Social and Literary Record.* New York: Holt, 1965.

Includes excerpts from more than a dozen midwestern historians and literary figures.

Blair, Walter, ed. *Native American Humor*. San Francisco: Chandler, 1960. Long introduction and scholarly notes; several early Midwest humorists are included.

Coggeshall, William T. *The Poets and Poetry of the West*. Columbus: Follett, 1861.
Includes a strong plea for the advancement of local literature.

Durham, Philip and Everett L. Jones, eds. *The Frontier in American Literature*. New York: Odyssey, 1969.
A section on "The Midwest Frontier."

Gallagher, William D. *Selections from the Poetical Literature of the West*. Cincinnati: James, 1841.
Like Coggeshall, Gallagher emphasizes the need for regional writing.

Greenberg, David B., ed. *Land That Our Fathers Plowed: The Settlement of Our Country as Told by the Pioneers Themselves and Their Contemporaries*. Norman: U. Oklahoma, 1969.
Section on the Midwest includes excerpts from Garland, Quick, Croy, and others.

Bibliography

Carson, William G. "The Theatre of the American Frontier: A Bibliographical Essay." *ThR*, 1 (March 1958), 14–23.

3. STATES

A. THE DAKOTAS

Arvold, Alfred G. *The Little Country Theatre*. New York: Macmillan, 1922.
Informal discussion of the important Little Theatre movement.

Coursey, Oscar W. *Literature of South Dakota*. 4th ed. Mitchell: Educator Supply, 1925.
Intended basically as a school text.

Norell, Irene. "Prose Writers of North Dakota." *NDQ*, 26 (1958), 3–36.

Anthologies

Dakota Playmakers. *Dakota Playmaker Plays*. Boston: Baker, 1923.
This "first series" includes "four plays on colonial themes."

Jenney, Adeline M., ed. *Prairie Poets*. Minneapolis: Lund, 1949.

———. *Prairie Poets II*. Minneapolis: Lund, 1958.

Lindberg, James C., ed. *Fifteen South Dakota Poets*. New York: Harrison, 1930.

Lindberg, James C. and Gertrude B. Gunderson, eds. *An Anthology of South Dakota Poetry*. Pierre: Olander, 1928.

Milton, John R., ed. *The Literature of South Dakota*. Vermillion: Dakota Press, 1975.

Putnam, Grace B. and A. Ackerman, eds. *North Dakota Singing*. New York: Paebar, 1936.

South Dakota State Poetry Society. *Pasque Petals* (May 1927–   ).
Issued periodically.

Bibliography

Parmalee, Gertrude, comp. *A South Dakota Bibliography*. Sioux Falls: Library Association, 1959.
Pamphlet supplementing WPA's *Selected List of South Dakota Books* (1943).

B. ILLINOIS (EXCLUSIVE OF CHICAGO)

Hook, J. N. et al., eds. "Illinois Authors." *IEB*, 54 (1966).
Compiled under the auspices of the Illinois Assn. of Teachers of English; 56 pages of biographical sketches and titles.

Anthologies

Angle, Paul M., ed. *Prairie State: Impressions of Illinois, 1673–1967, by Travelers and Other Observers*. Chicago: U. Chicago, 1968.
Includes excerpts from the French explorers and missionaries and impressions of literary figures visiting and native to the state.

Illinois Poets. New York: Harrison, 1935.
  Sixty-four poets represented.
Quaife, Milo, ed. *Pictures of Illinois One Hundred Years Ago.* Chicago: Donnelley, 1918.
  Includes long excerpts from Birkbeck and Schoolcraft.
Stibitz, E. Earle, ed. *Illinois Poets: A Selection.* Carbondale: Southern Illinois U., 1968.
Webb, Howard W., ed. *Illinois Prose Writers: A Selection.* Carbondale: Southern Illinois U., 1968.

Bibliography

Angle, Paul M. *Suggested Readings in Illinois History: With a Selected List of Historical Fiction.* Springfield: State Historical Society, 1935.
  Pamphlet.
WPA, Illinois. *Bibliography of Illinois Poets Since 1900.* Chicago: Chicago Public Library Omnibus Project, 1942.
  This bound typescript includes lists of books of poetry, single poems in composite books, and biographical and critical information.
———. *Final Narrative Report . . . Bibliography of Illinois Writers.* Chicago: Chicago Teachers College, 1940.

C. INDIANA

Banta, Richard E., comp. *Indiana Authors and Their Books, 1816–1916: Biographical Sketches of Authors Who Published During the First Century of Indiana Statehood, with Lists of Their Books.* Crawfordsville: Wabash College, 1949.
Beeson, Rebecca K. *Literary Indiana.* Indianapolis: Bobbs-Merrill, 1925.
  Short pamphlet of minor importance.
Brunvand, Jan H., comp. *A Dictionary of Proverbs and Proverbial Phrases from Books Published by Indiana Authors Before 1890.* Bloomington: Indiana U., 1961.
Nicholson, Meredith. *The Hoosiers.* New York: Macmillan, 1900.
  Discussion of writers from the "Hoosier school" including Riley, Tarkington, Thompson, Wallace, and others, by one who knew many of them well.
Shumaker, Arthur W. *A History of Indiana Literature: With Emphasis on the Authors . . . Writing Prior to World War II.* Indianapolis: Indiana Historical Bureau, 1962.
  This valuable compendium was also published as vol. 42 of the Indiana Historical Collections.

Anthologies

Banta, Richard E., ed. *Hoosier Caravan: A Treasury of Indiana Life and Lore.* Bloomington: Indiana U., 1951.
Indiana Poets. New York: Harrison, 1935.
Lindley, Harlow, ed. *Indiana as Seen by Early Travelers.* Indianapolis: Indiana Historical Commission, 1916.
  Coverage to 1830; excerpts from Birkbeck, Faux, Flint, Sealsfield, and others.
Parker, Benjamin S. and Enos B. Heiney, eds. *Poets and Poetry of Indiana.* New York: Silver, 1900.
Snyder, June, comp. *Hoof Marks in the Sod.* Indianapolis: Author, 1946.
Wetmore, Thomas H., ed. *Indiana Sesquicentennial Poets.* Muncie: Ball State U., 1967.
Williams, M. D. *Indiana Authors.* Indianapolis: Bobbs-Merrill, 1916.

Bibliography

Russo, Dorothy R. and Thelma L. Sullivan. *Bibliographical Studies of Seven Authors of Crawfordsville, Indiana.* Indianapolis: Historical Society, 1952.
  The seven authors are Lew and Susan Wallace, Maurice and Will Thompson, Mary Hannah, Caroline Virginia Krout, and Meredith Nicholson.

D. IOWA

Andrews, Clarence. *A Literary History of Iowa.* Iowa City: U. Iowa, 1972.
  Solidly researched and well written; a model for future state literary histories.

Brigham, Johnson, ed. *A Book of Iowa Authors by Iowa Authors*. Des Moines: Iowa State Teachers Assn., 1930.
  Essays about Iowa writers of the period.
Frederick, John T. "Early Iowa in Fiction." *Palimpsest*, 36 (1955), 389–420.
——. "The Farm in Iowa Fiction." *Palimpsest*, 32 (1951), 121–52.
——. "Town and City in Iowa Fiction." *Palimpsest*, 35 (1954), 49–96.
Hoeltje, Hubert H. "Iowa Literary Magazines." *Palimpsest*, 11 (1930), 87–94.
Mott, Frank L. "Iowa Literary Magazines." *Palimpsest*, 44 (1963), 285–380.
——. *Literature of Pioneer Life in Iowa*. Iowa City: State Historical Society, 1923.
  Originally an address; includes a partly annotated bibliography.
Smith, Jessica W. *What of the Iowa Poets*. New York: Harrison, 1941.

Anthologies

Gildner, Gary and Judith Gildner, eds. *Out of this World: Poems from the Hawkeye State*. Ames: Iowa State U., 1975.
Iowa Poets: An Anthology of 69 Contemporaries. New York: Harrison, 1935.
Luke, Lou M., ed. *Who's Who Among Prairie Poets*. Des Moines: Kuhne, 1938.

Bibliography

Marple, Alice. *Iowa Authors and Their Works*. Des Moines: Historical Dept. of Iowa, 1918.
  Not restricted to literature.
Paluka, Frank. *Iowa Authors: A Bio-Bibliography of Sixty Native Writers*. Iowa City: Friends of the U. Iowa Libraries, 1967.

E. KANSAS

Barker, Nettie G. *Kansas Women in Literature*. 2d ed. Kansas City, Kan.: Meseraull, 1915.
  Short biographical sketches of often deservedly obscure writers; not particularly valuable.
Callahan, James P. "Kansas in the American Novel and Short Story." *KSHSC*, 17 (1926–28), 139–88.
Carl, Sister Mary T. *A Survey of Kansas Poetry*. Seneca, Kan.: Courier-Tribune Press, 1938.
  A well researched, if not particularly sophisticated treatment.
Carruth, William H., comp. *Kansas in Literature*. 2 vols. Topeka: Crane, 1900.
  Intended as a text for schools; historical sketch plus bibliography and representative poems.
Cutler, Bruce, ed. *The Arts at the Grass Roots: The First Kansas State Conference of the Arts*. Lawrence: U. Kansas, 1968.
Festival of Kansas Arts and Crafts: Catalog Arts and Crafts of Kansas: Lawrence: U. Kansas, 1948.
Fox, C. Maynard. *Book Length Fiction by Kansas Writers, 1915–1938*. Topeka: Kansas State Printing, 1944.
  A good survey, including solid critical commentary and bibliography.
Streeter, Floyd B. *The Kaw*. New York: Farrar, 1941.
  Rivers of America series; on Kansas literature, pp. 337–46.
Van Schaak, Elizabeth D. "The Arts in Kansas." *Kansas, the First Century*. 4 vols. New York: Lewis, 1956.
  See vol. 2, pp. 241–66.

Anthologies

Hoopes, Helen R., ed. *Contemporary Kansas Poets*. Lawrence: Watts, 1927.
Hull, Myra. *Kansas Prose Writers*. Lawrence, 1936.
Kansas Poets. New York: Harrison, 1935.
Kliewer, Warren and Stanley K. Solomon, eds. *Kansas Renaissance*. Lindsborg, Kan.: Coronado, 1961.
  Verse and prose by contemporary Kansans.
Wattles, Willard A., ed. *Sunflowers: A Book of Kansas Poems*. 2d ed. Chicago: McClurg, 1916.

Bibliography

Cochrane, Mary E. *A Bibliography of Kansas History, Biography, and Fiction*. Pittsburgh, Kan.: Pittcraft, 1965.

Fuson, Ben W. *Centennial Bibliography of Kansas Literature, 1854–1961*. Salina, Kan.: Kansas Wesleyan, 1961.

———. *Kansas Literature in the Nineteen Sixties*. Salina, Kan.: Kansas Wesleyan, 1970.
An extension of Fuson's *Centennial Bibliography*.

F. MICHIGAN

Foster, Bernice M. *Michigan Novelists*. Ann Arbor: Wahr, 1928.
Pamphlet.

Gillard, Kathleen I. *Our Michigan Heritage*. New York: Pageant, 1955.
Popular examination of history, literature, and cultural life of the state.

Hilbert, Rachel M., ed. *Michigan Authors*. Ann Arbor: Michigan Assn. School Librarians, 1960.
Author lists, biographical information, and titles.

———. *Michigan Poets, with Supplement to Michigan Authors, 1960*. Ann Arbor: Michigan Assn. School Librarians, 1964.

Hilberry, Conrad et al., eds. *The Third Coast: Contemporary Michigan Poetry*. Detroit: Wayne, 1976.

Miller, James. *The Detroit Yiddish Theater: 1920–1937*. Detroit: Wayne, 1967.
Scholarly account.

Anthologies

Burklund, Carl E., ed. *New Michigan Verse*. Ann Arbor: U. Michigan, 1940.

Elliott, Margaret, ed. *Michigan Poets*. Rev. ed. Ann Arbor: 1960.

Lamport, Warren W., comp. *Michigan Poets and Poetry with Portraits and Biographies*. Detroit: Mason, 1904.

Michigan Poets: An Anthology of 36 Contemporaries. New York: Harrison, 1936.

Michigan Poets and Poetry. Leslie, Mich.: Michigan Publ. Co., 1904.

Mosher, Edith and Nella Williams, eds. *From Indian Legends to the Modern Bookshelf: An Anthology of Prose and Verse by Michigan Authors*. Ann Arbor: Wahr, 1931.
"Prepared for the youth of the state."

Rowe, Kenneth T., ed. *University of Michigan Plays*. 3 vols. Ann Arbor: Wahr, 1929–32.

Warner, Robert and C. Warren Vander Hill, eds. *Michigan Reader*. Grand Rapids: Eerdmans, 1974.

Bibliography

Black, Albert G. *Michigan Novels: An Annotated Bibliography*. Ann Arbor: Michigan Council of Teachers of English, 1963.
Omits juveniles and out-of-print novels.

Bullock, Penelope L. *Michigan Bibliographies and Indexes*. Ypsilanti: Eastern Michigan U., 1960.

Goodrich, Madge V. *A Bibliography of Michigan Authors*. Richmond, Va.: Richmond Press, 1928.

Streeter, Floyd B. *Michigan Bibliography . . . to July 1, 1917*. 2 vols. Lansing: Michigan Historical Commission, 1921.

G. MINNESOTA

Flanagan, John T. "Early Literary Periodicals in Minnesota." *MH*, 26 (1945), 293–311.

———. "Folklore in Minnesota Literature." *MH*, 36 (1958), 73–83.

———. "Some Minnesota Novels, 1920–1950." *MH*, 31 (1950), 145–47.

———. "Thirty Years of Minnesota Fiction." *MH*, 31 (1950), 129–44.

Gray, James. *Pine, Stream and Prairie: Wisconsin and Minnesota in Profile*. New York: Knopf, 1945.
Basically an historical volume, in Knopf's "American Scene" series, this perceptive look at the two states includes a good chapter on literature and the arts.

Guthrie, Tyrone. *A New Theatre*. New York: McGraw-Hill, 1964.
An entertaining narrative which outlines the reasons for choosing the Midwest, and Minneapolis particularly, as site of a major repertory theatre.

Nute, Grace L. *A History of Minnesota Books and Authors.* Minneapolis: U. Minnesota, 1958.
  Pamphlet; originally published in *A History of the Arts in Minnesota* (1958) ed. by William
  Van O'Connor.
Richards, Carmen N., ed. *Minnesota Writers: A Collection of Autobiographical Stories by
  Minnesota Prose Writers.* Minneapolis: Denison, 1961.
  Not comprehensive.
Richards, Carmen N. and Genevieve R. Breen, eds. *Minnesota Writes: A Collection of Auto-
  biographical Stories by Minnesota Prose Writers.* Minneapolis: Lund, 1945.
  Employs the autobiographical sketch technique of *Minnesota Writers;* includes authors not
  found in the later collection.

Anthologies

Anderson, Chester G., ed. *Growing Up in Minnesota: Ten Writers Remember Their Child-
  hoods.* Minneapolis: U. Minnesota, 1976.
League of Minnesota Poets. *Voices of the Arrowhead: Anthology of Poems About the Minne-
  sota Arrowhead Country and Its People.* Duluth, 1948.
Leighton, Louise, ed. *Poems by Arrowhead Writers.* Virginia, Minn.: 1935.
Minnesota and Nebraska Poets: An Anthology of Verse by 39 Contemporaries. New York:
  Harrison, 1937.
Richards, Carmen N., ed. *Minnesota Skyline: Anthology of Poems About Minnesota.* 13th ed.
  St. Cloud: Times, 1953.
Schliplin, Maude C., ed. *Minnesota Verse: An Anthology.* Rev. ed. St. Cloud: Times, 1938.

Bibliography

Minnesota Dept. of Education, Library Division. *Minnesota Authors.* Rev. ed. St. Paul: 1949.
Shove, Raymond et al., eds. *A Selected Bio-Bibliography: Minnesota Authors.* St. Paul: Centennial Commission, 1958.

H. Missouri

Bailey, Eutopia O. "The Small Town in Twentieth Century Missouri Fiction." *MHR,* 49
  (1955), 230–48, 328–41.
Brashear, Minnie M. "Missouri Literature Since the First World War." *MHR,* Part I, "Verse,"
  40 (1945), 1–20; Part II, "Drama, Juvenilia and Non-Fiction," 40 (1946), 330–48; Part III,
  "The Novel," 41 (1947), 241–65.
———. "Missouri Verse and Verse-Writers." *MHR,* 18 (1923), 315–44; 19 (1924–25), 36–84,
  85–91.
  Solid treatment.
DeMenil, Alexander N. *A Century of Missouri Literature.* Columbia: Historical Society, 1920.
  Reprinted from *Missouri Historical Review,* vol. 15, pp. 74–125.
Jacobs, Elijah L. and Forrest E. Wolverton. *Missouri Writers: A Literary History of Missouri,
  1780–1955.* St. Louis: State Publ. Co., 1955.
  Most extensive work on Missouri literary history; depends a good deal on Brashear's work.
Jesse, Richard H. and Edward A. Allen, eds. *Missouri Literature.* Columbia: Stephens, 1901.
McCullough, Florence, comp. *Living Authors of the Ozarks and Their Literature.* 2d ed.
  Joplin: 1945.
Putzel, Max. *The Man in the Mirror: William Marion Reedy and His Magazine.* Cambridge:
  Harvard U., 1963.
Spotts, Carle B. *The Development of Fiction in the Missouri Frontier (1830–1860).* Columbia:
  Author, 1935.
  Reprinted from articles in the *Missouri Historical Review* of 1934 and 1935.

Anthologies

Marsh, Susan L. and Charles G. Vannest, eds. *Missouri Anthology.* Boston: Christopher,
  1932.
Mott, Frank L., ed. *Missouri Reader.* Columbia: U. Missouri, 1964.
Shodly, James S., ed. *A Little Book of Missouri Verse.* Kansas City: Hudson, 1897.

Bibliography

Kraus, Joe W. "Missouri in Fiction: A Review and a Bibliography." *MHR*, 42 (1948), 209–25, 310–24.

I. NEBRASKA

Harvey, Alice G. *Nebraska Writers*. Rev. ed. Omaha: Citizen Printing Co., 1964.
Biographical sketches and bibliography.
Kauffman, Bernice, comp. *Nebraska Centennial Literary Map and Guide to Nebraska Authors*. Lincoln: Nebraska, 1967.

Anthologies

Faulkner, Virginia, ed. *Roundup: A Nebraska Reader*. Lincoln: U. Nebraska, 1957.
Humphrey, Frederick B., ed. *Poems by Nebraska Poets*. Lincoln: Marshall, 1940.
Minnesota and Nebraska Poets: An Anthology of Verse by 39 Contemporaries. New York: Harrison, 1937.
Poets and Poetry of Nebraska. Chicago: American, 1902.
Smith, Carl, ed. *Nebraska Poets: One Hundred Pages of Prairie Poems*. Omaha: Megeath, 1893.
Wimberly, L. C., ed. *Prairie Schooner Caravan*. Lincoln: U. Nebraska, 1943.
Collections of materials first published in the *Prairie Schooner*.

Bibliography

Lammers, S. J. *Provisional List of Nebraska Authors*. Lincoln: U. Nebraska, 1918.

J. OHIO

Coyle, William, ed. *Ohio Authors and Their Books* . . . *1796–1950*. Cleveland: World, 1962.
Includes entries on nearly 5,000 authors.

Anthologies

Abbe, George, ed. *Contemporary Ohio Poetry: An Anthology* . . . . New York: Poets of America, 1959.
Martzolff, Clement L., comp. *Poems on Ohio*. Columbus: State Historical Society, 1911.
Ohio Poets: An Anthology of 90 Contemporaries. New York: Harrison, 1934.
Ohio Department of Education. *Anthology of Ohio Verse*. Columbus, 1946.
Venable, Emerson, ed. *Poets of Ohio*. Cincinnati: Stewart & Kidd, 1909; 1912.

Bibliography

Janeway, W. Ralph. *A Selected List of Ohio Authors and Their Books*. Columbus: Hedrick, 1933.

K. WISCONSIN

Rounds, Charles R., ed. *Wisconsin Authors and Their Works*. Madison: Parker, 1918.
Titus, William A. *Wisconsin Writers: Sketches and Studies*. Rev. ed. Ann Arbor: Plutarch, 1971.
Biographical sketches and selections from published works; the author published an earlier edition of this work in 1930.

Anthologies

Derleth, August, ed. *A Wisconsin Harvest*. Sauk City, Wisc.: Stanton & Lee, 1966.
Derleth, August and Raymond E. Larsson, eds. *Poetry Out of Wisconsin by Wisconsin Poets*. New York: Harrison, 1937.
Dickinson, Thomas H., ed. *Wisconsin Plays*. New York: Huebsch, 1914.
First series: three plays.
———. *Wisconsin Plays*. New York: Huebsch, 1918.
Second series: four plays.

Gard, Robert E. et al., eds. *We Were Children: Ninety Wisconsin Writers, Age Six to Ninety-Six*. Madison: Wisconsin House, 1976.

Morehouse, Ruth, ed. *Northern Spring: An Anthology of Poems*. Minneapolis: Lund, 1956.

Rosenblum, Martin, ed. *Brewing: 20 Milwaukee Poets*. Lyme Center, N.H.: Giligia, 1972.

Rounds, Charles S. and Henry S. Hippensteel, eds. *Wisconsin in Story and Song*. Madison: Parker, 1916.

Shay, F. et al., eds. *Wisconsin Writings: An Anthology*. New York: Mohawk, 1931.

Totten, Maude et al., eds. *Poems Out of Wisconsin*. 3 vols. N.p. 1956–67.
Wisconsin Fellowship of Poets has sponsored these occasional anthologies, viz. vol. 1 (1956), vol. 2 (1961), vol. 3 (1967).

Wisconsin Community Plays. Chicago: Dramatic Publishing, 1935.
Six plays. Wisconsin was a leader in the community theatre movement.

Wisconsin Rural Plays. Chicago: Dramatic Publishing, 1931.
Five plays.

Bibliography

Hazeltine, Mary E. *One Hundred Years of Wisconsin Authorship, 1836–1937: A Contribution to a Bibliography of Books by Wisconsin Authors*. Madison: Wisconsin Library Assn., 1937.
――――. "Wisconsin Authors: Supplement." *WLB*, 34 (1938), 117–25.

Schlinkert, Leroy. *Subject Bibliography of Wisconsin History*. Madison: Historical Society, 1947.
Includes sections on literature and fiction.

Wisconsin Verse: A Compilation of the Titles of Volumes of Verse Written by Authors Born or Residing in the State of Wisconsin. Bibliographical Society of America, 1914.

4. COMPOSITE BOOKS

Aaron, Daniel. *Men of Good Hope: A Story of American Progressives*. New York: Oxford, 1951.
Although more social history than literary study, the writer does include chapters on Howells and Veblen.

Ahnebrink, Lars. *The Beginnings of Naturalism in American Fiction*. Cambridge: Harvard, 1950.
An extended study of Garland, Norris, and Stephen Crane, "with special reference to some European influences." Includes a short chapter on "Realism in the Middle West," with discussion of Eggleston, Howe, and Joseph Kirkland.

Allen, Walter. *The Urgent West: The American Dream and Modern Man*. London: Baker, 1969.
"West" means simply "America" to Britisher Allen, although there is a good deal of commentary on Midwest writers throughout.

Auchincloss, Louis. *Pioneers and Caretakers: A Study of American Women Novelists*. Minneapolis: U. Minnesota, 1965.
Has a chapter on Cather.

Bernard, Harry. *Le Roman Régionalist aux États Unis, 1913–1940*. Montreal: Fides, 1949.
A general survey chapter on "Le Centre-Quest."

Berthoff, Warner. *The Ferment of Realism: American Literature, 1884–1919*. New York: Free Press, 1965.
General literary history of the period. Includes chapters on Howells, Dreiser, Twain, et al., and extended treatment of regional and local color writing and the Chicago Renaissance.

Blake, Nelson M. *Novelists' America: Fiction as History, 1910–1940*. Syracuse: Syracuse U., 1969.
Chapters on Sinclair Lewis, Farrell, and Richard Wright.

Bluefarb, Sam. *The Escape Motif in the American Novel: Mark Twain to Richard Wright*. Columbus: Ohio State U., 1972.
Chapters on Twain, Sherwood Anderson, and Richard Wright.

Bostwick, Arthur E. *The Different West: As Seen by a Transplanted Easterner*. Chicago: McClurg, 1913.
Sophisticated, rambling collection of essays on the "West," including chapters on "Art in

the West"; "The Speech and Manners of the West"; and "Society in the West." An entertaining and suggestive book.

Bowden, Edwin T. *The Dungeon of the Heart: Human Isolation and the American Novel.* New York: Macmillan, 1961.

Chapters on "Frontier Isolation" (which treats Twain and Cather among others) and on "The Commonplace and the Grotesque" (deals with Sherwood Anderson and three others).

Boynton, Percy H. *The Rediscovery of the Frontier.* Chicago: U. Chicago, 1931.

Treats many Midwest writers. An important early work.

_____. *Some Contemporary Americans.* Chicago: U. Chicago, 1924.

Chapters on Masters and Sandburg; Tarkington; Dreiser.

_____. *More Contemporary Americans.* Chicago: U. Chicago, 1927.

Companion to the survey mentioned directly above. Chapters on Sherwood Anderson and Sinclair Lewis.

Bridgman, Richard. *The Colloquial Style in America.* New York: Oxford, 1966.

Takes quite a bit of space examining the relationship between prose and speech in the West and Midwest; chapters on "Nineteenth Century Talk," Twain, Hemingway, and Stein (this last examines Sherwood Anderson's writing as well).

Brodin, Pierre. *Le Roman Régionalist Américain.* Paris: Librairie G.-P. Maisonneuve, 1937.

A long survey chapter on "Le Middle-West."

Brooks, Van Wyck. *America's Coming of Age.* New York: Huebsch, 1915.

Emphasizes the double evil of Puritanism and pioneer life, both of which had repressed the creative spirit.

_____. *The Confident Years: 1885-1915.* New York: Dutton, 1952.

This final volume of the "Makers and Finders" series treats midwestern writers extensively, especially those who were part of the Chicago literary scene.

_____. *Opinions of Oliver Allston.* New York: Dutton, 1941.

In a chapter on "Nationalism and Regionalism," Allston (Brooks) discusses the necessity of clinging to the American soil in order to stave off personality disintegration. Brooks's early critical work, e.g., *America's Coming of Age* and *The Ordeal of Mark Twain,* had emphasized the negative effects of frontier life on American cultural pretensions. In later work, like the "Makers and Finders" series and *Allston,* Brooks reversed that position.

Cady, Edwin H. *The Light of Common Day: Realism in American Fiction.* Bloomington: Indiana U., 1971.

Essays on Twain and Howells, but the larger thrust of this recent critical study is away from midwestern writers.

Cargill, Oscar. *Intellectual America: Ideas on the March.* New York: Macmillan, 1941.

In this "survey of ideologies in American culture," Cargill discusses naturalism, veritism, and primitivism, movements particularly strong among Midwest writers. Garland, Dreiser, and Hemingway get a good deal of attention. A landmark in intellectual history and literary criticism.

Carter, Everett. *Howells and the Age of Realism.* Philadelphia: Lippincott, 1954.

Particular emphasis on Howells as a key figure, but also contains an abundance of literary criticism on writers like Twain, Eggleston, and Garland. There is a chapter on "Local Color" as well.

Clough, Wilson O. *The Necessary Earth: Nature and Solitude in American Literature.* Austin: U. Texas, 1964.

Studies the impact of untamed nature on American literature; writers of the frontier receive more than passing attention.

Commager, Henry Steele. *The American Mind: An Interpretation of American Thought and Character Since the 1880's.* New Haven: Yale, 1950.

Commager emphasizes the importance of the Midwest as a seed bed for the development of the modern American mind; extended discussion of Dreiser, Sinclair Lewis, Louis Sullivan, and Frederick Jackson Turner.

Cowie, Alexander. *The Rise of the American Novel.* New York: American, 1948.

Includes a long chapter on "Local-Color, Frontier, and Regional Fiction," plus chapters on Twain and Howells. A solid survey of nineteenth-century fiction.

Davidson, Donald. *The Attack on Leviathan: Regionalism and Nationalism in the United States.* Chapel Hill: U. North Carolina, 1938.

This emphatic defense of regional literature (primarily Southern) devotes several chapters to the literature and culture of the Midwest.

Fiedler, Leslie A. *The Return of the Vanishing American*. New York: Stein & Day, 1968.
This third volume of his "literary anthology" series is concerned with the advent of a "New Western" based on the myth of the Indian; the relationship between frontier attitudes and the literature of the "West" is imaginatively explored.

Fiske, Horace S. *Provincial Types in American Fiction*. New York: Chautauqua, 1903.
Includes a chapter on "Provincial Types in the Mississippi Valley."

Flanagan, Hallie. *Arena*. New York: Duell, 1940.
A long section (pp. 131–79) on Midwest Federal Theatre from 1935–1939.

Fussel, Edwin. *Frontier: American Literature and the American West*. Princeton: Princeton U., 1965.
The image of the West in the writings of Cooper, Melville, Thoreau, Poe, Hawthorne, and Whitman.

Galinsky, Hans et al. *The Frontier in American History and Literature*. Frankfurt am Main: Diesterweg, 1961.

Gard, Robert. *Grassroots Theatre: A Search for Regional Arts in America*. Madison: U. Wisconsin, 1955.

Gard, Robert and Gertrude S. Burley. *Community Theatre: Idea and Achievement*. New York: Duell, 1959.
A history and assessment of the movement with an especially detailed picture of Wisconsin and other Midwest theatres.

———. *Down in the Valleys: Wisconsin Back Country Lore and Humor*. Madison: Wisconsin-House, 1971.

Geismar, Maxwell. *The Last of the Provincials: The American Novel, 1915–1925*. Boston: Houghton Mifflin, 1947.
Extensive coverage of important Midwest writers, including Lewis, Cather, Anderson, and Fitzgerald.

———. *Rebels and Ancestors: The American Novel, 1890–1915*. Boston: Houghton Mifflin, 1953.
Includes essays on Norris and Dreiser.

Hakutoni, Yoshinobu and Lewis Fried, eds. *American Literary Naturalism: A Reassessment*. Heidelberg: Carl Winter, 1975.
Includes essays on Algren, Dreiser, Farrell, Herrick, Howe, Norris, and Richard Wright.

Hazard, Lucy L. *The Frontier in American Literature*. New York: Crowell, 1927.
A still valuable early work; last two chapters especially concerned with Midwest urban and rural frontiers.

Herron, Ima H. *The Small Town in American Literature*. Durham: Duke U., 1939.
Thorough survey of the subject; several chapters on the rural Midwest Realists, the "Village Apologists," and the "Revolt from the Village."

———. *The Small Town in American Drama*. Dallas: S. Methodist U., 1969.
Extensive treatment of little known dramatists and their plays, especially those coming out of the regional theatre movement.

Hilfer, Anthony C. *The Revolt from the Village, 1915–1930*. Chapel Hill: U. North Carolina, 1969.
A survey of the "revolt" phenomenon; examines the work of five midwestern writers (Cather, Gale, Masters, Anderson, and Lewis) among others.

Jensen, Merrill, ed. *Regionalism in America.* Madison: U. Wisconsin, 1951.
The Midwest is well covered; includes an excellent essay on "Regionalism in American Literature" by Benjamin T. Spencer.

Jones, Howard Mumford. *The Frontier in American Fiction*. Jerusalem: Magnes, 1956.
Essays on Cooper, Twain, and Cather.

Kamman, William F. *Socialism in German American Literature*. Philadelphia: Americana Germanica, 1917.
A valuable older study dealing with the generally neglected subject of German-American literature. Much of this literature, and the social thought it often reflects, is centered in Midwest German communities.

Karolides, Nicholas J. *The Pioneer in the American Novel, 1900–1950*. Norman: U. Oklahoma, 1967.
A general survey of the subject; the Midwest is treated throughout.

Knight, Grant C. *The Strenuous Age in American Literature*. Chapel Hill: U. North Carolina, 1954.
Studies the first decade of the twentieth century; treats several Midwest writers throughout.

Lee, Robert Edson. *From West to East: Studies in the Literature of the American West*. Urbana: U. Illinois, 1966.
Examines the divergent views of East and West in creating the mythic American West.

Lynn, Kenneth. *The Dream of Success: A Study of the Modern American Imagination*. Boston: Little, Brown, 1955.
Includes lengthy essays on Dreiser, Norris, and Herrick which attempt to show how their works reflect affirmation of the popular democratic feeling of the late nineteenth century.

McWilliams, Carey. *The New Regionalism in American Literature*. Seattle: U. Washington Book Store, 1930.
Pamphlet.

Martin, Jay. *Harvests of Change: American Literature, 1865–1914*. Englewood Cliffs, N.J.: Prentice-Hall, 1967.
Chapters on the national epic, regionalism, and utopian fiction of the period; particularly strong coverage of Twain, Howells, and Dreiser among midwestern figures.

May, Henry F. *The End of American Innocence: A Study of the First Years of Our Own Time, 1912–1917*. New York: Knopf, 1959.
Included is a brief examination of the role played by midwestern writers in modern social and literary revolutions; see especially pp. 90–106 and 252–69.

Millgate, Michael. *American Social Fiction: James to Cozzens*. New York: Barnes & Noble, 1964.
This survey includes essays on Howells, Norris, Dreiser, Anderson, Lewis, and Fitzgerald.

Morgan, H. Wayne. *American Writers in Rebellion: From Mark Twain to Dreiser*. New York: Hill & Wang, 1965.
Surveys the literary revolutions of that formative period when midwestern writers were particularly influential.

―――――. *Writers in Transition: Seven Americans*. New York: Hill & Wang, 1963.
This examination of the uses writers make of the "past" includes essays on Cather, Anderson, and Hart Crane.

Noble, D. W. *The Eternal Adam and the New World Garden: The Central Myth in the American Novel Since 1830*. New York: Braziller, 1968.
The "frontier thesis" as symbol of our national ideal; Noble explores the myth through American historians in *Historians Against History* and here continues with an examination of American literature; Twain, Howells, Dreiser, Hemingway, Fitzgerald, and Bellow are among the featured midwestern writers.

Odum, Howard W. and Harry E. Moore. *American Regionalism: A Cultural Historical Approach to National Integration*. New York: Holt, 1938. Includes a chapter on Midwest regionalism and a number of references throughout to Midwest culture.

Ossman, David. *The Sullen Art: Interviews with Modern American Poets*. New York: Corinth, 1963.
Poets Paul Carroll, Robert Bly, John Logan, and Edward Dorn are among those interviewed.

Parrington, Vernon L. *Main Currents in American Thought: An Interpretation of American Literature from the Beginnings to 1920*. 3 vols. New York: Harcourt, 1927–30.
Volume 3, *The Beginnings of Critical Realism in America, 1860–1920*, is especially valuable. Parrington interprets American thought as it is reflected in literature. The primary value of literature appears to be its convenience as an index to cultural values.

Pattee, Fred L. *The New American Literature 1890–1930*. New York: Century, 1930.
A long chapter on "The Prairie Poets."

Pizer, Donald. *Realism and Naturalism in Nineteenth Century American Literature*. Carbondale: Southern Illinois U., 1966.
Special consideration for theoreticians like Garland and Norris, but does not neglect other Midwest writers of the period who were involved in these movements.

"Regional Theatre: U.S.A." *TA*, 33 (Aug. 1949), 17–56, 102–05; 34 (Aug. 1950), 24–66, 93–96.

Rideout, Walter B. *The Radical Novel in the United States, 1900–1954*. Cambridge: Harvard U., 1956.

Discusses a number of midwestern social novelists in some detail, including Farrell, Conroy, Dreiser, Anderson, and others.

Rourke, Constance M. *American Humor: A Study of the National Character*. New York: Harcourt, 1931.

In this pioneering work, and in those of Rourke's cited below, the author attempts to discover the center of American culture in its folk traditions and pre-literary forms. The Midwest frontier becomes a key breeding ground for this cultural life.

_____. *Audubon*. New York: Harcourt, 1936.

Biography intended for juveniles which transcends that limited audience.

_____. *The Roots of American Culture, and Other Essays*. New York: Harcourt, 1942.

Essays, notes, and fragments edited by Van Wyck Brooks after the author's death; valuable for regionalists.

_____. "The Significance of Sections." *NR*, 26 (Sept. 20, 1933), 148–51.

Royce, Josiah. "Provincialism: Based Upon a Study of Early Conditions in California." *PM*, 7 (1909), 232–40.

A seminal essay on the subject.

Schneider, Robert W. *Five Novelists of the Progressive Era*. New York: Columbia U., 1965.

Among the five are three midwesterners (Dreiser, Howells, and Churchill), one quasi-midwesterner (Norris), and Stephen Crane.

Slotkin, Richard. *Regeneration Through Violence: The Mythology of the American Frontier*. Middletown, Conn.: Wesleyan U., 1973.

Especially valuable are chapter 10, "Evolution of the National Hero: Farmer to Hunter to Indian (1784–1855)," and chapter 12, "The Fragmented Image: The Boone Myth and Sectional Cultures (1820–1850)."

Smith, Henry Nash. *The Virgin Land: The American West as Symbol and Myth*. Cambridge: Harvard U., 1950.

A landmark in "myth criticism."

_____. "Western Chroniclers and Literary Pioneers." *Literary History of the United States*. Ed. by Robert Spiller et al. 3d rev. ed. New York: Macmillan, 1963.

Spencer, Benjamin T. *The Quest for Nationality: An American Literary Campaign*. Syracuse: Syracuse U., 1957.

Chapter on "Nationality Through Region and Locale (1815–1892)" treats a number of Midwest figures.

Sper, Felix. *From Native Roots: A Panorama of Our Regional Drama*. Caldwell, Idaho: Caxton, 1948.

Survey of regional and folk drama in the U.S.; includes chapters on "The Northern Border," "Hill Folk," "Plains and Prairies," all of which touch on the Midwest.

Spiller, Robert et al., eds. *The Literary History of the United States*. 3d rev. ed., New York: Macmillan, 1963.

In addition to the chapter by Henry Nash Smith cited above, sections 6–9 contain a wealth of material on Midwest writers and literary history.

Taylor, Walter F. *The Economic Novel in America*. New York: Octagon, 1964.

Allots a good deal of space to discussion of midwestern economic and social conditions as they are reflected in writers of the region; chapters on Twain, Howells, and Norris, plus a chapter on "Lesser Novelists."

Trent, William et al., eds. *The Cambridge History of American Literature*. New York: Putnam, 1917–1921.

Van Doren, Carl. *Many Minds*. New York: Knopf, 1924.

Treats Ade, Howe, Sandburg, Lindsay, and Lardner among others; personal and scholarly insights from an historian native to the Midwest.

Walcutt, Charles C. *American Literary Naturalism: A Divided Stream*. Minneapolis: U. Minnesota, 1956.

An important literary history; chapters on Garland, Norris, Churchill, Dreiser, Anderson, and Farrell.

Wentz, John C. "American Regional Drama, 1920–1940 . . . ," *MD*, 6 (1963), 286–93.

West, Thomas R. *Flesh of Steel: Literature and the Machine in American Culture*. Nashville: Vanderbilt U., 1967.
Essays on Anderson, Lewis, Veblen, and others.

Yates, Norris W. *The American Humorist*. Ames: Iowa State U., 1964.
Ade, Hubbard, and Lardner, are among those discussed.

Yatron, Michael. *America's Literary Revolt*. New York: Philosophical Library, 1959.
Sandburg, Lindsay, and Masters are featured.

Ziff, Larzer. *The American 1890's: Life and Times of a Lost Generation*. New York: Viking, 1966.
The author relies a good deal on midwestern writers to fill in his portrait of the literary generation. The chapter on "The Midwestern Imagination" is particularly valuable. Other chapters focus on Howells, Twain, Garland, Fuller, Norris, and Dreiser.

5. LINGUISTIC STUDIES

Allen, Harold B. *The Linguistic Atlas of the Upper Midwest*. 3 vols. Minneapolis: U. Minnesota, 1973–76.
A part of the still to be completed *Linguistic Atlas of the United States*, Hans Kurath, gen. ed. Allen's *Atlas*, a labor of many years in editing and field work, is the single most important publication in Midwest language study to date.

Allen, Harold B. and Gary N. Underwood, eds. *Readings in American Dialectology*. New York: Appleton, 1971.
Includes a section on "Area Studies" with several articles on Midwest language.

Brenni, Vito J., comp. *American English: A Bibliography*. Philadelphia: U. Pennsylvania, 1964.

Davis, Alva L. *"A Word Atlas of The Great Lakes Region."* Diss. U. Michigan, 1948.

Haugen, Einar. *The Norwegian Language in America: A Study in Bilingual Behavior*. 2 vols. Philadelphia: U. Pennsylvania, 1953.
Volume 1 includes material on the "historical and sociological aspects behind the linguistic problems of the Norwegian-American communities."

———. "Bilingualism in the Americas: A Bibliography and Research Guide." *PADS*, 26 (1956).

Kurath, Hans. "Dialect Areas, Settlement Areas, and Cultural Areas in the United States." In C. F. Ware, ed. *The Cultural Approach to History*. New York, 1940. Pp. 331–45.

———. "Linguistic Regionalism." In Merrill Jensen, ed. *Regionalism in America*. Madison, 1951. Pp. 297–310.

———. "Interrelation between Regional and Social Dialects." In H. G. Hunt, ed. *Ninth International Congress of Linguists*. The Hague, 1964. Pp. 135-44.

———. *Studies in Area Linguistics*. Bloomington: Indiana U., 1972.
Includes discussion of Midwest language research; an excellent bibliography is appended.

McDavid, Raven I., Jr., and Virginia G. and Alva L. Davis, eds. *A Compilation of the Work Sheets of the Linguistic Atlas of the United States and Canada and Associated Projects*. 2d ed. Chicago: U. Chicago, 1969.

Marckwardt, Albert H. "Principal and Subsidiary Dialect Areas in the North-Central States." *PADS*, 27 (1957), 3–15.

Mencken, H. L. *The American Language: An Inquiry into the Development of English in the United States*. 3d ed. New York: Knopf, 1930.
Classic study. Raven I. McDavid, Jr., published an abridged, annotated and supplemented edition in 1963.

Pederson, L. A. "The Pronunciation of English in Chicago." Diss. U. Chicago, 1964.

Shuy, Roger W. et al. *Field Techniques in an Urban Language Study*. Washington: Center for Applied Linguistics, 1968.
Detroit dialects study.

Wolfram, Walter A. *A Sociolinguistic Description of Detroit Negro Speech*. Washington: Center of Applied Linguistics, 1969.

Gerald C. Nemanic
Northeastern Illinois University
Chicago, Illinois

HISTORY AND SOCIETY

THERE HAS BEEN, to date, no definitive history of the Middle West which covers activities in the region from exploration to modern times. A few general histories of the Middle West have been published, e.g., Dan Clark's *The Middle West in American History* (1937), Sidney Glazer's *The Middle West* (1962), and Kenneth Walker's *History of the Middle West* (1972), but these serve best as introductory outlines to the subject. The various periods of midwestern history have been extended thorough treatment. Francis Parkman's classic *France and England in North America* (1865–84) remains a key document for the era of exploration. The frontier period (ca. 1780–1860) has attracted a vast historical literature. Probably the most intensive and thoroughgoing treatment of the midwestern frontier can be found in several works by Ray Allen Billington, especially his *Westward Expansion: A History of the American Frontier* (1949). Surveys of American history often include substantial treatment of the Middle West, especially for the nineteenth century. Among the most important in this category are Daniel Boorstin's *The Americans: The National Experience* (1965), Morison and Commager's *The Growth of the American Republic* (5th ed., 1962), Allan Nevins's *The Emergence of Modern America, 1865–1878* (1927), and Charles and Mary Beard's *The Rise of American Civilization* (1927), Richard Hofstadter's *The Age of Reform: From Bryan to F.D.R.* (1955) includes a good deal on late nineteenth- and twentieth-century Midwest history, especially with reference to the agrarian and populist movements.

Indeed, the number of volumes devoted to the various aspects of midwestern history and social organization run into the thousands. In the bibliographical lists which follow are included: (1) works most nearly definitive, exhaustive, or otherwise most satisfactory, (2) works which include substantial commentary on literature and cultural life, (3) works which, of themselves, constitute a contribution to *belle lettres*. It is entirely possible that works appearing under one of the following subdivisions might just as easily have been placed in one or more of the others as well. But since the lists are not that formidably extensive, and to save space, each work has been limited to a single entry in the category which seemed most appropriate.

1. GENERAL BIBLIOGRAPHY

Grob, Gerald N. *American Social History Before 1860*. New York: Appleton, 1970.
   Goldentree bibliography.

Howes, Wright. *U.S.-iana (1650–1950): A Selective Bibliography in Which are Described 11,620 Uncommon and Significant Books* . . . . Rev. ed. New York: Bowker, 1962.

Knox College. *Finley Collection on the History and Romance of the Northwest.* 2d ed. Galesburg: Knox College, 1928.
Catalogs over 2,500 books, pamphlets, and maps.

Ludewig, Herman E. *The Literature of American Local History: A Bibliographical Essay.* New York: Craighead, 1846.

Mugridge, Donald H. *American History and Civilization: A List of Guides and Annotated or Selective Bibliographies.* Rev. ed. Washington: GPO, 1951.
Pamphlet.

Mugridge, Donald H. and Blanche P. McCrum. *A Guide to the Study of the U.S.A.* Washington: GPO, 1960.
Valuable annotated lists of books dealing with American culture.

Peterson, Clarence S. *Consolidated Bibliography of County Histories in Fifty States in 1961.* Consolidated 1935–61. Baltimore: Author, 1961.

Rader, Jesse L. *South of Forty: From the Mississippi to the Rio Grande: A Bibliography.* Norman: U. Oklahoma, 1947.
Important for those areas of the region south of the fortieth parallel and west of the Mississippi River.

Sabin, Joseph. *Bibliotheca Americana: A Dictionary of Books Relating to America, from its Discovery to the Present Time.* Completed by Wilberforce Eames and R. W. G. Vail. 29 vols. New York: Sabin (later Bibliographical Society of America), 1868–1936.

Stevens, Harry R. *The Middle West.* New York: Macmillan, 1958.
Pamphlet discussing the historical literature of the Midwest.

Tanselle, G. Thomas. *Guide to the Study of United States Imprints.* 2 vols. Cambridge: Harvard U., 1971.
Extremely valuable work. Contains many state and regional literary bibliographies, individual author bibliographies, and guides to imprint bibliographies for all Midwest states.

Vail, R. W. G. *The Voice of the Old Frontier.* Philadelphia: U. Pennsylvania, 1949.
Bibliographical essays and lists dealing with the literature of the first American settlements to 1800. Omits materials by "nonresidents" and "Jesuit Relations."

Weimer, David R. *Bibliography of American Culture, 1493–1875.* Ann Arbor: University Microfilms, 1957.

Writings on American History. Compiled by the National Historical Publications Commission, 1902– .
Includes sections on regional, state, and local history.

2.   GENERAL

Beard, Charles A. and Mary R. *The Rise of American Civilization.* Rev. and enl. ed. New York: Macmillan, 1966.
First published in 1927, this influential work lays particular stress on the economic forces that helped create American society; Marxist in viewpoint; early midwestern radical movements in agriculture and labor become crucial factors in the rise of American social consciousness.

Boorstin, Daniel. *The Americans: The National Experience.* New York: Random, 1965.
This second of three volumes in the distinguished historian's interpretive history of the U. S. covers the Midwest frontier period and includes a detailed, valuable bibliographical essay.

Carman, Harry J., Harold C. Syrett, and Bernard W. Wishy. *A History of the American People.* 2d rev. ed. 2 vols. New York: Knopf, 1960.
A socio-political history.

Clark, Daniel E. *The Middle West in American History.* New York: Crowell, 1966.
Originally published as part of Clark's *The West in American History* (1937). Particularly strong on the frontier period.

Drury, John. *Midwest Heritage.* New York: Wyn, 1948.
A short survey of Midwest history, illustrated with old engravings.

Glazer, Sidney. *The Middle West: A Study of Progress.* New York: Bookman, 1962.
Short historical survey of the region.

Havighurst, Walter. *The Heartland: Ohio, Indiana, Illinois*. New York: Harper, 1962.
A fast-paced volume in the popular Regions of America series.

Hofstadter, Richard. *The Age of Reform: From Bryan to F.D.R.* New York: Knopf, 1955.
This Pulitzer Prize winning history is incisive in its treatment of the agrarian and populist movements in the Middle West.

Hutton, Graham. *Midwest at Noon*. Chicago: U. Chicago, 1946.
Stimulating, informal social history by an English writer who resided in the Midwest for a number of years. Particularly valuable as an evaluation of the modern Midwest by a non-American.

Lawrence College. *The Culture of the Middle West*. Appleton, Wisc.: Lawrence College, 1944.
This Faculty Lecture Series from 1942–43 includes papers on Midwest geography, the political and social development of the region, and its literary heritage.

McLaughlin, Robert. *The Heartland: Illinois, Indiana, Michigan, Ohio, Wisconsin*. New York: Time, 1967.
Part of the Time-Life Library of America Series, which also includes *The Plains States* (1968) by Evan Jones. These lushly illustrated "coffee table" histories are generally well written and contain a number of excellent photographs, drawings, and maps.

Morison, Samuel E. and Henry S. Commager. *The Growth of the American Republic*. 2 vols. New York: Oxford, 1962.
An unbiased and perspicuous political history with extensive treatment of the Midwest in the nineteenth century.

Nevins, Allan. *The Emergence of Modern America, 1865–1878*. New York: Macmillan, 1927.
Probably the best social history of this particular era, it treats sectionalism and regionalism at length.

Nye, Russel B. *The Cultural Life of the New Nation, 1776–1830*. New York: Harper, 1960.
This volume of the New American Nation series surveys the cultural development of the Midwest and other regions.

Schlesinger, Arthur M. and Dixon R. Fox, gen. eds. *A History of American Life*. 13 vols. New York: Macmillan, 1927–44.
The relevant volumes include: Fish, Carl R. *The Rise of the Common Man, 1830–1850* (1927). Vol. 6; Nevins, Allan. *The Emergence of Modern America, 1865–1878* (1927). Vol. 8; Schlesinger, Arthur M. *The Rise of the City, 1878–1898* (1933). Vol. 10; Faulkner, Harold U. *The Quest for Social Justice, 1898–1914* (1931). Vol. 11.

Seymour, Ralph F. *Our Midwest: Episodes in the Lives of Some Individuals Who Helped Shape the Growth of Our Midwest*. Chicago: Author, 1954.
An informal short history, beautifully illustrated.

Waitley, Douglas. *Portrait of the Midwest*. New York: Abelard-Schulman 1963.
Informal history of the Midwest "from the ice age to the industrial revolution."

Walker, Kenneth R. *A History of the Middle West, From the Beginning to 1970*. Little Rock: Pioneer, 1972.
Most recent history of the region; competent survey with short sections on the arts.

3.   DISCOVERY AND EXPLORATION (ca. 1500–1800)

Bakeless, John. *The Eyes of Discovery: The Pageant of North America as Seen by the First Explorers*. New York: Lippincott, 1950.
Interesting popular work. Bakeless tries to recreate the various wilderness areas as they were when explorers first saw them. He includes chapters on Midwest explorers Coronado, Vérendrye, and LaSalle, general treatments on both the Mississippi and Missouri Rivers, and a piece on "The Wild Middle West."

————. *Lewis and Clark, Partners in Discovery*. New York: Morrow, 1947.
Well-paced narrative examines both men and expedition.

Brebner, John B. *The Explorers of North America, 1492–1806*. New York: Macmillan, 1933.
Strong narrative history which remains fundamentally sound scholarship.

Burpee, Lawrence J. *The Search for the Western Sea: The Story of the Exploration of North-Western America*. Toronto: Musson, 1908.
Chapters on Radisson and Grosseilliers, Vérendrye, Carver, and others.

Burroughs, Raymond D., ed. *The Natural History of the Lewis and Clark Expedition*. East Lansing: Michigan State U., 1961.

A volume of particular interest to biologists and zoologists.

Butterfield, Consul W. *History of the Discovery of the Northwest by John Nicollet in 1634*. Cincinnati: Clarke, 1881.

Well-regarded pioneer work.

Caldwell, Norman W. *The French in the Mississippi Valley, 1740–1750*. Urbana: U. Illinois, 1941.

Short monograph.

Carse, Robert. *The River Men*. New York: Scribner, 1969.

Popular account of the "exploits of the men who first voyaged the rivers of North America"; of limited value.

Chesnel, Paul. *History of Cavelier de la Salle, 1643–1687: Explorations in the Valleys of the Ohio, Illinois and Mississippi . . . .* Tr. A. C. Meany. New York: Putnam, 1932.

Controversial short life of LaSalle; French edition first published in 1901.

Cutright, Paul R. *Lewis and Clark: Pioneering Naturalists*. Urbana: U. Illinois, 1969.

Close examination of the scientific data contained within the Lewis and Clark narratives; excellent descriptions of the flora and fauna discovered on the trip.

Delanglez, Jean. *Life and Voyages of Louis Jolliet, 1645–1700*. Chicago: Institute of Jesuit History, 1948.

Condensation of ten articles appearing between 1944 and 1946. Most of the originals were published in *Mid-America*.

————. *. . . . Some LaSalle Journeys*. Chicago: Institute of Jesuit History, 1938.

————. *Hennepin's Description of Louisiana: A Critical Essay*. Chicago: Institute of Jesuit History, 1941.

Scholarly monograph on Fr. Hennepin's controversial book.

Donnelly, Joseph P. *Jacques Marquette, S.J., 1637–1675*. Chicago: Loyola U., 1968.

Strong, opinionated biography.

————. *Pierre Gibault, Missionary, 1737–1802*. Chicago: Loyola U., 1971.

Biography of the Mississippi Valley cleric.

————. *Thwaites' Jesuit Relations: Errata and Addenda*. Chicago: Loyola U., 1967.

Includes a bibliography which updates Thwaites's.

Eggleston, Edward. *The Transit of Civilization from England to America in the Seventeenth Century*. New York: Appleton, 1901.

Actually broke new ground by showing the need for studying the early cultural development of the American people.

Finley, John H. *The French in the Heart of America*. New York: Scribner, 1915.

Vividly impressionistic narrative history; includes a good deal on the later history of the original French settlements.

Gilbert, Edmund W. *The Exploration of Western America, 1800–1850: An Historical Geography*. Cambridge: Harvard U., 1933.

History, with geographical analysis.

Hamilton, Raphael N. *Marquette's Explorations: The Narratives Reexamined*. Madison: U. Wisconsin, 1970.

Examines the contemporary documentation dealing with Marquette's discovery of the Mississippi; sound and scholarly.

Hollon, W. Eugene. *The Lost Pathfinder: Zebulon Montgomery Pike*. Norman: U. Oklahoma, 1949.

The best book on Pike.

Isely, Bliss. *Blazing the Way West*. New York: Scribner, 1939.

Popular history on Midwest exploration.

Jackson, Donald, ed. *Letters of the Lewis and Clark Expedition, with Related Documents, 1783–1854*. Urbana: U. Illinois, 1962.

Kennedy, John H. *Jesuit and Savage in New France*. New Haven: Yale, 1950.

Scholarly; mainly concerned with Canadian missions.

Lyon, E. Wilson. *Louisiana in French Diplomacy, 1759–1804*. Norman: U. Oklahoma, 1934.

Although mainly concerned with European political maneuverings, this scholarly work clearly relates the crucial events which led up to the sale of Louisiana.

Mirsky, Jeannette. *The Westward Crossings: Balboa, Mackenzie, Lewis and Clark*. New York: Knopf, 1946.

Striking narratives, yet maintaining sound scholarship throughout.

Moore, Charles. *The Northwest Under Three Flags, 1635–1796*. New York: Harper, 1900.
Older narrative history which still reads decently. The "Three Flags" are, of course, those of France, Britain, and the United States.

Nute, Grace L. *Caesars of the Wilderness*. New York: Appleton, 1945.
On Radisson and Grosseilliers.

Parkman, Francis. *France and England in North America*. Boston: Little, Brown, 1865–1884. Seven parts.
For breadth of scope, scholarly thoroughness and stylistic vigor, Parkman is unequaled as a chronicler of the pre-frontier Midwest. The relevant sections of his seven-part series include *The Discovery of the Great West* (1869) and *The Jesuits in North America . . .* (1867). Another relevant historical work, *The History of the Conspiracy of Pontiac . . .* (1851), is not formally a part of the series.

Phillips, Paul C. *The Fur Trade*. 2 vols. Norman: U. Oklahoma, 1961.
Most comprehensive history of the North American fur trade.

Severin, Timothy. *Explorers of the Mississippi*. London: Routledge, 1967.
An entertaining popular account of the men who explored the great river, from the earliest French and Spanish expeditions to the nineteenth century.

Thwaites, Reuben G. *Father Marquette*. New York: Appleton, 1902.
Short but sound early biography.

———. *France in America, 1497–1763*. New York: Harper, 1905.
Exceptional pioneering study by the indefatigable editor of the *Jesuit Relations*.

Tomkins, Calvin. *The Lewis and Clark Trail*. New York: Harper, 1965.
Short, entertaining recreation of the expedition by means of background texts, photos, paintings, maps, and excerpts from the original narratives.

Vandiveer, Clarence A. *The Fur Trade and Early Western Exploration*. Cleveland: Clark, 1929.
Although hardly a model of scholarship, this is a decent popular narrative.

Volwiler, Albert T. *George Croghan and the Westward Movement 1741–1782*. Cleveland: Clark, 1926.
Examines the activities of the traders in the pre-frontier Midwest, especially the romantic Indian agent, trader, speculator, and adventurer of the early Ohio country.

4.   FRONTIER PERIOD (ca. 1800–60)

Abernethy, Thomas. *Western Lands and the American Revolution*. New York: Appleton-Century, 1937.
Deals primarily in the importance of land speculation in the exploration and settlement of the frontier.

———. *The Burr Conspiracy*. New York: Oxford, 1954.
Detailed account of Aaron Burr's fantastic attempt to create a new nation in the frontier Middle West.

Atherton, Lewis. *The Pioneer Merchant in Mid-America*. Columbia U.: Missouri, 1939.
Short monograph which examines the role of St. Louis area merchants on the frontier. Reissued in 1971 as *The Frontier Merchant in Mid-America* by the U. Missouri Press.

Baldwin, Leland D. *The Keelboat Age on Western Waters*. Pittsburgh: U. Pittsburgh, 1941.
Detailed study. Title refers to early "western waters," i.e., those navigated before 1800.

Barnhart, John D. *Valley of Democracy: The Frontier vs. the Plantation in the Ohio Valley, 1775–1818*. Bloomington: Indiana U., 1953.
Barnhart, a student and disciple of Frederick Jackson Turner, defends his mentor's "thesis" in terms of the development of the Ohio Valley.

Benson, Lee. *Turner and Beard: American Historical Writing Reconsidered*. New York: Free Press, 1965.
Analyzes the theses and impact of two seminal American historians.

Berwanger, Eugene H. *The Frontier Against Slavery: Western Anti-Negro Prejudice and the Slavery Extension Controversy*. Urbana: U. Illinois, 1967.
Scholarly examination of anti-black feeling on the pre-Civil War frontier, especially in the Old Northwest. The author finds that Negro prejudice and anti-slavery were far from mutually exclusive.

Beveridge, Albert J. *Abraham Lincoln, 1809–1858*. 2 vols. Boston: Houghton Mifflin, 1928.
Well researched and written, albeit uncompleted biography which carries Lincoln's life
down to 1858. The picture of Lincoln's frontier years in the Midwest is comparable in value
to the more imaginative treatment by Carl Sandburg.

Billington, Ray A. *Westward Expansion: A History of the American Frontier*. 4th ed. New
York: Macmillan, 1974.
Most detailed and thorough treatment of the frontier.

———. *The Westward Movement in the United States*. Princeton: Van Nostrand, 1959.
Brief survey.

———. *America's Frontier Heritage*. New York: Holt, 1966.
Brilliant examination of the application of the "frontier thesis" in a variety of social and
behavioral disciplines. Makes a strong case for the validity of Turner's thesis.

———. *The American Frontier*. New York: Macmillan, 1958.
Pamphlet; evaluation of the writings about Turner's "frontier thesis."

———, ed. *The Frontier Thesis: Valid Interpretation of American History?* New York: Holt,
1966.
Collection of seminal essays on the "thesis," pro and con. Includes a good introduction by
Billington.

Billington, Ray A. and Martin Ridge, eds. *America's Frontier Story: A Documentary History
of Westward Expansion*. New York: Holt, 1969.

Branch, E. Douglas. *The Hunting of the Buffalo*. New York: Appleton, 1929.
Imaginative, dramatic rendition of the systematic extermination of the buffalo, not only on
the western plains but in the Middle West and South as well.

———. *Westward, the Romance of the American Frontier*. New York: Appleton, 1930.
Strong narrative history by a long-ignored but vital historian.

Buley, Roscoe C. and Madge E. Pickard. *The Midwest Pioneer, His Ills, Cures, and Doctors*.
Crawfordsville, Ind.: Banta, 1945.
Popular account of frontier medical practices.

Burnette, O. Lawrence, Jr., comp. *Wisconsin Witness to Frederick Jackson Turner: A Collection of Essays on the Historian and the Thesis*. Madison: State Historical Society, 1961.

Clark, Thomas D. *Frontier America: The Story of the Westward Movement*. 2d ed. New York:
Scribner, 1969.
Textbook. Includes a chapter on "Frontier Arts and Sciences," and several chapters on the
Midwest frontier.

———. *Three American Frontiers: Writings of Thomas D. Clark*. Ed. Holman Hamilton.
Lexington: U. Kentucky, 1970.
Selections from the writings of an historian who wrote mostly on the South, but also a good
deal on the Midwest frontier.

Cleaves, Freeman. *Old Tippecanoe: William Henry Harrison and His Times*. New York:
Scribner, 1939.
A scholarly biography of the old Indian fighter and later President of the United States.

Dunbar, Seymour. *A History of Travel in America*. Indianapolis: Bobbs-Merrill, 1915.
The best work of its kind. Includes a great deal of detailed description of travel conditions
on the frontier.

Ellis, David et al., eds. *The Frontier in American Development: Essays in Honor of Paul
Wallace Gates*. Ithaca: Cornell U., 1969.
Mainly essays on the distribution of frontier land by the government.

Fernow, Berthold. *The Ohio Valley in Colonial Days*. Albany: Munsell's, 1890.
Valuable early volume in Munsell's Historical series; extended coverage of the French and
Indian War, 1755–63.

Fox, Dixon R., ed. *Sources of Culture in the Middle West: Backgrounds vs. Frontier*. New
York: Appleton, 1934.
An iconoclastic and "brilliant young Easterner" (Benjamin Wright) enters the list with the
three "Turnerians" (Avery Craven, John Hicks, and Marcus Hansen). The result is this
interesting collection of conflicting views on the development of Midwest cultural life.

Garraghan, Gilbert J. *Chapters in Frontier History: Research Studies in the Making of the
West*. Milwaukee: Bruce, 1934.
Emphasis on the history of Catholic Church activity in the Midwest.

Grinnell, George B. *Trails of the Pathfinder*. New York: Scribner, 1911.
Discusses travel narrative writers of the frontier.

Goodwin, Cardinal L. *The Trans-Mississippi West (1803–1853): A History of Its Acquisition and Settlement*. New York: Appleton, 1922.
Solid, scholarly work.

Graham, Philip. *Showboats: The History of an American Institution*. Austin: U. Texas, 1951.
Showboats plied the large rivers of the Midwest and South in the nineteenth century. A unique book dealing with a singular cultural phenomenon.

Hale, John P. *Trans-Allegheny Pioneers* . . . . 2d ed. Charleston, W. Va.: Kanawha, 1931. [1st ed., 1886.]
Valuable older history; a narrative of selected pioneer families, including the author's own.

Havighurst, Walter. *George Rogers Clark: Soldier in the West*. New York: McGraw-Hill, 1952.
Popular biography.

_____. *Wilderness for Sale: The Story of the First Western Land Rush*. New York: Hastings, 1956.
Readable account. Part of the American Procession series.

Hine, Robert V. and Edward R. Bingham, eds. *The Frontier Experience: Readings in the Trans-Mississippi West*. Belmont, Cal.: Wadsworth, 1963. Enl. ed. published as *The American Frontier: Readings and Documents*. Boston: Little, Brown, 1972.
Anthology. Includes excerpts from the writings of F. J. Turner, Josiah Gregg, and others.

Hofstadter, Richard and Seymour Lipset, eds. *Turner and the Sociology of the Frontier*. New York: Basic Books, 1968.
Collected essays.

Holbrook, Stewart H. *Holy Old Mackinaw: A Natural History of the American Lumberjack*. New York: Macmillan, 1938.
Zesty, informal history. Covers the north woods of the Midwest, as well as the nation from Maine to Washington.

_____. *The Yankee Exodus: An Account of Migration from New England*. New York: Macmillan, 1950.
Colorful stories of New Englanders on the frontier. Emphasizes the influence of Yankee character in the development of the West.

Hubbart, Henry C. *The Older Middle West, 1840–1880*. New York: Appleton, 1936.
History of the southern Midwest, i.e., those southern portions of Indiana, Illinois, and Ohio which make up "the region of the river valleys." Hubbart emphasizes the southern character of these areas and the struggle for political domination between North and South before the Civil War.

Hunter, Louis C. *Steamboats on the Western Rivers: An Economic and Technical History*. Cambridge: Harvard U., 1949.
Standard work on the subject.

Jacobs, Wilbur R. et al. *Turner, Bolton and Webb: Three Historians of the Western Frontier*. Seattle: U. Washington, 1965.
Lectures originally delivered at the 1963 meeting of the Western History Association.

James, James A. *The Life of George Rogers Clark*. Chicago: U. Chicago, 1928.
Not only an excellent study of Clark, but a fine history of the American Revolution in the Middle West.

Jones, Robert Huhn. *The Civil War in the Northwest: Nebraska, Wisconsin, Iowa, Minnesota, and the Dakotas*. Norman: U. Oklahoma, 1960.

Jordan, Philip D. *Frontier Law and Order: Ten Essays*. Lincoln: U. Nebraska, 1970.
Well-researched, entertaining essays full of information on frontier jails, riverboat gambling, etc.

_____. *National Road*. Indianapolis: Bobbs-Merrill, 1948.
Narrative history of the great Cumberland road which brought settlers to and through the Middle West.

Kennedy, Roger G. *Men on the Moving Frontier*. Palo Alto, Calif.: American West, 1969.
Provocative essays focusing on romantic, visionary figures of the frontier (men like Beltrami, Sibley, and Donnelly). Their practical, rather dull counterparts (Long, Ramsey, and Burnham among others) are treated with a bit less enthusiasm.

Kaser, David. *Joseph Charless: Printer in the Western Country*. Philadelphia: U. Pennsylvania, 1963.
Scholarly study of the important St. Louis printer emphasizes his importance in the development of the western book trade.
Keyes, Nelson B. *American Frontier: Our Unique Heritage*. New York: Garden City Books, 1954.
Popular general history with a Turnerian flavor.
Klement, Frank L. *The Copperheads in the Middle West*. Chicago: U. Chicago, 1960.
Argues against the traditional view that the Copperheads were subversive, anti-union, and pro-Southern.
Klose, Nelson. *Concise Study Guide to the American Frontier*. Lincoln: U. Nebraska, 1964.
Valuable introduction and handbook. The extensive bibliography is especially worthwhile.
Krout, John A. and Dixon R. Fox. *The Completion of Independence, 1790–1830*. New York: Macmillan, 1944.
Sound general history with attention to social life on the western frontier.
Lavender, David. *The Fist in the Wilderness*. New York: Doubleday, 1964.
Strong narrative history of the American fur trade. The main focus is on dynastic Astor's American Fur Company, which operated extensively in the northern Midwest.
Leyburn, James. *Frontier Folkways*. New Haven: Yale U., 1935.
Challenges Turner's "frontier thesis."
Ludewig, Herman E. *The Literature of American Local History: A Bibliographical Essay*. New York: Craighead, 1846.
Important early compilation.
McCaleb, Walter F. *The Aaron Burr Conspiracy*. Exp. ed. New York: Argosy-Antiquarian, 1966.
McDermott, John F., ed. *The Frontier Re-examined*. Urbana: U. Illinois, 1967.
Papers from a 1965 conference in which historians used Turner "as a springboard . . . to examine new aspects of the frontier which Turner did not consider in his original thesis."
———. *Travelers on the Western Frontier*. Urbana: U. Illinois, 1970.
Papers contributed to the Conference on Travelers on the Western Frontier. Includes material of literary interest.
McMurtrie, Douglas C. *Beginnings of Printing in the Middle West*. Chicago, 1930.
McMurtrie has written voluminously in this field. Among his other works are histories of early printing in Wisconsin, Minnesota, Nebraska, and Illinois. Most are of pamphlet length.
Miller, James M. *The Genesis of Western Culture: The Upper Ohio Valley, 1800–1825*. Columbus: Historical Society, 1938.
Scholarly.
Myers, John M. *Print in a Wild Land*. Garden City, N.Y.: Doubleday, 1967.
Reconstructs the lives of frontier printers, a hardy and romantic breed of men.
Nasatir, Abraham P., ed. *Before Lewis and Clark: Documents Illustrating the History of the Missouri, 1785–1804*. 2 vols. St. Louis: Historical Documents Foundation, 1952.
Scholarly editing by Nasatir, who includes a thorough introductory narrative.
Noble, David W. *Historians Against History* . . . . Minneapolis: U. Minnesota, 1965.
Examines the theoretical assumptions of six so-called "covenant" historians: Bancroft, Turner, Beard, Becker, Parrington, and Boorstin.
Paxson, Frederic L. *History of the American Frontier, 1763–1893*. Boston: Houghton Mifflin, 1924.
This elaboration of Turner's ideas is still considered a standard textbook.
———. *The Last American Frontier*. New York: Macmillan, 1911.
Deals with the trans-Mississippi West.
———. *When the West is Gone*. New York: Holt, 1930.
These Colver lectures, delivered at Brown in 1929, provide a concise summary of the various American frontiers. Paxson speculates on the effect of the frontier's closing on future American patterns of life.
Peattie, Donald C. *Singing in the Wilderness*. New York: Putnam, 1935.
Affectionate sketch of Audubon's life and travels through America.
———, ed. *Audubon's America*. Boston: Houghton Mifflin, 1940.

Beautifully illustrated selection of Audubon's narratives of the frontier.

Philbrick, Francis S. *The Rise of the West, 1754–1830*. New York: Harper, 1965.
Volume in the New American Nation series.

Phillips, Paul C. *The West in the Diplomacy of the American Revolution*. Urbana: U. Illinois, 1913.

Porter, Kenneth W. *John Jacob Astor, Business Man*. 2 vols. Cambridge: Harvard U., 1931.
Definitive biography of Astor, whose role in the development of the upper Midwest was crucial.

Power, Richard L. *Planning Corn Belt Cultures: The Impress of the Upland Southerner and Yankee in the Old Northwest*. Indianapolis: Indiana Historical Society, 1953.
Emphasizes the cultural conflict between North and South in the creation of the Midwest mind.

Richmond, Robert W. and Robert W. Mardock, eds. *Nation Moving West: Readings in the History of the American Frontier*. Lincoln: U. Nebraska, 1966.
Collection of readings covering a broad spectrum of frontier life.

Riegel, Robert E. *America Moves West*. 3d. ed. New York: Holt, 1956.
Brief history of the westward expansion from the Appalachians to the Pacific.

Roosevelt, Theodore. *The Winning of the West*. 4 vols. New York: Putnam, 1889–96.
Although dated, these volumes exude the vigor and style of the man. Deals with the drama of expansion up to 1807.

Spence, Clark C. *The American West: A Source Book*. New York: Crowell, 1966.
Anthology. Concerned more with the Far West than the Midwest.

Stern, Madeleine B. *Imprints on History: Book Publishers and American Frontiers*. Bloomington: Indiana U., 1956.
Detailed, readable history of nineteenth-century publishing in America.

Still, Bayrd. *The West: Contemporary Records of America's Expansion Across the Continent, 1607–1890*. New York: Capricorn, 1961.

Sutton, Walter. *The Western Book Trade: Cincinnati as a Nineteenth Century Publishing and Book-Trade Center*. Columbus: Ohio State U., 1961.

Taylor, George R., ed. *The Turner Thesis Concerning the Role of the Frontier in American History*. Rev. ed. Boston: Heath, 1956.
Collected essays which reflect differing views of the "thesis."

Thwaites, Reuben G., ed. *Early Western Travels, 1748–1846: A Series of Annotated Reprints*. 32 vols. Cleveland: Clark, 1904–07.
Includes writings by a number of Midwest frontier travelers, among whom are Brackenridge, Faux, Gregg, and Flagg. Vols. 31 and 32 are indexes.

Tunis, Edwin. *Frontier Living*. New York: World, 1961.
Nicely illustrated portrayal of the implements and customs of frontier life.

Turner, Frederick Jackson. *The Rise of the New West, 1819–1829*. New York: Harper, 1906.
In this and other works cited below Turner elaborates the famous "Turner thesis" which had been first articulated in a paper delivered to the American Historical Society convention in 1893. The paper was entitled "The Significance of the Frontier in American History," and has been reprinted several times.

_____. *The Frontier in American History*. New York: Holt, 1920.

_____. *The Significance of the Sections in American History*. New York: Holt, 1932.

_____. *The United States, 1830–1950: The Nation and its Sections*. New York: Holt, 1935.

_____. *Frontier and Section: Selected Essays*. Englewood Cliffs, N.J.: Prentice-Hall, 1961.
Includes an introduction by Billington.

_____. *America's Great Frontiers and Sections: Frederick Jackson Turner's Unpublished Essays*. Ed. William R. Jacobs. Lincoln: U. Nebraska, 1969.

Van Every, Dale. *Men of the Western Waters: A Second Look at the First Americans*. Boston: Houghton Mifflin, 1956.
Popular history of the Ohio Valley frontier.

_____. *A Company of Heroes: The American Frontier, 1775–1783*. New York: Morrow, 1962.
Popular continuation of the author's Forth to the Wilderness series, this volume deals with the Old Northwest. Other volumes in Van Every's series of frontier history include *The Ark of Empire: The American Frontier, 1784–1803* (1963), and *The Final Challenge: The American Frontier, 1804–1845* (1964).

Wade, Richard C. *The Urban Frontier: The Rise of Western Cities, 1790–1830*. Cambridge: Harvard U., 1959.
  Important ground-breaking study of American urban history.
Waggoner, Madeline S. *The Long Haul West: The Great Canal Era, 1817–1850*. New York: Putnam, 1958.
  Particularly strong on upper New York State. This scholarly work emphasizes the economic import of the canals and the culture they helped to create along their routes.
Winther, Oscar O. *The Transportation Frontier: Trans-Mississippi West*. New York: Holt, 1964.
  A study of western transportation "from the advent of overland freighting to the era of the automobile."
Wright, Louis B. *Culture on the Moving Frontier*. Bloomington: Indiana U., 1955.
  Includes a chapter on the Midwest.
––––––. *Everyday Life on the American Frontier*. New York: Putnam, 1968.
  Information on Midwest frontier living.
Wright, Richardson L. *Hawkers and Walkers in Early America*. Philadelphia: Lippincott, 1927.
  Especially valuable as a study of the rise and fall of the Yankee peddlar, a breed frequently seen on the Midwest frontier.
Wyman, Walker D. and C. B. Kroeber, eds. *The Frontier in Perspective*. Madison: U. Wisconsin, 1957.
  Collected essays dealing with the Turner "thesis" and other matters. Includes a section on "Classics on the Midwest Frontier."
Yoder, Paton. *Taverns and Travelers: Inns of the Early Midwest*. Bloomington: Indiana U., 1969.
  Well-researched and entertaining; deals with the period from 1800–50.

5. OLD NORTHWEST

Bond, Beverly W., Jr. *The Civilization of the Old Northwest . . . 1788–1812*. New York: Macmillan, 1934.
  Detailed, scholarly history of political, social, and economic development.
Boyd, Thomas. *Mad Anthony Wayne*. New York: Scribner, 1929.
  Well-researched biography of the frontier Indian fighter.
Buley, Roscoe C. *The Old Northwest Pioneer Period, 1815–1840*. 2 vols. Indianapolis: History Society, 1950.
  Pulitzer Prize winning history; vol. 2, ch. 15 is "Literature, Science, Reform."
Caruso, John A. *The Great Lakes Frontier: An Epic of the Old Northwest*. Indianapolis: Bobbs-Merrill, 1961.
  Great Lakes region history, 1673–1848; second of a projected six volume study of the American frontier.
Cole, Harry E. *Stage Coach and Tavern Tales of the Old Northwest*. Cleveland: Clark, 1930.
  An entertaining history of the Old Northwest road taverns and inns.
Gilpin, Alec R. *The War of 1812 in the Old Northwest*. East Lansing: Michigan State U., 1958.
  Detailed scholarly treatment which centers especially on effects of the war on Michigan Territory.
Havighurst, Walter. *Land of Promise: The Story of the Northwest Territory*. New York: Macmillan, 1946.
  Popular narrative history.
Hinsdale, Burke A. *The Old Northwest: With a View of the Thirteen Colonies as Constituted by the Royal Charters*. New York: MacCoun, 1888.
  Valuable early study.
Ogg, Frederic A. *The Old Northwest: A Chronicle of the Ohio Valley and Beyond*. New Haven: Yale, 1920.
  Narrative history in the Chronicles of America series. Treats mainly the half century between Pontiac's conspiracy and the War of 1812.
O'Meara, Walter. *The Last Portage*. Boston: Houghton Mifflin, 1962. Fast-paced, informative biography of John Tanner based on "The Narrative of the Captivity and Adventures of John Tanner" (1830). Depicts the Great Lakes region and the Old Northwest.

Scheiber, Harry N., ed. *The Old Northwest: Studies in Regional History, 1787–1910*. Lincoln: U. Nebraska, 1969.
Sixteen essays on the historical development of the region chosen to emphasize the importance of "community-building" on the frontier.

6. MISSISSIPPI VALLEY

Alvord, Clarence. *The Mississippi Valley in British Politics*. 2 vols. Cleveland: Clark, 1917.
Exhaustive scholarly work.

Blair, Walter A. *A Raft Pilot's Log: A History of the Great Rafting Industry on the Upper Mississippi, 1840–1915*. Cleveland: Clark, 1930.
Richly mined history by a veteran pilot.

Blegen, Theodore C. *The Land Lies Open*. Minneapolis: U. Minnesota, 1949.
Short but authoritative history of the people who explored and settled the Upper Mississippi Valley in Minnesota and Wisconsin.

Croy, Homer. *Corn Country*. New York: Duell, 1947.
Folksy history of the Corn Belt by the Midwest humorist; American Folkways series.

Gray, James. *Pine, Stream and Prairie: Wisconsin and Minnesota in Profile*. New York: Knopf, 1945.
Sensitive profile of these Upper Mississippi Valley states. Includes a strong chapter on the artistic life of the region.

Hartsough, Mildred L. *From Canoe to Steel Barge on the Upper Mississippi*. Minneapolis: U. Minnesota, 1934.
Anecdotal narrative history of navigation on the upper river.

Havighurst, Walter. *Upper Mississippi: A Wilderness Saga*. New York: Farrar, 1937.
Rivers of America series.

_____. *Voices on the River: The Story of the Mississippi Waterways*. New York: Macmillan, 1964.
Vintage Havighurst, i.e., popular history with emphasis on dramatic incident.

Holbrook, Stewart H. *Iron Brew: A Century of American Ore and Steel*. New York: Macmillan, 1939.
Popular account.

Keating, Ben. *The Mighty Mississippi*. Washington: National Geographic, 1971.

LeSueur, Meridel. *North Star Country*. New York: Duell, 1945.
Volume in the American Folkways series pays special attention to immigration and the life of ordinary people in Minnesota and Wisconsin. Written with a strong literary flavor.

McDermott, John F., ed. *The French in the Mississippi Valley*. Urbana: U. Illinois, 1965.
Essays on aspects of French civilization in the region.

_____. *Frenchmen and French Ways in the Mississippi Valley*. Urbana: U. Illinois, 1969.
Papers presented at the 1967 Conference of the French in the Mississippi Valley.

Milburn, William H. *The Lance, Cross, and Canoe, Flatboat, Rifle and Plow in the Valley of the Mississippi*. New York: Thompson, 1892.
This and the following title represent vigorous early history of the region by a pioneer preacher. Milburn's autobiography, *Ten Years of Preacher Life* (1859), is also of interest.

_____. *The Pioneers, Preachers, and People of the Mississippi Valley*. New York: Derby, 1860.

Petersen, William J. *Steamboating on the Upper Mississippi*. Iowa City: State Historical Society, 1937.
Thorough history.

Quick, Herbert. *Mississippi Steamboatin': A History of Steamboating on the Mississippi and Its Tributaries*. New York: Holt, 1926.
Novelist's lively recreation of a romantic era.

Saxon, Lyle. *Father Mississippi*. New York: Century, 1927.
Popular history of river exploration, settlement, and traffic by a native of Louisiana.

7. EASTERN PLAINS

Athearn, Robert G. *High Country Empire*. New York: McGraw-Hill, 1960.
History of a region which comprises the states of Montana, Wyoming, Colorado, Nebraska, Kansas, and North and South Dakota.

Chittenden, Hiram M. *History of Early Steamboat Navigation on the Missouri River: Life and Adventure of Joseph LaBarge*. 2 vols. New York: Harper, 1903.
Exceptionally well-written and well-researched early study woven around the reminiscences of LaBarge, a pioneer river pilot.

Crabb, Richard. *Empire on the Platte*. New York: World, 1967.
History of the Platte Valley of Nebraska from the Civil War to the 1880s.

DeVoto, Bernard. *Across the Wide Missouri*. Boston: Houghton Mifflin, 1947.
Middle volume of DeVoto's trilogy of western history (the other two are *The Year of Decision: 1846* (1943) and *The Course of Empire* (1952)). All are solid narrative history.

Dick, Everett N. *The Sod House Frontier, 1854–1890: A Social History of the Northern Plains . . . .* New York: Appleton, 1937.
Engaging chronicle of the common man which emphasizes the development of frontier society on the Plains.

———. *Vanguards of the Frontier: A Social History of the Northern Plains and Rocky Mountains . . . .* New York: Appleton, 1941.
Companion to *The Sod House Frontier*.

Hafen, Leroy R. and Carl C. Rister. *Western America: The Exploration, Settlement and Development of the Region Beyond the Mississippi*. 2d ed. Englewood Cliffs, N.J.: Prentice-Hall, 1950.
Textbook.

Hooker, William F. *The Prairie Schooner*. Chicago: Saul, 1918.
Portrait of pioneer life in the West.

Jones, Evan. *The Plains States: Iowa, Kansas, Minnesota, Missouri, Nebraska, North Dakota and South Dakota*. New York: Time-Life, 1968.
Short survey; nicely illustrated.

Lass, William E. *A History of Steamboating on the Upper Missouri*. Lincoln: U. Nebraska, 1962.
Steamboats and life on the Missouri River between Sioux City and Ft. Benton, Mont., in the nineteenth century.

Milburn, George. *Black Jack Country*. New York: Duell, 1943.
Outlawry in parts of Kansas, Missouri, Arkansas, and Texas in the nineteenth century.

Monaghan, James (Jay). *Civil War on the Western Border, 1854–1865*. Boston: Little, Brown, 1955.
Deals with Kansas and Nebraska.

Paden, Irene D. *The Wake of the Prairie Schooner*. New York: Macmillan, 1943.
History of the western overland trails.

Sandoz, Mari. *The Buffalo Hunters: The Story of the Hide Men*. New York: Hastings, 1954.
Strong narrative in the American Procession series.

Steckmesser, Kent L. *The Western Hero in History and Legend*. Norman: U. Oklahoma, 1965.
Treats several figures who are associated with the Middle West as well as the West. Among them are Kit Carson, Billy the Kid, and Wild Bill Hickock.

Streeter, Floyd B. *The Kaw*. New York: Farrar, 1941.
Rivers of America series. Includes a short section on Kansas literature.

Vestal, Stanley, pseud. [Walter S. Campbell]. *The Missouri*. New York: Farrar, 1945.
Rivers of America series.

Webb, Walter Prescott. *The Great Plains*. Boston: Ginn, 1931.
Deals primarily with the Plains west of the 100th meridian; includes a chapter on literature of the Plains.

8.   GREAT LAKES

Barcus, Frank. *Freshwater Fury: Yarns and Reminiscences of the Greatest Storm in Inland Navigation*. Detroit: Wayne, 1960.
On the "Great Storm" of 1913; factual accounts of survivors assimilated into the narrative.

Beasley, Norman. *Freighters of Fortune: The Story of the Great Lakes*. New York: Harper, 1930.
Popular narrative history of the development of commerce on the lakes.

Bowen, Dana T. *Lore of the Lakes: Told in Story and Picture*. Daytona Beach, Fla.: Author, 1940.

This and the following two titles are anecdotal popular histories.

_____. *Memories of the Lakes: Told in Story and Picture*. Daytona Beach, Fla.: Author, 1946.

_____. *Shipwrecks of the Lakes: Told in Story and Picture*. Daytona Beach, Fla.: Author, 1952.

Boyer, Dwight. *Great Stories of the Great Lakes*. New York: Dodd, Mead, 1966.

This and the following two books are historical narrative in the popular manner.

_____. *Ghost Ships of the Great Lakes*. New York: Dodd, Mead, 1968.

_____. *True Tales of the Great Lakes*. New York: Dodd, Mead, 1971.

Channing, Edward and Marion F. Lansing. *The Story of the Great Lakes*. New York: Macmillan, 1910.

Though a bit dated, still a readable short history.

Curwood, James O. *The Great Lakes: The Vessels that Plough Them*. New York: Putnam, 1909.

Entertaining historical survey.

Cuthbertson, George A. *Freshwater: A History and Narrative of the Great Lakes*. Toronto: Macmillan, 1931.

A Canadian emphasis; popular, well-illustrated history of the Great Lakes ships.

Ellis, William D. *Land of the Inland Seas*. Palo Alto: American West, 1974.

Coffee table book, but a fine example of the type.

Hatcher, Harlan. *The Great Lakes*. New York: Oxford, 1944.

Narrative history in one volume; good popular reading.

_____. *Lake Erie*. Indianapolis: Bobbs-Merrill, 1945.

American Lakes series.

Hatcher, Harlan and Erich A. Walter. *A Pictorial History of the Great Lakes*. New York: Crown, 1963.

Havighurst, Walter. *The Long Ships Passing: The Story of the Great Lakes*. New York: Macmillan, 1942.

Includes fine illustrations by John O'Hara Cosgrave II.

Karlen, Arno, ed. *Superior: Portrait of a Living Lake*. New York: Harper, 1970.

Beautiful photography by Charles Steinhacker with a text drawn by Karlen from regional narratives, 1650–1880.

Landon, Fred. *Lake Huron*. Indianapolis: Bobbs-Merrill, 1944.

American Lakes series.

Malkus, Alida. *Blue-Water Boundary: Epic Highway of the Great Lakes and the St. Lawrence River*. New York: Hastings, 1960.

Lively history of the waterways from the French explorers to the Seaway.

Mansfield, John B., ed. *History of the Great Lakes* . . . . 2 vols. Chicago: Beers, 1899.

Important early history.

McKee, Russell. *Great Lakes Country*. New York: Crowell, 1966.

Short popular treatment.

Nute, Grace L. *Lake Superior*. Indianapolis: Bobbs-Merrill, 1944.

American Lakes series.

Plumb, Ralph G. *Lake Michigan*. Manitowoc, Wisc.: Brandt, 1941.

The author also produced an early short *History of the Navigation of the Great Lakes* (1911).

Pound, Arthur. *Lake Ontario*. Indianapolis: Bobbs-Merrill, 1945.

American Lakes series.

Quaife, Milo M. *Lake Michigan*. Indianapolis: Bobbs-Merrill, 1944.

American Lakes series. Quaife served as general editor for the series in ten volumes (five of which deal with the Great Lakes).

Waldron, Webb. *We Explore the Great Lakes*. New York: Century, 1923.

Basically a personal narrative of a trip between Buffalo and Duluth; contains a certain amount of history and lore.

9. STATES

A. ILLINOIS

Angle, Paul M. and Richard L. Beyer. *A Handbook of Illinois History*. Springfield: Historical Society, 1943.

Somewhat dated, but still a valuable introduction to the subject.

Boewe, Charles. *Prairie Albion: An English Settlement in Pioneer Illinois*. Carbondale: Southern Illinois U., 1962.

Scholarly study of the Birkbecks in Illinois.

Bonnell, Clarence. *The Illinois Ozarks*. Harrisburg, Ill.: Register, 1946.

Guide to the Southern Illinois region.

Calkins, Earnest E. *They Broke the Prairie* . . . . New York: Scribner, 1937.

A strong effort at local history features Galesburg, Ill., and Knox College.

Centennial History of Illinois. 6 vols. Springfield: Publications of the Centennial Commission, 1917–20. Ed. in chief, Clarence W. Alvord.

This was the first of the multi-volume, scholarly state histories. Produced by eminent scholars, it became a model for later productions in other states. The six volumes, all good, are dated but remain the most complete history of Illinois: Alvord, Clarence W. *The Illinois Country, 1818–1848* (1918). Vol. 1; Pease, Theodore C. *The Frontier State, 1818–1848* (1918). Vol. 2; Cole, Arthur C. *The Era of the Civil War, 1848–1870* (1919). Vol. 3; Bogart, Ernest L. and Charles M. Thompson. *The Industrial State, 1870–1893* (1920). Vol. 4; Bogart, Ernest L. and John M. Mathews. *The Modern Commonwealth, 1893–1913* (1920). Vol. 5. An introductory volume, *Illinois in 1818* (1917) by Solon J. Buck, was published in a second revised edition by the University of Illinois Press in 1967.

Drury, John. *Old Illinois Houses*. Springfield: State Historical Society, 1941.

Of more historical than architectural interest.

Gray, James. *The Illinois*. New York: Farrar, 1940.

Rivers of America series.

Howard, Robert P. *Illinois: A History of the Prairie State*. Grand Rapids: Eerdmans, 1972.

Masters, Edgar Lee. *The Sangamon*. New York: Farrar, 1942.

Rivers of America series.

Monaghan, James (Jay). *This is Illinois: A Pictorial History*. Chicago: U. of Chicago, 1949.

A 50th anniversary publication of the Illinois State Historical Society.

Morrison, Olin D. *Illinois "Prairie State": A History, Social, Political, Economic*. 3 vols. Athens, Ohio: Morrison, 1960–64.

Typescript published by the author.

Nevins, Allan. *Illinois*. New York: Oxford, 1917.

In American College and University series.

Pease, Theodore C. and Marguerite J. *George Rogers Clark and Revolution in Illinois, 1763–1787*. Springfield: State Historical Library, 1929.

Brief treatment.

————. *The Story of Illinois*. 3d ed. Chicago: U. Chicago, 1965.

Best one-volume history of the state. First two editions completed by Theodore alone (1925; 1949) and the third revised by Marguerite.

Solberg, Winton U. *The University of Illinois, 1867–1894: An Intellectual and Cultural History*. Urbana: U. Illinois, 1968.

Sutton, Robert. *Illinois Reader*. 2 vols. Grand Rapids: Eerdmans, 1976.

————. *The Prairie State: A Documentary History of Illinois*. 2 vols. Grand Rapids: Eerdmans, 1976.

Thomson, Gladys S. *A Pioneer Family: The Birkbecks in Illinois, 1818–1827*. London: Cape, 1953.

Short, well-written monograph which recounts the adventures of the Birkbeck family from their days in Surrey to the trying years on the frontier.

Sutton, Robert M. *History of Illinois in Paintings*. Urbana: U. Illinois, 1968.

Text by Sutton; illustrations by Robert Thom, George Parrish, Jr., and Douglas Parrish.

Walton, Clyde C., ed. *An Illinois Reader*. DeKalb, Ill.: Northern Illinois U., 1970.

Anthology of essays on Illinois history, including pieces by Allan Nevins, Jane Addams, Ray Billington, and others.

Whitney, Ellen M., ed. *The Black Hawk War, 1831–1832*. Springfield: State Historical Society, 1970.

Selections from manuscripts in the Illinois State Historical Library.

WPA Federal Writers' Project. *Illinois: A Descriptive and Historical Guide*. Ed. Harry Hansen. New rev. ed. New York: Hastings, 1974.

Sound introduction to the state.

B. INDIANA

Barnhart, John D. and Donald F. Carmony. *Indiana, from Frontier to Industrial Commonwealth.* 4 vols. New York: Lewis, 1954.
Outstanding. Vols. 3 and 4 are personal and family history. Literature: vol. 2, ch. 28.
Bowman, Heath. *Hoosier.* Indianapolis: Bobbs-Merrill, 1944.
Popular history of the state, illustrated by the author.
Clark, Thomas. *Indiana University: Midwest Pioneer.* 3 vols. Bloomington: Indiana U., 1977.
Dunn, Jacob P. *Greater Indianapolis: The History, the Industries, the Institutions, and the People of a City of Homes.* 2 vols. Chicago: Lewis, 1910.
Still the best history of the city.
Esarey, Logan. *A History of Indiana.* 2 vols. 3d. ed. Fort Wayne: Hoosier Press, 1924.
An older but still valuable history, both scholarly and affectionate, by a native. Includes a chapter on "Literature of the Century."
————. *The Indiana Home.* 2d ed. Bloomington: Indiana U., 1953.
Essays on pioneer life in the state.
History of Indiana. 5 vols. Indianapolis: Indiana Historical Bureau and Indiana Historical Society.
When this cooperative project is completed, Indiana should have a definitive state history. Volumes already published are: Barnhart, John D. and Dorothy Riker. *Indiana to 1816* (1971). Vol. 1; Thornbrough, Emma Lou. *Indiana in the Civil War, 1850–1880* (1965). Vol. 3; Phillips, Clifton J. *Indiana in Transition, 1880–1920* (1968). Vol. 4.
Leary, Edward A. *Indianapolis, Story of a City.* Indianapolis: Bobbs-Merrill, 1971.
A good recent one-volume history.
Leibowitz, Irving. *My Indiana.* Englewood Cliffs, N.J.: Prentice-Hall, 1964.
Fast-moving essays on varieties of life in the adopted state of the Indianapolis *Times* columnist.
Martin, John B. *Indiana: An Interpretation.* New York: Knopf, 1947.
Journalist Martin, through interviews and research, creates a lively picture of "the Hoosier character, the Hoosier thought, the Hoosier way of living." Includes a chapter on Indiana literature.
Nolan, Jeannette C. *Hoosier City: The Story of Indianapolis.* New York: Messner, 1943.
Popular history in the Cities of America Biography series.
Thornbrough, Gayle and Dorothy Riker, comps. *Readings in Indiana History.* Indianapolis: Indiana Historical Bureau, 1956.
Anthology of both scholarly and primary sources; based on an earlier (1914) edition.
Troyer, Byron. *Yesterday's Indiana.* Miami: Seemann, 1975.
Largely pictorial.
Wilson, William E. *Indiana: A History.* Bloomington: Indiana U., 1966.
Informal; includes a chapter on literature.
————. *The Wabash.* New York: Farrar 1940.
Rivers of America series; includes a chapter on literature.
WPA Federal Writers' Project. *Indiana: A Guide to the Hoosier State.* New York: Oxford, 1941.
Good survey of state history and cultural life.

C. IOWA

Christensen, Thomas P., ed. *Sagas of the Hawkeyes: Being Stories and Incidents of Early Iowa.* Iowa City: Mercer, 1945.
Material taken from local histories, biographies, and old periodicals.
Cole, Cyrenus. *Iowa Through the Years.* Iowa City: State Historical Society, 1940.
Popular history.
————. *A History of the People of Iowa.* Cedar Rapids: Torch Press, 1921.
Best history of Iowa to date, but not definitive.
Hake, Herbert V. *Iowa Inside Out.* Ames: Iowa State U., 1968.
Houlette, William. *Iowa, the Pioneer Heritage.* Des Moines: Wallace-Homestead, 1970.
Popular history.
Mills, George S. *Rogues and Heroes from Iowa's Amazing Past.* Ames: Iowa State U., 1972.

Iowa history told through the biographical sketches of famous and infamous Iowans; popular style.

Petersen, William J. *The Story of Iowa*. New York: Lewis, 1952. 4 vols.
Last two volumes are biographical.

──────. *Iowa History Reference Guide*. Iowa City: U. Iowa, 1952.

Sage, Leland. *A History of Iowa*. Ames: Iowa State U., 1974.
Primarily a political history.

Schweider, Dorothy, comp. *Patterns and Perspectives on Iowa History*. Ames: Iowa State U., 1973.

Stong, Phil. *Hawkeyes: A Biography of the State of Iowa*. New York: Dodd, Mead, 1940.
Colorful "biography" by a novelist and native son; includes a section on Iowa letters.

WPA Federal Writers' Project. *Iowa: A Guide to the Hawkeye State*. New York: Viking, 1938.
Sound entry in the American Guide series.

D. KANSAS

Abels, Jules. *Man on Fire: John Brown and the Cause of Liberty*. New York: Macmillan, 1971.
Detailed biography.

Andreas, Alfred T. *History of the State of Kansas . . . .* Chicago, 1883.
Solid early history.

Bracke, William B. *Wheat Country*. New York: Duell, 1950.
History of the state in American Folkways series.

Bright, John D. et al., eds. *Kansas: The First Century*. 4 vols. New York: Lewis, 1956.
Closest thing to a definitive history; Elizabeth D. Van Schaack contributed a section on "The Arts in Kansas."

Cochran, Mary E. *A Bibliography of Kansas History, Biography, and Fiction*. Pittsburg, Kans.: Pittcraft, 1965.
Pamphlet.

Connelley, William E. *A Standard History of Kansas and Kansans*. 5 vols. Chicago: Lewis, 1918.

Davis, Clyde B. *The Arkansas*. New York: Farrar, 1940. Rivers of America series.

Davis, Kenneth S. *River on the Rampage*. New York: Doubleday, 1953.
Well-written review of water control problems in the Missouri Valley; centers on Kansas River flood of 1950; Davis is also a novelist (*Morning in Kansas*) and editor (*Kansas Magazine*).

──────. *Kansas*. New York: Norton, 1976.
Volume in the State and Nation series.

Griffin, Clifford. *The University of Kansas: A History*. Lawrence: U. Kansas, 1974.

Howes, Charles C. *This Place Called Kansas*. Norman: U. Oklahoma, 1952.
This story of the "events and people who made Kansas great" is a pleasant blend of provincial Americana.

Ise, John, ed. *Sod-House Days: Letters from a Kansas Homesteader, 1877–78*. New York: Columbia U., 1937.
Letters written by Howard Ruede. Ise also wrote *Sod and Stubble: The Story of a Kansas Homestead* (1936).

Langsdorf, Edgar et al. *Kansas: A Pictorial History*. Topeka: Kansas Centennial Commission, 1961.

Malin, James C. *John Brown and the Legend of Fifty-Six*. Philadelphia: American Philosophical Society, 1942.
Exhaustive scholarly examination of the political climate in Kansas during the 1850s, of the Brown legend, and of the Potawatomie massacre of 1856.

Nichols, Alice. *Bleeding Kansas*. New York: Oxford, 1954.
Covers the turbulent years before the Civil War with an admittedly pro-Southern bias. For an earlier, pro-Northern "history" of that time, see Leverett W. Spring's *Kansas: The Prelude to the War for the Union* (1907).

Rich, Everitt, ed. *The Heritage of Kansas: Selected Commentaries on Past Times*. Lawrence: U. Kansas, 1960.
Anthology presents a panorama of Kansas life up to 1900.

Socolofsky, Homer E. and Huber Self. *Historical Atlas of Kansas*. Norman: U. Oklahoma, 1972.

Streeter, Floyd B. *The Kaw*. New York: Farrar, 1941.
Rivers of America series; short section on Kansas literature.

Vestal, Stanley, pseud. [Walter S. Campbell]. *Short Grass Country*. New York: Duell, 1941.
American Folkways series. Includes some material on eastern Kansas.

Whittemore, Margaret. *Historic Kansas: A Centenary Sketchbook*. Lawrence: U. Kansas, 1954.

WPA Federal Writers' Project. *Kansas: A Guide to the Sunflower State*. New York: Viking, 1939.
Good coverage of history and cultural life.

Zornow, William F. *Kansas: A History of the Jayhawk State*. Norman: U. Oklahoma, 1957.
One-volume general history; a perfunctory chapter on the arts, "Culture with Agriculture."

E. MICHIGAN

Angelo, Frank. *Yesterday's Detroit*. Miami: Seemann, 1974.
Largely pictorial. Popular account in the Historic Cities series.

Bald, F. Clever. *Michigan in Four Centuries*. Rev. ed. New York: Harper, 1961.
Decent, but not definitive one-volume history prepared under the auspices of the Michigan Historical Commission.

Beasley, Norman and George W. Stark. *Made in Detroit*. New York: Putnam, 1957.
Nostalgic account of Detroit industry from 1900–30 by two Detroit journalists.

Bullock, Penelope L. *Michigan Bibliographies and Indexes*. Ypsilanti: Eastern Michigan U., 1960.
Pamphlet.

Catton, Bruce. *Michigan's Past and the Nation's Future*. Detroit: Wayne State U., 1960.
Published in the Lewis Cass Lecture series; Catton, the Civil War historian, is a native of the state.

Dunbar, Willis F. *Michigan: A History of the Wolverine State*. 2d ed. Grand Rapids: Eerdmans, 1970.
Another sound one-volume history; chapter on "The Enrichment of Cultural Life" deals with literature and related arts.

Fuller, George N., ed. *Michigan: A Centennial History of the State and Its People*. 5 vols. Chicago: Lewis, 1939.
A valuable older history. Vol. 2, ch. 70 on Michigan literature.

Gilpin, Alec R. *The Territory of Michigan (1805–1837)*. East Lansing: Michigan State U., 1970.

Glazer, Sidney. *Detroit: A Study of Urban Development*. New York: Bookmans, 1965.

Glazer, Sidney and Milo M. Quaife. *Michigan: From Primitive Wilderness to Industrial Commonwealth*. New York: Prentice-Hall, 1948.
Good one-volume history in the Prentice-Hall series.

Havighurst, Walter. *Three Flags at the Straits: The Forts of Mackinac*. Englewood Cliffs, N.J.: Prentice-Hall, 1966.
Popular volume in the American Forts series.

Lochbiler, Don. *Detroit's Coming of Age, 1873–1973*. Detroit: Wayne, 1974.

Martin, John B. *Call it North Country: The Story of Upper Michigan*. New York: Knopf, 1944.
Folk history of the Peninsula country.

Olson, David. *Life on the Upper Michigan Frontier*. Boston: Branden, 1974.

Pound, Arthur. *Detroit: Dynamic City*. New York: Appleton, 1940.
Popular narrative by a veteran journalist.

Quaife, Milo M. *This is Detroit, 1701–1951*. Detroit: Wayne, 1951.
Pictorial history.

Quaife, Milo M. and Joseph and Estelle Bayliss. *River of Destiny: The St. Marys*. Detroit: Wayne, 1955.
Quaife writes Part I, a history of this northern Michigan river, and the Baylisses, local residents, write Part II, on "Local History with Recollections of Persons, Places and Events."

Sagendorph, Kent. *Michigan: The Story of the University*. New York: Dutton, 1948.
Streeter, Floyd B. *Michigan Bibliography . . . to July 1, 1917*. 2 vols. Lansing: Historical
Commission, 1921.
Utley, Henry M. and Byron M. Cutcheon. *Michigan as a Province, Territory and State*. 4 Vols.
New York: Publishing Society of Michigan, 1906.
Good older history.
WPA Federal Writers' Project. *Michigan: A Guide to the Wolverine State*. New York: Oxford,
1941.
Solid introduction to the state's history, culture, geography, etc.

F. MINNESOTA

Bjornson, Valdimar. *The History of Minnesota*. 4 vols. West Palm Beach, Fla.: Lewis, 1969.
Last two volumes are biographical sketches and institutional histories.
Blegen, Theodore C. *Grass Roots History*. Minneapolis: U. Minnesota, 1947.
Local history writing at its best; Blegen uses letters, diaries, songs, and ballads of the folk to
illuminate their history.
―――. *The Kensington Rune Stone: New Light on an Old Riddle*. St. Paul: Historical Soci-
ety, 1968.
Includes a bibliography on the subject by Michael Brook.
―――. *Minnesota: A History of the State*. Minneapolis: U. Minnesota, 1963.
Good one-volume history which includes much information on cultural life in the state.
Blegen, Theodore C. and Philip D. Jordan, eds. *With Various Voices: Recordings of North
Star Life*. St. Paul: Itasca, 1949.
An attempt to "relate the history of the North Star State in the words of those who actually
took part in the making of that history."
Blegen, Theodore C. and Theodore L. Nydahl. *Minnesota History: A Guide to Reading and
Study*. Minneapolis: U. Minnesota, 1960.
A revision of *Minnesota: Its History and People* (1937).
Brings, Lawrence M. *Minnesota Heritage*. Minneapolis: Denison, 1960.
Popular survey. Includes discussion of theatre and literature.
Brink, Carol R. *The Twin Cities*. New York: Macmillan, 1961.
Popular introduction to the area.
Brooks, Michael, comp. *Reference Guide to Minnesota: A Subject Bibliography of Books,
Pamphlets, and Articles in English*. St. Paul: Historical Society, 1974.
Excellent and useful compilation.
Castle, Henry A. *History of St. Paul and Vicinity . . . .* 3 vols. Chicago: Lewis, 1912.
About half devoted to biographical sketches.
Castle. Henry A. *Minnesota: Its Story and Biography*. 3 vols. Chicago: Lewis, 1915.
Vᴏ   2 and 3 are biographical; good early history.
Crouse, Nellis M. *La Vérendrye: Fur Trader and Explorer*. Ithaca: Cornell U., 1956.
Details the life of the explorer in New France.
DeKruif, Paul. *Seven Iron Men*. New York: Harcourt, 1934.
On the Merritt family and development of iron mining in the northern part of the state.
Drache, Hiram M. *The Challenge of the Prairie: Life and Times of the Red River Pioneers*.
Fargo: North Dakota Institute for Regional Studies, 1970.
Most detailed study of the Red River Valley frontier.
Dunn, James T. *The St. Croix: Midwest Border River*. New York: Holt, 1965.
Rivers of America series.
Flandrau, Charles E. *The History of Minnesota and Tales of the Frontier*. St. Paul: Porter,
1900.
Well-written early narrative history.
Folwell, William W. *A History of Minnesota*. 4 vols. St. Paul: Historical Society, 1921–30.
Thorough, scholarly history begun by Folwell at the age of 74 and completed before his
death at 96. The best history of the state to date. Vol. 1 of a new edition was issued in 1946.
Gilman, Rhoda R. and Hune D. Holmquist, eds. *Selections from "Minnesota History": A
Fiftieth Anniversary Anthology*. St. Paul: Historical Society, 1965.
Twenty-six outstanding articles.

Gray, James. *The University of Minnesota, 1851–1951*. Minneapolis: U. Minnesota, 1951.
Detailed history.
———. *Open Wide the Door: The Story of the University of Minnesota*. Minneapolis: U. Minnesota, 1958.
Hansen, Marcus L. *Old Fort Snelling, 1819–1858*. Iowa City: State Historical Society, 1917.
History of the pioneer fort at the junction of the Mississippi and Minnesota Rivers.
Heilbron, Bertha L. *The Thirty-Second State: A Pictorial History of Minnesota*. 2d ed. St. Paul: Historical Society, 1966.
———, ed. *With Pen and Pencil on the Frontier in 1851: The Diary and Sketches of Frank Blackwell Mayer*. St. Paul: Historical Society, 1932.
Mayer was a young Baltimore artist. Nearly 50 sketches are included.
Jones, Evan. *The Minnesota: Forgotten River*. New York: Holt, 1962.
Rivers of America series.
———. *Citadel in the Wilderness*. New York: Coward-McCann, 1966.
Popular history of Fort Snelling and the Old Northwest frontier.
Kavanagh, Martin. *La Vérendrye: His Life and Times . . . a Biography and a Social Study of a Folklore Figure, Soldier, Fur Trader, Explorer*. Brandon, Man.: Author, 1967.
Larsen, Erling. *Minnesota Trails: A Sentimental History*. Minneapolis: Denison, 1958.
Mitau, G. Theodore. *Politics in Minnesota*. 2d rev. ed. Minneapolis: U. Minnesota, 1970.
Handbook.
Nute, Grace L. *The Voyageur*. St. Paul: Historical Society, 1931.
Authoritative account of the French-Canadian voyageurs who engaged in the fur trade.
———. *The Voyageur's Highway: Minnesota's Border Lake Land*. St. Paul: Historical Society, 1941.
History of the Superior-Quetico canoe country and adjoining areas.
———. *Rainy River Country: A Brief History of the Region Bordering Minnesota and Ontario*. St. Paul: Historical Society, 1950.
Pritchett, John P. *The Red River Valley, 1811–1849: A Regional Study*. New Haven: Yale U., 1942.
Scholarly and detailed.
Shutter, Marion D., ed. *History of Minneapolis*. 3 vols. Chicago: Clarke, 1923.
Vols. 2 and 3 are biographical sketches.
Wahlgren, Erik. *The Kensington Stone: A Mystery Solved*. Madison: U. Wisconsin, 1958.
Persuasive attack on the genuineness of the Stone; scholarly.
Walker, Charles R. *American City: A Rank-and-File History*. New York: Farrar, 1937.
On Minneapolis.
WPA Federal Writers' Project. *Minnesota: A State Guide*. Rev. ed. New York: Hastings, 1954.
Good introduction to the state.

G. Missouri

Brown, A. Theodore. *Frontier Community: Kansas City to 1870*. Columbia: U. Missouri, 1963.
Sound and recent, but limited to the early years.
Garwood, Darrell. *Crossroads of America: The Story of Kansas City*. New York: Norton, 1948.
Short narrative history in the popular style.
Gill, McCune. *The St. Louis Story*. 3 vols. Hopkinsville, Ky.: Historical Record Assn., 1952.
Popular volume combines history and biographical sketches; tends toward boosterism.
Kirschten, Ernest. *Catfish and Crystal*. New York: Doubleday, 1960.
Informal history of St. Louis by a journalist of that city.
McCurdy, Frances L. *Stump, Bar, and Pulpit: Speechmaking on the Missouri Frontier*. Columbia: U. Missouri, 1969.
Stresses the element of "frontier rhetoric" in Missouri public address of the mid-nineteenth century.
McReynolds, Edwin C. *Missouri: A History of the Crossroads State*. Norman: U. Oklahoma, 1962.
Strong one-volume history.
March, David. *History of Missouri*. 4 vols. New York: Lewis, 1967.
Most recent history of the state; last two volumes are biographical.

Meyer, Duane. *Heritage of Missouri: A History*. Rev. ed. St. Louis: State Publishing, 1970.
Short history used in schools and colleges.

Sesquicentennial History of Missouri. 5 vols. Gen. ed., William E. Parrish. Columbia: U.
Missouri, 1971–
This project, when completed, should provide a definitive history of the state. Volumes
already published: Foley, William. *A History of Missouri, Vol. I: 1673–1820* (1971);
McCandless, Perry. *A History of Missouri, Vol. II: 1820–1860* (1972); Parrish, William E. *A
History of Missouri, Vol. III: 1860–1875* (1973).

Settle, William A., Jr. *Jesse James was His Name: Or Fact and Fiction Concerning the Careers
of the Notorious James Brothers of Missouri*. Columbia: U. Missouri, 1966.
Most scholarly of the many books devoted to the James legend.

Shoemaker, Floyd C. *Missouri and Missourians*. 5 vols. Chicago: Lewis, 1943.
Valuable older work, last three volumes are biographical.

Stephens, Frank F. *A History of the University of Missouri*. Columbia: U. Missouri, 1962.

Vestal, Stanley, pseud. [Walter S. Campbell]. *The Missouri*. New York: Farrar, 1945.
Rivers of America series.

Violette, Eugene M. *A History of Missouri*. Boston: Heath, 1920.
Excellent older history.

WPA Federal Writers' Project. *Missouri: A Guide to the "Show Me" State*. New York: Duell,
1941.
Guide to history, culture, and travel in the state.

H. NEBRASKA

Manley, Robert N. *Centennial History of the University of Nebraska. Vol. I: Frontier University, 1868–1919*. Lincoln: U. Nebraska, 1969.

Morton, J. Sterling and Albert Watkins. *Illustrated History of Nebraska*. 3 vols. Lincoln:
North, 1905–13.
Old but useful political history.

Olson, James C. *History of Nebraska*. Rev. and enl. ed. Lincoln: U. Nebraska, 1966.
Best state history to this time, but hardly definitive; one-volume study for the general reader.

Sawyer, R. McLaren. *Centennial History of the University of Nebraska*. Lincoln: U. Nebraska, 1974.

Sheldon, Addison E. *Nebraska: The Land and the People*. Chicago: Lewis, 1931.
Covers the settlement and populist periods well.

WPA Federal Writers' Project. *Nebraska: A Guide to the Cornhusker State*. New York: Viking,
1939.
Typically informative WPA guidebook.

I. NORTH DAKOTA

Crawford, Lewis F. *History of North Dakota*. 3 vols. Chicago: American Historical Society,
1931.
Good older history; last two volumes are biographical.

Drache, Hiram M. *The Challenge of the Prairie: Life and Times of the Red River Pioneers*.
Fargo: North Dakota Institute for Regional Studies, 1970.
Detailed history of the frontier along the North Dakota–Minnesota border.

Kazeck, Melvin E. *North Dakota: A Human and Economic Geography*. Fargo: Institute for
Regional Studies, 1956.

Kelsey, Vera. *Red River Runs North!* New York: Harper, 1951.
Short history of the Red River and the country it traverses, from the Dakotas to Hudson's
Bay.

Lamar, Howard R. *Dakota Territory, 1861–1889: A Study of Frontier Politics*. New Haven:
Yale U., 1956.
Intensive and scholarly.

Lounsberry, Clement A. *Early History of North Dakota: Essential Outlines of American History*. Washington: Liberty Press, 1919.
Valuable early history.

Nelson, Bruce. *Land of the Dacotahs*. Minneapolis: U. Minnesota, 1946.
 Unusually well-written history and evocation of the Dakota country.
Pritchett, John P. *The Red River Valley, 1811–1849: A Regional Study*. New Haven: Yale U.,
 1942.
 Scholarly and detailed.
Robinson, Elwyn B. *History of North Dakota*. Lincoln: U. Nebraska, 1966.
 Most comprehensive and accurate history of the state.
Rolfsrud, Erling N. *Lanterns Over the Prairies*. 2 vols. Brainerd, Minn.: Lakeland, 1949–50.
 Social and cultural history.
WPA Federal Writers' Project. *North Dakota: A Guide to the Northern Prairie State*. Fargo:
 Knight, 1938.

J. OHIO

Banta, Richard E. *The Ohio*. New York: Rinehart, 1949.
 Rivers of America series.
Condit, Carl. *The Railroad and the Cities: A Technological and Urbanistic History of Cin-
 cinnati*. Columbus: Ohio State U., 1976.
Condon, George E. *Yesterday's Cleveland*. Miami: Seemann, 1976.
 Largely pictorial.
DeChambrun, Clara L. *The Story of the Queen City*. New York: Scribner, 1939.
 Popular history of the city.
Ellis, William D. *The Cuyahoga*. New York: Holt, 1967.
 Rivers of America series.
Feck, Luke. *Yesterday's Cincinnati*. Miami: Seemann, 1976.
 Largely pictorial.
Galloway, William A. *Old Chillicothe: Shawnee and Pioneer History*. Xenia: Buckeye Press,
 1934.
 Scholarly history of the region gathered from Shawnee chronicles and later documents.
 Includes sketches of three famous residents: George Rogers Clark, Simon Kenton, and Dan-
 iel Boone.
Harlow, Alvin F. *The Serene Cincinnatians*. New York: Dutton, 1950.
 Harlow sees the serenity of Cincinnati as a product of "the experience and philosophical
 composure of age, informed by historical consciousness, and with a strong blend of German
 imperturbability." A volume in the Society of America series.
Hatcher, Harlan. *The Buckeye Country*. New York: Kinsey, 1940.
 Breezy treatment.
––––––. *The Western Reserve: The Story of New Connecticut in Ohio*. Indianapolis: Bobbs-
 Merrill, 1949.
 Deals with that area of northeastern Ohio which was a "reserve" of Connecticut until 1800.
 Hatcher emphasizes the unique mixture of old New England and later European immi-
 grant culture in that part of the state.
Havighurst, Walter. *River to the West: Three Centuries of the Ohio*. New York: Putnam, 1970.
 Informal and readable story of the Ohio River.
Howe, Henry. *Historical Collections of Ohio*. Cincinnati: Derby, 1847.
 Important early work by one who personally experienced much of frontier history.
Meade, David. *Yankee Eloquence in the Middle West: The Ohio Lyceum, 1850–1870*. East
 Lansing: Michigan State U., 1951.
 Sound historical study.
Miller, James M. *The Genesis of Western Culture: The Upper Ohio Valley, 1800–1825*. Co-
 lumbus: Historical Society, 1938.
 Scholarly.
Roseboom, Eugene H. and Francis P. Weisenburger. *A History of Ohio*. 2d ed. Columbus:
 Historical Society, 1967.
 Best one-volume history of the state.
Scheiber, Harry N. *Ohio Canal Era: A Case Study of Government and the Economy
 1820–1861*. Athens: Ohio U., 1968.
 Detailed scholarship.

Sesquicentennial History of the State of Ohio. 6 vols. Gen. ed. Carl F. Wittke. Columbus: Historical Society, 1941–44.
  The definitive history of the state. This is one of the earlier cooperative scholarly histories and remains one of the best. Bond, Beverly W., Jr. *The Foundations of Ohio* (1941). Vol. 1; Utter, William T. *The Frontier State, 1803–1825* (1942). Vol. 2; Weisenburger, Francis P. *The Passing of the Frontier, 1825–1850* (1941). Vol. 3; Roseboom, Eugene H. *The Civil War Era, 1850–1873* (1944). Vol. 4; Jordan, Philip D. *Ohio Comes of Age, 1873–1900* (1943). Vol. 5; Lindley, Harlow, comp. *Ohio in the Twentieth Century* (1942). Vol. 6.

Vexler, Robert, ed. *Cincinnati: A Chronological and Documentary History.* Dobbs Ferry, N.Y.: Oceana, 1975.

WPA Federal Writers' Project. *The Ohio Guide.* New York: Oxford, 1940.
  Good introduction to history and culture of the state.

K.   SOUTH DAKOTA

Cummins, Cedric. *The University of South Dakota, 1862–1966.* Vermillion: U. South Dakota, 1975.

Kingsbury, George W. *History of Dakota Territory.* 5 vols. Chicago: Clarke, 1915.
  Detailed early history.

Jennewein, J. Leonard and Janet Boorman, eds. *Dakota Panorama.* Sioux Falls: Midwest-Beach, 1961.
  Especially good for the territorial period.

Parmelee, Gertrude, comp. *A South Dakota Bibliography.* Rapid City: Library Assn., 1960.
  Pamphlet.

Robinson, Doane. *South Dakota, Sui Generis.* 3 vols. Rev. ed. New York: American Historical Society, 1930.
  Best early history of the state.

Sampson, York, ed. *South Dakota: Fifty Years of Progress.* Sioux Falls: Golden Anniversary Book Club, 1939.
  Includes a section on South Dakota literature.

Schell, Herbert S. *History of South Dakota.* 2d rev. ed. Lincoln: U. Nebraska, 1975.
  Good one-volume history; only work that covers the state's history from the territorial period to the present.

WPA Federal Writers' Project. *South Dakota: A Guide to the State.* Rev. ed. New York: Hastings, 1952.
  Solid introduction to the state.

L.   WISCONSIN

Austin, H. Russell. *The Wisconsin Story: The Building of a Vanguard State.* Rev. ed. Milwaukee: Milwaukee Journal, 1957.
  Popular journalist's account.

Bogue, Allan and Robert Taylor, eds. *The University of Wisconsin: 125 Years.* Madison: U. Wisconsin, 1975.

Curti, Merle E. and Vernon Carstensen. *The University of Wisconsin: A History, 1848–1925.* Madison: U. Wisconsin, 1949.
  Excellent history of this most vital of early Midwest institutions.

Gara, Larry. *A Short History of Wisconsin.* Madison: Historical Society, 1962.
  Sound, readable survey.

The History of Wisconsin. 6 vols. Madison: Historical Society, 1973–
  A cooperative effort sponsored by the State Historical Society. The volumes are scheduled to be published as follows: Smith, Alice E. *From Exploration to Statehood* (1973). Vol. 1; Current, Richard N. *Wisconsin in the Civil War Era, 1848–1873.* Vol. 2; Nesbit, Robert C. *Wisconsin in the Late Nineteenth Century, 1873–1893.* Vol. 3; Cronon, E. David. *Wisconsin in the Progressive Era, 1893–1915.* Vol. 4; Glad, Paul W. *Wisconsin Between the Wars, 1915–1940.* Vol. 5; Thompson, William F. *Wisconsin at Mid-Century, 1940–1965.* Vol. 6; Volumes 2–6 are scheduled to be published between 1974 and 1976.

Kellogg, Louise P. *The British Regime in Wisconsin and the Northwest.* Madison: Historical Society, 1935.
  Scholarly.

_____. *The French Regime in Wisconsin and the Northwest.* Madison: Historical Society, 1925.

Companion to Kellogg's *British Regime.*

Legler, Henry E. *Narratives of Early Wisconsin Travellers Prior to 1800.* Madison: Historical Society, 1906.

A somewhat misleading title, since this is not an anthology nor collection of narratives. Legler's discussion of early Wisconsin visitors is informative and scholarly.

Lesy, Michael, comp. *Wisconsin Death Trip.* New York: Pantheon, 1973.

Photos and texts of the bad old days.

Lord, Clifford L. and Carl Ubbelohde. *Clio's Servant: The State Historical Society of Wisconsin, 1846–1954.* Madison: Historical Society, 1967.

Detailed account of this prototypical midwestern historical society.

Nesbit, Robert C. *Wisconsin: A History.* Madison: Historical Society, 1973.

Good recent one-volume history.

Quaife, Milo M. *Wisconsin: Its History and Its People, 1634–1924.* 4 vols. Chicago: Clarke, 1924.

A good, early history.

Raney, William F. *Wisconsin: A Story of Progress.* New York: Prentice-Hall, 1940.

Outdated, but still in general use.

Still, Bayrd. *Milwaukee: The History of a City.* Madison: Historical Society, 1948.

The definitive history of the city.

Thwaites, Reuben G. *The French Regime in Wisconsin, 1727–48.* Madison: Historical Society, 1906.

Solid early work.

_____. *Wisconsin: The Americanization of a French Settlement.* Boston: Houghton, Mifflin, 1908.

Short but excellent early history.

_____. *Stories of the Badger State.* New York: American, 1900.

Wells, Robert W. *This is Milwaukee.* New York: Doubleday, 1970.

Informal history by a Milwaukee journalist.

_____. *Yesterday's Milwaukee.* Miami: Seemann, 1976.

Largely pictorial.

Whyte, Bertha K. *Wisconsin Heritage.* Boston: Branford, 1954.

Popular illustrated work.

WPA Federal Writers' Project. *Wisconsin: A Guide to the Badger State.* New York: Duell, 1941.

One of the stronger American Guide books. A good introduction to the state.

10. ECONOMIC AND POLITICAL LIFE

Buck, Solon J. *The Agrarian Crusade: A Chronicle of the Farmer in Politics.* New Haven: Yale U., 1920.

Considers the influence of the Populists and Grangers in Midwest and American politics.

_____. *The Granger Movement: A Study of Agricultural Organization and its Political, Economic, and Social Manifestations, 1870–1880.* Cambridge: Harvard U., 1913.

Standard work on the movement.

The Economic History of the United States. 10 vols. New York: Holt, 1951.

Relevant volumes: Nettles, Curtis P. *The Emergence of a National Economy, 1775–1815* (1962). Vol. 2; Gates, Paul. *The Farmer's Age: Agriculture, 1815–1860* (1960). Vol. 3; Taylor, George. *The Transportation Revolution: Industry, 1815–1860* (1951). Vol. 4.

Dorfman, Joseph. *Thorstein Veblen and His America.* New York: Viking, 1934.

Scholarly biography.

Elazar, Daniel J. *Cities of the Prairie: The Metropolitan Frontier and American Politics.* New York: Basic Books, 1970.

Intensive study of "the impact of federalism on the political institutions" of several middle-sized Midwest cities, including Duluth, Minn., and seven Illinois metropolitan areas.

Fenton, John H. *Midwest Politics.* New York: Holt, 1966.

General essays on six states: Michigan, Wisconsin, Ohio, Indiana, Illinois, and Minnesota.

Henderson, James M. and Anne O. Krueger. *National Growth and Economic Change in the Upper Midwest*. Minneapolis: U. Minnesota, 1965.

Hicks, John D. *The Populist Revolt: A History of the Farmer's Alliance and the People's Party*. Minneapolis: U. Minnesota, 1931.
  Excellent study of the movement which gained considerable power in the Midwest in the last years of the nineteenth century.

Jensen, Richard J. *The Winning of the Midwest: Social and Political Conflict, 1888–1896*. Chicago: U. Chicago, 1971.
  Close study of Midwest political campaigns.

Kleppner, Paul. *The Cross of Culture: A Social Analysis of Midwestern Politics, 1850–1900*. New York: Free Press, 1970.
  Examines the role of conflicting social groups in Midwest political life.

Kramer, Dale. *The Wild Jackasses: The American Farmer in Revolt*. New York: Hastings, 1956.
  Popular volume in the American Procession series.

Merrill, Horace S. *Bourbon Democracy of the Middle West 1865–1896*. Baton Rouge: Louisiana State U., 1953.
  Studies the conservative "Bourbon" leaders of the Democratic Party in a period of alliance between big business and Midwest Democratic politicians. Scholarly history.

Nichols, Jeannette P. and James G. Randall, eds. *Democracy in the Middle West*. New York: Appleton, 1941.
  Five scholarly essays.

Nye, Russel B. *Midwestern Progressive Politics, 1870–1958*. Rev. ed. East Lansing: Michigan State U., 1959.
  Standard treatment of the subject.

Pollack, Norman. *The Populist Response to Industrial America: Midwestern Populist Thought*. Cambridge: Harvard U., 1962.
  Author sees Populism as essentially radical and progressive rather than reactionary; scholarly and detailed.

Saloutos, Theodore and John D. Hicks. *Agricultural Discontent in the Middle West, 1900–1939*. Madison: U. Wisconsin, 1951.
  Scholarly work; reprinted in 1965 under the title *Twentieth Century Populism*.

Sharkansky, Ira. *Regionalism in American Politics*. Indianapolis: Bobbs-Merrill, 1970.
  Statistical analysis of how different regions diverge politically.

Steffens, Lincoln. *The Shame of the Cities*. New York: McClure, 1904.
  Influential social reporter and muckraker examines conditions in three Midwest cities: Chicago, Minneapolis, and St. Louis. Steffens also discusses the making of this book in his *Autobiography* (1931).

Youngdale, James M., ed. *Third Party Footprints: An Anthology from Writings and Speeches of Midwest Radicals*. Minneapolis: Ross & Haines, 1966.
  Includes pronouncements from Ignatius Donnelly, Henry Wallace, Charles Lindbergh, Sr., Robert LaFollette, and others.

11. RELIGION

Andrews, Edward D. *The People Called Shakers: A Search for the Perfect Society*. Enl. ed. New York: Oxford, 1963.
  A comprehensive history. Since the 1930s Andrews has been chief chronicler of Shaker life and art.

Asbury, Herbert. *A Methodist Saint: The Life of Bishop Asbury*. New York: Knopf, 1927.
  A descendant of the good bishop waxes irreverent in this satirical portrait of frontier religion and life.

Billington, Ray A. *The Protestant Crusade, 1800–1860: A Study of American Nativism*. New York: Macmillan, 1938.
  Excellent history of anti-Catholic, anti-foreign movement in America.

Burr, Nelson R. et al. *A Critical Bibliography of Religion in America*. Princeton: Princeton U., 1961.

_____. *Religion in American Life*. New York: Appleton, 1971.
  A Goldentree bibliography.

Clark, Elmer T. *The Small Sects in America*. Rev. ed. New York: Abingdon, 1949.
Includes a good deal on Midwest sects (Shakers, Amana Society, etc.).

Cleveland, Catharine C. *The Great Revival in the West 1797–1805*. Chicago: U. Chicago, 1916.
Detailed study of the Kentucky-Ohio revival in its historic context.

Elmen, Paul. *Wheat Flour Messiah: Eric Jansson of Bishop Hill*. Carbondale: Southern Illinois U., 1976.

Flanders, Robert B. *Nauvoo: Kingdom on the Mississippi*. Urbana: U. Illinois, 1965.
A history of Nauvoo and the early Mormons.

Garraghan, Gilbert J. *The Jesuits of the Middle United States*. 3 vols. New York: American, 1938.
Solid historical writing. Garraghan emphasizes the early missions and carries the story in detail to about 1860.

Gaustad, Edwin S. *Historical Atlas of Religion in American*. New York: Harper, 1962.

Goodykoontz, Colin B. *Home Missions on the American Frontier*. Caldwell, Idaho: Caxton, 1939.
Scholarly examination of the role played by Eastern Congregational and Presbyterian "missionaries" in the cultural development of the frontier.

Johnson, Charles A. *The Frontier Camp Meetings, Religion's Hardest Time*. Dallas: Southern Methodist U., 1955.
History of that peculiar frontier phenomenon which flourished in the Midwest.

MacLean, John P. *Shakers of Ohio: Fugitive Papers*. Columbus: Heer, 1907.
Scholarly treatment.

McKinsey, Elizabeth. *The Western Experiment: New England Transcendentalists in the Ohio. Valley*. Cambridge: Harvard U., 1973.

Miyakawa, T. Scott. *Protestants and Pioneers: Individualism and Conformity on the American Frontier*. Chicago: U. Chicago, 1964.
Detailed sociological study of the impact of four Protestant sects (Baptists, Methodists, Presbyterians, and Friends) on frontier culture.

Mode, Peter G. *The Frontier Spirit in American Christianity*. New York: Macmillan, 1923.

Nottingham, Elizabeth K. *Methodism and the Frontier: Indiana Proving Ground*. New York: Columbia U., 1941.
Readable popular history of this powerful cultural force in frontier Indiana.

Obenhaus, Victor. *The Church and Faith in Mid-America*. Philadelphia: Westminster, 1963.
Report based on 1200 interviews by University of Chicago School of Theology students and faculty in their attempt to assess religious life in the Midwest. A sociological as well as religious study.

Piercy, Caroline B. *The Valley of God's Pleasure: A Saga of the North Union Shaker Community*. New York: Stratford, 1951.
Account of the community that existed from 1822 to 1889 in an area now part of Cleveland.

Rudolph, L. C. *Hoosier Zion: The Presbyterians in Early Indiana*. New Haven: Yale U., 1963.
Study of erudite eastern ministers and their roughnecked, unlettered flocks.

Schroeder, W. Widick and Victor Obenhaus. *Religion in American Culture: Unity and Diversity in a Midwestern County*. New York: Free Press, 1964.
Sociological study of religious behavior "in an area considered to be typical of the Midwestern Corn Belt farming region."

Shambaugh, Bertha M. *Amana That Was and Amana That Is*. Iowa City: Historical Society, 1932.
Thorough history of the German communistic colony in Iowa.

Sweet, William W. *Religion on the American Frontier*. 4 vols. New York: Cooper Square, 1964.
Definitive study. In this and the following titles, Sweet has proved to be a knowledgeable and prolific writer on Midwest religion.

————. *Revivalism in America, its Origin, Growth, and Decline*. New York: Scribner, 1944.

————. *The Story of Religion in America*. 2d rev. ed. New York: Harper, 1950.

————. *Religion in the Development of American Culture, 1765–1840*. New York: Scribner, 1952.

————. *Circuit-Rider Days Along the Ohio*. New York: Methodist Book Concern, 1923.

————. *Circuit-Rider Days in Indiana*. Indianapolis: Stewart, 1916.

Weisberger, Bernard A. *They Gathered at the River: The Story of the Great Revivalists and their Impact Upon Religion in America*. Boston: Little, Brown, 1958.

Emphasizes the interrelationships of frontier and revivalist religion. Zestfully written and entertaining, yet also sound scholarship.

12. SOCIOLOGY

Bertrand, Alvin L. et al., eds. *Rural Sociology: An Analysis of Contemporary Rural Life*. New York: McGraw-Hill, 1958.

Reference to the Midwest *passim*.

Blouet, Brian and Merlin Lawson, eds. *Images of the Plains: The Role of Human Nature in Settlement*. Lincoln: U. Nebraska, 1975.

Carr, Lowell J. and James E. Stermer. *Willow Run: A Study of Industrialization and Cultural Inadequacy*. New York: Harper, 1952.

Sociological study emphasizes poor working and living conditions at a wartime airplane factory near Detroit.

Curti, Merle. *The Making of an American Community: A Case Study of Democracy in a Frontier Community*. Palo Alto: Stanford U., 1959.

Deals with the cultural development of Trempealeau County, Wisconsin.

Eden, Lynn. *Crisis in Watertown: The Polarization of an American Community*. Ann Arbor: U. Michigan, 1972.

College undergraduate conducted interviews with the populace of Watertown, Wisc.

Engler, Richard E., Jr. *The Challenge of Diversity*. New York: Harper, 1964.

Explores differing cultural patterns in various regions of the U.S., including Racine, Wisc., and Bremer County, Iowa.

Gallaher, Art, Jr. *Plainville Fifteen Years Later*. New York: Columbia U., 1961.

Follow up to *Plainville, U.S.A.* by James West (q.v.).

Harrison, Shelby M. *Social Conditions in an American City: A Summary of the Findings of the Springfield Survey*. New York: Sage Foundation, 1920.

Part of a unique series meticulously examining a small American city. The entire series takes up nos. 7–16 (1914–29) of the Russell Sage Foundation Publications.

Havighurst, Robert J. and Hugh G. Morgan. *The Social History of a War-Boom Community*. New York: Longmans, 1951.

Describes the impact of social change on Seneca, Ill., during World War II when that small town became an important center of armaments manufacture.

Kirschner, Don S. *City and Country: Rural Responses to Urbanization in the 1920s*. Westport, Conn.: Greenwood, 1970.

Solid study examines attitudes about urbanization held by rural Corn Belt folk.

Kolb, John H. *Emerging Rural Communities: Group Relations in Rural Society*. Madison: U. Wisconsin, 1959.

An enlightening review of research on the subject conducted over the past half century at the University of Wisconsin.

Kornhauser, Arthur. *Detroit as the People See It*. Detroit: Wayne, 1952.

Survey of social attitudes.

Lantz, Herman R. and J. S. McCrary. *The People of Coal Town*. New York: Columbia U., 1958.

Strong study of a southern Illinois town based on 250 interviews with local residents.

LeMasters, E. E. *Blue-Collar Aristocrats: Life Styles at a Working Class Tavern*. Madison: U. Wisconsin, 1975.

Loomis, Charles P. and Allan J. Beegle. *Rural Social Systems*. New York: Prentice-Hall, 1950.

Scholarly textbook.

————. *Rural Sociology: The Strategy of Change*. Englewood Cliffs, N.J.: Prentice-Hall, 1957.

Popular revision of *Rural Social Systems*.

Lyford, Joseph P. *The Talk in Vandalia*. Santa Barbara: Center for the Study of Democratic Institutions, 1962.

Under the auspices of the Center and the Fund for the Republic, political journalist Lyford conducted revealing taped interviews with residents of "small town America" (Vandalia, Ill.).

Lynd, Robert S. and Helen M. *Middletown: A Study in Contemporary American Culture.* New York: Harcourt, 1929.
  Classic study of Muncie, Ind. A model of sociological inquiry followed in many subsequent studies of provincial America.
———. *Middletown in Transition.* New York: Harcourt, 1937.
  Reevaluation of Muncie life during the Depression.
Nelson, Lowry. *American Farm Life.* Cambridge: Harvard U., 1954.
  Readable survey.
———. *The Minnesota Community: Country and Town in Transition.* Minneapolis: U. Minnesota, 1960.
  Study of changes in rural Minnesota as the state has changed from an agricultural society to a predominantly urban and industrial one.
———. *Rural Sociology: Its Origin and Growth in the United States.* Minneapolis: U. Minnesota, 1969.
  Important history of this discipline.
Schafer, Joseph. *The Social History of American Agriculture.* New York: Macmillan, 1936.
  Comprehensive economic and social history.
Sorokin, Pitirim and Carle C. Zimmerman. *Principles of Rural-Urban Sociology.* New York: Holt, 1929.
  Good, older textbook.
Taylor, Carl C. et al. *Rural Life in the United States.* New York: Knopf, 1949.
  Extensive and valuable text in rural sociology; covers Midwest rural culture well.
Vogt, Evon Z. and Ray Hyman. *Water Witching, U.S.A.* Chicago: U. Chicago, 1959.
  Well-researched and entertaining study of "dowsers" (water diviners), in America.
West, James, pseud. (Carl Withers). *Plainville, U.S.A.* New York: Columbia U., 1945.
  Pioneering study of a small Missouri town. Art Gallaher returned to write *Plainville Fifteen Years Later* (q.v.).

13. ETHNIC STUDIES

For studies of Blacks and Indians in the Midwest, see specific subject bibliographies in this volume. Studies of ethnic communities in Chicago appear in the Chicago bibliography.

Babcock, Kendric C. *The Scandanavian Element in the United States.* Urbana: U. Illinois, 1914.
  Tells the story of Norwegian, Danish, and Swedish immigration to the Midwest.
Barton, H. Arnold, ed. *Letters from the Promised Land: Swedes in America, 1840–1914.* Minneapolis: U. Minnesota, 1975.
Benson, Adolph B. and Naboth Hedin. *American From Sweden.* Philadelphia: Lippincott, 1950.
  Midwest Swedes considered *passim.* Peoples of America series.
Blegen, Theodore C., ed. *The Land of Their Choice: The Immigrants Write Home.* Minneapolis: U. Minnesota, 1936.
  Letters written by Norwegian immigrants to the U.S. between 1824–77.
Blegen, Theodore C. and Martin B. Ruud, eds. *Norwegian Emigrant Songs and Ballads.* Minneapolis: U. Minnesota, 1936.
  Provides English prose translations and the original Norwegian.
———. *Norwegian Migration to America.* 2 vols. Northfield, Minn.: Norwegian-American Historical Assn., 1931 and 1940.
  Vol. 2 deals more specifically with adjustment to American life. Great numbers of Norwegians settled in the Upper Midwest.
Commager, Henry S., ed. *Immigration and American History: Essays in Honor of Theodore C. Blegen.* Minneapolis: U. Minnesota, 1961.
  Eleven strong essays honoring a pioneer in American immigration history. Includes an essay on "The Immigrant in Western Fiction," by John Flanagan.
Dinnerstein, Leonard and Frederic C. Jaher, eds. *Aliens: A History of Ethnic Minorities in America.* New York: Appleton, 1970.
Esslinger, Dean. *Immigrants and the City: Ethnicity and Mobility in a Nineteenth Century Midwestern Community.* Port Washington, N.Y.: Kennikat, 1975.
  Study of South Bend, Indiana.

Gerlach, Russel L. *Immigrants in the Ozarks: A Study in Ethnic Geography.* University of Missouri Studies Series. Vol. 64. Columbia: U. Missouri, 1976.

Hansen, Marcus L. *The Atlantic Migration, 1607–1860: A History of the Continuing Settlement of the United States.* Cambridge: Harvard U., 1940.

Emphasizes European conditions which forced migration to America. Strong scholarship.

———. *The Immigrant in American History.* Cambridge: Harvard U., 1940.

A suggestive survey.

Hoglund, A. William. *Finnish Immigrants in America, 1880–1920.* Madison: U. Wisconsin, 1960.

A good deal on Midwest Finns, especially in the Upper Midwest.

Iverson, Noel. *Germania, U.S.A.: Social Change in New Ulm, Minnesota.* Minneapolis: U. Minnesota, 1966.

Sociological and historical examination of this small ethnic community.

Larson, Laurence M. *The Changing West.* Northfield, Minn.: Norwegian-American Historical Assn., 1937.

Fine collection of essays; includes an essay on Norwegian-American fiction and others on Norwegian culture in the U.S.

———. *The Log Book of a Young Immigrant.* Northfield, Minn.: Norwegian-American Historical Assn., 1939.

Perhaps the most substantial written account of Norwegian immigrant life in the Midwest outside of O. E. Rölvaag's books.

Lucas, Henry S. *Netherlanders in America.* Ann Arbor: U. Michigan, 1955.

Treats Dutch immigration to the U.S. and Canada between 1789–1950. Includes a good deal about Dutch culture in the Midwest, especially in the author's home state of Michigan.

Mann, Arthur, comp. *Immigrants in American Life, Selected Readings.* Boston: Houghton Mifflin, 1968.

Anthology of Life in America series.

Mulder, Arnold. *Americans From Holland.* Philadelphia: Lippincott, 1947.

A history and commentary on Dutch life in the U.S. by the Michigan novelist.

Nelson, Helge. *The Swedes and the Swedish Settlements in North America.* 2 vols. Lund, Sweden: Gleerup, 1943.

Extended treatment of Midwest Swedes.

Pochmann, Henry A. *German Culture in America: Philosophical and Literary Influences, 1600–1900.* Madison: U. Wisconsin, 1957.

This monumental study deals extensively with German life in the Midwest.

Russell, John A. *The Germanic Influence in the Making of Michigan.* Detroit: U. Detroit, 1929.

Detailed study.

———. *Bibliography of German Culture in America to 1940.* Madison: U. Wisconsin, 1953.

Qualey, Carlton C. *Norwegian Settlement in the United States.* Northfield, Minn.: Norwegian-American Historical Assn., 1938.

Thorough history.

Simirenko, Alex. *Pilgrims, Colonists, and Frontiersmen: An Ethnic Community in Transition.* New York: Free Press, 1964.

Russians in Minneapolis.

Tolzmann, Don. *German-Americana: A Bibliography.* Metuchen, N.J.: Scarecrow, 1975.

Wheeler, Thomas C., ed. *The Immigrant Experience: The Anguish of Becoming an American.* New York: Dial, 1971.

Nine essays, predominantly by poets and novelists.

Wittke, Carl F. *We Who Built America: The Saga of the Immigrant.* New York: Prentice-Hall, 1939.

Historical survey of immigration to the U.S.

———. *Refugees of Revolution: The German Forty-Eighters in America.* Philadephia: U. Pennsylvania, 1952.

Many intellectuals who fled Germany settled in the Midwest; scholarly study.

14.   UTOPIAN COMMUNITIES

Arndt, Karl J. *George Rapp's Harmony Society, 1785–1847.* Philadelphia: U. Pennsylvania, 1965.

Sound study of the Pietist community on the Wabash. The buildings and lands were later taken over by Robert Owen, who created "New Harmony."

Bestor, Arthur E. *Backwoods Utopias: The Sectarian and Owenite Phases of Communitarian Socialism in America, 1663–1829*. Philadelphia: U. Pennsylvania, 1950.
Excellent survey, especially strong on Owenism and the New Harmony community; includes extensive bibliographies.

Calverton, Victor F. *Where Angels Dared to Tread*. Indianapolis: Bobbs-Merrill, 1941.
Vigorous prose highlights this entertaining survey of utopias in America.

Egbert, Donald D. and Stow Persons, eds. *Socialism and American Life*. 2 vols. Princeton, N.J.: Princeton U., 1952.
Outstanding scholarly work on communitarian socialism; includes extended discussion of Midwestern communities. Vol. 2 is an exhaustive bibliography by T. D. Seymour Bassett.

Harrison, John F. *Quest for the New Moral World: Robert Owen and the Owenites in Britain and America*. New York: Scribner, 1969.
Excellent.

_____, ed. *Utopianism and Education: Robert Owen and the Owenites*. New York: Teachers College Press, 1968.
Scholarly edition of Owen's essays, lectures, etc., dealing with the subject.

Hertzler, Joyce O. *The History of Utopian Thought*. New York: Macmillan, 1923.
A popular but challenging work.

Holloway, Mark. *Heavens on Earth: Utopian Communities in America, 1680–1880*. Rev. ed. New York: Dover, 1966.
Readable survey of American utopias.

Lockwood, George B. *The New Harmony Communities*. Marion, Ind.: Chronicle, 1902.
Book-length history of the New Harmony experiment revised in a 1905 edition, *The New Harmony Movement*. Of limited value now.

Mumford, Lewis. *The Story of Utopias*. New York: Boni & Liveright, 1922.
Informed and perceptive survey from Plato to the present.

Nordhoff, Charles. *The Communistic Societies of the United States*. New York: Harper, 1875.
Thorough account by a journalist who had the advantage of seeing many of the communities first hand.

Noyes, John H. *History of American Socialisms*. Philadelphia: Lippincott, 1870.
Valuable because of the author's experience as leader of a sectarian community.

Owen, Robert Dale. *Twenty-Seven Years of Autobiography: Threading My Way*. New York: Carleton, 1874.
Although his father wrote little about his American experiences, Robert Dale Owen has provided us with an important historical document of New Harmony.

Parrington, Vernon L. *American Dreams: A Study of American Utopias*. Providence: Brown U., 1947.
Sound survey of utopian fiction and other writings.

Pease, William H. and Jane H. *Black Utopia: Negro Communal Experiments in America*. Madison: State Historical Society, 1963.

Seldes, Gilbert V. *The Stammering Century: Minor Movements, Cults, Manias, Fads, Sects and Religious Excitements in 19th Century America*. New York: Day, 1928.
Entertaining, irreverent social history. Sections on Harmony, New Harmony, Zion, Frances Willard, and Dwight Moody.

Shaw, Albert. *Icaria: A Chapter in the History of Communism*. New York: Putnam, 1884.
Study of the Icarian communities, two of which were in the Midwest (at Nauvoo, Ill., and in Iowa).

Webber, Everett. *Escape to Utopia: The Communal Movement in America*. New York: Hastings, 1959.
Not very scholarly but valuable as a general survey, particularly of the more eccentric communal experiments; American Procession series.

Wilson, William E. *The Angel and the Serpent: The Story of New Harmony*. Bloomington: Indiana U., 1964.
Popular history.

Young, Marguerite. *The Angel in the Forest*. New York: Scribner, 1945. Rpt. 1966 with an introduction by Mark Van Doren.
Imaginative history of New Harmony by a novelist and poet.

15. INTELLECTUAL LIFE

Atherton, Lewis E. *Main Street on the Middle Border*. Bloomington: Indiana U., 1954.
  A gold mine of information on popular culture in the Midwest from frontier times to the twentieth century. Includes a chapter which analyzes the relatively meager acceptance of the fine arts in the region.

Bode, Carl. *The American Lyceum: Town Meeting of the Mind*. New York: Oxford, 1956.
  Scholarly study of a vanished American institution.

Cargill, Oscar. *Intellectual America: Ideas on the March*. New York: Macmillan, 1941.
  This survey of American ideologies discusses naturalism, veritism, primitivism, and a number of Midwest writers like Garland, Dreiser, and Hemingway. Valuable both as an intellectual history and as literary criticism.

Case, Robert O. and Victoria. *We Called it Culture: The Story of Chatauqua*. New York: Doubleday, 1948.
  Popular account of this movement for "self improvement" in small-town America.

Commager, Henry S. *The American Mind: An Interpretation of American Thought and Character since the 1880s*. New Haven: Yale U., 1950.
  Good chapters on Veblen, Turner, and the development of literary realism.

Curti, Merle. *The Growth of American Thought*. 3rd ed. New York: Harper, 1964.
  Sections 4 and 5 on the rise of democracy and nationalism are especially relevant.

————. *Probing Our Past*. New York: Harper, 1955.
  An excellent short survey of American intellectual traditions.

Dorfman, Joseph. *The Economic Mind in American Civilization*. 5 vols. New York: Viking, 1946–59.
  Thorough and detailed; five volumes arranged chronologically.

Ginger, Ray, ed. *American Social Thought*. New York: Hill & Wang, 1961.
  Includes chapters on Dewey, Veblen, Turner, Debs, and Addams.

Harrison, Harry P. *Culture Under Canvas: The Story of Tent Chatauqua as told to Karl Detzer*. New York: Hastings, 1958.
  Colorful first-hand account of a cultural movement which flourished in the Midwest during the first third of the twentieth century.

Hofstadter, Richard and Wilson Smith. *American Higher Education: A Documentary History*. 2 vols. Chicago: U. Chicago, 1961.
  References to Midwest educational history throughout.

Lerner, Max. *America as a Civilization: Life and Thought in the United States Today*. New York: Simon & Schuster, 1957.
  Ambitious one-volume survey.

Mosier, Richard D. *The American Temper: Patterns of Our Intellectual Heritage*. Berkeley: U. California, 1952.
  Sees four "phases of growth" in American intellectual history: Puritanism, Enlightenment, Romanticism, and Modern.

Nicholson, Meredith. *The Valley of Democracy*. New York: Scribner, 1918.
  Emphasizes the democratic origins and bourgeois spirit of the region, especially in its core of small towns and cities.

Parrington, Vernon L. *Main Currents in American Thought: An Interpretation of American Literature from the Beginnings to 1920*. 3 vols. New York: Harcourt, 1927–30.
  Vol. 3, *The Beginnings of Critical Realism in America, 1860–1920*, is the relevant volume. Parrington interprets American thought as it is mirrored in literature, and thus includes a good deal on the Midwest naturalists. Chapters on Dreiser, Rölvaag, Norris, Anderson, Lewis et al.

Perry, Charles M. *The St. Louis Movement in Philosophy: Some Source Material*. Norman: U. Oklahoma, 1931.
  Discusses the Movement and its members: H. C. Brokmeyer, W. T. Harris, and Denton J. Snider.

Snider, Denton J. *The St. Louis Movement in Philosophy, Literature, Education, Psychology . . . .* St. Louis: Sigma, 1920.
  Partly autobiographical story of the Movement, by a participant.

Wish, Harvey. *Society and Thought in America*. 2 vols. New York: Longmans, 1950–52.
  Extended sections on the frontier, immigration, politics, economics, and literary activity.

White, Morton G. *Social Thought in America: The Revolt Against Formalism*. New York: Viking, 1949.
Treats the "historicism" and "cultural organicism" of Veblen, Dewey, Beard, Holmes, and J. H. Robinson.

Gerald C. Nemanic
Northeastern Illinois University
Chicago, Illinois

FOLKLORE

THE CREATION OF the American Folklore Society in 1888, along with its pioneering journal, was a primary encouragement to scholarship in the field. Among the regional magazines spawned by the parent Society was *Midwest Folklore* and numerous smaller journals devoted to state and local materials. In the Midwest, pioneering efforts and leadership have come from a few key individuals. Richard Dorson of Indiana University has written *American Folklore* (1959), *Buying the Wind: Regional Folklore in the United States* (1964), and several regional titles which have provided models for scholarship. Dorson has been instrumental in placing Indiana University and its University Press in the vanguard of folklore scholarship in the region. John T. Flanagan has been active in midwestern folklore and literary scholarship of the region, indeed often combining the two disciplines in his articles and books. Walter Blair's thorough scholarship can be seen in a number of important contributions to midwestern folklore, including books on Mike Fink and regional humor. Vance Randolph has been the most prolific of midwestern folklorists, as evidenced by his shelf of titles concentrating on the cultural life of the Missouri Ozarks.

Of the midwestern literary artists whose bibliographies appear in this volume the majority can be said to incorporate folklore or folkways into their work. The following is a highly selective list of writers who have made extensive use of midwestern folklore or folkways.

Humor: Ade, Clemens, Dunne, Hubbard, Lardner, Locke.

Frontier society: Garland, Hall, Hay, C. Kirkland, Richter, Sandoz*, Sandburg.

North Country: Ostenso*, Sarett, Stevens*.

Ethnic groups: Dunbar, Hughes (Blacks); Catherwood, Woolson (French); DeJong* (Dutch); Petrakis* (Greeks); Algren (Poles); Bellow, Levin (Jews); Suckow (Germans); DeCapite, M. and R.* (Italians); Rölvaag (Norwegians); Cather (Czechs).

Small town and farm life: J. Kirkland, Lindsay, Masters (Illinois); Lockridge, West (Indiana); Aldrich, Quick (Iowa); Howe, Inge (Kansas); Lutes, Moore (Michigan); Krause, Manfred (Minnesota); Croy*, Dorrance (Missouri); Johnson*, Morris, Sandoz* (Nebraska); Cahill, Hudson* (North Dakota); Anderson, Bromfield (Ohio); Lane, L. Wilder* (South Dakota); Conkle*, Derleth*, Garland (Wisconsin).

* See Appendix A.

1.   GENERAL TREATMENTS: ANTHOLOGIES

Botkin, Benjamin A., ed. *Folk-Say: A Regional Miscellany.* 4 vols. Norman: U. Oklahoma, 1929–32.
  Vol. 4 of this anthology includes selections from Midwest writers like Vance Randolph, E. P. Conkle, and Virgil Geddes.
————. *Sidewalks of America.* Indianapolis: Bobbs-Merrill, 1954.
  The folklore of the American city; Chicago is accorded thorough treatment and other Midwest cities come in for passing attention.
————. *A Treasury of American Folklore: Stories, Ballads, and Traditions of the People.* New York: Crown, 1944.
  Midwest figures spotlighted are Mike Fink, Jesse James, Paul Bunyan, and Johnny Appleseed.
————. *A Treasury of Mississippi River Folklore: Stories, Ballads, Traditions, and Folkways of the Mid-American River Country.* New York: Crown, 1955.
  Diverse anthology covers material from Minnesota to the Gulf.
————. *A Treasury of Western Folklore.* New York: Crown, 1951.
  Includes material from the eastern Plains States.
Botkin, Benjamin A. and A. F. Harlow, eds. *A Treasury of Railroad Folklore: The Stories, Tall Tales, Traditions, Ballads and Songs of the American Railroad Man.* New York: Crown, 1953.
  No specific section on the Midwest, but contains plenty of reference to midland railroads and railroaders.
Brunvand, Jan H. *The Study of American Folklore: An Introduction.* New York: Norton, 1968.
  Aims to be a "basic guidebook to the types of folklore found in the United States."
Carmer, Carl L., ed. *Songs of the Rivers of America.* New York: Farrar, 1942.
  This songbook is part of the Rivers of America series.
Clough, Benjamin C., ed. *The American Imagination at Work: Tall Tales and Folk Tales.* New York: Knopf, 1947.
  This large collection of American folk tales and tall tales includes a good amount of midwestern material.
Doerflinger, William M., comp. *Shanty Men and Shanty Boys: Songs of the Sailor and Lumberman.* New York: Macmillan, 1951.
  Traces and development of shanty songs and ballads and shows how they spread from the Northeast Coast to the Great Lakes region.
Dorson, Richard M. *American Folklore.* Chicago: U. Chicago, 1959.
  Includes chapters on "Regional Folk Cultures" and "Immigrant Folklore," and other material important for midwestern culture.
————. *American Folklore and the Historian.* Chicago: U. Chicago, 1971.
  General, but includes many allusions to the Midwest, Dorson's particular area of expertise.
————. *Buying the Wind: Regional Folklore in the United States.* Chicago: U. Chicago, 1964.
  A chapter on "Illinois' Egyptians."
————. *Folklore: Selected Essays.* Bloomington: U. Illinois, 1972.
Emrich, Duncan. *American Folk Poetry: An Anthology.* Boston: Little, Brown, 1974.
  Several Midwest items.
————. *Folklore on the American Land.* Boston: Little, Brown, 1972.
  Popular treatment.
Flanagan, John T. and Arthur P. Hudson, eds. *American Folklore Reader.* New York: Barnes, 1958.

This anthology includes excerpts from Schoolcraft, Stevens, Lindsay, and others from all sections. A text edition was published as *Folklore in American Literature*.

Korson, George G., ed. *Coal Dust on the Fiddle: Songs and Stories of the Bituminous Industry*. Philadelphia: U. Pennsylvania, 1943.

Material on Ohio, Indiana, and Illinois, as well as Pennsylvania and the Southern states.

Kramer, Frank R. *Voices in the Valley: Mythmaking and Folk Belief in the Shaping of the Middle West*. Madison: U. Wisconsin, 1964.

Interesting study, both imaginative and scholarly, which examines the myths of various ethnic and social groups in the region.

Laws, George M. *Native American Balladry: A Descriptive Study and a Bibliographical Syllabus*. Philadelphia: American Folklore Society, 1950.

Sections on pioneers and lumberjacks are especially relevant.

Lomax, Alan, ed. *Folk Songs of North America, in the English Language*. Garden City: Doubleday, 1960.

The Lomaxes, father and son, have made the most noteworthy collections of American folk music. References to Midwest materials appear *passim* in this and in the following volumes.

Lomax, John A. and Alan, eds. *American Ballads and Folk-Songs*. New York: Macmillan, 1934.

——. *Cowboy Songs and Other Frontier Ballads*. Rev. & enl. ed. New York: Macmillan, 1945.

——. *Folk Songs U.S.A.: The 111 Best American Ballads*. New York: Duell, 1947.

——. *Our Singing Country: A Second Volume of American Ballads and Folk Songs*. New York: Macmillan, 1941.

Miller, Olive B. *Heroes, Outlaws, and Funny Fellows of American Popular Tales*. New York: Doubleday, 1939.

The Midwest is represented by stories about Johnny Appleseed, Mike Fink, Cahokia, Paul Bunyan, and Febold Feboldson. Popular.

Odum, Howard W. *Folk, Region, and Society: Selected Papers*. Chapel Hill: U. North Carolina, 1965.

Selections from the writings of Odum edited by Katherine Jocher and others. Quite a bit on regionalism and folklore.

Paredes, Américo and Ellen J. Stekert, eds. *The Urban Experience and Folk Tradition*. Austin: U. Texas, 1971.

Papers from a symposium held at Wayne State in 1968. Midwest cities are examined extensively.

Rickaby, Franz, coll. and ed. *Ballads and Songs of the Shanty-Boy*. Cambridge: Harvard U., 1926.

Scholarly; 84 songs and ballads collected "from men who worked in the woods of Michigan, Wisconsin, and Minnesota" during the "Golden Age of American Lumbering (1870 to 1900)."

Sandburg, Carl, coll. and ed. *American Songbag*. New York: Harcourt, 1927.

Includes a number of songs originating in the region.

Wright, Robert L. *Swedish Emigrant Ballads*. Lincoln: U. Nebraska, 1965.

With texts, music, and annotation.

2. FRONTIER

Beath, Paul R., comp. *Febold Feboldson: Tall Tales of the Great Plains*. Lincoln: U. Nebraska, 1948.

Selection of short tales told in a manner suitable for juveniles; nonetheless, the volume provides a valuable compilation of stories centering on the fabled plainsman.

Blair, Walter. *Tall Tale America: A Legendary History of our Humorous Heroes*. New York: Coward-McCann, 1944.

Delightful tongue-in-cheek "history"; among the heroes of the Midwest, Blair features Mike Fink, Paul Bunyan, and Johnny Appleseed.

Blair, Walter and Franklin J. Meine. *Half Horse, Half Alligator: The Growth of the Mike Fink Legend*. Chicago: U. Chicago, 1956.

Collects all available original stories about Fink, the legendary raftsman hero of the Mississippi and Ohio Rivers; includes a scholarly introduction.

————. *Mike Fink, King of Mississippi Keelboatmen*. New York: Holt, 1933.
   Earlier, more popular handling of the material in *Half Horse, Half Alligator*.
Boatright, Mody C. *Folk Laughter on the American Frontier*. New York: Macmillan, 1949.
   Contains both a collection of tales and a theory of frontier humor. Unlike Van Wyck Brooks and others who saw frontier humor arising as an antidote to grim living conditions, the author finds in the distinctive "frontier laughter" signs of a great and spirited people.
Chittick, V. L. O., ed. *Ring-Tailed Roarers: Tall Tales of the American Frontier 1830–1860*. Caldwell, Ida: Caxton, 1941.
   Mostly southern, but has a section of Mike Fink stories and another on "Mississippi Steamboatin'."
Clark, Thomas D. *The Rampaging Frontier: Manners and Humors of Pioneer Days in the South and the Middle West*. Indianapolis: Bobbs-Merrill, 1939.
   Folklore and social history of the frontier.
Dick, Everett N. *Tales of the Frontier*. Lincoln, U. Nebraska, 1963.
   Retells interesting tales and legends of frontier life; of value to folklorists.
Felton, Harold V. *Legends of Paul Bunyan*. N.Y.: Knopf, 1947.
   Collects more than 100 of the best tales.
Finger, Charles J., coll. *Frontier Ballads*. Garden City, N.Y.: Doubleday, 1927.
   Running narrative accompanies this collection of about 65 songs.
Hartshoren, Millor. *Paul Bunyan: A Study in Folk Literature*. Los Angeles: Occidental College, 1934.
Hoffman, Daniel. *Paul Bunyan: Last of the Frontier Demigods*. Philadelphia: U. Pennsylvania, 1952.
   Hoffman sees the Bunyan legends originating in professional letters, not in an authentic oral tradition.
Price, Robert. *Johnny Appleseed: Man and Myth*. Bloomington: U. Indiana, 1954.
   Best scholarly treatment of this Midwest folk hero. The author attempts to separate fact and legend, but pays homage to the creative forces which bred the myth.
Rourke, Constance M. *American Humor: A Study of the National Character*. New York: Harcourt, 1931.
   Examines the relationship between folk and literary art in the development of a native tradition.

See also: The sources of popular books which incorporate the Paul Bunyan legends would require an extensive bibliography in itself. For detailed information on the most prolific of the Bunyan myth makers, see the author entry on James Stevens.

3.   BLACKS

Dorson, Richard M., ed. *Negro Folktales in Michigan*. Cambridge: Harvard U., 1956.
   The first scholarly collection of black folklore materials outside the South.
————. *Negro Tales from Pine Bluff, Arkansas, and Calvin, Michigan*. Bloomington: Indiana U., 1958.
Owen, Mary A. *Voodoo Tales: As Told Among the Negroes of the Southwest*. New York: Negro Universities, 1969.
   Includes a chapter on Missouri folklore.
Wheeler, Mary. *Steamboatin' Days: Folk Songs of the River Packet Era*. Baton Rouge: Louisiana State U. 1944.
   "Rouster songs" and tales of black dock workers along the Ohio, Mississippi, and Tennessee Rivers.

4.   STATES

A.   ILLINOIS

Allen, John W. *Legends and Lore of Southern Illinois*. Carbondale: Southern Illinois U., 1963.
   Selections from Allen's weekly newspaper column.
————. *It Happened in Southern Illinois*. Carbondale, Southern Illinois U., 1968.
   More folkways and regional history.

Carrière, Joseph M., and Anna C. O'Flynn, colls. and eds. *Life and Customs in the French Villages of the Old Illinois Country (1763–1939)*. Ottawa: Canadian Historical Assn., 1939. Pamphlet.

Hyatt, Harry M. *Folklore from Adams County, Illinois*. 2d ed. New York: Hyatt Foundation, 1965.
  Collection of sayings, superstitions, old wives' cures, etc., gathered from the inhabitants of one Illinois county; remarkably comprehensive (16,537 items).

Lewis, Lloyd. *Myths After Lincoln*. New York: Harcourt, 1929.
  The "Railsplitter" has generated a folk legend which Lewis details admirably.

Korson, George G., ed. *Coal Dust on the Fiddle: Songs and Stories of the Bituminous Industry*. Philadelphia: U. Pennsylvania, 1943.
  Includes material on Ohio, Indiana, and Illinois, as well as on Pennsylvania and the southern states.

McIntosh, David. *Folk Songs and Singing Games of the Illinois Ozarks*. Carbondale: Southern Illinois U., 1974.

Neely, Charles, coll. *Tales and Songs of Southern Illinois*. Ed. John W. Spargo. Menasha, Wisc.: Banta, 1938.
  Sections on folktales and on ballads and songs.

B. INDIANA

Brewster, Paul G., coll. and ed. *Ballads and Songs of Indiana*. Bloomington: Indiana U., 1940.
  First volume of the Indiana University Folklore Series; scholarly edition of one hundred ballads and songs.

Carrière, Joseph M. and Anna C. O'Flynn, eds. *Folk Songs of Old Vincennes*. Chicago: Fitzsimons, 1946.
  Thirty-eight songs in both French and English which reflect the early French civilization in the region.

Federal Writers' Project. Indiana. *Hoosier Tall Stories*. Indianapolis, 1937.
  Mimeographed pamphlet.

Korson, George G., ed. *Coal Dust on the Fiddle: Songs and Stories of the Bituminous Industry*. Philadelphia: U. Pennsylvania, 1943.
  Includes material on Ohio, Indiana, and Illinois, as well as on Pennsylvania and the southern states.

C. IOWA

Stout, Earl J., ed. *Folklore from Iowa*. New York: Stechert, 1936.
  Includes ballads, folk songs, cures, etc.

Van Vechten, Carl. *In the Garrett*. New York: Knopf, 1920.
  Includes "Folksongs of Iowa." This chapter is also included in the author's *Sacred and Profane Memories* (1932).

D. KANSAS

Sackett, Samuel J. and William E. Koch, eds. *Kansas Folklore*. Lincoln: U. Nebraska, 1961.
  Includes selections of folktales, legends, dialects, customs, etc.; *the* book on Kansas folklore.

Snow, Florence L. *Pictures on My Wall: A Lifetime in Kansas*. Lawrence: U. Kansas, 1945.
  Memorabilia of late nineteenth-century Kansas; contains folkloric material.

E. MICHIGAN

Barnes, Al. *Vinegar Pie and Other Tales of the Grand Traverse Region*. Detroit: Wayne, 1959.
  Folk history memorabilia collected from the columns of the Traverse City newspaperman.

Beck, Earl C. *Lore of the Lumber Camps*. Rev. and enl. ed. Ann Arbor: U. Michigan, 1948.
  In its original edition (1941) called *Songs of the Michigan Lumberjacks*.

Burroughs, Raymond D. *Peninsular Country*. Grand Rapids: Eerdmans, 1965.
  Unfancy but clean cut sketches of Michigan life and lore by the well-known naturalist and ecologist.

Dorson, Richard M. *Bloodstoppers and Bearwalkers: Folk Traditions of the Upper Peninsula*. Cambridge: Harvard U., 1952.
  Sound scholarship.

————. *Negro Folktales in Michigan*. Cambridge: Harvard U., 1956.
First scholarly edition of non-southern black folklore.

————. *Negro Tales from Pine Bluff, Arkansas, and Calvin, Michigan*. Bloomington: Indiana U., 1958.

Drier, Roy W., ed. *Copper Country Tales*. Calumet, Mich.: Author, 1967.
A "compendium of fact, fiction, and poetry" about the copper mining region of the upper peninsula.

Drier, Roy W. and Alfred Nicholls, eds. *More Copper Country Tales*. Calumet, Mich.: Author, 1968.

Gardner, Emelyn E. and Geraldine J. Chickering, eds. *Ballads and Songs of Southern Michigan*. Ann Arbor: U. Michigan, 1939.
201 pieces. A fine collection of drawings depicting Michigan rural life accompanies the text.

Hamlin, Marie C. W. *Legends of Le Detroit*. Detroit: Nourse, 1884.
Legends and stories of the French at Detroit.

Hoogasian-Villa, Susie. *Armenian Tales and their Folkloristic Relevance*. Detroit: Wayne, 1966.
Includes tales of second generation Armenians in the state.

Rickaby, Franz, ed. *Ballads and Songs of the Shanty-Boy*. Cambridge: Harvard U., 1926.
Scholarly collection of 84 songs and ballads of the lumber industry in Michigan, Wisconsin, and Minnesota, 1870–1900.

Schoolcraft, Henry R. See author bibliography.

F. MINNESOTA

Blegen, Theodore C. and Martin Ruud, eds. *Norwegian Emigrant Songs and Ballads*. Minneapolis: U. Minnesota, 1936.
The originals with prose translations.

Dean, M. C. *Flying Cloud and One Hundred and Fifty Other Old Time Songs and Ballads*. Virginia, Minn.: Quickprint, n.d.

Rickaby, Franz, ed. *Ballads and Songs of the Shanty-Boy*. Cambridge: Harvard U., 1926.
Scholarly collection of 84 songs and ballads of the lumber industry in Michigan, Wisconsin, and Minnesota, 1870–1900.

G. MISSOURI

Belden, Henry M., ed. *Ballads and Songs Collected by the Missouri Folklore Society*. 2d ed. Columbia: U. Missouri, 1955.
Collections begun in 1903.

Broadfoot, Lennis L. *Pioneers of the Ozarks*. Caldwell, Ida.: Caxton, 1944.
Interesting drawings and character sketches of Missouri mountain folk.

Carrière, Joseph M., ed. *Tales from the French Folklore of Missouri*. Evanston: Northwestern U., 1937.
The author did extensive field work at Old Mines, Mo., a community settled by the French in the eighteenth century.

Collins, Earl. *Folktales of Missouri*. Boston: Christopher, 1935.
A substantial collection.

Lyon, Marguerite. *Take to the Hills: A Chronicle of the Ozarks*. Indianapolis: Bobbs-Merrill, 1941.
A personal narrative with chapters on "Home Remedies," "Ozark Vittles," "Well Witching," etc.

————. *Fresh From the Hills*. Indianapolis: Bobbs-Merrill, 1945.

————. *And Green Grass Grows All Around*. Indianapolis: Bobbs-Merrill, 1942.

Moore, Tom. *Mysterious Tales and Legends of the Ozarks*. Philadelphia: Dorrance, 1938.

Randolph, Vance, ed. *The Devil's Pretty Daughter, and Other Ozark Folk Tales*. New York: Columbia U., 1955.

————. *From an Ozark Holler: Stories of Ozark Mountain Folk*. New York: Vanguard, 1933.

———. *Hot Springs and Hell, and Other Folk Jests and Anecdotes From the Ozarks*. Hatboro, Pa.: Folklore Associates, 1965.

———. *An Ozark Anthology*. Caldwell, Ida.: Caxton, 1940.

———. *Ozark Folksongs*. 4 vols. Columbia: State Historical Society of Missouri, 1946–1950.
A large collection (833 songs) which supplements Belden's volume cited above.

———. *Ozark Ghost Stories*. Girard, Kan.: Haldeman-Julius, 1944.
Pamphlet.

———. *Ozark Mountain Folks*. New York: Vanguard, 1932.

———. *Ozark Superstitions*. New York: Columbia U., 1947.

———. *The Ozarks: An American Survival of Primitive Society*. New York: Vanguard, 1931.

———. *Sticks in the Knapsack, and Other Ozark Folk Tales*. New York: Columbia, 1958.

———. *Tall Tales From the Ozarks*. Girard, Kan.: Haldeman-Julius, 1944.
Pamphlet.

———. *The Talking Turtle, and Other Ozark Folk Tales*. New York: Columbia, 1957.

———. *We Always Lie to Strangers: Tall Tales From the Ozarks*. New York: Columbia U., 1951.

———. *Who Blowed Up the Church House? and Other Ozark Folk Tales*. New York: Columbia U., 1952.

———. *Pissing in the Snow and Other Ozark Folktales*. Urbana: U. Illinois, 1976.

Randolph, Vance and Guy W. Von Schriltz, eds. *Ozark Outdoors: Hunting and Fishing Stories of the Ozarks*. New York: Vanguard, 1937.

Randolph, Vance and George P. Wilson. *Down in the Holler: A Gallery of Ozark Folk Speech*. Norman: U. Oklahoma, 1953.
A study of Ozark dialect.

Rayburn, Otto E. *Ozark Country*. New York: Duell, 1941.
Part of American Folklore series.

Wilson, Charles M. *Backwoods America*. Chapel Hill: U. North Carolina, 1934.
Examines the history, life, and customs of the Ozark people.

———. *The Bodacious Ozarks: True Tales of the Back Hills*. New York: Hastings, 1959.
Deals mainly with Arkansas life, but includes some Missouri material.

———, comp. *Stars in God's Lanterns: An Offering of Ozark Tellin' Stories*. Norman: U. Oklahoma, 1969.

H. NEBRASKA

Cannell, Margaret. "Signs, Omens, Portents, in Nebraska Folklore." *University of Nebraska Studies in Language, Literature, and Criticism*. No. 13 (1933), 7–50.

Federal Writers' Project, Nebraska. *Nebraska Folklore Pamphlets*. Lincoln, 1937–40.
Includes cowboy songs, Indian legends, tall tales, etc.; nos. 1–40 published between 1937–40.

Pound, Louise. "Folk-Songs of Nebraska and the Central West: A Syllabus." *Nebraska Academy of Science Publications*. Vol. 10, no. 3 (1915).

———. *Nebraska Folklore*. Lincoln: U. Nebraska 1959.

Snapp, Emma L. "Proverbial Lore in Nebraska." *University of Nebraska Studies in Language, Literature, and Criticism*. No. 13 (1933), 53–112.

Welsch, Roger L., ed. *Shingling the Fog and Other Plains Lies*. Chicago: Swallow, 1972.
Emphasis on the tall tale in Nebraska.

———. *A Treasury of Nebraska Pioneer Folklore*. Lincoln: U. Nebraska, 1966.

I. OHIO

Eddy, Mary O., comp. *Ballads and Songs From Ohio*. New York: Austin, 1939.
Contains collected versions of 25 English and Scottish popular ballads and almost 300 European and native American folksongs.

Korson, George G., ed. *Coal Dust on the Fiddle: Songs and Stories of the Bituminous Industry*. Philadelphia: U. Pennsylvania, 1943.

Includes material on Ohio, Indiana, and Illinois, as well as on Pennsylvania and the southern states.

Margolis, Ellen. *Idy the Fox-Chasing Cow, and Other Stories*. Cleveland: World, 1962.
Seven stories gathered from the Ohio hill country.

J. Wisconsin

Brown, Charles E. *Collected Tales and Legends of Wisconsin*. Madison: 1923–45.
Pamphlets of the Wisconsin Folklore Society.

_____. "A Record of Wisconsin Antiquities." *Wisconsin Archaeologist*, 5 (1906), 289–429.

Chapin, Earl V. *Earl Chapin's Tales of Wisconsin*. River Falls, Wisc.: U. Wisconsin, River Falls Press, 1973.

Gard, Robert. *This is Wisconsin*. Spring Green: Wisconsin House, 1969.
Sketches of ordinary people and places by one who traveled up and down the state gathering impressions.

_____. *Wisconsin is My Doorstep: A Dramatist's Yarn Book of Wisconsin Lore*. New York: Longmans, 1948.
Combination of folklore and history.

Gard, Robert and L. G. Sorden. *Wisconsin Lore: Antics and Anecdotes of Wisconsin People and Places*. New York: Duell, 1962.
Material similar to the *Doorstep* volume.

Gard, Robert and Elaine Reetz, comps. *The Trail of the Serpent: The Fox River Valley: Lore and Legend*. Madison: Wisconsin House, 1937.

Gleason, Margaret. *Wisconsin Folklore and Tall Tales: A Selected List*. Madison, 1950.

Holmes, Fred L. *Old World Wisconsin: Around Europe in the Badger State*. Eau Claire: Hale, 1944.
Popular excursion into the cultural multiplicity of the state. Chapters on Germans, Cornishmen, Belgians, Icelanders, and other groups.

Kearney, Luke S. *The Hodag, and Other Tales of Logging Camps*. Wausau: Author, 1938.

Rickaby, Franz, ed. *Ballads and Songs of the Shanty-Boy*. Cambridge: Harvard U., 1926.
Scholarly collection of 84 songs and ballads of the lumber industry in Michigan, Wisconsin, and Minnesota, 1870–1900.

Sorden, Leland G. *Lumberjack Lingo*. Spring Green: Wisconsin House, 1969.
Not confined to the Midwest.

Wyman, Walker D. *Mythical Creatures of the North Country*. River Falls, Wisc.: State University Press, 1969.
Volume in the North Country Lore series.

NOTE: There have as yet been no full-length studies of folklore from the eastern Dakotas. Those wishing to introduce themselves to the subject should consult Haywood (cited in the following bibliography section) or the WPA Guides for those states. Indeed, the WPA Guides provide a good introduction to folklore in all Midwest states.

5. BIBLIOGRAPHY

Davidson, Levette J. *A Guide to American Folklore*. Denver: U. Denver, 1951.
Excellent handbook; reviews folklore research and presents an overview of scholarship.

Haywood, Charles. *A Bibliography of North American Folklore and Folksong*. 2 vols. Rev. ed. New York: Dover, 1961.
Arranged by state; valuable annotated lists, but complete only down to about 1950.

Lawless, Ray M. *Folksingers and Folksongs of America*. Rev. ed. New York: Duell, 1965.
Not particularly convenient in organization, but includes detailed annotations on many Midwest titles.

Leach, Maria, ed. *Funk and Wagnalls Standard Dictionary of Folklore, Mythology and Legend*. New York: Funk, 1949–50.

Lomax, Alan and Sidney R. Cowell. *American Folk Song and Folk Lore: A Regional Bibliography*. New York: Progressive Education Assn., 1942.
Pamphlet.

Mugridge, Donald H. and Blanche F. McCrum. *A Guide to the Study of the United States of*

America: Representative Books Reflecting the Development of American Life and Thought. Washington: Library of Congress, 1960.
Selective, annotated lists; includes a section on "Folklore, Folk Music, Folk Art."
Tallman, Marjorie. *Dictionary of American Folklore.* New York: Philosophical Library, 1959.

Gerald C. Nemanic
Northeastern Illinois University
Chicago, Illinois

PERSONAL NARRATIVES

AN IMMENSE VOLUME of material, much of it with scant literary value, has come down to us in the form of journals, travel sketches, personal reminiscences, and the like. All such personal accounts have been grouped under this heading, from the jottings of seventeenth-century Jesuit missionaries such as Marquette to the contemporary accounts of canoe trips on the northern lakes. Until recently, publishers have had little inclination to re-edit or reprint the narratives of early explorers, pioneers, and adventurers. Now, with ambitious reprint series such as University Microfilms' *March of America*, these documents are becoming available to the scholar and general reader.

Those interested in approaching the early midwestern narratives in an organized way should consult Hubach's *Early Midwestern Travel Narratives 1634–1830: An Annotated Bibliography* (1961).

1. BIBLIOGRAPHY

Buck, Solon J. *Travel and Description, 1765–1865* . . . . Springfield: Historical Library, 1914.
An exhaustive bibliography of early books on Illinois.
Cox, Edward. *A Reference Guide to the Literature of Travel.* Seattle: U. Washington, 1938.
Not complete after 1800; vol. 2 contains a section on North America.
Haywood, Charles. *A Bibliography of North American Folklore and Folksong.* 2d ed. New York: Dover, 1961.
Haywood's broad definition of "folklore" allows him to include plenty of personal narratives in his lists; since Hubach goes only to 1850, this work is especially valuable for materials in the last half of the nineteenth century; vol. 1 includes chapters on the Midwest and on the individual midwestern states.
Hubach, Robert R. *Early Midwestern Travel Narratives: An Annotated Bibliography 1634–1850.* Detroit: Wayne, 1961.
Invaluable reference work; contains substantial bibliographies on early midwestern literary history and concise resumes of hundreds of narratives; supercedes most of the work done earlier.
Kaplan, Louis et al. *A Bibliography of American Autobiographies.* Madison: U. Wisconsin, 1961.

Indexes by geographical area, e.g., "West North Central States," etc., but this doesn't prove too useful; supposedly complete to 1946, but many holes exist.

Klyberg, Albert T. *A Critical Bibliography for the March of America Series*. Ann Arbor: University Microfilms, 1966.

This series has reprinted, among other things, about twenty Midwest narratives written over the past 300 years, many of them long out of print.

Lillard, Richard G. *American Life in Autobiography: A Descriptive Guide*. Stanford: Stanford U., 1956.

Annotated bibliography of these autobiographies which reflect life in the U.S. and its regions; includes a section on writers and other artists.

Matthews, William. *American Diaries: An Annotated Bibliography of American Diaries Written Prior to the Year 1861*. Berkeley: U. California, 1945.

Includes a number of obscure Midwest items not readily found elsewhere. Arranged chronologically.

Monaghan, Frank, comp. *French Travellers in the United States, 1765–1932*. New York: New York Public Library, 1933.

Especially valuable for the period since 1850 not covered by Hubach.

Nevins, Allan, ed. *America Through British Eyes*. New York: Oxford, 1948.

Not much midwestern material in this anthology, but it does include an annotated bibliography of British travel writing on America. Originally published as *American Social History as Recorded by British Travellers* (1923).

Rader, Jesse L. *South of Forty: From the Mississippi to the Rio Grande: A Bibliography*. Norman: U. Oklahoma, 1947.

Most valuable for the literature of the Southwest, but does include most of Kansas and Missouri in its coverage.

Rusk, Ralph. *The Literature of the Middle Western Frontier*. New York: Columbia U., 1925.

Vol. 2 of this pioneering work is a bibliography of midwestern literature to 1840; much of it is superceded by Hubach.

Spiller, Robert et al. *The Literary History of the United States: Bibliography*. 3d rev. ed. New York: Macmillan, 1963.

Section on "Chronicles of the Frontier" provides a general survey of personal narratives for that period.

Trent, William P. et al. *Cambridge History of American Literature*. 4 vols. New York: Putnam, 1917–1921.

Includes a checklist, "Travellers and Explorers, 1846–1900," in vol. 4; this list provides some supplement to Hubach but it is not annotated or complete.

Wagner, Henry R. *The Plains and the Rockies: A Bibliography of Original Narratives of Travel and Adventure, 1800–1865*. 3d ed. rev. and enl. by Charles L. Camp. Columbus, Ohio: Long's, 1953.

Adds only fifteen years to Hubach and, for our purposes, is only valuable in that period for materials on the Plains states.

2. ANTHOLOGIES

Angle, Paul M., ed. *Prairie State: Impressions of Illinois, 1637–1967: by Travellers and Other Observers*. Chicago: U. Chicago, 1968.

Includes excerpts ranging from the French explorers and missionaries to the present. Among those represented are Marquette, Jolliet, Hennepin, Birkbeck, Bryant, Dickens, Anthony Trollope, de Beauvoir, and Peattie.

Brockway, Wallace and Bart K. Winer, eds. *Homespun America* . . . . New York: Simon and Shuster, 1958.

Material by Cartwright, Cobbett, F. Trollope, Marryat, Dickens, A. Trollope, Eggleston, Beecher, Twain, Riley, Field, Dunne, Hubbard, E. W. Howe, W. A. White, Ade, S. Anderson, Lardner, Sandburg, Cedric Adams, others.

Cox, Isaac J., ed. *The Journals of René-Robert Cavalier, Sieur de la Salle* . . . . 2 vols. New York: Barnes, 1905.

The various narratives of the LaSalle expeditions brought together, including those of Tonty, Hennepin, Membré, LaSalle, and others.

Flanagan, John T., ed. *America is West: An Anthology of Middlewestern Life and Literature.* Minneapolis: U. Minnesota, 1945.
    Includes excerpts from Schoolcraft, Hennepin, Carver, Cartwright, Smart, Henry, and more. Perhaps the best general anthology of all periods in midwestern writing.

Greenberg, David B., ed. *Land That Our Fathers Plowed.* Norman: U. Oklahoma, 1969.
    The section on the Midwest includes excerpts from Burland, Muir, Garland, Quick, Croy, and Hedrick.

Havighurst, Walter. *The Great Lakes Reader.* New York: Macmillan, 1966.
    Among the personal narrative excerpted are works by Jean Claude Allouez, Hennepin, Schoolcraft, de Kruif, Hoffman, Lanman, Henry Howe, Whitlock, Hedrick, Thwaites, Henry, Bryant, and others.

_____, ed. *Land of the Long Horizons.* New York: Coward-McCann, 1960.
    Nicely illustrated collection of Midwest narratives including excerpts from Marquette, Hennepin, Birkbeck, Muir, Audobon, Dreiser, Peattie, and many more.

Kellogg, Louise P., ed. *Early Narratives of the Old Northwest, 1634–1698.* New York: Scribner, 1917.
    Contains a long and valuable introduction; included are narratives (in English translation) of Nicolet, Allouez, Marquette, Jolliet, Tonty and many others; part of Original Narratives of Early American History series.

Kenton, Edna., ed. *The Indiana of North America . . . .* New York: Harcourt, Brace, 1927.
    A volume of excerpts from the generally unobtainable seventy-three volume work edited by Thwaites (*The Jesuit Relations*), with an introduction by Thwaites; includes writings by Lalemont, Vimont, and Marquette.

Lindley, Harlow, ed. *Indiana as Seen by Early Travellers.* Indianapolis: Historical Commission, 1916.
    Coverage to 1830. Includes excerpts from Birkbeck, Faux, Flint, Sealsfield, and others.

McDermott, John F., ed. *Before Mark Twain: A Sampler of Old, Old Times on the Mississippi.* Carbondale: Southern Illinois U., 1968.
    First volume of an ambitious Southern Illinois Press project which will edit and reprint early travel narratives of the midwestern rivers (Travels on Western Waters). This volume includes excerpts from Flint, Latrobe, Featherstonhaugh, and others.

McFarling, Lloyd, ed. *Exploring the Northern Plains.* Caldwell, Ida.: Caxton, 1955.
    Excerpts from Lewis and Clark, Brackenridge, Catlin, Parkman, Fremont, Joseph Nicolet, Audubon, and others. Includes a chronology and bibliography.

McIlvaine, Mabel and Milo M. Quaife, eds. *Lakeside Press Classics of Western Exploration and Travel.* Chicago: Donnelley, 1903.
    This great series of reprints and new editions has included a number of anthologies, among them *Reminiscences of Early Chicago* (1912) and *Pictures of Illinois One Hundred Years Ago* (1918).

Mealing, S. R. *Jesuit Relations and Allied Documents: A Selection.* Toronto: McClelland, 1963.

Neider, Charles, ed. *The Great West.* New York: Coward-McCann, 1958.
    Particularly strong on the Far West and Southwest, but some materials on the Prairies and Plains are included; excerpts from Irving, Stevenson, and others.

Pierce, Bessie, ed. *As Others See Chicago: Impressions of Visitors, 1673–1933.* Chicago: U. Chicago, 1933.
    Goes well together with Angle's book (see above). Excerpts from the writings of Marquette, Latrobe, Hoffman, Martineau, Kipling, Chesterton, and many more.

Quaife, Milo, ed. *Pictures of Illinois One Hundred Years ago.* Chicago: Donnelley, 1918.
    Part of the Lakeside Classics series; includes long excerpts from Birkbeck and Schoolcraft.

Shea, John D. G., ed. *Discovery and Exploration of the Mississippi Valley.* New York: Redfield, 1852.
    An old and hard to get item, but one containing a long introduction and narratives by Marquette, Allouez, Hennepin, and others.

Thwaites, Reuben G., ed. *Early Western Travels (1748–1846): A Series of Annotated Reprints.* 32 vols. Cleveland: Clark, 1904–07.
    What the *Jesuit Relations* did for the literature of French exploration, this volume did for

the later travel literature in English: notable among the reprints included are works by
Brackenridge, Faux, Long, Gregg, Flagg, Michaux, and Flower.

_____. *The Jesuit Relations and Allied Documents: Travels and Explorations of the Jesuit
Missionaries in New France, 1610–1791 . . . . The Original French Latin and Italian
Texts, with English Translations and Notes . . . .* 73 vols. Cleveland: Clark,
1896–1901.
This monumental edition stands as the single most important scholarly project in its field.
Extensive introductions and bibliographies throughout.

Tryon, Warren S., ed. *A Mirror for Americans.* Chicago: U. Chicago, 1952.
Excerpts "the works of native Americans" who traveled through the country. A long section
on the Midwest includes materials from Brackenridge, Flagg, Gregg, and others. Reprinted
in an abridged edition as *My Native Land* (1961).

Washburn, Wilcomb, ed. *Narratives of North American Indian Captivities.* 111 vols. New
York: Garland, 1975.
311 titles are included.

Wright, Louis B. and Elaine Fowler, eds. *The Moving Frontier.* New York: Delacorte, 1972.
Part of Great Explorers series; excerpts from the writings of Nicolet, Allouez, Marquette,
Hennepin, LaSalle, Washington, Henry, Lewis and Clark, and others.

3. SOME PROMINENT NARRATIVES

Personal Narratives by authors included in the author bibliographies appear there. Consult
appropriate subject bibliographies (e.g., Blacks, Chicago, Indians) for additional narrative
entries.

From among the hundreds of published personal narratives that deal with
life in the Midwest, we have tried to choose the most important for inclusion here. Among them are narratives by well-known literary figures, especially those written or available in English. Among the rest, we include
those that seem especially well written or thoughtful, keeping in mind that
differences in taste might dictate a different choice by others.

A. FRENCH EXPLORERS AND MISSIONARIES
(SEVENTEENTH AND EIGHTEENTH CENTURIES).

The French domain, headquartered at Quebec and extending into the low-
er Mississippi Valley, was responsible for virtually all literary activity in
the Midwest from the 1640s until the founding of the Republic. The Spanish remained to the south and southwest of the region, except for the mo-
mentary incursion of Coronado into Kansas. Thus it is the journals of
French missionaries like Jolliet and LaSalle which provide a portrait of
conditions in the region. Some of these, e.g., those of Marquette, Hennepin, and others listed below, made valid contributions to literature. The
great majority of the narratives served strictly utilitarian functions. The
collection and translation of these documents in the *Jesuit Relations* (see
Anthologies above) is one of the monuments of American scholarship.

Charlevoix, Pierre Francois Xavier de. *Histoire et Description Generale de la Nouvelle France,
avec le Journal Historique d'un Voyage Fait par Ordre du Roi dans l'Amérique Septen-
trionnele.* 3 vols. Paris: Nyon Fils, 1744. English translations: *Journal of a Voyage to North
America . . . .* 2 vols. London, 1761. (This translation reprinted in a modern edition by
Louise P. Kellogg for the Caxton Club. 2 vols. Chicago, 1923.); *History and General Description of New France.* New York: Harper, 1900 (tr. and ed. by John D. G. Shea).
Although the bulk of the Jesuit Charlevoix' work deals with Canada (he was professor of

rhetoric at the college at Quebec), he did take a long canoe voyage through the Great Lakes, the Illinois country, and on down the Mississippi to the Gulf in 1721. This scholar-adventurer's description of Indian life and the Mississippi Valley wilderness are vivid and precise.

Galineé, Rene Brehan de. *Voyage . . . de Galineé, 1669–70*. Montreal: Societe Historique, 1875. English translation: *Exploration of the Great Lakes 1669–70, by Dollier de Casson and de Brehant de Galineé*. Tr. and ed. by James H. Coyne. Toronto: Ontario Historical Society, 1903.

Fr. Galineé's account of his Great Lakes journey has real charm; plenty of descriptive writing.

Hennepin, Louis. *Description de la Louisiane . . . .* Paris: Huré, 1683.

Several later editions. This and the following item are perhaps the best written narratives of the French explorations; Hennepin, a wily and bombastic cleric who traveled with LaSalle, was an extremely popular writer in his day. Many of his stories are downright falsehoods, but he comes off as a talented writer and an engaging eccentric.

————. *Nouvelle decouverte d'un très grand pays dans l'Amerique . . . .* Utrecht: Broedelet, 1697. English translation in *A New Discovery of a Vast Country in America . . . .* Ed. by Reuben G. Thwaites. Chicago: McClurg, 1903.

Jolliet, Louis. *Journal*. Paris: Thévenot, 1681. English translation in Shea (q.v.).

A short memoir by the celebrated merchant-explorer who discovered the Mississippi River with Marquette in 1673. Jolliet's original journal, kept during the journey, was lost.

Lahontan, Louis-Armand de Lom d'Ares, Baron de. *Nouveaux Voyages . . . dans l'Amérique Septentrionale*. 2 vols. The Hague, 1703. English translation, *New Voyages to North America . . . .* 2 vols. London, 1703.

Soldier-adventurer and litterateur, Lahontan fought Indians and explored the West between 1683–1692. His well-written and popular accounts sparked interest in primitive life among literary Frenchmen.

LaSalle, René-Robert Cavalier, Sieur de. *Relation of the Discovery and Voyages of Cavalier de la Salle, from 1679–1681 . . . .* Translated by M. B. Anderson for the Caxton Club edition. Chicago, 1901.

This most interesting and famous of French explorers found no time to write a formal narrative, but many of his papers relating to the expeditions have been collected in the *Relation*. Forceful leader, egomaniac, daring adventurer, his exploits have been retold in the powerful narrative by Francis Parkman (q.v.).

LaVèrendrye, Pierre Gaultier de Varennes, Sieur de. *Mémoir . . . au Sujet des Etablissements pour Parvenu à la Découverte de la Mer de l'Ouest*. In *Decouvertes et Etablissements des Francais dans le Sud de l'Amerique Septentrionale (1615–1754)*. Ed. Pierre Margry. 6 vols. Paris, 1879–88. English translation in *Journals and Letters of Pierre Gaultier de la Vèrendrye and his Sons*. Ed. by Lawrence J. Burpee. Toronto, 1927.

One of the most imaginative writers and explorers among the French. LaVèrendrye, Canadian born, explored northern Minnesota and North Dakota in search of a Northwest Passage between 1731 and 1743. He and his sons were the first whites to explore the upper Missouri River.

Marquette, Jacques. *Voyage et Découverte du P. Marquette et Sr. Jolliet dans l'Amerique Septentrionale*. In *Recueil de Voyage . . . .* Paris: Thévenot, 1681.

Marquette's intense missionary zeal and feeling for nature combine in what is perhaps the most beautifully written of early French narratives. A companion of Jolliet, he explored the Mississippi with him in 1673. After attempting to convert the Illinois Indians he died near Lake Michigan in 1675. Complete English translations appear in Thwaites (q.v.) and Shea (q.v.); there is a partial translation in Kellogg (q.v.).

Radisson, Pierre Esprit. *Voyages of Pierre Esprit Radisson . . . from 1652–1684*. London, 1885.

Radisson explored the upper regions of the Mississippi River with Groseilliers in 1659 and composed five narratives in English covering a period of thirty-two years. The manuscripts of this fur-trader's work remained unpublished for two hundred years. Excerpts are reprinted in Kellogg's anthology (q.v.).

Vimont, Fr. Barthelemy. *Relation de ce que s'est Passé en la Nouvelle France en . . . 1642*. Paris, 1643. English translation in Thwaites and Kellogg. Vimont wrote the first narrative of French exploration in the Midwest, an account of his friend Jean Nicolet's travels to

Wisconsin in 1634. Nicolet, a *coureur de bois* (illegal fur trader, literally "woods runner") thought when reaching Wisconsin that he was in the Orient. He thereupon clothed himself in a Chinese robe to meet the Winnebagos.

B.   ACCOUNTS OF LATER SCIENTIFIC, MILITARY, AND EXPLORATORY MISSIONS

The French presence in the Mississippi Valley was effectively ended during the last half of the eighteenth century, and accounts by the French missionaries in *The Jesuit Relations* ended by 1791. President Jefferson's purchase of "Louisiana" from Napoleon in 1803 gave America the midwestern lands between the Mississippi and Missouri Rivers. The business of exploration was then carried on by Americans, who, like the French, kept journals along the way. Most of these writings are matter-of-fact notations about the topography, climate, Indian life, etc., of the region, but several do rise above unadorned technical language to give vivid, imaginative substance to the haunting wilderness. Among the more important and interesting narratives are the following:

Audubon, John. *Ornithological Biography . . . Interspersed with Delineations of American Scenery and Manners.* 5 vols. Edinburgh: Black, 1831–39.
    The famed ornithologist traveled up and down the Mississippi and Missouri Rivers observing the birds, countryside, and people of those regions. Besides the *Biography*, other relevant writings by Audubon include his *Journal . . . Made During his Trip to New Orleans in 1820–1821.* Boston: Club of Odd Volumes, 1929, and his *Journal . . . Made While Obtaining Subscriptions to his "Birds of America" 1840–1843.* Boston: Club of Odd Volumes, 1929.
Carver, Jonathan. *Travels Through the Interior Parts of North-America, in the Years, 1766, 1767, and 1768.* London: Author, 1778.
    Carver was an American adventurer who explored the Minnesota country and other areas west of the Mississippi. He had difficulty publishing his *Travels*, but once launched they proved extremely popular.
Clark, George Rogers. *The Conquest of the Illinois.* Chicago: Donnelley, 1920.
    This modern edition gathers the Clark journals which had appeared earlier in periodicals. The adventures of Colonel Clark and his band of American "Long Knives" among the French and Indians of Vincennes, Kaskaskia, and Cahokia are told in a straight forward, unadorned manner, but the fantastic events speak for themselves.
Clark, William and Meriwether Lewis. *History of the Expedition of Captains Lewis and Clark, to the Sources of the Missouri, Thence Across the Rocky Mountains, and down the River Columbia to the Pacific Ocean.* 2 vols. Philadelphia and New York, 1814. Reprinted many times (including a modern condensed version in one volume edited by Bernard DeVoto), this work details the historic and dramatic voyage from Pittsburgh on the Ohio to the Pacific Ocean between 1803–1806. Although long dull stretches occur in the narrative, the wonder and scope of the vast American heartland are recorded in this epic work. The 1965 edition by Elliot Coues is best. A volume of photographs by Ingvard H. Eide, with excerpts, was published as *American Odyssey* (1970).
Fremont, John Charles. *Memoirs of My Life.* 2 vols. Chicago: Bedford, Clarke, 1887.
    One of the great romantic figures of the early West, Colonel Fremont explored extensively between the Mississippi and Missouri Rivers in the 1830s. His *Memoirs* contain many vivid descriptions of life on the prairies.
Henry, Alexander. *New Light on the Early History of the Great Northwest.* Ed. Elliott Coues. 3 vols. New York: Harper, 1897.
    Henry was an English fur trader in the Northern lakes region between 1761 and 1808. His life in the Minnesota country is recorded in this careful journal. In another journal, *Travels and Adventures in Canada and the Indian Territories, Between the Years 1760 and 1776*

(New York, 1809) and reprinted in an edition by Milo M. Quaife (Chicago, 1921), Henry tells of his capture by Chippewa Indians at Fort Mackinac in 1763.

Long, Stephen H. *Voyage in a Six Oared Skiff to the Falls of Saint Anthony. Collections of the Minnesota Historical Society II* (1889, report of 1860–1867). See pp. 9–83.
Major Long was involved in a number of exploratory expeditions in the North country during the 1810s and 1820s. His diary of the "six-oared skiff" voyage represents his best writing. The dogged Long was involved in a famous set-to with the romantic Italian Giacomo Beltrami (q.v.) during an expedition to the Red River in 1823.

Nicollet, Joseph Nicholas. *Journals.* Ed. by Martha Bray. St. Paul: Historical Society, 1970.
This important work by the French scientist and descendant of Jean Nicolet was finally published as a book, in English, by the Minnesota Historical Society. It recounts Nicollet's 1836–37 travels among the Indians of the upper Mississippi and contains a good deal of information about their folkways.

Pike, Zebulon M. *An Account of Expeditions . . . During the Years 1805, 1806, and 1807 . . . .* Philadelphia and Baltimore, 1810. A standard edition is *The Expedition of Zebulon Montgomery Pike, to Head Waters of the Mississippi River, through Louisiana Territory, and in New Spain, During the Years 1805–6-7.* Ed. by Elliot Coues. 3 vols. New York, 1895.
Leading a military expedition, Pike surveyed and explored the upper Mississippi near its source. His journal is thorough and appealing, giving many valuable glimpses of Indian life and strong descriptions of the country.

Rogers, Robert. *Journals . . . .* London: Author, 1765. Exp. ed. Albany: Munsell's, 1883.
Rogers was the American-born leader of the fabled "Rogers Rangers," a British force which fought the French. Rogers led a mercurial life in the western wilderness. He worked closely with Jonathan Carver (q.v.). His journals give a lively sense of life in the Great Lakes region during the 1760s.

Washington, George. *George Washington and the West.* New York: Century, 1905.
Certainly not a literary piece, this diary of Washington's search for a link between the Atlantic and the Great Lakes, a trip undertaken in 1784, reveals the author's interest in the growth of the West.

C. Literary accounts of the Midwestern frontier by travelers

The literary travel account was already established as a popular genre when the midwestern frontier opened in the nineteenth century. Among the renowned authors who traveled to and wrote impressions of the midwestern landscape and its social structures were Dickens, Bryant, Irving, Whitman, Stevenson, Marryat, Anthony and Frances Trollope, Harriet Martineau, and others. Cooper, who wrote of the region in novels (*Oak Openings, The Prairie*), never visited it.

Beltrami, Giacomo C. *A Pilgrimage in Europe and America . . . .* 2 vols. London: Hunt, 1828.
This interesting narrative was partly reprinted in *A Pilgrimage to America* (1962). An Italian disciple of Rousseau, Beltrami bungled through an incredible journey in the wilds of northern Minnesota. After leaving the relative safety of Major Stephen Long's expedition, Beltrami, hardly a woodsman, wandered alone in the region near the Mississippi headwaters. Pulling a canoe through miles of swamp (he never learned to paddle), Beltrami stumbled upon Indians and was finally led back to civilization. His romantic account of the American woods influenced many a visionary European bent on adventure.

Bird, Robert. *Peter Pilgrim: or, a Rambler's Recollections.* 2 vols. Philadelphia: Lea, 1838.
Bird is best known for his novels of Kentucky border life, such as *Nick of the Woods* (1837). The "Pilgrim" sketches are products of his travels on the southern and midwestern frontier.

Brackenridge, Henry. *Views of Louisiana.* Pittsburgh: Cramer, 1814.
Second edition expanded and retitled *Journal of a Voyage Up the River Missouri* (Baltimore: Coole, 1816). *Journal* was reprinted in Thwaites's *Early Western Travels*, vol. 1 (q.v.).
_____. *Recollections of Persons and Places in the West.* Philadelphia: Kay, 1834.

Son of Hugh Henry Brackenridge, he spent a good deal of time traveling the Midwest between 1811 and 1821. Brackenridge presents a vivid portrait of frontier life in *Recollections* . . . (his autobiography) and in his *Journal* of a Missouri River trip in 1811.

Bradbury, John. *Travels in the Interior of America* . . . . 2d ed. London: Sherwood, 1819.
Excerpted in *Early Western Travels*. The straightforward narrative of this English botanist is especially valuable for its observations of Indian life in the great river valleys of this region.

Bremer, Fredrika. *The Homes of the New World*. 3 vols. Stockholm, 1853. (In Swedish.) Tr. by Mary Howitt. 2 vols. New York: Harper, 1853.
Thoughtful and sensitive pictures of mid-century Chicago, the prairies, family life on the frontier, etc. Miss Bremer was a well-known Swedish writer who published a number of travel pieces on Europe and America. Selections from *Homes* were published as *America of the Fifties*, ed. Adolph B. Benson. New York, 1924.

Bryant, William Cullen. "Illinois Fifty Years Ago." In *Prose Writings of William Cullen Bryant*. New York: Appleton, 1889. *Letters of a Traveller*. New York: Putnam, 1850. (Reprinted from the New York *Post*.)
The author of the "The Prairies" had extensive first-hand knowledge of the Midwest gleaned on several trips to visit his family in Illinois. His attitude toward the frontier is positive and optimistic.

Catlin, George. *Life Among the Indians*. Edinburgh, 1867.
First person narrative by the famous ethnologist and painter of Indians. An earlier volume, *North American Indians* (New York, 1841) is a collection of letters written during his explorations among the Indians between 1832–40. Much Midwest material in both works.

Dickens, Charles. *American Notes for General Circulation*. 2 vols. London: Chapman, 1842.
Already famous, Dickens took a trip to Illinois in 1842, primarily to look after his land investments. Disillusioned by the "detestable morass" of Cairo, Ill., Dickens's general impression of the midwestern frontier was one of disgust. He called the Mississippi River "that intolerable river dragging its slimy length and ugly freight abruptly off towards New Orleans."

Faux, William. *Memorable Days in America*. London: Simpkin, 1823. Reprinted in Thwaites's *Early Western Travels*, vol. 11.
Satirical, rough and tumble account by a remarkable English character. Faux summed up his feeling for the midwestern frontier succinctly: "I hate the prairies, all of them."

Featherstonhaugh, George W. *A Canoe Voyage up the Minnay Sotor*. 2 vols. London: Bentley, 1847.
An English geologist, Featherstonhaugh traveled extensively in the northern Mississippi Valley between 1835 and 1837. His narrative is hardly technical; there are excellent descriptions of nature and reflective comments on frontier life.

Flagg, Edmund. *The Far West* . . . . 2 vols. New York: Harper, 1838.
Romantic young poet and journalist waxes rapturous over the frontier in his letters describing journeys on the Ohio and Mississippi rivers. Certainly one of the more dazzling accounts of the early Midwest.

Fuller, Sarah M. *Summer on the Lakes in 1843*. Boston: Little, Brown, 1844.
Miss Fuller took a short respite from her feverish intellectual life in Boston to make a short tour of the Great Lakes region in 1843. Her descriptions of Chicago and Milwaukee life are especially interesting. In general, she reflected mixed enthusiasm and dismay over the crude circumstances prevalent in the Old Northwest.

Gladstone, Thomas H. *The Englishman in Kansas* . . . . New York: Miller, 1857.
Collected reports of London *Times* correspondent dealing with the "Bloody Kansas" warfare of the 1850s. One of the best dispassionate accounts of those troubled times on the frontier. Includes interesting sketches of frontier life.

Hoffman, Charles F. *A Winter in the West*. 2 vols. New York: Harper, 1835. Reprinted with new notes, Chicago: Fergus, 1882.
Engaging romantic accounts of the Midwest frontier by a talented New York writer and editor. Many comments on customs and manners of the region, as well as impassioned descriptions of nature.

———. *Wild Scenes in the Forest and Prairie*. 2 vols. London: Bentley, 1839.

Imlay, Gilbert. *A Topographical Description of the Western Territory of North America* . . . . London: Debratt, 1792.

Precise language of his title misrepresents the rhapsodic intensity and questionable authenticity of Imlay's impressions. It is possible that most of his "description" of midwestern life was gleaned from other sources. A sophisticated adventurer, Imlay was involved in a plot to take over Louisiana. His novel *The Emigrants* (1793) romanticized the westering movement in America.

Irving, John T. *Indian Sketches* . . . . 2 vols. Philadelphia: Carey, 1835.

Irving traveled from St. Louis to Pawnee Indian country on the western prairies in 1833. His sympathetic and accurate descriptions of Indian life are especially valuable. Irving was the nephew of the celebrated American writer.

Irving, Washington. *A Tour on the Prairies*. Philadelphia: Carey, 1835.

The first treatment of the Midwest by a noted American writer. Irving's trip with Paulding, Latrobe, and Pourtales provided material for later works on the frontier. Irving's *Journals* (1819) and *Western Journals* (1844) provide more of his generally positive reflections on the Midwest.

Jameson, Anna B. *Winter Studies and Summer Rambles in Canada*. 3 vols. London, 1838.

Engaging account of travels in the Great Lakes region by the Irish writer.

Lanman, Charles. *Essays for Summer Hours*. Boston: Hilliard, 1841.

This professional travel writer and artist made several excursions into the Midwest. A number of his pieces on the northern wilderness are notable for vivid descriptions of the country and people.

————. *A Summer in the Wilderness* . . . . New York: Appleton, 1847.

————. *Adventures in the Wilds of the United States and British American Provinces*. 2 vols. Philadelphia: Moore, 1856.

Latrobe, Charles J. *The Rambler in North America, 1832–1833*. 2 vols. London: Seeley, 1835.

Delightful, casual account of western travels by the British writer who traveled America with Washington Irving and Count Pourtales.

Lewis, Henry. *Making a Motion Picture in 1848*. Ed. by Bertha Heilbron. St. Paul: Minnesota Historical Society, 1936.

Painter and panoramist, Lewis wrote two excellent books on his impressions of the frontier river country. This title (which refers to the panoramas) tells of a canoe voyage from Minneapolis to St. Louis.

————. *The Valley of the Mississippi Illustrated*. Tr. by A. H. Poatgieter. Ed. by Bertha Heilbron. St. Paul: Minnesota Historical Society, 1967.

First published in Germany in 1854. The 1967 English version includes Lewis's fine original illustrations.

Marryat, Frederick. *A Diary in America, with Remarks on its Institutions*. 2 vols. Philadelphia: Carey, 1839; 3 vols. London: Longmans, 1839.

English sea-writer visited America in 1837–38, spending considerable time in the Midwest. His *Diary* is well paced, often quite funny. His feelings about the frontier were generally negative. The Mississippi River struck him as "The Great Sewer."

Martineau, Harriet. *Society in America* . . . . 2 vols. New York: Saunders, 1837.

Perceptive commentary on American manners, especially on the frontier, by a hardy Englishwoman who roamed the forests and prairies in the 1830s. Her portrait of the rough life in a young Chicago has particular interest.

————. *Retrospect of Western Travel*. 3 vols. London: Saunders, 1838; 2 vols. New York: Harper, 1838.

Moore, Nathaniel F. *A Trip from New York to the Falls of St. Anthony in 1845*. Ed. Stanley Pargellis and Ruth L. Butler. Chicago: U. Chicago, 1946.

Belatedly published through the Newberry Library. Moore was president of Columbia University and a leader in American education. He vividly describes Indian customs in the Upper Midwest and writes well throughout.

Oliphant, Laurence. *Minnesota and the Far West*. Edinburgh: Blackwood, 1855.

British traveler and Superintendent of Indian Affairs for Canada; his urbane observations were first published in *Blackwood's Magazine*.

Parkman, Francis. *The California and Oregon Trail: Being Sketches of Prairie and Rocky Mountain Life*. New York: Putnam, 1849.

The great historian of the "forest" kept a journal of his trip to the prairies and mountains in 1846. This is perhaps the best written account of the prairie frontier and the human traffic on its trails into the West.

Pourtales, Count Alfred de. *On the Western Tour with Washington Irving*. Ed. by George F. Spaulding. Norman: U. Oklahoma, 1968.

This recently discovered material throws more light on the western tour of Irving, Latrobe, and Pourtales in the 1830s. Pourtales, something of a Swiss dandy, describes the frontier in entertaining fashion.

Rich, Virtulon. *Western Life in the Stirrups*. Ed. by Dwight Smith. Chicago: Caxton Club, 1965.

This manuscript was found in 1963. It contains lively descriptions of the Indiana and Ohio frontier observed by an obscure gentleman during a western trip of 1832.

Sealsfield, Charles. *Die Vereinigten Staaten von Nord Amerika* . . . . Stuttgart: Cotta, 1827. Abr. English tr. in *The Americans as They Are* . . . . London: Hurst, 1828.

A descriptive analysis of the Midwest frontier by the German novelist (real name, Karl Postl). His generally favorable impressions encouraged many Germans to emigrate. Sealsfield also wrote fiction, in German, with Midwest settings.

Shirreff, Patrick. *A Tour through North America* . . . . Edinburgh: Oliver, 1835.

Written as a handbook for British farmers who wished to emigrate, this book turns out to be much more. Shirreff paints an accurate and absorbing picture of Mississippi Valley and Chicago life in the 1830s.

Smith, Solomon F. *Theatrical Apprenticeship* . . . . Philadelphia: Carey, 1846.

Lively adventures of a theatrical impresario on the frontier. Together with Joseph Jefferson's *Autobiography*, this provides the best first hand picture of early theatre in the Midwest.

Stevenson, Robert Louis. *Across the Plains*. New York: Scribner, 1892. Included in *From Scotland to Silverado*. Ed. by James D. Hart. Cambridge: Harvard, 1966.

Hart's is the first complete edition, the earlier ones having been bowdlerized. Stevenson's Scotland to California trip in 1879 resulted in his interesting chapters on "The Nebraska Plains" and "By Way of Council Bluffs." His view of Chicago: "a great and gloomy city."

Thoreau, Henry D. *The First and Last Journeys of Thoreau* . . . . Ed. by Franklin B. Sanborn. 2 vols. Boston: Bibliophile Society, 1905.

The journal of Thoreau's visit to Minnesota (1861) is in vol. 2.

————. *Thoreau's Minnesota Journey: Two Documents. Thoreau's Notes on the Journey West and the Letters of Horace Mann, Jr*. Ed. by Walter Harding. *Thoreau Society Booklet 16*. Geneseo, N.Y., 1962.

Tocqueville, Alexis C. H. M. C. de. *De Tocqueville's Voyage en Amerique*. Ed. by R. Clyde Ford. Boston: Heath, 1909. English tr. George Lawrence. *Journey to America*. New Haven: Yale, 1959.

Famed author of *Democracy in America* visited the western Great Lakes and the Mississippi Valley in 1831. His descriptions of social conditions on the frontier are acute.

Trollope, Anthony. *North America*. London: Chapman, 1862.

The famous English novelist made his way to America thirty years after his mother had infuriated the American reading public with her book (see below). His view of the rapidly disappearing Midwest frontier was hardly inspiring. A dull book, *North America* is of interest mainly because of the author's reputation.

Trollope, Frances M. *Domestic Manners of the Americans*. 2 vols. London: Whittaker, 1832.

This cantankerous lady wrote one of the most popular and controversial accounts of midwestern (especially Cincinnati) life in the nineteenth century. She excited the consternation of American patriots by lambasting the vulgarity of frontier society.

Whitman, Walt. "Excerpts from a Traveller's Note Book—Nos. 1, 2, and 3." In *The Uncollected Poetry and Prose of Walt Whitman*. Ed. by Emery Holloway. 2 vols. New York: Doubleday, 1921.

Whitman's impressions of the Mississippi Valley and Great Lakes region (including Chicago) from a trip made in 1848. The vast, wild country excited him, and echoes of his trip can be found laced through *Leaves of Grass*.

Wilkey, Major Walter, pseud. [Ebenezer Deming]. *Western Emigration* . . . . New York: Claiborne, 1839.

Possibly the best piece of satirical writing about the Midwest frontier. Wilkey describes himself as "an Honest Yeoman of Mooseboro, State of Maine." He writes of a trip to a town called "Edensburgh" Illinois, which, as one can imagine, proves to be anything but Edenic.

D. PIONEER NARRATIVES OF SPECIAL INTEREST (NINETEENTH CENTURY)

Few frontier settlers, hunters, or guides were literary men. For that matter, not many were even literate. But there was an indigenous literature growing up in this country, much of it written, at first, in the form of journals, diaries, and letters. Europeans and New England intellectuals like Birkbeck, Flower, and Robert Owen came West to experiment with farming and communal living. Circuit preachers such as Dow and Cartwright rode among frontier settlements observing the ways of sinners. Teachers, lawyers, and journalists settled in the Midwest and commenced writing about the place. Even a few yeomen took up the pen, recording the dramatic simplicity of their lives in a new country, far away from the old ties in Sweden, Germany, or Devonshire. Of the incredible volume of such writing only a few of the better examples can be mentioned here. Many of these pieces are being made available for general readers in such reprints as the *Lakeside Classics* or University Microfilm's *March of America* series.

Birkbeck, Morris. *Letters from Illinois*. Boston: Wells, 1818.
An Englishman of good education, Birkbeck helped found an English settlement in Edwards County, Illinois. His *Letters* are sophisticated and very readable. His enthusiasm over the possibilities of the frontier led him to urge others to follow from England. Another relevant book, *Notes on a Journey in America . . .* , was published in 1817.
Burlend, Rebecca. *A True Picture of Emigration*. London: Berger, 1848. Reprint, Chicago: Donnelley, 1936.
The Burlend family emigrated from England to Illinois in 1831. They farmed in Pike County, where Mrs. Burlend's account, as related to her son Edward, gives a careful and sensitive picture of rural midwestern life in that time.
Carson, Christopher (Kit). *Kit Carson's Story of His Own Life*. Ed. by Blanche C. Grant. Taos, N.M.: Carson Memorial Foundation, 1926.
Most of Carson's adventurous career was spent in the Rockies, but he had been raised in Missouri. This autobiography reflects a good deal of Missouri life in the 1820s and 1830s.
Cartwright, Peter. *Autobiography of Peter Cartwright, the Backwoods Preacher*. Ed. by W. P. Strickland. Cincinnati: Cranston, 1856.
A rough and ready circuit preacher, Cartwright writes with bravado and charm about his rugged life traveling the Midwest, especially Illinois, beginning in the 1820s.
Dow, Lorenzo. *Perambulations of a Cosmopolite . . . .* Rochester: Printed for the Publisher, 1842.
Another circuit riding preacher, Dow roamed the Midwest in the early years of the nineteenth century. Like Cartwright, Dow gives a vivid picture of religious life on the frontier.
Drake, Dr. Daniel. *Pioneer Life in Kentucky . . . .* Ed. by Charles D. Drake. Cincinnati: Clark, 1870.
Behind this somewhat misleading title we find a text consisting of letters written by Drake, a sometime Cincinnatian, to his children. Drake wrote and lectured about the developing frontier and was a notable personality in Ohio and Kentucky during the first half of the nineteenth century.
Flower, Richard. *Letters from Lexington and the Illinois . . . .* London: Ridgway, 1819.
This son of George Flower (who had come to the frontier with Birkbeck) wrote persuasively about the potential of the Midwest. His positive picture of Illinois life was sharply contrast-

ed with that of eastern interests who were discouraging western settlement. Flower's *Letters* was written partly to counter attacks on the frontier written by William Cobbett and others.

Gregg, Josiah. *Commerce of the Prairies* . . . . 2 vols. New York: Langley, 1844.
  Reprinted many times, Gregg's reflectively poetic narrative deals mainly with the origin and development of the Santa Fe Trail.

Hall, Baynard R. *The New Purchase, or Seven and a Half Years in the Far West.* New York: Appleton, 1843.
  Describes frontier life in southern Indiana, where Hall became a professor at the new state university. Hall emphasizes his disappointment with life in the Midwest.

Heckewelder, John G. *A Narrative of the Mission of the United Brethren Among the Delaware and Mohegan Indians* . . . . Philadelphia: McCarty, 1820.
  This Moravian missionary lived an adventurous life on the frontier. The narrative covers the period 1740–1810.

Hedrick, Ulysses P. *The Land of the Crooked Tree.* New York: Oxford, 1948.
  An intimate and engaging account of pioneer life in the L'Arbe Croche region of northern Michigan, by an early settler.

Howells, William Cooper. *Recollections of Life in Ohio, 1813–1840.* Cincinnati: Clarke, 1895.
  Father of the famous novelist, W. C. Howells's memoirs are interesting for that reason alone. Yet this dignified Ohio pioneer writes well himself and gives a valuable picture of a less rambunctious side of the frontier.

Kennerly, William C. and Elizabeth Russell. *Persimmon Hill.* Norman: U. Oklahoma, 1948.
  Colorful and nostalgic rendition of nineteenth century life in a young St. Louis. "Persimmon Hill" was the old Kennerly home, now destroyed.

Kinzie, Juliette. *Wau-bun, the "Early Day" in the North-West.* New York: Derby, 1856.
  Wife of Chicago pioneer John Kinzie, Juliette writes of her travels on the Great Lakes in the 1830s and describes the traders and Indians in early Chicago. Her narrative includes a second-hand account of the Indian massacre at Fort Dearborn in 1812.

Nowlin, William. *The Bark Covered House* . . . . Detroit: Author, 1876.
  Absorbing account of pioneer Nowlin's life in the Michigan woods. Excellent portrait of the simple and hardy life—planting, building, dealing with the natural hazards of weather, wild animals, and Indians.

Robinson, Sara. *Kansas* . . . . Cincinnati: Blanchard, 1856.
  Beautifully-written picture of Kansas in the troubled 1850s. Mrs. Robinson shows a fine lyric sense and, at the same time, is able to write bitterly of the terrors in "bleeding Kansas."

Sanford, Mollie D. *Mollie.* Lincoln: U. Nebraska, 1959.
  Only recently published, this pioneer woman's journal covers a period from 1857–66 in the Colorado and Nebraska Territories; this is a nicely reflective and well-written narrative.

E. MODERN NARRATIVES

Modern narratives of the Midwest have reflected both the diversity and complexity of life in the region. By 1900 most of the rural Midwest had been homesteaded and settled. The new frontier became urban, with burgeoning cities like Chicago, Cleveland, Detroit, Kansas City, Minneapolis, and Milwaukee attracting millions from eastern Europe, Germany, Scandinavia, and Italy. Blacks from the South and Jews from Russia helped create immense ghettoes in Chicago, and smaller ones in other cities.

The narratives mirror both the turmoil and the nostalgia associated with twentieth-century life. The rich mixture of ethnicity and social strife in an urban setting characterize the narratives of Oscar Ameringer, Ernst Meyer, "Mezz" Mezzrow, and others. The great majority of modern midwestern narratives are associated with small town and rural life, or with incursions into wilderness areas. Nostalgic memoirs abound, e.g., those of Mary Austin, Ray Stannard Baker, Thomas Hart Benton, Bruce Catton, and Mackinlay Kantor. Quietly insightful observations of small town life are provided in many an obscure volume by chroniclers like Albert Britt, Loula Erdman, "Jake Falstaff," Francis Grierson, Charles Tenney Jackson, Della Lutes, Hugh Orchard, Helen Santmyer, and William Venable. Indians (narratives by Crashing Thunder, Mountain Wolf Woman, Charles Eastman) and Blacks (Ruby Goodwin, Langston Hughes, and Era Bell Thompson) provide insights into the rural experiences of those minorities. There are the tales of movement back to the land, literally and/or emotionally, in the books of Jerry Apps, Curtis Stadtfeld, and others. Natural history (Donald C. Peattie, John Muir) or reflective observations of wilderness (Helen Hoover, Florence Jaques) are to be found in abundance. The list that follows will give some idea of the variety and scope of these writings.

Ameringer, Oscar. *If You Don't Weaken . . . the Autobiography of Oscar Ameringer.* New York: Holt, 1940.
   Wisconsin socialist and labor leader tells of his experiences with strikes, German Americans, and the panoply of Midwest life in the late nineteenth century.
Anderson, Chester, ed. *Growing Up in Minnesota: Ten Writers Remember Their Childhoods.* Minneapolis: U. Minnesota, 1976.
   The ten include: Anderson, Meridel Le Sueur, Harrison Salisbury, Gerald Vizenor, Keith Gunderson, Shirley Schoonover, Toyse Kyle, Robert Bly, Edna & Howard Hong, and Mary Hong Loe.
Apps, Jerry. *The Land Still Lives.* Madison: Wisconsin House, 1970.
   Simple, strong description of an experience in moving "back to the land" on a farm north of Madison.
Austin, Mary. *Earth Horizon.* Boston: Houghton Mifflin, 1932.
   Although the novelist spent most of her life in the Southwest, she writes here, with zest, of her childhood at Nolinwood, Illinois. Her impressions of the sober, religious life of the rural Midwest are especially vivid.
Baker, Ray Stannard. *Native American: The Book of My Youth.* New York: Scribner, 1941.
   First volume of an autobiography continued in American Chronicle (1945); a charming, nostalgic account of his Wisconsin boyhood.
Benton, Thomas Hart. *An Artist in America.* 3d rev. ed. Columbia: U. Missouri, 1968.
   Excellent autobiography by the painter and muralist who spearheaded the Regional movement; chapters on Benton's youth in Missouri are especially delightful.
Bissell, Richard. *My Life on the Mississippi, or Why I am Not Mark Twain.* Boston: Little, Brown, 1973.
   Humorous, witty concoction by the popular novelist and travel writer.
Blegen, Theodore C. *The Saga of Saga Hill.* St. Paul: Minnesota Historical Society, 1971.
   Scholar's reminiscence of boyhood summers on Lake Minnetonka in the 1890s and early 1900s.
Bolz, J. Arnold. *Portage into the Past: By Canoe along the Minnesota-Ontario Boundary Waters.* Minneapolis: U. Minnesota, 1960.
   Solid nature writing; includes drawings by Lee Jaques.
Britt, Albert. *An America That Was.* Barre, Mass.: Barre, 1964.
   Recollections of life on an Illinois farm at the turn of the century. Britt writes well and with real sympathy for the old life.
Burman, Ben L. *Big River to Cross.* New York: Day, 1948.
   This Kentuckian has written a great deal about the southern Mississippi River, but in this book he describes the modern river scene from the Twin Cities to New Orleans.
Caldwell, Erskine. *Afternoons in Mid-America.* New York: Dodd, 1976.
   Descriptive sketches collected in the form of seventeen letters. With drawing by Virginia Caldwell.
Catton, Bruce. *Waiting for the Morning Train.* New York: Doubleday, 1972.
   Reminiscence of the author's early years in Michigan.

Chapman, William M. *Remember the Wind: A Prairie Memoir*. Philadelphia: Lippincott, 1965.
Sensitive portrayal of Sioux ways and prairie tonalities by an easterner forced to move west because of his son's health. Chapman spent three years on the Standing Rock Indian Reservation in South Dakota.

Cole, Cyrenus. *I Remember, I Remember*. Iowa City: State Historical Society, 1936.
Historian's autobiography of early life in Iowa.

Darrow, Clarence. *The Story of My Life*. New York: Scribner, 1932.
Straight forward narrative of the celebrated lawyer's youth in Kinsman, Ohio, and at the University of Michigan. Later chapters center on the Chicago scene of his great legal struggles.

Davenport, Eugene. *Timberland Times*. Urbana: U. Illinois, 1950.
Pioneer life in Michigan.

DeKruif, Paul. *The Sweeping Wind*. New York: Harcourt, 1962.
Deals mostly with the author's writing career, love life, and scientific adventures; includes a section on the writing of *Seven Iron Men*, the story of iron mining development in Minnesota.

Douglas, Lloyd C. *Time to Remember*. Boston: Houghton Mifflin, 1951.
This son of an Ohio Valley clergyman writes tellingly, perhaps more so than he intends, of the "nice" life in small towns of the Midwest, circa 1890. The author later went on to write best selling novels like *The Robe*.

Eiseley, Loren. *All the Strange Hours*. New York: Harper, 1975.
Anthropologist and nature writer tells of his unhappy youth in Nebraska and of his lifelong fascination with the Great Plains.

Eifert, Virginia L. *Journeys in Green Places: The Shores and Woods of Wisconsin's Door Peninsula*. New York: Dodd, 1963.
Lyrical nature writing; the author has produced other books in a similar vein, including *Delta Queen* (1960) and *River World* (1959).

Falstaff, Jake, pseud. [Herman Fetzer]. *Jacoby's Corners*. Boston: Houghton Mifflin, 1940.
The *Corners* books (see also *The Big Snow*, 1941) are popular and nostalgic portraits of life in the rural Midwest.

Firestone, Clark B. *Sycamore Shores*. New York: McBride, 1936.
Nicely wrought narrative of the author's explorations on the tributaries of the Ohio River. A similar book on the Mississippi River by the same author is *Flowing South* (1941).

Folwell, William W. *W. W. Folwell: The Autobiography and Letters of a Pioneer of Culture*. Ed. by Solon J. Buck. Minneapolis: U. Minnesota, 1933.
Important narrative by a famous early historian.

Fugina, Frank J. *Lore and Lure of the Upper Mississippi River* . . . . Winona, Minn.: Author, 1945.
Story of a river captain's observations; tends to be a bit dry in parts, but still a valuable document.

Glazier, William. *Headwaters of the Mississippi* . . . . Chicago: Rand McNally, 1893.
Entertaining travel book and good representative of the "Mississippi Madness" which victimized adventurer-explorers of the late nineteenth century. The author claims, in the midst of his colorful descriptions of Mississippi River life, to have finally discovered the true source of that stream. Glazier also penned that all-time favorite, *Ocean to Ocean on Horseback*.

Goodwin, Ruby B. *It's Good to be Black*. Garden City: Doubleday, 1953.
Black writer tells of her happy childhood in DuQuoin, Ill., where she grew up in the family of a coal miner. Her emphasis on the pleasant side of black life in the region makes an interesting contrast to the impressions of Malcolm X, Richard Wright, and others.

Grierson, Francis. *The Valley of Shadows*. 5th ed. Boston: Houghton Mifflin, 1948.
These "recollections of scenes and episodes of my early life in Illinois and Missouri" have a haunting, mystical aura appropriate to a man who wrote and lectured for many years on theosophy and the occult. Van Wyck Brooks and Edmund Wilson, among others, have praised this forgotten book and tried to revive interest in Grierson. First published in 1909.

Hall, James N. *My Island Home: An Autobiography*. Boston: Little, Brown, 1952.

The "island" is Papeete, but adventure novelist Hall takes up the first one-third of his memoir with scenes of his youth at Colfax, Iowa, and at Grinnell College.

Hall, Leonard. *Stars Upstream: Life Along an Ozark River.* Chicago: U. Chicago, 1958.
Decent nature writing centered on the Current River country, by a naturalist and long-time resident of the Ozarks. Other books by Hall include *Possom Trot Farm* (1949) and *Country Year* (1957), both concerned with life in the Ozarks.

Hapgood, Hutchins. *A Victorian in the Modern World.* New York: Harcourt, 1939.
Autobiography details the author's life amidst the left-wing political swirls of his times. His description of youth in Alton, Ill., and of his later years in Chicago are handled well.

Hapgood, Norman. *The Changing Years.* New York: Farrar, 1930.
Brother of Hutchins, he also writes tellingly of early years in Alton.

Hastings, Robert J. *A Nickel's Worth of Skim Milk: A Boy's View of the Great Depression.* Carbondale: Southern Illinois U., 1972.
On growing up in Marion, a southern Illinois mining town.

Hawkinson, John E. *The Brothers.* Washington: Author, 1969.
Swedish family life in Minnesota.

Hoover, Helen. *The Long Shadowed Forest.* New York: Crowell, 1963.
Pleasant if unexceptional nature writing; Hoover and her husband have lived in the northeastern Minnesota wilderness for many years. Her later titles include *The Gift of the Deer* (1966) and *A Place in the Woods* (1969).

Hubbard, Harlan. *Shanty Boat.* New York: Dodd, 1953.
Artist Hubbard describes a three-year trip down the Ohio and Mississippi rivers; some fine descriptive writing and illustrations by the author.

Humphreys, John R. *The Last of the Middle West.* New York: Doubleday, 1966.
Affectionate, well-written account of a rambling rediscovery of the region by a native who sees the old country disappearing.

Hunt, Frazier. *One American and His Attempt at Education.* New York: Simon & Schuster, 1938.
Memoir of the midwestern journalist whose boyhood on a series of farms is recreated with a strong human touch.

Jackson, Charles Tenney. *The Buffalo Wallow.* Indianapolis: Bobbs-Merrill, 1953.
Folksy, often humorous account of the novelist's youth in central Nebraska.

Jaques, Florence P. *The Geese Fly High.* Minneapolis: U. Minnesota, 1939.
Concerns the flight of ducks and geese down the Mississippi flyway. Illustrated by Lee Jaques. This husband-wife team has collaborated on other similar works, including *Snowshoe Country* (1944) and *Canoe Country* (1938).

Jensen, Carl C. *An American Saga.* Boston: Little, Brown, 1927.
Sensitively written account of a young Dane's assimilation into midwestern life. Jensen later became a prominent sociologist.

Johnson, Alvin S. *Pioneer's Progress.* New York: Viking, 1952.
By the founder of New School for Social Research, who grew up on a Nebraska farm.

Johnson, Henry. *The Other Side of Main Street.* New York: Columbia U., 1943.
This educator writes well of his early years at Sauk Centre, Minn. (the setting for Sinclair Lewis's *Main Street*).

Johnson, Josephine. *The Inland Island.* New York: Simon & Schuster, 1969.
Highly literate depiction of farm life in southern Ohio by the author of *Now in November* and other novels.

Jonk, Clarence. *River Journey.* New York: Stein & Day, 1964.
Journal account of a house boat excursion on the upper Mississippi.

Larson, Laurence M. *The Log Book of a Young Immigrant.* Northfield, Minn.: Norwegian-American Historical Assn., 1939.
Outside of Rolvaag's books, this is perhaps the most substantial account of Norwegian immigrant life in America.

Leopold, Aldo. *A Sand County Almanac.* Enl. ed. New York: Oxford, 1966.
Wisconsin naturalist and ecologist writes beautifully of his experiences in the wilds of the state. A similar book by Leopold is *Round River* (1953) which, like the *Almanac*, is material published posthumously from the author's journals.

Lighty, Kent and Margaret. *Shanty-Boat*. New York: Century, 1930.
    One of the best accounts of the eccentric "river people" on and near the Mississippi.
Lindbergh, Charles A. *Boyhood on the Upper Mississippi: A Reminiscent Letter*. St. Paul: Minnesota Historical Society, 1972.
    Aviator recalls his boyhood on a farm near Little Falls, Minn.
Logan, Ben. *The Land Remembers: The Story of a Farm and Its People*. New York: Viking, 1975.
    Memoir of farm life in Wisconsin.
McKenney, Ruth. *Industrial Valley*. New York: Harcourt, 1939.
    Author of the popular novel *My Sister Eileen* writes here of her life in Akron, Ohio.
Mathews, John J. *Talking to the Moon*. Chicago: U. Chicago, 1945.
    An Osage Indian educated in the white man's world, Mathews returned to live ten years alone on a Kansas prairie.
Malcolm X [Malcolm Little]. *The Autobiography of Malcolm X*. New York: Grove, 1965.
    Black Muslim leader recounts his small-town Michigan boyhood.
Mead, Robert D. *Reunion: Twenty-five Years Out of School*. New York: Saturday Review, 1972.
    Basically a memoir of Evanston, Ill., in the 1940s.
Merrick, George B. *Old Times on the Upper Mississippi*. Cleveland: 1909.
    Not really literary, this memoir of a steamboat pilot is rich in the language and culture of the river. Chapters on "The Art of Steering," "Bar and Barkeepers," "Gamblers and Gambling," "Music and Art," others.
Meyer, Ernst L. *"Hey! Yellowbacks!": The War Diary of a Conscientious Objector*. New York: Day, 1930.
    Narrative of the author's experiences before and after his expulsion from the University of Wisconsin. Especially interesting are the descriptions of the atmosphere in Madison during the 1910s and of contacts with various fundamentalist sects in conscientious objector camps. Meyer also wrote a memoir of German immigrant life in Milwaukee, *Bucket Boy* (1947).
Mezzrow, Milton ("Mezz"). *Really the Blues*. New York: Random, 1946.
    Written in a rich patois of underground life in Chicago, this is probably the best narrative of the Chicago jazz era.
Mott, Frank Luther. *Time Enough: Essays in Autobiography*. Chapel Hill: U. North Carolina, 1962.
    Fifteen evocative essays ranging from the author's Quaker youth in rural Iowa to his years as a professor of journalism at the University of Missouri.
Muir, John. *The Story of My Boyhood and Youth*. Boston: Houghton Mifflin, 1913.
    The great naturalist's life from the beginnings in Scotland through his student years at the University of Wisconsin; several beautifully written chapters are given over to his boyhood on a Wisconsin farm.
Nelson, Joseph. *Backwoods Teacher*. Philadelphia: Lippincott, 1949
    Experiences of a school teacher in the Ozarks; slightly reminiscent of James Agee's evocations of the rural South.
Olson, Sigurd F. *The Singing Wilderness*. New York: Knopf, 1956.
    Good nature writing on the Superior-Quetico country of Minnesota and Ontario by a well-known naturalist; among Olson's later titles dealing with the same region: *Listening Point* (1958); *Open Horizons* (1969); *Sigurd F. Olson's Wilderness Days* (1972).
Orchard, Hugh A. *Old Orchard Farm*. Ames: Iowa State U., 1952.
    Richly anecdotal autobiography of a lifetime farmer and clergyman from Des Moines County, Ia.
Parks, Gordon. *A Choice of Weapons*. New York: Harper, 1966.
    Angry autobiography of a black man growing up in Kansas and Minnesota. Author of *The Learning Tree* and one-time *Life* photographer, Parks has made a number of Hollywood films featuring black actors.
Peattie, Donald C. *A Prairie Grove*. New York: Simon & Schuster, 1938.
    Well-written account of the prairie tree groves of Illinois, by a famous naturalist and native son.
Peattie, Roderick. *The Incurable Romantic*. New York: Macmillan, 1941.

Autobiography of the American geographer is filled with a deep feeling for the natural world of his Nebraska youth.

Price, Willard. *The Amazing Mississippi*. New York: Day, 1962.

Perhaps the best popular travel book on the river.

Purcell, William Gray. *St. Croix Trail Country: Recollections of Wisconsin*. Minneapolis: U. Minnesota, 1967.

Good nature writing and character sketches; Purcell was an architectural colleague of Wright and Sullivan.

Rand, Austin L. and Rheua M. *A Midwestern Almanac*. New York: Ronald, 1961.

Observations of the Indiana dunes over the course of a year by two Chicago naturalists who made their home in the area.

Reed, Earl H. *The Dune Country*. New York: Lane, 1916.

Reed has put together several books of description and sketch work on Midwest byways. In *Dune Country* he explores the isolated people and places at the southern end of Lake Michigan. Other similar collections: *Sketches in Duneland* (1918); *Sketches in Jacobia* (1919), on Michigan; *Tales of a Vanishing River* (1920), on the Kankakee River region.

Reishus, Martha. *The Rag Rug*. New York: Vantage, 1955.

Norwegians in Minnesota.

Rhodes, Richard. *The Inland Ground*. New York: Atheneum, 1970.

One of the best contemporary accounts of the region. The chapters inspired by the author's experiences at the Iowa Writers' Workshop and on a coyote hunt in Kansas are especially fine narrative writing.

Ross, Edward A. *Seventy Years of It*. New York: Appleton, 1936.

Opinionated and engaging memoirs of a controversial sociologist who spent his youth on farms in Kansas and Iowa. He writes a good deal about his academic life at the University of Wisconsin.

Runyon, Tom. *In for Life: A Convict's Story*. New York: Norton, 1953.

Perhaps the best memoir of a "Depression bandit," of whom there were many in the Midwest. Runyon took up bank robbery after a sanguine South Dakota boyhood. Written at the Iowa State Penitentiary.

Russell, Charles E. *A-rafting on the Mississip'*. New York: Century, 1928.

Entertaining combination of river history and personal reminiscence by one who grew up along the frontier Mississippi.

Santmyer, Helen H. *Ohio Town*. Columbus: Ohio State U., 1962.

Nostalgic reminiscence of Xenia, Ohio. Santmyer went on to an academic career at Wellesley and at Cedarville College.

Sauter, Van Gordon and Stephen Feldman. *Fabled Land/Timeless River*. Chicago: Quadrangle, 1970.

Photo-text product of a Mississippi River excursion. Sauter writes well and Feldman's photography is excellent.

Schurz, Carl. *The Reminiscences of Carl Schurz*. 3 vols. New York: McClure, 1907–08.

Among the very best memoirs by a midwestern public figure. Schurz's political life had breadth and color, from his early years as a German republican through his participation in the political arenas of Washington, D.C., Missouri, and Wisconsin.

Sevareid, Eric. *Not So Wild a Dream*. New York: Knopf, 1946.

Accounts of the journalist's youth in North Dakota and of his years at the University of Minnesota. Sevareid wrote of a canoe trip through Minnesota and Ontario in *Canoeing With the Cree* (1935).

Smart, Charles A. *R.F.D.* New York: Norton, 1938.

Born in Cleveland, Smart moved to New York in 1917, wrote two novels and decided to return to a small farm inheritance in rural Ohio. He handles the threadbare theme of city boy on the farm with real grace and humor.

Stadtfeld, Curtis K. *From the Land and Back*. New York: Scribner, 1972.

Nicely realized story of the author's farming forefathers in central Michigan.

Stallard, John. *Four in a Wild Place*. New York: Norton, 1971.

City folk in the wilds again (Wisconsin), but carried along by some sound writing.

Street, Julian L. *Abroad at Home*. New York: Century, 1914.

Literary, urbane travel book mostly on the Midwest.

Thomas, William. *The Country in the Boy*. Nashville: Nelson, 1976.
 Lyric evocation of Ohio youth in the early twentieth century.
Thompson, Era Bell. *American Daughter*. Chicago: U. Chicago, 1946.
 Ebony editor writes of her childhood among Blacks in the rural Midwest.
Thwaites, Reuben G. *On the Storied Ohio*. Rev. ed. Chicago: McClurg, 1903 [original title: *Afloat on the Ohio*].
 The great scholar and editor of *The Jesuit Relations* traveled the Midwest water routes himself, by canoe. Here and in *Down Historic Waterways* (rev. ed., 1926) he presents a good mix of history and personal narrative.
Traver, Robert, pseud. [John D. Voelker]. *Trout Madness*. New York: St. Martin's, 1960.
 Former judge has written good fishing yarns of upper Michigan. Another similar volume is *Trout Magic* (1974). Traver penned the popular novel *Anatomy of a Murder* (1958) and other narratives of his experiences as a lawyer and judge, including *Small Town D.A.* (rev. ed. 1956) and *Troubleshooters* (1943).
Ueland, Andreas. *Recollections of an Immigrant*. New York: Minton, 1929.
 Norwegian immigrants in Minnesota.
Van Doren, Carl. *Three Worlds*. New York: Harper, 1936.
 This oldest son of a famous Midwest family covers his boyhood at Hope, Ill., and his years at the University of Illinois in Part One, "First World." The first section of Part One, "Village," was reprinted as *An Illinois Boyhood* (1939).
Van Goetham, Larry. *The Fifth Horseman is Riding*. New York: Macmillan, 1974.
 Interesting essays on the natural history of Wisconsin.
Venable, William H. *A Buckeye Boyhood*. Cincinnati: Clarke, 1911.
 Good, old-fashioned, romantic idyll of mid-nineteenth century boyhood by the chronicler of early literary history in the Ohio Valley.
Wallace, Lew. *Lew Wallace: An Autobiography*. 2 vols. New York: Harper, 1906.
 Classic document of Midwest American life and values. Lawyer, Civil War general and diplomat as well as author of an early best-seller, *Ben Hur* (1880), Wallace writes extensively of his early life in Indiana.
Werkley, Caroline E. *Mister Carnegie's Library*. New York: American Heritage, 1970.
 Humorous, pungent account of life in Moberly, Mo.
Woodward, Mary D. *The Checkered Years*. Caldwell, Ida.: Caxton, 1937.
 Perceptive diary of a young woman living on a bonanza farm near Fargo in the 1880s.
Wright, Frank Lloyd. *An Autobiography*. Rev. ed. New York: Duell, 1943.
 One of the best autobiographies to come out of the region; the architect's youth in Wisconsin and his Chicago years are evoked with real brilliance.
Xan, Erna O. *Wisconsin My Home*. Madison: U. Wisconsin, 1950.
 Simple, charming story of Norwegian immigrants.

Gerald C. Nemanic
Northeastern Illinois University
Chicago, Illinois

ARCHITECTURE AND GRAPHICS

ASIDE FROM FICTION, architecture is the art form most often associated with the Midwest. To be accurate, it was Chicago, rather than the Midwest region, which provided the capital and receptive environment necessary to encourage the emerging leaders of a new architecture. Thus, it is appropriate that the majority of items devoted to this subject be found in the Chicago bibliography. One is referred there for books about the "Chicago School" and for studies of individual architects like Wright, Sullivan, and Mies.

Of course the influence of these men did spread through the region, notably in the development of a "Prairie School," which Wright helped found. In general, the urban Midwest has been particularly interested in architectural innovation, and the titles listed here reflect that interest.

In graphics, the Midwest has provided very little leadership. Paris and New York have been the center of creative activity in the field since the nineteenth century, and the Midwest has produced no school comparable to the many (Impressionist, Post-Impressionist, Barbizon, Ash-Can, etc.) which have dominated the art world of the last hundred years. One school of regional painters, headed by Thomas Hart Benton, John Steuart Curry, and Grant Wood, managed to cause a stir, especially in the 1930s when themes of social realism were popular. Unlike its architectural and literary counterparts in the region, this movement was essentially reactionary. Another group of painters, those limners of Indian and frontier life such as George Catlin, George Caleb Bingham, and Seth Eastman, has maintained a reputation for ingenuity and vigor.

1. ARCHITECTURE: MIDWEST

For books dealing primarily with Chicago architecture and architects, consult the Chicago bibliography in this volume.

Andrews, Wayne. *Architecture in Chicago and Mid-America: A Photographic History*. New York: Atheneum, 1968.
  Section on major Chicago and other Midwest architects.
———. *Architecture in Michigan: A Representative Photographic Survey*. Detroit: Wayne, 1967.
  With a short introduction.
Brooks, H. Allen. *The Prairie School: Frank Lloyd Wright and his Midwest Contemporaries*. Toronto: U. Toronto, 1972.
  Detailed introduction and commentary accompanies photographs and drawings.
Bryan, John A. *Missouri's Contribution to American Architecture: A History of the Architectural Achievements in this State . . . .* St. Louis: Architectural Club, 1928.
  Short introductions to each of five chapters in this photographic chronology.
Campen, Richard N. *The Architecture of the Western Reserve, 1800–1900*. Cleveland: Case Western Reserve U., 1971.
  Excellent discussion of the distinctive architecture in "Ohio's New England."
———. *Ohio—An Architectural Portrait*. Chagrin Falls, Ohio: West Summit Press, 1973.
  Valuable introductory essay and commentary on individual photographic illustrations.
Drury, John. *Historic Midwest Houses*. Minneapolis: U. Minnesota, 1947.
  This, like all of Drury's architectural books, is interesting as much for its historical material as for its commentary on architecture.
———. *Old Illinois Houses*. Springfield: Historical Society, 1941.
Duncan, Hugh D. *Culture and Democracy—The Struggle for Form and Architecture in Chicago and the Middle West during the Life and Times of Louis H. Sullivan*. Totowa, N.J.: Bedminster Press, 1965.
  A pioneering cultural history of the region, marred at times by scientific jargon; lengthy discussions of Midwest architecture.

Ferry, W. Hawkins. *The Buildings of Detroit: A History*. Detroit: Wayne, 1969.
Survey of the city's architecture from the eighteenth century to the present.

Frary, Ihna T. *Early Homes of Ohio*. Richmond, Va.: Garrett, 1936.
Discusses the transplanting of architectural forms from the East into Ohio.

Kennedy, Roger G. *Minnesota Houses: An Architectural and Historical View*. Minneapolis: Dillon, 1967.

Keyes, Margaret N. *Nineteenth Century Home Architecture*. Iowa City: U. Iowa, 1967.
On the architecture of Iowa City.

Koeper, Frederick. *Illinois Architecture: From Territorial Times to the Present—a Selective Guide*. Chicago: U. Chicago, 1968.
Published under the auspices of the Illinois Sesquicentennial Commission.

———. *Historic St. Paul Buildings: A Report of the Historic Sites Committee*. St. Paul: City Planning Board, 1964.

Lafore, Laurence D. *American Classic*. Iowa City: Iowa State Historical Dept., 1975.
Focuses on the architecture of Iowa City as a museum setting.

McClure, Harlan E., ed. *Twin Cities Architecture: Minneapolis and St. Paul, 1820–1955*. New York: Reinhold, 1955.
Informative pamphlet.

McCue, George. *The Building Art in St. Louis: A Guide to the Architecture of the City and its Environs*. St. Louis: American Institute of Architects, 1964.

Madden, Betty I. *Arts, Crafts, and Architecture in Early Illinois*. Urbana: U. Illinois, 1975.
Extensive cultural history of the state to 1860.

Meyer, Katharine M., ed. *Detroit Architecture: American Institute of Architects Guide*. Detroit: Wayne, 1971.

Newcomb, Rexford G. *Architecture of the Old Northwest Territory*. Chicago: U. Chicago, 1950.
Best introduction to nineteenth century building in the Midwest.

Peat, Wilbur D. *Indiana Houses of the Nineteenth Century*. Indianapolis: Indiana Historical Society, 1962.
Study of domestic architecture in the state.

Perrin, Richard W. *Historic Wisconsin Buildings: A Survey of Pioneer Architecture, 1835–1870*. Milwaukee: Public Museum Press, 1962.
This, and the following titles by the same author, provide an excellent introduction to the architecture of Wisconsin.

———. *Wisconsin Architecture: A Catalog of Buildings Represented in the Library of Congress*. Washington: GPO, 1966.

———. *The Architecture of Wisconsin*. Madison: State Historical Society, 1967.

———. *Milwaukee Landmarks: An Architectural Heritage*. Milwaukee: Public Museum Press, 1968.

Torbert, Donald R. *A Century of Art and Architecture in Minnesota*. Minneapolis: U. Minnesota, 1958.
Originally published as a section of *A History of the Arts in Minnesota*, edited by William Van O'Connor.

Western Architect. *The Work of Purcell and Elmslie, Architects*. Park Forest, Ill.: Prairie School Press, 1965.
Includes all texts and plates from relevant 1913–15 issues of *Western Architect;* with a new introduction by David Gebhard.

2. GRAPHICS

A. General Studies

Baigell, Matthew. *The American Scene: American Painting of the 1930's*. New York: Praeger, 1974.
Treats Benton, Wood, and other Midwest painters.

Barr, Paul. *North Dakota Artists*. Grand Forks: U. North Dakota Library Studies, 1954.
Short survey of the field.

Barton, John R. *Rural Artists of Wisconsin*. Madison: U. Wisconsin, 1948.
Describes the origin and development of the rural art movement in Wisconsin.

Battaglia, Elio L. *The Face of Missouri*. Columbia: U. Missouri, 1960.
Photographic essay.

Brill, Charles. *Indian and Free: A Contemporary Portrait of Life on a Chippewa Reservation*. Minneapolis: U. Minnesota, 1974.
Photographs and text.

Brown, Stirling W. *In the Limestone Valley: Pen Pictures of Early Days in Wisconsin*. West Salem, Wisc.: 1900.

Bucklin, Clarissa, ed. *Nebraska Art and Artists*. Lincoln: U. Nebraska, 1932.
Short (82 p.) illustrated survey, with biographical sketches.

Burnet, Mary Q. *Art and Artists of Indiana*. New York: Century, 1921.
An extensive history.

Butts, Porter. *Art in Wisconsin*. Madison: Democratic Printing, 1936.
History of art on the Wisconsin frontier.

Chamberlin, Mary W. *Guide to Art Reference Books*. Chicago: American Library Assn., 1959.
Basic and comprehensive.

Clark, Edna M. *Ohio Art and Artists*. Richmond, Va.: Garrett, 1932.
Extensive illustrated survey with biographical data.

Coen, Rena. *Painting and Sculpture in Minnesota, 1820–1914*. Minneapolis: U. Minnesota, 1976.

Dawdy, Doris O. *Artists of the American West: A Biographical Dictionary*. Chicago: Swallow, 1973.

──────. *Annotated Bibliography of American Indian Painting*. New York: Museum of the American Indian, 1968.
Pamphlet.

Engle, Paul. *Portrait of Iowa*. Minneapolis: Adams, 1974.
Photographs of the state by John Zielinski and others; good extended introduction by poet Engle.

Flexner, James T. *That Wilder Image: The Painting of America's Native School from Thomas Cole to Winslow Homer*. Boston: Little, Brown, 1962.
Sections on Bingham, Bodmer, Catlin, and Miller. The following titles by the same author include some material on Midwest frontier art.

──────. *The Light of Distant Skies, 1760–1835*. New York: Harcourt, 1954.

──────. *Nineteenth Century American Painting*. New York: Putnam, 1970.

Getlein, Frank. *The Lure of the Great West*. Waukesha, Wisc.: Country Beautiful, 1973.
Sound survey of Western American art from the aborigines to Georgia O'Keefe; excellent color reproductions of artists like Bingham, Miller, Bodmer, and Catlin.

Gibson, Arthur H. *Artists of Early Michigan: A Biographical Dictionary of Artists Native to or Active in Michigan, 1701–1900*. Ann Arbor: U. Michigan, 1975.

Goodman, Bernard. *Readings and Writings in the Arts: A Handbook*. Detroit: Wayne, 1972.

Haberland, Wolfgang. *The Art of North America*. New York: Greystone, 1968.
Includes material on Great Plains art and an extensive Indian bibliography.

Hallmark editors. *Kansas City*. Kansas City: Hallmark, 1973.
Lush pictorial essay on the city.

Heller, Nancy and Julia Williams. *The Regionalists*. Cincinnati: Watson-Guptill, 1976.

Keating, Bern and James L. Stanfield. *The Mighty Mississippi*. Washington: National Geographic Society, 1971.
Prose by Keating is straightforward and factual; illustrated with photographs by Stanfield, and with reproductions of painters like Audubon, Henry Lewis, and J. S. Curry.

Klitgaard, Kaj. *Through the American Landscape*. Chapel Hill: U. North Carolina, 1941.
Includes sections on the various Midwest states.

Lefebvre, Mark E., ed. *Wisconsin Sketches*. Madison: Wisconsin House, 1974.

Lesy, Michael, comp. *Wisconsin Death Trip*. New York: Random House, 1973.
Photos and text revealing the sordid aspects of the Wisconsin frontier, 1885–1900.

Lewis, Henry. *The Valley of the Mississippi Illustrated*. Tr. by A. H. Poatgieter. Ed. by Bertha Heilbron. St. Paul: Historical Society, 1967.

Good introduction by Heilbron; this excellent work first appeared in German in 1854. Lewis was best known as a river panoramist.

Lieberman, Archie. *Farm Boy*. New York: Abrams, 1974.
Photographic essay on two generations of an Illinois farm family.

Liebling, Jerome. *The Face of Minneapolis*. Minneapolis: Dillon, 1966.
Photography by Liebling; text by Don Morrison.

Lucas, E. Louise. *Art Books: A Basic Bibliography on the Fine Arts*. Greenwich, Conn.: New York Graphic Society, 1968.
Includes a section on U.S. art.

Lynes, Russell. *The Art-Makers of Nineteenth Century America*. New York: Atheneum, 1970.
Popular social history.

McCracken, Harold. *Portrait of the Old West: With a Biographical Check List of Western Artists*. New York: McGraw-Hill, 1952.
Coffee-table art book with valuable notes and lists.

McDermott, John F. *The Lost Panoramas of the Mississippi*. Chicago: U. Chicago, 1958.
Fine study of the panorama art of the nineteenth century.

McKinzie, Richard D. *The New Deal for Artists*. Princeton: Princeton U., 1973.
Sound history of federally sponsored projects for artists in the 1930s.

McManigal, J. W. *Farm Town: A Memoir of the 1930's*. Brattleboro, Vt: Green, 1974.
Photographs of rural Kansas taken in the 1930s.

Mead, Howard et al., comps. *Portrait of the Past: A Photographic Journey Through Wisconsin*. Madison: Wisconsin Tales and Trails, 1971.

Mendelowitz, Daniel M. *A History of American Art*. 2d ed. New York: Holt, 1973.
A standard history; material on folk art, frontier art, and Midwest figures.

Moses, George. *Minnesota in Focus*. Minneapolis: U. Minnesota, 1974.
Photographic essay.

Ness, Zenobia B., comp. *Iowa Artists of the First Hundred Years*. Des Moines: Wallace, 1939.
Survey, with biographical sketches of the artists.

O'Connor, Francis V., ed. *Art for the Millions: Essays from the 1930's by Artists and Administrators of the WPA Federal Art Project*. Greenwich, Conn.: New York Graphic Society, 1973.
Several essays deal with the WPA projects in the Midwest.

———. *The New Deal Art Projects: An Anthology of Memoirs*. Washington: Smithsonian, 1972.
Memoirs of ten people involved in creating and administering projects between 1933 and 1943. The essay by Edward Laning on "New Deal Mural Projects" is of particular interest for the Midwest.

Parry, Ellwood. *The Image of the Indian and the Black Man in American Art, 1590–1900*. New York: Braziller, 1974.
Emphasizes tendency toward stereotyped depiction of these American minorities; illustrated.

Patten, Marjorie. *The Arts Workshop in Rural America: A Study of the Rural Arts Program of the Agricultural Extension Service*. New York: Columbia, 1937.
States examined include Wisconsin, Iowa, North Dakota, and Ohio; chapters on the Little Theater movement and on the arts and crafts movement.

Seymour, Paul, ed. *The Living River*. Kansas City: Hallmark, 1973.
Pictorial study of the Missouri River.

Seymour, Ralph F. *Some Went This Way*. Chicago: Seymour, 1945.
Reminiscences of Chicago artists, publishers, printers, etc., from the first half of the twentieth century.

Sherman, John K. *Art and Culture in Minneapolis*. Minneapolis: U. Minnesota, 1964.
Originally published as part of *A History of the Arts in Minnesota* (1958) edited by William Van O'Connor.

Taft, Robert. *Artists and Illustrators of the Old West, 1850–1900*. New York: Scribner, 1953.
Trans-Mississippi art.

Tilden, Freeman. *Following the Frontier: With F. Jay Haynes, Pioneer Photographer of the Old West*. New York: Knopf, 1964.

Most of Haynes's excellent photography deals with western subjects, but this volume contains some exposures of St. Paul and the Red River Valley. Haynes's studio was in St. Paul.

Watkins, Tom. *Mark Twain's Mississippi: A Pictorial History of America's Greatest River*. Palo Alto: American West, 1974.

Wayman, Norbury L. *Life on the River: A Pictorial History of the Mississippi, the Missouri, and the Western Rivers*. New York: Crown, 1971.

B. INDIVIDUAL ARTISTS

1. Thomas Hart Benton

Baigell, Matthew. *Thomas Hart Benton*. New York: Abrams, 1974.
Fine reproductions.
_____, ed. *A Thomas Hart Benton Miscellany: Selections from His Published Opinions, 1916–1960*. Lawrence: U. Kansas, 1971.
Comments on regionalism and the Midwest *passim*.

Benton, Thomas Hart. *An Artist in America*. 3d rev. ed. Columbia: U. Missouri, 1968.
Classic American autobiography first published in 1937.
_____. *An American in Art: A Professional and Technical Autobiography*. Lawrence: U. Kansas, 1969.
Reprints his famous article on "American Regionalism: A Personal History of the Movement," from *University of Kansas City Review*, 18 (1951), 41–75.
:_____. *Drawings*. Columbia: U. Missouri, 1968

2. George Caleb Bingham

Bloch, E. Maurice. *George Caleb Bingham: The Evolution of an Artist*. 2 vols. Berkeley: U. California, 1967.
Definitive study of the artist.

Christ-Janer, Albert. *George Caleb Bingham of Missouri: The Story of an Artist*. New York: Dodd, Mead, 1940.
Includes a preface by T. H. Benton.

Larkin, Lew. *Bingham: Fighting Artist*. St. Louis: State Publishing Co., 1955.
A biography.

McDermott, John F. *George Caleb Bingham: River Portraitist*. Norman: U. Oklahoma, 1959.
Includes reproductions of 79 paintings and 112 genre drawings.

3. Charles Burchfield

Baur, John I. *Charles Burchfield*. New York: Macmillan, 1956.
Volume of reproductions, with a biographical sketch.

Burchfield, Charles. *The Drawings of Charles Burchfirld*. Ed. Edith H. Jones. New York: Praeger, 1968.
Mainly reproductions, but includes autobiographical notes and comments on the drawings by the Ohio artist.

Charles Burchfield. New York: American Artists Group, 1945.
Short (63 p.) monograph in the A.A.G. series.

4. George Catlin.

Catlin, George. *George Catlin: Episodes from "Life Among the Indians" and "Last Rambles," with 152 Scenes and Portraits by the Artist*. Ed. by Marvin E. Ross. Norman: U. Oklahoma, 1959.
Narrative by Catlin first published in 1867.
_____. *George Catlin: Letters and Notes of the North American Indians*. Ed. by Michael M. Mooney. New York: Potter, 1975.
Originally published in 1841, in 2 volumes.
_____. *North American Indian Portfolio*. London: Catlin, 1844.
Drawings and notes.

Haberly, Lloyd. *Pursuit of the Horizon: A Life of George Catlin, Painter and Recorder of the American Indian.* New York: Macmillan, 1948.
Popular biography.

Haverstock, Mary S. *Indian Gallery: The Story of George Catlin.* New York: Four Winds Press, 1973.
Chronicle of Catlin's travels in the West; includes illustrations.

McCracken, Harold. *George Catlin and the Old Frontier.* New York: Dial, 1959.
Biography; illustrated.

Plate, Robert. *Palette and Tomahawk: The Story of George Catlin.* New York: McKay, 1962.
Popular dramatization of the artist's western adventures.

Roehme, Marjorie Catlin, ed. *The Letters of George Catlin and His Family: A Chronicle of the American West.* Berkeley: U. California, 1966.
An extensive and important collection.

5.   John Steuart Curry

John Steuart Curry. New York: American Artists Group, 1945.
Monograph no. 14 in the A.A.G. series.

Schmeckebier, Laurence E. *John Steuart Curry's Pageant of America.* New York: American Artists Group, 1943.
Biography and analysis of his work; includes eight color plates and 341 illustrations.

6.   Seth Eastman

McDermott, John F. *Seth Eastman: Pictorial Historian of the Indian.* Norman: U. Oklahoma, 1961.
Introduction to the work of the army captain who painted scenes of life on the upper Mississippi.

———. *Seth Eastman's Mississippi: A Lost Portfolio Recovered.* Urbana: U. Illinois, 1973.
Author discusses the importance of lately discovered watercolors which depict life along the Mississippi.

7.   Alfred Jacob Miller

Miller, Alfred Jacob. *Braves and Buffalo: Plains Indian Life in 1837.* Toronto: U. Toronto, 1973.
Watercolors and descriptive notes by the artist; introduction by Michael Bell.

———. *The West of Alfred Jacob Miller (1837).* Rev. and enl. ed. Norman: U. Oklahoma, 1968.
Excellent reproductions of this frontier painter's work.

8.   Grant Wood

Brown, Hazel E. *Grant Wood and Marvin Cone.* Ames: Iowa State U., 1972.
Homely biography of two Iowa painters who grew up together in Cedar Rapids and collaborated often over the years; by a friend of both artists.

Garwood, Darrell. *Artist in Iowa: A Life of Grant Wood.* New York: Norton, 1944.
Popular biography.

Wood, Grant. *Revolt Against the City.* Iowa City: Clio, 1935.
Essay on the development of regional and rural consciousness in the arts.

9.   Others

Gag, Wanda. *Growing Pains: Diaries and Drawings for the Years 1908–1917.* New York: Coward-McCann, 1940.
Unaffected account of the artist's early years in Minnesota.

Milton, John. *Oscar Howe: The Story of an American Indian.* Minneapolis: Dillon, 1971.
Short monograph on the Sioux painter.

Scott, Alma. *Wanda Gag: The Story of an Artist.* Minneapolis: U. Minnesota, 1949.
Biography of the printmaker and illustrator, by a personal friend.

Taft, Ada B. *Lorado Taft: Sculptor and Citizen.* Greensboro, N.C.· Smith, 1946.

Short biography and memoir of the sculptor, by his wife; deals briefly with his early years at Elmwood, Ill., and includes several chapters on his Chicago years.

Wakefield, Robert. *Schwiering and the West*. Aberdeen, S.D.: North Plains Press, 1973.
Biography of Conrad Schwiering and examination of his western paintings; fine illustrations.

Gerald C. Nemanic
Northeastern Illinois University
Chicago, Illinois

CHICAGO

CHICAGO WAS UNDENIABLY the literary capital of the Middle West, and perhaps of the United States, from 1890 to about 1920. In recent decades the city's role as a conduit for the artistic talents of the region has been greatly modified. With the establishment of New York and Los Angeles as the major centers of the communications media (including, most importantly, the publishing industry), Chicago has found its influence in developing literary movements steadily diminishing. On the other hand, the city as paradoxical symbol both of human possibility and violent degeneration remains viable. Chicago persists not only as a vivid memory of our national spirit; it has endured as that most American of cities, consistently intriguing to American and foreigner alike.

An examination of the cultural life of Chicago will yield important insights into the development of the arts in urban America, but as importantly it will reveal the undercurrents of taste in mid-America. For Chicago has always had an atmosphere distinctively flavored by the agrarian and small-town life which surrounds this city to which still comes a steady flow of provincial youth from a radius of 500 miles. New York, Boston, Los Angeles, San Francisco—their determined isolation from parochial forces which press in only from one direction has made them unique islands of culture. From their entrenched positions they manufacture both serious and popular culture for the nation and the world. For better or worse, this detachment has never made much headway in Chicago. The city remains, except for its few sophisticated enclaves, a concentration of "the people."

There are a half dozen works with which the student of Chicago cultural life will want to begin. The standard scholarly history of the city is *A History of Chicago*, 3 vols. (1937–57) by Bessie Pierce. Unfortunately, the third volume carries the story only through 1893. A proposed fourth volume, if completed, will fill a critical need. There is no literary history of Chicago, but the period of greatest literary activity in the city is amply covered in

Bernard Duffey's *Chicago Renaissance in American Letters* (1954). Another general treatment is available in Dale Kramer's *Chicago Renaissance: The Literary Life of the Midwest, 1900–1930* (1966). Carl Condit has written a valuable history of *The Chicago School of Architecture* (1964). Hugh Duncan's synthesizing study of midwestern cultural life and Chicago architecture, *Culture and Democracy* (1965), is uneven but stimulating. The premier study of urban Negro life in America is *Black Metropolis* (1945), an exhaustive sociological research into black society in Chicago by St. Clair Drake and Horace Cayton.

Architecture is an art form for which Chicago has maintained an international reputation. The fantastic growth of the city in the late nineteenth century ran parallel to breakthroughs in construction technique and a growing awareness of the social function of architecture in an expanding, money-oriented society. Chicago, and other midwestern cities to a lesser degree, symbolized the dawning "age of the dynamo" prophesied by Henry Adams. Architectural leaders such as Frank Lloyd Wright, Louis Sullivan, and later Ludwig Mies van der Rohe, found in Chicago both a receptivity to innovation and the working capital which allowed for the construction of numerous pioneer landmarks in modern architecture. As a museum of modern architecture, no city of the world is so important as Chicago. At the same time Wright, a Wisconsin native, was heading the formation of a "Prairie School" of architects which was to provide dominant ideas in the art of residence building during the first two-thirds of the twentieth century.

1. LITERARY STUDIES

For discussions of Chicago Literature in composite books, see Literature and Language bibliography in this volume. For studies of individual Chicago writers, see the following author bibliographies: Ade; Algren; Anderson; Barnes; Bellow; Brooks; Burnett; Dell; Dreiser; Dunne; Farrell; Field; Fuller; Garland; Halper; Hansberry; Hecht; Herrick; Lardner; Levin; Monroe; Morris; Motley; Powers; Roe; Sandburg; Wright. Also consult appendices for additional Chicago writers and literature.

Anderson, Margaret, ed. *The Little Review Anthology*. New York: Hermitage, 1953.
    Miss Anderson was the original and indefatigable editor of this important outlet for writers of the "Robin's Egg Renaissance" of the 1910s; writers featured in this collection are Sherwood Anderson (no relation), Arthur D. Ficke, Vachel Lindsay, Carl Sandburg, and others.
Angle, Paul M. *Suggested Readings in Illinois History, with a Selected List of Historical Fiction*. Springfield: State Historical Society, 1935.
    Pamphlet; dated now, but still good for lists of earlier works.
Blanden, Charles G., ed. *The Chicago Anthology: A Collection of Verse from the Work of Chicago Poets*. Chicago: Roadside Press, 1916.
    Contains a good deal of "genteel" verse, but includes poems by Sandburg, Tietjens, Garland, and Bodenheim; an interesting introduction on the merits of the "old" and "new" poetry by Llewellyn Jones.
Coan, Otis and Richard G. Lillard. *America in Fiction: An Annotated List of Novels that Interpret Aspects of Life in the U.S.* 5th ed. Stanford: Pacific, 1967.
    Includes many Chicago novels.

Duffey, Bernard I. *The Chicago Renaissance in American Letters*. East Lansing: Michigan State U., 1954.
  Best single study of Chicago literature and the influences which combined to make the city a literary center between 1890–1920.
Duncan, Hugh D. *The Rise of Chicago as a Literary Center from 1885–1920: A Sociological Essay in American Culture*. Totowa, N.J.: Bedminster, 1964.
  Mixture of literary history and social science often proves frustrating, but this title, together with the author's *Culture and Democracy* (q.v.), provides a stimulating cultural overview of Chicago and the Midwest.
Dunbar, Olivia. *A House in Chicago*. Chicago: U. Chicago, 1947.
  The "House" is the literary salon of Harriet C. Moody, wife of the poet and dramatist William Vaughn Moody; the book includes a good deal of commentary on Chicago literary life during the early years of the twentieth century.
Field, Eugene. *Culture's Garland: Being Memoranda of the General Rise of Literature, Art, Music and Society in Chicago and Other Western Ganglia*. Boston: Ticknor, 1887.
  Informal and entertaining notes of a Chicago poet and newspaper celebrity; important for a view of Chicago and Midwest letters in the "genteel" period.
Fiske, Horace S., ed. *Chicago in Picture and Poetry*. Chicago: Seymour, 1903.
  Anthology.
_____. *Poems on Chicago and Illinois*. Boston: Stratford, 1927.
  Anthology.
Fleming, Herbert E. *Magazines of a Market-Metropolis: Being a History of the Literary Periodicals and Literary Interest of Chicago*. Chicago: U. Chicago, 1906.
  Papers first printed in the American Journal of Sociology, vols. 11 and 12.
Fuller, Henry B. "The Upward Movement in Chicago." *Atl*, 30 (1897), 534–47.
  Overview of the "genteel" movement in Chicago.
Gelfant, Blanche. *The American City Novel*. 2d ed. Norman: U. Oklahoma, 1970.
  Chicago is well covered; includes a selective list of city novels.
Gohdes, Clarence. *Literature and Theater of the States and Regions of the U.S.A.: An Historical Bibliography*. Durham: Duke U., 1967.
  See section on Illinois.
Hahn, Emily. *Romantic Rebels: An Informal History of Bohemianism in America*. Boston: Houghton Mifflin, 1967.
  Discussion of many Chicago figures.
Halper, Albert, ed. *This is Chicago, an Anthology*. New York: Holt, 1952.
  Only recent anthology devoted exclusively to Chicago literature.
Hansen, Harry. *Midwest Portraits: A Book of Memories and Friendships*. New York: Harcourt, 1923.
  Combines personal memoirs and biographical sketches of several Midwest writers and Midwest scenes.
Joost, Nicholas. *Years of Transition: The Dial, 1912–1920*. Barre, Mass.: Barre, 1967.
  Historical study of the magazine, including its last years in Chicago.
Kramer, Dale. *Chicago Renaissance: The Literary Life of the Midwest, 1900–1930*. New York: Appleton, 1966.
  More of a popular study than Duffey's work but informative nonetheless.
Kramer, Sidney. *A History of Stone and Kimball and Herbert S. Stone and Co., with a Bibliography of their Publications, 1893–1905*. Chicago: U. Chicago, 1940.
  Valuable history of the early Chicago publishing firms.
Logasa, Hannah, comp. *Regional United States: A Subject List*. Boston: Faxon, 1942.
  Includes a section on Chicago; selective checklists.
Mencken, Henry L. "The Literary Capital of the United States." *NA*, 27 (Apr. 17, 1920), 90–92.
  "In Chicago a spirit broods upon the face of the waters" intones Mencken, who argues that Chicago and the Midwest produced the great writers of the day.
_____. *The Bathtub Hoax and Other Blasts and Bravos from the Chicago Tribune*. Ed. by Robert McHugh. New York: Knopf, 1958.
  Selections of Mencken's writing for the *Tribune* from 1924–27.
Morgan, Anna. *My Chicago*. Chicago: Seymour, 1918.
  History of the growth of the art and literary colony in Chicago, with short biographical sketches; especially valuable for information on "The Little Room."

Payne, William M. "Chicago's Higher Evolution." *Dial* (Oct. 1, 1892).
  Brief survey of Chicago genteelism by the *Dial* editor.
———. "Literary Chicago." *NEM* (July 1893).
  Surveys Chicago literature of the period.
Shackleton, Robert. *The Book of Chicago*. Philadelphia: Penn, 1920.
  This general portrait of the city includes chapters on literature, art, and music.
Sherman, Robert L. *Chicago Stage: Its Records and Achievements*. Chicago: Author, 1947.
  A record of Chicago theaters and performances between 1834–1871.
Stratman, Carl J. *Bibliography of the American Theater, Excluding New York City*. Chicago:
  Loyola U., 1965.
  A section on Chicago.
Williams, Kenny J. *In the City of Men: Another Story of Chicago*. Nashville: Townsend, 1974.
  Discussion of Chicago cultural life, with emphasis on literature and architecture. Includes a
  checklist of Chicago fiction.

2. HISTORY

See also "Illinois" in History and Society bibliography.

Ahern, M. L. *The Political History of Chicago*. Chicago: Donohue, 1886.
  Valuable early study.
Andreas, Alfred T. *History of Chicago*. 3 vols. Chicago: Author, 1884–86.
  Includes three chapters on early literature (vol. 2, pp. 483–501; vol. 3, pp. 684–92 and
  692–93).
Andrews, Wayne. *The Battle for Chicago*. New York: Harcourt, 1946.
  Depicts the city's history in terms of the power struggles which have developed within it.
Asbury, Herbert. *Gem of the Prairie: An Informal History of the Chicago Underworld*.
  Garden City, N.Y.: Knopf, 1940.
  Breezy journalism; also published under the title *Chicago Underworld* (1940).
Beadle, Muriel et al. *The Fortnightly of Chicago*. Chicago: Regnery, 1973.
  Excellent history of the venerable club; important for insight into women's history in the
  city.
Becker, Stephen D. *Marshall Field III*. New York: Simon and Schuster, 1964.
  Popular history of the liberal publisher (Chicago *Sun*) whose grandfather was the Chicago
  department store magnate.
Bright, John. *Hizzoner Big Bill Thompson: An Idyll of Chicago*. New York: Dape and Smith,
  1930.
  Popular study of the grafting mayor and Chicago in the Jazz Age.
Burg, David. *Chicago's White City of 1893*. Lexington: U. Kentucky, 1976.
  "White City" refers to the site of the Columbian Exposition.
Butt, Ernest. *Chicago Then and Now*. Chicago: Aurora, 1933.
  Pictorial; includes a reprint of the first city directory.
Casey, Robert J. *Chicago Medium Rare: When We Were Both Younger*. Indianapolis: Bobbs-
  Merrill, 1950.
  Chicago journalist writes engagingly about the period of his youth (1890–1910) in the city;
  includes a chapter on "Culture and the Arts."
Coughlan, Neil. *Young John Dewey: An Essay in Intellectual History*. Chicago: U. Chicago,
  1975.
Cromie, Robert A. *The Great Chicago Fire*. New York: McGraw-Hill, 1958.
  Crackling popular history.
Cromie, Robert A. and Arthur Haug. *Chicago*. Chicago: Ziff-Davis, 1948.
  Pictorial, with text by Cromie and photographs by Haug.
David, Henry. *The History of the Haymarket Affair*. 2d ed. New York: Russell and Russell,
  1958.
  Thoroughgoing history of the 1886 bombing, placed in its historical context.
Dedmon, Emmett. *Fabulous Chicago*. New York: Random House, 1953.
  Includes quite a bit of cultural material and brings the history up to the post–World War II
  period.

Farr, Finis. *Chicago, a Personal History of America's Most American City*. New Rochelle, N.Y.: Arlington House, 1973.
A readable popular history similar to Dedmon's *Fabulous Chicago* (q.v.).

Fehrenbacher, Don E. *Chicago Giant: A Biography of "Long John" Wentworth*. Madison: U. Wisconsin, 1957.
Sound scholarly biography of this important nineteenth century publisher, journalist, and politician.

Ginger, Ray. *Altgeld's America: The Lincoln Ideal Versus Changing Realities*. New York: Funk and Wagnall, 1958.
Dramatizes the struggle to rekindle Lincolnian ideals in turn-of-the-century Chicago; emphasizes the influence of several cultural heroes: Altgeld, Addams, Dreiser, Veblen, Wright, Sullivan, Dewey, and others.

Gottfried, Alex. *Boss Cermak of Chicago: A Study of Political Leadership*. Seattle: U. Washington, 1962.
Scholarly study combining history and political science.

Grant, Bruce. *Right for a City: The Story of the Union League Club of Chicago and Its Times, 1880–1955*. Chicago: Rand, McNally, 1955.
Story of the patriotic organization in Chicago.

Hamilton, Henry R. *The Epic of Chicago*. Chicago: Willett, 1932.
Traces the city's industrial, civic, and political development.

Hansen, Harry. *The Chicago*. New York: Farrar, 1942.
Rivers of America series.

Hutchinson, William T. *Cyrus Hall McCormick*. 2 vols. New York: Appleton, 1930–35.
Scholarly biography of the Chicago inventor and industrial leader.

Kinsley, Philip. *The Chicago Tribune: Its First Hundred Years*. 2 vols. New York: Knopf, 1943–46.
Detailed history of the influential Chicago newspaper to 1880.

Kirkland, Joseph. *The Story of Chicago*. 2 vols. Chicago: Dibble, 1892–94.
Good early history.

Kirkland, Joseph and John Moses. *History of Chicago, Illinois*. Chicago: Munsell, 1895.
By Kirkland and Moses, "aided by eminent local writers."

Kogan, Herman and Robert Cromie. *The Great Fire: Chicago 1871*. New York: Putnam, 1971.
Popular illustrated history of the fire.

Kogan, Herman and Lloyd Wendt. *Lords of the Levee: The Story of Bathhouse John and Hinky Dink*. Indianapolis: Bobbs-Merrill, 1943.
Popular story of Chicago political shennanigans. Reprinted as *Bosses in Lusty Chicago* (1967).

————. *Give the Lady What She Wants!* Chicago: Rand McNally, 1952.
History of Marshall Field's retail operations.

————. *Big Bill of Chicago*. Indianapolis: Bobbs-Merrill, 1953.
Popular history of Big Bill Thompson's reign as mayor of Chicago.

————. *Chicago: A Pictorial History*. New York: Dutton, 1958.

Kogan, Herman and Rick Kogan. *Yesterday's Chicago*. Miami: Seemann, 1976.
Largely pictorial. In the Historic Cities series.

Kupcinet, Irv. *Kup's Chicago*. New York: World, 1962.
Selected columns by the popular Chicago journalist; a guide to popular culture in the city.

Leech, Harper and John C. Carroll. *Armour and His Times*. New York: Appleton, 1938.
History of the meat-packing magnate and the business world of turn-of-the-century Chicago.

Lewis, Lloyd and Henry J. Smith. *Chicago: The History of Its Reputation*. New York: Blue Ribbon, 1933.
Readable one volume history which includes material on the 1920s and early '30s.

Lindsey, Almont. *The Pullman Strike*. Chicago: U. Chicago, 1942.
History of the calamitous labor upheaval of 1894.

Longstreet, Stephen. *Chicago, 1860–1919*. New York: McKay, 1973.
Popular history.

MacPhaul, Jack. *Johnny Torrio: First of the Gang Lords*. New Rochelle: Arlington House, 1970.

Popular portrait of the Chicago racketeer.

Masters, Edgar Lee. *The Tale of Chicago*. New York: Putnam, 1933.
Vivid and contentious narrative history by the poet.

Mayer, Harold M. and Richard C. Wade. *Chicago: Growth of a Metropolis*. Chicago: U. Chicago, 1969.
Sumptuous pictorial history with extensive text; an excellent example of its kind.

Meeker, Arthur. *Chicago, with Love: A Polite and Personal History*. New York: Knopf, 1955.
Engaging portrait of the city by a native novelist.

Murray, George. *The Madhouse on Madison Street*. Chicago: Follett, 1965.
Journalist's story of the Chicago *American*, the Hearst paper in the city; much on Hearst, his sensational brand of journalism, and on Chicago newspaper life in general.

Pasley, Fred D. *Al Capone*. New York: Washburn, 1930.
Exciting popular biography of the Chicago racketeer by a journalist.

Pierce, Bessie L. *A History of Chicago*. 3 vols. New York: Knopf, 1937–57.
Most complete history of the city through 1893.

Poole, Ernest. *Giants Gone: Men Who Made Chicago*. New York: McGraw-Hill, 1943.
Novelist Poole writes of the grand figures in a romantic story of Chicago's development. Sections on Palmer, McCormick, Armour, and others.

Quaife, Milo M. *Chicago and the Old Northwest, 1673–1835*. Chicago: U. Chicago, 1913.
Thorough, scholarly work.

———. *Checagou: From Indian Wigwam to Modern City, 1673–1835*. Chicago: U. Chicago, 1933.
Shorter, more popular account than the above title.

———. *Chicago's Highways Old and New*. Chicago: Keller, 1923.
Describes early trails, roads, stage coaches, and inns during the second quarter of the nineteenth century.

———. *Lake Michigan*. Indianapolis: Bobbs-Merrill, 1944.
American Lakes series.

Rucker, Darnell. *The Chicago Pragmatists*. Minneapolis: U. Minnesota, 1969.
History of the development of the pragmatists' philosophic "School" at the University of Chicago.

Smith, Henry J. *Chicago: A Portrait*. New York: Century, 1931.
Leisurely, readable paean to the city by a Chicagoan; emphasis on the contemporary period.

———. *Chicago's Great Century, 1833–1933*. Chicago: Consolidated, 1933.
Brief history written as a guide for visitors at the Century of Progress.

Storr, Richard J. *Harper's University: The Beginnings*. Chicago: U. Chicago, 1966.
First volume is a detailed, scholarly history of the University of Chicago.

Stuart, William A. *Twenty Incredible Years*.
Study of Big Bill Thompson's career as mayor of Chicago.

Tebbel, John W. *American Dynasty: Story of the McCormicks, Medills, and Pattersons*. New York: Greenwood, 1968.
Examination of powerful families who developed industry in Chicago and in America.

———. *The Marshall Fields: A Study in Wealth*. New York: Dutton, 1947.
Biography of Marshall Fields I and III, the department store magnate and his publisher grandson.

Wagenknecht, Edward C. *Chicago*. Norman: U. Oklahoma, 1964.
Brief guidebook to the history and cultural life of the city.

Waldrop, Frank C. *McCormick of Chicago*. Englewood Cliffs, N.J.: Prentice-Hall, 1966.
Popular biography of Colonel Robert McCormick, controversial Chicago *Tribune* publisher from 1912–55.

Washburn, Charles. *Come into My Parlor: A Biography of the Aristocratic Everleigh Sisters of Chicago*. New York: National Library Press, 1936.
Story of the stylish madames who ran one of the world's most fabulous bordellos.

Wille, Lois. *Forever Open, Clear and Free: The Historic Struggle for Chicago's Lakefront*. Chicago: Regnery, 1972.
Chicago *Daily News* journalist's historical account.

WPA Federal Writers' Project. *Chicago in Periodical Literature: A Summary of Articles*. Chicago, 1940.
Pamphlet.

3. ARCHITECTURE

A. WORKS ON CHICAGO

Andrews, Wayne. *Architecture in Chicago and Mid-America: A Photographic History*. New York: Atheneum, 1968.
Includes sections on major Chicago architects.
Architectural Forum. May, 1962; Jan., 1974.
Issues devoted entirely to Chicago architecture.
Bach, Ira J. *Chicago on Foot: Walking Tours of Chicago's Architecture*. 2d ed. Chicago: O'Hara, 1973.
Popular guidebook.
Blake, Peter. *The Master Builders*. New York: Knopf, 1960.
Chapters on Wright, LeCorbusier, and Mies Van der Rohe.
Burnham, Daniel H. et al. *Chicago: World's Columbian Exposition*. 10 vols. New York: Appleton, 1893–95.
Elaborate record of the exotic opulence which produced the "White City" abhorred by Sullivan.
Burnham, Daniel H. and Edward H. Bennett. *Plan of Chicago* . . . . Ed. Charles Moore. Chicago: Commercial Club, 1909.
Blueprint of the plan, masterminded by Burnham and others, which was to provide a model for an efficient and liveable environment in the industrial city; a landmark of modern city planning.
Burnham, Daniel H., Jr., and Robert Kingery. *Planning the Region of Chicago*. Eds. John B. Morrill and Paul O. Fischer. Chicago: 1956.
Prepared under the direction of the Chicago Regional Planning Association.
Cohen, Stuart. *Chicago Architects: A Revisionist View of Chicago Architecture*. Chicago: Swallow, 1976.
Condit, Carl W. *The Chicago School of Architecture: A History of Commercial and Public Building in the Chicago Area, 1875–1925*. Chicago: U. Chicago, 1964.
Expanded version of *The Rise of the Skyscraper* (1952).
———. *Chicago Since 1910: Building, Planning and Urban Technology, 1910–1970*. 2 vols. Chicago: U. Chicago, 1973–74.
Scholarly, detailed record.
Drury, John. *Old Chicago Houses*. Chicago: U. Chicago, 1941.
Brief histories of about ninety important Chicago structures, "from pioneer farm houses to magnificent mansions."
Duncan, Hugh D. *Culture and Democracy: The Struggle for Form and Architecture in Chicago and the Middle West during the Life and Times of Louis H. Sullivan*. Totowa, N.J.: Bedminster, 1965.
As much cultural study of Chicago as it is architectural history.
Gilbert, Paul and Charles L. Bryson. *Chicago and its Makers*. Chicago: Mendelsohn, 1929.
Big (1985 pages), valuable combination of history and biographical sketches of leading Chicagoans.
Hasbrouck, W. R., ed. *Architectural Essays from the Chicago School, 1900–1909*. Park Forest, Ill.: Prairie School Press, 1967.
Jones, John H. and Fred A. Birtten, eds. *A Half Century of Chicago's Buildings*. Chicago: Authors, 1910.
Detailed, early reference guide.
Mendelsohn, Felix. *Chicago—Yesterday and Today*. Chicago: Mendelsohn, 1932.
Mainly a descriptive work.

National Park Service. *Historic American Buildings Survey: Chicago and Nearby Illinois Areas*. Ed. J. William Rudd. Park Forest, Ill.: Prairie School Press, 1966.
    Valuable pamphlet serves as an index to architecture in Chicago.
Peisch, Mark L. *The Chicago School of Architecture: Early Followers of Sullivan and Wright*. New York: Random, 1964.
    Particular attention paid to Walter Burley Griffin.
Poesch, Jessie J. *The Chicago School in Print: An Annotated Bibliography*. Charlottesville, Va.: American Assn. of Architectural Bibliographers, 1959.
Randall, Frank A. *History of the Development of Building Construction in Chicago*. Urbana: U. Illinois, 1949.
    Detailed history of Chicago structures.
Randall, John D. *A Guide to Significant Chicago Architecture of 1872–1922*. Glencoe, 1958.
    Pamphlet.
Ranney, Victoria P. *Olmsted in Chicago*. Chicago: Open Lands Project, 1972.
    Valuable pamphlet on the landscape architect.
Root, John Wellborn. *The Meanings of Architecture*. Ed. Donald Hoffman. New York: Horizon, 1967.
    Collection of twenty-one articles by the Chicago architect; most originally appeared in *Inland Architect* between 1885–1891.
Siegel, Arthur S., ed. *Chicago's Famous Buildings*. Chicago: U. Chicago, 1965.
    Guidebook.
Tallmadge, Thomas E. *Architecture in Old Chicago*. Chicago: U. Chicago, 1941.
    Valuable historical account, from the building of Ft. Dearborn to the Columbian Exposition of 1893. Author's untimely death prevented completion of the entire history.
Tunnard, Christopher. *The City of Man*. New York: Scribner, 1970.
    Important study in urban planning; material on the Columbian Exposition.
Wester, James C. *Architecture of Chicago and Vicinity*. Media, Pa.: Society of Architectural Historians, 1965.
    Guidebook.
Williams, Kenny J. *In the City of Men: Another Story of Chicago*. Nashville: Townsend, 1974.
    Emphasis on literature and architecture in the city.

B. AMERICAN ARCHITECTURE

Andrews, Wayne. *Architecture, Ambition and America*. New York: Harper, 1955.
    Includes a long chapter on "The Chicago Story: 1883–1955."
Bragdon, Claude. *Architecture and Democracy*. New York: Knopf, 1926.
    Includes a chapter on Sullivan.
Brownell, Baker and Frank Lloyd Wright. *Architecture and Modern Life*. New York: Harper, 1937.
    Valuable discussion of contemporary society by social philosopher and practicing architect.
Burchard, John E. and Albert Bush-Brown. *The Architecture of America: A Social and Cultural History*. Boston: Little, Brown, 1961. Abr. & rev. ed., 1966.
    Sound general history; Chicago material in plenty.
Coles, William A., ed. *Architecture in America: A Battle of Styles*. New York: Appleton, 1961.
Condit, Carl. *American Building Art*. 2 vols. New York: Oxford, 1960–61.
    An important history of non-domestic building techniques in America.
———. *American Building: Materials and Techniques from the Beginning of the Colonial Settlements to the Present*. Chicago: U. Chicago, 1968.
    Excellent one-volume survey.
Eaton, Leonard K. *American Architecture Comes of Age: European Reaction to H. H. Richardson and Louis Sullivan*. Cambridge: MIT, 1972.
    Discusses the influence of these two important architects on building in Europe.
Fitch, James M. *American Building—The Forces that Shape It*. Rev. & enl. ed. Boston: Houghton Mifflin, 1966.
    Survey of American architectural history, emphasizing its development along functional lines.

Giedion, Siegfried. *Space, Time and Architecture: The Growth of a New Tradition.* Cambridge: Harvard, 1954.
Good section on Chicago.

Gifford, Don, ed. *The Literature of Architecture: The Evolution of Architectural Theory and Practice in Nineteenth Century America.* New York: Dutton, 1966.
Anthology of American architectural writings.

Hamlin, Talbot F. *The American Spirit in Architecture.* New Haven: Yale, 1926.
Volume in the Pageant of America series.

Heyer, Paul, ed. *Architects on Architecture: New Directions in America.* New York: Walker, 1966.
Taped interviews with leading architects.

Hitchcock, Henry R. *American Architectural Books . . . Published in America before 1895.* 3d rev. ed. Minneapolis: U. Minnesota, 1946.
Standard reference.

Jordy, William and Ralph Coe, eds. *American Architecture and Other Writings.* Cambridge: Harvard U., 1961.
Includes bibliography of periodicals dealing with Midwest architecture.

Kimball, S. Fiske. *American Architecture.* New York: Bobbs-Merrill, 1928.
Popular historical survey; sound and readable.

McCallum, Ian R. *Architecture U.S.A.* New York: Reinhold, 1959.
Historical survey, with emphasis on the major figures, by the British architectural critic.

Mumford, Lewis. *The Brown Decades: A Study of the Arts in America, 1865–1895.* 2d ed. New York: Dover, 1955.
Includes a discussion of Chicago architecture.

––––––. *Sticks and Stones: A Study of American Architectural Civilization.* 2d ed. New York: Dover, 1955.
Recognizes the importance of Chicago as leader of architectural development in U.S. Cities.

––––––, ed. *The Roots of Contemporary Architecture.* New York: Reinhold, 1952.
Collected essays, with an introduction by Mumford.

O'Neal, William B., ed. *American Association of Architectural Bibliographies.* Charlottesville, Va.: U. Virginia, 1966.

Pierson, William H. *American Buildings and Their Architects.* 2 vols. Garden City, N.Y.: Doubleday, 1970–72.

Roos, Frank J. *Bibliography of Early American Architecture: Writings on Architecture Constructed before 1860 in Eastern and Central United States.* Rev. ed. Urbana: U. Illinois, 1968.

Scully, Vincent J. *American Architecture and Urbanism.* New York: Praeger, 1969.
Scholarly history of American urban development and the architectural solutions which accompanied it.

Sturgis, Russell. *A Dictionary of American Architecture and Building: Biographical, Historical, and Descriptive.* Detroit: Gale, 1966.

Tallmadge, Thomas E. *The Story of American Architecture.* Rev. & enl. ed. New York: Norton, 1936.
Eminently readable history, by an architect.

Whiffen, Marcus. *American Architecture since 1780: A Guide to the Styles.* Cambridge: MIT, 1969.
Popular work; classifies American architecture into thirty-eight styles, from "Jeffersonian classical" to "Brutalism."

C. INDIVIDUAL ARCHITECTS

1. Frank Lloyd Wright

a. *Writings about:*

Blake, Peter. *Frank Lloyd Wright: Architecture and Space.* Baltimore: Penguin, 1964.
Introductory monograph originally published as a section of the author's *Master Builders* (1961).

Brooks, H. Allen. *The Prairie School: Frank Lloyd Wright and his Midwest Contemporaries.* Toronto: U. Toronto, 1972.
Detailed introduction and commentary accompanies photographs and drawings.
Drexler, Arthur. *The Drawings of Frank Lloyd Wright.* New York: Harper, 1962.
Eaton, Leonard K. *Two Chicago Architects and Their Clients: Frank Lloyd Wright and Howard Van Doren Shaw.* Cambridge: MIT, 1969.
Includes some history of Chicago architecture.
Farr, Finis. *Frank Lloyd Wright: A Biography.* New York: Scribner, 1961.
Popular biography.
"Frank Lloyd Wright." *Architectural Forum,* 68 (Jan. 1938).
Issue devoted to Wright's career.
Hitchcock, Henry R. *In the Nature of Materials: The Buildings of Frank Lloyd Wright, 1887–1941.* New York: Duell, 1942.
Substantial commentary accompanies photographs and drawings.
Karpel, Bernard. *What Men Have Written about Frank Lloyd Wright: A Bibliography* . . . . New York, 1959.
Pamphlet.
Manson, Grant C. *Frank Lloyd Wright to 1910.* New York: Reinhold, 1958.
Thorough treatment of the period covered.
Miller, Richard A. et al., eds. *Four Great Makers of Modern Architecture: Gropius, Mies Van der Rohe, Le Corbusier, and Wright.* New York: Columbia, 1963.
Verbatim record of a symposium held at the Columbia School of Architecture.
Scully, Vincent J. *Frank Lloyd Wright.* New York: Braziller, 1960.
Short introductory essay.
Smith, Norris K. *Frank Lloyd Wright: A Study in Architectural Content.* Englewood Cliffs, N.J.: Prentice-Hall, 1966.
Sees Wright in an American romantic tradition; suggestive work by an historian of ideas.
Storrer, William A. *The Architecture of Frank Lloyd Wright, A Complete Catalog.* Cambridge: MIT, 1974.
Twombly, Robert C. *Frank Lloyd Wright: An Interpretive Biography.* New York: Harper, 1973.
Scholarly and detailed.
Wright, John L. *My Father Who is on Earth.* New York: Putnam, 1946.
Short book of reminiscences by the architect's son.
Wright, Olgivanna L. *Our House.* New York: Horizon, 1959.
Reminiscences by the architect's wife; "Our House" refers to their homes, Taliesen East (in Wisconsin) and Taliesen West (in Arizona). The following titles continue Olgivanna's memoirs of her husband: *The Shining Brow* (1960), *The Roots of Life* (1963), and *Frank Lloyd Wright: His Life, His Work, His Words* (1966).

b. Writings by (chronological list):

Modern Architecture. Princeton: U. Princeton, 1931.
Kahn lectures for 1930.
Architecture and Modern Life. New York: Harper, 1937.
With Baker Brownell.
When Democracy Builds. Chicago: U. Chicago, 1945.
Genius and the Mobocracy. New York: Duell, 1949.
Memoir and study of Louis Sullivan, his mentor.
Taliesin Drawings. New York: Wittenborn, 1952.
The Future of Architecture. New York: Horizon, 1953.
The Natural House. New York: Horizon, 1954.
An American Architecture. Ed. Edgar Kaufmann. New York: Horizon, 1955.
The Story of the Tower. New York: Horizon, 1956.
The Living City. New York: Horizon, 1958.
Drawings for a Living Architecture. New York: Horizon, 1959.
Architecture: Man in Possession of his Earth. New York: Doubleday, 1962.
Includes a biographical sketch by his daughter, Iovanna.

The Industrial Revolution Runs Away. New York: Horizon, 1969.
  Revised edition of *The Disappearing City* (1932).
An Autobiography. Rev. & exp. ed. New York: Horizon, 1974.
  Classic American autobiography first published in 1932.

c. Collections:

Gutheim, Frederick. ed. *Frank Lloyd Wright on Architecture: Selected Writings, 1895–1940.*
  New York: Duell, 1941.
Kaufmann, Edgar, ed. *Frank Lloyd Wright: Writings and Buildings.* New York: Horizon,
  1960.
  Selected writings, with illustrations.

2. Louis H. Sullivan

a. Writings about:

Bush-Brown, Albert. *Louis Sullivan.* New York: Braziller, 1960.
  Short introductory essay on Sullivan's career.
Connely, Willard. *Louis Sullivan as He Lived.* New York: Horizon, 1960.
  Best biographical source.
Duncan, Hugh D. *Culture and Democracy: The Struggle for Form and Architecture in Chica-
  go and the Middle West during the Life and Times of Louis H. Sullivan.* Totowa, N.J.:
  Bedminster, 1965.
  Extensive discussion of Sullivan as culture hero.
Morrison, Hugh S. *Louis Sullivan, Prophet of Modern Architecture.* New York: Norton, 1955.
  Thorough evaluation of Sullivan's work and influence; standard critique.
Paul, Sherman. *Louis Sullivan: An Architect in American Thought.* Englewood Cliffs, N.J.:
  Prentice-Hall, 1962.
  Study of Sullivan as philosopher and literary artist.
Szarkowski, John. *The Idea of Louis Sullivan.* Minneapolis: U. Minnesota, 1956.
  Photographic album with quotes from Sullivan and others; includes a biographical profile.
Wright, Frank Lloyd. *Genius and the Mobocracy.* New York: Duell, 1949.
  Short appreciation of the master, by his former pupil.

b. Writings by (chronological list):

The Autobiography of an Idea. New York: Institute of Architects, 1924.
  Zesty and moving autobiography which carries the author from his early hopeful days in
  Boston and Paris through his tumultuous Chicago period and into the disillusionment of
  later years.
Kindergarten Chats and Other Writings. New York: Wittenborn, 1947.
  First published serially in 1901–02 and later edited for book publication (1934).
Democracy: A Man-Search. Detroit: Wayne, 1961.
  A philosophical study of democracy.

c. Collections:

English, Maurice. *The Testament of Stone: Themes of Idealism and Indignation from the
  Writings of Louis Sullivan.* Evanston: Northwestern U., 1963.

3. Mies Van der Rohe

Blake, Peter. *Mies Van der Rohe, Architecture and Structure.* Baltimore: Penguin, 1960.
  First published as a section of the author's *Master Builders* (1961).
Blaser, Werner. *Mies Van der Rohe: The Art of Structure.* Tr. D. Q. Stephenson. New York:
  Praeger, 1965.
  Mainly pictorial; by the Swiss architect and colleague of Mies.
Drexler, Arthur. *Ludwig Mies Van der Rohe.* New York: Braziller, 1960.
  Brief introduction to the architect's work.

Hilberseimer, Ludwig. *Mies Van der Rohe*. Chicago: Theobald, 1956.
Photographs, drawings, sketches; with a short introductory text.
Miller, Richard A., et al., eds. *Four Great Makers of Modern Architecture: Gropius, Mies Van der Rohe, Le Corbusier, and Wright*. New York: Columbia, 1963.
Verbatim record of a symposium held at the Columbia School of Architecture.
Pawley, Martin. *Mies Van der Rohe*. New York: Simon & Schuster, 1970.
Introduction and notes by Pawley; photographs by Yukio Futagawa.
Speyer, A. James. *Mies Van der Rohe*. Chicago: Art Institute, 1968.
Catalog of a retrospective exhibition at the Art Institute of Chicago in 1968.

4.   Daniel H. Burnham

Hines, Thomas S. *Burnham of Chicago: Architect and Planner*. New York: Oxford, 1974.
Moore, Charles. *Daniel H. Burnham, Architect, Planner of Cities*. 2 vols. Boston: Houghton Mifflin, 1921.
Important early biography.

5.   John Wellborn Root

Hoffman, Donald. *The Architecture of John Wellborn Root*. Baltimore: Johns Hopkins, 1973.
————, ed. *The Meanings of Architecture: Buildings and Writings of John Wellborn Root*. New York: Horizon, 1967.
Collection of twenty-one articles by the Chicago architect; most originally appeared in *Inland Architect* between 1885–91.
Monroe, Harriet. *John Wellborn Root: A Study of his Life and Work*. Boston: Houghton Mifflin, 1896.
Able biography by the later editor of *Poetry* magazine.

6.   Henry H. Richardson

Hitchcock, Henry R. *The Architecture of H. H. Richardson and his Times*. Rev. ed. Hamden, Conn.: Anchor, 1961.
Excellent portrait of this "Victorian" American architect and his nineteenth century milieu.
Van Rennselaer, Marianna G. *Henry Hobson Richardson and his Works*. Boston: Houghton Mifflin, 1888.
Short biography.

4.   THE ARTS (Exclusive of Literature)

Cook, Bruce. *Listen to the Blues*. New York: Scribner, 1973.
Readable introductory survey.
Davis, Ronald L. *A History of Opera in the American West*. Englewood Cliffs, N.J.: Prentice-Hall, 1965.
Evans, Walker. "Chicago: A Camera Exploration of the Huge, Energetic Sprawl of the Midlands." *Fortune*, 35 (Feb. 1947), 112–21.
Perhaps the best of the many photo essays on Chicago which have appeared in periodicals and pictorial volumes.
Jacobson, Jacob Z., ed. *Art of Today—Chicago*. Chicago: Stein, 1932.
Reproductions and "artist's statements" by fifty-two Chicago painters and sculptors; with an introduction and biographical sketches by the editor.
Kiel, Charles. *Urban Blues*. Chicago: U. Chicago, 1966.
Stresses the importance of Chicago and other Midwest cities in the development of that music which came north with the black migrations.
Korth, Fred. *The Chicago Book: Photographs*. Chicago: n.p., 1949.
Perhaps second only to Evans's work in this genre.
Moore, Edward C. *Forty Years of Opera in Chicago*. New York: Liveright, 1930.
Anecdotal history by a veteran Chicago *Tribune* music critic; begins with the Auditorium opening in 1889.

Oliver, Paul. *Story of the Blues*. Philadelphia: Chilton, 1969.
  Short but valuable illustrated history, by an English scholar.
Ramsey, Frederic, Jr. and Charles E. Smith, eds. *Jazzmen*. New York: Harcourt, 1939.
  A long section on Chicago jazz, with chapters on Armstrong, Beiderbecke, the "Austin
  (H.S.) Gang," blues and boogie-woogie.
Rowe, Mike. *Chicago Breakdown*. New York: Drake, 1975.
  Blues history.
Schulze, Franz. *Fantastic Images: Chicago Art Since 1945*. Chicago: Follett, 1972.
  Covers the movements and major figures in the city.
Smith, Alson J. *Chicago's Left Bank*. Chicago: Regnery, 1953.
  Informal history of the arts in Chicago.
Thomas, Theodore. *A Musical Autobiography*. Ed. George P. Upton. 2 vols. Chicago:
  McClurg, 1905. Reprint, New York: Da Capo, 1964; includes some new material.
  Memoirs of Chicago's symphony leader at the turn-of-the-century.
Wagenknecht, Edward. *Chicago*. Norman: U. Oklahoma, 1964.
  Centers of Civilization series; cultural overview which includes information on literature
  and the arts.

5. SOCIETY

Abbott, Edith. *Tenements of Chicago, 1908–1935*. Chicago: U. Chicago, 1936.
  Perceptive early analysis of the relationship between housing and urban problems; author
  was a close associate of Jane Addams.
Adamic, Louis. *Dynamite: The Story of Class Violence in America*. New York: Viking, 1931.
  Labor history with a left-wing bias; includes a good deal on conditions in Chicago and the
  Midwest.
Addams, Jane. *Twenty Years at Hull House*. New York: Macmillan, 1910.
  Written in a style invariably clear and penetrating, a revelation of the strength of personali-
  ty which characterizes her career of social work in Chicago. This volume also contains
  reminiscences of the author's early years in Cedarville, Ill.
_____. *The Second Twenty Years at Hull House*. New York: Macmillan, 1930.
_____. *The Spirit of Youth and the City Street*. New York: Macmillan, 1909.
Allswang, John M. *A House for All Peoples: Ethnic Politics in Chicago, 1890–1936*. Lexing-
  ton: U. Kentucky, 1971.
  Scholarly study of nine Chicago ethnic groups and their influence on local politics.
Amory, Cleveland. *Who Killed Society?* New York: Harper, 1960.
  An entertaining history of American "High Society." Examines the cultural aspirations of
  Chicago's *nouveau riche* at the turn of the century.
Anderson, Nels. *The Hobo: The Sociology of the Homeless Man*. Chicago: U. Chicago, 1923.
  Close study of Chicago hoboes, derelicts, migratory workers, etc. Examines districts and
  outlying "jungles" where the men congregate; some description of hobo "folklore."
Appel, Benjamin. *The People Talk*. New York: Dutton, 1930.
  Mixed interviews and descriptive writing reveals an urgent socialist message; sections on
  Detroit, Chicago, and rural Wisconsin life.
Aschenbrenner, Joyce. *Lifelines: Black Families in Chicago*. New York: Holt, 1975.
Banfield, Edward C. *Political Influence*. Glencoe, Ill.: Free Press, 1961.
  Study of political pressure groups in Chicago.
Banish, Roslyn. *City Families: Chicago and London*. New York: Pantheon, 1976.
Beijbom, Ulf. *Swedes in Chicago: A Demographic and Social Study of the 1846–1880 Immi-
  gration*. Tr. Donald Brown. Stockholm: Läromedeisförlager, 1971.
  Scholarly.
Bogue, Donald J. *Skid Row in American Cities*. Chicago: Community and Family Study
  Centers, U. Chicago, 1963.
  Sociological study; includes detailed information on Chicago.
Bogue, Donald J. and Ernest W. Burgess, eds. *Contributions to Urban Sociology*. Chicago: U.
  Chicago, 1964.
  Collected essays. An abridged version is *Urban Sociology* (1967).
Bontemps, Arna and Jack Conroy. *Anyplace But Here*. Rev. and enl. ed. New York: Hill and
  Wang, 1966.

Study of black migrations from the South (Chicago was the destination of great numbers). This volume was originally published as *They Seek a City* (1945).

Chicago Commission on Race Relations. *The Negro in Chicago.* Chicago: U. Chicago, 1922.
Commission report in aftermath of 1921 race riots.

Davis, Allen F. *American Heroine: The Life and Legend of Jane Addams.* New York: Oxford, 1973.
Biography which attempts to separate the real woman from the mythic historical figure she has become.

Davis, Allen F. and Mary L. McCree. *Eighty Years at Hull House.* Chicago: Quadrangle, 1969.
Interviews with fifty-seven people who lived there or observed it closely; includes essays by Edmund Wilson, Studs Terkel, and other lights.

Dees, Jesse W. *Flophouse.* Francetown, N.H.: M. Jones, 1948.
"Undercover" study of conditions among the "unattached" men of Chicago.

Demaris, Ovid. *Captive City: Chicago in Chains.* New York: Lyle Stuart, 1969.
Often sensational study of interrelations between politicians, racketeers, and businessmen; by a journalist.

Drake, St. Clair and Horace Cayton. *Black Metropolis.* New York: Harcourt, 1945.
Premier study of urban Negro life in America; exhaustive sociological analysis of Chicago Blacks.

Duncan, Hugh D. *Culture and Democracy: The Struggle for Form and Architecture in Chicago and the Middle West during the Life and Times of Louis H. Sullivan.* Totowa, N.J.: Bedminster, 1965.
Extended treatment of social life in the city.

Faris, Robert E. *Chicago Sociology, 1920–1932.* San Francisco: Chandler, 1967.
Discusses the extensive work generated by sociologists at the University of Chicago.

Fish, John H. *Black Power/White Control: The Struggle of the Woodlawn Organization in Chicago.* Princeton: Princeton U., 1973.
Scholarly study.

Frazier, E. Franklin. *Black Bourgeoisie.* New York: Free Press, 1957.
Excellent sociological study of black middle class in America; includes material on Chicago life.

———. *Negro Family in Chicago.* U. Chicago, 1932.
Sociological study; emphasizes the difficulty of Southern black families in adjusting to urban life.

Fuchs, Lawrence H. *American Ethnic Politics.* New York: Harper, 1968.

Gitlin, Todd and Nanci Hollander. *Uptown: Poor Whites in Chicago.* New York: Harper, 1970.
Taped interviews with transplanted Appalachian whites in Chicago.

Gosnell, Harold F. *Machine Politics: Chicago Model.* 2d ed. Chicago: U. Chicago, 1968.
Detailed piece of political science reportage, first edition published in 1937.

Gregory, Susan. *Hey, White Girl.* New York: Norton, 1970.
Diary of the only white student at Marshall High School.

Halper, Albert, ed. *Chicago Crime Book.* New York: World, 1967.
Anthology of twenty-four journalistic pieces on crime in the city.

Heise, Kenan. *They Speak for Themselves: Interviews with the Destitute in Chicago.* Chicago: Young Christian Worker, 1965.
By a Chicago journalist.

———. *Is There Only One Chicago?* Richmond, Va.: Westover, 1973.
Selections from Heise's question-answer column in the Chicago *American.*

———. *The Chicagoization of America.* Chicago: O'Hara, 1976.

Hillman, Arthur and Robert J. Casey. *Tomorrow's Chicago.* Chicago: U. Chicago, 1953.
A plea for city planning by two Chicago journalists.

Hofmeister, Rudolph. *The Germans of Chicago.* Champaign: Stipes, 1976.

Horowitz, Helen. *Culture and the City: Cultural Philanthropy in Chicago from the 1880s to 1917.* Lexington: U. Kentucky, 1976.

Kantowicz, Edward R. *Polish-American Politics in Chicago, 1888–1940.* Chicago: U. Chicago, 1975.

Kirschner, Don S. *City and Country: Rural Responses to Urbanization in the 1920's*. Westport, Conn.: Greenwood, 1970.

Kornblum, William. *Blue Collar Community*. Chicago: U. Chicago, 1974.
Study of ethnic and political life in South Chicago.

Lasch, Christopher, ed. *The Social Thought of Jane Addams*. Indianapolis: Bobbs-Merrill, 1965.
Selections from her writings.

Levine, Daniel. *Jane Addams and the Liberal Tradition*. Madison: Historical Society, 1971.
Biography.

Merriam, Charles E. *Chicago: A More Intimate View of Urban Politics*. New York: Macmillan, 1929.
A history of Chicago politics since 1871, by a political scientist and alderman.

Murphy, William and D. J. R. Bruckner, eds. *The Idea of the University of Chicago*. Chicago: U. Chicago, 1976.

Nelli, Humbert. *Italians in Chicago, 1880–1930: A Study in Ethnic Mobility*. New York: Oxford, 1970.
Detailed examination of this important Chicago ethnic group.

O'Connor, Len. *Clout: Mayor Daley and His City*. Chicago: Regnery, 1975.
Solid reportage by popular Chicago television commentator.

Peterson, Virgil W. *Barbarians in Our Midst: A History of Chicago Crime and Politics*. Boston: Little, Brown, 1952.
Excellent and readable history by the director of the Chicago Crime Commission.

Rather, Ernest R. *Chicago Negro Almanac and Reference Book*. Chicago: Negro Publishing Co., 1973.

Rakove, Milton. *Don't Make No Waves—Don't Back No Losers: An Insider's Analysis of the Daley Machine*. Bloomington: Indiana U., 1976.

Reckless, Walter C. *Vice in Chicago*. Chicago: U. Chicago, 1933.
Sociological study of prostitution in the city since the closing of the red light district in 1912.

Royko, Mike. *Up Against It*. Chicago: Regnery, 1967.
Collection of Chicago *Daily News* columns by the local humorist and political observer. Two other collections have followed: *I May be Wrong, but I Doubt It* (1968) and *Slats Grobnik and Some Other Friends* (1973).
_____. *Boss: Richard J. Daley of Chicago*. New York: Dutton, 1971.
Debunking portrait of "Hizzoner, the Mare."

Sandburg, Carl. *The Chicago Race Riots of July, 1919*. New York: Harcourt, 1969.
Reprint of 1919 edition with a new preface by Ralph McGill.

Shiavo, Giovanni E. *The Italians of Chicago: A Study in Americanization*. Chicago: Italian American, 1928.
Includes a preface by Jane Addams.

Sennett, Richard. *Families against the City: Middle Class Homes of Industrial Chicago, 1872–1890*. New York: Vintage Books, 1974 (ca. 1970).

Shaw, Clifford R., ed. *The Jack-Roller: A Delinquent Boy's Own Story*. Chicago: U. Chicago, 1930.
Both autobiography and sociological case study of a young Chicago delinquent.

Short, James F., Jr., ed. *The Social Fabric of the Metropolis: Contributions of the "Chicago School of Urban Sociology*." Chicago: U. Chicago, 1971.
Collected essays by various hands.

Sinclair, Upton. *The Jungle*. New York: Doubleday, 1906.
Most famous of fictionalized accounts of social conditions in Chicago.

Smith, Alson J. *Syndicate City: The Chicago Crime Cartel and What to do About it*. Chicago: Regnery, 1954.
Readable history which emphasizes contemporary problems.

Smith, Joseph R. *Sin Corner and Joe Smith: A Story of Vice and Corruption in Chicago*. New York: Exposition, 1964.

Spear, Allan H. *Black Chicago: The Making of a Negro Ghetto, 1890–1920*. Chicago: U. Chicago, 1967.
Sound social history.

Stead, William T. *If Christ Came to Chicago*. Chicago: Laird, 1894.
Muckraking indictment of Old Chicago's degenerate ways, by a crusading English publisher, journalist, and social reformer.

Steffens, Lincoln. *The Shame of the Cities*. New York: McClure, 1904.
Includes a section on Chicago, "Half Free and Fighting On." Strong attack on urban life in the Midwest.

Steiger, Brad. *Psychic Chicago: Doorway to Another Dimension*. New York: Doubleday, 1976.

Suttles, Gerald D. *The Social Order of the Slum: Ethnicity and Territory in the Inner City*. Chicago: U. Chicago, 1968.
Examines the struggles within and among four West Side Chicago groups: Blacks, Puerto Ricans, Mexicans, and Italians.

Tarr, Joel A. *A Study in Boss Politics: William Lorimer of Chicago*. Urbana: U. Illinois, 1971.
Close study of the powerful turn-of-the-century Republican politician, by a political scientist.

Taylor, Graham. *Pioneering on Social Fronts*. Chicago: U. Chicago, 1931.
Important Chicago reformer and settlement house director discusses his career in social work.

Terkel, Louis ("Studs"). *Division Street: America*. New York: Pantheon, 1967.
Taped interviews with Chicagoans famous and obscure; an excellent collection of reflections on modern urban society. Terkel, a well-known Chicago radio-TV personality, has made two other similar collections: *Hard Times* (1970), reminiscences of the Great Depression, and *Working* (1974), interviews with American workers of all descriptions.

Thrasher, Frederick M. *The Gang: A Study of 1,313 Gangs in Chicago*. Rev. ed. Chicago: U. Chicago, 1936. Abr. ed., 1963, with new introd. by James F. Short, Jr.
Detailed sociological analysis.

Vynne, Harold R. *Chicago by Day and Night*. Chicago: Thomson, 1892.
One of the first "vice guides" to Chicago, and possibly the most entertaining; folk material galore.

Wade, Louise C. *Graham Taylor: Pioneer for Social Justice, 1851–1938*. Chicago: U. Chicago, 1964.
Biography of the founder and director of Chicago Commons Settlement House.

Walker, Daniel. *Rights in Conflict: Chicago's Seven Brutal Days*. New York: Grosset, 1969.
Important detailed report of the tumultuous Chicago Democratic Convention of 1968.

Wirth, Louis. *The Ghetto*. Chicago: U. Chicago, 1928.
Sociologist's history of the Jewish ghettoes, with detailed reference to Chicago.

Zorbaugh, Harvey W. *The Gold Coast and the Slum*. Chicago: U. Chicago, 1929.
Stresses the extremes of wealth and poverty side-by-side on the near North Side.

6. PERSONAL NARRATIVES

A number of additional personal narratives will be found in the author bibliographies.

Algren, Nelson. *Chicago: City on the Make*. Garden City, N.Y.: Doubleday, 1951.
Poetic, often turbulent portrait of the city Algren has loved and hated for half a century.
————. *Who Lost an American?* New York: Macmillan, 1963.
This travel book, mostly on Europe, includes a long section on Chicago.

Anderson, Margaret. *My Thirty Years' War*. New York: Covici, 1930.
Important autobiography by the editor of *Little Review*.

Andrews, Robert H. *A Corner of Chicago*. Boston: Little, Brown, 1963.
Journalist's sprightly account of his young working years in Chicago during the 1920s and 30s; some light is thrown on the literary scene.

Angle, Paul M., ed. *The Great Chicago Fire . . . Described by Eight Men and Women Who Experienced its Horrors and Testified to the Courage of its Inhabitants*. Chicago: Historical Society, 1971.
————. *Prairie State: Impressions of Illinois, 1673–1967*. Chicago: U. Chicago, 1968.
Includes excerpts from a number of narratives focusing on Chicago and environs.

Anton, Rita. *Pleasant Company Accepted*. New York: Doubleday, 1963.
Light reminiscences of Catholic family life in Chicago.

Beauvoir, Simone de. *America Day by Day*. Tr. Patrick Dudley. London: Duckworth, 1952.

Strong impressionistic chapters on the city, emphasizing the two sides of Chicago—glittering facade and squalor behind it; the French novelist's trip to Chicago was the occasion which initiated her celebrated friendship with Nelson Algren (she writes much more of this in her novel, *The Mandarins*).

Beck, Frank O. *Hobohemia*. Rindge, N.H.: Smith, 1956.
Freewheeling memoirs of literary and low life during the Chicago "Renaissance."

Bennett, Arnold. *Your United States: Impressions of a First Visit*. New York: Harper, 1912.
Unpretentious, pleasant travel book by the English novelist; materials on Chicago and the Midwest woven throughout.

Bowen, Louise de Koven. *Growing up with a City*. New York: Macmillan, 1926.
Personal reminiscences by a leading socialite.

Browne, Maurice. *Too Late to Lament*. Bloomington: Indiana U., 1956.
Autobiography of the Chicago theatre champion.

Bunin, Ed. *Hack #777*. Evanston: Regency, 1963.
Often hilarious escapades of a Chicago cab driver who "takes you with him on a wild ride through the fleshpots and back streets of America's fastest city, and straight into America's most significant labor trouble."

Butcher, Fanny. *Many Lives—One Love*. New York: Harper, 1972.
Richly anecdotal memoirs of a Chicago newspaperwoman who mixed with the literary crowd for half a century; interesting portraits of Sandburg, Dreiser, Sinclair Lewis, Harriet Monroe, and many others.

Chatfield-Taylor, Hobart C. *Chicago*. Boston: Houghton Mifflin, 1917.
Intimate portrait of the city by a literary man; illustrated by Lester Hornby.

_____. *Cities of Many Men*. Boston: Houghton Mifflin, 1925.
"A wanderer's memories of . . . Chicago during half a century."

Chesterton, Gilbert K. *What I Saw in America*. New York: Dodd, 1922.
This, plus an essay "Mr. Chesterton Looks Us Over" (*New York Times Magazine*, Feb. 11, 1931), represents some very entertaining impressions of Chicago and America by the English writer.

Cook, Frederick F. *Bygone Days in Chicago*. Chicago: McClurg, 1910.
Recollections of the "Garden City" before the Fire, by a prominent Chicago journalist. Includes a section on Chicago theatre.

Dubkin, Leonard. *Wolf Point: An Adventure in History*. New York: Putnam, 1953.
This Chicago businessman has mixed personal narrative and natural history writing in a simple, agreeable way in several volumes. "Wolf Point" refers to a secluded area on the Chicago River, in the city's center, where the writer observed the continuance of natural phenomena—bird activity, growth of flowers and grasses, etc. Among his other titles, similar in scope, are *The Natural History of a Yard* (1955), *The White Lady* (about a white albino bat—1952), *The Murmur of Wings* (1944), and *Enchanted Streets* (1947).

Garden, Mary. *Mary Garden's Story*. New York: Simon and Schuster, 1951.
Autobiography of the English opera star and controversial public "character." Her comments on Chicago life in the World War I era capture a certain zany spirit of the times.

Harrison, Carter H. *Stormy Years*. Indianapolis: Bobbs-Merrill, 1935.
Five times mayor of Chicago writes with first-hand knowledge of the city's roughneck days. The author also produced a second volume, *Growing Up with Chicago* (1939).

Kipling, Rudyard. *From Sea to Sea: Letters of Travel*. Authorized ed. New York: Doubleday, 1917.
Contains "American Notes," in which Kipling begins his impressions of Chicago with the following blast: "Having seen it, I urgently desire never to see it again. It is inhabited by savages. Its water is the water of the Hooghly, and its air is dirt." First published in 1899.

Kirkland, Caroline, ed. *Chicago Yesterdays*. Chicago: Daughaday, 1919.
A collection of memoirs, including essays by the editor, Mrs. Arthur Meeker, Mrs. B. F. Ayer, Carter Harrison, H. C. Chatfield-Taylor, and others.

Lakeside Classics Series. Mabel McIlvaine (1912–15) and Milo M. Quaife (1916–52), eds. Chicago: R. R. Donnelley, 1912–
The Lakeside Press of R. R. Donnelley and the Caxton Club of Chicago collaborated on this privately issued series of frontier narratives. Those volumes dealing with frontier life in Chicago include the first four in the series, edited by McIlvaine: *Reminiscences of Early*

Chicago (1912); *Reminiscences of Chicago During the 40's and 50's* (1913); *Reminiscences . . . Civil War* (1914); and *Reminiscences . . . Great Fire* (1915). An edition of Juliette Kinzie's *Wau-bun* was issued in 1932 under Quaife's editorship.

Lewis, Lloyd and Henry J. Smith, eds. *Oscar Wilde Discovers America: 1882.* New York: Harcourt, 1936.
Wilde's opinions of the Midwest, especially Chicago, are recorded mainly in Book Three. Wilde did not write a formal narrative; the editors have gleaned most of his impressions from newspapers, magazines, etc. Wilde's comment on the revered Chicago Water Tower: "a castellated monstrosity with pepper-boxes stuck all over it."

Liebling, A. J. *Chicago: The Second City.* New York: Knopf, 1952.
A delightful, pungent book in which a New Yorker tweeks the collective noses of pretentious Chicagoans. One of the best pieces of satirical writing on the city.

Lovett, Robert Morss. *All Our Years.* New York: Viking, 1948.
Perhaps the best memoir of the early excitement associated with the beginnings of the University of Chicago, by a professor and critic. Excellent portraits of William Vaughn Moody and Robert Herrick.

McPhaul, John J. *Deadlines and Monkeyshines.* Englewood Cliffs, N.J.: Prentice-Hall, 1962.
Memoir of the hectic Chicago newspaper scene, by a journalist.

Mailer, Norman. *Miami and the Siege of Chicago.* New York: New American Library, 1968.
Best narrative of the 1968 Democratic Convention; Mailer ranges beyond the Convention to give us a trenchant view of this "tough" city.

Meeker, Arthur. *Chicago, with Love: A Polite and Personal History.* New York: Knopf, 1955.
Novelist's memoirs include portraits of many of the city's most important people: the Palmers, Armours, Fields, and leaders of the arts community during the first half of the twentieth century.

Monroe, Harriet. *A Poet's Life: Seventy Years in a Changing World.* New York: Macmillan, 1938.
The founder and editor of *Poetry* captures Chicago literary life from the 1880s on into the 1930s.

Morley, Christopher. *Old Loopy: A Love Letter for Chicago.* Chicago: Argus, 1935.
Delightful short piece, with photos by Guy Ederheimer.

Morris, James [Jan]. *Places.* London: Faber, 1972.
Includes an evocative piece on Chicago, by the fine English travel writer.

Newberry, Julia. *Julia Newberry's Diary.* New York: Norton, 1933.
Charming record of Chicago "high society" in the nineteenth century, by an adolescent girl of family. With an introduction by Margaret Ayer Barnes and Janet Ayer Fairbanks.

O'Faolain, Sean. "The Three Chicagos." *Holiday,* 28 (Dec. 1960), 74–87, 180–89.
Vigorous impressions by the Irish writer, who sees the "three Chicagos" as the "ruthless barons on the top and the ruthless brigands below, with the mass of honest burghers crushed between them."

Pierce, Bessie L., ed. *As Others See Chicago.* Chicago: U. Chicago, 1933.
Excellent older anthology. Used together with Angle's *Prairie State* (q.v.), it will provide a broad spectrum of personal narratives dealing with Chicago.

Rascoe, Burton. . . . *Before I Forget.* Garden City, N.Y.: Doubleday, 1937.
Tribune journalist carries his autobiography up to 1920, when he left Chicago for New York.

Read, Opie. *I Remember.* New York: Smith, 1930.
Autobiography of the novelist, humorist, and journalist. His time in Chicago during the late nineteenth century is covered well.

Seymour, Ralph F. *Some Went This Way: A Forty Year Pilgrimage Among Artists, Bookmen and Printers.* Chicago: Seymour, 1945.
Covers nearly the first half of the twentieth century.

Sienkiewicz, Henryk. *Portrait of America: Letters.* Ed. & tr. by Charles Morley. New York: Columbia U., 1959.
Selection of the Nobel laureate's letters home during a visit to the U.S. in 1876–78. He describes life in Chicago's Polish community and notes his impressions of the Midwest as viewed through a train window.

Starrett, Vincent. *Born in a Bookshop: Chapters from the Chicago Renascence*. Norman: U. Oklahoma, 1965.

Memoirs of the ubiquitous Chicago bookman.

Stone, Melville E. *Fifty Years a Journalist*. Garden City, N.Y.: Doubleday, 1921.

Stone began the *Daily News* in 1875 and was the first to bring first-rate journalism to Chicago. Eugene Field, George Ade, and Finley Peter Dunne all worked for him.

Sullivan, Louis H. *The Autobiography of an Idea*. New York: American Institute of Architects, 1924.

The great architect came to Chicago at seventeen in 1873. The *Autobiography* carries his life up to the Exposition in 1893, and contains some strong impressions of the hustling life of the city in the twenty years after the Fire.

Tietjens, Eunice. *The World at My Shoulder*. New York: Macmillan, 1938.

This autobiography by a Chicago writer and frequenter of literary circles is particularly important for its picture of the art world of the city.

Thomas, Theodore. *Theodore Thomas, A Musical Autobiography*. Ed. by George P. Upton. 2 vols. Chicago: McClurg, 1905. Reprint, New York: Da Capo, 1964; includes some new materials.

The orchestra leader's career in Chicago during the late nineteenth century is well covered. Thomas was a pioneer in attempting to bring serious music to the new cities of the American West.

Thompson, Slason. *Way Back When*. Chicago: Koch, 1931.

Editor and newspaperman's memoirs of the early days of Chicago literature, publishing, and newspaper life. Thompson edited the "genteel" magazine *America* from 1888–91.

Wilkie, Franc B. *Walks about Chicago, 1871–1881*. Chicago: Belford, 1882.

Valuable picture of Chicago in the decade following the Fire, by a local journalist.

Wright, Frank Lloyd. *An Autobiography*. Rev. & exp. ed. New York: Horizon, 1974.

First published in 1932, this absorbing and passionate autobiography is one of the very best by an American. Wright's Chicago years are well covered.

Gerald C. Nemanic
Northeastern Illinois University
Chicago, Illinois

BLACK LITERATURE

IN *BLACK BOY*, Richard Wright describes his move from the South to Chicago as an attempt to "transplant" his experience "in alien soil, to see if it could grow differently, if it could drink of new and cool rains, bend in strange winds, respond to the warmth of other suns, and perhaps, to bloom." Wright's images signal the beginning of a consciously midwestern black literature that has become as diversified as the plains, small towns, and cities to which southern blacks migrated. This essay is intended as a brief survey of historical and literary patterns; appended to it is a checklist of significant critical works, periodicals, bibliographies, and other aids for the scholar beginning a study of black literature of the Midwest. I shall not repeat references to major figures who are considered individually elsewhere in this volume. Neither shall I attempt to provide any list of the increasing number of full-length studies of Afro-American literature on the whole.

The history of midwestern black literature has yet to be written. When such a chronicle appears, it will need to address itself to poetry from Paul Laurence Dunbar, Fenton Johnson, and Langston Hughes to Robert Hayden, Gwendolyn Brooks, Don L. Lee, and younger poets too numerous to mention here; drama from Lorraine Hansberry to sharp contrasts in the most recent community workshop productions in Detroit and Chicago; and fiction from Richard Wright to Toni Morrison. Such a history must also consider the influence of life in the Midwest on Malcolm X and other important figures not usually thought of as midwesterners. Close study is needed, too, of the black poetry in the Midwest that has emerged from the increased opportunity afforded by black-owned and operated presses, journals, and centers for study located principally in midwestern cities. Most influential over the past decade has been Dudley Randall's Broadside Press in Detroit, which publishes not only books of poems but also collections representing young poets and an extended series of Broadsides.

The literary roots of midwestern black writers are in folk literature, the slave narrative, the black sermon, the spirituals, and a range of literary forms in the oral tradition. A study of the oral tradition maps one directly into patterns of migration from the southern agrarian to the northern, and more particularly midwestern, urban environments. Often, the writers' debts to black experience in non-southern settings have gone unnoticed. I shall include in this checklist many of the studies readily available as introductions to these crucial influences. My selection is offered as a sample, with no polemics intended. General bibliographies (see Part II) detail each of these topics in at least one section or chapter.

A student approaching the study of midwestern black writers faces an especially difficult task. He must at once look deep into the origins of black people in and around the Midwest of nineteenth-century America and examine, at the same time, an increasing number of critical studies of the whole Afro-American literary tradition.

1. BLACK LITERATURE AND LIFE IN THE MIDWEST

Berwanger, Eugene H. *The Frontier Against Slavery: Western Anti-Negro Prejudice and the Slavery Extension Controversy.* Urbana: U. Illinois, 1967.

Barrett, Leonard F. *Soul Force: African Heritage in Afro-American Religion.* Garden City, N.Y.: Doubleday, 1974.

Bontemps, Arna and Jack Conroy. *Anyplace But Here.* New York: Hill & Wang, 1966.

Botkin, B. A. *Lay My Burden Down: A Folk History of Slavery.* Chicago: U. Chicago, 1945.

Brazier, Arthur M. *Black Self-determination: The Story of the Woodlawn Organization* [Chicago]. Grand Rapids: Eerdmans, 1969.

Brooks, Gwendolyn et al., eds. *A Capsule Course in Black Poetry Writing.* Detroit: Broadside, 1975.

Campbell, Rex R. and Peter R. Robertson. *Negroes in Missouri: A Compilation of Statistical*

Data from the 1960 U.S. Census of Population. Jefferson City: Missouri Commission on Human Rights, 1967.

Chicago Commission on Race Relations. *The Negro in Chicago: A Study of Race Relations and a Race Riot.* Chicago: U. Chicago, 1922.

Clapsy, Everett. *The Negro in Southwestern Michigan: Negroes in the North in a Rural Environment.* Dowagiac, Mich.: n.p., 1967.

Dabny, Wendell P. *Cincinnati's Colored Citizens.* Cincinnati: Dabny, 1926.

Dillard, J. L. *Black English.* New York: Random House, 1972.

Dorson, Richard M. *American Negro Folktales.* Greenwich, Conn.: Fawcett, 1970.

_____. *Negro Folk Tales in Michigan.* Cambridge, Mass.: Harvard U., 1956.

_____. *Negro Tales from Pine Bluff, Arkansas, and Calvin, Michigan.* Bloomington: Indiana U., 1958.

Drake, St. Clair and Horace R. Cayton. *Black Metropolis: A Study of Negro Life in a Northern City.* New York: Harcourt, 1945.

Duncan, Otis D. and Beverly Duncan. *Chicago's Negro Population.* Chicago: U. Chicago, 1956.

Durham, Philip and Everett L. Jones. *The Negro Cowboys.* New York: Dodd, Mead, 1965.

Elazar, Daniel J. *Cities of the Prairie: The Metropolitan Frontier and American Politics.* New York: Basic Books, 1970.

Frazier, E. Franklin. *The Negro Church in America.* New York: Schocken, 1964.

_____. *The Negro Family in Chicago.* Chicago: U. Chicago, 1932.

Gara, Larry. *The Liberty Line: The Legend of the Underground Railroad.* Lexington: U. Kentucky, 1961.

Grant, Robert B. *The Black Man Comes to the City: A Documentary Account from the Great Migration to the Great Depression, 1915 to 1930.* Chicago: Nelson-Hall, 1972.

Groh, George W. *The Black Migration: The Journey to Urban America.* New York: Weybright and Talley, 1972.

Hamilton, Charles V. *The Black Preacher in America.* New York: Morrow, 1972.

Harris, Norman D. *The Study of Negro Servitude in Illinois, and of the Slavery Agitation in that State, 1719–1864.* Chicago: McClurg, 1904.

Henderson, Stephen, ed. *Understanding the New Black Poetry: Black Speech and Black Music as Poetic References.* New York: Morrow, 1973.

Herskovits, Melville J. *The Myth of the Negro Past.* New York: Harper, 1941.

Hickok, Charles T. *The Negro in Ohio, 1802–1870.* Cleveland: F. C. Butler Publ. Fund, 1896.

Hines, Burleigh and Van Gordon Sauter. *Nightmare in Detroit: A Rebellion and Its Victims.* Chicago: Regnery, 1968.

Hughes, Langston and Arna Bontemps, eds. *The Book of Negro Folklore.* New York: Dodd, Mead, 1958.

Johnson, James Weldon and J. Rosamond Johnson, eds. *The Books of Negro Spirituals.* New York: Viking, 1956.

Johnson, Joseph A. *The Soul of the Black Preacher.* Philadelphia: Pilgrim, 1971.

Johnson, Philip A. *Call Me Neighbor, Call Me Friend: The Case History of the Integration of a Neighborhood on Chicago's South Side.* Garden City, N.Y.: Doubleday, 1965.

Jones, LeRoi [Imamu Baraka]. *Blues People: Negro Music in White America.* New York: Morrow, 1963.

Katz, William L. *The Black West.* Garden City, N.Y.: Doubleday, 1971.

Katzman, David M. *Before the Ghetto: Black Detroit in the Nineteenth Century.* Urbana: U. Illinois, 1973.

Keil, Charles. *Urban Blues.* Chicago: U. Chicago, 1966.

Kennedy, Louise V. *The Negro Peasant Turns Cityward: Effects of Recent Migrations to Northern Cities.* New York: Columbia U., 1930.

Kirschner, Don S. *City and Country: Rural Responses to Urbanization in the 1920s.* Westport, Conn.: Greenwich, 1970.

Lafcadio, Hearn. *Children of the Levee.* Lexington: U. Kentucky, 1957.

Liebow, Elliott. *Tally's Corner: A Study of Negro Streetcorner Men.* Boston: Little, Brown, 1967.

Lee, Alfred McL. and Norman D. Humphrey. *Race Riot* [Detroit]. New York: Dryden, 1943.

Liwack, Leon F. *North of Slavery: The Negro in the Free States, 1790–1860.* Chicago: U. Chicago, 1961.

Loeb, Charles H. *The Future is Yours: The History of the Future Outlook League, 1935–1946.* Cleveland: Future Outlook League, 1947.

Lovell, John. *Black Song: The Forge and the Flame.* New York: Macmillan, 1972.

Lynch, Hollis R. *The Black Urban Condition: A Documentary History 1866–1971.* New York: Crowell, 1973.

Mark, Mary L. *Negroes in Columbus.* Columbus: Ohio State U., 1928.

Mays, Benjamin E. *The Negro's God as Reflected in His Literature.* Boston: Chapman and Grimes, 1938.

The Midwest Journal. Jefferson City: Lincoln U., 1948–56.

Millender, Dolly. *Yesterday in Gary: A Brief History of the Negro in Gary.* Gary, Ind.: Author, 1967.

Nelsen, Hart M., Raytha L. Yoklen, and Anne K. Nelsen, eds. *The Black Church in America.* New York: Basic Books, 1971.

Osofsky, Gilbert. "The Significance of the Slave Narratives." Introduction to *Puttin' on Ole Massa: The Slave Narratives of Henry Bibb, William Wells Brown, and Solomon Northrup.* New York: Harper, 1969.

Porter, Kenneth W. *The Negro in the American Frontier.* New York: Arno, 1970.

Primeau, Ronald. "Slave Narrative Turning Midwestern: Deadwood Dick Rides into Difficulties." In *MidAmerica I: The Yearbook of the Society for the Study of Midwestern Literature,* ed. David D. Anderson. East Lansing: Midwest Press, 1974. Pp. 16–35.

Quarles, Benjamin. *Black Abolitionists.* New York: Oxford, 1969.

Quillen, Frank U. *The Color Line in Ohio: A History of Race Prejudice in a Typical Northern State.* Ann Arbor: Wahr, 1913.

Rainwater, Lee. *Behind Ghetto Walls: Black Families in a Federal Slum* [St. Louis]. Chicago: Aldine, 1970.

Randall, Dudley. *Broadside Memories: Poets I Have Known.* Detroit: Broadside, 1975.

Robb, John M. *The Black Coal Miner of Southeast Kansas.* Topeka: Commission on Civil Rights, 1969.

Rossi, Peter H. and Robert A. Dentler. *The Politics of Urban Renewal: The Chicago Findings.* New York: Free Press, 1961.

Rudwick, Elliott M. *Race Riot at East St. Louis, July 2, 1917.* Carbondale: Southern Illinois, 1964.

Sherman, Richard B., ed. *The Negro and the City.* Englewood Cliffs, N.J.: Prentice-Hall, 1970.

Sidran, Ben. *Black Talk: How the Music of Black America Created a Radical Alternative to the Values of Western Literary Tradition.* New York: Holt, 1971.

Southern, Eileen. *The Music of Black Americans: A History.* New York: Norton, 1971.

Spangler, Earl. *The Negro in Minnesota.* Minneapolis: Denison, 1961.

Spear, Allan H. *Black Chicago: The Making of a Negro Ghetto, 1890–1920.* Chicago: U. Chicago, 1967.

Strickland, Arvath E. *History of the Chicago Urban League.* Urbana: U. Illinois, 1966.

Sullenger, Thomas Earl and J. Harvey Kerns. *The Negro in Omaha: A Social Study of Negro Development.* Omaha: U. Omaha, 1931.

Taeuber, Karl E. and Alma F. Taeuber. *Negroes in Cities: Residential Segregation and Neighborhood Change.* New York: Atheneum, 1965.

Thornbrough, Emma Lou. *The Negro in Indiana: A Study of a Minority.* Indianapolis: Indiana Historical Bureau, 1957.

Todd, Edwin S. *A Sociological Study of Clark County, Ohio.* Springfield, Ohio: Springfield Publ. Co., 1904.

Tolson, Arthur L. *The Negro in Oklahoma Territory, 1889–1907.* Ann Arbor: Univ. Microfilms, 1972.

Voegeli, V. Jacque. *Free But Not Equal: The Midwest and the Negro During the Civil War.* Chicago: U. Chicago, 1967.

Warner, William Lloyd et al. *Color and Human Nature: Negro Personality Development in a Northern City* [Chicago]. Washington, D.C.: American Council on Education, 1941.

Wesley, Charles n. *Ohio Negroes in the Civil War.* Columbus: Vanguard, 1962.
Woodson, Carter G. *A Century of Negro Migration.* Washington, D.C.: Assn. for the Study of Negro Life and History, 1918.
———. *Negro Orators and Their Orations.* Washington, D.C.: Associated Publ., 1925.
Woofter, Thomas J., Jr. *Negro Migration.* New York: Gray, 1920.
Woodward, C. Vann. *The Strange Career of Jim Crow.* Rev. ed. New York: Oxford, 1966.
Work, John W., ed. *American Negro Songs and Spirituals.* New York: Howell, Soskin, 1940.
Wright, Richard. "How Bigger Was Born." *SatR,* 22 (June 1, 1940), 3–4, 17–20.

2. BIBLIOGRAPHY

Bailey, Leeonead, ed. *Broadside Authors: A Bibliographical Directory.* Detroit: Broadside, 1971.
Baskin, Wade and Richard N. Runes. *Dictionary of Black Culture.* New York: Philosophical Library, 1973.
Bell, Barbara L. *Black Biographical Sources: An Annotated Bibliography.* New Haven: Yale U. Library, 1970.
Black List: The Concise Reference Guide to Publishers and Broadcasting Media of Black America, Africa, and the Caribbean. New York: Panther House, 1971.
Boone, Dorothy D. *A Historical Review and A Bibliography of Selected Negro Magazines 1910–1969.* Ann Arbor: Univ. Microfilms, 1972.
Brown, Warren H. *Check List of Negro Newspapers in the United States (1827–1946).* Jefferson City: School of Journalism, Lincoln U., 1946.
Chapman, Abraham. *The Negro in American Literature and A Bibliography of Literature by and about Negro Americans.* Oshkosh, Wisc.: Council of Teachers of English, 1966.
Cromwell, Otelia. *Readings from Negro Authors for Schools and Colleges, with A Bibliography of Negro Literature.* New York: Harcourt, 1931.
Davis, John P., ed. *The American Negro Reference Book.* Englewood Cliffs, N.J.: Prentice-Hall, 1966.
Davis, Lenwood G. *The Black Family in Urban Areas in the United States.* Monticello, Ill.: Council of Planning Librarians, 1973.
A Dictionary Catalog of the Schomburg Collection of Negro Literature and History. 9 vols. Boston: Hall, 1962; 2 vols. suppl., 1967.
Directory of Black Literary Magazines. Washington, D.C.: Negro Bibliographic and Research Center, 1970–
Dodds, Barbara. *Negro Literature for High School Students.* Champaign: National Council of Teachers of English, 1968.
Dumond, Dwight L. *Bibliography of Anti-Slavery in America.* Ann Arbor: U. Michigan, 1961.
Fontvieille, Jean R. *Guide Bibliographique du Monde noir.* Yaounde: Direction des affaires culturelles, 1970.
Fuller, Juanita B. *An Annotated Bibliography of Biographies and Autobiographies of Negroes, 1839–1961.* Microcard. Rochester, N.Y.: Association of College and Research Libraries, 1964.
Gardner, Henry L. *Readings in Contemporary Black Politics: An Annotated Bibliography.* Carbondale: Public Affairs Research Bureau, Southern Illinois 1969.
Gross, Seymour L. and John E. Hardy, eds. *Images of the Negro in American Literature.* Chicago: U. Chicago, 1966.
Hatch, James V. *Black Image on the American Stage: A Bibliography of Plays and Musicals, 1770–1970.* New York: DBS Publ., 1970.
Homer, Dorothy R. *The Negro in the United States: A List of Significant Books.* 9th ed. New York: New York Public Library, 1965.
Homer, Dorothy R. and Ann M. Swarthout. *Books About the Negro: An Annotated Bibliography.* New York: Praeger, 1966.
Index to Periodical Articles by and about Negroes. Boston: Hall, 1950, 1959–   .
Irwin, Leonard B. *Black Studies: A Bibliography.* Brooklawn, N.J.: McKinley, 1973.
Jackson, Bruce. *The Negro and His Folklore in Nineteenth-Century Periodicals.* Austin: U. Texas, 1967.

Jackson, Clara O. *A Bibliography of Afro-American and Other American Minorities Represented in Libraries and Library Listings.* New York: American Institute for Marxist Studies, 1970.

Jahn, Janheinz. *A Bibliography of Neo-African Literature from Africa, America, and the Caribbean.* New York: Praeger, 1965.

Klotman, Phyllis R. and Wilmer H. Baatz. *The Black Family and the Black Woman: A Bibliography.* Bloomington: Indiana U. Library, 1972.

Lawson, Hilda J. *The Negro in American Drama: A Bibliography of Contemporary Drama.* Ph.D. diss., U. Illinois, 1939.

Marshall, Albert P. *A Guide to Negro Periodical Literature.* 4 vols. Winston-Salem, N.C.: Winston-Salem State College, 1941–46.

McPherson, James M. et al. *Blacks in America: Bibliographical Essays.* Garden City, N.Y.: Doubleday, 1971.

Meyer, Jon K. *Bibliography on the Urban Crisis.* Chevy Chase, Md.: Institutes of Mental Health. 1969.

Miller, Elizabeth W. and Mary L. Fisher. *The Negro in America: A Bibliography.* 2d ed. Cambridge, Mass.: Harvard U., 1970.

The Negro Handbook. Chicago: Johnson, 1966.

The Negro in Print: Bibliographic Survey. Washington, D.C.: Negro Bibliographic and Research Center, 1965– .

Penn, Joseph E. et al. *The American Negro in Paperback: A Selected List.* Washington, D.C.: National Education Association, 1967.

Ploski, Harry A. and Roscoe C. Brown, Jr. *The Negro Almanac.* New York: Bellwether, 1967.

Porter, Dorothy B. *The Negro in the United States.* Washington, D.C.: Library of Congress, 1970.

———. *North American Negro Poets: A Bibliographical Checklist of their Writings, 1760–1944.* Hattiesburg, Miss.: Book Farm, 1945.

———. *A Working Bibliography on the Negro in the U.S.* Ann Arbor: Univ. Microfilms, 1969.

Pride, Armistead S. *The Black Press: A Bibliography.* Jefferson City, Mo.: Association for Education in Journalism, 1968.

Querry, Ronald, and Robert E. Fleming. "A Working Bibliography of Black Periodicals." *Studies in Black Literature,* 3 (Summer 1972), 31–36.

Ross, Frank A. and Louise V. Kennedy. *A Bibliography of Negro Migration.* New York: Columbia U., 1934.

Ryan, Pat. *Black Writing in the U.S.A.: A Bibliographical Guide.* Brockport, N.Y.: Drake Memorial Library, 1969.

Schneider, Joyce B. *A Selected List of Periodicals Relating to Negroes, with Holdings in the Libraries of Yale University.* New Haven: Yale U. Library, 1970.

Spalding, Henry D. *Encyclopedia of Black Folklore and Humor.* Middle Village, N.Y.: Jonathan David, 1972.

Spangler, Earl. *Bibliography of Negro History: Selected and Annotated Entries, General and Minnesota.* Minneapolis: Ross and Haines, 1963.

Swisher, Robert. *Black American Biography.* Bloomington: Indiana U. Library, 1969.

Thompson, Edgar T. and Alma M. Thompson. *Race and Region: A Descriptive Bibliography Compiled with Special Reference to the Relations Between Whites and Negroes in the U.S.* Chapel Hill: U. North Carolina, 1949.

Turner, Darwin T. *Afro-American Writers.* New York: Appleton, 1970.

Welsch, Erwin K. *The Negro in the United States: A Research Guide.* Bloomington: Indiana U., 1965.

West, Earle H. *A Bibliography of Doctoral Research on the Negro, 1933–1966.* Washington, D.C.: Xerox, 1969.

Whiteman, Maxwell. *A Century of Fiction by Negroes: A Descriptive Bibliography (1853–1952).* Philadelphia: Jacobs, 1955.

Whitlow, Roger. *Black American Literature: A Critical History with a 1,520 Title Bibliography of Works Written by and about Black Americans.* Chicago: Nelson-Hall, 1973.

Williams, Daniel T. *Eight Negro Bibliographies.* New York: Kraus, 1970.

Williams, Ethel L. and Clifton L. Brown. *Afro-American Religious Studies: A Comprehensive Bibliography with Locations in American Libraries*. Metuchen, N.J.: Scarecrow, 1972.
Williams, Ora. *American Black Women in the Arts and Social Sciences: A Bibliographical Survey*. Metuchen, N.J.: Scarecrow, 1973.
Work, Monroe. *A Bibliography of the Negro in Africa and America*. New York: Wilson, 1928.

Ronald Primeau
Central Michigan University
Mt. Pleasant, Michigan

INDIANS

IF THE NUMBER of new titles and reprints is a valid index, interest in the cultural life of midwestern Indians has increased markedly in the last decade. Paralleling the popular rediscovery of the Indian has come a renewed scholarly interest, with major studies completed in physical and cultural anthropology, linguistics, and history.

What is a midwestern Indian? There is no simple answer. The nomandic activities of many tribes in the prehistoric period complicate the matter, as do the later, often forced movements of whole peoples from one region to another. For example, in the prehistorical and early historical periods, the Sioux are native to the Upper Midwest. By the second half of the nineteenth century, they have been forced substantially into the northern plains west of the 100th meridian. If we go strictly by the geography of the moment, the Sioux of Charles Eastman are midwestern and those of Sitting Bull are not. The same problem is faced when we consider the movements of the Pawnee, the Cree, the Kickapoo, the Chippewa, and other tribes. Our solution, admittedly an inadequate one, is to include only those studies dealing with Indians at the time of their sojourn in the Midwest. We have not included tribes which had only brief contact with the Midwest or those which are generally associated with areas outside the region (e.g., the Delaware, Ottawa, Wyandotte, and various branches of the western Sioux).

Frederick W. Hodge published his encyclopedic *Handbook of American Indians North of Mexico* in two volumes between 1907 and 1910. This compendium remains an extremely valuable scholarly contribution. The midwestern tribes—Sioux, Chippewa (or Ojibwa), Winnebago, Sauk, et al. are given thorough treatment. The Bureau of American Ethnology reports on Amerindian tribes, many of which were issued in the World War I era, also remain valuable.

In general, the midwestern Indians can be divided into two groups: those of the western Great Lakes and of the eastern Great Plains. W. Vernon

Kinietz has provided a scholarly survey of *The Indians of the Western Great Lakes, 1615–1760* (1940). The Chippewa is the most prominent tribe of this region. For the layman, readable and sound introductions can be found in George I. Quimby's *Indian Life in the Upper Great Lakes: 11,000 B.C. to A.D. 1800* (1960) and in *The Woodland Indians of the Western Great Lakes* by Robert E. and Pat Ritzenthaler (1970). Two books by Clark Wissler, *North American Indians of the Plains* (1934) and *The American Indians* (3d ed., 1950), provide a good introduction to the anthropological investigations of the American tribes, and in particular to Plains tribes like the Sioux. A number of George E. Hyde's monographs, e.g., *Indians of the Woodlands* (1962), provide valuable surveys.

Among intensive studies of single tribes, their history, folklore, language, etc., are those models provided by Ruth Landes, who has recently contributed volumes on the Sioux, Ojibwa, and Potawatomi tribes. Paul Radin's *Winnebago Tribe* (1923) is a classic ethnological work.

Grant Foreman has provided several scholarly works dealing with the clash between Indian and white on the frontier, and with the inevitable removal of the red men to ever more westerly areas.

Midwestern Indian life in the period of exploration is most fully reflected, of course, in the voluminous reports of French explorers and missionaries which make up the *Jesuit Relations*. For the frontier period, first hand accounts of midwestern tribes are plentiful (see also Personal Narratives), the most notable being those of Schoolcraft, John Treat Irving, Parkman, and the painter Catlin.

The "General and Reference" list includes discussions of tribes in the various states; bibliographies; anthologies; and other Amerindian titles containing extensive materials on midwestern tribes. Predominantly technical treatises are not included.

Consult also the following sections of this book: History and Society; Folklore; Personal Narrative.

For extensive treatment of the Indian in literary works, consult the following author bibliographies: Berger; Catherwood; Flint; Garland; Hemingway; Manfred; Neihardt; Richter; Sarett; Schoolcraft; and Woolson.

1. GENERAL AND REFERENCE WORKS

*Indicates important bibliographical source.

Alexander, Hartley B. *North American Mythology*. Boston: Marshall Jones, 1916.
_____. *The World's Rim: Great Mysteries of the North American Indians*. Lincoln: U. Nebraska, 1953.
Astrov, Margot, ed. *The Winged Serpent: An Anthology of American Indian Prose and Poetry*. New York: Day, 1946.
Barrett, Stephen M. *Sociology of the American Indians*. Kansas City: Burton, 1946.
Bettarel, Robert L. and Hale G. Smith. *The Moccasin Bluff Site and the Woodland Cultures of Southwestern Michigan*. Ann Arbor: U. Michigan, 1973.
Bird, Harrison. *War for the West, 1790–1813*. New York: Oxford, 1971.
Blair, Emma H., ed. *The Indian Tribes of the Upper Mississippi Valley and the Region of the Great Lakes*. 2 vols. Cleveland: Clark, 1911.

*Boas, Franz. *Handbook of American Indian Languages.* Washington: GPO, 1911.

*Bonnerjen, Biren, ed. *Index to Bulletins 1–100 of the Bureau of American Ethnology: With Index to Contributions to North American Ethnology, Introductions and Miscellaneous Publications.* Washington: GPO, 1963.

Brady, Cyrus T. *Indian Fights and Fighters.* Garden City, N.Y.: Doubleday, 1916.

Brandon, William, ed. *The Magic World: American Indian Songs and Poems.* New York: Morrow, 1972.

Brennan, Louis A. *No Stone Unturned: An Almanac of American Prehistory.* New York: Random, 1959.

Britt, Albert. *Great Indian Chiefs: A Study of Indian Leaders in the Two Hundred Year Struggle to Stop the White Advance.* New York: McGraw-Hill, 1938.

Brower, Jacob V. *Memoirs of Explorations in the Basin of the Mississippi.* 8 vols. St. Paul: Author, 1898–1904.

Brown, Dee. *Bury My Heart at Wounded Knee: An Indian History of the American West.* New York: Holt. 1970.

Burland, Cottie A. *North American Indian Mythology.* New ed. Feltham, Mass.: Hamlyn, 1968.

Burns, Robert I. *The Jesuits and the Indian Wars of the Northwest.* New Haven: Yale, 1966.

Bushnell, David I. *Villages of the Algonquian, Siouan, and Caddoan Tribes West of the Mississippi.* Washington: GPO, 1922.

Callender, Charles. *Social Organization of the Central Algonkian Indians.* Milwaukee: Public Museum, 1962.

Cash, Joseph and Herbert T. Hoover, eds. *To Be an Indian: An Oral History.* New York: Holt, 1971.

Catlin, George. See Architecture and Graphics section.

Ceram, C. W. *The First American.* New York: New American Library, 1971.

Chapman, Carl H. and Eleanor F. *Indians and Archaeology of Missouri.* Columbia: U. Missouri, 1964.

Cottier, Randy L., comp. *A Selected Bibliography of Missouri Archaeology.* Columbia: U. Missouri College of Arts & Sciences, 1973.

David, Jay, ed. *The American Indian: The First Victim.* New York: Morrow, 1972.

*Dawdy, Doris O. *Annotated Bibliography of American Indian Painting.* New York: Museum of the American Indian, 1968.

Day, A. Grove. *The Sky Clears: Poetry of the American Indians.* New York: Macmillan, 1951.

Debo, Angie. *A History of the Indians of the United States.* 2 vols. Norman: U. Oklahoma, 1970–71.

Deuel, Thorne. *American Indian Ways of Life.* Springfield: State of Illinois, 1968.

Dewdney, Selwyn H. and Kenneth E. Kidd. *Indian Rock Paintings of the Great Lakes.* 2d rev. ed. Toronto: U. Toronto, 1962.

Dobyns, Henry F. *Native American Historical Demography: A Critical Bibliography.* Bloomington: Indiana U., 1976.

*Dockstader, Frederick. *The American Indian in Graduate Studies: A Bibliography of Theses and Dissertations.* New York: Museums of the American Indian, 1973–74.

*_____. *Books About Indians.* 2d rev. ed. New York: Museum of the American Indian, 1972.

_____. *Indian Art in North America.* New York: N.Y. Graphic Society, 1973.

Douglas, John M. *The Indians in Wisconsin's History.* Milwaukee: Public Museum, 1954.

Downes, Randolph C. *Council Fires on the Upper Ohio: A Narrative of Indian Affairs in the Upper Ohio Valley Until 1795.* Pittsburgh: U. Pittsburgh, 1940.

Driver, Harold E. *Indians of North America.* 2d rev. ed. Chicago: U. Chicago, 1969.

Dunn, Jacob P. *True Indian Stories, with a Glossary of Indiana Indian Names.* Indianapolis: Sentinel, 1908.

Eggan, Fred, ed. *Social Anthropology of the North American Tribes.* Enl. 2d ed. Chicago: U. Chicago, 1955.

Erdoes, Richard. *The Sun Dance Indians: Their Past and Present.* New York: Knopf, 1972.

Erdman, Joyce M. *Handbook on Wisconsin Indians.* Madison: Commission on Human Rights, 1966.

*Fay, George E. *Bibliography of the Indians of Wisconsin.* Oshkosh: Wisconsin State U., 1965.

Federal Writers' Project. Wisconsin. *Wisconsin Indian Place Legends.* Madison, 1936.

Fitting, James E. *The Archaeology of Michigan: A Guide to the Pre-history of the Great Lakes Region.* Garden City: Natural History Press, 1970.

———. *Late Woodland Cultures of Southeastern Michigan.* Ann Arbor: U. Michigan, 1965.

———, ed. *The Development of North American Archeology: Essays in the History of Regional Tradition.* Garden City, N.Y.: Anchor, 1973.

Fletcher, Alice C. *Indian Games and Dances with Native Songs: Arranged from American Indian Ceremonials and Sports.* Boston: Birchard, 1915.

———. *Indian Story and Song from North America.* Boston: Birchard, 1900.

Flint, Timothy. *Indian Wars of the West.* Cincinnati: E. H. Flint, 1833.

Folsom, Franklin. *America's Ancient Treasures.* New York: Rand, McNally, 1971.

Foreman, Grant. *Advancing the Frontier, 1830–1860.* Norman: U. Oklahoma, 1933.

———. *Indians and Pioneers.* Rev. ed. Norman: U. Oklahoma, 1936.

———. *The Last Trek of the Indians.* Chicago: U. Chicago, 1946.

Gates, Charles M., ed. *Five Fur Traders of the Northwest.* Minneapolis: U. Minnesota, 1933.

Glubok, Shirley. *The Art of the Woodland Indians.* New York: Macmillan, 1976.

Greenman, Emerson F. *The Indians of Michigan.* Lansing: Historical Commission, 1961.

Gridley, Marion E. *American Indian Landmarks.* Chicago: Swallow, 1972.

Griffin, James B., ed. *Archaeology of the Eastern United States.* Chicago: U. Chicago, 1952.

Hall, Robert L. *The Archeology of Carcajou Point: With an Interpretation of the Development of Oneota Culture in Wisconsin.* 2 vols. Madison: U. Wisconsin, 1962.

Hallowell, A. Irving. *Culture and Experience.* Philadelphia: U. Pennsylvania, 1955.

Hamilton, Charles, ed. *Cry of the Thunderbird: The American Indian's Own Story.* Norman: U. Oklahoma, 1972.

Hanzeli, Victor E. *Missionary Linguistics in New France: A Study of 17th and 18th Century Descriptions of American Indian Languages.* New York: Humanities Press, 1970.

Harkins, Arthur M. *Attitudes and Characteristics of Selected Wisconsin Indians.* Minneapolis: U. Minnesota, 1969.

*Haywood, Charles, ed. *A Bibliography of North American Folklore and Folksong.* 2 vols. Rev. ed. New York: Dover, 1961.
  See volume 2.

Hinsdale, Wilbert B. *The First People of Michigan.* Ann Arbor: U. Michigan, 1930.

———. *Primitive Men in Michigan.* Ann Arbor: U. Michigan, 1925.

*Hirschfelder, Arlene B. *American Indian Authors: A Representative Bibliography.* New York: Assn. on American Indian Affairs, 1970.

Hodge, Frederick W., ed. *Handbook of American Indians North of Mexico.* 2 vols. Washington: GPO, 1907–10.

Holder, Preston. *The Hoe and the Horse on the Plains: A Study of Cultural Development Among North American Indians.* Lincoln: U. Nebraska, 1970.

Holmes, William H. *Handbook of Aboriginal American Antiquities.* Washington: GPO, 1919– .

Hunter, John D. *Manners and Customs of Several Indian Tribes Located West of the Mississippi.* Philadelphia: Maxwell, 1823.

———. *Memoirs of a Captivity Among the Indians of North America.* London: Longman, 1823.

Hyde, George E. *Indians of the High Plains: From the Prehistoric Period to the Coming of the Europeans.* Norman: U. Oklahoma, 1959.

———. *Indians of the Woodland: From Prehistoric Times to 1725.* Norman: U. Oklahoma, 1962.

Jackson, Helen Hunt. *A Century of Dishonor: A Sketch of the U.S. Government's Dealing with some of the Indian Tribes.* New York: Harper, 1881.

Jennings, Jesse D. *Prehistory in North America.* 2d ed. New York: McGraw-Hill, 1974.

——— and Edward Norbeck, eds. *Prehistoric Man in the New World.* Chicago: U. Chicago, 1964.

Johnson, Elden, ed. *Aspects of Upper Great Lakes Anthropology: Papers in Honor of Lloyd A. Wilford.* St. Paul: Minnesota Historical Society, 1974.

Johnson, Frederick, ed. *Man in Northeastern North America*. Andover, Mass.: Peabody Foundation, 1946.

Jones, Hettie, comp. *The Trees Stand Shining: Poetry of the North American Indians*. New York: Dial, 1971.

Judson, Katherine B. *Myths and Legends of the Great Plains*. Chicago: McClurg, 1913.

————. *Myths and Legends of the Mississippi Valley and the Great Lakes*. Chicago: McClurg, 1914.

Kane, Grace F. *Myths and Legends of the Mackinacs and Lake Region*. Cincinnati: Editor Publ. Co., 1897.

Keiser, Albert. *The Indian in American Literature*. New York: Oxford, 1933.

Keller, James H. *An Introduction to the Prehistory of Indiana*. Indianapolis: Indiana Historical Society, 1973.

Kennedy, John H. *Jesuit and Savage in New France*. New Haven: Yale U., 1950.

Kenton, Edna, ed. *The Indians of North America*. New York: Harcourt, 1927.
A selection of materials from the *Jesuit Relations* (q.v.).

Kinietz, W. Vernon. *The Indians of the Western Great Lakes: 1615–1760*. Ann Arbor: U. Michigan, 1940.

Klein, Bernard and Daniel Icolari. *Reference Encyclopedia of the American Indian*. 2d rev. ed. Rye, N.Y.: Klein, 1970.

Knopf, Richard. *Indians of the Ohio Country*. Columbus: Modern Methods, 1959.

Kroeber, Alfred L. *Cultural and Natural Areas of Native North Americans*. Berkeley: U. California, 1939.

Kubiak, William J. *Great Lakes Indians: A Pictorial Guide*. Grand Rapids: Baker, 1970.

Lincoln, Jackson S. *The Dream in Primitive Cultures*. London: Cresset, 1935.

Linderman, Frank B. *Indian Lodge-Fire Stories*. New York: Scribner, 1918.

————. *Indian Old-Man Stories*. New York: Scribner, 1920.

————. *Indian Why Stories*. New York: Scribner, 1915.

Longstreet, Stephen. *War Cries on Horseback: The Story of the Indian Wars on the Great Plains*. Garden City: Doubleday, 1970.

Lowie, Robert H. *Indians of the Plains*. New York: McGraw-Hill, 1954.

————. *Plains Indian Age Societies*. New York: Museum of Natural History, 1916.

————. *Studies in Plains Indians Folklore*. Berkeley: U. California, 1932.

McDermott, John F. *Seth Eastman: Pictorial Historian of the Indian*. Norman: U. Oklahoma, 1961.

McGowan, Kenneth and Joseph A. Hester, Jr. *Early Man in the New World*. Rev. ed. New York: Doubleday, 1962.

McKusick, Marshall B. *The Davenport Conspiracy*. Iowa City: State Archaeologist, 1970.

————. *Men of Ancient Iowa, as Revealed by Archaeological Discoveries*. Ames: Iowa State U., 1964.

McLuhan, T. C., comp. *Touch the Earth: A Self-Portrait of Indian Existence*. New York: Dutton, 1971.

MacNeish, Richard S., ed. *Early Men in America: Readings from Scientific American*. San Francisco: Freeman, 1973.

McNitt, Frank. *The Indian Traders*. Norman: U. Oklahoma, 1962.

*Marken, Jack W. *The Indians and Eskimos of North America: A Bibliography of Books in Print Through 1972*. Vermillion, S.D.: Dakota Press, 1973.

Mails, Thomas E. *The Mystic Warriors of the Plains*. Garden City, N.Y.: Doubleday, 1972.

Marquis, Arnold. *A Guide to America's Indians: Ceremonies, Reservations, and Museums*. Norman: U. Oklahoma, 1974.

Miller, Alfred J. *Braves and Buffalo: Plains Indian Life in 1837*. Toronto: U. Toronto, 1973.

————. *The West of Alfred Jacob Miller (1837)*. Rev. & enl. ed. Norman: U. Oklahoma, 1968.

Milton, John, ed. "The American Indian." *SDR*, 7 (Summer 1969) [special issue].

————. "American Indian II." *SDR*, 9 (Summer 1971) [special issue].

Mooney, James. *The Aboriginal Population of America North of Mexico*. Washington: GPO, 1928.

Morgan, L. H. *The Indian Journals, 1859–62*. Ann Arbor: U. Michigan, 1959.

————. *Systems of Consanguinity and Affinity*. Washington: GPO, 1871.

*Mugridge, Donald H. and Blanche P. McCrum. *A Guide to the Study of the United States of America: Representative Books Reflecting the Development of American Life and Thought.* Washington: Library of Congress, 1960.
Section 7 on the American Indian.
*Murdock, George P. *Ethnographic Bibliography of North America.* 3d ed. New Haven: Human Relations Area Files, 1960.
Murphy, James L. *An Archaeological History of the Hocking Valley.* Athens: Ohio U., 1974.
Nasatir, Abraham P., ed. *Before Lewis and Clark: Documents Illustrating the History of the Missouri, 1785–1804.* 2 vols. St. Louis: St. Louis Historical Documents Foundation, 1952.
*Newberry Library. *Dictionary Catalog of the Edward E. Ayer Collection of Americana and American Indians.* 16 vols. Boston: G. K. Hall, 1961.
*_____. *Narratives of Captivity Among the Indians of North America: A List of Books and Manuscripts on the Subject in the Edward E. Ayer Collection of the Newberry Library.* With Supplement. Chicago: Newberry Library, 1938.
*Owen, Roger C., comp. *The North American Indian: A Sourcebook.* New York: Macmillan, 1967.
Parry, Elwood. *The Image of the Indian and the Black Man in American Art, 1590–1900.* New York: Braziller, 1974.
Petersen, Karen D. *Plains Indian Art from Fort Marion.* Norman: U. Oklahoma, 1971.
Parsons, Elsie C., ed. *American Indian Life.* Lincoln: U. Nebraska, 1967.
Pearce, Roy H. *The Savages of America: A Study of the Indian and the Idea of Civilization.* Baltimore: Johns Hopkins, 1965.
Peckham, Howard H. *Captured by Indians: True Tales of Pioneer Survivors.* New Brunswick: Rutgers, 1954.
Peters, Joseph P., comp. *Indian Battles and Skirmishes on the American Frontier 1790–1898.* New York: Arno, 1966.
Quimby, George I. *Indian Culture and European Trade Goods: The Archaeology of the Historic Period in the Western Great Lakes Region.* Madison: U. Wisconsin, 1966.
_____. *Indian Life in the Upper Great Lakes: 11,000 B.C. to A.D. 1800.* Chicago: U. Chicago, 1960.
Potter, Martha A. *Ohio's Prehistoric Peoples.* Columbus: Ohio Historical Society, 1968.
Ritzenthaler, Robert E. and George I. Quimby. *The Red Ocher Culture of the Upper Great Lakes and Adjacent Areas.* Chicago: Natural History Museum, 1962.
Ritzenthaler, Robert E. and Pat Ritzenthaler. *The Woodland Indians of the Western Great Lakes.* Garden City, N.Y.: Natural History Press, 1970.
Sanders, Thomas E. and Walter W. Peek, comps. *Literature of the American Indian.* New York: Glencoe, 1973.
Saum, Lewis. *The Fur Trader and the Indian.* Seattle: U. Washington, 1965.
Sibley, Henry H. *Iron Face: The Adventures of Jack Frazer, Frontier Warrior, Scout, and Hunter.* Ed. Theodore Blegen and Sarah A. Davidson. Chicago: Caxton Club, 1950.
Shetrone, Henry C. *The Indians of Ohio.* Columbus: Ohio Archaeological, 1918.
Silverberg, Robert. *Mound Builders of Ancient America: The Archaeology of a Myth.* New York: Graphic, 1968.
Popular survey of nineteenth century speculations and investigations concerning the mysterious "mounds" in the Mississippi Valley.
Skinner, Alanson. *Medicine Ceremony of the Menomini, Iowa and Wahpeton Dakota. With Notes on the Ceremony Among the Ponca, Bungi, Ojibwa and Potawatomi.* New York: Museum of the American Indian, 1920.
Snelling, William J. *Tales of the North-West.* Boston: Hilliard, 1830.
South Dakota. *Indians of South Dakota.* Brookings: State Planning Bd., 1937.
*Stensland, Anna L. *Literature By and About the American Indian.* Urbana: NCTE, 1973.
Stoltman, James B. *The Laurel Culture in Minnesota.* St. Paul: Historical Society, 1973.
Stout, David B. et al. *Indians of E. Missouri, W. Illinois, and S. Wisconsin, from the Proto-Historic Period to 1804.* New York: Garland, 1974.
Stoutenbrugh, John L., Jr. *Dictionary of the American Indian.* New York: Philosophical Library, 1960.
Swanton, John R. *Indian Tribes of North America.* Washington: GPO, 1952.
Terrell, John U. *American Indian Almanac.* New York: World, 1971.

Thompson, Stith, ed. *Tales of the North American Indians*. Bloomington: Indiana U., 1966.

Thwaites, Reuben G., ed. *Jesuit Relations*. [See Personal Narratives section.]

Turner, Frederick J. *The Character and Influence of the Indian Trade in Wisconsin: A Study of the Trading Post as an Institution*. New York: Franklin, 1970.

*Ullom, Judith C. *Folklore of the North American Indians: An Annotated Bibliography*. Washington: GPO, 1969.

Underhill, Ruth M. *Red Man's America: A History of Indians in the United States*. Chicago: U. Chicago, 1953.

_____. *Red Man's Religion: Beliefs and Practices of the Indians North of Mexico*. Chicago: U. Chicago, 1965.

Utley, Robert. *Frontiersmen in Blue: The United States Army and the Indian, 1848–1865*. New York: Macmillan, 1967.

Vandergriff, James H., comp. *The Indians of Kansas*. Emporia: Teachers College Press, 1973.

Vestal, Stanley, pseud. [Walter S. Campbell]. *Warpath and Council Fire: The Plains Indians' Struggle for Survival in War and in Diplomacy, 1851–1891*. New York: Random, 1948.

Voegelin, Charles F. and F. M. Voegelin. *Map of North American Indian Languages*. Rev. ed. Seattle: U. Washington, 1967.

Wedel, Waldo R. *Prehistoric Man on the Great Plains*. Norman: U. Oklahoma, 1961.

_____. *An Introduction to Kansas Archeology*. Washington: GPO, 1959.

Will, George F. and George E. Hyde. *Corn Among the Indians of the Upper Missouri*. St. Louis: Miner, 1917.

Willey, Gordon R. *An Introduction to American Archaeology*. Englewood Cliffs, N.J.: Prentice-Hall, 1966.

Wilcox, Frank N. *Ohio Indian Trails*. Cleveland: Gates, 1933.

Winslow, Charles S., ed. *Indians of the Chicago Region*. Chicago: n.p., 1946.

Wissler, Clark. *The American Indian: An Introduction to the Anthropology of the New World*. 3d ed. New York: P. Smith, 1950.

_____. *Indians of the United States: Four Centuries of Their History and Culture*. Garden City, N.Y.: Doubleday, 1946.

_____. *North American Indians of the Plains*. New York: American Museum of Natural History, 1934.

Witt, Shirley H., comp. *The Way: An Anthology of American Indian Literature*. New York: Knopf, 1972.

Wormington, H. Marie. *Ancient Man in North America*. 4th rev. ed. Denver: Museum of Natural History, 1957.

Wright, John C. *The Crooked Tree: Indian Legends of Northern Michigan*. Harbor Springs, Mich.: Author, 1917.

2. TRIBES

A. CHIPPEWA (OJIBWA)

Banér, Johan G. *Kitch-iti-ki-pi, the "Big Spring"* . . . *Ojibway and Chippewa Indian Legends* . . . . Manistique, Mich.: n.p., 1933.

Baraga, Friedrich. *A Dictionary of the Otchipwe Language*. 2 vols. 2d ed. Montreal: Beauchemin, 1878.

Barnouw, Victor. *Acculturation and Personality Among the Wisconsin Chippewa*. Menasha, Wisc.: American Anthropological Assn., 1950.

Barrett, Samuel A. *The Dream Dance of the Chippewa and Menominee Indians of Northern Wisconsin*. Milwaukee: Public Museum, 1911.

Bartlett, William W. *History, Tradition and Adventure in the Chippewa Valley*. Chippewa Falls, Wisc.: Chippewa Printery, 1929.

Blackbird, Andrew J. *History of the Ottawa and Chippewa Indians of Michigan*. Harbor Springs, Mich.: Babcock, 1897.

Bloomfield, Leonard. *Eastern Ojibwa*. Ann Arbor: U. Michigan, 1957.

Brill, Charles. *Indian and Free: A Contemporary Portrait of Life on a Chippewa Reservation*. Minneapolis: U. Minnesota, 1974.

   Good photo-text study.

Burton, Frederick R. *American Primitive Music with Especial Attention to the Songs of the Ojibways*. New York: Moffat, 1909.

Calkins, Franklin W. *Two Wilderness Voyagers: A True Tale of Indian Life*. Chicago: F. H. Revell, 1902.

Cappel, Jeanne L. *Chippewa Tales, Retold by Wa-be-no*. Los Angeles: Wetzel, 1928.

Coleman, Sister Bernard. *Decorative Designs of the Ojibwa of Northern Minnesota*. Washington: Catholic U., 1947.

———. *The Religion of the Ojibwa of Northern Minnesota*. Washington: Catholic Anthropological Conference, 1937.

——— et al. *Ojibwa Myths and Legends*. Minneapolis: Ross and Haines, 1961.

Copway, George. *Life, History and Travels of Kah-ge-ga-gah-bowh, Indian Chief of the Ojibwa Nation*. Albany: Weed and Parsons, 1847.

———. *Traditional History and Characteristic Sketches of the Ojibwa Nation. By Kah-ge-ga-gah-bowh, Chief of the Ojibwa Nation*. London: Gilpin, 1850.

Davidson, John N. *In Unnamed Wisconsin*. Milwaukee: Chapman, 1895.

Densmore, Frances. *Chippewa Customs*. Washington: GPO, 1929.

———. *Chippewa Music*. Washington: GPO, 1913.

———. *Chippewa Music II*. Washington: GPO, 1913.

Gilfillan, Joseph. *The Ojibway: A Novel of Indian Life of the Period of the Early Advance of the Civilization in the Northwest*. New York: Neala, 1904.

Gilman, Chandler R. *Life on the Lakes: Being Tales and Sketches Collected during a Trip to the Pictured Rocks of Lake Superior*. 2 vols. New York: Dearborn, 1836.

Gordon, Hanford. *Legend of the Northwest . . . Containing the Ojibwa Legend of the Pictured Rock of Lake Superior*. St. Paul: St. Paul Book and Stationery, 1881.

Henry, Thomas R. *Wilderness Messiah: The Story of Hiawatha and the Iroquois*. New York: Sloane, 1955.

Hickerson, Harold. *The Chippewa and their Neighbors: A Study in Ethnohistory*. New York: Holt, 1970.

———. *Ethnohistory of the Chippewa of Lake Superior*. New York: Garland, 1974.

———. *The Southwestern Chippewa: An Ethnohistorical Study*. Menasha, Wisc.: American Anthropological Assn., 1962.

Hilger, Sister M. Inez. *Chippewa Child Life and its Cultural Background*. Washington: GPO, 1951.

———. *A Social Study of One Hundred Fifty Chippewa Indian Families of the White Earth Reservation in Minnesota*. Washington: Catholic University of America Press, 1939.

Hoffman, Walter J. *The Midewiwin or Grand Medicine Society of the Ojibwa*. Washington: GPO, 1891.

Jameson, Anna. *Sketches in Canada, and Rambles Among the Red Men*. London: Longmans, 1852.

Jones, James. *Tales of an Indian Camp*. 2 vols. London: Colburn, 1829.

Jones, Rev. Peter. *History of the Ojibway Indians: With Special Reference to their Conversion to Christianity*. London: A. W. Bennett, 1861.

Jones, William. *Ojibway Texts*. Ed. Truman Michelson. New York: Stechert, 1917–19.

Johnston, Basil H. *Ojibway Heritage*. New York: Columbia U., 1976.

Kinietz, W. Vernon. *Chippewa Village: The Story of Katikitegon*. Bloomfield Hills, Mich.: Cranbrook, 1947.

Kohl, Johann G. *Kitchi-Gami: Wanderings 'Round Lake Superior*. Tr. Lascelles Wraxhall. London: Chapman and Hall, 1860.

Landes, Ruth. *Ojibway Religion and the Midewiwin*. Madison: U. Wisconsin, 1968.

———. *Ojibway Sociology*. New York: Columbia U., 1937.

———. *Ojibway Woman*. New York: Columbia U., 1938.

Levi, Carolissa. *Chippewa Indians of Yesterday and Today*. New York: Pageant, 1956.

Lyford, Carrie A. *Ojibway Crafts*. Washington: GPO, 1943.

McKenney, Thomas L. *Sketches of a Tour to the Lakes . . . . Also, a Vocabulary of the Algic, or Chippeway Language*. Baltimore: Lucas, 1827.

Minnesota Historical Society. *Chippewa and Dakota Indians: A Subject Catalog of Books, Pamphlets, Periodical Articles, and Manuscripts in the Minnesota Historical Society*. St. Paul: Historical Society, 1969.

Morriseau, Norval. *Legends of My People, the Great Ojibway.* Ed. by Selwyn Dewdney. Toronto: Ryerson, 1965.

Nicollet, Joseph N. *The Journals of Joseph N. Nicollet: A Scientist on the Mississippi Headwaters. With notes on Indian Life, 1836–37.* Ed. by Martha C. Bray. St. Paul: Historical Society, 1970.

O'Meara, Walter. *The Sioux are Coming.* Boston: Houghton Mifflin, 1971.
Fiction.

Osborn, Chase S. and Stellanova Osborn. *"Hiawatha" with its Original Indian Legends.* Lancaster, Pa.: Cattel, 1944.

Paredes, Anthony, ed. *Six Studies of the Chippewa Indians.* Gainesville: U. Florida, 1977.

Piper, William. *The Eagle of Thunder Cape.* New York: Knickerbocker Press, 1924.

Reid, Dorothy M. *Tales of Nanabozho.* New York: Walck, 1963.
Nanabozho is the original for Longfellow's Hiawatha.

Roddis, Louis H. *The Indian Wars of Minnesota.* Cedar Rapids: Torch Press, 1956.

Schoolcraft, Henry R. [See Author Entry.]

Smith, Huron H. *Ethnobotany of the Ojibwe Indians.* Milwaukee: Public Museum, 1932.

Tanner, John. *A Narrative of the Captivity of John Tanner . . . during Thirty Years Residence among the Indians in the Interior of North America.* Ed. Edwin James. Minneapolis: Ross & Haines, 1956.

Tanner, Helen. *The Ojibwas: A Critical Bibliography.* Bloomington: Indiana U., 1976.

United States Indian Claims Commission. *Commission Findings on the Chippewa Indians.* New York: Garland, 1947.

Vizenor, Gerald R., ed. *Escorts to White Earth, 1868–1968, 100 Year Reservation: Selected Readings.* Minneapolis: Four Winds, 1968.

_____. *The Everlasting Sky: New Voices from the People Named the Chippewa.* New York: Crowell, 1972.

*_____. *A Selected Bibliography of the Dakota and Ojibway Indians of Minnesota . . . .* Minneapolis: Curriculum Resource Center, 1967.

Voeglin, Erminie. *An Ethnohistorical Report on the . . . Chippewa of Northwest Ohio.* New York: Garland, 1974.

Warren, William W. *History of the Ojibway Nation.* Minneapolis: Ross & Haines, 1957.
Originally published in Minnesota Historical Collections of 1885.

Wilson, Edward F. *The Ojibway Language.* Toronto: Rowell & Hutchinson, 1874.

Winchell, Newton H. *The Aborigines of Minnesota.* St. Paul: Historical Society, 1911.

Wright, John C. *The Great Myth.* Lansing: Michigan Education Supply, 1922.

Young, Egerton R. *Algonquin Indian Tales.* New York: Eaton and Mains, 1903.

_____. *Stories from Indian Wigwams and Northern Camp-Fires.* New York: Hunt and Eaton, 1893.

B. ILLINOIS

Brown, James A., ed. *Illinois Archaeology.* Urbana: U. Illinois, 1961.

Illinois Natural History Museum. *Prehistoric People of Illinois.* Chicago: NHM, 1963.

Montet-White, Onta. *The Lithic Industries of the Illinois Valley in the Early and Middle Woodland Period.* Ann Arbor: U. Michigan, 1968.

Peithmann, Irvin M. *Echoes of the Red Man: An Archaeological and Cultural Survey of the Indians of Southern Illinois.* New York: Exposition, 1955.

_____. *Indians of Southern Illinois.* Springfield: Thomas, 1964.

Roundy, William N. *The Last of the Illini.* Chicago: Author, 1916.

Temple, Wayne C. *Indian Villages of the Illinois Country.* Springfield: Illinois State Museum, 1958.

C. IOWA

Adams, Ephraim. *The Iowa Band.* Boston: Pilgrim Press, 1902.

Christensen, Thomas P. *The Iowa Indians: A Brief History.* Iowa City: Athens Press, 1954.

Hamilton, William and S. M. Irvin. *An Ioway Grammar, Illustrating the Principle of the Language used by the Ioway, Otoe, and Missouri Indians.* N.P.: Ioway and Sac Mission Press, 1848.

Fulton, Alexander R. *The Red Men of Iowa*. Des Moines: Mills, 1882.
Miner, William H. *The Iowa*. Cedar Rapids: Torch Press, 1911.
Skinner, Alanson. *Ethnology of the Ioway Indians*. Milwaukee: Public Museum, 1926.
_____. *Societies of Iowa, Kansa, and Ponca Indians*. New York: Museum of Natural History, 1895.
_____. "Traditions of Iowa Indians." *JAF*, 38 (1925), 425–506.

D.   KICKAPOO

Gibson, Arrell M. *The Kickapoos: Lords of the Middle Border*. Norman: U. Oklahoma, 1963.
Hoad, Louise G. *Kickapoo Indian Trails*. Caldwell, Ida.: Caxton, 1944.
Hunter, John D. *Memoirs of a Captivity Among the Indians of North America*. London: Longman, 1823.
Jones, William. *Kickapoo Tales*. New York: Columbia U., 1915.
Kohl, Johann G. *Kitche-Gami, Wanderings 'Round Lake Superior*. Tr. Lascelles Wraxhall. London: Chapman, 1860.
Lilly, Eli. *Prehistoric Antiquities of Indiana*. Indianapolis: Indiana Historical Society, 1937.
Voorhis, Paul. *Introduction to the Kickapoo Language*. Bloomington: Indiana U., 1974.

E.   MENOMINEE

Banér, Johan. *Medicine-Water. Menominee and Chippeway Indian Legends and Myths*. Manistique, Mich.: n.p., 1933.
Barrett, Samuel A. *The Dream Dance of the Chippewa and Menominee Indians of Northern Wisconsin*. Milwaukee: Public Museum, 1911.
_____. *Ancient Aztalan*. Milwaukee: Public Museum, 1933.
Bloomfield, Leonard. *Menomini Texts*. New York: Stechert, 1928.
Brown, Charles E. *Wigwam Tales*. Madison: Author, 1920.
Cooper, L. R. *The Red Cedar River Variant of the Wisconsin Hopewell Culture*. Milwaukee: Public Museum, 1933.
Davidson, John N. *In Unnamed Wisconsin*. Milwaukee: Chapman, 1895.
Densmore, Frances. *Menominee Music*. Washington: GPO, 1932.
Hoffman, Walter J. *The Menomini Indians*. Washington: GPO, 1896.
Keesing, Felix M. *The Menomini Indians of Wisconsin*. Philadelphia: American Philosophical Society Memoir 10, 1939.
   Reprinted in 1971 with new introduction.
Lapham, Increase A. *The Antiquities of Wisconsin*. Washington: GPO, 1852.
Nichols, Phebe. *Sunrise of the Menominees*. Boston: Humphries, 1944.
_____. *Tales from an Old Indian Lodge*. Boston: Humphries, 1944.
Skinner, Alanson. *Material Culture of the Menomini*. New York: Museum of the American Indian, 1921.
_____. "The Menomini Indian." *SW*, 40 (1911), 372–579.
_____. *Social Life and Ceremonial Bundles of the Menomini Indians*. New York: American Museum of Natural History, 1913.
_____ and John V. Satterlee. *Folklore of the Menominee Indians*. New York: Museum of Natural History, 1915.
Slotkin, James S. *Menomini Peyotism* . . . . Philadelphia: American Philosophical Society, 1952.
_____. *The Menomini Powwow: A Study in Cultural Decay*. Milwaukee: Public Museum, 1957.
Smith, Huron H. *Ethnobotany of the Menomini Indians*. Milwaukee: Public Museum, 1923.
Spindler, George D. *Sociological and Psychological Processes in Menomini Acculturation*. Berkeley: U. California, 1955.

F.   MIAMI

Anson, Bert. *The Miami Indians*. Norman: U. Oklahoma, 1970.
Hill, Leonard U. *John Johnston and the Indians in the Land of the Three Miamis: With Recollections of Sixty Years by John Johnston*. Piqua, Ohio: 1957.

Hundley, Will M. *Squawtown: My Boyhood Among the Last Miamis.* Caldwell, Ida.: Caxton, 1939.
Lilly, Eli. *Prehistoric Antiquities of Indiana.* Indianapolis: Indiana Historical Society, 1937.
Trowbridge, Charles C. *Meearmeear Traditions.* Ed. Vernon Kinietz. Ann Arbor: U. Michigan, 1938.
Voegelin, Erminie W. et al. *An Anthropological Report on the Miami, Wea, and Eel-River Indians.* New York: Garland, 1974.
Winger, Otho. *The Last of the Miamis.* Elgin, Ill.: Elgin Press, 1936.
_____. *Lost Sister Among the Miamis.* N. Manchester, Ind.: Schultz, 1936.
Young, Calvin M. *Little Turtle, the Great Chief of the Miami Indian Nation.* Indianapolis: Sentinel, 1917.

G. OMAHA

Allis, Rev. Samuel. *Forty Years Among the Indians and on the Eastern Borders of Nebraska.* Lincoln: State Historical Society, 1887.
Dorsey, J. Owen. *Omaha and Ponka Letters.* Washington: GPO, 1891.
_____. *Omaha Sociology.* Washington: GPO, 1884.
Fletcher, Alice C. *Tribal Structure: A Study of the Omaha and Cognate Tribes.* New York: Stechert, 1909.
_____. *The Omaha Tribe.* Washington: GPO, 1911.
_____. *A Study of Omaha Indian Music . . . .* Cambridge: Harvard U., 1893.
Fortune, Reo F. *Omaha Secret Societies.* New York: Columbia U., 1932.
Giffin, Fannie R. *Oa-Mah-Ha-Ta-Wa-Tha (Omaha City).* Lincoln, Neb.: Author, 1898.
Gilmore, Melvin R. *Uses of Plants by the Indians of the Missouri River Region.* Washington: GPO, 1919.
_____. *Prairie Smoke . . . A Collection of Lore of the Prairies.* New York: Columbia U., 1929.
La Flesche, Francis. *The Middle Five: Indian Boys at School.* Boston: Small, Maynard, 1900.
_____. *The Middle Five: Indian Schoolboys of the Omaha Tribe.* Madison: U. Wisconsin, 1963.
Mead, Margaret. *The Changing Culture of an Indian Tribe.* New York: Columbia U., 1932.
Welsch, Roger. *Omaha Indian Myths and Trickster Tales.* Chicago: Swallow, 1975.
Wilson, Dorothy C. *Bright Eyes: The Story of Susette La Flesche, an Omaha Indian.* New York: McGraw-Hill, 1974.

H. OSAGE

Barrett, Stephen M. *Skinkah, the Osage Indian.* Oklahoma City: Harlow, 1916.
Chapman, Carl H. *The Origin of the Osage Indian Tribe.* New York: Garland, 1974.
Dickerson, Philip J. *History of the Osage Nation.* Pawhuska, Okla.: n.p., 1906.
Drinnon, Richard. *White Savage: The Case of John Dunn Hunter.* New York: Schocken, 1972.
   Examination of an Osage captivity.
Fitzgerald, Macy P. *Beacon on the Plains.* Leavenworth, Kan.: St. Mary College, 1939.
Hunter, John D. *Memoirs of a Captivity Among the Indians of North America.* London: Longman, 1823.
La Flesche, Francis. *Dictionary of the Osage Language.* Washington: GPO, 1932.
_____. *The Osage Tribe: Rite of the Chiefs, Sayings of the Ancient Men.* Washington: GPO, 1921.
_____. *The Osage Tribe: Rite of Vigil.* Washington: GPO, 1925.
_____. *The Osage Tribe: Two Versions of the Child Naming Rite.* Washington: GPO, 1928.
_____. *The Osage Tribe: Rite of the Wa-xo-be.* Washington: GPO, 1930.
_____. *War Ceremony and Peace Ceremony of the Osage Indians.* Washington: GPO, 1939.
McDermott, John F., ed. *Tixier's Travels of the Osage Prairies.* Norman: U. Oklahoma, 1940.
Marriott, Alice L. *Osage Research Report and Bibliography of Basic Research Influences.* New York: Garland, 1974.
Mathews, John J. *The Osages, Children of the Middle Waters.* Norman: U. Oklahoma, 1961.

————. *Talking to the Moon.* Chicago: U. Chicago, 1945.
   Narrative of an Osage who spent ten solitary years on the Kansas prairie.
————. *Wah-Kon-Tah: The Osage and the White Man's Road.* Norman: U. Oklahoma, 1932.
Neihardt, John G. [See Author Entry.]
Nuttall, Thomas. *A Journal into the Arkansa Territory.* Philadelphia: Palmer, 1821.
Voget, Fred W. *Osage Research Report.* New York: Garland, 1974.
White Horse Eagle. *We Indians: The Passing of a Great Race.* Tr. Christopher Turner. London: Butterworth, 1931.
Will, George F. *Archaeology of the Missouri Valley.* New York: Museum of Natural History, 1924.

I.   PAWNEE

Alexander, Hartley B. *The Mystery of Life. A Poetization of "The Hako"—a Pawnee Ceremony.* Chicago: Open Court, 1913.
Barrett, Stephen M. *Beaver, the Pawnee Indian.* Oklahoma City: Harlow, 1918.
Carleton, Lt. J. Henry. *The Prairie Logbooks.* Ed. Louis Pelzer. Chicago: Caxton Club, 1944.
Clayton, William, ed. *Traditions of the Skidi Pawnee.* Boston: Houghton Mifflin, 1904.
————. *William Clayton's Journal.* Salt Lake City: Deseret News, 1921.
Densmore, Frances. *Pawnee Music.* Washington: GPO, 1929.
Dorsey, George A. *The Pawnee: Mythology (Part I).* Washington: Carnegie Institute of Washington, 1906.
Dunbar, John B. *The Pawnee Indians, a Sketch.* Morrisania, N.Y.: Author, 1882.
Fletcher, Alice C. *The Hako: A Pawnee Ceremony.* Washington: GPO, 1904.
————. *Indian Story and Song From North America.* Boston: Birchard, 1900.
Grinnell, George B. *Pawnee, Blackfoot, and Cheyenne: History and Folklore of the Plains; from the Writings of George B. Grinnell.* New York: Scribner, 1961.
————. *Pawnee Hero Stories and Folk Tales . . . .* New York: Forest and Stream, 1889.
   Many later editions.
Hazen, Reuben W. *History of the Pawnee Indians.* Fremont, Neb.: Fremont Tribune, 1893.
Hyde, George E. *The Pawnee Indians.* Denver: U. Denver, 1951.
Irving, John T. *Indian Sketches: Taken During an Expedition to the Pawnee Tribes (1833).* Ed. John F. McDermott. Norman: U. Oklahoma, 1955. (First ed., Philadelphia: Carey, 1835.)
Lesser, Alexander. *The Pawnee Ghost Dance Hand Game. A Study of Cultural Change.* New York: Columbia U., 1933.
Murie, James R. *Pawnee Indian Societies.* New York: The Trustees, 1914.
Murray, Sir Charles. *Travels in North America: Including a Summer Residence with the Pawnee Tribe of Indians, in the Remote Parts of Missouri.* London: Bentley, 1854.
Strong, William D. *Introduction to Nebraska Archaeology.* Washington: GPO, 1935.
Wedel, Waldo R. *An Introduction to Pawnee Archeology.* Washington: GPO, 1936.
Weltfish, Gene. *Caddoan Texts: Pawnee, South Bend Dialect.* New York: Augustin, 1937.
————. *The Lost Universe, with a Closing Chapter on the Universe Regained.* New York: Basic Books, 1965.

J.   POTAWATOMI

Landes, Ruth. *The Prairie Potawatomi: Tradition and Ritual in the Twentieth Century.* Madison: U. Wisconsin, 1970.
Lawson, Publius V. "The Potawatomi." *WA*, 19 (1920), 41–116.
Ritzenthaler, Robert E. *The Potawatomi Indians of Wisconsin.* Milwaukee: Public Museum, 1954.
Skinner, Alanson. *The Mascoutens or Prairie Potawatomi Indians.* Milwaukee: Public Museum, 1924.
Smith, Huron H. *Ethnobotany of the Forest Potawatomi Indians.* Milwaukee: Public Museum, 1933.
Voegelin, Erminie. *An Ethnohistorical Report on the Wyandot, Potowatomi, Ottawa and Chippewa of Northwest Ohio.* New York: Garland, 1974.

West, George A. *The Aboriginal Pipes of Wisconsin*. Milwaukee: Wisconsin Archaeological Society, 1905.
Winter, Otho. *The Potawatomi Indians*. Elgin, Ill.: Elgin Press, 1939.

K. SAC (SAUK) AND FOX (MESQUAKI)

Anonymous. *Cha-ka-ta-ko-si: A Collection of Meskwaki Manuscripts*. Iowa City: n.p., 1907.
Armstrong, Perry A. *The Piasa, or the Devil among the Indians*. Morris, Ill.: Fletcher, 1887.
_____. *The Sauks and the Black Hawk War, with Biographical Sketches, etc.* Springfield, Ill.: Rokker, 1887.
Barrett, Samuel A. *Ancient Aztalan*. Milwaukee: Public Library, 1933.
Beals, Frank L. *Chief Black Hawk*. Chicago: Wheeler, 1943.
Beckhard, Arthur J. *Black Hawk*. New York: Messner, 1957.
Beech, Mervyn. *The Sauk, their Language and Folklore*. Oxford: Clarendon, 1911.
Black Hawk. *Black Hawk: An Autobiography*. Ed. by Donald Jackson. Urbana: U. Illinois, 1955.
   There are numerous earlier editions of this classic going back to 1833.
Brown, Charles E. *Wigwam Tales*. Madison: Author, 1920.
Busby, Allie B. *Two Summers Among the Musquakies*. Vinton: Herald Book, 1886.
Cole, Cyrenus. *I Am a Man: The Indian Black Hawk*. Iowa City: State Historical Society, 1938.
Davidson, John N. *In Unnamed Wisconsin*. Milwaukee: Chapman, 1958.
Drake, Benjamin. *The Great Indian Chief of the West, or the Life and Adventures of Black Hawk*. New York: U.S. Book Co., 1848.
   Many later editions.
Fuller, Iola. *The Shining Trail*. New York: Duell, 1943.
   A novel of Chief Black Hawk.
Gearing, Frederick O. *The Face of the Fox*. Chicago: Aldine, 1970.
_____, ed., with R. M. Netting, and L. R. Peattie. *Documentary History of the Fox Project, 1948–1959*. Chicago: Dept. of Anthropology, U. Chicago, 1960.
Gussnow, Zachary. *An Anthropological Report on the Sac, Fox, and Iowa Indians*. New York: Garland, 1974.
Hagan, William T. *The Sac and Fox Indians*. Norman: U. Oklahoma, 1958.
Harrington, Mark R. *Sacred Bundles of the Sac and Fox*. Philadelphia: U. Pennsylvania, 1914.
James, William. *Algonquin (Fox)*. Washington: GPO, 1911.
Joffe, Natalie F. *Acculturation in Seven Indian Tribes*. New York: Appleton, 1940.
_____. *The Fox of Iowa*. New York: Appleton, 1940.
Jones, William. *Ethnography of the Fox Indians*. Ed. by Margaret W. Fisher. Washington: GPO, 1939.
_____. *Fox Tests*. Ed. by Franz Boas. Leiden: Brill, 1907.
Lapham, Increase A. *The Antiquities of Wisconsin*. Washington: GPO, 1852.
Lockwood, Myra. *Indian Chief*. New York: Oxford, 1943.
   On Sauk Chief Keokuk.
Michelson, Truman. *The Autobiography of a Fox Indian Woman*. Washington: GPO, 1925.
_____. *Contributions to Fox Ethnology*. Washington: GPO, 1927.
_____. *Fox Miscellany*. Washington: GPO, 1924.
_____. *Notes on the Buffalo-head Dance of the Thunder Gens of the Fox Indians*. Washington: GPO, 1928.
_____. *Notes on Fox Mortuary Customs and Beliefs*. Washington: GPO, 1925.
_____. *Notes on the Fox Society Known as Those Who Worship the Little Spotted Buffalo*. Washington: GPO, 1925.
_____. *Notes on the Fox Wapanonowiweni*. Washington: GPO, 1932.
_____. *Observations on Thunder Dance of Bear Gens of Fox Indians*. Washington: GPO, 1929.
_____. *The Owl Sacred Pack of the Fox Indians*. Washington: GPO, 1921.
_____. *The Traditional Origin of the Fox Society Known as "The Singing Around Rite."* Washington: GPO, 1925.
Owen, Mary A. *Folk-Lore of the Musquakie Indians of North America*. London: Nutt, 1904.

Owen, Mary A. and Truman Michelson. *The Mythical Origin of the White Buffalo Dance of the Fox Indians.* Washington: GPO, 1918.

Skinner, Alanson. *Observations on the Ethnology of the Sauk Indians.* Milwaukee: Public Museum, 1923–25.

Smith, Huron H. *Ethnobotany of the Meskwaki Indians.* Milwaukee: Public Museum, 1928.

Steward, John F. *Lost Maramech and Earliest Chicago: A History of the Foxes and their Downfall . . . .* Chicago: Revell, 1903.

Tax, Sol. *The Social Organization of the Fox Indians.* Chicago: n.p., 1937.

West, George A. *The Aboriginal Pipes of Wisconsin.* Milwaukee: Wisconsin Archaeological Society, 1905.

Whitney, Ellen M., comp. and ed. *The Black Hawk War, 1831–1832.* Springfield: Illinois Historical Society, 1970.

L. SHAWNEE

Creighton, Luella S. *Tecumseh: The Story of the Shawnee Chief.* London: Macmillan, 1965.

Drake, Benjamin. *Life of Tecumseh and of His Brother the Prophet: With a Historical Sketch of the Shawnee Indians.* Cincinnati: Morgan, 1841.
Many later editions.

Galloway, William A. *Old Chillicothe: Shawnee and Pioneer History.* Xenia, O.: Buckeye, 1934.

Klinck, Carl F., ed. *Tecumseh: Fact and Fiction in Early Records.* Englewood Cliffs, N.J.: Prentice-Hall, 1961.

Oskison, John M. *Tecumseh and His Times: The Story of a Great Indian.* New York: Putnam, 1938.

Trowbridge, Charles C. *Shawnese Traditions.* Ed. Vernon Kinietz and Erminie Voegelin. Ann Arbor: U. Michigan, 1939.

Tucker, Glenn. *Tecumseh: Vision of Glory.* Indianapolis: Bobbs-Merrill, 1956.

M. SIOUX (DAKOTA): EASTERN TRIBES

Andrist, Ralph K. *The Long Death: The Last Days of the Plains Indian.* New York: Macmillan, 1964.

Artichoker, John. *Indians of South Dakota.* Pierre: Dept. of Public Instruction, 1956.

Bishop, Harriet E. *Dakota War Whoop: Or, Indian Massacres and War in Minnesota, 1862–'63.* Rev. ed. St. Paul: Author, 1864.

Blackthunder, Elijah et al. *Ehanna Woyakapi: History of the Sisseton Wahpeton Sioux Tribe.* Sisseton, S.D.: Tribal Publications, 1972.

Brownlee, Fred L. and Charles B. Johnson. *The Indians of North and South Dakota.* Nashville: Fisk U., 1941.

Bryant, Charles S. and Abel B. Murch. *A History of the Great Massacre by the Sioux Indians in Minnesota, Including the Personal Narratives of Many Who Escaped.* Cincinnati: Rickey, 1864.
Many later editions.

Buck, Daniel. *Indian Outbreaks.* Mankato, Minn.: n.p., 1904.

Carley, Kenneth A. *The Sioux Uprising of 1862.* St. Paul: Historical Society, 1961.

Deloria, Ella. *Dakota Texts.* New York: Stechert, 1932.

Dorsey, James O. *A Study of Siouan Cults.* Washington: GPO, 1894.

Eastman, Charles. *From the Deep Woods to Civilization: Chapters in the Autobiography of an Indian.* Boston: Little, Brown, 1916.

_____. *Indian Boyhood.* New York: McClure, 1902.

_____. *Indian Child Life.* Boston: Little, Brown, 1913.

_____. *Indian Heroes and Great Chieftains.* Boston: Little, Brown, 1918.

_____. *Old Indian Days.* New York: McClure, 1907.

_____. *Red Hunters and the Animal People.* New York: Harper, 1904.

_____. *The Soul of the Indian.* Boston: Houghton Mifflin, 1911.

Eastman, Charles and Elaine G. Eastman. *Wigwam Evenings.* Boston: Little, Brown, 1909.

Eastman, Mary H. *Dahcotah: Or Life and Legends of the Sioux Around Fort Snelling.* New York: Wiley, 1849.

Federal Writers' Project. South Dakota. *Legends of the Mighty Sioux*. Chicago: Whitman, 1941.

Fiske, Frank B. *The Taming of the Sioux*. Bismarck: Tribune, 1917.

Hans, Frederic M. *The Great Sioux Nation: A Complete History of Indian Life and Warfare in America*. Chicago: Donohue, 1907.

Hassrick, Royal B. *The Sioux: Life and Customs of a Warrior Society*. Norman: U. Oklahoma, 1964.

Heard, Isaac V. *History of the Sioux War and Massacres of 1862 and 1863*. New York: Harper, 1864.

Hickerson, Harold. *Adewakanton Band of Sioux Indians*. New York: Garland, 1974.

Holley, Frances C. *Once Their Home: Or, Our Legacy from the Dahkotahs* . . . . Chicago: Donohue, 1890.

Hughes, Thomas. *Indian Chiefs of Southern Minnesota*. Mankato: Free Press, 1927.

Jones, Robert H. *The Civil War in the Northwest: Nebraska, Wisconsin, Iowa, Minnesota, and the Dakotas*. Norman: U. Oklahoma, 1960.

Kelly, Fanny. *My Captivity Among the Sioux Indians*. New ed. New York: Corinth, 1962. First edition 1871.

Landes, Ruth. *The Mystic Lake Sioux: Sociology of the Mdewakantonwan Santee*. Madison: U. Wisconsin, 1969.

LaPointe, Frank. *The Sioux Today*. New York: Crowell, 1972.

LaPointe, James. *Legends of the Lakota*. San Francisco: Historical Press, 1974.

McLaughlin, James. *My Friend the Indian*. Boston: Houghton Mifflin, 1910.

McLaughlin, Marie. *Myths and Legends of the Sioux*. Bismarck: Tribune, 1916.

Manfred, Frederick [Feike Feikema]. [See Author Entry.]

Mayer, Frank B. *With Pen and Pencil on the Frontier in 1851: The Diary and Sketches of Frank B. Mayer*. Ed. Bertha Heilbron. St. Paul: Historical Society, 1932.

Meyer, Roy W. *History of the Santee Sioux: United States Indian Policy on Trial*. Lincoln: U. Nebraska, 1967.

Minnesota Historical Society. . . . *The Aborigines of Minnesota: A Report* . . . . St. Paul: Pioneer, 1911.

————. *Chippewa and Dakota Indians: A Subject Catalog of Books, Pamphlets, Periodical Articles, and Manuscripts in the Minnesota Historical Society*. St. Paul: Historical Society, 1969.

Mooney, James . . . . *The Siouan Tribes of the East*. Washington: GPO, 1894.

Niehardt, John G. [See Author Entry.]

Neill, Edward D. *Dahkotah Land and Dahkotah Life, with the History of the Fur Traders of the Extreme Northwest during the French and British Dominions*. Philadelphia: Lippincott, 1859.

Nelson, Bruce. *Land of the Dahcotahs*. Minneapolis: U. Minnesota, 1946.

Nurge, Ethel, ed. *The Modern Sioux: Social Systems and Reservation Culture*. Lincoln: U. Nebraska, 1970.

Oehler, Chester M. *The Great Sioux Uprising*. New York: Oxford, 1959.

Olden, Sarah E. *The People of Tipi Sapa (the Dakotas)* . . . . Milwaukee: Morehouse, 1918.

Riggs, Stephen R. *A Dakota-English Dictionary*. Washington: GPO, 1890.

Robinson, Doane. *History of the Dakota or Sioux Indians* . . . . Aberdeen: State of South Dakota, 1904.

Roddis, Louis H. *The Indian Wars in Minnesota*. Cedar Rapids: Torch Press, 1956.

Sandoz, Mari. [See Appendix A.]

Satterlee, Marion P. *A Detailed Account of the Massacre by the Dakota Indians of Minnesota in 1862*. 2d ed. Minneapolis: Author, 1925.

Sharp, Abigail S. *History of the Spirit Lake Massacre and Captivity of Miss Abbie Gardner*. 7th ed. Arnolds Park, Ia.: Author, 1918.

Shetrone, Henry C. *The Mound-Builders*. New York: Appleton, 1930.

Sibley, Henry H. *Iron Face: The Adventures of Jack Frazer, Frontier Warrior, Scout, and Hunter*. Chicago: Caxton Club, 1950.

Teakle, Thomas. *The Spirit Lake Massacre*. Iowa City: State Historical Society, 1918.

Terrell, John U. *Sioux Trail*. New York: McGraw-Hill, 1974.

Thorson, Alice O. *The Tribe of Pezhekee: A Legend of Minnesota*. Minneapolis: Heywood, 1901.

Vizenor, Gerald R. *A Selected Bibliography of the Dakota and Ojibway Indians of Minnesota* . . . . Minneapolis: Curriculum Resource Center, 1967.

Wall, Oscar G. *Recollections of the Sioux Massacre* . . . . Lake City, Minn.: Home Printery, 1909.

Willand, John. *Lac Qui Parle and the Dakota Mission*. Madison, Minn.: Lac Qui Parle Historical Society, 1964.

Winchell, Newton H. *The Aborigines of Minnesota*. St. Paul: Historical Society, 1911.

Zitkala-Sa. *Old Indian Legends*. New York: Ginn, 1901.

N. WINNEBAGO

Barrett, Samuel A. *Ancient Aztalan*. Milwaukee: The Public Museum, 1933.

Bowman, James C. *Winabojo, Master of Life*. Racine, Wisc.: Whitman, 1941.

Brown, Charles E. *Lake Mendota Indian Legends*. Madison: Author, 1927.

_____. *Wigwam Tales*. Madison: Author, 1930.

Cooper, L. R. *The Red Cedar River: Variant of the Wisconsin Hopewell Culture*. Milwaukee: Public Museum, 1933.

Davidson, John N. *In Unnamed Wisconsin*. Milwaukee: Chapman, 1895.

Jones, John A. *Winnebago Ethnology*. New York: Garland, 1974.

LaMere, Oliver and Harold B. Shinn. *Winnebago Stories*. New York: Rand McNally, 1928.

Lapham, Increase A. *The Antiquities of Wisconsin*. Washington: GPO, 1852.

Lilly, Eli. *Prehistoric Antiquities of Indiana*. Indianapolis: Indiana Historical Society, 1937.

Lurie, Nancy O., ed. *Mountain Wolf Woman, Sister of Crashing Thunder: The Autobiography of a Winnebago Indian*. Ann Arbor: U. Michigan, 1961.
    Taped and translated memoirs; well-told, interesting incidents. Paul Radin had done a memoir with Crashing Thunder in the 1920s (q.v.).

Radin, Paul. *The Evolution of an American Prose Epic: A Study in Comparative Literature*. 2 vols. Baltimore: Waverly, 1954–56.

_____. *The Road of Life and Death: A Ritual Drama of the American Indian*. Foreword by Mark Van Doren. New York: Pantheon, 1945.

_____. *A Semi-historical Account of the War of the Winnebago and the Foxes*. Madison: State Historical Society, 1915.

_____. *The Winnebago Culture as Described by Themselves*. Baltimore: Waverly, 1950.

_____. *Winnebago Hero Cycles*. Bloomington: Indiana U., 1948.

_____. *The Winnebago Tribe*. Washington: GPO, 1916.

_____, ed. *The Autobiography of a Winnebago Indian*. Berkeley: U. California, 1920.
    Autobiography of Sam Blowsnake, in two parts. Part I was published in 1926 under the title *Crashing Thunder: The Autobiography of an American Indian*.

Radin, Paul, Karl Kerenyi, and Carl G. Jung. *The Trickster: A Study in American Indian Mythology*. New York: Bell, 1956.

West, George A. *The Aboriginal Pipes of Wisconsin*. Milwaukee: Wisconsin Archaeological Society, 1905.

O. OTHER TRIBES

Davidson, John N. *Muh-he-ka-ne-ok, a History of the Stockbridge Nation*. Milwaukee: Chapman, 1893.

DeVoe, Carrie. *Legends of the Kaw*. Kansas City: Hudson, 1904.

Dorsey, George A., comp. *The Mythology of the Wichita*. Washington: Carnegie Institution, 1904.

Skinner, Alanson. *Societies of Iowa, Kansa, and Ponca Indians*. New York: Museum of Natural History, 1895.

Tibbles, Thomas H. *The Ponca Chiefs: An Account of the Trial of Standing Bear*. Ed. by Kay Graber. Lincoln: U. Nebraska, 1972.

Unrau, William E. *The Kansa Indians: A History of the Wind People, 1673–1873*. Norman: U. Oklahoma, 1971.

Voegelin, Erminie. *An Ethnohistorical Report on the Wyandot, Potowatomi, Ottawa and Chippewa of Northwest Ohio.* New York: Garland, 1974.

Gerald C. Nemanic
Northeastern Illinois University
Chicago, Illinois

LITERARY PERIODICALS

1. BEGINNING

One might begin a study of a specific midwestern periodical published before 1930 by consulting appropriate sections of Frank Luther Mott's comprehensive study, *A History of American Magazines.* Mott provides informative sketches and publishing data for many midwestern periodicals, and places them within their historical contexts. For twentieth-century magazines consult the general studies by Theodore Peterson, John Tebbel, and James Playsted Wood.

A next step would have to include a glance at Rusk's two volume *The Literature of the Middle Western Frontier* and Oscar Winther's *A Classified Bibliography of the Trans-Mississippi West 1811–1967* for further details and a beginning bibliography.

At this point the student of midwestern periodicals must begin consulting the special studies related to his field: a surprising number of dissertations, a number of books or parts of books, and a significant number of articles.

2. CATEGORIES

Midwestern literary periodicals divide themselves into three categories which occasionally overlap: (1) academic or critical reviews almost always associated with a university; (2) magazines devoted primarily to the publication of creative writing. In the past this type of magazine was not associated with a university, but now it is almost always the case. (3) The "little" magazine devoted to creative writing and usually only tangentially identified with a university.

The first category is immediately recognizable and ranges in the Midwest from *Classical Philology*, published at the University of Chicago, to *Science-Fiction Studies* from Indiana State University. The second category would include established, good-looking, usually university-subsidized magazines devoted largely to "quality" writing by well-known or up-and-coming mainstream writers. Examples would include *Prairie Schooner* from the University of Nebraska, *New Letters* from the University of Missouri at Kansas City, and the *Chicago Review* from the University of Chicago. The third category is most difficult to pin down. It includes numerous magazines which have sprung up as a result of the "mimeo revolution" —the technological development which made widely available inexpensive word-reproduction processes. These magazines are published by individuals or small groups generally without financial aid from institutional sources. A majority of them have a homemade quality, limited subscriptions, and favor publishing experimental or anti-establishment literature. Because of their underground nature, they are not always readily at hand. Until its demise, *Trace* (1952–70) kept a running checklist of these little magazines. Now *The Small Press Review* (ed. and pub. Len Fulton, Paradise, California, 1966–   ) and *Margins* (ed. and pub. Tom Montag, Milwaukee, Wisconsin, 1972–   ) maintain columns of information and notes regarding little magazine activities and publications. In addition, since 1964 Len Fulton has published an annual *Directory of Little Magazines, Small Presses and Underground Newspapers*.

The original sense of the term little magazine—that created through the practice of Margaret Anderson, Harriet Monroe, and Ezra Pound—meant to imply that a particular magazine was not part of the publishing Establishment, that it did not have a "respectable" audience which it had to please, that it was devoted solely to the expression of art regardless of popular taste. It was considered an alternative source of publication for new writers who because of their experimentalism or bold philosophical and aesthetic positions, were ignored or misunderstood by editors and publishers committed to the expression of a particular level and quality of taste in their magazines. This sense of the radical in little magazine publishing is alive today in the Midwest in such magazines as the *Ann Arbor Review* (ed. Fred Wolven, Ann Arbor, Mich., 1967–   ), *December* (ed. Curt Johnson, Western Springs, Ill., 1958–   ), *Ghostdance* (ed. Hugh Fox, East Lansing, Mich., 1968–   ), and *Mojo Navigator(e)* (ed. John Jacob, Oak Park, Ill., 1969–   ).

3. LIBRARIES

Among the standard published guides to library holdings, of special interest to midwestern scholars is the *Union List of Little Magazines*. This book, published through a cooperative effort, lists the literary periodical holdings of six midwestern universities: Indiana, Northwestern, Ohio State, Iowa, Chicago, and Illinois.

Besides the Library of Congress and The New York Public Library, the University of Wisconsin Library has one of the largest collections in the country of twentieth-century magazines, including little and literary magazines. Of special note should be the reprints of older magazines made available by such corporations as AMS, Johnson, Kraus, and William

Dawson. Xerox University Microfilms is presently engaged in microfilming some 1,200 periodicals of eighteenth- and nineteenth-century America.

4.   THE CHECKLISTS

These checklists are selective and meant to be work aides for the scholar and student beginning a study of midwestern periodicals and periodical literature.

The first category is divided into two parts and lists essentially the standard reference works that must be consulted as a matter of course to locate specific midwestern periodicals and to obtain a working bibliography.

The second category is also divided into two parts. The first contains a long list, arranged alphabetically by author, of studies relating to midwestern periodicals. Most of these are of a broad or generalized nature, although a few are on quite specific subjects. The second part contains specific studies relating to five of the more well-known midwestern literary periodicals.

The last category, also divided into two parts—creative and critical—lists representative midwestern periodicals, their places of origin, dates of publication, and, where significant, their first editor or publisher. This last category is by no means exhaustive. It is meant to merely suggest the variety and scope of midwestern periodical publication.

1.   GENERAL STUDIES

A.   SELECTED GUIDES TO LIBRARY HOLDINGS OF PERIODICALS

Downs, Robert B. *American Library Resources: A Bibliographical Guide.* Chicago: American Library Assn., 1951. *Supplement 1950–1961.* Chicago, 1962. *Supplement 1961–1970.* Chicago, 1972.

Freitag, Ruth S. *Union List of Serials: A Bibliography.* Washington, D.C.: Library of Congress, 1964.

New Serial Titles: A Union List of Serials Commencing Publication After December 31, 1949. Washington, D.C.: Library of Congress, 1953–

Titus, Edna B. *Union List of Serials in Libraries of the U.S. and Canada.* New York: H. W. Wilson, 1965.

Ulrich's International Periodical Directory: A Classified Guide to a Selected List of Current Periodicals, Foreign and Domestic. Ed. by Marietta Chicorel. 2 vols. New York: Bowker, 1967–68. Annual *Supplements.*

Union List of Little Magazines. Chicago: Midwest Inter-library Center, 1956.

B.   SELECTED SOURCES FOR LOCATING STUDIES OF MIDWESTERN LITERARY PERIODICALS

American Literature, bibliography, 1929–   .

Comprehensive Dissertation Index 1861–1972. Vol. 29–30. Language and Literature. Ann Arbor: Xerox Univ. Microfilms, 1973.

Dissertation Abstracts. Ann Arbor: Univ. Microfilms Library Services, 1955–   .

Gohdes, Clarence, comp. *Bibliographical Guide to the Study of the Literature of the U.S.A.* Durham, N.C.: Duke U., 1970.

Leary, Lewis. *Articles on American Literature 1900–1950, 1950–1967.* Durham N.C.: Duke U., 1954 and 1970.

Mid-America: Yearbook of the Society for the Study of Midwestern Literature, annual bibliography.

PMLA, annual bibliography.

Winchell, Constance M. *Guide to Reference Books*. Chicago: American Library Association, 1967.

Winther, Oscar O. *A Classified Bibliography of the Periodical Literature of the Trans-Mississippi West (1811–1957)*, and with Richard A. Van Orman, *Supplement (1957–1967)*. Bloomington: Indiana U., 1961 and 1970.

Woodress, James. *Dissertations in American Literature 1891–1966*. Durham, N.C.: Duke U., 1968.

2. STUDIES OF MIDWESTERN LITERARY PERIODICALS

A. SELECTED STUDIES

Allen, Charles. "Regionalism and the Little Magazines." *CE*, 7 (1945), 10–16.

Calkins, Earnest E. "The Chap-Book." *Colophon*, pt. 10 (1932), n.p.

Callahan, J. P. "Kansas Magazines." *KM* (1933), 56.

Doepke, Dale K. "St. Louis Magazines before the Civil War, 1832–1860." Ph.D. diss., Washington U., 1963.

Duffey, Bernard. *The Chicago Renaissance in American Letters: A Critical History*. East Lansing, Mich.: Michigan State College, 1954.

Dunn, Edgar C. "Settlers' Periodicals: Eugene Smalley and the *Northwest Magazine*." *MH*, 33 (1952), 29–34.

Ferlazzo, Paul J. "A Checklist of Midwestern Literary Magazines." *SSMLN*, 2 (Spring 1972), 4–9.

Flanagan, John T. "A Soil for the Seeds of Literature." In *The Heritage of the Middle West*. Ed. by John J. Murray. Norman: U. Oklahoma, 1958. Pp. 198–233.

⸺. "Early Literary Periodical in Minnesota." *MH*, 26 (1945), 293–311.

⸺. "Some Middlewestern Literary Magazines." *PLL*, 3 (Summer 1967), 237–53.

⸺. "Some Projects in Midwest Cultural History." *IMH*, 47 (Sept. 1951), 239–250.

Fleming, Herbert E. "The Literary Interests of Chicago." *AmJSoc*, 11, 12 (1905–06, 1906–07), 377–408, 499–531, 784–816, 68–118.

Garwood, Irving. *American Periodicals from 1850 to 1860*. Macomb, Ill.: Commercial Art Press, 1931.

Harmon, Susanna M. "Periodicals Publishing Literary Scholarship in the Midwest." *SSMLN*, 4 (Summer 1974), 10–11.

Henry, David D. "An Editor's Troubles 80 Years Ago." *MHM*, 19 (Autumn 1935), 399–403.

Hoeltje, H. H. "Iowa Literary Magazines." *Palimpsest*, 11 (1930), 87–94.

Hoffman, Frederick J., Charles Allen, and Carolyn F. Ulrich. *The Little Magazine: A History and Bibliography*. Princeton, N.J.: Princeton U., 1947.

Hounchell, Saul. "The Principal Literary Magazines of the Ohio Valley to 1840." Ph.D. diss., George Peabody U., 1934.

Janssens, G. A. M. *The American Literary Review: A Critical History 1920–50*. The Hague: Mouton, 1968.

Kramer, Dale. *Chicago Renaissance*. New York: Appleton, 1966.

Kramer, Sidney. *A History of Stone & Kimball and Herbert S. Stone & Company*. Chicago: N. W. Forgue, 1940.

Lundegaard, Bob. "Sizing Up the Little Magazines." *Minneapolis Tribune*, 17 Apr. 1966, pp. E–1, 5.

Milton, John R. "Inside the *South Dakota Review*." *MASJ*, 10 (1969), 68–78.

Mott, David C. "Thomas Gregg, Local Historian and Author." *AnIowa*, 3d series, 14 (Apr. 1924), 263–71.

Mott, Frank Luther. *A History of American Magazines*. 5 vols. Cambridge, Mass.: Harvard U., 1938–68.

⸺. "Iowa Magazines—Series 1." *Palimpsest*, 44 (1963), 285–316.

⸺. "Iowa Magazines—Series 2." *Palimpsest*, 44 (1963), 317–79.

Peterson, Theodore. *Magazines in the Twentieth Century*. Urbana, Ill.: U. Illinois, 1964.

Radke, Merle L. "Local-Color Fiction in Middle-Western Magazines, 1865–1900." Ph.D. diss., Northwestern U., 1965.

Rusk, Ralph Leslie. *The Literature of the Middle Western Frontier*. 2 vols. New York: Columbia U., 1926.
Scott, F. W. *Newspapers and Periodicals of Illinois 1814–79*. Springfield, Ill.: Illinois State Historical Library, 1910.
Shoemaker, Floyd C. "Forty-Five Years as Editor and Author of Missouri History, 1915–1960." *MHR*, 54 (1959–60), 225–30.
Stewart, Paul R. *The Prairie Schooner Story. A Little Magazine's First Twenty-five Years*. Lincoln: U. Nebraska, 1955.
Tebbel, John. *The American Magazine: A Compact History*. New York: Hawthorn, 1969.
Venable, W. H. *Beginnings of Literary Culture in the Ohio Valley: Historical and Biographical Sketches*. Cincinnati: Clarke, 1891.
[Wheeler, Edward J.] "An Illinois Art Revivalist." *CurLit*, 50 (Mar. 1911), 320–23.
Whittemore, Reed. *Little Magazines*. Minneapolis: Minnesota, 1963.
Wood, James P. *Magazines in the United States*. New York: Ronald Press, 1956.
Wright, Luella M. "Johnson Brigham." *Palimpsest*, 33 (Aug. 1952), 225–56.
———. "The Midland Monthly." *IJHP*, 45 (Jan. 1947), 2–61.

B. Five Midwestern Periodicals

1. The Dial

Allen, Charles. "The Dial," *UR*, 10 (Winter 1943), 101–8.
Fc rier, Ruth G. "The Literary Criticism of the *Dial* 1920–1929." Ph.D. diss., Vanderbilt, 1959.
Gohdes, Clarence. "The *Western Messenger* and *The Dial*." *SP*, 26 (Jan. 1929), 67–84.
Joost, Nicholas. "*The Dial* in Transition: The End of the Browne Family's Control, 1913–1916." *JISHS*, 59 (Autumn 1966), 272–88.
———. *Years of Transition: The Dial, 1912–1920*. Barre, Mass.: Barre Publishers, 1967.
Marshall, H. E. "The Story of the *Dial*." *NMQ*, 1 (May 1931), 147–65.
Moore, Marianne. "*The Dial*: A Retrospect." *PR*, 9 (Jan.–Feb., 1942), 52–58.
Mosher, Frederic J. "Chicago's 'Saving Remnant': Francis Fisher Browne, William Morton Payne, and the *Dial* (1880–1892)." Ph.D. diss., U. Illinois, 1950.

2. The Little Review

Allen, Charles. "American Little Magazines: II. *The Little Review*." *AmPref*, 3 (Jan. 1938), 54–59.
Anderson, Margaret C. *My Thirty Years' War: An Autobiography*. New York: Covici, Friede, 1930.
Bryer, Jackson R. "A Trial-Track for Racers: Margaret Anderson and the *Little Review*." Ph.D. diss., U. Wisconsin, 1964.
Todd, Ruthven. "The Little Review." *TCV*, nos. 15–16 (1939), 159–62.

3. The Midland

Allen, Charles. "American Little Magazines: IV. *The Midland*." *AmPref*, 3 (June 1938), 136–40.
Hartley, Lois. "The Midland." *IJHP*, 47 (October 1949), 325–44.
Riegelman, Milton M. *The Midland: A Venture In Literary Regionalism*. Iowa City: U. Iowa, 1975.

4. Poetry

Allen, Charles. "American Little Magazines: I. *Poetry: A Magazine of Verse*." *AmPref*, 3 (Nov. 1937), 28–32.
Gregory, Horace. "The Unheard of Adventure—Harriet Monroe and *Poetry*." *ASch*, 6 (1937), 195–200.
Hansen, Harry. *Midwest Portraits: A Book of Memories and Friendships*. New York: Harcourt, 1923.

Jackson, Mabel Ella. "A Critical Analysis of *Poetry: A Magazine of Verse* 1912–1922." Ph.D. diss., Pittsburgh U., 1971.
Monroe, Harriet. *A Poet's Life*. New York: Macmillan, 1938.
Williams, Ellen. "Harriet Monroe and the Poetry Renaissance—the First Ten Years of *Poetry: A Magazine of Verse* 1912–1922." Ph.D. diss., U. Chicago, 1970.

5.   Reedy's Mirror

Flanagan, John T. "Reedy of the Mirror," *MHR*, 43 (1949), 128–44.
Fox, Marjorie Eileen. "William Marion Reedy and the *St. Louis Mirror*." M.A. thesis, U. Illinois, 1947.
King, Ethel M. *Reflections of Reedy: A Biography of William Marion Reedy of Reedy's Mirror*. Brooklyn: Rickard, 1961.
Masters, Edgar Lee. "Literary Boss of the Middle West," *AmMerc*, 34 (1934), 450–55.
———. "William Marion Reedy," *AmS*, 9 (1934), 96–98.
———. "William Marion Reedy: Feaster." *Esquire*, 12 (Oct. 1939), 67, 148, 150.
Putzel, Max. "American Verse in *Reedy's Mirror*." Ph.D. diss., Yale U., 1958.
———. *The Man in the Mirror: William Marion Reedy and His Magazine*. Cambridge, Mass.: Harvard U., 1963.
Winkler, Jean. "William Marion Reedy," *StLouisR*, 2, no. 7 and 8 (Jan. 28, 1933 and Feb. 11, 1933), 5–7, 7–10.
Wolf, Fred Wilhelm. "William Marion Reedy: A Critical Biography." Ph.D. diss., Vanderbilt U., 1951.

3.   SELECTED MIDWESTERN PERIODICALS

A.   PRIMARILY CREATIVE

The Illinois Monthly Magazine, later *The Western Monthly Magazine*. 1830–37. James Hall. Vandalia and Cincinnati.
Western Messenger. 1835–41. Ephraim Peabody. Cincinnati.
Wellman's Literary Miscellany, later *Monthly Literary Miscellany*. 1849–54. D. F. Quimby. Detroit.
Literary Budget. 1852–56. W. W. Dannenhower. Chicago.
Genius of the West. 1853–56. Howard Durham. Cincinnati.
The Western Monthly, later *The Lakeside Monthly*. 1869–74. H. V. Reed and F. F. Browne. Chicago.
The Dial. 1880–1929 (moved to New York, 1916). F. F. Browne. Chicago.
Current. 1883–88. Edgar L. Wakeman. Chicago.
Reedy's Mirror. 1893–1920. William Marion Reedy. St. Louis.
The Chap-Book. 1894–98. Herbert Stuart Stone. Chicago.
Midland Monthly. 1894–99. Johnson Brigham. Des Moines.
Bellman. 1906–19. William C. Edgar. Minneapolis.
Poetry: A Magazine of Verse. 1912–   . Harriet Monroe et al. Chicago.
Little Review. 1914–29 (left Chicago 1917). Margaret C. Anderson. Chicago.
Midland. 1915–33. John T. Frederick. Iowa City (1915–29); Chicago (1930–33).
The Chicago Literary Times. 1923–24. Ben Hecht. Chicago.
Prairie Schooner. 1927–   . Lowry C. Wimberly. Lincoln, Nebraska.
The Anvil. 1933–35. Jack Conroy. Moberly, Missouri.
American Prefaces. 1935–43. Wilbur L. Schramm and Paul Engle. Iowa City.
Accent. 1940–60. Kerker Quinn. Urbana, Illinois.
Chicago Review. 1946–   . Carolyn Dillard and J. Radcliffe Squires. Chicago.
Perspective. 1947–   . Sherman Conrad, Mona Van Duyn, Jarvis Thursten. St. Louis.
Beloit Poetry Journal. 1949–65. Chad Walsh and Robert H. Glauber. Beloit, Wisconsin.
South Dakota Review. 1963–   . John R. Milton. Vermillion.

B.   PRIMARILY CRITICAL

Journal of English and Germanic Philology. 1897–   . University of Illinois.
Modern Philology. 1903–   . University of Chicago.

Philological Quarterly. 1921– . University of Iowa.
The University of Kansas City Review, then *The University Review*, later *New Letters*.
  1934– . University of Missouri at Kansas City.
Iowa Review. 1970– . University of Iowa.
Kenyon Review. 1939–70. John Crowe Ransom. Kenyon College.
Midwest Folklore. 1951–63. Indiana University.
Modern Fiction Studies. 1955– . Purdue University.
Victorian Studies. 1957– . Indiana University.
Centennial Review. 1957– . Michigan State University.
Papers on Language and Literature. 1964– . Southern Illinois University.
Criticism. 1959– . Wayne State University.
Tri-Quarterly. 1964– . Northwestern University.
Journal of Popular Culture. 1967– . Bowling Green University.
Great Lakes Review. 1974– . Northeastern Illinois University.
The Old Northwest. 1975– . Miami (Ohio) University.

Paul J. Ferlazzo
Michigan State University
East Lansing, Michigan

PART 2

AUTHOR BIBLIOGRAPHIES

GEORGE ADE (1866–1944)

George Ade, the Indiana-born author and dramatist, was a genial satirist who made America roar with laughter through his syndicated fables and theatrical comedies. His style, which continued the tradition of the western humorists and reflected both the rise of realism and the increasing use of colloquial language in literature, enjoyed widespread contemporary popularity. However, his once-towering reputation has suffered from the rapid obsolescence of his language.

Anyone interested in studying Ade has ample criticism at hand. Bibliographically, Ade is splendidly preserved in Russo's book, which still contains the most complete list of secondary material. Kolb's bibliographical essay is also excellent. Kelly's biography is the only full-scale effort, and it is therefore indispensable even though largely adulatory and uncritical.

One useful avenue for future research on Ade would be in the social and intellectual atmosphere of his times. He both represents and documents many significant aspects of midwestern life between 1890 and 1920, e.g., the movement from rural provincialism to a pseudo-sophisticated urban provincialism; the development of Chicago; the tension between realism and romance; and the development of American journalism. Although Ade will never be considered a great writer, perhaps he does deserve to be placed, as Mencken put it, in "the second rank" of writers whose literary achievements, though often narrowly based and unsustained, do have a measure of excellence.

Major Works

Artie. Chicago: H. S. Stone, 1896. [sketches]
Pink Marsh. Chicago: H. S. Stone, 1897. [sketches]
Doc Horne. Chicago: H. S. Stone, 1899. [sketches]
Fables in Slang. Chicago: H. S. Stone, 1900. [fables]
More Fables. Chicago: H. S. Stone, 1900. [fables]
Forty Modern Fables. New York: R. H. Russell, 1901. [fables]
The Girl Proposition. New York: R. H. Russell, 1902. [fables]
In Babel. New York: McClure, Phillips, 1903. [fables]
People You Know. New York: R. H. Russell, 1903. [fables]
Sultan of Sulu. New York: R. H. Russell, 1903. [play]
Circus Day. Akron: Saalfield, 1903. [sketches]
Breaking Into Society. New York: Harper, 1904. [fables]
True Bills. New York: Harper, 1904. [fables]
In Pastures New. New York: McClure, Phillips, 1906. [fables]
The Slim Princess. Indianapolis: Bobbs, Merrill, 1907. [novel]
Verses and Jingles. Indianapolis: Bobbs, Merrill, 1911. [verses]
Knocking the Neighbors. New York: Doubleday, 1912 [fables]
Ade's Fables. New York: Doubleday, 1914. [fables]

Hand-Made Fables. New York: Doubleday, 1920. [fables]
Single Blessedness and Other Observations. New York: Doubleday, 1922. [essays]
The College Widow. New York: Samuel French, 1924. [play]
The County Chairman. New York: Samuel French, 1924. [play]
Just Out of College. New York: Samuel French, 1924. [play]
Bang! Bang! New York: J. H. Sears, 1928. [stories]
The Old-Time Saloon. New York: Long and Smith, 1931. [historical essay]
Letters of George Ade. Ed. by Terence Tobin. Lafayette, Ind.: Purdue U., 1973.

CHECKLIST OF SECONDARY SOURCES

Burke; *CB; CHAL; DAB*; Herzberg; *LHUS; OCAL; TCA & Supp.*

Bauerle, Richard F. "A Look at the Language of George Ade." *AS*, 33 (Feb. 1958), 77–79.
Brenner, Jack. "Howells and Ade." *AL*, 38 (May 1966), 198–207.
Clark, John Abbott. "Ade's Fables in Slang: An Appreciation." *SAQ*, 46 (Oct. 1947), 537–44.
Coyle, Lee. *George Ade.* New York: Twayne, 1964.
Crowder, Richard. "American Nestor: Six Unpublished Letters from Howells to Ade." *BuR*, 7 (Mar. 1958), 144–49.
Daniels, Balfour. "George Ade As Social Critic." *MissQuart*, 12 (Fall 1959), 194–204.
DeMuth, James. "Small Town Chicago: The Comic Perspective of Finley Peter Dunne, George Ade, and Ring Lardner (1890–1920)." *DAI*, 36:3711A.
Dickinson, Thomas H. *Playwrights of the New American Theater.* New York: Macmillan, 1925.
Eaton, Ernest Riley. "George Ade—American Author and Fabulist." *PAGQuart* (May 1934), 57.
Evans, Bergen. "George Ade: Rustic Humorist." *AmMerc*, 70 (Mar. 1950), 312–29.
"George Ade Memorial Issue." *Mag Sigma Chi* (Oct.–Nov. 1944), 1–176.
Hasley, Louis. "George Ade, Realist, Fabulist." *FQ*, 19 (1970), 25–32.
Howells, William Dean. "Certain of the Chicago School of Fiction." *NAR*, 176 (May 1903), 734–46.
———. "Editor's Easy Chair." *Harper*, 134 (Feb. 1917), 442–45.
Kelly, Fred C. *George Ade: Warmhearted Satirist.* Indianapolis: Bobbs-Merrill, 1947.
Kolb, Harold H., Jr. "George Ade." *AmLitR*, 4 (Spring 1971), 157–69.
Masson, Thomas. *Our American Humorists.* New York: Moffat, Yard, 1922.
Matson, Lowell. "Ade—Who Needed None." *LitRev*, 5 (Autumn 1961), 99–114.
McKee, James H. "The Ade Family and Newton County." *IHB*, 39 (Feb. 1962), 27–32.
Mencken, H. L. *Prejudices: First Series.* New York: Knopf, 1919.
Nordhus, Philip. "George Ade: A Critical Study." Ph.D. diss., U. Iowa, 1957.
Pattee, Fred Lewis. *The New American Literature 1890–1930.* New York: Century, 1930.
Russo, Dorothy R. *A Bibliography of George Ade.* Indianapolis: Indiana Historical Society, 1947.
Tarkington, Booth. "George and John Liven Things Up." *SEPost* (Aug. 23, 1941), 27.
Van Doren, Carl. "Old Wisdom in a New Tongue: George Ade: Moralist in Slang." *Century* (Jan. 1923), 471.
Yates, Norris W. "George Ade, Student of 'Success'." In *The American Humorist.* Ames, Iowa: Iowa State U., 1964.

Carl Demarkowski
University of Toledo
Toledo, Ohio

BESS STREETER ALDRICH (1881–1954)

Iowan Bess Streeter Aldrich is the author of thirteen novels and anthologies, and some 160 stories whose basic theme is "the rearing of an empire in the rich, fertile Middle West." Always a very popular author, she has not, however, caught the attention of serious literary critics and no book-length studies have been produced. As one critic noted, she may seem "falsely optimistic" to serious minds, or else her writing "is not so realistic as that of Hamlin Garland."

The most detailed biographical study is that of Meier, *Bess Streeter Aldrich: Her Life and Work* (1968), which is based on her Kearney State College (Nebraska) master's thesis. "I Remember," a memoir of Aldrich's childhood in Waterloo and Cedar Falls, Iowa, was published in *A Bess Streeter Aldrich Treasury*. The introduction to that book has a summary commentary on her work written by her son, Robert. Shorter items are listed below.

Paluka has the definitive bibliography of books and editions. The major portion of her papers is located in the Nebraska State Historical Society in Lincoln.

MAJOR WORKS

Mother Mason. New York: Appleton, 1924. [novel]
The Rim of the Prairie. New York: Appleton, 1925. [novel]
The Cutters. New York: Appleton, 1926. [novel]
A Lantern in Her Hand. New York: Appleton, 1928. [novel]
A White Bird Flying. New York: Appleton, 1931. [novel]
Miss Bishop. New York: Appleton, 1933. [novel]
Spring Came on Forever. New York: Appleton, 1935. [novel]
The Man Who Caught the Weather, and Other Stories. New York: Appleton, 1936.
Song of Years. New York: Appleton, 1939. [novel]
The Drum Goes Dead. New York: Appleton, 1941. [novel]
The Lieutenant's Lady. New York: Appleton, 1942. [novel]
Journey Into Christmas, and Other Stories. New York: Appleton, 1949.
The Bess Streeter Aldrich Reader. New York: Appleton, 1950. [anthology]
A Bess Streeter Aldrich Treasury. New York: Appleton, 1959. [anthology]

CHECKLIST OF SECONDARY SOURCES

TCA; Warfel.

Aldrich, Bess Streeter. "Mid-Western Writers." *PrS*, 1 (Jan. 1927), 80–81.
———. "The Story Germ." *Writer*, 54 (Dec. 1941), 355–57. [about the writing of *Miss Bishop*]
———. "Why I Live in a Small Town." *LadiesHJ* 80, (June 1933), 21ff.
———. "Working Backward." *Writer*, 63 (Nov. 1950), 350–53. [about the writing of "Stars Across the Tracks"]
Aldrich, Robert Streeter. "Introduction." *A Bess Streeter Aldrich Treasury*. New York: Appleton, 1959. Pp. vii–x.

Andrews, Clarence A. *A Literary History of Iowa.* Iowa City: U. Iowa, 1972. Pp. 27–30.

Annals of Iowa, 32 (1953–55). [Obituary and brief estimate]

Frederick, John Towner. "The Town in Iowa Fiction." *Palimpsest,* 35 (Feb. 1954), 64–65.

Lambert, Lillian Vitalique. "Bess Streeter Aldrich." In *A Book of Iowa Authors,* ed. Johnson Brigham. Des Moines: Iowa State Teachers Association, 1930.

Marble, Annie R. *A Daughter of Pioneers, Bess Streeter Aldrich and Her Books.* New York: Appleton, n.d. [pamphlet]

Meier, A. Mabel. "Bess Streeter Aldrich: A Literary Portrait." *NH,* 50 (Spring 1969), 66–100.

Mendelsohn, Eleanor H. *Bess Streeter Aldrich.* Unpublished MS. Louisiana State U., Baton Rouge, La. [See fn. 101 in Meier, *supra.*]

Paluka, Frank. "Bess Streeter Aldrich." *Iowa Authors: A Bio-Bibliography of Sixty Native Writers.* Iowa City: Friends of the University of Iowa Libraries, 1967. Pp. 57–59.

Rosse, James C. "Midwestern Writers: Bess Streeter Aldrich." *PrS,* 1 (Jan. 1927), 226–29.

Clarence A. Andrews
University of Iowa
Iowa City, Iowa

NELSON ALGREN (1909–81)

Most critics call Nelson Algren a realist or a naturalist and identify him with Chicago, particularly the West Side, which has been the location and inspiration for much of his work. Eisinger discusses Algren as a naturalist who writes with compassion and sensibility; Belfast sees him as an ecological novelist, whose protagonists search for a common background of disorder; Geismar concludes that Algren's work represents an extreme phase of native American realism, a world where human beings caught in the trap of social circumstances find prison, "an iron sanctuary," the safest place to be. Bluestone, however, in perhaps the most perceptive criticism of Algren's work yet published, contends that Algren is not a naturalist and is only secondarily an urban writer. He discusses the importance of the love and death themes in Algren's fiction and lauds the poetry and art with which they are presented. Algren says that both Geismar and Bluestone "cut in close" to the truth about his work.

Algren has produced four novels, more than fifty short stories, numerous sketches, essays, poems, travel books, book reviews, and other literary criticism during nearly four decades of writing. His books are all in print, some in several editions. They have been highly successful abroad, and, in translation by Sartre and others, are available in several languages. Yet only two full-length publications on the man or his work have appeared: one, the transcriptions of taped conversations Donohue made with Algren, though unstructured, could, as Donohue suggests, be accurately subtitled *Notes Toward a Biography*; the other, the Cox and Chatterton study in the Twayne series, is an introduction to and examination of Algren's fiction.

The latter also contains a long introductory biographical chapter checked by the author himself.

The only extensive manuscript collection of Algren's work, including typescripts of four versions of *The Man with the Golden Arm*, the galley proof, and the proof copy—in addition to numerous other works, is in the collections of the Ohio State University Libraries.

Algren's position and influence in American literature is difficult for critics to assess at this time. Some complain that he has wasted his time since 1956, when his last novel, *A Walk on the Wild Side*, was published. They consider the subsequent travel books, sketches, and stories below the stature of his earlier achievements and unworthy of his talents. Yet others praise these later works, finding in them greater control of prose, mood, comic sense, and message.

MAJOR WORKS

Somebody in Boots. New York: Farrar, 1935. [novel]
Never Come Morning. New York: Harper, 1942. [novel]
The Neon Wilderness. Garden City, N.Y.: Doubleday, 1947. [stories]
The Man with the Golden Arm. Garden City, N.Y.: Doubleday, 1949. [novel]
Chicago: City on the Make. New York: Doubleday, 1951. [prose poem]
A Walk on the Wild Side. New York: Farrar, 1956. [novel]
Nelson Algren's Own Book of Lonesome Monsters. New York: Lancer, 1962. [stories introduced and edited by Algren]
Who Lost an American? New York: Macmillan, 1963. [travel book]
Conversations with Nelson Algren. (With H. E. F. Donohue). New York: Hill & Wang, 1964. [transcriptions of typed interviews about Algren's life and work]
Notes from a Sea Diary: Hemingway All the Way. New York: Putnam's, 1965. [travel book and personal reflections]
The Last Carousel. New York: Putnam, 1973. [stories and sketches]

CHECKLIST OF SECONDARY SOURCES

Allsop, K., ed. "A Talk on the Wild Side." *Sp*, 203 (Oct. 16, 1959), 509–10. [interview]
Anderson, Alston and Terry Southern. "Nelson Algren." *ParisR*, 11 (Winter 1955), 37–58. Reprinted in *Writers at Work: The Paris Review Interviews*. New York: Viking, 1958. [interview]
Bluestone, George. "Nelson Algren." *WR*, 22 (Autumn 1957), 27–44.
Breit, Harvey. "The Writer Observed." *NYTBR*, Oct. 2, 1949, p. 33. Reprinted as "Nelson Algren" in *The Writer Observed*. Cleveland: World, 1956. [interview]
Corrington, John W. "Nelson Algren Talks with NOR's Editor-at-Large." *NOR*, 1 (Winter 1969), 130–32. [interview]
Cox, Martha Heasley and Wayne Chatterton. *Nelson Algren*. Boston: Twayne, 1975.
De Beauvoir, Simone. "An American Rendezvous: The Question of Fidelity." *Harper*, 229 (Dec. 1964), 111–22.
Donohue, H. E. F. *Conversations with Nelson Algren*. New York: Hill & Wang, 1964.
Eisinger, Chester E. "Nelson Algren: Naturalism as the Beat of the Iron Heart." *Fiction of the Forties*. Chicago: U. Chicago, 1963.
Geismar, Maxwell, "Nelson Algren: The Iron Sanctuary." *CE*, 14 (Mar. 1953), 311–15. Reprinted in *EJ*, 42 (Mar. 1936), 121–25, and in *American Moderns: From Rebellion to Conformity*. New York: Hill & Wang, 1958.
Gelfant, Blanche. *The American City Novel*. Rev. ed. Norman: U. Oklahoma, 1970.
Lipton, Lawrence. "A Voyeur's View of the Wild Side: Nelson Algren and His Reviewers." *ChiR* (Winter 1957), 31–41.
McCollum, Kenneth. *Nelson Algren: A Checklist*. Detroit: Gale, 1973.

Omick, Robert. "Compassion in the Novels of Nelson Algren." Ph.D. diss., U. Iowa, 1967.
Ray, David. "Talk on the Wild Side: A Bowl of Coffee with Nelson Algren." *Rptr*, 20 (June 11, 1959), 31–33.
Studing, Richard. "A Nelson Algren Checklist." *TCL*, 19 (Jan. 1973), 27–39.

Martha Heasley Cox
San Jose State University
San Jose, California

SHERWOOD ANDERSON (1876–1941)

Born in the small town of Camden, Ohio, Sherwood Anderson epitomized in his own life the achievement of material success and spiritual frustration inherent in the Horatio Alger myth of late nineteenth-century America. He went on to a literary career initially successful and increasingly frustrating. Finally he returned in spirit, and partially in fact, to the small-town values and way of life that he had left, presumably forever, as they presumably vanished forever when the nineteenth century became the twentieth.

This, in essence, is the course of Anderson's life and careers, all of them irretrievably one as they fuse into a unified whole, a search, at times confident and at others desperate, for a life and work at once meaningful and fulfilling. During the course of this search Anderson became one of the most influential writers of his generation; he wrote with the eloquence and compassion of those who, like himself, sought to understand other human lives at their most intimate moments; and he wrote with a faith in the ability of man to transcend the material and achieve that understanding. In his search he demolished the popular American myth with which he had been imbued, and he constructed one of his own; in seeking understanding, he found much misunderstanding of what he wrote; uniquely among significant prose writers of his time, he was a romantic idealist who sought an ultimate unity beyond appearance, and in the process he was called a naturalist, a primitive, a Freudian, and a realist, all of which, in the conventional critical sense he was not, but all of which were, in ways peculiarly his own, techniques or ideas which he used for his own ends.

Anderson was most of all a conscious literary craftsman and an equally conscious seeker of an American ideal beyond that defined by America's post-Civil War myth-makers. In these two phases of his life, he contributed, first of all, a style that from its origins in the Midwest heartland has, through Hemingway and others, come to dominate American fiction of this century; and in his search for a new reality of compassion, identification, and empathy, he anticipated the new romantic search that has become a characteristic of the second half of the twentieth century.

Major Works

Windy McPherson's Son. London: John Lane, 1916. Rev. ed. New York: Huebsch, 1921.
[novel]
Marching Men. London: John Lane, 1917. [novel]
Mid-American Chants. London: John Lane, 1918. [poems]
Winesburg, Ohio. New York: Huebsch, 1919. [novel]
Poor White. New York: Huebsch, 1921. [novel]
The Triumph of the Egg. New York: Huebsch, 1921. [stories]
Many Marriages. New York: Huebsch, 1923. [novel]
Horses and Men. New York: Huebsch, 1923. [stories]
A Story Teller's Story. New York: Huebsch, 1924. [autobiography]
Dark Laughter. New York: Liveright, 1925. [novel]
The Modern Writer. San Francisco: Gelber, Lilienthal, 1925. [criticism]
Tar: A Midwest Childhood. New York: Liveright, 1926. [autobiography]
Sherwood Anderson's Notebook. New York: Liveright, 1926. [criticism]
A New Testament. New York: Liveright, 1927. [poems]
Hello Towns! New York: Liveright, 1929. [journalism]
Nearer the Grass Roots. San Francisco: Westgate, 1929. [essay]
Alice and The Lost Novel. London: Elkin Mathews and Marrot, 1929. [stories]
The American County Fair. New York: Random House, 1930. [essay]
Perhaps Women. New York: Liveright, 1931. [essays]
Beyond Desire. New York: Liveright, 1932. [novel]
Death In the Woods. New York: Liveright, 1933. [stories]
No Swank. Philadelphia: Centaur, 1934. [essays]
Puzzled America. New York: Scribner, 1935. [essays]
Kit Brandon. New York: Scribner, 1936. [novel]
Plays: Winesburg and Others. New York: Scribner, 1937.
Home Town. New York: Alliance, 1940. [essay]
Sherwood Anderson's Memoirs. New York: Harcourt, 1942. [autobiography]
Letters of Sherwood Anderson. Eds. Howard Mumford Jones and Walter P. Rideout. Boston:
Little, Brown, 1953.

Checklist of Secondary Sources

Books and Special Issues

Bibliographies

Gozzi, Raymond D. "A Bibliography of Sherwood Anderson's Contributions to Periodicals,
1914–1946." *NLB*, 2d series (Dec. 1948).
Jessup, Mary E. "A Checklist of the Writings of Sherwood Anderson." *ABC*, 5 (1928), 157–58.
Rogers, Douglas. *Sherwood Anderson: A Selective, Annotated Bibliography.* Metuchen, N.J.:
Scarecrow, 1976.
Sheehy, Eugene P. and Kenneth A. Lohf, comp. *Sherwood Anderson: A Bibliography.* Los
Gatos, Calif.: Talisman, 1960.
White, Ray Lewis. *The Merrill Checklist of Sherwood Anderson.* Columbus, Ohio: Merrill,
1969.

Critical and Biographical Studies

Anderson, David D. *Sherwood Anderson: An Introduction and Interpretation.* New York:
Holt, 1967.
————, ed. *Sherwood Anderson: Dimensions of His Literary Art: A Collection of Critical
Essays.* East Lansing: Michigan State U., 1976.
Appel, Paul P., ed. *Homage to Sherwood Anderson: 1876–1941.* Mamaroneck, N.Y.: Appel,
1970.
Asselineau, Roger. *Configuration Critique de Sherwood Anderson. La Revue des Lettres Mo-
dernes,* nos. 78–80 (1963).
Burbank, Rex. *Sherwood Anderson.* New York: Twayne, 1964.

Campbell, Hilbert and Charles Modlin, eds. *Sherwood Anderson: Centennial Studies*. Troy, N.Y.: Whitston, 1976.

Chase, Cleveland B. *Sherwood Anderson*. New York: McBride, 1927.

Curry, Martha, ed. *The "Writer's Book": A Critical Edition*. Metuchen, N.J.: Scarecrow, 1975.

Fagin, Bryllion N. *The Phenomenon of Sherwood Anderson*. Baltimore: Johns Hopkins U., 1927.

Fanning, Michael. *France and Sherwood Anderson: Paris Notebook, 1921*. Baton Rouge: Louisiana State U., 1976.

Howe, Irving. *Sherwood Anderson*. New York: Sloane, 1951.

Newberry Library Bulletin, 2d series, (Dec. 1948).

Newberry Library Bulletin, 6 (July 1971).

Rideout, Walter B., ed. *Sherwood Anderson: A Collection of Critical Essays*. Englewood Cliffs, N.J.: Prentice-Hall, 1974.

Schevill, James. *Sherwood Anderson, His Life and Works*. Denver: U. Denver, 1951.

Shenandoah. 13 (Spring 1972).

Story, 19 (Sept.–Oct., 1941).

Sutton, William A. *The Road to Winesburg: A Mosaic of the Imaginative Life of Sherwood Anderson*. Metuchen, N.J.: Scarecrow, 1972.

White, Ray Lewis, ed. *The Achievement of Sherwood Anderson: Essays in Criticism*. Chapel Hill: U. North Carolina, 1966.

Articles and Chapters in Books

Adams, Mildred. "A Small-town Editor Airs His Mind." *NYTMS* (Sept. 22, 1929), pp. 3, 20.

Almy, Robert F. "Sherwood Anderson: The Nonconforming Rediscoverer." *SatR*, 28 (Jan. 6, 1945), 17–18.

Anderson, David D. *Critical Studies in American Literature: A Collection of Critical Essays*. Karachi, Pakistan: U. Karachi, 1964. Pp. 99–141.

———. "Emerging Awareness in Sherwood Anderson's 'Tar.' " *Ohioana*, 4 (Summer 1961), 40–42, 51

———. "Sherwood Anderson and the Coming of the New Deal." *Criticism and Culture*, 88–96. Papers of the Midwest Modern Language Association, no. 2 (1972).

———. "Sherwood Anderson and the Two Faces of America." *Critical Studies in American Literature*. Karachi, Pakistan: U. Karachi, 1964. Pp. 99–107.

———. "Sherwood Anderson's Idea of the Grotesque." *Ohioana*, 6 (Spring 1963), 12–13.

———. "Sherwood Anderson's Moments of Insight." *Critical Studies in American Literature*. Karachi, Pakistan: U. Karachi, 1964. Pp. 108–31.

———. "Sherwood Anderson's Larger View." *Critical Studies in American Literature*. Karachi, Pakistan: U. Karachi, 1964. Pp. 132–41.

———. "Sherwood Anderson's Use of the Lincoln Theme." *LH*, 64 (Spring 1962), 28–32.

Anderson, Karl. "My Brother, Sherwood Anderson." *SatR*, 31 (Sept. 4, 1948), 6–7, 26–27.

Babb, Howard S. "A Reading of Sherwood Anderson's 'The Man Who Became a Woman,' " *PMLA*, 33 (Sept. 1965), 432–35.

Barker, Russell H. "The Storyteller Role." *CE*, 3 (Feb. 1942), 433–42.

Berland, Alwyn. "Sherwood Anderson and the Pathetic Grotesque." *WR*, 15 (Winter 1951), 135–38.

Birney, Earle. "Sherwood Anderson: A Memory." *CanF*, 21 (June 1941), 82–83.

Bishop, John Peale. "This Distrust of Ideas (D. H. Lawrence and Sherwood Anderson)." *VF*, 22 (Dec. 1921), 10–12, 118.

Bowden, Edwin T. *The Dungeon of the Heart: Human Isolation and the American Novel*. New York: Macmillan, 1961. Pp. 114–24.

Bridgman, Richard. *The Colloquial Style in America*. New York: Oxford, 1966. Pp. 152–64.

Brossard, Chandler. "Sherwood Anderson: A Sweet Singer, 'A Smooth Son of a Bitch.' " *AmMerc*, 72 (May 1951), 611–16.

Bucco, Martin. "A Reading of Sherwood Anderson's 'Hands.' " *ColSR*, 1 (Spring 1966), 5–8.

Buchanan, Annabel Morris. "Sherwood Anderson: Country Editor." *WT*, 53 (Feb. 1929), 249–53.

Budd, Louis J. "The Grotesque of Anderson and Wolfe." *MFS*, 5 (Winter 1959–60), 304–10.

Burrow, Trigant. "Psychoanalytic Improvisations and the Personal Equation." *PsyR*, 13 (Apr. 1926), 173–86.

Calverton, V. F. "Sherwood Anderson: A Study in Sociological Criticism." *ModQ*, 2 (Fall 1924), 82–118.

Cargill, Oscar. *Intellectual America*. New York: Macmillan, 1941. Pp. 311–98.

Ciancio, Ralph. " 'The Sweetness of the Twisted Apples': Unity of Vision in Winesburg, Ohio." *PMLA*, 87 (Oct. 1972), 994–1006.

Clark, Edward. "*Winesburg, Ohio*: An Interpretation." *DNS*, 8 (Dec. 1959), 547–52.

Crane, Hart. "Sherwood Anderson." *DD*, 2 (July 1921), 42–45.

Crawford, Nelson Antrim. "Sherwood Anderson, the Wistfully Faithful." *Midland*, 8 (Nov. 1922), 297–308.

Daugherty, George. "Anderson, Advertising Man." NLB, series 2, 2 (Dec. 1948), 30–43.

Dell, Floyd. "How Sherwood Anderson Became an Author." *NYHTBR*, 18 (Apr. 12, 1942), pp. 1–2.

———. "On Being Sherwood Anderson's Literary Father." *NLB*, 5 (Dec. 1961), 315–21.

Dickie, Francis. "From Forest Fire to France." *ABC*, 10 (Oct. 1959), 23–24.

Dickinson, L. R. "Smyth County Items." *Outlook*, 148 (Apr. 11, 1928), 581–83.

Fadiman, Clifton. "Sherwood Anderson: The Search for Salvation." *Nation*, 135 (Nov. 9, 1932), 454–56.

Farrell, James T. "A Memoir on Sherwood Anderson." *Perspective*, 7 (Summer 1954), 83–88.

Faulkner, William. "Prophets of the New Age: Sherwood Anderson." *PULC*, 18 (1957), 89–94.

Faulkner, William and William Spratling. *Sherwood Anderson and Other Famous Creoles*. New Orleans: Pelican Bookshop, 1926. [Foreword]

Feldman, Eugene. "Sherwood Anderson's Search." *Psychoanalysis*, 3 (1955), 44–51.

Flanagan, John T. "Hemingway's Debt to Sherwood Anderson." *JEGP*, 54 (Oct. 1955), 507–20.

———. "The Permanence of Sherwood Anderson," *SWR*, 35 (Summer 1950), 170–177.

Geismar, Maxwell David. "Anderson's *Winesburg*." *NYTBR*, July 18, 1943, p. 4.

———. *The Last of the Provincials*. Boston: Houghton Mifflin, 1947.

Gerhard, Joseph. "The American Triumph of the Egg: Anderson's 'The Egg' and Fitzgerald's *The Great Gatsby*." *Criticism*, 7 (Spring 1965), 131–40.

Gildzen, Alex. "Sherwood Anderson, Elyria, and the Escape Hunch." *Serif*, 5 (Mar. 1968), 3–10.

Gochburg, Donald. "Stagnation and Growth: The Emergence of George Willard." *Expression*, 4 (Winter 1960), 29–35.

Gold, Herbert. "*Winesburg, Ohio*: The Purity and Cunning of Sherwood Anderson." *HudR*, 10 (Winter 1957–58), 548–57.

Gregory, Alyse. "Sherwood Anderson." *Dial* 75 (Sept. 1923), 243–46.

Gross, Seymour L. "Sherwood Anderson's Debt to *Huckleberry Finn*." *MTJ*, 11 (Summer 1960), 3–5, 24.

Guerin, Wilfried. " 'Death in the Woods': Sherwood Anderson's 'Cold Pastoral.' " *CEA*, 30 (May 1968), 4–5.

Hilton, Earl Raymond. "The Evolution of Sherwood Anderson's 'Brother Death.' " *NOQ*, 24 (Summer 1952), 125–30.

———. "Sherwood Anderson and Heroic Vitalism." *NOQ*, 29 (Spring 1957), 97–107.

Hoffman, Frederick J. "Sherwood Anderson: A 'Groping, Artistic, Sincere Personality.' " *WR*, 18 (Winter 1954), 159–62.

Hovey, Richard B. "*The Torrents of Spring*: Prefigurations in the Early Hemingway." *CE*, 26 (Apr. 1965), 460–64.

Huebsch, Benjamin W. "Footnotes to a Publisher's Life." *Colo.*, n.s., 11 (Summer 1937), 415–17.

Johnson, A. Theodore. "Realism in Contemporary American Literature: Notes on Dreiser, Anderson, Lewis." *SwB*, n.s., 16 (Sept. 1929), 3–16.

Jones, Howard M. "Introduction." *Dark Laughter*. New York: Liveright, 1960.

Joselyn, Sister M. "Sherwood Anderson and the Lyric Short Story." In Richard E. Langford and William E. Taylor, eds. *The Twenties: Prose and Poetry*. DeLand, Fla.: Everett, 1966. Pp. 70–73.

————. "Some Artistic Dimensions of Sherwood Anderson's 'Death in the Woods.' " *SSF*, 4 (Spring 1967), 252–59.

Kirchwey, Freda. "Sherwood Anderson." *Nation*, 152 (Mar. 22, 1941), 313–14.

Kramer, Dale. *Chicago Renaissance: The Literary Life in the Midwest, 1900–1930*. New York: Appleton, 1966. Pp. 37–51ff.

Laughlin, Rosemary M. "Godliness and the American Dream in *Winesburg, Ohio*." *TCL*, 13 (July 1967), 97–103.

Lawry, Jon S. "The Artist in America: The Case of Sherwood Anderson." *BSUF*, 7 (Spring 1966), 15–26.

————. " 'Death in the Woods' and the Artist's Self in Sherwood Anderson." *PMLA*, 74 (June 1959), 306–11.

Lewis, Wyndham. "Paleface (12): Sherwood Anderson." *Enemy* (Sept. 1928), 26–27.

Love, Glen A. "*Winesburg, Ohio* and the Rhetoric of Silence." *AL*, 40 (Mar. 1968), 38–57.

Lovett, Robert Morss. "The Promise of Sherwood Anderson." *Dial*, 72 (Jan. 1922), 79–83.

————. "Sherwood Anderson." *EJ*, 13 (Oct. 1924), 531–39.

————. "Sherwood Anderson." *NR*, 89 (Nov. 25, 1936), 103–5.

————. "Sherwood Anderson, American." *VQR*, 17 (Summer 1941), 379–88.

Lucow, Ben. "Mature Identity in Sherwood Anderson's 'The Sad Horn-Blowers,' " *SSF*, 2 (Spring 1965), 291–93.

McAleer, John J. "Christ Symbolism in *Winesburg, Ohio*." *Discourse*, 4 (Summer 1961), 168–81.

McCole, Camille John. "Sherwood Anderson—Congenital Freudian." *CathW*, 130 (Nov. 1929), 129–33.

MacDonald, Dwight. "Sherwood Anderson." *YLM*, 93 (July 1928), 209–43.

Mahoney, John J. "An Analysis of *Winesburg, Ohio*." *JAAC*, 15 (Dec. 1956), 245–52.

Mellard, J. M. "Narrative Forms in *Winesburg, Ohio*." *PMLA*, 83 (Oct. 1968), 1304–12.

Mencken, H. L. "America's Most Distinctive Novelist—Sherwood Anderson." *VF*, 27 (Dec. 1926), 88.

Miller, William V. "In Defense of Mountaineers: Sherwood Anderson's Hill Stories." *BSUF*, 15 (Spring 1974), 51–58.

————. "Earth Mothers, Succubi, and Other Ectoplasmic Spirits: The Women in Sherwood Anderson's Short Stories." In David D. Anderson, ed. *M–A I*. East Lansing, Mich.: Center for the Study of Midwestern Literature, 1974. Pp. 64–81.

Murphy, G. D. "The Theme of Sublimation in Anderson's *Winesburg, Ohio*." *MFS*, 13 (Summer 1967), 237–46.

Parish, John E. "The Silent Father in Anderson's 'I Want to Know Why.' " *RUS*, 51 (Winter 1965), 49–57.

Pearson, Norman Holmes. "Anderson and the New Puritanism." *NLB*, series 2 (Dec. 1948), 52–63.

Phillips, William L. "The First Printing of Sherwood Anderson's *Wineburg, Ohio*." *SB*, 4 (1951–52), 211–13.

Picht, Douglas R. "Anderson's Use of Tactile Imagery in *Winesburg, Ohio*." *RSWSU*, 35 (June 1967), 176–78.

Raymund, Bernard. "The Grammar of Notreason: Sherwood Anderson." *ArQ*, 12 (Spring-Summer 1956), 136–48.

Richardson, H. Edward. "Anderson and Faulkner." *AL*, 36 (Nov. 1964), 298–314.

————. "Faulkner, Anderson, and Their Tall Tale." *AL*, 34 (May 1962), 287–91.

Rideout, Walter B. "Introduction." *Beyond Desire*. New York: Liveright, 1961. Pp. vii–xiii.

————. "Introduction." *Poor White*. New York: Viking, 1966. Pp. ix–xx.

————. "Sherwood Anderson's 'Mid-American Chants.' " In *Aspects of American Poetry: Essays Presented to Howard Mumford Jones*, ed. Richard M. Ludwig. Columbus: Ohio State U., 1962. Pp. 149–70.

Rideout, Walter B. and James B. Meriwether. "On the Collaboration of Faulkner and Anderson." *AL*, 35 (Mar. 1963), 85–87.

Robinson, Eleanor M. "A Study of 'Death in the Woods.' " *CEA*, 30 (Jan. 1968), 6.

Rohrberger, Mary. "The Man, the Boy, and the Myth: Sherwood Anderson's 'Death in the Woods.' " *MASJ*, 3 (Fall 1962), 48–54.

Rosenfeld, Paul. *Port of New York.* New York: Harcourt, 1924. Pp. 175–98.

San Juan, Epifanio, Jr. "Vision and Reality: A Reconsideration of Sherwood Anderson's *Winesburg, Ohio.*" *AL*, 35 (May 1963), 137–55.

Smith, Rachel. "Sherwood Anderson: Some Entirely Arbitrary Reactions." *SR*, 37 (Apr. 1929), 159–63.

Somers, Paul P., Jr. "Anderson's Twisted Apples and Hemingway's Crips." In David D. Anderson, ed. *M-A I.* East Lansing, Mich.: Center for the Study of Midwestern Literature, 1974. Pp. 82–97.

Spencer, Benjamin T. "Sherwood Anderson: American Mythopoeist." *AL*, 41 (Mar. 1969), 1–18.

Stein, Gertrude. "Idem the Same—A Valentine to Sherwood Anderson." *LittleR*, 9 (Spring 1923), 5–9.

Stewart, Maaja A. "Scepticism and Belief in Chekkov and Anderson." *SSF*, 9 (Winter 1972), 29–40.

Sullivan, John A. "Winesburg Revisited." *AR*, 20 (Summer 1960), 213–21.

Sutton, William A. "The Diaries of Sherwood Anderson's Parents." In Ray Lewis White, ed. *Tar: A Midwest Childhood, A Critical Text.* Cleveland: Case Western Reserve U. 1969. Pp. 219–30.

_____. "Sherwood Anderson: The Advertising Years, 1900–1906." *NOQ*, 22 (Summer 1950), 129–57.

_____. "Sherwood Anderson: The Cleveland Year, 1906–1907." *NOQ*, 22 (Winter 1949–50), 39–44.

_____. "Sherwood Anderson: The Clyde Years, 1884–1896." *NOQ*, 19 (July 1947), 99–114.

_____. "Sherwood Anderson: The Spanish-American War Year." *NOQ*, 20 (Jan. 1948), 20–36.

_____. "Sherwood Anderson's Second Wife." *BSUF*, 7 (Spring 1966), 39–46.

Tanner, Tony. *The Reign of Wonder: Naivety and Reality in American Literature.* Cambridge: Cambridge U., 1965.

Tanselle, G. Thomas. "Anderson Annotated by Brooks." *N&Q*, 15 (Feb. 1968), 60–61.

_____. "Letters of Sherwood Anderson and August Derleth." *N&Q*, 12 (July 1965), 266–73.

_____. "Realist or Dreamer: Letters of Sherwood Anderson and Floyd Dell." *MLR*, 58 (Oct. 1963), 532–37.

Thurston, Jarvis A. "Anderson and 'Winesburg': Mysticism and Craft." *Accent*, 15 (Spring 1956), 107–28.

Van Doren, Carl. "Sinclair Lewis and Sherwood Anderson: A Study of Two Moralists." *Century*, 110 (July 1925), 362–69.

Weber, Brom. "Anderson and 'The Essence of Things.' " *SR*, 59 (Autumn 1951), 678–92.

West, Michael D. "Sherwood Anderson's Triumph: 'The Egg.' " *AQ*, 20 (Winter 1968), 675–93.

West, Thomas Reed. *Flesh of Steel: Literature and the Machine in American Culture.* Nashville: Vanderbilt U., 1967. Pp. 21–34.

Whipple, Thomas K. *Spokesmen: Modern Writers and American Life.* New York: Appleton, 1928. Pp. 115–38.

White, Ray Lewis. "Hemingway's Private Explanation of *The Torrents of Spring.*" *MFS*, 13 (Summer 1967), 261–63.

_____. "The Original for Sherwood Anderson's *Kit Brandon.*" *NLB*, 6 (Dec. 1965), 196–99.

_____. "Sherwood Anderson's First Published Story." *RW*, 1 (Apr. 1968), 32–38.

Winther, S.K. "The Aura of Loneliness in Sherwood Anderson." *MFS*, 5 (Summer 1959), 145–52.

Wright, Donald M. "A Mid-western Ad Man Remembers: Sherwood Anderson, Advertising Man." *AdS*, 28 (Dec. 17, 1936), 35, 68.

David D. Anderson
Michigan State University
East Lansing, Michigan

HARRIETTE ARNOW (1908–   )

Except for one book-length study, Harriette Simpson Arnow has unfortunately received little critical attention. Her fictional world is that of the southern hill white, often displaced to Midwest cities such as Detroit. Her works exhibit little literary experimentation and are marked by a straightforward, realistic style that reflects a penetrating insight into the various characters and situations that she examines.

MAJOR WORKS

Mountain Path. New York: Covici Friede, 1936. [novel]
Hunter's Horn. New York: Macmillan, 1949. [novel]
The Dollmaker. New York: Macmillan, 1954. [novel]
Seedtime in the Cumberland. New York: Macmillan, 1960. [social history]
Flowering of the Cumberland. New York: Macmillan, 1963. [social history]
The Weedkiller's Daughter. New York: Knopf, 1970. [novel]

CHECKLIST OF SECONDARY SOURCES

CA; CB; Warfel.

Bradbury, John. *Renaissance in the South.* Chapel Hill: U. North Carolina, 1963. Pp. 20, 171–72.
Davidson, Donald. "The Cumberland's Great Past in a Stirring Portrait." *NYHTBR*, Sept. 4, 1960, pp. 1–2. [rev. of *Seedtime*]
Duckworth, Lois. "When the Cumberland Pioneer Turned to Better Things." *Louisville Courier Journal*, Dec. 8, 1963, pp. 20–23. [rev. of *Flowering*]
Eckley, Wilton. *Harriette Arnow.* Boston: Twayne, 1974.
Hass, Victor. "A Way of Life Down South." *SatR*, 32 (June 25, 1949), 20. [rev of *Hunter's Horn*]
Havighurst, Walter. "Hillbilly D.P.'s." *SatR*, 37 (Apr. 24, 1954), 12. [rev. of *The Dollmaker*]
Hazard, Eloise Perry. "Notes on a Baker's Dozen." *SatR*, 33 (Feb. 11, 1950), 12. [biog. sketch]
Hobbs, Glenda. "Harriette Arnow's Kentucky Novels: Beyond Local Color." *Kate Chopin Newsletter*, 2 (1976), 27–32.
Oates, Joyce Carol. "Afterword." *The Dollmaker.* 4th printing. New York: Macmillan, 1954. Pp. 601–08. [crit. appraisal]
Ulman, Ruth. "Harriette Arnow." *WLB*, 29 (Sept. 1954), 20. [biog. sketch]

Wilton Eckley
Drake University
Des Moines, Iowa

MARGARET AYER BARNES (1886–1967)

In 1931 Margaret Ayer Barnes, at forty-five, dramatically launched her literary career by receiving the Pulitzer Prize for her first novel, *Years of Grace*. When her fiction first appeared, it gained a most enthusiastic critical and popular response. Today, however, literary histories contain only fleeting references to her work, and her fiction lies unread on library shelves.

Perhaps the most obvious reason for this neglect of Mrs. Barnes, who retains her reputation as "a good storyteller," is the narrow scope of her work. All of her fiction centers on the upper middle class in America during the forty-year span from the 1890s through the 1930s. The novels from the era of the 1930s that still win critical acclaim often have strong sociopolitical overtones. While her work sometimes fits into the category of social protest and always must be judged as social commentary, it is a far cry from the viewpoint of social critics such as Dos Passos or Steinbeck.

Although she generally chose Chicago as the principal locale for her novels, she cannot be classified as a regionalist in the usual sense of that designation. Barnes's essential concern was the portrayal of a social class as a whole. She used a fictional approach to write a social history of the upper middle class in America during that important transitional period from the Spanish-American War through the Great Depression.

Within the very restricted domain that she set for herself, Barnes succeeded in re-creating vividly one segment of the social scene of late nineteenth- and early twentieth-century America. Thus for the student of American social history her fiction will remain a limited but important record.

MAJOR WORKS

Prevailing Winds. Boston: Houghton Mifflin, 1928. [stories]
Years of Grace. Boston: Houghton Mifflin, 1930. [novel]
Westward Passage. Boston: Houghton Mifflin, 1931. [novel]
Within This Present. Boston: Houghton Mifflin, 1933. [novel]
Edna His Wife. Boston: Houghton Mifflin, 1935. [novel]
Wisdom's Gate. Boston: Houghton Mifflin, 1938. [novel]

CHECKLIST OF SECONDARY SOURCES

Burke; *CA; CAA; CB*; Herzberg; *OCAL; TCA* & Supp.

Brown, Elizabeth L. Review of *Within This Present*. *NYTBR*, Nov. 12, 1933, p. 8.
Davenport, Russell. Review of *Westward Passage*. *SatR*, 7 (Dec. 5, 1931), 345.
Field, Louise M. Review of *Wisdom's Gate*. *NYTBR*, Nov. 6, 1938, p. 6.
Hawkins, Ethel W. Review of *Westward Passage*. *Atl*, 149 (Feb. 1932), 18.

Lawrence, Margaret. *The School of Femininity*. New York: Stokes, 1936. Reissued by Kennikat Press, Port Washington, N.Y., 1966, pp. 222–26. [criticism]

Lovett, Robert M. Review of *Years of Grace*. *NR*, 63 (July 23, 1930), 298.

Lowrie, Rebecca. Review of *Edna His Wife*. *SatR*, 13 (Nov. 9, 1935), 7.

Protens. Review of *Years of Grace*. *NS*, 35 (Aug. 16, 1930), 596.

Ross, Virgilia P. Review of *Westward Passage*. *OI*, 159 (Dec. 9, 1931), 473–74.

Stuckey, William J. *The Pulitzer Prize Novels: A Critical Backward Glance*. Norman: U. Oklahoma, 1966. Pp. 86–89. [crit. of *Years of Grace*]

Taylor, Lloyd C., Jr. *Margaret Ayer Barnes*. Boston: Twayne, 1974.

Van Doren, Dorothy. Review of *Years of Grace*. *Nation*, 130 (Aug. 6, 1930), 158.

Walton, Edith H. Review of *Edna His Wife*. *NYTBR*, Nov. 10, 1935.

Lionel C. Taylor, Jr.
Texas A&M University
College Station, Texas

THOMAS BEER (1889–1940)

Thomas Beer, an Iowa native, attracted a considerable amount of attention in the 1920s with novels, short stories, and studies in biography and culture. The "Mrs. Egg" stories were his main contribution to the chronicle of rural life in the Midwest. Beer's outstanding feature was his brilliant and highly-mannered style. He was a friend of James Branch Cabell, Joseph Hergesheimer, and Carl Van Vechten and was often associated with them as—in Alfred Kazin's phrase—an "American exquisite." The critical label which has most often been applied to Beer is impressionist, and his close association with writers like Stephen Crane, Joseph Conrad, and James G. Huneker gives credence to that description. Because he wrote distinguished literary works and at the same time turned out a steady flow of popular short stories, mostly for the *Saturday Evening Post*, William Peden has called him a brilliant dualist.

In the twenties, Beer's name was in book columns and reviews constantly, and at the time of his death there was a flurry of respectful articles by critics such as Bernard De Voto and Lewis Mumford. Thomas Wolfe drew admiring portraits of Beer in *The Web and the Rock* and *You Can't Go Home Again*. William Faulkner cited Beer as an important influence on his style and method of characterization. But Beer has been virtually neglected since his death. The only full-length study of his work is Harrington's dissertation in 1968. Follett's introduction to *Mrs. Egg and Other Americans* has very valuable insights into the author and all the published work.

MAJOR WORKS

The Fair Rewards. New York: Knopf, 1922. [novel]
Stephen Crane: A Study in American Letters. New York: Knopf, 1923. [biography]

Sandoval: A Romance of Bad Manners. New York: Knopf, 1924. [novel]
The Mauve Decade: American Life at the End of the Nineteenth Century. New York: Knopf, 1926. [cultural history]
The Road to Heaven: A Romance of Morals. New York: Knopf, 1928. [novel]
Hanna. New York: Knopf, 1929. [biography]
Mrs. Egg and Other Barbarians. New York: Knopf, 1933. [short stories]
Mrs. Egg and Other Americans. New York: Knopf, 1947. [short stories]

CHECKLIST OF SECONDARY SOURCES

DAB; *LHUS*; *OCAL*; *TCA*.

Basso, Hamilton. "Thomas Beer and Others." *NY*, 32 (Oct. 11, 1947), 120. [rev.]
Beer, Alice B. "Recollections of a Writer: Thomas Beer." [MS. in the Thomas Beer Papers, Yale]
Boyd, Ernest. *Portraits: Real and Imaginary.* New York: Doran, 1924.
Canby, H. S. "The Mauve Decade." *SRL*, 2 (Apr. 17, 1926), 717. [rev.]
Chamberlain, John. "Mr. Beer's Character Parts." *SRL*, 10 (Aug. 19, 1933), 53.
Clark, Emily. "Thomas Beer." *SRL*, 10 (May 12, 1934), 689.
Connolly, Cyril. Review of *The Road to Heaven. NS*, 31 (July 21, 1928), 484.
Davis, Robert G. Review of *Mrs. Egg and Other Americans. NYTBR*, Oct. 5, 1947, p. 28.
De Voto, Bernard. "Even in the 'Twenties' He Remained Himself." *NYHTBR*, Aug. 24, 1941, p. 6. [rev.]
Follett, Wilson, ed. "Introduction." In *Mrs. Egg and Other Americans.* New York: Knopf, 1947.
Frank, Waldo. "Thomas Beer, Esq're." *NR*, 47 (June 9, 1926), 88. [rev.]
Harrington, Evans. "The Work of Thomas Beer: Appraisal and Bibliography." Ph.D. diss., U. Mississippi, 1968.
Kazin, Alfred. *On Native Ground.* New York: Reynal and Hitchcock, 1942.
Lane, James W. "Thomas Beer." *Bookman*, 79 (Nov. 1931), 241–46.
Mumford, Lewis. "Thomas Beer: Aristocrat of Letters." *SRL*, 22 (May 4, 1940), 3–4, 17.
Peden, William. "Brilliant Dualist." *SRL*, 30 (Nov. 15, 1947), 12–13. [rev.]
Rascoe, Burton. "Contemporary Reminiscences." *Arts and Decoration*, 25 (June 1926), 29, 80–82.
Sherman, Stuart Pratt. *The Main Stream.* New York: Scribner, 1927.
Whipple, Margaret. "Mr. Beer's Backdrops." *Bookman*, 67 (June 1928), 538–41. [rev.]
Wooley, Monty and Cary Abbot. "Thomas Beer." *SRL*, 24 (Sept. 13, 1941), 12–13.

Evans Harrington
University of Mississippi
University, Mississippi

SAUL BELLOW (1915–   )

Saul Bellow, winner of the Nobel Prize, the Pulitzer Prize, and three National Book Awards, is America's most honored and respected living American novelist. His literary art has been the subject of nine books, two collections of critical essays and two pamphlets. There exists a portable edition of his fiction and a critical edition of *Herzog*. In addition to numerous articles about every facet of his canon, analyses of Bellow's work have figured prominently in the major studies of the contemporary American novel.

After Bellow completed his second novel, *The Victim*, he claimed he was a "Jew who happened to be a writer"; after he received national and international recognition for *Herzog* and *Mr. Sammler's Planet*, he claimed he was a "writer who happened to be a Jew." With the postwar emergence of pride in ethnicity, many of the Jewish critics, ignoring the distinction Bellow made about himself, chose to dwell upon the Jewish aspects of his fiction. Guttmann sees Bellow as the Jewish "explorer of marginality," depicting characters who are displaced persons trying to find themselves. Rovit states that "spoken or argued Yiddish" is the chief influence in Bellow's style. Howe, reviewing *Mr. Sammler's Planet*, believes that Bellow is the most Jewish and serious of the American Jewish writers, in whom "the tradition of immigrant Jewishness . . . survives with a stern dignity." Alter stresses the relationship between Herzog's Jewishness and his denunciation of the "Wasteland" pessimism.

Certain non-Jewish critics have been struck by the spiritual dimensions of Bellow's work, but have not found them to be exclusively Jewish. Opdahl maintains that Bellow's perspective is essentially a religious one, akin to the American Transcendentalists' view. Porter's study, though primarily a new critical analysis of Bellow's novels, also places his fiction in the tradition of "neo-transcendentalism" reaffirming "human possibilities of the dream despite the power of the dread." Detweiler analyzes Bellow's literature in terms of a Christian point of view, comparing the Bellow hero to the Christian man of faith and the course of his life to the Christian pattern of redemption. Tanner, the English critic, sees the Bellow hero anchored to no particular theological moorings, but in need of some "sacred affirmative" to give life meaning. Scott considers Bellow's fiction to be man-centered rather than God-centered, concerned with consecrating the "human bond." Clayton employs psychoanalytic criticism to show that Bellow's heroes want to commit themselves to a "holy brotherhood of people," but that they, as well as Bellow himself, are alienatees and masochists, overwhelmed with guilt and the fear of death.

Bellow, in a 1965 *Paris Review* interview, the longest and most informative of his interviews, revealed that he preferred complaint over comedy. The comic in his works has also received critical attention. Shulman notes the similarities between Bellow's antic erudite style and the comic encyclopedic style of Rabelais, Burton, Sterne, Melville, and Joyce. Cohen explores both the function and evolution of Bellow's comedy and demonstrates the progressively sophisticated and versatile use of the comic mode in his work.

MAJOR WORKS

Dangling Man. New York: Vanguard, 1944. [novel]
The Victim. New York: Vanguard, 1947. [novel]
"Address by Gooley MacDowell to the Hasbeens Club of Chicago," *HudR*, 4 (Summer 1951), 222–27. [short story]
The Adventures of Augie March. New York: Viking Press, 1953. [novel]

Seize the Day. New York: Viking Press, 1956. [novel]
"Illinois Journey," *Holiday*, 22 (Sept. 1959), 62, 102–07. [article]
Henderson the Rain King. New York: Viking Press, 1959. [novel]
Herzog. New York: Viking Press, 1964. [novel]
The Last Analysis. New York: Viking Press, 1965. [play]
Mosby's Memoirs and Other Stories. New York: Viking Press, 1968. [novel]
Mr. Sammler's Planet. New York: Viking Press, 1970. [novel]
Humboldt's Gift. New York: Viking Press, 1975. [novel]
To Jerusalem and Back. New York: Viking Press, 1976. [travel]

CHECKLIST OF SECONDARY SOURCES

Alter, Robert. "The Stature of Saul Bellow." *Midstream*, 10 (Dec. 1964), 3–15. Reprinted in Alter. *After the Tradition: Essays on Modern Jewish Writing.* New York: Dutton, 1971. Pp. 95–115.
Baker, Sheridan. "Saul Bellow's Bout with Chivalry." *Criticism*, 9 (Spring 1967), 109–22.
Baumbach, Jonathan. "The Double Vision: *The Victim* by Saul Bellow." In *The Landscape of Nightmare.* New York: New York U., 1965. Pp. 35–54.
Bradbury, Malcolm. "Saul Bellow and the Naturalist Tradition." *REL*, 4 (Oct. 1963), 80–92.
Clayton, John J. *Saul Bellow: In Defense of Man.* Bloomington: Indiana U., 1968.
Cohen, Sarah Blacher. *Saul Bellow's Enigmatic Laughter.* Urbana: U. Illinois, 1974.
Detweiler, Robert. *Saul Bellow: A Critical Essay.* Grand Rapids: Eerdmans, 1967. [pamphlet]
Dommergues, Pierre. *Saul Bellow.* Paris: Grasset, 1967.
Dutton, Robert R. *Saul Bellow.* New York: Twayne, 1971.
Eisinger, Chester E. "Saul Bellow: Love and Identity." *Accent*, 18 (Summer 1958), 179–203. Reprinted in Eisinger. *Fiction of the Forties.* Chicago: U. Chicago, 1963.
Galloway, David D. "The Absurd Man as Picaro: The Novels of Saul Bellow." *TSLL*, 6 (Summer 1964), 226–54. Reprinted in Galloway. *The Absurd Hero in American Fiction*, rev. ed. Austin: U. Texas, 1970. Pp. 82–139.
————. "*Mr. Sammler's Planet*: Bellow's Failure of Nerve." *MFS*, 19 (Spring 1973), 17–28.
Guerard, Albert. "Saul Bellow and the Activists: On *The Adventures of Augie March*." *SouR*, 3 (July 1967), 582–96.
Guttmann, Allen. "Mr. Bellow's America." In *The Jewish Writer in America: Assimilation and the Crisis of Identity.* New York: Oxford U., 1971. Pp. 178–221.
Hassan, Ihab. *Radical Innocence: Studies in the Contemporary American Novel.* New York: Harper & Row, 1966. Pp. 290–324.
Hoffman, Michael. "From Cohn to Herzog." *YR*, 58 (Spring 1969), 342–58.
Howe, Irving. "Odysseus, Flat on His Back." *NR*, 151 (Sept. 19, 1964), 21–26.
————. "Review of *Mr. Sammler's Planet*." *Harpers*, 240 (Feb. 1970), 106–14.
Howe, Irving. ed. *Saul Bellow, Herzog, Text and Criticism.* New York: Viking Press, 1976.
Josipovici, Gabriel, ed. *The Portable Saul Bellow.* New York: Viking, 1974.
Kazin, Alfred. "My Friend Saul Bellow." *Atl*, 215 (Jan. 1965), 51–54.
————. "The World of Saul Bellow." *In Contemporaries.* Boston: Little, Brown, 1962. Pp. 217–23.
Malin, Irving, ed. *Saul Bellow and the Critics.* New York: New York U., 1967.
————. *Saul Bellow's Fiction.* Carbondale: Southern Illinois U., 1969.
Opdahl, Keith M. *The Novels of Saul Bellow: An Introduction.* University Park: Pennsylvania State U., 1967.
Overbeck, Pat T. "The Women in *Augie March*." *TSLL*, 10 (Fall 1968), 471–84.
Pinsker, Sanford. "The Psychological Schlemiels of Saul Bellow." In *The Schlemiel as Metaphor: Studies in the Yiddish and American Jewish Novel.* Carbondale: Southern Illinois U., 1971. Pp. 125–57.
Podhoretz, Norman. "The Adventures of Saul Bellow." In *Doings and Undoings.* New York: Farrar, Straus and Giroux, 1964. Pp. 205–27.
Porter, M. Gilbert. *Whence the Power? The Artistry and Humanity of Saul Bellow.* Columbia: U. Missouri, 1974.
Rovit, Earl. *Saul Bellow.* Minneapolis: U. Minnesota Pamphlets on American Writers, No. 65. Minnesota: U. Minnesota, 1967.

———, ed. *Saul Bellow: A Collection of Critical Essays*. Englewood Cliffs: Prentice-Hall, 1974.

Scheer-Schazler, Brigitte. *Saul Bellow*. New York: Frederick Unger, 1972.

Schulz, Max F. "Saul Bellow and the Burden of Selfhood." In *Radical Sophistication: Studies in Contemporary Jewish-American Novelists*. Athens: Ohio U., 1969. Pp. 110–53.

Scott, Nathan A., Jr. "Bellow's Vision of the 'Axial Lines.' " In *Three American Moralists: Mailer, Bellow, Trilling*. Notre Dame: U. Notre Dame, 1973. Pp. 101–49.

Shulman, Robert. "The Style of Bellow's Comedy." *PMLA*, 83 (Mar. 1968), 109–17.

Sokoloff, B. A. *Saul Bellow: A Comprehensive Bibliography*. Folcroft, Penn.: Folcroft Library Editions, 1972.

Stasio, Marilyn. "On *The Last Analysis*." In *Broadway's Beautiful Losers*. New York: Delacorte, 1972. Pp. 238–61.

Stock, Irwin. "The Novels of Saul Bellow." *SouR*, 3 (Winter 1967), 13–42.

Tanner, Tony. *Saul Bellow*. Edinburgh: Oliver & Boyd, 1965.

Trachtenberg, Stanley. "Saul Bellow's *Luftmenschen:* The Compromise with Reality." *Critique*, 9 (Summer 1967), 37–61.

Weber, Ronald. "Bellow's Thinkers." *WHR*, 22 (Autumn 1968), 305–13.

Weinberg, Helen. "The Heroes of Saul Bellow's Novels." In *The New Novel in America: The Kafkan Mode in Contemporary Fiction*. Ithaca: Cornell U., 1970. Pp. 55–107.

Sara Blacher Cohen
State University of New York at Albany
Albany, New York

ROBERT BLY (1926–   )

Criticism of Robert Bly's poetry generally identifies three bright strands: the mystical, the surreal, and the unrhetorical. Reconciling these diversities is challenging enough; Bly's ownership of his own press only complicates the finished fabric. He published his earlier work and that of others under the label of The Sixties Press, Madison, Minnesota. Now his own books are published by major presses, but what Bly renamed The Seventies Press is still a going business.

At least three critics emphasize Bly's mystic vision. Hall, reminded of Thomas Hardy and Wallace Stevens, characterizes Bly as "mysterious, of the mouth and imagination." For Heyen, Bly is "symbolic and mystical"; in a Yeatsian sense there is a "moving inward"—being able to talk to a tree, a leaf of grass, a grain of sand. Piccione describes the process as a mode of thinking, an arrival at an "inner vision." In his dissertation he analyzes Bly's poetry in order to define and exemplify the "deep image . . . a re-creation of conditions through which the unconscious is engaged and communicated . . . a mystical awareness." Elsewhere Piccione describes Bly's language as a kind of "sensory epiphany," or what Libby calls "a sense of apocalyptic crisis . . . [using] surrealist imagery." Hall talks about "fantastic images . . . developed irrationally, with intensity

. . . ." Friedman notes Bly's use of experimental devices "to embody . . . an intensely imagined world."

What Heyen has called "unrhetorical" in Bly, Poulin calls sparsity of "wit or literary allusion . . . topical allusion abounds . . . . Myth is made rather than drawn upon." Zweig calls it "the sort of low-brow poetry that Whitman and Crane wrote." Others, in what Rosenthal has identified as "the Bly group," who have turned away from the arcane, highly allusive poetry of Eliot and Pound, are echoing Whitman instead of Donne. Poulin views this as a waning of the influence of the New Criticism.

This moving away from the literary to the topical allusion coincides, perhaps, with Bly's own keen political and social awareness. The businessman-poet refused a $5,000 grant offered to his Sixties Press by the National Foundation on the Arts and Humanities because of his opposition to government policies; accepting the National Book Award for his *The Light Around the Body*, Bly spoke out vehemently against the war in Vietnam.

Major Works

Twenty Poems. Madison, Minn.: Sixties Press, 1961. [poetry of Georg Trakl, tr. by Bly and James Wright]
The Lion's Tail and Eyes; Poems Written out of Laziness and Silence. Madison, Minn.: Sixties Press, 1962. [poetry by Bly, James Wright, and William Duffy]
Silence in the Snowy Fields. Middletown, Conn.: Wesleyan U., 1962. New enlarged edition, London: Cape, 1967. [poetry]
Light Around the Body. Scranton: Harper, 1967. [poetry]
I Do My Best Alone at Night. Washington: Charioteer, 1968. [poetry of Gunnar Ekelöf, tr. by Bly and Christina Paulsten]
The Morning Glory. Another thing that will never be my friend. Santa Cruz, Calif.: Kayak, 1969. [poetry]
Shadow Mothers: Poetry. Scranton: Harper, 1970. [poetry]
The Teeth-Mother Naked at Last. San Francisco: City Lights, 1970. [poetry]
Neruda and Vallejo: Selected Poems. Boston: Beacon, 1971. [tr. by Bly, John Knoepfle, and James Wright]
Night Vision. Northwood Narrows, N.H.: Lillabulero, 1971. London: London Magazine Editions, 1972. [poetry of Thomas Tranströmer, tr. by Bly]
Poems for Tennessee. Martin, Tenn.: Tennessee Poetry Press, 1971. [poetry by Bly, William Stafford, and William Matthews]
Jumping Out of Bed. Barre, Mass.: Barre, 1972. [poetry]
Lorca and Jiminez: selected poems. Boston: Beacon, 1973. [tr. by Bly]
Sleepers Joining Hands. Scranton: Harper, 1973. [poetry]
Leaping Poetry: An Idea with Poems and Translation. Boston: Beacon, 1975.
The Morning Glory. New York: Harper, 1975. [prose poems]
Old Man Rubbin' His Eyes. Greensboro, N.C.: Unicorn, 1975. [poetry]
Friends, You Drank Some Darkness. Boston: Beacon Press, 1975. [poetry of Harry Martinson, Gunnar Ekelöf, and Tomas Tranströmer, tr. by Bly]

Checklist of Secondary Sources

Burke; *CA; CP.*

Alexander, Franklyn. "Robert Bly/Bibliography." *GLR*, 3 (Summer 1976), 66–69.
Calhoun, Richard. "On Robert Bly's Protest Poetry." *TPJ*, 2 (Winter 1969). [this and other entries listed below appear in a special Bly number of *TPJ*]
Hall, Donald. "The Expression Without the Song." *MQR*, 8, 4 (1969), 223–25.

———. "American Expressionist Poetry." *Serif*, 1 (Apr. 1, 1964), 18–19.

Heyen, William. "Inward to the World." *FarP*, 3 (Fall/Winter 1969), 42–50.

Janssens, G. A. M. "The Present State of American Poetry: Robert Bly and James Wright." *ES*, 51 (Apr. 1970), 112–37.

Lensing, George and Ronald Moran. *Four Poets and the Emotive Imagination: Robert Bly, James Wright, Louis Simpson, and William Stafford.* Baton Rouge: Louisiana State U., 1976.

Libby, Anthony. "Fire and Light, Four Poets to the End and Beyond." *IR*, 4 (Spring 1973), 111–26. [Bly, Ted Hughes, James Dickey, W. S. Merwin]

Poulin, A., Jr. "Contemporary American Poetry: The Radical Tradition." *ConcP*, 3 (Fall 1970), 5–21.

Piccione, Anthony. "Robert Bly and the Deep Image." Ph.D. diss., Ohio U., 1969.

Rosenthal, M. L. *The New Poets. American and British Poetry since World War II.* London, Oxford and New York: Oxford, 1967. [identifies "the Bly group"]

Sage, Frances. "Robert Bly: His Poetry and Literary Criticism." *DAI* 35:5423A .

Scheele, Roy. "On Bly." *TPJ*, 2 (Winter 1969).

Steele, Frank. "Three Questions Answered." *TPJ*, 2 (Winter 1969).

Zweig, Paul. "The American Outsider." *MA*, 12 (Fall 1968), 517–19.

Franklyn Alexander
Northeastern Illinois University
Chicago, Illinois

VANCE N. BOURJAILY (1922–   )

Iowan Vance Bourjaily's critical reputation has never reached the heights it seemed destined for when Aldridge spoke of Bourjaily's first novel, *The End of My Life,* as "the most neglected but, in many ways, the most promising" of all the novels about World War II. Aldridge backed his judgment by giving Bourjaily more than twice the space he devoted to Mailer's *The Naked and the Dead,* but it was not a judgment other critics would share, nor would Aldridge maintain it for long. Bourjaily's work has received very little serious critical attention since Aldridge's early book. While each of his novels has been widely reviewed, only one has received a strongly favorable reception. Ironically, that one is probably his least skillful and most sentimental novel, *The Man Who Knew Kennedy.*

Reviewers have often found fault with what they regard as Bourjaily's verbosity and with the apparent lack of structure of the last four of his six novels; Mailer described his besetting sin as slickness. Less seriously, he has been accused of a preoccupation with sex and a trendy interest in ecology. His subject has been the generation which grew to maturity during World War II and its subsequent difficulties, and reviewers have recognized Bourjaily as an accurate and sometimes moving delineator of that generation as well as a skillful manager of dramatic scenes. But only recently has serious attention been paid to Bourjaily's interesting experiments with narrative which reached a climax with the publication of *Now Playing at Canterbury* in 1976.

MAJOR WORKS

The End of My Life. New York: Scribner, 1947. [novel]
The Hound of Earth. New York: Scribner, 1955. [novel]
The Violated. New York: Dial, 1958. [novel]
Confessions of a Spent Youth. New York: Dial, 1960. [novel]
The Unnatural Enemy. New York: Dial, 1963. [on hunting]
The Man Who Knew Kennedy. New York: Dial, 1967. [novel]
Brill Among the Ruins. New York: Dial, 1970. [novel]
Country Matters. New York: Dial, 1973. [essays]
Now Playing at Canterbury. New York: Dial, 1976. [novel]

CHECKLIST OF SECONDARY SOURCES

Burke; *CA;* Herzberg; *LLC; OCAL.*

Aldridge, John W., *After the Lost Generation*. New York: McGraw-Hill, 1951. Pp. 117–32.
Bourjaily, Vance N. "A Certain Kind of Work." In *Afterwords*, ed. Thomas McCormack. New York: Harper, 1969. Pp. 176–91. [essay on the writing of *Confessions of a Spent Youth*]
Dienstfrey, Harris. "The Novels of Vance Bourjaily." *Commentary* (Apr. 30, 1961), 360–63.
Frakes, James R. Review of *Brill among the Ruins. NYTBR,* Nov. 1, 1970, p. 5.
Francis, William A. "The Motif of Names of Bourjaily's *The Hound of Earth." Critique,* 17 (1976), 64–72.
———. "The Novels of Vance Bourjaily: A Critical Analysis." *DAI,* 36:4487A–88A.
Hicks, Granville. "The Generation of the Assassination." *SatR,* 50 (Feb. 4, 1967), 35.
Madden, Charles E. "Vance Bourjaily." In *Talks With Authors*. Carbondale: Southern Illinois U., 1968. Pp. 204–14.
Mailer, Norman. *Advertisements for Myself*. New York: Putnam, 1959. Pp. 468–69.
McMillen, William. "The Public Man and the Private Novel: Bourjaily's *The Man Who Knew Kennedy." Critique,* 17 (1976), 86–95.
——— and John Muste. "A Vance Bourjaily Checklist . . . ." *Critique,* 17 (1976), 105–10.
Muste, John M., "The Second Major Subwar: Four Novels of Vance Bourjaily." In *The Shaken Realist*, ed. Melvin Friedman and John W. Vickery. Baton Rouge: Louisiana State U., 1970. Pp. 311–26.
———. "The Fractional Man as Hero: Bourjaily's *Confessions of a Spent Youth." Critique,* 17 (1976), 73–85.
Nichols, Lewis. "Interview." *New York Times,* Aug. 31, 1958, p. 8.
Towner, Daniel. "Brill's Ruins and Henderson's Rains." *Critique,* 17 (1976), 96-104.

John Muste
Ohio State University
Columbus, Ohio

LOUIS BROMFIELD (1896–1956)

During his long career Bromfield wrote thirty books—novels, collections of short stories and of nature pieces, and practical farming treatises. Throughout his life he remained one of America's most prolific, widely read, and financially successful writers, and he managed to acquire new audiences without losing the old. He earned more than a million dollars by his writing, much of which went into his agricultural enterprises.

Bromfield's early fiction was regarded by his contemporary critics as brilliant; he was considered the most promising of his contemporaries, and in 1926 he received the Pulitzer Prize. Nevertheless, by the early 1930s his reputation deteriorated under the onslaught of critics of the *Nation* and the *New Republic*, and it has not recovered to any great extent, largely because academic critics have refused to consider the few reassessments that have appeared.

Actually, Bromfield's work, from his early fiction to his last farming studies, has been remarkably consistent in theme and philosophy as well as in remarkably lucid prose. In philosophy, Bromfield was a Jeffersonian democrat, seeking to define the Jeffersonian ideal that had been destroyed by what he considered Hamiltonian industrialism of the late nineteenth century. His farming ventures in Ohio and the works that grew out of them were based upon his conviction that Jeffersonianism was a valid philosophy, even in the industrial twentieth century. A successful proponent of the eighteenth-century ideal throughout his career, he recognized at the end of his life that he had not made it a reality, and his last years were marked by personal and philosophical frustration.

MAJOR WORKS

The Green Bay Tree. New York: Stokes, 1924. [novel]
Possession. New York: Stokes, 1925. [novel]
Early Autumn. New York: Stokes, 1926. [novel]
A Good Woman. New York: Stokes, 1927. [novel]
The Strange Case of Miss Annie Spragg. New York: Stokes, 1928. [novel]
Awake and Rehearse. New York: Stokes, 1929. [stories]
Twenty-Four Hours. New York: Stokes, 1930. [novel]
A Modern Hero. New York: Stokes, 1932. [novel]
The Farm. New York: Harper, 1934. [novel]
Here Today and Gone Tomorrow. New York: Harper, 1934. [stories]
The Man Who Had Everything. New York: Harper, 1935. [novel]
The Rains Came. New York: Harper, 1937. [novel]
It Takes All Kinds. New York: Harper, 1939. [stories]
Night in Bombay. New York: Harper, 1940. [novel]
Wild Is the River. New York: Harper, 1941. [novel]
Until the Day Break. New York: Harper, 1942. [novel]
Mrs. Parkington. New York: Harper, 1943. [novel]
The World We Live In. New York: Harper, 1944. [stories]
What Became of Anna Bolton. New York: Harper, 1944. [novel]
Pleasant Valley. New York: Harper, 1945. [essays]
A Few Brass Tacks. New York: Harper, 1946. [essays]
Kenny. New York: Harper, 1947. [novel]
Colorado. New York: Harper, 1947. [novel]
Malabar Farm. New York: Harper, 1948. [essays]
The Wild Country. New York: Harper, 1948. [novel]
Out of the Earth. New York: Harper, 1950. [essays]
Mr. Smith. New York: Harper, 1951. [novel]
A New Pattern for a Tired World. New York: Harper, 1954. [essays]
From My Experience. New York: Harper, 1955. [essays]
Animals and Other People. New York: Harper, 1955. [essays]

CHECKLIST OF SECONDARY SOURCES

Anderson, David D. "Dimensions of the Midwest." In *MidAmerica I*. East Lansing, Mich.: Center for the Study of Midwestern Literature, 1974. P. 13.

―――. *Louis Bromfield*. New York: Twayne, 1964.

Anon. *"Here Today and Gone Tommorrow."* *Nation*, 137 (Apr. 25, 1934), 486. [rev.]

Bongartz, Roy. "Malabar Farm: Louis Bromfield's Paradise Lost." *New York Times*, May 19, 1974, p. 9.

Bromfield, Mary. "The Writer I Live With." *Atl*, 166 (Aug. 1950), 77–79.

Brown, Morrison. *Louis Bromfield and His Books*. Fair Lawn, N.J.: Essential, 1957.

Caldwell, Erskine. "Brilliant and Tedious." *Nation*, 137 (Sept. 6, 1933), 277.

Canby, Henry Seidel. "America Concentrated." *SatR*, 7 (Sept. 20, 1930), 137.

Cargill, Oscar. *Intellectual America*. New York: Macmillan, 1948.

Carter, John. "A Middle Western Factory Town." *NYTBR*, Mar. 30, 1924, p. 5.

Commager, Henry Steele. "Louis Bromfield Looks Backward." *SatR*, 9 (Aug. 19, 1933), 49.

Fadiman, Clifton. "A Modern Novelist." *Nation*, 135 (July 13, 1932), 40.

Geld, Ellen Bromfield. *The Heritage: A Daughter's Memories of Louis Bromfield*. New York: Harper, 1962.

Hutchinson, Percy. "Mr. Bromfield's Story of a Philanderer." *NYTBR*, May 1, 1932, p. 6.

Lohrke, Eugene. "Satirist—and Victim." *Nation*, 131 (Nov. 5, 1930), 503.

Lord, Russell. "Afterword." In Louis Bromfield, *The Farm*. New York: New American Library, 1961.

Marble, Annie Russell. "Louis Bromfield." In *A Study of the Modern Novel*. New York: Appleton, 1928.

Meyer, Roy W. *The Middle Western Farm Novel in the Twentieth Century*. Lincoln, Neb.: U. Nebraska, 1965.

Smith, Harrison. "Babbitt of a New Generation." *SatR* (Aug. 25, 1951), 12.

Stein, Gertrude. *The Autobiography of Alice B. Toklas*. New York: Harcourt, 1933.

Wagenknecht, Edward. *Cavalcade of the American Novel*. New York: Holt, 1952.

White, E. B. Review of *Malabar Farm*. *NY*, 24 (May 8, 1948), 104.

Wilson, Edmund. "What Became of Louis Bromfield." *NY*, 20 (Apr. 1, 1944), 80.

David D. Anderson
Michigan State University
East Lansing, Michigan

GWENDOLYN BROOKS (1917–   )

Scholarship has not yet caught up with the vigorous career of Gwendolyn Brooks. In spite of the extraordinary range of her accomplishments, no full-length study of her works has yet appeared. She is widely acclaimed as recipient of the Pulitzer Prize for *Annie Allen* in 1949 and later was named Poet Laureate of Illinois. But until recently, with few exceptions, critical reception of her writings had been limited to reviews, newspaper articles, and brief mentions in more general studies.

Recent commentary is identifying the "new" Gwendolyn Brooks with the Black Renaissance of the sixties and seventies, and at the same time discovering what has always been central in her works. Critics now see that her move into the "new" scene was natural. Her acknowledged influence today on almost all black writers is stimulating closer study of her complex career. Foremost in recognition of Brooks's achievements are tributes by her students and fellow poets (like Lee and Rivers). Lee and others recently edited *To Gwen With Love* (Chicago: Johnson, 1971), an anthology dedicated to Brooks. Loff's checklist is useful and detailed.

MAJOR WORKS

A Street in Bronzeville. New York: Harper, 1945. [poems]
Annie Allen. New York: Harper, 1949. [poems]
Maud Martha. New York: Harper, 1953. [novel]
Bronzeville Boys and Girls. New York: Harper, 1956. [poems]
The Bean Eaters. New York: Harper, 1960. [poems]
Selected Poems. New York: Harper, 1963.
In the Mecca. New York: Harper, 1968. [poems]
Riot. Detroit: Broadside, 1969. [poems]
Aloneness. Detroit: Broadside, 1971. [poems]
A Broadside Treasury. Detroit: Broadside, 1971. [anthol.]
Family Pictures. Detroit: Broadside, 1971. [poems]
Jump Bad: A New Chicago Anthology. Detroit: Broadside, 1971.
The World of Gwendolyn Brooks. New York: Harper, 1971. [includes *A Street in Bronzeville*, *Annie Allen*, *Maud Martha*, *The Bean Eaters*, and *In the Mecca*]
The Black Position. Detroit: Broadside, 1971. [periodical]
Report From Part One: An Autobiography. Detroit: Broadside, 1972.

CHECKLIST OF SECONDARY SOURCES

Burke; *CA; CB; CP*; Herzberg; *LLC; OCAL; TCA Supp.*

Angle, Paul M. *We Asked Gwendolyn Brooks about the Creative Environment in Illinois*. Chicago: Bell Telephone, n.d. [interview]
Baker, Houston A. "The Achievement of Gwendolyn Brooks." *CLA*, 16 (Sept. 1972), 23–31.
Bird, Leonard G. "Gwendolyn Brooks: Educator Extraordinaire." *Discourse*, 12 (1969), 158–66.
Brown, Frank London. "Chicago's Great Lady of Poetry." *ND*, 11 (Dec. 1961), 53–57.
"The Creative Person: Gwendolyn Brooks." Film by WTTW, Chicago, for NET (Bloomington, Indiana: Indiana U., n.d.)
Crockett, Jacqueline. "An Essay on Gwendolyn Brooks." *NHB*, 19 (Nov. 1955), 37–39.
Davis, Arthur P. "The Black-and-Tan Motif in the Poetry of Gwendolyn Brooks." *CLA*, 6 (1962), 90–97.
———. "Gwendolyn Brooks: A Poet of the Unheroic." *CLA*, 7 (1963), 114–25.
Drotning, Phillip T. and Wesley W. South. "Gwendolyn Brooks: Poet Laureate." In *Up From the Ghetto*. New York: Cowles, 1970. Pp. 170–76.
Furman, Marva Riley. "Gwendolyn Brooks: The 'Unconditioned' Poet." *CLA*, 17 (1973), 1–10.
Garland, Phyl. "Gwendolyn Brooks: Poet Laureate." *Ebony*, 23 (July 1968), 48–50.
Hansell, William H. "Aestheticism Versus Political Militancy in Gwendolyn Brooks's 'The Chicago Picasso' and 'The Wall.' " *CLA*, 17 (1973), 11–15.
———. "Positive Themes in the Poetry of Four Negroes: Claude McKay, Countee Cullen, Langston Hughes, and Gwendolyn Brooks." Ph.D. diss., U. Wisconsin, 1972.
Hudson, Clenora F. "Racial Themes in the Poetry of Gwendolyn Brooks." *CLA*, 17 (1973), 16–20.
Jaffe, Dan. "Gwendolyn Brooks: An Appreciation from the White Suburbs." In *The Black American Writer, II: Poetry and Drama*, ed. C. W. E. Bigsby. DeLand, Fla.: Everett/Edwards, 1969. Pp. 89–98.
Kent, George E. "Gwen's Way." Preface to *Report From Part One: An Autobiography*. Detroit: Broadside, 1972. Pp. 31–35.
———. "The Poetry of Gwendolyn Brooks." Parts I and II, *BW*, 20 (Sept. and Oct., 1971), 30–43; 36–48, 68–71.
Loff, John M. "Gwendolyn Brooks: A Bibliography." *CLA*, 17 (Sept. 1973), 21–32.

Lee, Don L. "The Achievement of Gwendolyn Brooks." *BlS*, 3 (Summer 1972), 32–41.

———. "Gwendolyn Brooks: Beyond the Wordmaker—The Making of an Afro-American Poet." Preface to *Report From Part One: An Autobiography*. Detroit: Broadside, 1972.

Lewis, Ida. "Conversation: Gwen Brooks and Ida Lewis." *Essence*, 1 (Apr. 1971), 26–31. [interview]

Miller, Jeanne Marie A. "Poet Laureate of Bronzeville, U.S.A." *Freedomways*, 10 (1970), 63–75.

Newquist, Roy., ed. "Gwendolyn Brooks." In *Conversations*. New York: Rand McNally, 1967. [interview]

Rivers, Conrad K. "The Poetry of Gwendolyn Brooks." *ND*, 13 (June 1964), 67–68.

Shands, Annette Oliver. "Gwendolyn Brooks as Novelist." *BW*, 22 (June 1973), 22–30.

Stavros, George. "An Interview with Gwendolyn Brooks." *ConL*, 2 (Winter 1970), 1–20.

Ronald Primeau
Central Michigan University
Mt. Pleasant, Michigan

WILLIAM RILEY BURNETT (1899–   )

Aside from periodical and newspaper reviews, Burnett's nearly three dozen novels have received scant critical attention. There is no suitable bibliography of primary or secondary sources, and Marsh's reviews, which span a quarter of a century, are the most penetrating discussion of Burnett's fiction.

In his first novel, *Little Caesar*, a study of the Chicago underworld, Burnett established patterns he was to follow later. His trademark became a hard-boiled realistic style characterized by objective observation, vernacular diction, concise sentences, and fast-paced action. A succession of tough, Midwestern-born protagonists (gangsters, prize fighters, petty gamblers, jazz musicians, crooked politicians, con men, and drifters) encountered the big city and, more often than not, retreated to their Ohio (Burnett's home state), Indiana, or Kentucky homes. The sensational success of *Little Caesar* and the film made from it led Burnett to Hollywood and a second career as screenwriter. Most of his subsequent novels have been made into films—some more than once. Although literary historians and critics have ignored his fiction, Burnett has had an important role in shaping the conventions of gangster films and fiction.

MAJOR WORKS

Little Caesar. New York: Dial, 1929. [novel]
Iron Man. New York: Dial, 1930. [novel]
The Giant Swing. New York: Harper, 1932. [novel]
Dark Hazard. New York: Harper, 1933. [novel]
High Sierra. New York: Knopf, 1940. [novel]
The Asphalt Jungle. New York: Knopf, 1949. [novel]

CHECKLIST OF SECONDARY SOURCES

CA; CAB; TCA & Supp.

Anon. "W. R. Burnett." *WLB*, 7 (1932), 284–86. [biography]
Corliss, Richard, ed. "W. R. Burnett." In *The Hollywood Screenwriters*. New York: Avon, 1972. Pp. 297–98. [filmography]
Gorman, Herbert. Review of *Iron Man. NYHTBR*, Jan. 5, 1930, p. 4.
Grella, George. "The Gangster Novel: The Urban Pastoral." In *Tough Guy Writers of the Thirties*, ed. by David Madden. Carbondale: Southern Illinois U., 1968. Pp. 186–98. [criticism]
Kazin, Alfred. "King Cole." *NHTBR*, Oct. 4, 1936, p. 9. [rev.]
Marsh, Fred T. Review of *The Giant Swing. NYTBR*, Sept. 4, 1932, p. 7.
———. "Goodbye to the Past." *NYTBR*, Sept. 9, 1934, p. 7. [rev.]
———. "The Goodhues of Sinking Creek." *NYTBR*, Nov. 11, 1934, p. 6. [rev.]
———. Review of *High Sierra. NYTBR*, Mar. 10, 1940, p. 6.
———. "Underdog." *NYHTBR*, Feb. 17, 1957, p. 3. [rev.]
Poore, C. B. Review of *Dark Hazard. NYTBR*, Sept. 3, 1933, p. 7.
Terry, C. V. "Tomorrow's Another Day." *NYTBR*, Nov. 18, 1945, p. 12. [rev.]

Jon F. Patton
University of Toledo
Toledo, Ohio

HOLGER CAHILL (1893–1960)

Opinions differ sharply on Cahill's work. The anonymous critic for *NYTBR* sees *Profane Earth* as "rather hewn out—a strong, honest, ungainly novel that has a great deal of turbulence and some beauty." The reviewer for the *Nation* thinks it might have been a reasonably satisfactory naturalistic novel if Dreiser had never existed.

Hass finds *The Shadow of My Hand* rich in both characterization and in the description of the land, with its sights and smells. For him that novel is comparable with Rolvaag's *Giants in the Earth* in terms of elemental strength. On the other hand, Willingham thinks *Shadow*, albeit reflecting a strong love of the northern prairie land, fails because it is loaded down with a trite, romantic, love story. Van Ghent sees Cahill failing in an attempt to do for Illinois (but the story is laid in North Dakota!) what Hardy did for Wessex.

Meyer notes that Cahill brought sexual frankness (and even the subject of homosexuality) to the farm novel, where it had been notably absent before 1920. Milton thinks that the writer has gone beyond physical description to the influence of the land on the development of man's spirit. Jacobson, who has made a study of the novels of North Dakota, finds *Shadow* "vividly imbued with the feel, sight, sound, and smell of farming . . . a novel in which the soil itself becomes more important than plot and character."

Major Works

Profane Earth. New York: Macaulay, 1927. [novel]
A Yankee Adventurer: The Story of Ward and the Taiping Rebellion. New York: Macaulay, 1930. [historical account]
Look South to the Polar Star. New York: Harcourt, 1947. [novel]
The Shadow of My Hand. New York: Harcourt, 1947. [novel]
[Cahill also wrote and edited a number of works on American art.]

Checklist of Secondary Sources

Burke; Warfel.

Anon. Review of *Profane Earth. NYTBR,* Oct. 2, 1927, p. 8.
_____. Review of *Shadow of My Hand. Time,* 67 (Mar. 5, 1956), 117–18.
_____. Review of *Profane Earth. Nation,* 125 (Nov. 2, 1927), 484.
Hass, Victor P. "It's the Land that Counts." *NYTBR,* Mar. 4, 1956, p. 5. [rev. of *Shadow*]
Jacobson, Harvey K. "A Study of Novels about North Dakota." Master's thesis, U. North Dakota, 1956.
Meyer, Roy W. *The Middle Western Farm Novel in the Twentieth Century.* Lincoln: U. Nebraska, 1965. Pp. 196–97, 204.
Milton, John. "The Dakota Image." *SDR,* 8 (Autumn 1970), 16–17. [criticism]
Vanderhoff, Jack. *A Bibliography of Novels Related to American Frontier and Colonial History.* Troy, N.Y.: Whitston, 1971.
Van Ghent, Dorothy. "Technique and Vision: Some Recent Fiction." *YR,* 45 (1955–56), 633.
Willingham, John R. "Technique Above Comment." *Nation,* 182 (June 16, 1956), 516–17. [rev. of *Shadow*]

Mary Ellen Caldwell
University of North Dakota
Grand Forks, North Dakota

WILL[IAM MCKENDREE] CARLETON (1845–1912)

Carleton attained local prominence in 1868 with readings of his campaign poem "Fax," and national prominence in 1871 through the widely-circulated "Betsey and I are Out." Carleton's poetry, including "Over the Hill to the Poorhouse," has suffered almost complete eclipse in the twentieth century. Once a valued property of the publishing firm of Harper, Carleton was treated respectfully by contemporary critics and lauded by biographers for his stress on Victorian virtues and pious sentimentality. Later critics, particularly Pattee, have found his use of midwestern dialect contrived and his agrarian localism debased. Sloane has recently argued that realistic elements of dialect and agrarian and urban setting give his poetry historical importance. Carleton, a Michigan native, spent most of his later life in Boston and New York, publishing verse and plays.

Major Works

Farm Ballads. New York: Harper, 1873. [poems]
Farm Legends. New York: Harper, 1876. [poems]

Young Folks' Centennial Rhymes. New York: Harper, 1876. [poems]
Farm Festivals. New York: Harper, 1881. [poems]
City Ballads. New York: Harper, 1885. [poems]
City Legends. New York: Harper, 1890. [poems]
City Festivals. New York: Harper, 1892 [poems]
Rhymes of Our Planet. New York: Harper, 1895. [poems]
Songs of Two Centuries. New York: Harper, 1902. [poems]
Drifted In. New York: Moffat, Yard, 1908. [poems]

CHECKLIST OF SECONDARY SOURCES

Blanck; *CHAL; DAB;* Herzberg; *LHUS.*

Anon. "World Biographies." *Literary World,* 15 (Jan. 15, 1884), 28–29. [bio-bibliography]
Bolton, Sarah K. *Famous American Authors.* New York: Crowell, 1887. Pp. 326–44.
Corning, A. Elwood. *Will Carleton: A Biographical Study.* New York: Lanmere, 1917.
Finney, Byron A. *Will Carleton.* Lansing: Michigan Historical Commission, 1917.
M'Alpine, Frank. *Our Album of Authors: A Cyclopedia of Popular Literary People.* Philadelphia: Elliot & Beezley, 1886. Pp. 69–73.
Pattee, Fred L. *A History of American Literature since 1870.* New York: Century, 1916. Pp. 322-23, 352.
Sloane, David E. E. "In Search of a Realist Poetic Tradition." *ALR,* 5 (Fall 1972), 489–91.
———. "Will Carleton: Toward Poetic Realism." *MarkR,* 4 (1975), 81–85.
[Trowbridge, J. T.] "Will Carleton." *Harper,* 68 (Mar. 1884), 572–79.

David E. E. Sloane
University of New Haven
West Haven, Connecticut

ALICE (1820–71) AND PHOEBE (1824–71) CARY

Since the inseparable Cary sisters died the same year, their work has been generally left undisturbed by literary archaeologists, except Fred Lewis Pattee, who admired especially Alice's two early series of "Clovernook" sketches about life on a midwestern farm. He describes these as "the first piece of Hamlin Garland-like realism to come out of the Middle Border lands . . . some ten years before Hamlin Garland was born." Onderdonk— the only historian of American poetry to give the sisters more than passing notice—was less interested in their writings than in their having established in the Sunday evening receptions that they held for fifteen years in their little house on Twentieth Street in New York City what their memorialist, novelist Mary Clemmer Ames, calls "the nearest approach to the first ideal blue-stocking reception ever reached in this country." Pattee also considers these Sunday nights that Horace Greeley and others attended, "so famous indeed that no treatise on the literary 1850s and 1860s can neglect" them. Mrs. Ames reports that Edgar Allan Poe pronounced Alice's "Pictures of Memory," "one of the most musically perfect lyrics in the English language," but Onderdonk calls the remark "perhaps only another instance of that critic's indiscriminate use of the superlative in treating of female poets." Onderdonk himself observes that "Alice's song was tender, musical, and deep, with a touch of mysticism; Phoebe's was buoyant, hopeful, and vigorous." Perhaps the Carys could scarcely have been expected to appeal to times beyond their own if we can trust Mrs. Ames's observation that in hundreds of notices of Alice's death, "the remarkable feature is that no matter how remote the journal in which each was published, it was more an expression of individual sorrow at the departure of a beloved friend, than of mere regret at the death of an author." Their collected works were last reprinted in 1903, though they are represented in anthologies such as Alfred Kreymborg's *Lyric America* as late as 1930.

MAJOR WORKS

[Completely separating the productions of the Carys is difficult because bits of Phoebe's verse keep cropping up in Alice's books. The following arrangement suggests as nearly as possible their shared and separate achievements. For many contributions to gift-books and lyrics for sheet music, consult Blanck.]

Joint Publications:

The Poems of Alice and Phoebe Cary. Philadelphia: Moss and Brother, 1850.
The Josephine Gallery. New York: Derby and Jackson, 1856. [biographical sketches]
Eds. *From Year to Year: A Token of Remembrance.* New York: Leavitt, 1869. [gift book]
The Last Poems of Alice and Phoebe Cary. Ed. by Mary Clemmer Ames. New York: Hurd and Houghton, 1873.
Ballads for Little Folks. Ed. by Mary Clemmer Ames. New York: Hurd and Houghton, 1874.
Early and Late Poems of Alice and Phoebe Cary. Boston: Houghton Mifflin, 1887.

Major Works of Alice Cary:

Clovernook, or Recollections of Our Neighborhood in the West. New York: Redford, 1852. Second series, 1853. [stories and sketches]
Lyra and Other Poems. New York: Redford, 1852.
Hagar, A Story of Today. New York: Redford, 1852. [novel]
Clovernook's Children. Boston: Ticknor and Fields, 1855. [sketches]
Poems. Boston: Ticknor and Fields, 1855.
Married, Not Mated; or, How They Lived at Woodside and Throckmorton Hall. New York: Derby and Jackson, 1856. [novel]
Pictures of Country Life (announced as "Clovernook Revisited"). New York: Derby and Jackson, 1856. [stories and sketches]
The Adopted Daughter, and Other Tales. Philadelphia: Smith, 1859.
Ballads, Lyrics, and Hymns. New York: Hurd and Houghton, 1866.
The Bishop's Son. New York: Carleton, 1867. [novel]
Snow-Berries, A Book for Young Folks. Boston: Ticknor and Fields, 1867.
A Lover's Diary. Boston: Ticknor and Fields, 1868. [poems]
"The Born Thrall," 17 chapters in *The Revolution* (women's suffrage weekly), New York, 1870. [unfinished novel].

Major Works of Phoebe Cary:

Poems and Parodies. Boston: Ticknor and Fields, 1854.
Poems of Faith, Hope and Love. New York: Hurd and Houghton, 1868.

CHECKLIST OF SECONDARY SOURCES

BDAL; Blanck; Burke; *DAB; OCAL.*

Ames, Mary Clemmer. *A Memorial of Alice and Phoebe Cary.* New York: Hurd and Houghton, 1873.

Coggeshall, William T. *The Poets and Poetry of the West: With Biographical and Critical Notes.* Columbus: Follett, Soter, 1860.

Greeley, Horace. "Alice and Phoebe Cary." In *Eminent Women of the Age.* Hartford: Betts, 1868. Pp. 164–72.

Griswold, Rufus. *The Female Poets of America.* Philadelphia: Carey and Hart, 1859.

Onderdonk, James J. *History of American Verse (1610–1897).* Chicago: McClurg, 1901. Pp. 263–64.

Pattee, Fred Lewis. *The Feminine Fifties.* New York: Appleton, 1940.

Pulsifer, Janice G. "Alice and Phoebe Cary: Whittier's Sweet Singers of the West." *Essex Historical Institute Coll.,* 109 (Jan. 1973), 9–59.

Warren French
Indiana University–Purdue University
Indianapolis, Indiana

WILLA CATHER (1873–1947)

Significant recognition came to Willa Cather after 1915 when critics and fellow artists (e.g., Bourne and Mencken, Lewis, and Dell) praised her for painting the landscape of the West genuinely and peopling it with flesh and blood characters. After 1920 Cather was impelled to stress a dual theme: the sunset of the pioneer, and the victory of a repugnant industrial materialism. The elegiac tone then adopted was not out of keeping with the widespread disillusion of the postwar years. As the decade progressed, the nation arrived at an unusual degree of unanimity concerning the quality of Cather's work, particularly in regard to its artistry, which usually meant an unqualified admiration for her style, called "classic."

Critics of the Depression decade, concerned more with content than art, and valuing message above style, seized upon Cather's attention to the American past as evidence of a major and debilitating failure to cope with contemporary themes. Led by Marxists, the effort attempted a direct reversal of the Cather cult, and criticism during the decade took on its most strident, negative tone. "Escape" and "retreat" became common epithets in the process of assigning Cather and her works to an era dead and buried and of no interest to the living. Her essay "The Novel Démeublé" was not immune to the charge of irrelevance to the times. Ironically, Cather's public reputation and popularity were then attaining their peaks.

These extremes notwithstanding, no study of the American literary scene after 1920 was complete without a chapter estimating Cather's contribution. Prior to her death, only one book, the Rapin study, had been devoted solely to her; but after 1947 a number of indispensable works appeared. Valuable memoirs came from Sergeant, Lewis, and Moorhead. Even more notable was Bennett's study of Cather in the Red Cloud years, which provided a base for future source criticism. The critical biography by Brown and Edel set a standard for future examinations of Cather's life and art.

More recent criticism has been concerned with identifying unities of theme and idea in the total sweep of Cather's work. This has been a goal of both Greene and Edel, while Randall has given voice to the same concern, Cather's "search for value," in subtitling his volume. Critics interested in the biographical strand have been hampered by Cather's outright destruction of letters and her refusal to allow other correspondence to be printed. Nevertheless, substantial collections of letters have survived and been put to profitable use, most notably in Woodress's comprehensive introduction to Cather.

Cather's inclusion as the sole woman in Bryer's *Fifteen Modern American Authors* (1969) reflected the author's respected position and encouraged a further wave of interest. Prior to this, in Red Cloud, the Willa Cather Pioneer Memorial had dedicated itself to preserving sites employed in the fiction and to collecting Cather correspondence, editions, and other memorabilia. More recently, the University of Nebraska Press has nourished scholars with bountiful collections of early Cather fiction and journalism, with original studies, and with reprints of essential critical/biographical volumes.

One value of current scholarship is its tendency to restore proportion by turning from heavily studied novels (*My Ántonia, Death Comes for the Archbishop*) toward redefining the place of neglected works such as *My Mortal Enemy*. In addition, two fresh strands of criticism show promise: one involves itself with Cather in relationship to feminism; the other explores the mythic dimensions of her fiction. The significance of viewing Cather as a woman will surely depend upon further biographical discoveries and/or disclosures. Myth criticism, already a provocative vein of inquiry, revitalizes the suggestion that Cather is concerned less with topicalities than with universals.

MAJOR WORKS

April Twilights. Boston: Badger, 1903. [poems]
The Troll Garden. New York: McClure, Phillips, 1905. [stories]
Alexander's Bridge. Boston: Houghton Mifflin, 1912. [novel]
O Pioneers! Boston: Houghton Mifflin, 1913. [novel]
My Autobiography. New York: Stokes, 1914. (Ostensibly by S. S. McClure, but actually by Cather.) [biography]
The Song of the Lark. Boston: Houghton Mifflin, 1915. [novel]
My Ántonia. Boston: Houghton Mifflin, 1918. [novel]
Youth and the Bright Medusa. New York: Knopf, 1920. [stories]
One of Ours. New York: Knopf, 1922. [novel]
A Lost Lady. New York: Knopf, 1923. [novel]
The Professor's House. New York: Knopf, 1925. [novel]
My Mortal Enemy. New York: Knopf, 1926. [novel]
Death Comes for the Archbishop. New York: Knopf, 1927. [novel]
Shadows on the Rock. New York: Knopf, 1931. [novel]

Obscure Destinies. New York: Knopf, 1932. [stories]
Lucy Gayheart. New York: Knopf, 1935. [novel]
Not Under Forty. New York: Knopf, 1936. [essays]
Sapphira and the Slave Girl. New York: Knopf, 1940. [novel]
The Old Beauty and Others. New York: Knopf, 1948. [stories]
Willa Cather on Writing. New York: Knopf, 1949. [essays]
Writings from Willa Cather's Campus Years. Ed. by James R. Shively. Lincoln: Nebraska, 1950. [essays and stories]
Five Stories by Willa Cather. New York: Knopf, 1956.
Willa Cather in Europe. New York: Knopf, 1956. [journalism]
Early Stories of Willa Cather. New York: Dodd, Mead, 1957.
The Kingdom of Art. Ed. by Bernice Slote. Lincoln: U. Nebraska, 1966. [journalism]
Collected Short Fiction 1892–1912. Ed. by Virginia Faulkner. Lincoln: U. Nebraska, 1970.
The World and the Parish. Ed. by William M. Curtin. 2 vols. Lincoln: U. Nebraska, 1970. [journalism]
Uncle Valentine and Other Stories. Ed. by Bernice Slote. Lincoln: U. Nebraska, 1973.

CHECKLIST OF SECONDARY SOURCES

Adams, J. Donald. *The Shape of Books to Come*. New York: Viking, 1944. Pp. 120–25.
Andes, Cynthia J. "The Bohemian Folk Practice in 'Neighbour Rosicky.' " *WAL*, 7 (1972), 63–64.
Auchincloss, Louis. *Pioneers and Caretakers*. Minneapolis: U. Minnesota, 1964. Pp. 92–122.
Baker, Bruce, II. "Nebraska Regionalism in Selected Works of Willa Cather." *WAL*, 3 (1968), 19–35.
Baum, Bernard. "Willa Cather's Waste Land." *SAQ*, 48 (Oct. 1949), 589–601.
Beer, Thomas. "Miss Cather." *The Borzoi 1925*. New York: Knopf, 1925. Pp. 23–30.
Bennett, Mildred R. "How Willa Cather Chose her Names." *Names*, 10 (Mar. 1962), 29–37.
_____. *The World of Willa Cather*. New York: Dodd, Mead, 1951. (Reprinted, Lincoln: U. Nebraska, 1961). [biography]
Bloom, Edward A. and Lillian D. Bloom. *Willa Cather's Gift of Sympathy*. Carbondale: Southern Illinois U., 1962.
Bogan, Louise. "American Classic." *NY*, 7 (Aug. 8, 1931), 19–22.
Bourne, Randolph. "Morals and Art from the West." *Dial*, 65 (Dec. 14, 1918), 556–57. [review essay]
Boynton, Percy H. *America in Contemporary Fiction*. Chicago: U. Chicago, 1940. Pp. 150–63.
Brooks, Van Wyck. *The Confident Years: 1885–1915*. New York: Dutton, 1955. Pp. 527–33.
Brown, E. K. and Leon Edel. *Willa Cather: A Critical Biography*. New York: Knopf, 1953.
Brown, Marion M. and Ruth Crone. *Willa Cather: The Woman and Her Works*. New York: Scribner, 1970.
Butcher, Fanny. *Many Lives—One Love*. New York: Harper, 1972.
Carroll, Latrobe. "Willa Sibert Cather." *Bookman*, 54 (May 1921), 212–14. [interview]
Canby, H. S. "Willa Cather (1876–1947)." *SatR*, 30 (May 10, 1947), 22–24.
Charles, Sr., Isabel, O. P. "Love and Death in Willa Cather's *O Pioneers!*" *CLAJ*, 9 (1965), 140–50.
_____. "*My Ántonia*: A Dark Dimension." *WAL*, 2 (1967), 91–108.
Connolly, Francis X. "Willa Cather: Memory as Muse." In *Fifty Years of the American Novel*. Ed. Harold C. Gardiner, S.J. New York: Scribner, 1951. Pp. 69–87.
Daiches, David. *Willa Cather: A Critical Introduction*. Ithaca: Cornell U., 1951.
Edel, Leon. *Willa Cather: The Paradox of Success*. Washington: Library of Congress, 1960. [pamphlet]
Fadiman, Clifton. "Willa Cather: The Past Recaptured." *Nation*, 135 (Dec. 7, 1932), 563–65.
Feger, Lois. "The Dark Dimension of Willa Cather's *My Ántonia*." *EJ*, 69 (Sept. 1970), 775–79.
Ferguson, J. M. " 'Vague Outlines': Willa Cather's Enchanted Bluffs." *WR*, 7 (1970), 61–64.
Fisher, Dorothy Canfield. "Daughter of the Frontier." *NYHT* Magazine Section, May 28, 1933, p. 7.
Folsom, James K. *The American Western Novel*. New Haven: College and University Press, 1966. Pp. 189–91.

Footman, Robert H. "The Genius of Willa Cather." *AL*, 10 (May 1938), 123–41.

Forman, Henry J. "Willa Cather: A Voice from the Prairie." *SwR*, 47 (1962), 248–58.

Fox, Maynard. "Two Primitives: Huck Finn and Tom Outland." *WAL*, 1 (1966), 26–33.

Gale, Robert L. "Willa Cather and the Usable Past." *NR*, 42 (1961), 181–90.

Geismar, Maxwell. *The Last of the Provincials*. Boston: Houghton Mifflin, 1947. Pp. 153–222.

Gelfant, Blanche H. "The Forgotten Reaping-Hook: Sex in *My Ántonia*." *AL*, 60 (Mar. 1971), 60–82.

Gerber, Philip L. *Willa Cather*. Boston: Twayne, 1975.

———. "Willa Cather and the Big Red Rock." *CE*, 19 (Jan. 1958), 152–57.

Giannone, Richard. *Music in Willa Cather's Fiction*. Lincoln: U. Nebraska, 1966.

Greene, George. "Willa Cather at Mid-Century." *Thought*, 32 (1957), 577–92.

Harper, Marion. "The West of Twain and Cather." *DilR*, 14 (1966), 60–80.

Hart, Clive. "*The Professor's House*: A Shapely Story." *MLR*, 67 (1972), 271–81.

Hartwick, Harry. *The Foreground of American Fiction*. New York: American, 1934. Pp. 389–404.

Hatcher, Harland. *Creating the Modern American Novel*. New York: Farrar, 1935. Pp. 58–71.

Helmick, Evelyn T. "Myth in the Works of Willa Cather." *MASJ*, 9 (1968), 63–69.

Herron, Ima H. *The Small Town in American Literature*. Durham: Duke U., 1939. Pp. 394–403.

Hilfer, Anthony C. *The Revolt from the Village 1915–1930*. Chapel Hill: U. North Carolina, 1969. Pp. 84–110.

Hinz, Evelyn J. "Willa Cather's Technique and the Ideology of Populism." *WAL*, 7 (1972), 47–61.

Hinz, John. "A Lost Lady and 'The Professor's House.' " *VQR*, 29 (Winter 1953), 70–85.

———. "Willa Cather in Pittsburgh." *New Colophon*, 3 (1950), 198–207.

———. "Willa Cather—Prairie Spring." *PrS*, 23 (1949), 82–89.

Hoffman, Frederick J. *The Modern Novel in America*. Chicago: Regnery, 1951. Pp. 52–65.

———. *The Twenties*. Rev. ed. New York: Free Press, 1962. Pp. 181–90.

Jobes, Lavon M. "Willa Cather's *The Professor's House*." *UR*, 34 (1967), 154–60.

Jones, Howard Mumford. *The Bright Medusa*. Urbana: U. Illinois, 1952.

———. "The Novels of Willa Cather." *SatR*, 18 (Aug. 6, 1938), 3–4.

Kazin, Alfred. *On Native Grounds*. New York: Reynall and Hitchcock, 1942. Pp. 247–64.

Kronenberger, Louis. "Willa Cather." *Bookman*, 74 (Oct. 1931), 134–40.

Lathrop, JoAnna, comp. *Willa Cather: A Checklist of Her Published Writing*. Lincoln: U. Nebraska, 1975.

Lee, Robert Edson. *From East to West*. Urbana: U. Illinois, 1966. Pp. 112–35.

Lewis, Edith. *Willa Cather Living*. New York: Knopf, 1953. [memoir]

Lewisohn, Ludwig. *Expression in America*. New York: Harper, 1932. Pp. 538–43.

Martin, Terence. "The Drama of Memory in *My Ántonia*." *PMLA*, 84 (Mar. 1969), 304–11.

McFarland, Dorothy T. *Willa Cather*. New York: Ungar, 1972.

McNamara, Robert. "Phases of American Religion in Thornton Wilder and Willa Cather." *CathW*, 135 (Sept. 1932), 641–49.

Mencken, H. L. "Willa Cather." *The Borzoi 1925*. New York: Knopf, 1925. Pp. 28–31.

Meyer, Roy W. *The Middle Western Farm Novel in the Twentieth Century*. Lincoln: U. Nebraska, 1965. Pp. 38–47.

Miller, James E., Jr. "*My Ántonia*: A Frontier Drama of Time." *AQ*, 10 (1958), 476–84.

———. "The Nebraska Encounter: Willa Cather and Wright Morris." *PrS*, 41 (1967), 165–67.

Moorhead, Elizabeth. *These Too Were Here*. Pittsburgh: U. Pittsburgh, 1950. [memoir]

Morris, Lloyd. "Willa Cather." *NAR*, 219 (Apr. 1924), 641–52.

Murphy, John J., ed. *Five Essays on Willa Cather*. North Andover, Mass.: Merrimack College, 1974.

———. "The Respectable Romantic and the Unwed Mother: Class Consciousness in *My Ántonia*." *CLQ*, 10 (1973), 149–56.

Nyquist, Edna. "The Significance of the Locale in the Nebraska Fiction of Willa Cather, Especially in *My Ántonia*." *WSL*, 2 (1965), 81–89.

Overton, Grant. *An Hour of the American Novel*. Philadelphia: Lippincott, 1929. Pp. 148–152.

_____. *The Women Who Make Our Novels*. New York: Moffat, Yard, 1918. Pp. 254–66.
Pers, Mona. *Willa Cather's Children*. Stockholm: Almqvist, 1975.
Quinn, Arthur Hobson. *American Fiction*. New York: Appleton, 1936. Pp. 683–97.
Randall, John H., III. *The Landscape and the Looking Glass*. Boston: Houghton Mifflin, 1960.
_____. "Willa Cather and the Decline of Greatness." *The Twenties: Poetry and Prose*. Eds. Richard E. Langford and William E. Taylor. Deland: Everett Edwards, 1966. Pp. 78–81.
Rapin, René. *Willa Cather*. New York: McBride, 1930.
Rascoe, Burton. "Contemporary Reminiscences." *Arts and Decoration*, 20 (Apr. 1924), p. 28. [interview]
_____. *We Were Interrupted*. New York: Doubleday, 1947. Pp. 316–19. [portrait]
Schneider, Sr., Lucy, C.S.J. "*O Pioneers!* in the light of Willa Cather's 'Land Philosophy.' " *CLQ*, 8 (1968), 55–70.
Schroeter, James, ed. *Willa Cather and Her Critics*. Ithaca: Cornell U., 1967. [criticism]
Seibel, George. "Willa Cather and the Village Atheist." *PrS*, 41 (1967), 168–71.
Sergeant, Elizabeth Shepley. *Fire Under the Andes*. New York: Knopf, 1927. Pp. 261–82.
Sherman, Stuart. *Critical Woodcuts*. New York: Scribner, 1926. Pp. 32–48.
Slote, Bernice. "Willa Cather." *Sixteen Modern American Authors*. Ed. Jackson Bryer. Durham: Duke U., 1974. Pp. 29–73. [bibliography, criticism]
_____. *Willa Cather: A Pictorial Memoir*. Lincoln: U. Nebraska, 1974.
_____. "Willa Cather as a Regional Writer." *KQ*, 2 (1970), 7–15.
Slote, Bernice and Virginia Faulkner, eds. *The Art of Willa Cather*. Lincoln: U. Nebraska, 1975. [essays]
Snell, George. *The Shapers of American Fiction*. New York: Dutton, 1947. Pp. 140–55.
Stegner, Wallace. "Willa Cather, *My Ántonia*." In *The American Novel*. New York: Basic Books, 1965. Pp. 144–53.
Stouck, David. *Willa Cather's Imagination*. Lincoln: U. Nebraska, 1975.
Stuckey, William J. "*My Ántonia*: A Rose for Miss Cather." *SNNTS*, 4 (1972), 473–83.
Sullivan, Patrick. "Willa Cather's Southwest." *WAL*, 7 (1972), 25–37.
Tittle, Walter. "Glimpses of Interesting Americans: Willa Cather." *Century*, 110 (July 1925), 309–13. [interview]
Van Doren, Carl. *The American Novel 1789–1939*. New York: Macmillan, 1940. Pp. 281–93.
Van Ghent, Dorothy. *Willa Cather*. Minneapolis: U. Minnesota, 1964.
Wagenknecht, Edward. *Cavalcade of the American Novel*. New York: Holt, 1952. Pp. 319–38.
Walker, Don D. "The Western Humanism of Willa Cather." *WAL*, 1 (1966), 75–90.
West, Rebecca. *The Strange Necessity*. New York: Doubleday, Doran, 1928. Pp. 233–48.
White, George L. "Willa Cather." *SR*, 50 (Jan. 1942), 18–25.
Winsten, Archer. "A Defense of Willa Cather." *Bookman*, 74 (Mar. 1932), 634–40.
Woodress, James. *Willa Cather: Her Life and Art*. New York: Western, 1970.
Yongue, Particia Lee. "*A Lost Lady:* The End of the First Cycle." *WAL*, 7 (1972), 3–12.
Zabel, Morton Dauwen. "Willa Cather." *Nation*, 164 (June 14, 1947), 713–16.

Philip L. Gerber
State University of New York
Brockport, New York

MARY HARTWELL CATHERWOOD (1847–1902)

Mary Hartwell Catherwood was highly regarded in her own time for historical fiction and realistic representation, but her affinities for sentimentality and sheer romance obscure her genuine worth as a writer. Simonds and

McMahon reflect the tone of the criticism of the turn of the century; reviews of her work as it appeared are numerous and lavish in their praise. Pattee points out that she was among the first to attempt to set down in a realistic manner details of rural life in a belt of the Midwest roughly bisected by the Old National Trail through Ohio, Indiana, and Illinois. Banta gives her prominence as a regionalist for two areas, the Midwest and the Great Lakes–St. Lawrence complex. Fullerton cites the approval of Parkman (introduction to *Dollard*) as evidence of her accurate knowledge and careful research but notes her unfortunate tendency to melodrama. Her eminent success as a writer of juveniles is established by Dondore.

Modern scholarship devoted to Catherwood is extremely limited. Price lists her short stories as examples of the best work ever done in their peculiar areas of local color; she emerges as a forerunner of the school of realism. The novels themselves draw little attention these days; they suffer from sentimentality and melodrama, but they are historically sound. Shumaker agrees with Price and Banta that a main fault is the attempt to fictionalize historical personages rather than to fictionalize around them. Shumaker maintains that because of her pioneering in local color, regionalism, realism, and romance, and since she was the first woman writer of prominence west of the Alleghenies and the first with a college degree, she deserves a re-evaluation in the history of American fiction.

MAJOR WORKS

A Woman in Armor (Mary Hartwell). New York: G. W. Carleton, 1875. [novel]
Craque-o'-Doom. Philadelphia: Lippincott, 1881. [novel]
The Romance of Dollard. Introd. by Francis Parkman. New York: Century, 1889. [novel]
The Story of Tonty. Chicago: McClurg, 1890. [novel]
The Lady of Fort St. John. Boston: Houghton Mifflin, 1891. [novel]
Old Kaskaskia. Boston: Houghton Mifflin, 1893. [novel]
The White Islander. New York: Century, 1893. [novel]
The Chase of Saint-Castin and Other Stories of the French in the New World. Boston: Houghton Mifflin, 1894.
The Spirit of an Illinois Town, and The Little Renault: Two Stories of Illinois at Different Periods. Boston: Houghton Mifflin, 1897. [novelettes]
The Days of Jeanne D'Arc. New York: Century, 1897. [novel]
Spanish Peggy; A Story of Young Illinois. Chicago: Stone, 1899. [novel]
The Queen of the Swamp, and Other Plain Americans. Boston: Houghton Mifflin, 1899. [stories]
Mackinac and Lake Stories. New York: Harper, 1899. [stories]
Lazarre. Indianapolis: Bowen-Merrill, 1901. [novel]

CHECKLIST OF SECONDARY SOURCES

Blanck; *CHAL; DAB; LHUS.*

Banta, R. E. *Hoosier Caravan, A Treasury of Indiana Life and Love*. Bloomington: Indiana U., 1951. P. 309.
———. *Indiana Authors and Their Books, 1816–1916*. Crawfordsville, Ind.: Wabash College, 1949. Pp. 54–56.
Catherwood, Mary H., ed. "Western Association of Writers, Souvenir No. 2: Proceedings of the Fifth Annual Convention." N.p., n.d.
Dennis, Charles H. *Eugene Field's Creative Years*. Garden City: Doubleday, 1924. Pp. 130–34.

Dondore, Dorothy. *The Prairie and the Making of Middle America.* Cedar Rapids, Iowa: Torch Press, 1926. Pp. 370–71.

Earle, M. T. *"Lazarre,* a Review." *Book Buyer,* 23 (1901), 235–36.

Fullerton, Bradford M. *Selective Bibliography of American Literature, 1775–1900.* New York: Payson, 1932. Pp. 46–47.

Kunitz, Stanley J. and Howard Haycraft. *American Authors, 1600–1900.* New York: Wilson, 1938. Pp. 138–39.

Leary, Edward A. "Hoosier Woman Among Earliest Female Writers." *Indianapolis Star,* Nov. 14, 1971, p. 47.

McMahon, Helen. *Criticism of Fiction: A Study of Trends in the* Atlantic Monthly, *1857–1898.* New York: Bookman, 1952.

Pattee, Fred Lewis. *A History of American Literature since 1870.* New York: Century, 1917. Pp. 258–59.

———, ed. *Century Readings in the American Short Story.* New York: Century, 1927. P. 394. [preface to "Windigo"]

Price, Robert. "A Critical Biography of Mary Hartwell Catherwood: A Study of Middle Western Regional Authorship, 1847–1902." Ph.D. diss., Ohio State U., 1943.

———. "Mary Hartwell Catherwood: A Bibliography." *ISHSJ,* 33 (1940), 68–77.

———. "Mrs. Catherwood's Early Experiments with Critical Realism." *AL,* 17 (1945), 140–51.

Quinn, Arthur H. *American Fiction.* New York: Appleton, 1936. Pp. 488–89.

Scudder, H. E. "Mary Hartwell Catherwood's *Romance of Dollard." Atl,* 65 (1890), 125. [rev.]

Shumaker, Arthur W. *A History of Indiana Literature.* North Manchester: Indiana Historical Society, 1962. Pp. 300–10.

Simonds, W. E. "Mary Hartwell Catherwood as a Writer." *Critic,* 42 (1903), 169–71.

Warfel, Harry, and G. Harrison Orians. *American Local Color Stories.* New York: American Book, 1941. Pp. xxiii, 383.

Weggand, James L. *Winona Holiday: The Story of the Western Association of Writers.* Nappanee, Ind.: Author, 1948. Pp. 1–45.

Wilson, Milton L. *Biography of Mary Hartwell Catherwood.* Newark, Ohio: American Tribune Printery, 1904.

Bertrand F. Richards
Indiana State University
Terre Haute, Indiana

WINSTON CHURCHILL (1871–1947)

Winston Churchill, a native of St. Louis, was one of the most popular American novelists between 1900 and 1920. Four or five decades ago he was taken seriously by a group of literary scholars largely nurtured in the genteel tradition, most of whom concentrated on his early contributions in the historical romance (Cooper, Pattee, Quinn). Churchill's reputation had slipped precipitously, however, long before his death in 1947. Since World War II, he has become little more than a footnote in literary studies.

Students of cultural history and historians of ideas have provided the bulk of the more recent scholarship on Churchill. The Hofstadters consider his novels as social documents reflecting the conflict between business and moral values. Walcutt shows Churchill struggling vainly to reconcile his basic romantic, genteel proclivities with the new science of the Progressive era. Titus's Twayne study is a brief survey of the man's life and writing that presents him as a barometer of popular reading tastes as well as a popularizer of ideas that marked the Progressive mind from 1900 to 1917. Schneider's biography was written with the advantage of access to Churchill papers unavailable to previous scholars; it sheds new light on Churchill's retirement from active authorship but does not alter the basic portrait of his role in the Progressive era. Two studies (Speare and Milne) have been concerned with Churchill solely as a political novelist. Despite some renewed scholarly interest in his problem novels, the only Churchill works currently in print are the two best-selling historical romances, *Richard Carvel* and *The Crisis*.

Major Works

The Celebrity. New York: Macmillan, 1898. [novel]
Richard Carvel. New York: Macmillan, 1899. [novel]
The Crisis. New York: Macmillan, 1901. [novel]
The Crossing. New York: Macmillan, 1904. [novel]
The Title-Mart. New York: Macmillan, 1905. [play]
Coniston. New York: Macmillan, 1906. [novel]
Mr. Crewe's Career. New York: Macmillan, 1908. [novel]
A Modern Chronicle. New York: Macmillan, 1910. [novel]
The Inside of the Cup. New York: Macmillan, 1913. [novel]
A Far Country. New York: Macmillan, 1915. [novel]
The Dwelling-Place of Light. New York: Macmillan, 1917. [novel]
A Traveller in War-Time. New York: Macmillan, 1918. [essays]
Dr. Jonathan. New York: Macmillan, 1919. [play]
The Uncharted Way. Philadelphia: Dorrance, 1940. [essay]

Checklist of Secondary Sources

Burke; *CAA;* Herzberg; *OCAL; TCA & Supp.*

Chapman, E. J. "Winston Churchill: Popularizer of Progressivism." *DartColLibBul*, 8 (Apr. 1968), 43–50.

Clemens, Cyril. "A Visit with the American Winston Churchill." *Hobbies*, 52 (May 1947), 144–45. [interview]

Cooper, Frederic T. "Some Representative American Story Tellers: XII—Winston Churchill." *Bookman*, 31 (May 1910), 246–53.

Crapa, Joseph. "Progressives in Search of a Usable Past: The Role of a Native Tradition of Idealism in the Social Novels of David Graham Phillips, Winston Churchill, and Robert Herrick, 1900–1917." *DAI*, 36:4484A.

Ellis, J. Breckenridge. "Missourians Abroad—No. 11, Winston Churchill." *MHR*, 16 (July 1922), 517.

Griffin, Lloyd W. "Winston Churchill, American Novelist." *MB*, 23 (Nov. 1948), 331–38.

Hofstadter, Richard and Beatrice. "Winston Churchill: A Study in the Popular Novel." *AQ*, 2 (Spring 1950), 12–28.

Irvin, Frederic B. "The Didacticism of Winston Churchill." Ph.D. diss. U. Pittsburgh, 1947.

Killat, Johannes. *Das Amerikabild des Romanschriftstellers Winston Churchill*. Berlin: Junker and Dunnhaupt, 1940.

Milne, Gordon. *The American Political Novel*. Norman: U. Oklahoma, 1966. Pp. 87–95.

Noble, David W. *The Eternal Adam and the New World Garden*. New York: Braziller, 1968. Pp. 140–44.

Noble, David W., Robert W. Schneider, and Miriam M. Heffernan. "Two Novelists and Progressivism." *MQ*, 3 (Jan. 1962), 149–82.

Oi, Koji. "The Railroad and the Pastoral Ideal in Winston Churchill's Political Novels." *SEL* (Japan), 43 (Mar. 1967), 229–44.

Parsons, H. V. *"The Tory Lover, Oliver Wiswell, and Richard Carvel."* *CLQ*, 9 (Dec. 1971), 220–31.

Pattee, Fred Lewis. *The New American Literature, 1890–1930*. New York: Century, 1930. Pp. 93–98.

Quinn, Arthur H. *American Fiction*. New York: Appleton, 1936. Pp. 496–501.

——. *Novelist to a Generation: The Life and Thought of Winston Churchill*. Bowling Green: Bowling Green U. Popular Press, 1976.

Speare, Morris E. *The Political Novel: Its Development in England and in America*. New York: Oxford U., 1924.

Titus, Warren I. "The Progressivism of the Muckrakers: A Myth Re-examined Through Fiction." *JCMVASA*, 1 (Spring 1960), 10–16.

——, ed. "The Senator and the Author: Beveridge—Churchill Correspondence." *IMH*, 55 (June 1959), 169–78.

——. *Winston Churchill*. New York: Twayne, 1963.

——. "Winston Churchill, American: A Critical Biography." Ph.D. diss. New York U. 1957.

——. "Winston Churchill." *AmLitR*, 1 (Fall 1967), 26–31. [biblio-essay]

Underwood John. *Literature and Insurgency*. New York: Kennerley, 1914.

Walcutt, Charles C. *American Literary Naturalism, A Divided Stream*. Minneapolis: U. Minnesota, 1956. Pp. 157–179.

——. *The Romantic Compromise in the Novels of Winston Churchill*. U. Michigan Contributions in Modern Philology, No. 18 (1951).

Warren I. Titus
George Peabody College for Teachers
Nashville, Tennessee

SAMUEL LANGHORNE CLEMENS [MARK TWAIN] (1835–1910)

Three attitudes often stand out among Mark Twain critics. Some of the more visceral keep their gusto for both the unique man and his writings, for every personal squabble or literary by-blow that gets exhumed; so much material is available now that they dream of assuming his psyche vicariously. Other critics have grown wary, weary, and even lax about keeping up with the still rising flood of commentary. Others, more aggressively, are getting impatient with his continuing resistance to formulas and with the radiating gaps in what was once simply a DeVoto-Brooks polarity. For whatever reasons surprisingly few overall readings of his work have shouldered forward in recent years.

The busiest lines of scholarship are concentrating on some segment of his career. Also, two projects have lured at least fifty specialists into dogged prospecting, much of it over ground they thought they already knew. The Mark Twain Papers edition, which has already issued nine volumes, will bring out many fresh letters, the full notebooks, more autobiography, and the remaining manuscript; eventually it will make stay-at-home expertise feasible. The Iowa/California edition, which has produced two volumes thus far, will not only refurbish the texts of his standard books but set up the canon of his newspaper and magazine pieces. These editions may swing his last decade into the right perspective within a writing career of practically fifty years. Even in that privately tormented decade he led a banqueting outer life. Recently he has drawn homage from both the establishment and the counter-cultures. In the search for reassurances that personality matters more than electronic tape, Mark Twain most eminently pulses with a fallible yet tenacious vitality.

MAJOR WORKS

The Celebrated Jumping Frog of Calaveras County, and Other Sketches. New York: Webb, 1867. [humorous pieces]
The Innocents Abroad. Hartford: American, 1869. [travel]
Roughing It. Hartford: American, 1872. Also, Franklin R. Rogers, ed. In *The Works of Mark Twain*, II. Berkeley: U. California, 1972. [travel]
The Gilded Age (with Charles Dudley Warner). Hartford: American, 1873. [novel]
Mark Twain Speaking, Paul Fatout, ed. Iowa City: U. Iowa, 1976. [speeches]
Mark Twain's Sketches, New and Old. Hartford: American, 1875. [humorous pieces]
The Adventures of Tom Sawyer. Hartford: American, 1876. [novel]
A Tramp Abroad. Hartford: American, 1880. [travel]
The Prince and the Pauper. Boston: Osgood, 1882. [novel]
The Stolen White Elephant. Boston: Osgood, 1882. [humorous pieces]
Life on the Mississippi. Boston: Osgood, 1883. [travel]
Adventures of Huckleberry Finn. New York: Webster, 1885. [novel]
A Connecticut Yankee in King Arthur's Court. New York: Webster, 1889. [novel]
The American Claimant. New York: Webster, 1892. [novel]
The £1,000,000 Bank Note and Other New Stories. New York: Webster, 1893. [fiction]
Tom Sawyer Abroad. New York: Webster, 1894. [novel]
The Tragedy of Pudd'nhead Wilson and the Comedy of Those Extraordinary Twins. Hartford: American, 1894. [novel]
Personal Recollections of Joan of Arc. New York: Harper, 1896. [biography]
Tom Sawyer, Detective, and Other Stories. New York: Harper, 1896. [fiction]
Following the Equator. Hartford: American, 1897. [travel]
How to Tell a Story and Other Essays. New York: Harper, 1897. [literary essays]
The Man That Corrupted Hadleyburg and Other Stories and Essays. New York: Harper, 1900. [miscellany]
What Is Man? Privately printed, 1906. Also, Paul Baender, ed. *"What Is Man?" and Other Philosophical Writings.* In *The Works of Mark Twain*, XIX. Berkeley: U. California, 1973. [philosophical dialogue]
The $30,000 Bequest and Other Stories. New York: Harper, 1906. [fiction]
Christian Science. New York: Harper, 1907. [polemic]
Extract from Captain Stormfield's Visit to Heaven. New York: Harper, 1909. [moral fable]
The Mysterious Stranger. New York: Harper, 1916. But see William M. Gibson, ed. *Mark Twain's Mysterious Stranger Manuscripts.* Berkeley: U. California, 1969. [moral fable]

CHECKLIST OF SECONDARY SOURCES

Bibliographical Guides

Blanck; *LHUS*, and *Supp.*

Baldanza, Frank. *MT: An Introduction and Interpretation.* New York: Barnes & Noble, 1961. Pp. 141–46.
Beebe, Maurice and John Feaster. "Criticism of MT: A Selected Checklist." *MFS*, 14 (1968), 93–139.

Budd, Louis J. "A Listing of and Selection from Newspaper and Magazine Interviews with Samuel L. Clemens, 1874–1910." *AmLitR*, 10 (Winter 1977), 1–100.
Clark, Harry Hayden. "MT." *Eight American Authors: A Review of Research and Criticism*. Ed. James Woodress. Rev. ed. New York: Norton, 1971. Pp. 273–320.
Gale, Robert L. *Plots and Characters in the Works of MT*. 2 vols. Hamden, Conn.: Archon, 1973.
Gerber, John C. (Hamlin Hill for 1969 to 1975; Louis J. Budd for 1976–   ). "MT." Ed. James Woodress (or at times Albert E. Robbins). *American Literary Scholarship: An Annual*. Durham: Duke U., 1965–   .
Hill, Hamlin. "Who Killed MT?" *AmLitR*, 7 (1974), 119–24.
Johnson, Merle. *A Bibliography of the Works of MT*. Rev. ed. New York: Harper, 1935.
Leary, Lewis. *Articles on American Literature, 1900–1950*. Durham: Duke U., 1954. Pp. 43–55.
_____. *Articles on American Literature, 1950–1967*. Durham: Duke U., 1970. Pp. 56–77.
Tenney, Thomas Asa. *MT: A Reference Guide*. Boston: Hall, 1977.

Biography and Criticism

Anderson, Frederick, et al. eds. *MT's Notebooks and Journals*. 2 vols. Berkeley: U. California, 1975.
Andrews, Kenneth R. *Nook Farm: MT's Hartford Circle*. Cambridge: Harvard U., 1950.
Asselineau, Roger. *The Literary Reputation of MT from 1910–1950: A Critical Essay and a Bibliography*. Paris: Didier, 1954.
Baender, Paul. "The 'Jumping Frog' as a Comedian's First Virtue." *MP*, 60 (1963), 192–200.
Baetzhold, Howard G. "The Course of Composition of *A Connecticut Yankee*: A Reinterpretation." *AL*, 33 (1961), 195–214.
_____. *MT & John Bull*. Bloomington: Indiana U., 1970.
Barchilon, Jose and Joel S. Kovel. "Huckleberry Finn: A Psychoanalytic Study." *JAPA*, 14 (1966), 775–814.
Bellamy, Gladys C. *MT as a Literary Artist*. Norman: U. Oklahoma, 1950.
Benson, Ivan. *MT's Western Years*. Stanford: Stanford U., 1938.
Blair, Walter. "MT." *Native American Humor (1800–1900)*. New York: American, 1937. Reprint San Francisco: Chandler, 1960. Pp. 147–62.
_____. *MT & Huck Finn*. Berkeley and Los Angeles: U. California, 1960.
_____. "MT's Other Masterpiece: 'Jim Baker's Blue-Jay Yarn'." *SAH*, 1 (Jan. 1975), 132–47.
_____. "On the Structure of *Tom Sawyer*." *MP*, 37 (1939), 75–88.
Blues, Thomas. *MT & the Community*. Lexington: U. Kentucky, 1970.
Branch, Edgar M. *The Literary Apprenticeship of MT*. Urbana: U. Illinois, 1950.
_____. " 'My Voice is Still for Setchell': A Background Study of 'Jim Smiley and His Jumping Frog'." *PMLA*, 82 (1967), 591–601.
Brashear, Minnie M. *MT, Son of Missouri*. Chapel Hill: U. North Carolina, 1934.
Bridgman, Richard. "Henry James and MT." *The Colloquial Style in America*. New York: Oxford U., 1966. Pp. 106–30.
Brodwin, Stanley. "MT's Masks of Satan: The Final Phase." *AL*, 45 (1973), 206–27.
_____. "The Humor of the Absurd: Mark Twain's Adamic Diaries." *Criticism*, 14 (1972), 49–64.
Brooks, Van Wyck. *The Ordeal of MT*. Rev. ed. New York: Dutton, 1933.
Budd, Louis J. "MT and the Upward Mobility of Taste." Ed. Ray B. Browne. *New Voices in American Studies*. West Lafayette: Purdue U. Studies, 1966. Pp. 21–34.
_____. *MT: Social Philosopher*. Bloomington: Indiana U., 1962.
Canby, Henry Seidel. *Turn West, Turn East: MT and Henry James*. Boston: Houghton Mifflin, 1951.
Cardwell, Guy A. "Samuel Clemens' Magical Pseudonym." *NEQ*, 48 (June 1975), 175–93.
_____. *Twins of Genius*. East Lansing: Michigan State U., 1953.
Carrington, George C., Jr. *The Dramatic Unity of "Huckleberry Finn."* Columbus: Ohio State U., 1976.
Covici, Pascal, Jr. *MT's Humor: The Image of a World*. Dallas: Southern Methodist U., 1962.
Cox, James M. *MT: The Fate of Humor*. Princeton: Princeton U., 1966.
_____. "Remarks on the Sad Initiation of Huckleberry Finn." *SR*, 62 (1954), 389–405.
Cummings, Sherwood. "MT's Acceptance of Science." *CR*, 6 (1962), 245–61.

David, Beverly R. "The Pictorial *Huck Finn:* MT and His Illustrator, E. W. Kemble." *AQ*, 26 (Oct. 1974), 331–51.

DeVoto, Bernard. *MT at Work*. Cambridge: Harvard U., 1942.

———. *MT's America*. Boston: Little, Brown, 1932.

Duckett, Margaret. *MT and Bret Harte*. Norman: U. Oklahoma, 1964.

Dyson, A. E. "Huckleberry Finn and the Whole Truth." *CQ*, 3 (1961), 29–40.

Ensor, Allison. *MT & the Bible*. Lexington: U. Kentucky, 1969.

Fatout, Paul. *MT in Virginia City*. Bloomington: Indiana U., 1964.

———. *MT on the Lecture Circuit*. Bloomington: Indiana U., 1960.

Ferguson, J. DeLancey. *MT: Man and Legend*. Indianapolis: Bobbs-Merrill, 1943.

Fetterley, Judith. "Disenchantment: Tom Sawyer in *Huckleberry Finn*." *PMLA*, 87 (1972), 69–74.

Fiedler, Leslie A. "*Huckleberry Finn*: Faust in the Eden of Childhood." In *Love and Death in the American Novel*. Cleveland: World, 1960. Pp. 553–91.

Foner, Philip S. *MT: Social Critic*. New York: International, 1958.

French, Bryant Morey. *MT and "The Gilded Age": The Book That Named an Era*. Dallas: Southern Methodist U., 1965.

Ganzel, Dewey. *MT Abroad: The Cruise of the "Quaker City."* Chicago: U. Chicago, 1968.

Gerber, John C. "The Relation between Point of View and Style in the Works of MT." *Style in Prose Fiction: English Institute Essays, 1958*. Ed. Harold C. Martin. New York: Columbia U., 1959. Pp. 142–71.

Gibson, William M. *The Art of MT*. New York: Oxford U., 1976.

Gribben, Alan. "The Dispersal of Samuel L. Clemens' Library Books." *RALS*, 5 (Autumn 1975), 147–65.

Hansen, Chadwick. "The Character of Jim and the Ending of *Huckleberry Finn*." *MassR*, 5 (1963), 45–66.

Hemminghaus, Edgar H. *MT in Germany*. New York: Columbia U., 1939.

Hill, Hamlin. *MT and Elisha Bliss*. Columbia: U. Missouri, 1964.

———. *MT: God's Fool*. New York: Harper, 1973.

Hoffman, Daniel G. "MT." *Form and Fable in American Fiction*. New York: Oxford U., 1961. Pp. 317–50.

Howells, William Dean. *My MT: Reminiscences and Criticisms*. New York: Harper, 1910.

Hubbell, Jay B. "MT." *The South in American Literature, 1607–1900*. Durham: Duke U., 1954. Pp. 822–36.

Kaplan, Justin. *Mr. Clemens and MT*. New York: Simon and Schuster, 1966.

Kaul, A. N. "*Huckleberry Finn*: A Southwestern Statement." In *The American Vision: Actual and Ideal Society in Nineteenth-Century Fiction*. New Haven: Yale U., 1963. Pp. 280–304.

Krause, Sydney J. *MT as Critic*. Baltimore: Johns Hopkins U., 1967.

———. "Twain's Method and Theory of Composition." *MP*, 56 (1959), 167–77.

Leary, Lewis. "MT and the Comic Spirit," "MT's Wound," "On Writing about Writers: Especially about MT," "The Bankruptcy of MT," and "Tom and Huck: Innocence on Trial." In *Southern Excursions*. Baton Rouge: Louisiana State U., 1971. Pp. 3–110.

Long, E. Hudson. *MT Handbook*. New York: Hendricks, 1958.

Lorch, Fred W. *The Trouble Begins at Eight: MT's Lecture Tours*. Ames: Iowa State U., 1968.

Lynn, Kenneth S. *MT and Southwestern Humor*. Boston: Little, Brown, 1959.

Martin, Jay. "MT: The Dream of Drift and the Dream of Delight." In *Harvests of Change: American Literature 1865–1914*. Englewood Cliffs, N. J.: Prentice-Hall, 1967. Pp. 165–201.

Marx, Leo. "Mr. Eliot, Mr. Trilling, and Huckleberry Finn." *ASch*, 22 (1953), 423–40.

———. "Two Kingdoms of Force." *The Machine in the Garden: Technology and the Pastoral Ideal in America*. New York: Oxford U., 1964. Pp. 319–40.

Mendel'son, Moris O. *MT*. 2d ed. Moscow: Molodaia Guardiia, 1958.

Mirizzi, Piero. *MT*. Rome: Edizioni di Storia e Letteratura, 1965.

Paine, Albert Bigelow. *MT: A Biography*. New York: Harper, 1912.

Parrington, Vernon L. "The Backwash of the Frontier—MT." *Main Currents in American Thought*. New York: Harcourt, Brace, 1927–30. Vol. 3, pp. 86–101.

Pettit, Arthur G. *MT & The South*. Lexington: U. Kentucky, 1974.

Poli, Bernard. *MT: Écrivain de l'Ouest: Régionalisme et Humour*. Paris: Presses Universitaires, 1965.

Ramsay, Robert L. and Frances G. Emberson. "A MT Lexicon." *University of Missouri Studies*, 13 (1938), i–cxix, 1–278.

Regan, Robert. *Unpromising Heroes: MT and His Characters*. Berkeley and Los Angeles: U. California Press, 1966.

Rogers, Franklin R. *MT's Burlesque Patterns: As Seen in the Novels and Narratives, 1855–1885*. Dallas: Southern Methodist U., 1960.

Rosa-Clot, Paola. *L'Angoscia di MT*. Milan: U. Mursia, 1968.

Rowlette, Robert. *MT's Pudd'nhead Wilson: The Development and Design*. Bowling Green: Bowling Green U. Popular Press, 1971.

Rubin, Louis D., Jr. "MT and the Postwar Scene." *The Writer in the South: Studies in a Literary Community*. Athens: U. Georgia, 1972. Pp. 34–81.

———. "MT Tonight." *The Teller in the Tale*. Seattle: U. Washington, 1967. Pp. 52–82.

Salomon, Roger B. "MT and Victorian Nostalgia." Ed. Marston LaFrance. *Patterns of Commitment in American Literature*. Toronto: U. Toronto, 1967. Pp. 73–91.

———. *Twain and the Image of History*. New Haven: Yale U., 1961.

Scott, Arthur L. *On the Poetry of MT with Selections from His Verse*. Urbana: U. Illinois, 1966.

Sloane, David E. E. "MT's Comedy: The 1870s." *SAH*, 2 (1976), 146–56.

Smith, Henry Nash. *MT's Fable of Progress: Political and Economic Ideas in "A Connecticut Yankee."* New Brunswick: Rutgers U., 1964.

———. *MT: The Development of a Writer*. Cambridge: Harvard U., 1962.

Spengemann, William C. *MT and the Backwoods Angel: The Matter of Innocence in the Works of Samuel L. Clemens*. Kent: Kent State U., 1966.

Stone, Albert E., Jr. *The Innocent Eye: Childhood in MT's Imagination*. New Haven: Yale U., 1961.

Tanner, Tony. "MT." *The Reign of Wonder: Naivety and Reality in American Literature*. Cambridge: Cambridge U., 1965. Pp. 97–183.

Tuckey, John S. *MT and Little Satan: The Writing of "The Mysterious Stranger."* West Lafayette: Purdue U. Studies, 1963.

———. "MT's Later Dialogues." *AL*, 41 (1970), 532–42.

Turner, Arlin. *MT and G. W. Cable: The Record of a Literary Friendship*. East Lansing: Michigan State U., 1960.

———. "MT and the South: An Affair of Love and Anger." *SR*, n.s. 4 (1968), 493–519.

Wadlington, Warwick. "MT: The Authority of the Courtier." In *The Confidence Game in American Literature*. Princeton: Princeton U., Pp. 181–284.

Wagenknecht, Edward. *MT: The Man and His Work*. Rev. ed. Norman: U. Oklahoma, 1967.

Webster, Samuel C., ed. *MT, Business Man*. Boston: Little, Brown, 1946.

Wecter, Dixon. *Sam Clemens of Hannibal*. Boston: Houghton, Mifflin, 1952.

Wiggins, Robert A. *MT: Jackleg Novelist*. Seattle: U. Washington, 1964.

Young, Philip. "Adventures of Huckleberry Finn." In *Ernest Hemingway: A Reconsideration*. Rev. ed. University Park: Pennsylvania State U., 1966. Pp. 211–41.

Louis J. Budd
Duke University
Durham, North Carolina

JACK CONROY (1899–   )

Although Missourian Jack Conroy has written or edited more than ten books, only his first novel, *The Disinherited*, has received any attention from critics. The year after the publication of *The Disinherited*, both

Brewster and Elistratova wrote of the book's autobiographical focus and of its position as one of the very best works of "revolutionary realism" in American literature. In the ensuing years, the novel has had its vehement detractors; but it also has continued to receive recognition as one of the very best novels to come out of the proletarian movement of the 1930s. Luccock (in *American Mirror*) praises it for the real people "who carry their lives on the printed page." Rideout, in his study of *The Radical Novel*, contends that its rambling structure notwithstanding, *The Disinherited* has a driving vitality which gives the reader a sense of the active but undirected life of migratory workers. Aaron notes that the book can be read as a "good example of the American picaresque novel and as a graphical document of the early Depression," while Beck, in a review of the reprint of *The Disinherited* (*Chicago Tribune Magazine of Books*, May 12, 1963), compares it favorably to works by Steinbeck and Dos Passos, finding it to be a book which is "permanently valuable and still interesting." This is a judgment also shared by Larsen and Pells (both of whom offer balanced and cogent assessments of the work), and to a lesser degree by Brooks, Lewis, and Warren, who despite their reservations, consider *The Disinherited* to be "virtually the only 'proletarian novel' that is still readable as a work of some literary appeal in its own right."

Despite Conroy's more than forty years of active and influential participation in the literary world, relatively little attention has been given to his place in the history of American letters. Mangione considers his involvement in the Federal Writers' Project, Gilbert discusses his part in the formation of *Partisan Review*, Fabre examines his role as an editor, and Salzman studies the literary relationship between Conroy and H. L. Mencken. However, there is no full-length study devoted to Conroy; there is no complete bibliography, and most of his work continues to remain unavailable. What biographical information there is must be culled from such sources as Warfel and Fried, while Burke's bibliography is only a preliminary checklist. Work currently being done, however, suggests that this dismal situation may change somewhat: a bibliography is being prepared by Ken McCollum, and Salzman and David Ray are editing a collection of Conroy's writings which will include most of his long-unavailable stories and essays.

Major Works

Unrest: The Rebel Poets Anthology. Ed. with Ralph Cheyney. London: Stockwell, 1929.
Unrest: The Rebel Poets Anthology. Ed. with Ralph Cheyney. London: Studies Publications, 1930.
Unrest: The Rebel Poets Anthology. Ed. with Ralph Cheyney. New York: Harrison, 1931.
The Disinherited. New York: Covici-Friede, 1933. [novel]
A World to Win. New York: Covici-Friede, 1935. [novel]
They Seek a City: A Study of Negro Migration. With Arna Bontemps. New York: Doubleday, 1945. Rev. ed. Anyplace But Here. New York: Hill & Wang, 1966.
Midland Humor: A Harvest of Fun and Folklore. Editor. New York: Wyn, 1947. [collection]
Writers in Revolt: The Anvil Anthology. Ed. with Curt Johnson. New York: Lawrence Hill, 1973.

CHECKLIST OF SECONDARY SOURCES

CA; CN; LHUS; OCAL; Warfel.

Aaron, Daniel. Introd. to reprint of *The Disinherited.* New York: Hill & Wang, 1963.

Brewster, Dorothy and Angus Burrell. *Modern Fiction.* New York: Columbia U., 1934. Pp. 296–300.

Brooks, Cleanth, R. W. B. Lewis, and Robert Penn Warren, eds. *American Literature: The Makers and the Making.* New York: St. Martin's, 1973. Pp. 2406–7.

Burke, John Gordon. "A Preliminary Checklist of the Writings of Jack Conroy." *ABC,* 21 (June 1971), 20–24.

Davis, Cheryl. "A Rhetorical Study of Selected Proletarian Novels of the 1930's: Vehicles for Protest and Engines for Change." *DAI,* 37:32A.

Elistratova, Anne. "Jack Conroy: American Worker-Writer." *IL,* 1 (1934), 112–18.

Fabre, Michel. "Jack Conroy as Editor." *NL,* 39 (Winter 1972), 115–37.

Fried, Lewis. "Conversation with Jack Conroy." *NL,* 39 (Fall 1972), 41–56. [interview]

Gilbert, James. *Writers and Partisans: A History of Literary Radicalism in America.* New York: Wiley, 1968.

Hagglund, Ben. " . . . akin to revelation . . . . " *Carleton Misc,* 6 (Winter 1965), 62–68.

Larsen, Erling. "Jack Conroy's 'The Disinherited' or The Way It Was." In *Proletarian Writers of the Thirties.* Ed. David Madden. Carbondale: Southern Illinois U., 1968. Pp. 85–95.

Mangione, Jerre. *The Dream and the Deal: The Federal Writers' Project, 1935–1943.* Boston: Little, Brown, 1972.

Pells, Richard. *Radical Visions and American Dreams: Culture and Social Thought in the Depression Years.* New York: Harper, 1973.

Rideout, Walter. *The Radical Novel in the United States 1900–1954: Some Interrelations of Literature and Society.* Cambridge, Mass.: Harvard U., 1956.

Salzman, Jack. "Conroy, Mencken, and *The American Mercury.*" *JPC,* 7 (Winter 1973), 524–28.

Stott, William. *Documentary Expression and Thirties America.* New York: Oxford, 1973.

Jack Salzman
Long Island University
Brooklyn, New York

ROBERT COOVER (1932–   )

Critics place the fiction of Robert Coover, an Iowa native, in the contemporary experimental tradition of Barth, Barthelme, Beckett, and Borges. Scholarly evaluations center around his defining notions of reality, the relationship between life and the fiction which orders it. Scholes adopts the term "metafiction" to describe Coover's manipulation of form and reality; Schultz emphasizes the "black humor" inherent in the author's mythic cosmology; Ricks cites a surrealism which takes its meaning from the "unignorable real" of the fictional events. Gado notes that the narrative of Coover's work is naturalistic, albeit composed of bizarre and absurd events. Gass suggests that the random arrangement and rearrangement of paragraphs in the short stories are exercises in myth-making imagination. Gilman sees Coover's work as a call to our senses to note the possible substitution of one world for another.

Critical reception of Coover's work has been mostly favorable, regarding him as a developing talent. All of his major works are in print. Several of the plays have been performed professionally—*The Kid* was nominated for an "Obie" in 1972. Currently Coover is working on several novels, one of which deals with the trial of Ethel and Julius Rosenberg.

Major Works

The Origin of the Brunists. New York: Putnam, 1966. [novel]
The Universal Baseball Association, Inc., J. Henry Waugh, Prop. New York: Random House, 1968. [novel]
Pricksongs and Descants. New York: Dutton, 1969. [stories]
A Theological Position. New York: Dutton, 1971. [plays]

Checklist of Secondary Sources

CA; CN.

Blachowicz, Camille. "Robert Coover/Bibliography." *GLR*, 3 (Summer 1976), 69–73.
Dillard, E. H. W. "The Wisdom of the Beast: The Fiction of Robert Coover." *HC*, 7 (1970), 1–11.
Gado, Frank. *First Person: Conversations on Writers and Writing*. Schenectady: Union College, 1973. Pp. 142–59. [interview]
Gass, William. *Fiction and the Figures of Life*. New York: Knopf, 1970. Pp. 104–9.
Gilman, Richard. "News from the Novel." *NR*, 7 (Aug. 7, 1968), 27–36.
Harris, Charles. *The Contemporary Novel of the Absurd*. New Haven: College and University Press, 1971. Pp. 131–34.
Heckard, Margaret. "Robert Coover, Metafiction, and Freedom." *TCL*, 22 (1976), 210–27.
Lahr, John. "Mystery on the Stage." *EvR*, 13 (Dec. 1969), 53–57.
Mahin, Linda. "Experiments in Fiction: The Poetic Visions of Samuel Beckett, Jorge Luis Borges, and Robert Coover." *DAI*, 37:298A.
McCaffery, Lawrence. "The Reliance of Man on Fiction-Making: A Study of the Works of Robert Coover." *DAI*, 36:2810A.
———. "Donald Barthelme, Robert Coover, William H. Gass: Three Checklists." *BB*, 21, (July-Sept. 1974), 101–6.
Ricks, Christopher. "The Unignorable Real." *NYRB*, Feb. 12, 1970, pp. 22–24.
Scholes, Robert. "Metafiction." *IR*, 1 (Fall 1970), 100–15.
Schultz, M.F. "The Politics of Parody; the Comic Apocalypses of Jorge Luis Borges, Thomas Berger, Thomas Pynchon, and Robert Coover." In *Black Humor of the 60's*. Athens: Ohio U., 1973. Pp. 66–90.
Sheed, Wilfred. *The Morning After*. New York: Farrar, 1971. Pp. 79–82.

Camille L. Blachowicz
Foster McGaw Graduate School
Evanston, Illinois

PAUL COREY (1903–   )

No booklength studies of Corey have yet appeared. There are brief estimates in Andrews, McCown, Meyer, Paluka, and Frederick. A doctoral dissertation, at least, is in order, for Corey's fiction constitutes an important addition to the rural literature of Iowa and the Midwest.

The University of Iowa has a large collection of Corey manuscripts and papers, including the manuscript of *Three Miles Square*. The definitive bibliography through 1967 is in Paluka.

MAJOR WORKS

Three Miles Square. Indianapolis: Bobbs-Merrill, 1939. [novel]
The Road Returns. Indianapolis: Bobbs-Merrill, 1940. [novel]
County Seat. Indianapolis: Bobbs-Merrill, 1941. [novel]
Acres of Antaeus. New York: Holt, 1946. [novel]
The Planet of the Blind. London: Hale, 1968. [novel]

CHECKLIST OF SECONDARY SOURCES

CA; CB; TCA & Supp; Warfel.

Andrews, Clarence A. *A Literary History of Iowa*. Iowa City: U. of Iowa, 1972. Pp. 132–40.
Frederick, John T. "The Farm in Iowa Fiction." *Palimpsest*, 32 (1951) 141–43.
———. "Town and City in Iowa Fiction." *Palimpsest*, 35 (Feb. 1954), 89–91.
McCown, Robert A. "Paul Corey's Mast Trilogy." *BIowa*, Friends of the U. Iowa Libraries, 17 (Nov. 1972), 15–19, 23–26.
Meyer, Roy W. *The Middle-Western Farm Novel in the Twentieth Century*. Lincoln: U. Nebraska, 1965. Pp. 94–100, 119–22, 206–7, *passim*.
Paluka, Frank. *Iowa Authors: A Bio-Bibliography of Sixty Native Writers*. Iowa City: Friends of the U. Iowa Libraries, 1967.
Seabrook, William. "Pioneer Spirit, '39." *RD*, 35 (Sept. 1939), 42–46.
———. "Move over, big boys, to make room for Iowa's Paul Corey." *Des Moines Register*, Oct. 13, 1940.

Clarence A. Andrews
University of Iowa
Iowa City, Iowa

HART CRANE (1899–1932)

The resources, both scholarly and critical, available for the study of Hart Crane are unusually rich. Apart from three major biographies, ten book-length studies exist. These include solid introductions such as Hazo; Leibowitz's profound study of Crane's use of the language; and an exhaustive and brilliant textual analysis by Lewis.

Studies exist of Crane as an American poet and midwestern poet in particular; of Crane and the affirmative Whitman tradition; of Crane and Nietzsche; of Crane and the late nineteenth-century French poets; of Crane and Eliot; and of Crane and Waldo Frank. His relationship to the period and the major figures of the period has been examined in detail by scholars and critics, as has his relationship to the Elizabethan poets, Christopher Marlowe in particular.

Crane's slender output of poetry has also drawn criticism from the most respected literary figures of our time, including Allen Tate, Yvor Winters, and R. P. Blackmur, the three critics who shaped the view of *The Bridge* as a "magnificent failure." *White Buildings* received mixed reviews, though it has come to be regarded as an unquestionably superb book of poems.

Recently, the Tate, Winters, and Blackmur view of *The Bridge* has been balanced by the belief that *The Bridge* is an unqualified masterpiece. This notion of *The Bridge* was first presented with serious impact in 1960 by Louis Dembo in *Hart Crane's Sanskrit Charge*, the first book-length study of Crane. This attitude toward *The Bridge* has been continued by Hazo, Quinn, Lewis, Leibowitz, and others, and seems today to be the prevailing one.

Key West, Crane's last and posthumous collection of poems, has not drawn the detailed critical attention given his first two books—except for "The Broken Tower," Crane's magnificent last lyric, which has been worked over mercilessly by the critics. Yet *Key West* has good staying power and may someday reach the stature of *White Buildings*.

Since Crane was the kind of poet whose life was tightly ensnarled with his words, biographies and letters reveal as much about the poetry as they do the poet. Unterecker's *Voyager*, the third and largest of the biographies of Crane, reveals information hitherto kept in the family closet. While not the artistic or literary triumph that is Horton's 1937 biography (one of the great biographies of American writers), it is an exhaustively detailed chart of this tragic poet's life. Of his letters, it can only be said that they are magnificent and deeply moving.

Most of the criticism rightly sees Crane as a midwestern writer who along with other early century intellectuals followed Sherwood Anderson out of the Midwest. Unquestionably Crane's consciousness and his idealistic sense of America are shaped by the Midwest, and his head-long dive into the Bohemian-intellectual life of New York was compelled by a reaction to the Midwest, that complex hub of the country which has given birth to so many great and complex American artists.

MAJOR WORKS

White Buildings. New York: Liveright, 1926.
The Bridge. New York: Liveright, 1930.
The Collected Poems of Hart Crane. Ed. Waldo Frank. New York: Liveright, 1933. Reprinted as *The Complete Poems of Hart Crane.* New York: Doubleday, 1958.
The Complete Poems and Selected Letters and Prose of Hart Crane. Ed. Brom Weber. New York: Liveright, 1966.
The Letters of Hart Crane and His Family. Ed. by Thomas S. Lewis. New York: Columbia U., 1974.

CHECKLIST OF SECONDARY SOURCES

Andreach, Robert J. "Hart Crane." In *Studies in Structure.* New York: Fordham U., 1964. Pp. 102–29.
Baird, Peggy. "The Last Days of Hart Crane." *Venture,* 4 (1961), 21–46.
Bewley, Marius. "Hart Crane's Last Poem." *Accent,* 19 (Spring 1959), 75–85.
Blackmur, R. P. "New Thresholds, New Anatomies: Notes on a Text of Hart Crane." In *Language as Gesture.* New York: Harcourt, 1952. Pp. 301–16.

Brown, Susan Jenkins. *Letters and Memories of Hart Crane*. Middletown, Conn.: Wesleyan U., 1968–69.

Butterfield, R. W. *The Broken Arc: A Study of Hart Crane*. Edinburgh: Oliver and Boyd, 1969.

Cowley, Malcolm. "A Preface to Hart Crane." *NR*, 62 (Apr. 23, 1930), 276–77.

———. "Remembering Hart Crane." *NR*, 104 (Apr. 14, 1941), 504–6.

———. "The Roaring Boy." In *Exile's Return*. New York: Viking, 1951. Pp. 221–34.

———. "The Roaring Boy." *NR*, 91 (June 9, 1937), 134.

Dembo, L. S. "Hart Crane's Early Poems." *UKCR*, 27 (Spring 1961), 181–87.

———. *Hart Crane's Sanskrit Charge: A Study of The Bridge*. Ithaca: Cornell U., 1960.

Frank, Waldo. "An Introduction to Hart Crane." *NR*, 74 (Feb. 15, 1933), 11–15.

Ghiselin, Brewster. "Bridge into the Sea." *PR* (July 1949), 679–86.

Grigsby, Gordon K. "Hart Crane's Doubtful Vision." *CE*, 24 (Apr. 1963), 518–23.

"Hart Crane: A Conversation with Samuel Loveman." New York: Interim, 1964.

Hazo, Samuel. *Hart Crane: An Introduction and Interpretation*. New York: Barnes and Noble, 1963.

Herman, Barbara. "The Language of Hart Crane." *SR*, 58 (Winter 1950), 52–67.

Horton, Philip. *Hart Crane: The Life of an American Poet*. New York: Norton, 1937.

Larrabee, Ankey. "The Symbol of the Sea in Crane's 'Voyages.' " *Accent*, 3 (Winter 1943), 117–19.

Leibowitz, Herbert A. *Hart Crane: An Introduction to the Poetry*. New York: Columbia U., 1968.

Lewis, R. W. B. *The Poetry of Hart Crane: A Critical Study*. Princeton: Princeton U., 1967.

Lewis, Thomas S. W., ed. *Letters of Hart Crane and His Family*. New York: Columbia U., 1974.

Martey, Herbert. "Hart Crane's 'The Broken Tower': A Study in Technique." *UKCR*, 18 (Spring 1952), 199–205.

Miller, James E., Karl Shapiro, and Bernice Slote. *Start With the Sun: Studies in the Whitman Tradition*. Lincoln: U. Nebraska, 1960.

Monroe, Harriet. "A Discussion with Hart Crane." *Poetry*, 29 (Oct. 1926), 34–41.

Moss, Howard. "Disorder as Myth." *Poetry*, 62 (Apr. 1943), 32–45.

Munson, Gorham B. "Hart Crane: Young Titan in the Sacred Wood." *Destinations: A Canvas of American Literature Since 1900*. New York: Sears, 1928. Pp. 160–77.

Paul, Sherman. *Hart's Bridge*. Urbana: U. Illinois, 1972.

Perry, Robert L. *The Shared Vision of Waldo Frank and Hart Crane*. Lincoln: U. Nebraska, 1966.

Quinn, Sister M. Bernetta. "Eliot and Crane: Protean Techniques." *The Metamorphic Tradition in Modern Poetry*. New Brunswick, N.J.: Rutgers U., 1955. Pp. 130–67.

Quinn, Vincent. *Hart Crane*. New York: Twayne, 1963.

Rupp, H. R. "Hart Crane: Vitality as Credo in 'Atlantis.' " *MQ*, 3 (Apr. 1962), 265–75.

Slote, Bernice. "The Structure of Hart Crane's *The Bridge*." *UKCR*, 24 (Spring 1958), 225–38.

———. "Transmutation in Crane's Imagery in The Bridge." *MLN*, 73 (Jan. 1958), 15–23.

Spears, Monroe K. *Hart Crane*. Minneapolis: U. Minnesota, 1965.

Swallow, Alan. "Hart Crane." *UKCR*, 16 (Winter 1949), 103–18.

Tate, Allen. "Hart Crane and the American Mind." *Poetry*, 40 (July 1932), 210–16.

———. "Hart Crane." In *Reactionary Essays on Poetry and Ideas*. New York: Scribner, 1936. Pp. 26–42.

———. "The Self-Made Angel." *NR*, 129 (Aug. 31, 1953), 17, 21.

Taylor, Frajam. "Keats and Crane: An Airy Citadel." *Accent*, 8 (Autumn 1947), 34–40.

Unterecker, John. *Voyager*. New York: Farrar, Straus, and Giroux, 1969.

———. "The Architecture of *The Bridge*." *WSCL*, 3 (Spring-Summer 1962), 5–20.

Van Nostrand, Albert. "*The Bridge* and Hart Crane's 'Span of Consciousness.' " *Aspects of American Poetry*. Ed. Richard M. Ludwig. Columbus: Ohio State U., 1962. Pp. 171–202.

Waggoner, Hyatt Howe. "Hart Crane: Beyond all Sesames of Science." *The Heel of Elohim: Science and Values in Modern American Poetry*. Norman: U. Oklahoma, 1950. Pp. 155–92.

———. "Hart Crane and the Broken Parabala." *UKCR*, 11 (Spring 1945), 173–77.

Weber, Brom. *Hart Crane: A Biographical and Critical Study*. New York: Bodley, 1948.

———, ed. *The Letters of Hart Crane, 1916–1932*. New York: Hermitage House, 1952. Berkeley: U. California, 1965.

Willingham, John R. " 'Three Songs' of Hart Crane's *The Bridge.*" *AL*, 27 (Mar. 1955), 62–68.
Winters, Yvor. "The Progress of Hart Crane." *Poetry*, 36 (June 1930), 153–65.
———. *Primitivism and Decadence: A Study of American Experimental Poetry*. New York: Arrow, 1937.
———. "The Significance of *The Bridge* by Hart Crane, or what are we to think of Professor X?" In *In Defense of Reason*. Denver: Swallow, 1947. Pp. 577–603.

Stanley Radhuber
Portland State University
Portland, Oregon

JAMES OLIVER CURWOOD (1878–1927)

From his first published short story about an Indian battle near Chesaning, Michigan, James Oliver Curwood ranged from the Great Lakes to the remote wilderness of Canada and Alaska to spin tales of romantic adventure that gave him enormous popularity at home and abroad. He was second · only to Jack London in French translations and had forty separate editions of novels in Russia as well as a wide following in Latin America. With a claim to have "never written an unwholesome word," Curwood's characters confronted harrowing events in which the good were rewarded and the evil killed or defeated. Among novels set in the region of the Great Lakes were his first published: *The Courage of Captain Plum* (1908), *The Country Beyond* (1922), *A Gentleman of Courage* (1924), and *Green Timber* (1930). This last, a novel about the reformation of a Detroit gangster, was published after his death, as was a collection of regional short stories entitled *Falkner of the Inland Seas* (1931), and his autobiography, *Son of the Forest* (1930). His nonfiction history, *The Great Lakes and the Vessels that Plough Them*, was originally written in 1909 and reprinted in 1967. This latter date marked a new era of appreciation for Curwood's early contribution to the preservation of forests and wildlife in Michigan, Canada, and the Alaskan wilderness. Curwood's popularity as a novelist had enabled him to champion new conservation laws, and the Michigan Department of Natural Resources' publication *Michigan Outdoors* paid tribute to Curwood's effort fifty years after he organized the Owosso, Michigan, chapter of the Izaak Walton League in 1923.

MAJOR WORKS

The Courage of Captain Plum. Indianapolis: Bobbs-Merrill, 1908 [novel]
The Wolf Hunters. Indianapolis: Bobbs-Merrill, 1908. [novel]
The Gold Hunters. New York: Cosmopolitan, 1909. [novel]
The Great Lakes and the Vessels That Plough Them. New York: Putnam, 1909. [historical account]
The Danger Trail. Indianapolis: Bobbs-Merrill, 1910. [novel]

The Honor of the Big Snows. Indianapolis: Bobbs-Merrill, 1911. [novel]
Philip Steele of the Royal Mounted. Indianapolis: Bobbs-Merrill, 1911. [novel]
Flower of the North. New York: Harper, 1912. [novel]
Isobel. New York: Harper, 1913. [novel]
Kazan. Indianapolis: Bobbs-Merrill, 1914. [novel]
God's Country and the Woman. Garden City, N.Y.: Doubleday, 1915. [novel]
The Hunted Woman. Garden City, N.Y.: Doubleday, 1916. [novel]
The Grizzly King. Garden City, N.Y.: Doubleday, 1916. [novel]
Baree, Son of Kazan. Garden City, N.Y.: Doubleday, 1917. [novel]
The Courage of Marge O'Doone. Garden City, N.Y.: Doubleday, 1918. [novel]
Nomads of the North. Garden City, N.Y.: Doubleday, 1919. [novel]
The River's End. New York: Cosmopolitan, 1919. [novel]
The Valley of Silent Men. New York: Cosmopolitan, 1920. [novel]
Back to God's Country. New York: Cosmopolitan, 1920. [novel]
The Flaming Forest. New York: Cosmopolitan, 1921. [novel]
The Golden Snare. New York: Cosmopolitan, 1921. [novel]
God's Country—Trail to Happiness. New York: Cosmopolitan, 1921. [essays]
The Country Beyond. New York: Cosmopolitan, 1922. [novel]
The Alaskan. New York: Cosmopolitan, 1923. [novel]
A Gentleman of Courage. New York: Cosmopolitan, 1924. [novel]
The Ancient Highway. New York: Cosmopolitan, 1925. [novel]
The Black Hunter. New York: Cosmopolitan, 1926. [historical novel]
Swift Lightning. New York: Cosmopolitan, 1926. [novel]
The Plains of Abraham. Garden City, N.Y.: Doubleday, 1928. [novel]
The Crippled Lady of Peribonka. Garden City, N.Y.: Doubleday, 1929. [novel]
Son of the Forests. Garden City, N.Y.: Doubleday, 1930. [autobiography]
Green Timber. Garden City, N.Y.: Doubleday, 1930. [novel]
Falkner of the Inland Seas. Indianapolis: Bobbs-Merrill, 1931. [stories]

CHECKLIST OF SECONDARY SOURCES

DAB; LHUS; OCAL; TCA.

Anon. "A Critic." *Owosso Evening-Argus,* Nov. 27, 1894.
Baldwin, C. C. "James Oliver Curwood." In *Men Who Made Our Novels.* New York: Dodd, Mead, 1924. Pp. 116–23.
Curwood, James Oliver. "Why I Write Nature Stories." *GoodH* (July 1918), 32.
Dickey, John E., "James Oliver Curwood." *Curwood Collector,* 2 (1973), 13–14.
Eastman, John. "J. O. Curwood Conservation's Holy Terror." *Michigan Outdoors* (July 1973), 10.
Farley, G. M. *"Zane Grey." Curwood Collector,* 2 (1974), 9–12.
Galantiere, L. "American Books in France." *AmMerc* (May 1924), 97–102.
Gamester, Stephen J. "The Man Who Invented God's Country." *MacLeans* (Feb. 22, 1964), 19.
Kinsey, H. C. "Jim Curwood of Owosso." *GoodH* (Nov. 1922), 40.
Long, Ray. "Jas. Oliver Curwood and His Far North." *Bookman* (Feb. 1921), 492–95.
Long, Ray. "Jim Curwood." *Bookman* (Nov. 1927), 289–91.
May, William Allen. "Owosso, Dream City of the Indians." *Owosso Argus Press,* Centennial Edition, July 1936.
Swiggett, Hobart D. *J. O. Curwood, Disciple of the Wilds.* New York: Paeber, 1943. [biography]

Patricia A. D'Itri
Michigan State University
East Lansing, Michigan

EDWARD DAHLBERG (1900–   )

The starting point for any study of Dahlberg's work should be Billings's bibliography, which offers a complete list of Dahlberg's publications through 1971 and includes a section entitled "Works About Dahlberg," and which lists the critical and biographical material available up to that year. The best critical essays on Dahlberg's work are collected in Billings's *Edward Dahlberg: American Ishmael of Letters* (1968). Items that have appeared since 1971 are relatively scattered, although the annotated bibliography in Moramarco's critical study (1972) may be consulted, as well as the entry on Dahlberg by Ryan in *Contemporary Novelists* (1972). In addition, much valuable biographical information as well as several insightful critical essays may be found in the special issue of *Tri-Quarterly* devoted entirely to Dahlberg.

Dahlberg's reputation has been enormously enhanced in the last decade since the publication of his masterpiece, *Because I Was Flesh*, which was widely hailed as a major American autobiography and surely one of the most eloquent accounts of coming of age in the American Midwest. Essentially a revision of his first novel, *Bottom Dogs*, the later work covers the same materials with the benefit of thirty-five years spent developing a prose style that is truly unique, embodying as it does mythical references, classical allusions, and the staggering erudition of a mind that ranges easily over a vast body of world literature. He is *"the* poet of sentence design," in Rosenthal's phrase, a rhetorical craftsman without equal in our literature.

The sheer range of Dahlberg's work makes a mockery of our traditional critical categories. He has written fiction, poetry, autobiography, critical essays, and, in works like *The Sorrows of Priapus* and *The Carnal Myth*, has invented genres that are distinctly his own. Because of his generic innovation, his work does not fit easily into courses in American fiction, poetry, or drama, and it has suffered years of neglect by academic critics. Nonetheless, as the entries in the Secondary Sources section below show, a substantial amount of critical commentary on that work is finally beginning to emerge.

Major Works

Bottom Dogs. London: Putnam, 1929. [novel]
From Flushing to Calvary. New York: Harcourt, 1932. [novel]
Those Who Perish. New York: John Day, 1934. [novel]
Do These Bones Live. New York: Harcourt, 1941. [critical essays]
Sing O Barren. London: George Routledge, 1947. [English edition of *Do These Bones Live*, revised.]

The Flea of Sodom. New York: New Directions, 1950. [allegorical novel]
The Sorrows of Priapus. Norfolk, Conn.: New Directions, 1957. [mythical essays]
Can These Bones Live. New York: New Directions, 1960. [A completely revised edition of *Do These Bones Live* with drawings by James Kearns.]
Truth Is More Sacred. New York: Horizon, 1961. [exchange of letters with Sir Herbert Read]
Because I Was Flesh. Norfolk, Conn.: New Directions, 1964. [autobiography]
Alms for Oblivion. Minneapolis: U. Minnesota, 1964. [memoir and critical essays]
Reasons of the Heart. New York: Horizon, 1965. [aphorisms]
Cinpango's Hinder Door. Austin: U. Texas, 1966. [poems]
Epitaphs of Our Times. New York: Braziller, 1967. [selected letters]
The Edward Dahlberg Reader. New York: New Directions, 1967. [anthology]
The Leafless American. Austin, Texas: Roger Beacham, 1967. [essays]
The Carnal Myth. New York: Weybright and Talley, 1968. [mythic essays]
The Confessions of Edward Dahlberg. New York: Braziller, 1971. [autobiography]
The Gold of Ophir. New York: Dutton, 1972. [travel narratives]
The Sorrows of Priapus. New York: Harcourt, 1972. [Reissue of *The Sorrows of Priapus* and *The Carnal Myth* in one volume.]
The Olive of Minerva or The Comedy of a Cuckold. New York: Crowell, 1976. [allegorical romance]
Bottom Dogs, From Flushing to Calvary, Those Who Perish. New York: Minerva, 1976. [Reissue of Dahlberg's first three novels, with introduction by Harold Billings.]

CHECKLIST OF SECONDARY SOURCES

Aaron, Daniel. *Writers on the Left: Episodes in American Literary Communism*. New York: Harcourt, 1961.
Allen, Walter. *The Modern Novel*. New York: Dutton, 1964.
Bedient, Calvin. "Anyone's Miserable Chagrin." *NR* (Feb. 6, 1971), 27–32.
Billings, Harold, ed. *Edward Dahlberg: American Ishmael of Letters*. Austin: Beacham, 1968. [collection of critical essays]
———. *A Bibliography of Edward Dahlberg*. Austin: U. Texas, 1971.
Boyle, Kay. "A Man in the Wilderness." *Nation* (May 29, 1967), 693–94.
Chech, John O. "Edward Dahlberg and Charles Olson: A Biography of a Friendship." Ph.D. diss., U. Connecticut, 1974.
Chametsky, Jules. "Edward Dahlberg: Early and Late." In *Proletarian Writers of the Thirties*. Ed. Donald Madden. Carbondale: Southern Illinois U., 1968.
Contemporary Literary Criticism, 1. Ed. Carolyn Riley. Detroit: Gale Research, 1973. Pp. 71–73.
DeWeese, Robert. "The Novels of Edward Dahlberg." Master's thesis, U. Texas, 1970.
Duncan, Robert. "Against Nature." *Poetry*, 94 (Apr. 1959), 54–59.
Farrell, James T. "In Search of the Image." *NM* (Dec. 4, 1934), 21–22.
Ford, Ford Madox. "The Fate of the Semiclassic." *Forum*, 97 (Sept. 1937), 126–28.
Hassan, Ihab. "The Sorrows of Edward Dahlberg." *MassR*, 5 (Spring 1964), 457–61.
Herbst, Josephine. "Edward Dahlberg's Because I was Flesh." *SouR*, 1, n.s. (Spring 1965), 337–51.
Hicks, Granville et al., eds. *Proletarian Literature in the United States*. New York: International, 1935.
Karlen, Arno. "The Wages of Risk." *Nation* (Mar. 30, 1964), 331–34.
Kazin, Alfred. "The Eloquence of Failure." *Reporter* (Aug. 13, 1964), 59–62.
———. *On Native Grounds. An Interpretation of Modern American Prose Literature*. New York: Reynal and Hitchock, 1942.
Kramer, Hilton. "The Confessions of Edward Dahlberg." *NYTBR*, Jan. 31, 1971, pp. 1, 30–31.
Kindrick, Robert. "Lizzie Dahlberg and Eula Varner: Two Modern Perspectives on the Earth Mother." *M-A II* (1975), 93–111.
Library of Literary Criticism. Eds. Dorothy N. Curley et al. *Modern American Literature, A-F*. 4th ed. New York: Ungar, 1969. Pp. 269–74.
Leibowitz, Herbert. "Stoking the Oedipal Furnace: Edward Dahlberg's *Because I Was Flesh*." *ASch*, 44 (Summer 1975), 473–83.

Lipton, Victor. "Cudgels and Distaffs, for the Rebirth." *PrS,* (Winter 1961), 286–88, 354–56.

Lyon, Melvin. "Man and his Sources." *PrS,* 44 (1970), 81–83.

MacShane, Frank. "Alms for Oblivion and Others." *SouR,* 3 (1967), 788–95.

Moramarco, Fred. "An Interview with Edward Dahlberg." *WHR,* 20 (Summer 1966), 249–53.

———. "Make Him a Legend in His Own Time: Writing About Edward Dahlberg." *UPLL,* 1 (1969), 21–32.

———. *Edward Dahlberg.* New York: Twayne, 1972.

Rideout, Walter. *The Radical Novel in the United States 1900–1954.* Cambridge: Harvard U. 1956.

Roditi, Edouard. "Prophet or Pedant." *Poetry,* 77 (Jan. 1951), 236–38.

Rosenthal, Irving. *Sheeper.* New York: Grove, 1968. Pp. 122–23.

Salzman, Jack. Review of *A Bibliography of Edward Dahlberg* and *The Confessions of Edward Dahlberg. RALS,* 2 (1972), 278–80.

Shapiro, Karl. *To Abolish Children and Other Essays.* Chicago: Quadrangle, 1968.

Sorrentino, Gilbert. "Poet of Absolute Inventions." *Nation* (Jan. 8, 1973), 54–56.

Spencer, Benjamin T. "American Literature as Black Mass; Edward Dahlberg." *TCL,* 21 (1975), 381–93.

Swados, Harvey, ed. *The American Writer and the Great Depression.* New York: Bobbs-Merrill, 1966.

Tate, Allen. "A Great Stylist: The Prophet as Critic." *SR* (Spring 1961), 314–17.

Unali, Lina Garegnani. "Introduzione a Edward Dahlberg." *SA,* 9 (1965), 271–308.

Wain, John. "Eating Fables." *NYRB* (Jan. 2, 1969), pp. 13–14.

White, Edmund. "The Dahlberg Dilemma." *NR* (Aug. 3, 1968), 19–21.

Whittaker, Edward Keith. "Touching Pitch: A Reader's Garland for Edward Dahlberg." Master's thesis, U. British Columbia, 1968.

Widmer, Kingsley. "American Poetic Naturalist: Edward Dahlberg." *Shenandoah,* 16 (1964), 69–72.

Williams, Jonathan, ed. *A Festschrift for Edward Dahlberg. NUTQ,* no. 19 (Fall 1970). [special issue devoted entirely to Dahlberg]

———, ed. *Edward Dahlberg: A Tribute.* New York: David Lewis, 1971. [reprint of *NUTQ,* no. 19]

———. "Edward Dahlberg's Book of Lazarus." *TQ,* 6 (Summer 1963), 35–49.

Wilson, Edmund. *The Shores of Light.* New York: Farrar, 1952.

Fred Moramarco
San Diego State University
San Diego, California

FLOYD DELL (1887–1969)

Editor, book-reviewer, bohemian, social critic, novelist, government employee, Floyd Dell received widespread recognition as "the greatest book-reviewer in America" (Paul Jordan-Smith) and as one of the best self-educated men in the United States (Max Eastman). His novels were widely reviewed for their celebration of youth and bohemian ways, for illicit love affairs and liberal social views. As plots and characters became repetitious, his popularity waned. *Moon-Calf,* his first and best novel, was compared to the work of Sinclair Lewis, F. Scott Fitzgerald, and Sherwood Anderson. His career ended abruptly in the mid-1930s.

Critics rediscovered Dell's contribution to intellectual and literary history in the mid-1950s: Duffey and Kramer focused on his role in the Chicago renaissance; May and Churchill identified his part as leader of rebellious young people and as Greenwich Village bohemian; Aaron untangled his relation with radical movements; Hahn presented him as a textbook case of romantic rebel.

Of the full-length studies, Tanselle stresses the dreamer-socialist conflict that ends in conventional views. Horberg emphasizes a return to traditional values. Smith traces the early feminism in the novels. In the only published study, Hart shows him as a liberal and rebellious spirit who, caught in a violent and changing world, continued to seek sensible and valid insights. Tanselle provides a complete bibliography. *Moon-Calf, Homecoming, Love in the Machine Age, Upton Sinclair,* and *Love in Greenwich Village,* are in print.

MAJOR WORKS

Women as World Builders. Chicago: Forbes, 1913. [essays]
The Angel Intrudes. New York: Arens, 1918. [play]
Were You Ever a Child? New York: Knopf, 1919; rev. ed. with new preface, 1921. [essays]
Moon-Calf. New York: Knopf, 1920. [novel]
The Briary-Bush. New York: Knopf, 1921. [novel]
Sweet and Twenty. Cincinnati: Kidd, 1921. [play]
King Arthur's Socks and Other Village Plays. New York: Knopf, 1922.
Looking at Life. New York: Knopf, 1924. [essays]
Janet March. New York: Knopf, 1923; rev. ed., New York: Doran, 1927. [novel]
This Mad Ideal. New York: Knopf, 1925. [novel]
Runaway. New York: Doran, 1925. [novel]
An Old Man's Folly. New York: Doran, 1926. [novel]
Intellectual Vagabondage: An Apology for the Intelligentsia. New York: Doran, 1926.
Love in Greenwich Village. New York: Doran, 1926. [essays, stories]
An Unmarried Father. New York: Doran, 1927. [novel]
Upton Sinclair: A Study in Social Protest. New York: Doran, 1927.
Souvenir. Garden City, N.Y.: Doubleday, 1929. [novel]
Love in the Machine Age: A Psychological Study of the Transition from Patriarchal Society. New York: Farrar, 1930.
Love Without Money. New York: Farrar, 1931. [novel]
Diana Stair. New York: Farrar, 1932. [novel]
Homecoming: An Autobiography. New York: Farrar, 1933.
The Golden Spike. New York: Farrar, 1934. [novel]

CHECKLIST OF SECONDARY SOURCES

Burke; *CAA;* Herzberg; *LHUS; LLC; OCM; TCA & Supp.*

Aaron, Daniel. *Writers on the Left: Episodes in American Literary Communism.* New York: Harcourt, 1961.
Churchill, Allen. *The Improper Bohemians: A Re-creation of Greenwich Village in Its Heyday.* New York: Dutton, 1959.
Duffey, Bernard. *The Chicago Renaissance in American Letters: A Critical History.* East Lansing: Michigan State, 1953.
Eastman, Max. *Enjoyment of Living.* New York: Harper, 1948.
_____. *Love and Revolution.* New York: Random House, 1964.
_____. *Art and the Life of Action with Other Essays.* New York: Knopf, 1934.
Freeman, Joseph. *An American Testament: A Narrative of Rebels and Romantics.* New York: Farrar, 1936.

Glaspell, Susan. *The Road to the Temple*. New York: Stokes, 1927.

Goist, Park. "Community and Self in the Midwest Town: Floyd Dell's *Moon Calf*." *M-A II* (1975), 88–92.

Hahn, Emily. *Romantic Rebels, an Informal History of Bohemianism in America*. Boston: Houghton Mifflin, 1967.

Hansen, Harry. *Midwest Portraits*. New York: Harcourt, 1923.

Hatcher, Harlan. *Creating the Modern American Novel*. New York: Farrar, 1935.

Hart, John E. *Floyd Dell*. New York: Twayne, 1971.

Herron, Ima H. *The Small Town in American Literature*. New York: Pageant, 1959.

Hoffman, Frederick J. *The Twenties, American Writing in the Postwar Decade*. New York: Viking, 1955.

Horberg, Richard O. "To the Twentieth Century and Back: A Round Trip with Floyd Dell." Ph.D. diss., U. Minnesota, 1968.

Kramer, Dale. *Chicago Renaissance: The Literary Life in the Midwest 1900–1930*. New York: Viking, 1955.

Marriner, Gerald. "Floyd Dell: Freedom or Marriage." In *M-A II* (1975), 63–79.

May, Henry F. *The End of American Innocence*. New York: Knopf, 1959.

O'Neill, William L., ed. *Echoes of Revolt: "The Masses" 1911–1917*. Introduction by Irving Howe. Afterword by Max Eastman. Chicago: Quadrangle, 1966.

Rideout, Walter B. *The Radical Novel in the United States, 1900–1954*. Cambridge: Harvard U., 1956.

Smith, John Thomas. "Feminism in the Novels of Floyd Dell." Ph.D. diss., U. Texas, 1970.

Tanselle, G. Thomas. "Faun at the Barricades. The Life and Work of Floyd Dell." Ph.D. diss., Northwestern U., 1959.

Witham, W. Tasker. *The Adolescent in the American Novel 1920–1960*. New York: Ungar, 1964.

Young, Art. *Art Young His Life and Times*. Ed. John N. Beffel. New York: Sheridan, 1939.

———. *On My Way: Being the Book of Art Young in Text and Picture*. New York: Liveright, 1928.

John E. Hart
Albion College
Albion, Michigan

IGNATIUS DONNELLY (1831–1901)

Most of the critics of Minnesotan Ignatius Donnelly's fiction have chosen to concentrate on the sociopolitical aspects of these works. Hofstadter finds them mildly anti-Semitic, full of suppressed lasciviousness, sadistic, nihilistic and, above all, thoroughly Populist. Jaher feels Donnelly is obsessed with violence and a paranoid, a man thirsting for revenge on his political enemies. Rideout, however, simply sees him as a man who frequently sounds more radical than he really was—a man more apt to give warning than to threaten. Pollack and Bovee have defended Donnelly against most of Hofstadter's charges and have shown him to be, in fact, a humanitarian and a reformer. Ridge has emphasized his role as an ombudsman.

Sold by the hundreds of thousands in his lifetime, Donnelly's works were largely ignored in the early part of this century. At least four have been reprinted in the last twenty years. Recently Donnelly has caught the interest of those attracted to such subjects as politics, flying saucers, sunken continents, science fiction as literature, and even Shakespearian research. His ability as an artist is usually either ignored or deprecated; the only study of Donnelly as a man of letters is Bovee's dissertation. The only biography, and a very good one, is Ridge's. Donnelly remains a figure fascinating to the tabloids and Sunday supplements as well as to the literary and historical journals.

MAJOR WORKS

Atlantis: The Antediluvian World. New York: Harper, 1882. [scientific study]
Caesar's Column. Chicago: Schulte, 1890. [novel]
Dr. Huguet. Chicago: Schulte, 1891. [novel]
The Golden Bottle. St. Paul: Merrill, 1892. [novel]
The Great Cryptogram. Chicago: Peale, 1887. [Shakespearean study]
Ragnarok: The Age of Fire and Gravel. New York: Appleton, 1883. [scientific study]

CHECKLIST OF SECONDARY SOURCES

BDAL; Blanck; Burke; *DAB*; Herzberg; *OCAL*.

Bovee, John R. *"Dr. Huguet*: Donnelly on Being Black." *MH* (Summer 1969), 286–94.
––––––. "Ignatius Donnelly as a Man of Letters." Ph.D. diss., Washington State U., 1968.
Hofstadter, Richard. *The Age of Reform*. New York: Random House, 1955.
Joher, Frederick C. *Doubters and Dissenters*. London: Collier-Macmillan, 1964.
O'Connor, W. D. *Mr. Donnelly's Reviewers*. Chicago: Belford, Clarke, 1889.
Patterson, John. "Alliance and Antipathy: Ignatius Donnelly's Ambivalent Vision in Dr. Huguet." *AQ*, 3 (Winter 1970), 824–45.
Pollack, Norman. "Ignatius Donnelly on Human Rights: A Study of Two Novels." *M-A* (Apr. 1965), 99–112.
Rideout, Walter B. *The Radical Novel in the United States: 1900–1954*. New York: Hill and Wang, 1956.
Ridge, Martin. *Ignatius Donnelly*. Chicago: U. Chicago, 1962.
Saxton, Alexander. *"Caesar's Column*: The Dialogue of Utopia and Catastrophe." *AQ*, 1 (1967), 224–38.
Wright, David. "The Art of Vision of Ignatius Donnelly." *DAI*, 35:6116A–17A.

John Bovee
St. Cloud State University
St. Cloud, Minnesota

WARD ALLISON DORRANCE (1904–   )

Dorrance has yet to receive critical attention beyond reviews of his large scale works: the novel, *The Sundowners*, and the record of a canoe trip down the Mississippi, *Where the Rivers Meet*. Response to *The Sundowners* stressed Dorrance's eye for local color more than his ability to create characters. Feld noted that "Dorrance is better at creating and fusing the drama of human beings and nature than he is with the ordinary relationships of men and women." *Where the Rivers Meet* was compared, not unfavorably, to Thoreau. While the style and evident love for his subject were praised, his "sectional pride" has limited his national appeal. His later novels have received virtually no notice. His short stories have been praised by Gordon for their "passion of observation."

Major Works

Where the Rivers Meet. New York: Scribner, 1939. [travel]
The Sundowners. New York: Scribner, 1942. [novel]
The White Hound: Stories by Ward Dorrance and Thomas Mabry. Columbia: U. Missouri, 1959.
The Party at Mrs. Purefoy's. New York: Delacorte, 1969. [novel]
A Man About the House. Columbia: U. Missouri, 1972. [novella]

Checklist of Secondary Sources

Burke.

Feld, Rose. Review of *The Sundowners. NYTBR*, Aug. 16, 1942, p. 7.
Gordon, Caroline. Introduction to *The White Hound*. Columbia: U. Missouri, 1959. Pp. ix–xiv.
Reynolds, Horace. Review of *Where the Rivers Meet. NYTBR*, Dec. 31, 1939, p. 2.

John Clum
Duke University
Durham, North Carolina

THEODORE DREISER (1871–1945)

Critical response to Dreiser frequently has centered on his writing style. His earliest detractors, such as Sherman and Boynton, insisted that Dreiser's work had neither moral value nor memorable beauty. This was an opinion echoed over the years by a number of critics, including Lewis Mumford (who, in *The Golden Day*, compared the artistic merits of Dreiser's work to the Sunday newspaper), Arthur Quinn, Dorothy Parker, and most recently and most notably, Lionel Trilling, who condemned not only Dreiser's style but all critics who defended it.

The Indiana novelist has had his defenders, of course, and they have been just as vociferous as his detractors. Mencken, for example, in responding to Sherman's attack, saw Dreiser as a phenomenon, standing alone in the desert of American fiction. Bourne explained that Dreiser's admirers excused his many faults because he was able to catch hold of the thread of human desire, and Sherwood Anderson apologized for Dreiser's crudity by noting that Dreiser was true to "something in the life about him." Sinclair Lewis, in his 1930 Nobel Prize acceptance speech, contended that Dreiser, more than any other man, had cleared the trail from Victorian and Howellsian timidity and gentility in American fiction to honesty and passion. And this was the position later taken by several of Dreiser's most ardent admirers: Farrell wrote that no other American writer had done more to free American literature; Cargill agreed that Dreiser was "the Hindenburg of the novel" and claimed that in Dreiser, rather than in Hardy or Zola, was to be found the very quintessence of naturalism; and Kazin best summed up the argument for Dreiser when he stated that it was an established part of our folklore that Dreiser lacked everything but genius.

There still are areas of Dreiser studies that need more work (see Pizer in *Dreiser Newsletter*, Spring, 1970); but, for the most part, Dreiser has been well-served by critics and scholars. Although Matthiessen's study remains one of the best books about Dreiser's writings, recent studies by Lehan, Markels, Moers, and Phillips have added considerably to our understanding of Dreiser's art. The biographies by Elias and Swanberg are excellent in their own ways: Swanberg's is the more exhaustive and Elias's is the more interesting and sympathetic. And to these, we now can add the more specialized books by Tjader and Kennell. With the exception of Pizer's checklist of Dreiser's publications, however, there is no good bibliography of either primary or secondary material. Hopefully, this will be corrected when G. K. Hall publishes Pizer's primary bibliography and the secondary bibliography now being prepared by Richard Dowell and Frederic Rusch. What then will most be needed is an edition of Dreiser's writing, but that seems unlikely to become a reality in the near future.

MAJOR WORKS

Sister Carrie. New York: Doubleday, 1900. [novel]
Jennie Gerhardt. New York: Harper, 1911. [novel]
The Financier. New York: Harper, 1912. [novel]
A Traveler at Forty. New York: Century, 1913. [nonfiction]
The Titan. New York: Lane, 1914. [novel]
The "Genius." New York: Lane, 1915. [novel]
Plays of the Natural and the Supernatural. New York: Lane, 1916. [plays]
A Hoosier Holiday. New York: Lane, 1916. [nonfiction]
Free and Other Stories. New York: Boni and Liveright, 1918. [stories]
The Hand of the Potter. New York: Boni and Liveright, 1918. [play]
Twelve Men. New York: Boni and Liveright, 1919. [sketches]
Hey Rub-a-Dub-Dub. New York: Boni and Liveright, 1920. [nonfiction]
A Book About Myself. New York: Boni and Liveright, 1922. [autobiography]
The Color of a Great City. New York: Boni and Liveright, 1923. [nonfiction]
An American Tragedy. New York: Boni and Liveright, 1925. [novel]
Chains: Lesser Novels and Stories. New York: Boni and Liveright, 1927. [stories]
Moods: Cadenced and Declaimed. New York: Boni and Liveright, 1928. [poems]
Dreiser Looks at Russia. New York: Liveright, 1928. [nonfiction]
A Gallery of Women. New York: Liveright, 1929. [sketches]
Epitaph. New York: Heron, 1929. [poem]
Fine Furniture. New York: Random House, 1930. [short story]
Dawn: A History of Myself. New York: Liveright, 1931. [autobiography]
Tragic America. New York: Horace Liveright, 1931. [nonfiction]
Moods, Philosophical and Emotional: Cadenced and Declaimed. New York: Simon and Schuster, 1931. [poems]

America Is Worth Saving. New York: Modern Age, 1941. [nonfiction]
The Bulwark. New York: Doubleday, 1946. [novel]
The Stoic. New York: Doubleday, 1947. [novel]
Letters of Theodore Dreiser, ed. by Robert H. Elias. 3 vols. Philadelphia: U. Pennsylvania, 1959.
Notes on Life. Ed. by Marguerite Tjader and John J. McAleer. University, Ala.: U. Alabama, 1974. [philosophy]

CHECKLIST OF SECONDARY SOURCES

Ahnebrink, Lars. "Dreiser's *Sister Carrie* and Balzac." *Symposium*, 7 (Nov. 1953), 306–22.
Anderson, Sherwood. "An Apology for Crudity." *Dial*, 63 (Nov. 8, 1917), 437–38.
Arnavon, Cyrille. "Theodore Dreiser and Painting." *AL*, 17 (May 1945), 113–26.
Asselineau, Roger. "Theodore Dreiser's Transcendentalism." *EST*, 2d series, 11 (1961), 233–46.
Beach, Joseph Warren. "The Realist Reaction: Dreiser." In *The Twentieth Century Novel*. New York: Century, 1932.
Becker, George. "The Realist as Social Critic." *TCL*, 1 (Oct. 1955), 117–27.
Berthoff, Warner. "Lives of the Americans: Theodore Dreiser." *The Ferment of Realism: American Literature 1884–1919*. New York: Free Press, 1965.
Blackstock, Walter. "Dreiser's Dramatization of Art, the Artist, and the Beautiful in American Life." *SQ*, 1 (1962), 63–86.
Bourne, Randolph. "The Art of Theodore Dreiser." In *History of a Literary Radical and Other Essays*. New York: Huebsch, 1920.
Boynton, Percy. "Theodore Dreiser." *Some Contemporary Americans*. Chicago: U. Chicago, 1924.
Brooks, Van Wyck. "Theodore Dreiser." *The Confident Years: 1885–1915*. New York: Dutton, 1952.
Brown, Deming. *Soviet Attitudes Toward American Writing*. Princeton: Princeton U., 1962.
Butler, Gerald J. "The Quality of Emotional Greatness." *Paunch*, 25 (Feb. 1966), 5–17.
Cargill, Oscar. *Intellectual America*. New York: Macmillan, 1941.
Cowley, Malcolm. "Sister Carrie's Brother." In *A Many-Windowed House*. Ed. by Henry Dan Piper. Carbondale: Southern Illinois U., 1970.
Dreiser, Helen. *My Life with Dreiser*. Cleveland: World, 1951.
Dreiser, Vera. *My Uncle Theodore: An Intimate Family Portrait of Theodore Dreiser*. New York: Nash, 1976.
Drummond, Edward J. "Theodore Dreiser: Shifting Naturalism." In *Fifty Years of the American Novel*. Ed. by Harold C. Gardiner. New York: Scribner, 1951.
Dudley, Dorothy. *Forgotten Frontiers: Dreiser and the Land of the Free*. New York: Harrison Smith, 1932.
Elias, Robert. *Theodore Dreiser: Apostle of Nature*. Emended ed. Ithaca: Cornell U., 1970.
————. "Theodore Dreiser." In *Sixteen Modern American Authors*. Ed. by Jackson R. Bryer. Durham, N.C.: Duke U., 1974.
Farrell, James T. "Dreiser's *Sister Carrie*." In *The League of Frightened Philistines*. New York: Vanguard, 1945.
————. "Some Correspondence with Theodore Dreiser." *General Magazine and Historical Chronicle of the University of Pennsylvania*, 53 (Summer 1951), 237–52.
Fiedler, Leslie A. *Love and Death in the American Novel*. Rev. ed. New York: Stein and Day, 1966.
Flanagan, John T. "Dreiser's Style in *An American Tragedy*." *TSLL*, 7 (Autumn 1965), 285–94.
Frohock, W. M. *Theodore Dreiser*. Minneapolis: U. Minnesota, 1972.
Geismar, Maxwell. "Theodore Dreiser: The Double Soul." In *Rebels and Ancestors: The American Novel, 1890–1915*. Boston: Houghton Mifflin, 1953.
Gelfant, Blanche H. "Theodore Dreiser: The Portrait Novel." *The American City Novel*. Norman, Okla.: U. Oklahoma, 1954.
Gerber, Philip L. *Theodore Dreiser*. New York: Twayne, 1964.
————. "Dreiser's Financier: A Genesis." *JML*, 1 (Mar. 1971), 354–74.

————. *Plots and Characters in the Fiction of Theodore Dreiser*. Hamden, Conn.: Archon, 1976.

Gilmer, Walker. *Horace Liveright: Publisher of the Twenties*. New York: Lewis, 1970.

Grebstein, Sheldon N. "Dreiser's Victorian Vamp," *MASJ*, 4 (1963), 3–12.

————. "*An American Tragedy*: Theme and Structure." In *The Twenties: Poetry and Prose: 20 Critical Essays*. Ed. by Richard E. Langford and William E. Taylor. Deland, Fla.: Edwards, 1966.

Griffin, Ernest G. "Sympathetic Materialism: A Rereading of Theodore Dreiser." *HAB*, 20 (Winter 1969), 59–68.

Hakutani, Yoshinobu. "Theodore Dreiser's Editorial and Free-Lance Writing." *LCUP*, 37 (Winter 1971), 70–85.

Handy, William J. "A Re-Examination of Dreiser's *Sister Carrie*." *TSLL*, 1 (Autumn 1959), 380–93.

Hartwick, Harry. "The Hindenburg of the Novel." In *The Foreground of American Fiction*. New York: American, 1934.

Hoffman, Frederick J. "The Scene of Violence: Dostoevsky and Dreiser." *MFS*, 6 (Summer 1960), 91–105.

Howe, Irving. "Dreiser: The Springs of Desire." In *The Decline of the New*. New York: Harcourt, 1970.

Jurnak, Sheila Hope. "Popular Art Forms in *Sister Carrie*." *TSLL*, 13 (Summer 1971), 313–20.

Katope, Christopher. "*Sister Carrie* and Spencer's *First Principles*." *AL*, 41 (Mar. 1969), 64–75.

Katz, Joseph. "Theodore Dreiser's *Ev'ry Month*." *LCUP*, 38 (Winter 1972), 46–66.

————. "Dummy: *The 'Genius'* by Theodore Dreiser." *Proof*, 1 (1971), 330–57.

Kazin, Alfred. "Two Educators: Edith Wharton and Theodore Dreiser." In *On Native Grounds*. New York: Reynal and Hitchcock, 1942.

Kazin, Alfred and Charles Shapiro, eds. *The Stature of Theodore Dreiser*. Bloomington: Indiana U., 1955, 1965.

Kennell. Ruth Epperson. *Theodore Dreiser and the Soviet Union, 1927–1945: A First-Hand Chronicle*. New York: International, 1969.

Kern, Alexander. "Dreiser's Difficult Beauty." *WR*, 16 (Winter 1952), 129–36.

Kwiat, Joseph J. "Dreiser and the Graphic Artist." *AQ*, 3 (Summer 1951), 127–41.

Lane, Lauriat, Jr. "The Double in *An American Tragedy*." *MFS*, 12 (Summer 1966), 213–20.

Lehan, Richard. *Theodore Dreiser: His World and His Novels*. Carbondale: Southern Illinois U., 1969.

Leonard, Neil. "Theodore Dreiser and Music." In *Challenges in American Culture*. Ed. Ray Browne et al. Bowling Green, Ohio: Bowling Green U., Popular Press, 1970.

Lundén, Rolf. *The Inevitable Equation: The Antithetic Pattern of Theodore Dreiser's Thought and Art*. Uppsala: n.p., 1973.

Lundquist, James. *Theodore Dreiser*. New York: Ungar, 1974.

Lydenberg, John. "Theodore Dreiser: Ishmael in the Jungle." *MR*, 7 (Aug. 1954), 124–36.

————, ed. *Dreiser: A Collection of Critical Essays*. Englewood Cliffs, N.J.: Prentice-Hall, 1971.

Lynn, Kenneth S. "Theodore Dreiser: The Man of Ice." In *The Dream of Success*. Boston: Little, Brown, 1955.

Markels, Julian. "Dreiser and the Plotting of Inarticulate Experience." *MassR*, 2 (Spring 1961), 431–48.

Martin, Jay. *Harvest of Change: American Literature 1865–1914*. Englewood Cliffs, N.J.: Prentice-Hall, 1967.

Matthiessen, F. O. *Theodore Dreiser*. New York: William Sloane, 1951.

McAleer, John J. *Theodore Dreiser: An Introduction and Interpretation*. New York: Holt, 1968.

Mencken, H. L. "Theodore Dreiser." In *A Book of Prefaces*. New York: Knopf, 1917.

Millgate, Michael. "Theodore Dreiser." *American Social Fiction: James to Cozzens*. New York: Barnes and Noble, 1964.

Moers, Ellen. *Two Dreisers*. New York: Viking, 1969.

Mookerjee, R. N. *Theodore Dreiser: His Thought and Social Criticism*. Delhi, India: National Publishing House, 1974.

Orton, Vrest. *Dreiserana: A Book About His Books*. New York: Chocorua, 1929.

Pavese, Cesare. "Dreiser and His Social Battle." *American Literature: Essays and Opinions*. Trans. Edwin Fussell. Berkeley: U. California, 1970.

Phillips, William L. "The Imagery of Dreiser's Novels." *PMLA*, 78 (Dec. 1963), 572–85.

Pizer, Donald. "Theodore Dreiser's 'Nigger Jeff': The Development of an Aesthetic." *AL*, 41 (Nov. 1969), 331–41.

———. *The Novels of Theodore Dreiser: A Critical Study*. Minneapolis: U. Minnesota, 1976.

———, Richard Dowell, and Frederic Rusch. *Theodore Dreiser: A Primary and Secondary Bibliography*. Boston: Hall, 1975.

Poirier, Richard. *A World Elsewhere: The Place of Style in American Literature*. New York: Oxford, 1966.

Purdy, Strother B. "*An American Tragedy* and *L'Étranger*." *CL*, 19 (Summer 1967), 252–68.

Rascoe, Burton. Theodore Dreiser. New York: McBride, 1926.

Salzman, Jack, ed. *The Merrill Studies in An American Tragedy*. Columbus, Ohio: Merrill, 1971.

———. *Theodore Dreiser: The Critical Reception*. New York: David Lewis, 1973.

———. "The Curious History of Dreiser's *The Bulwark*." *Proof*, 3 (1973), 21–61.

Samuels, Charles T. "Mr. Trilling, Mr. Warren, and *An American Tragedy*." *YR*, 53 (Summer 1964), 629–40.

Schneider, Robert W. "Theodore Dreiser: The Cry of Despair." *Five Novelists of the Progressive Era*. New York: Columbia U., 1965.

Shapiro, Charles. *Theodore Dreiser: Our Bitter Patriot*. Carbondale: Southern Illinois U., 1962.

———. *Guide to Theodore Dreiser*. Columbus, Ohio: Merrill, 1969.

Sherman, Stuart P. "The Naturalism of Mr. Dreiser." *Nation*, 101 (Dec. 2, 1915), 148–50.

———. "Mr. Dreiser in Tragic Realism." In *The Main Stream*. New York: Scribner, 1927.

Snell, George. "Theodore Dreiser: Philosopher." *The Shapers of American Fiction, 1708–1947*. New York: Holt, 1947.

Spatz, Jonas. "Dreiser's *Bulwark*: An Archaic Masterpiece." In *The Forties: Fiction, Poetry, Drama*. Ed. Warren French. Deland, Fla.: Everett/Edwards, 1969.

Stewart, Randall. "Dreiser and the Naturalistic Heresy." *VQR*, 34 (Winter 1958), 100–16.

Swanberg, W. A. *Dreiser*. New York: Scribner, 1965.

Taylor, Gordon O. "The Voice of Want: Frank Norris and Theodore Dreiser." In *The Passages of Thought: Psychological Representation in the American Novel 1870–1900*. New York: Oxford, 1969.

Tjader, Marguerite. *Theodore Dreiser: A New Dimension*. Norwalk, Conn: Silvermine, 1965.

Trilling, Lionel. "Reality in America." In *The Liberal Imagination*. New York: Viking, 1945.

Van Gelder, Robert. "An Interview with Theodore Dreiser." In *Writers and Writing*. New York: Scribner, 1946.

Vance, William C. "Dreiserian Tragedy." *SNNTS*, 4 (Spring 1972), 39–51.

Vivas, Eliseo. "Dreiser: An Inconsistent Mechanist." *Ethics*, 47 (July 1938), 498–508.

Wadlington, Warwick. "Pathos and Dreiser." *SouR*, 7 (Spring 1971), 411–29.

Wagenknecht, Edward. "Theodore Dreiser, The Mystic Naturalist." In *Cavalcade of the American Novel*. New York: Holt, 1954.

Wagner, Vern. "The Maligned Style of Theodore Dreiser." *WHR*, 19 (Spring 1965), 175–84.

Walcutt, Charles C. *American Literary Naturalism: A Divided Stream*. Minneapolis: U. Minnesota, 1956.

Warren, Robert Penn. *Homage to Theodore Dreiser*. New York: Random House, 1971.

Westlake, Neda. "Dummy: *Twelve Men*, by Theodore Dreiser." *Proof*, 2 (1972), 153–74.

Willen, Gerald. "Dreiser's Moral Seriousness." *UKCR*, 23 (Spring 1957), 181–87.

Wolfe, Don M. "Theodore Dreiser and the Human Enigma." In *The Image of Man in America*. Dallas: Southern Methodist U., 1957.

Wycherley, H. Alan. "Mechanism and Vitalism in Dreiser's Nonfiction." *TSLL*, 11 (Summer 1969), 1039–49.

Zassoursky, Yassen N. *Theodore Dreiser (on the 100th Anniversary of His Birth)*. Literature No. 8. Moscow: Znanie, 1971.

Ziff, Larzer. "A Decade's Delay: Theodore Dreiser." In *The American 1890's: Life and Times of a Lost Generation*. New York: Viking, 1966.

Jack Salzman
Long Island University
Brooklyn, New York

PAUL LAURENCE DUNBAR (1872–1906)

At the end of the nineteenth century Paul Laurence Dunbar of Dayton, Ohio, was considered to be one of the outstanding "younger" poets of his period. With the critical and well-intentioned aid of William Dean Howells, Dunbar became quite popular; however, he never achieved the financial independence which he thought should have accompanied his fame. His letters and comments to friends are full of recriminations about his work and about the American reading public. Yet even before his death in 1906, his dialect poetry had become so popular that his publisher (Dodd, Mead) began to issue it in "gift books" which sold well but which also reinforced the image of Dunbar as a writer of dialect. So associated was he with the plantation tradition that his poetry in standard English was frequently dismissed by critics as not being "representative." During his own lifetime he was accused of writing "white" novels when he did not specify the race of his characters. That judgment has prevailed among more recent critics.

Dunbar's work, however, cannot be simply dismissed as a product of a man who tried to please his audience at all costs. It is significant to remember that Dunbar wrote articles on the race issue for some of the major newspapers of the country, including the Chicago *Record* and the Chicago *Tribune*, during the early years of the twentieth century when to do so required far more courage than a similar act today. He published four novels, one of which—*The Sport of the Gods* (1902)—was an early exercise in naturalism. In addition to the five collections of short stories which were published during his lifetime, there appeared—especially during the period between 1901 and 1905—numerous short stories in the magazines of the day. And by 1906 he had written and published more than five hundred poems.

After his death he achieved "instant fame." Schools were named for him as well as housing projects and literary societies. This was partially due to the belief that he was the first member of his race to achieve recognition among the white reading public, who used him as an example of what could be accomplished by a person of "pure African descent" in America. The immediate result of this popularity is seen in the number of his works which have appeared in the years since his death.

Dunbar's reputation has gone through several cycles. During the 1920s he was increasingly associated with the plantation tradition and was rejected by those who eschewed such a tradition in literature. As time passed, Dunbar's fears that he might be remembered for his "jingle in a broken tongue" were coming true. In recent years, however, there has been a re-evaluation of his work which has attempted to place him in his proper perspective in terms of his time and place. Too frequently Dunbar has been dismissed as having been a romantic who idealized the pathos of the old slave-master relationship. Certainly many of his works are in this tradition, but it is injudicious to claim, as many critics from Howells to Robert Bone have done, that his "significance" rests merely in these works.

Major Works

Oak and Ivy. Dayton: United Brethren, 1893. [poetry]
Majors and Minors. Toledo: Hadley and Hadley, 1895. [poetry]
Lyrics of Lowly Life. New York: Dodd, Mead, 1896. [poetry]
Folks From Dixie. New York: Dodd, Mead, 1898. [short stories]
The Uncalled. New York: Dodd, Mead, 1898. [novel]
Lyrics of the Hearthside. New York: Dodd, Mead, 1899. [poetry]
Poems and Cabin and Field. New York: Dodd, Mead, 1899. [gift book]
The Strength of Gideon and Other Stories. New York: Dodd, Mead, 1900. [short stories]
The Love of Landry. New York: Dodd, Mead, 1900. [novel]
Candle-Lightin' Time. New York: Dodd, Mead, 1901. [gift book]
The Fanatics. New York: Dodd, Mead, 1901. [novel]
The Sport of the Gods. New York: Dodd, Mead, 1902. [novel]
Lyrics of Love and Laughter. New York: Dodd, Mead, 1903. [poetry]
In Old Plantation Days. New York: Dodd, Mead, 1903. [short stories]
The Heart of Happy Hollow. New York: Dodd, Mead, 1904. [short stories]
Li'l Gal. New York: Dodd, Mead, 1904. [gift book]
Lyrics of Sunshine and Shadow. New York: Dodd, Mead, 1905. [poetry]
Howdy, Honey, Howdy. New York: Dodd, Mead, 1905. [gift book]
Joggin Erlong. New York: Dodd, Mead, 1906. [gift book]
Chris'mus Is A-Comin'. New York: Dodd, Mead, 1907. [gift book]
The Complete Poems of Paul Laurence Dunbar. New York: Dodd, Mead, 1913.
The Best Short Stories of Paul Laurence Dunbar. New York: Dodd, Mead, 1938.

Checklist of Secondary Sources

Burke; *DAB; LHUS*.

Achille, Louis T. "Paul Laurence Dunbar, Poète Nègre." *RAA*, 2 (Aug. 1934), 504–19.
Arnold, Edward F. "Some Personal Reminiscences of Dunbar." *JNH*, 17 (Oct. 1932), 400–8.
Barton, Rebecca C. *Race Consciousness and American Negro Literature*. Griefswald, Germany: Dollmeyer, 1934.
Bontemps, Arna and Jack Conroy. *They Seek a City*. New York: Doubleday, 1945.
Brawley, Benjamin. *Negro Builders and Heroes*. Chapel Hill: U. North Carolina, 1937.
———. *The Negro Genius*. New York: Dodd, Mead, 1937.
———. *Paul Laurence Dunbar: Poet of His People*. Chapel Hill: U. North Carolina, 1936.
Brown, Hallie Q. *Homespun Heroines*. Xenia, Ohio: Aldine, 1926.
Brown, Sterling. *Negro in American Fiction*. Washington, D.C.: Association in Negro Folk Education, 1937.

_____. *Negro in American Poetry and Drama*. Washington, D.C.: Association in Negro Folk Education, 1937.

Burch, Charles Eaton. "The Plantation Negro in Dunbar's Poetry." *SW*, 50 (Oct. 1921), 227–29.

_____. "Dunbar's Poetry in Literary English." *SW*, 50 (Oct. 1921), 469–73.

Burris, Andrew M. "Bibliography of Works of Paul Laurence Dunbar." *ABC*, 5 (Nov. 1927), 69–73.

Conover, Charlotte Reeve. *Dayton and Montgomery County—Resources and People*. New York: Lewis Historical Publishing, 1932.

Cromwell, John. *The Negro in American History*. Washington, D.C.: American Negro Academy, 1914. Pp. 188–94.

Culp, Daniel, ed. *Twentieth Century Negro Literature, or Cyclopedia of Thought by 100 of America's Greatest Negroes*. Naperville, Ill.: J. L. Nichols, 1902.

Cunningham, Virginia. *Paul Laurence Dunbar and His Song*. New York: Dodd, Mead, 1947.

Daniel, Theodore W. "Paul Laurence Dunbar and the Democratic Ideal." *NHB*, 6 (June 1943), 206–8.

DuBois, William E. B. "The Negro in Literature and Art." *AAA* (Sept. 1913), 233–37.

Dunbar, Alice Nelson. "The Poet and His Song." *A.M.E. Church Review*, 31 (Oct. 1914), 121–35.

Ford, Thomas. "Howells and the American Negro." *TSLL*, 5 (1964), 530–37.

Fuller, Sara. *The Paul Laurence Dunbar Collection: An Inventory to the Microfilm Edition*. Columbus, Ohio: Ohio Historical Society Archives Library, 1972.

Gayle, Addison, Jr. *Oak and Ivy: A Biography of Paul Laurence Dunbar*. Garden City, N.Y.: Doubleday, 1971.

Hudson, Gossie H. *Biography of Paul Laurence Dunbar*. Ph.D. diss., Ohio State U., 1970.

Johnson, James Weldon. *Along This Way*. New York: Viking, 1933.

Johnson, Ralph Glasgow. "The Poetry of Dunbar and McKay: A Study." M.A. thesis, U. Pittsburgh, 1950.

Kerlin, Robert T. *Negro Poets and Their Poems*. Washington, D.C.: Associated Publishers, 1923.

Lawson, Victor. *Dunbar Critically Examined*. Washington, D.C.: Associated Publishers, 1941.

Locke, Alain, ed. *The New Negro*. New York: Boni and Liveright, 1925.

Loggins, Vernon. *The Negro Author: His Development in America*. New York: Columbia U., 1931. Pp. 318–24, 344–52.

Martin, Jay. " 'Jump Back, Honey': Paul Laurence Dunbar and the Rediscovery of American Poetical Traditions." *BMMLA*, 7 (Spring 1974), 40–53.

_____, ed. *A Singer in the Dawn: Reinterpretations of Paul Laurence Dunbar*. New York: Dodd, Mead, 1974.

Metcalf, Gene. *Paul Laurence Dunbar: A Bibliography*. Metuchen, N.J.: Scarecrow, 1975.

Morgan, Anna. *My Chicago*. Chicago: R. F. Seymour, 1918.

Ransom, Reverdy C. "Paul Laurence Dunbar." *A.M.E. Church Review*, 31 (Oct. 1914), 188–90.

Redding, J. Saunders. *To Make A Poet Black*. Chapel Hill: U. North Carolina, 1939.

Scarborough, William S. "The Poet Laureate of the Negro Race." *A.M.E. Church Review*, 31 (Oct. 1914), 135–43.

Stronks, James B. "Paul Laurence Dunbar and William Dean Howells." *OhioHQ*, 17 (Apr. 1958), 95–108.

Turner, Darwin T. *In a Minor Chord: Three Afro-American Writers and Their Search for Identity*. Carbondale: Southern Illinois U., 1971.

_____. "Paul Laurence Dunbar: The Rejected Symbol." *JNH*, 52 (Jan. 1967), 1–13.

Van Deusen, John G. *The Black Man in White America*. Washington, D.C.: Associated Publishers, 1944.

Venable, Emerson, ed. *Poets of Ohio*. Cincinnati: Robert Clarke, 1909.

Wagner, Jean. *Les Poètes Nègres des États-Unis: Le Sentiment Racial et Religieux dans la Poésie de Paul Laurence Dunbar à Langston Hughes*. Paris: Librarie Istra, 1963.

Walker, Allen. "Paul Laurence Dunbar: A Study in Genius." *PsyR*, 25 (Jan. 1938), 53–82.

Walker, Robert H. *The Poet and the Gilded Age: Social Themes in Late Nineteenth Century American Verse.* Philadelphia: U. Pennsylvania, 1963.

Weatherford, Willis D. and Charles S. Johnson. *Race Relations: Adjustment of Whites and Negroes in the United States.* Boston: Heath, 1934.

Whittle, Gilberta S. "Paul Dunbar." *A.M.E. Church Review,* 18 (Apr. 1902), 320–27.

Wiggins, Lida Keck. *The Life and Works of Paul Laurence Dunbar.* Naperville, Ill.: J. L. Nichols, 1907.

Williams, Kenny J. *They Also Spoke: An Essay on Negro Literature in America, 1787–1930.* Nashville: Townsend, 1970.

Young Pauline A. "Paul Laurence Dunbar: An Intimate Glimpse." *Freedomways,* 12 (1972), 319–29.

Kenny J. Williams
Duke University
Durham, North Carolina

FINLEY PETER DUNNE (1867–1936)

Although, according to his son, Philip, Finley Peter Dunne was "by far the highest-paid writer of his time," his work has not received extensive critical analysis. Most commentators on the "Mr. Dooley" sketches have discussed Dunne either as a social critic or as a social historian of the period between the Spanish-American War and World War I. In the former category, such critics as Blair, Yates, and Bier have followed Tandy's assignment of Dunne to the "crackerbox philosopher" tradition in American humor; the most emphatic claim for Dunne as chronicler of his times is Masson's contention that a social history of the U.S. between 1898–1910 could be recreated entirely from the Dooley sketches.

One recurrent area of controversy in discussions of the Chicago journalist's work concerns the continuing relevance of the Mr. Dooley pieces. Thus, while on the one hand Pattee found Dunne's humor dated over forty years ago, Hutchinson, on the other hand, called it pertinent in the 1960s. Perhaps the violent disruptions in American society in the last decade have rejuvenated Dunne's social criticism; increased social malaise could also be a factor in the comparative boom in Dunne reprints and collections in the last dozen years.

There has not been much systematic study of the political philosophy emerging from the Dooley sketches. Probably the most satisfactory effort in this area has been Harrison's; he finds Dunne a "genial anarchist," whose works imply an "easy-going progressivism." Seventy years ago Boynton suggested that the literary artistry of the Dooley sketches deserved serious study, but there has not been much detailed examination of Dunne's use of Irish-American dialect, nor (despite the work of Yates and Bier) of his development of Mr. Dooley as a character. In addition, except for brief comments by Philip Dunne, no critical attention has been given to Dunne's non-Dooley writings. It is to be hoped that E. J. Brander's forthcoming book-length study of Dunne (Twayne U.S. Authors series) will fill in some or all of these areas of critical neglect.

Schaaf's *Mr. Dooley's Chicago* provides a very illuminating commentary on Dunne's early work, setting it in its local Chicago context and discussing it in terms of national issues.

MAJOR WORKS

Mr. Dooley in Peace and War. Boston: Small, Maynard, 1898. [humorous sketches]
Mr. Dooley in the Hearts of His Countrymen. Boston: Small, Maynard, 1899. [humorous sketches]
What Dooley Says. Chicago: Kazmar, 1899. [humorous sketches]
Mr. Dooley's Philosophy. New York: Russell, 1900. [humorous sketches]
Mr. Dooley's Opinions. New York: Russell, 1901. [humorous sketches]
Observations by Mr. Dooley. New York: Russell, 1902. [humorous sketches]
Dissertations by Mr. Dooley. New York: Harper, 1906. [humorous sketches]
Mr. Dooley Says. New York: Scribner, 1910. [humorous sketches]
New Dooley Book. New York: Scribner, 1911. [humorous sketches]
Mr. Dooley on Making a Will. New York: Scribner, 1919. [humorous sketches]
Mr. Dooley at His Best. Ed. by Elmer Ellis. New York: Scribner, 1938.
Mr. Dooley: Now and Forever. Ed. by Louis Filler. Stanford: Academic Reprints, 1954.
The World of Mr. Dooley. Ed. by Louis Filler. New York: Collier, 1962.
Mr. Dooley on Ivrything and Ivrybody. Ed. by Robert Hutchinson. New York: Dover, 1963.
Mr. Dooley's Chicago. Ed. by Barbara C. Schaaf. Garden City, N.Y.: Doubleday, 1977. [a large selection of early Dunne sketches]

CHECKLIST OF SECONDARY SOURCES

CHAL; Herzberg; *LHUS: TCA.*

Adams, Franklin P. "Mr. Dooley." *NR*, 94 (May 4, 1938), 390–1. [review-memoir]
———. Foreword to *Mr. Dooley at His Best*. New York: Scribner, 1938. Pp. xiii–xix. [introduction by F. P. Dunne]
Bander, Edward J. Preface to *Mr. Dooley on the Choice of Law*. Charlottesville, Va.: Michie, 1963. Pp. v–xii.
Bier, Jesse. *The Rise and Fall of American Humor*. New York: Holt, 1968. Pp. 178–90.
Blair, Walter. *Horse Sense in American Literature*. Chicago: U. Chicago, 1942. Pp. 240–55.
Boynton, Henry W. "American Humor." In *Journalism and Literature*. Boston: Houghton Mifflin, 1904. Pp. 87–102.
Canby, Henry S. "Mr. Dooley and Mr. Hennessy." *SatR*, 14 (May 9, 1936), 3–4. [memoir]
Chamberlain, John. "Mr. Dooley on Mr. Dewey." *NR*, 97 (Nov. 23, 1938), 77–78. [rev.]
Daly, T. A. "I see be th' Pa-apers." *SatR*, 14 (May 9, 1936), 4–5. [memoir]
DeMuth, James. "Small Town Chicago: The Comic Perspective of Finley Peter Dunn, George Ade, and Ring Lardner (1890–1920)." *DAI*, 36:3711A.
Duffey, Bernard. "Humor, Chicago Style." In *The Comic Imagination in American Literature*. Ed. by Louis D. Rubin, Jr. New Brunswick, N.J.: Rutgers U., 1973. Pp. 207–16.
Dunne, Philip, ed. *Mr. Dooley Remembers: The Informal Memoirs of Finley Peter Dunne*. Boston: Little, Brown, 1963.
Ellis, Elmer. *Mr. Dooley's America: A Life of Finley Peter Dunne*. New York: Knopf, 1941.
Filler, Louis. Introduction to *The World of Mr. Dooley*. New York: Collier, 1962. Pp. 9–23.
Harrison, J. M. "Finley Peter Dunne and the Progressive Movement." *JQ*, 44 (Autumn 1967), 475–81.
Howells, William Dean. "Certain of the Chicago School of Fiction." *NAR*, 176 (May 1, 1903), 743–46.

Hutchinson, Robert. Introduction to *Mr. Dooley on Ivrything and Ivrybody*. New York: Dover, 1963. Pp. iii–viii.
Leacock, Stephen. *The Greatest Pages of American Humor*. Garden City, N.Y.: Doubleday, 1936. Pp. 172–74.
Masson, Thomas L. *Our American Humorists*. Enl. ed. Freeport, N.Y.: Books for Libraries, 1931. Pp. 110–19.
Pattee, Fred L. *The New American Literature*. New York: Century 1930. Pp. 107–10.
Tandy, Jennette. *Crackerbox Philosophers in American Humor and Satire*. New York: Columbia U., 1925. Pp. 160–63.
Yates, Norris W. *The American Humorist*. Ames, Iowa: Iowa State U., 1964. Pp. 81–100.

Terence Malley
Long Island University
Brooklyn, New York

EDWARD EGGLESTON (1837–1902)

Eggleston once called his *Hoosier School-master* the "file-leader in the procession of American dialect novels." *LHUS* sees his work as the "cornerstone of a school." Van Doren believes that midwestern naturalism "descends from Eggleston," and Shumaker states that Eggleston began "the Golden Age of Indiana literature." But for Pattee, Eggleston saw the frontier as a "world peopled by Dickens."

Rendel has done the best extended studies, but none of the novels other than *School-master* has received any extended critical attention. The best primary bibliography is to be found in Blanck; the most extended secondary list is in Rendel. The major manuscript repository is Cornell University; the letters have not been collected; a definitive biography is needed.

MAJOR WORKS

The Hoosier School-master. New York: Orange Judd, 1871. [novel]
The End of the World: A Love Story. New York: Orange Judd, 1872. [novel]
The Mystery of Metropolisville. New York: Orange Judd, 1873. [novel]
The Circuit Rider: A Tale of the Heroic Age. New York: Ford, 1874. [novel]
Roxy. New York: Scribner, 1878. [novel]
The Hoosier School-Boy. New York: Scribner, 1883. [novel]
The Graysons: A Story of Illinois. New York: Century, 1888. [novel]
A History of the United States and its People for the Use of Schools. New York: Appleton, 1888.
The Faith Doctor: A Story of New York. Appleton, 1891. [novel]

CHECKLIST OF SECONDARY SOURCES

BDAL; Blanck; Burke; *CHAL*; *DAB*; Herzberg; *LHUS*; *OCAL*.

Beard, Anne. "Games and Recreations in the Novels of EE." *MF*, 11 (1961), 85–104.
Brown, Clarence A. "EE is a Social Historian." *JISHS*, 54 (1961), 405–18.
Cowie, Alexander. *The Rise of the American Novel*. New York: American, 1948. Pp. 538–56.
Danner, Effa Morrison. "EE." *IMH*, 33 (1937), 435–53.

Eggleston, George Cary. *The First of the Hoosiers, Reminiscences of Edward Eggleston* . . . . Philadelphia: Drexel Biddle, 1903.
Flanagan, John T. M. "The Novels of EE." *CE*, 5 (1944), 250–54.
——. "The Hoosier Schoolmaster in Minnesota." *MH*, 18 (1937), 347–70.
Haller, John M. "EE, Linguis." *PQ*, 24 (1945), 175–86.
Hirschfeld, Charles. "EE: Pioneer in Social History." In *Historiography and Urbanization: Essays in Honor of W. Stull Holt*. Ed. by Eric F. Goldman. Baltimore: Johns Hopkins U., 1941. Pp. 189–210.
Johannsen, R. W. "Literature and History: The Early Novels of EE." *IMH*, 48 (1952), 37–54.
Logan, Harlan D. "An Unpublished Journal of Edward Eggleston's with Supplementary Letters." M.A. thesis, Indiana U., 1932.
Nicholson, Meredith. *The Hoosiers*. New York: Macmillan, 1915. Pp. 134–55.
Paine, Stephen. "A Critical Study of the Writings of Edward Eggleston." Ph.D. diss., Duke U., 1961.
Randel, William. *Edward Eggleston: Author of The Hoosier School-Master*. New York: King's Crown, 1946.
——. *Edward Eggleston*. New Haven: College and University Press, 1963.
Rawley, James A. "Some New Light on EE." *AL* (1940), 453–58.
——. "EE: Historian." *IMH*, 40 (1944), 341–52.
Roth, John D. "Down East and Southwestern Humor in the Western Novels of Edward Eggleston." Ph.D. diss., U. Alabama, 1971.
Shumaker, Arthur W. *A History of Indiana Literature*. Indianapolis: Indiana Historical Bureau, 1962. Pp. 261–72.
Smith, Henry Nash. *The Virgin Land*. Cambridge, Mass.: Harvard U., 1950. Pp. 233–42.
Stone, Edward. "EE's Religious Transit." *UTSE* (July 1939), 210–18.
Van Doren, Carl. *The American Novel: 1789–1939*. New York: Macmillan, 1940. Pp. 118–20.
Wilson, Jack H. "Eggleston's Indebtedness to George Eliot in Roxy." *AL*, 42 (1970), 38–49.
Wolford, Thorp L. "EE: The Evolution of an Historian?" *IMH*, 63 (1967), 17–48.

E. Bruce Kirkham
Ball State University
Muncie, Indiana

PAUL ENGLE (1908–   )

Paul Engle is well-known for his work as teacher and administrator in connection with the writing workshops at the University of Iowa. His career as a writer has, in recent years, been overlooked. It did not begin that way. His first book, a Yale Series of Younger Poets winner, also won qualified critical approval from Monroe and Benét. His second made him into a nationally recognized poet and aroused controversy. Adams reviewed it enthusiastically on page one of the *New York Times Book Review*. Cowley, however, while admiring Engle's ability to structure poems solidly and to keep them moving along, faulted him for over-blown patriotic rhetoric. Fletcher felt the poetry, though not great, was certainly competent, and said Engle needed to mature a "boyish pioneer dream."

Among later reviewers of his poetry (the prose has received scant attention), Zabel called the work monotonous and too full of "verbal barba-risms," although acknowledging "considerable equipment." Hillyer praised some poems but mainly found "distraught verses" with overstated meanings. Friar admired Engle's "affirmative and manly" tone but depre-cated provincialism in the Iowa subject-matter. Jacobson said many poems showed "grasp and vigor" but their praise of everything (in *Poems in Praise*) blurred the quality of praise. Meredith was also critical, yet recog-nized fine lines and good poems. On the other hand, Willingham found Engle to be a "generously gifted poet."

Nevertheless, the early promise of Engle's poetry has not been fulfilled for most reviewers, and less attention has been paid to it in recent years. Aside from Hasselmayer's sympathetic short essay, there has been only Weber's M.A. thesis, limited in focus. And several books have been pub-lished since they wrote. While Andrews devotes several pages to Engle, he naturally writes historical description more than any extended critical eval-uation. He is right in observing that an attempt at a final summing-up is premature. Engle is still writing. More extensive critical attention could be paid, however, to the work already done.

MAJOR WORKS

Worn Earth. New Haven: Yale, 1932. [poems]
American Song. New York: Doubleday, 1934. [poems]
Break the Heart's Anger. New York: Doubleday, 1936. [poems]
Corn. New York: Doubleday, 1939. [poems]
Always the Land. New York: Random House, 1941. [novel]
West of Midnight. New York: Random House, 1941. [poems]
American Child: A Sonnet Sequence. New York: Random House, 1945. [poems]
The Word of Love. New York: Random House, 1951. [poems]
American Child: Sonnets for My Daughters. New York: Dial, 1956. [poems]
For the Iowa Dead. Iowa City, Iowa: State of Iowa, 1956. [poems]
Poems in Praise. New York: Random House, 1959. [poems]
Prairie Christmas. New York: Longmans, 1960. [5 essays, and poem]
Golden Child. New York: Dutton, 1962. [opera libretto]
Song Cycle, The Word of Love (with Philip Bezanson, composer). New York: American
    Composers Alliance, 1962. [poems as song lyrics]
Old Fashioned Christmas. New York: Dial, 1963. [poems & sketches]
A Woman Unashamed and Other Poems. New York: Random House, 1965. [poems]
Embrace. New York: Random House, 1969. [poems]
Introduction to *Portrait of Iowa.* Photographs by John Zielinski and others. Minneapolis:
    Adams, 1974. Pp. 14–36.

CHECKLIST OF SECONDARY SOURCES

CA; CAA; CB; CP; Herzberg; OCAL.

Adams, J. Donald. "A New Voice in American Poetry." *NYTBR*, July 29, 1934, p. 1. [rev.]
Andrews, Clarence A. *A Literary History of Iowa.* Iowa City: U. Iowa, 1972. Pp. 143–44,
    195–203.
Benét, William Rose. "Round About Parnassus." *SatR*, 9 (Dec. 24, 1932), 344. [rev.]
Cowley, Malcolm. "Eagle Orator." *NR*, 80 (Aug. 29, 1934), 79. [rev.]
Fletcher, John Gould. "The American Dream." *Poetry*, 45 (Feb. 1935), 285–88. [rev.]
Friar, Kimon. In "From the Mystic to the Merry." *SatR*, 43 (Feb. 6, 1960), 22. [rev.]

Hasselmayer, Louis A. "Three Contemporary Poets in Iowa." *IEY* (Fall 1959), 2–4.
Hillyer, Robert. "The Search for Love." *NYTBR*, Sept. 30, 1951, p. 27. [rev]
Jacobson, Josephine. "Comment." *Poetry*, 96 (July 1960), 231. [rev]
Meredith, William. "Poetry Roundup." *NYTBR*, Dec. 27, 1959, p. 6. [rev.]
Monroe, Harriet. "Paul Engle's First Book." *Poetry*, 42 (July 1933), 220–22. [rev.]
Paluka, Frank. *Iowa Authors.* Iowa City: Friends of The University of Iowa Libraries, 1967. Pp. 214–16. [bio-bibliography]
Van Gelder, Robert. "An Interview with Iowa's Paul Engle." *NYTBR*, Mar. 22, 1942, p. 2. [rev.]
Weber, R. B. "Paul Engle: A Checklist." *BIowa* (Nov. 1966), 11–37.
_____. "The Sonnets of Paul Engle." M.A. thesis, U. Iowa, 1958.
Willingham, J. R. *LJ*, 90 (Mar. 1, 1965), 1123. [rev.]
Zabel, Morton D. "Because I Love You So." *Poetry*, 48 (July 1936), 228–31. [rev.]

R. B. Weber
Southampton College of Long Island
University
Southampton, New York

LOULA GRACE ERDMAN (ca. 1912–   )

The popularity of Miss Erdman's writings is demonstrated by the fact that in 1974 nine of her books, including her first novel published thirty years earlier, were in print. The authoritative study is that of Sewell, which contains a bibliography of all of Erdman's works up to 1970. Additional secondary material is scanty, consisting almost entirely of book reviews and notices of publication.

The novels fall into two classes: the contemporary, based upon the author's experiences, observation, and imagination; and the historical, based upon her family roots and childhood in Missouri, her interest in midwestern people and culture, and her long residence in and study of the Texas Panhandle region. *The Short Summer, The Far Journey, Lonely Passage, The Years of the Locust*, and the reminiscent sketches of *Life Was Simpler Then* are set in Missouri.

Erdman's works usually feature women as the central characters and some are classified as juveniles, but all of them deal maturely and competently with such significant themes as teaching, pioneering, writing, and the civilization of the great heartland of America.

MAJOR WORKS

Separate Star. New York: Longmans, Green, 1944. [novel]
Fair Is the Morning. New York: Longmans, Green, 1945. [novel]
The Years of the Locust. New York: Dodd, Mead, 1947. [novel]
Lonely Passage. New York: Dodd, Mead, 1948. [novel]
The Edge of Time. New York: Dodd, Mead, 1950. [historical novel]
The Wind Blows Free. New York: Dodd, Mead, 1952. [historical novel]

My Sky Is Blue. New York: Longmans, Green, 1953. [novel]
Three at the Wedding. New York: Dodd, Mead, 1953. [novel]
The Far Journey. New York: Dodd, Mead, 1955. [historical novel]
The Wide Horizon: A Story of the Texas Panhandle. New York: Dodd, Mead, 1956. [historical novel]
The Short Summer. New York: Dodd, Mead, 1958. [novel]
The Good Land. New York: Dodd, Mead, 1959. [historical novel]
Many a Voyage. New York: Dodd, Mead, 1960. [historical novel]
The Man Who Told the Truth, With Six Short Stories. New York: Dodd, Mead, 1962. [novella and stories]
Room to Grow. New York: Dodd, Mead, 1962. [novel]
Life Was Simpler Then. New York: Dodd, Mead, 1963. [reminiscences, sketches, stories]
A Wonderful Thing, and Other Stories. New York: Dodd, Mead, 1964. [stories]
Another Spring. New York: Dodd, Mead, 1966. [historical novel]
A Time to Write. New York: Dodd, Mead, 1969. [autobiography, views on writing]
A Bluebird Will Do. New York: Dodd, Mead, 1973. [historical novel]

Checklist of Secondary Sources

CA; Herzberg; Warfel.

Baker, Nina Brown. "Texas Pioneers." *NYTBR*, Nov. 23, 1952, p. 54. [rev.]
Birney, Hoffman. "Sodbuster." *NYTBR*, Nov. 26, 1950, p. 37. [rev.]
Buckman, Gertrude. "Thurley Renfro." *NYTBR*, Jan. 16, 1949, p. 21. [rev.]
Campbell, Walter S. ("Stanley Vestal"). *The Book Lover's Southwest: A Guide to Good Reading*. Norman: U. Oklahoma, 1955. P. 249. [reading guide]
E. L. B. "One-Room Schoolhouse." *NYTBR*, Oct. 4, 1953, p. 28. [rev.]
Gross, Sarah Crokla. "The Youngest." *NYTBR*, Sept. 27, 1959, p. 48. [rev.]
Karolides, Nicholas J. *The Pioneer in the American Novel, 1900–1950*. Norman: U. Oklahoma, 1967. Pp. 77, 188, 129ff.
Meyer, Roy W. *The Middle Western Farm Novel in the Twentieth Century*. Lincoln: U. Nebraska, 1965. Pp. 192, 210.
Nordyke, Lewis. "The Long Trail to Texas." *NYTBR*, Sept. 18, 1955, p. 30. [rev.]
Parke, Andrea. "Wedding-Blues Trio." *NYTBR*, Jan. 31, 1954, p. 21. [rev.]
Sewell, Ernestine P. *Loula Grace Erdman*. Southwest Writers Series, No. 33. Austin: Steck-Vaughn, 1970. [biog.-critical pamphlet]
Taylor, Pamela. "Old Dade Dies." *SatR*, 30 (Sept. 20, 1947), 30–31. [rev.]

Don R. Swadley
University of Texas at Arlington
Arlington, Texas

JAMES T. FARRELL (1904–79)

The Farrell collection at the Charles Patterson Van Pelt Library of the University of Pennsylvania is an indispensable resource for Farrell scholars. As of May 1977, it contained approximately two hundred volumes of Farrell's publications in various editions; over seven hundred boxes of Farrell's letters, other manuscripts, and short published writings, all of these now listed in six volumes of descriptive entries; a voluminous collection of letters to Farrell, reviews of his books, interviews, articles about him, and other relevant newspaper clippings; sixty boxes of similar materials in various stages of preparation for the inventory; and over two hundred cartons of as yet unsorted manuscripts, letters, and materials. Westlake's article describes the resources of the collection in greater detail. Farrell also has given copies of some publications and manuscripts to the University of Chicago Library, the University of Kentucky Library, and the Milwaukee Public Library. Relatively extensive collections of his correspondence may be found in the Beinecke Library at Yale, the New York Public Library, and the university libraries at Columbia, Harvard, Indiana, Oregon, Princeton, Syracuse, and Virginia.

As of May 1977, Farrell had completed first drafts of three volumes of his autobiography entitled "Since I Began," twelve novels in "A Universe of Time" series, and numerous short stories and novelettes. He has recorded several score of his lectures. There is no full scale biography.

With reference to the checklist of secondary sources below, Beach and Gelfant provide excellent and extensive introductory studies of Farrell's fiction and its place in twentieth-century urban literature. Dyer and Reiter give detailed consideration, respectively, to the Studs Lonigan and Danny O'Neill novels, and to Farrell's short stories. Gelfant, Matthiessen, Kligerman, and Eisinger supply valuable commentary on the Bernard Carr books. Lynch and Wolfe judiciously assess Farrell's critical writings. A majority of the listed critics characterize—each from his own perspective—Farrell's literary naturalism; and Owen, Mitchell, Branch ("Freedom and Determinism . . ."), and Fried study its basic relationship to the thought of American pragmatists. Wald provides a comprehensive account of the evolution of Farrell's socialist political thought and affiliations. *Twentieth Century Literature* for February 1976 provides a sampling of contemporary estimates of Farrell's accomplishment. Branch supplies a checklist of Farrell's writings and a book-length critical study of Farrell's works that centers chiefly on the novels.

MAJOR WORKS

Young Lonigan. New York: Vanguard, 1932. [novel]
Gas-House McGinty. New York: Vanguard, 1933. [novel]
The Young Manhood of Studs Lonigan. New York: Vanguard, 1934. [novel]
Calico Shoes and Other Stories. New York: Vanguard, 1934.
Judgment Day. New York: Vanguard, 1935. [novel]
Guillotine Party and Other Stories. New York: Vanguard, 1935.
Studs Lonigan: A Trilogy. New York: Vanguard, 1935. [includes *Young Lonigan, The Young Manhood of Studs Lonigan, Judgment Day*]
A Note on Literary Criticism. New York: Vanguard, 1936. [polemical literary criticism]
A World I Never Made. New York: Vanguard, 1936. [novel]
Can All This Grandeur Perish? and Other Stories. New York: Vanguard, 1937.
The Short Stories of James T. Farrell. New York: Vanguard, 1937. [includes *Calico Shoes, Guillotine Party, Can All This Grandeur Perish?*]
No Star Is Lost. New York: Vanguard, 1938. [novel]
Tommy Gallagher's Crusade. New York: Vanguard, 1939. [novella, reprinted in *To Whom It May Concern and Other Stories*]

Father and Son. New York: Vanguard, 1940. [novel]
Ellen Rogers. New York: Vanguard, 1941. [novel]
$1,000 a Week and Other Stories. New York: Vanguard, 1942.
My Days of Anger. New York: Vanguard, 1943. [novel]
To Whom It May Concern and Other Stories. New York: Vanguard, 1944.
The League of Frightened Philistines and Other Papers. New York: Vanguard, 1945. [critical essays: literary, social, autobiographical]
Bernard Clare. New York: Vanguard, 1946. [novel]
When Boyhood Dreams Come True. New York: Vanguard, 1946. [stories]
Literature and Morality. New York: Vanguard, 1947. [critical essays: literary and social]
The Life Adventurous and Other Stories. New York: Vanguard, 1947.
The Road Between. New York: Vanguard, 1949. [novel]
A Misunderstanding. New York: House of Books, 1949. [novella, reprinted in *An American Dream Girl*]
The Name Is Fogarty: Private Papers on Public Matters. New York: Vanguard, 1950. [satirical social-political commentary by Jonathan Titulescu Fogarty, author's pseudonym]
An American Dream Girl. New York: Vanguard, 1950. [stories]
This Man and This Woman. New York: Vanguard, 1951. [novel]
Yet Other Waters. New York: Vanguard, 1952. [novel]
The Face of Time. New York: Vanguard, 1953. [novel]
Reflections at Fifty and Other Essays. New York: Vanguard 1954. [critical essays: literary, social, autobiographical]
French Girls Are Vicious and Other Stories. New York: Vanguard, 1955.
An Omnibus of Short Stories. New York: Vanguard, 1957. [reprints *$1,000 a Week, To Whom It May Concern, The Life Adventurous*]
A Dangerous Woman and Other Stories. New York: New American Library, 1957.
My Baseball Diary. New York: Barnes, 1957, [essays, reminiscences, and fiction on baseball]
It Has Come to Pass. New York: Herzl, 1958. [impressions of Israel]
Dialogue on John Dewey. Ed. Corliss Lamont. New York: Horizon, 1959. [conversation on John Dewey by Farrell and ten others]
Boarding House Blues. New York: Paperback Library, 1961. [novel]
Side Street and Other Stories. New York: Paperback Library, 1961.
Sound of a City. New York: Paperback Library, 1962. [stories]
The Silence of History. New York: Doubleday, 1963. [novel]
What Time Collects. New York: Doubleday, 1964. [novel]
The Collected Poems of James T. Farrell. New York: Fleet, 1965.
Lonely for the Future. New York: Doubleday, 1966. [novel]
When Time Was Born. New York: Horizon, 1966. [prose poem]
New Year's Eve/1929. New York: Horizon, 1967. [novel]
A Brand New Life. New York: Doubleday, 1968. [novel]
Judith. Athens, Ohio: Schneider, 1969. [novella, reprinted in *Judith and Other Stories*]
Childhood Is Not Forever. New York: Doubleday, 1969. [stories]
Invisible Swords. New York: Doubleday, 1971. [novel]
Judith and Other Stories. New York: Doubleday, 1973.
The Dunne Family. New York: Doubleday, 1976. [novel]
Literary Essays, 1954–1974. Ed. by Jack Alan Robbins. Port Washington, N.Y.: Kennikat Press, 1976.

CHECKLIST OF SECONDARY SOURCES

Alexis, Gerhard T. "Farrell Since *Our* Days of Anger." *CE*, 27 (1965), 221–26.
Beach, Joseph Warren. "James T. Farrell: Tragedy of the Poolroom Loafer" and "James T. Farrell: The Plight of the Children." *American Fiction, 1920–1940.* New York: Macmillan, 1941.
Berry, Newton. "A Preface to the Death Fantasy Sequence of 'Judgment Day.' "*NUTQ,* (Winter 1965), 124–26.
Branch, Edgar M. *A Bibliography of James T. Farrell's Writings, 1921–1957.* Philadelphia: U. Pennsylvania, 1959. [continued in *Am Bk Collector:* Summer 1961, pp. 42–48; May 1967, pp. 9–19; March-April 1971, pp. 13–18; January-February 1976, pp. 17–22.]

———. "American Writer in the Twenties: James T. Farrell and the University of Chicago." *ABC* (Summer 1961), 25–32.

———. "Freedom and Determinism in James T. Farrell's Fiction." In *Kent Studies in English, Number 1*. Ed. by Sydney J. Krause. Kent, Ohio: Kent State, 1964.

———. *James T. Farrell*. New York: Twayne, 1971.

Cargill, Oscar. "The Naturalists." *Intellectual America: Ideas on the March*. New York: Macmillan, 1948.

Chamberlin, John. "Introduction." *Studs Lonigan: A Trilogy*. New York: Modern Library, 1938.

The Coming of Age of a Great Book. New York: Vanguard, 1953. [commentary on Farrell and his work]

Curley, Thomas F. "Catholic Novels and American Culture." *Commentary*, 36 (1963), 34–42.

Davis, Robert Gorham. "New Chapter in the Farrell Story." *NYTBR*, May 12, 1963, pp. 1, 43. [rev. of *The Silence of History*]

———. "The Stuff of Life, Minus the Breath of Life." *NYTBR*, Nov. 2, 1947, p. 7. [rev. of *The Life Adventurous and Other Stories*]

DeVoto, Bernard. "Beyond Studs Lonigan." *SatR* (Oct. 24, 1936), 5–6. [rev. of *A World I Never Made*]

Dickstein, Felice Witztum. "James T. Farrell" in "The Role of the City in the Works of Theodore Dreiser, Thomas Wolfe, James T. Farrell, and Saul Bellow." Ph.D. diss., City U. New York, 1973.

Douglas, Wallace. "The Case of James T. Farrell." *NUTQ*, (Winter 1965), 105–23.

Dyer, Henry Hopper. "James T. Farrell's Studs Lonigan and Danny O'Neill Novels." Ph.D. diss., U. Pennsylvania, 1965.

Eisinger, Chester E. "The Survivors." *Fiction of the Forties*. Chicago: U. Chicago, 1963.

Fried, Lewis F. "James T. Farrell: Shadow and Act." *JA*, 17 (1972), 140–55.

———. "The Naturalism of James Farrell: A Study of His Major Novels." Ph.D. diss., U. Massachusetts, 1969.

Friedman, Philip Allan. "Afterword." *Studs Lonigan: A Trilogy*. Signet Classic ed., 5th printing, May 1965. New York: New American Library of World Literature, 1965.

Frohock, Wilbur M. "James T. Farrell: The Precise Content." *The Novel of Violence in America, 1920–1950*. 2d ed. Dallas: Southern Methodist U., 1958.

Gelfant, Blanche H. "James T. Farrell: The Ecological Novel." *The American City Novel*. Norman: U. Oklahoma, 1954.

Glicksberg, Charles I. "The Criticism of James T. Farrell." *SwR*, 35 (1950), 189–96.

Grattan, C. Hartley. "James T. Farrell: Moralist." *Harper*, 209 (Oct. 1954), 93–94, 96, 98. [rev. of *The Face of Time* and general essay]

Gregory, Horace. "James T. Farrell: Beyond the Provinces of Art." *New World Writing*. Fifth Mentor Selection. New York: New American Library of World Literature, 1954.

Hart, Robert Charles. "James T. Farrell: The Novelist as Sociological Realist." In "Writers on Writing: The Opinions of Six Modern American Novelists on the Craft of Fiction." Ph.D. diss., Northwestern U., 1954.

Hatfield, Ruth. "The Intellectual Honesty of James T. Farrell." *CE*, 3 (1942), 337–46.

Hobsbaum, Philip. "The Great American Novel: A Study of James T. Farrell." *Gemini*, 2 (Summer 1959), 39–42.

Howe, Irving. "James T. Farrell—The Critic Calcified." *PR*, 14 (1947), 545–46, 548, 550, 552.

Kazin, Alfred. "The Revival of Naturalism." In *On Native Grounds: An Interpretation of Modern American Prose Literature*. New York: Reynal & Hitchcock, 1942.

Klingerman, Jack. "The quest for Self: James T. Farrell's Character Bernard Carr." *UKCR*, 29 (1962), 9–16.

Lovett, Robert Morss. "James T. Farrell." *EJ*, 26 (1937), 347–54. [reprinted as "Introduction" to *The Short Stories of James T. Farrell*, 1937]

Lynch, William James. "The Theory and Practice of the Literary Criticism of James T. Farrell." Ph.D. diss., U. Pennsylvania, 1966.

Matthiessen, F. O. "James T. Farrell's Human Comedy." *NYTBR*, May 12, 1946, pp. 1, 35. [rev. essay of *Bernard Clare*]

Mitchell, Richard. "James T. Farrell's Scientific Novel." Ph.D. diss., Syracuse U., 1963.

_____. "Studs Lonigan: Research in Morality." *CR*, 6 (1962), 202–14. [revision of "Studs Lonigan: A Scientific Novel." *Thoth*, 1 (Fall 1959), 35–43]

Myers, Helen. "Farrell Is Voluble on Mental Biography: Ready and Willing to Talk of Own Aims and Standards." Poughkeepsie *Sunday New Yorker*, June 30, 1946, p. 2–A. [interview]

O'Malley, Frank. "James T. Farrell: Two Twilight Images." *Fifty Years of the American Novel: A Christian Appraisal.* Ed. by Harold C. Gardiner, S.J. New York: Scribner, 1951.

Owen, David H. "A Pattern of Pseudo-Naturalism: Lynd, Mead, and Farrell." Ph.D. diss., U. Iowa, 1950.

Posselt, Edith. "Das Charakterbild in den Werken James T. Farrells als Ausdruck seiner Weltanschauung." Ph.D. diss., U. Kiel, 1954.

Reiter, Irene Morris. "A Study of James T. Farrell's Short Stories and Their Relation to His Longer Fiction." Ph.D. diss., U. Pennsylvania, 1964.

Rosenthal, T. G. "Studs Lonigan and the Search for an American Tragedy." *BBAAS*, n.s. 7 (1963), 46–53.

Salzman, Jack. "James T. Farrell: An Essay in Bibliography." *RALS*, 6 (Autumn 1976), 131–63.

Schickel, Richard. "James T. Farrell: Another Time, Another Place." *Esquire*, 58 (Dec. 1962), 156–57, 272–75. [interview-article]

Shannon, William V. "The Irish in Literature." In *The American Irish*. Rev. ed. New York: Macmillan, 1966.

Shaughnessy, Edward L. "Oliver Alden and Studs Lonigan: Heirs to Spiritual Poverty." *MarkR*, 4 (1974), 48–52.

Stock, Irving. "Farrell and His Critics." *ArQ*, 6 (1950), 328–38.

Walcutt, Charles C. "James T. Farrell: Aspects of Telling the Whole Truth." *American Literary Naturalism, A Divided Stream*. Minneapolis: U. Minnesota, 1956.

Wald, Alan. "James T. Farrell: The Revolutionary Socialist Years." Ph.D. diss., U. California at Berkeley, 1974.

Wallenstein, Barry. "James T. Farrell: Critic of Naturalism." In *American Literary Naturalism: A Reassessment*. Ed. by Yoshinobu Hakutani and Lewis Fried. Heidelberg: Carl Winter U., 1976.

Westlake, Neda M. "The James T. Farrell Collection at the University of Pennsylvania." *ABC* (Summer 1961).

Wolfe, Don M. "Introduction: Notes on Farrell as Critic and Writer." *James T. Farrell Selected Essays*. Ed. by Luna Wolf. New York: McGraw-Hill, 1964.

Edgar M. Branch
Miami University
Oxford, Ohio

KENNETH FEARING (1902–61)

No book-length study of Fearing's work has yet been published, although Perkins has completed a dissertation on Fearing's poetry (1972) and in 1949 Rosenthal gave over part of his dissertation to an examination of the poetry in terms of the contribution it made to the "Depression literature" of the 1930s. Rosenthal, Kahn, Gregory, and Abbott have published substantial articles, Kahn dealing primarily with Fearing's themes, Gregory with his contributions to proletariat and leftist literature, and Abbott with the appropriateness of the writer's forms and techniques to his urban settings.

Little of critical substance exists on the novels, which have often been dismissed as entertaining thrillers. Thematic ties between the novels and the poetry remain to be examined. The same can be said of the possible relationship between Fearing's Midwest background (Oak Park, Ill., Chicago, and the University of Wisconsin) and his work.

MAJOR WORKS

Angel Arms. New York: Coward McCann, 1929. [poetry]
Poems. New York: Dynamo, 1935. [poetry]
Dead Reckoning. New York: Random House, 1938. [poetry]
The Hospital. New York: Random House, 1939. [novel]
Collected Poems. New York: Random House, 1940.
Dagger of The Mind. New York: Random House, 1941. [novel]
Clark Gifford's Body. New York: Random House, 1942. [novel]
Afternoon of a Pawnbroker, and Other Poems. New York: Harcourt, 1943.
The Big Clock. New York: Harcourt, 1946. [novel]
John Barry. (As Donald F. Bedford, pseud., with H. Bedford Jones and Donald Friede.) New York: Creative Age Press, 1947. [novel]
Stranger at Coney Island. New York: Harcourt, 1948. [poems]
Lonliest Girl in The World. New York: Harcourt, 1951. [novel]
The Generous Heart. New York: Harcourt, 1954. [novel]
New and Selected Poems. Bloomington: Indiana U., 1956.
The Crozart Story. New York: Doubleday, 1960. [novel]

CHECKLIST OF SECONDARY SOURCES

Burke; *CAA;* Herzberg; *LHUS; LLC; OCAL;* Warfel.

Aaron, Daniel. *Writers on The Left: Episodes in American Literary Communism*. New York: Harcourt, 1961.
Abbott, C. D. "The Poetics of Mr. Fearing." *UCSLL,* ser. 2B (Oct. 1945), 382–87.
Bishop, John Peale. *The Collected Essays of John Peale Bishop*. New York: Scribner, 1948.
———. "The Poet as an American." *Nation,* 151 (Oct. 12, 1940), 340–42. [rev.]
Dahlberg, Edward. "Introduction." In Kenneth Fearing's *Poems*. New York: Dynamo, 1935.
Gregory, Horace and Marya Zaturenska. "Critical Realism of Kenneth Fearing." *A History of American Poetry 1900–1940*. New York: Harcourt, 1942.
Guttman, Allen. "The Brief Embattled Course of Proletarian Poetry." In *Proletarian Writers of The Thirties*, ed. by David Madden. Carbondale: Southern Illinois U., 1968.
Kahn, Sy. "Kenneth Fearing and the Twentieth Century Blues." *The Thirties: Fiction, Poetry and Drama*. Deland, Fla.: Everett Edwards, 1967.
Kees, Weldon. "Fearing's Collected Poems." *Poetry,* 57 (Jan. 1941), 264–70. [rev.]
Kunitz, Stanley. "Private Eye." *SatR,* 40 (Jan. 29, 1957), 51–53. [rev.]
Perkins, James Ashbrook. "An American Rhapsody: The Poetry of Kenneth Fearing." Ph.D. diss., U. Tennessee, 1972.
Rahv, Phillip. "Proletarian Literature: A Political Autopsy." *SouR,* 4 (1939), 616–18.
Rosenthal, Macha Louis. "The Meaning of Kenneth Fearing's Poetry." *Poetry,* 64 (July 1944), 208–23.
———. "Chief Poets of the American Depression: Contributions of Kenneth Fearing, Horace Gregory, and Muriel Rukeyser to Contemporary American Poetry." Ph.D. diss., New York U., 1949.
Stephen, Ruth. "Fearing and the Art of Communication." *Poetry,* 63 (Dec. 1943), 163–65. [rev.]

Sy Kahn
University of the Pacific
Stockton, California

EDNA FERBER (1887–1968)

There are limited resources available to the scholar interested in Edna Ferber's writing. Although her work was at one time very popular, students of literature have not found it sufficiently provocative to treat it at length. No full-scale studies of Miss Ferber have yet been produced. There are, however, many reviews of her works, and some articles—Brenni identifies many of the more useful ones.

Critics have tended to concentrate on the social dimensions of Ferber's work. Overton speaks of her as a social critic, and White compares her to Dickens in this regard. White, in pointing out her intense interest in people of all sorts, echoes much of the commentary on her work. Williams remarks that although the structure of her stories is weak, the characters are vivid and realistic. He notes O. Henry's influence upon her style. Farrar comments upon the importance of her newspaper experience in developing the tendency to observe people closely and sympathetically. Parker, while granting that Ferber is a good storyteller with interesting perceptions into human nature, rejects the notion that she can be taken seriously as a critic of society.

An extremely prolific writer, Ferber received widespread attention from her contemporaries for her novels, plays, and short stories (often set in the Midwest of her youth), and for the nearly twenty films based on her work. Although her popularity has declined, several of her plays are still occasionally produced.

MAJOR WORKS

Buttered Side Down. New York: Stokes, 1912. [stories]
Roast Beef, Medium: The Business Adventures of Emma McChesney. New York: Stokes, 1913. [stories]
Personality Plus: Some Experiences of Emma McChesney and Her Son, Jock. New York: Stokes, 1914. [stories]
Emma McChesney and Co. New York: Stokes, 1915. [stories]
Fanny Herself. New York: Stokes, 1917. [novel]
Cheerful, By Request. Garden City, N.Y.: Doubleday, 1918. [stories]
$1200 a Year. With Newman Levy. Garden City, N.Y.: Doubleday, 1920. [play]
Half Portions. Garden City, N.Y.: Doubleday, 1920. [stories]
The Girls. Garden City, N.Y.: Doubleday, 1921. [novel]
Gigolo. Garden City, N.Y.: Doubleday, 1922. [stories]
So Big. Garden City, N.Y.: Doubleday, 1924. [novel]
Minick. With George S. Kaufman. Garden City, N.Y.: Doubleday, 1925. [play]
Show Boat. Garden City, N.Y.: Doubleday, 1926. [novel]
Mother Knows Best: A Fiction Book. Garden City, N.Y.: Doubleday, 1927. [stories]
Royal Family. With George S. Kaufman. Garden City, N.Y.: Doubleday, 1928. [play]
Cimarron. Garden City, N.Y.: Doubleday, 1930. [novel]

American Beauty. Garden City, N.Y.: Doubleday, 1931. [novel]
Dinner At Eight. With George S. Kaufman. Garden City, N.Y.: Doubleday, 1932. [play]
They Brought Their Women: A Book of Short Stories. Garden City, N.Y.: Doubleday, 1933.
Come and Get It. Garden City, N.Y.: Doubleday, 1935. [novel]
Stage Door. With George S. Kaufman. Garden City, N.Y.: Doubleday, 1936. [play]
Nobody's in Town. Garden City, N.Y.: Doubleday, 1938. [two short novels]
A Peculiar Treasure. Garden City, N.Y.: Doubleday, 1939. [autobiography]
Saratoga Trunk. Garden City, N.Y.: Doubleday, 1941. [novel]
Great Son. Garden City, N.Y.: Doubleday, 1945. [novel]
One Basket: Thirty-One Short Stories. New York: Simon and Schuster, 1947. [stories]
Bravo. With George S. Kaufman. New York: Dramatists Play Service, 1949. [play]
Giant. Garden City, N.Y.: Doubleday, 1952. [novel]
Ice Palace. Garden City, N.Y.: Doubleday, 1958. [novel]
A Kind of Magic. Garden City, N.Y.: Doubleday, 1963. [autobiography]

CHECKLIST OF SECONDARY SOURCES

CAA; LLC; OCAL; TCA & Supp; Warfel.

Allen, M. P. " 'The Odd Women' and 'The Girls.' " *NAR,* 216 (Nov. 1922), 691–94.
Banning, Margaret C. "Edna Ferber's America." *SatR,* 19 (Feb. 4, 1939), 5–6.
Bromfield, Louis. "Edna Ferber." *SatR,* 12 (June 15, 1935), 10–12.
Brenni, V. J. and B. L. Spencer. "Edna Ferber, A Selected Bibliography." *BB,* 22 (Sept.–Dec. 1958), 152–56.
Davidson, Donald. "Edna Ferber." In *The Spyglass: Views and Reviews.* Nashville: Vanderbilt U., 1963. Pp. 70–74.
Dickinson, Rogers. *Edna Ferber: A Biographical Sketch with a Bibliography.* New York: Doubleday, 1925.
Farrar, John C., ed. *The Literary Spotlight.* New York: Doran, 1924. Pp. 135–45.
Flagg, J. M. "Frills and Ednaferberlows." *AmM,* 77 (May 1914), 102–12.
Forestier, Marie. "L'Amérique se penche sur son passé." *RevN,* 8 (July–Aug. 1948), 92–95.
Gray, James. *On Second Thought.* Minneapolis: Minnesota, 1946. Pp. 158–61.
Johnson, Merle. "American First Editions . . . Edna Ferber." *PW,* 119 (May 21, 1931), 1611–12.
Nichols, Lewis. "Talk with Edna Ferber." *NYTBR,* Oct. 5, 1942, p. 30.
Overton, Grant. "The Social Critic in Edna Ferber." *Bookman,* 64 (Oct. 1926), 138–43.
———. *The Women Who Make Our Novels.* New York: Moffat, 1922. Pp. 126–38.
Parker, W. R. "Stranger's Story of Edna Ferber." *EJ,* 19 (June 1930), 447–49.
Patrick, Arnold. "Getting into Six Figures." *Bookman,* 61 (Apr. 1925), 164–68.
Plante, P. R. "Mark Twain, Ferber, and the Mississippi." *MTJ,* 13 (Summer 1966), 8–10.
Shaughnessy, Mary R. *Women and Success in American Society in the Works of Edna Ferber.* New York: Gordon, 1976.
Spitz, Leon. "Edna Ferber: An American Jewish Self-Portrait." *CJF,* 13 (Winter 1955), 100–3.
Van Gelder, R. *Writers and Writing.* New York: Scribner, 1946. Pp. 360–65.
White, W. A. "Edna Ferber." *WW,* 59 (June 1930), 36–38.
———. "Edna Ferber in the Forefront of the Reporters of Her Age." *WT,* 59 (Aug. 1930), 221-25.
———. "A Friend's Story of Edna Ferber." *EJ,* 19 (Feb. 1930), 101–6.
Williams, Blanche C. *Our Short Story Writers.* New York: Moffat, 1922. Pp. 277–78.

Robert E. Probst
Georgia State University
Atlanta, Georgia

EUGENE FIELD (1850–95)

In an attempt to check the popularity of rival newspapers, Melville Stone decided that Chicago needed a journalist of national reputation who could attract a number of readers to a morning edition of the *Daily News*. When Eugene Field, the successful managing editor of the Denver *Tribune,* was invited to come to Chicago, the *News* had already become important in the development of Chicago literature, for the newspapers had unconsciously taken the lead toward a new interpretation of urban life and urban symbols. The city was showing promise as a possible literary center when Field arrived in 1883.

The twelve years which Field spent in Chicago were quite productive. His humorous column, "Sharps and Flats," was well-known. It often attacked without mercy the pretensions of Chicago society and Chicago culture. But more important in a study of regional literature is the fact that Field's column served as the immediate model and source of inspiration for an entire generation of younger newspapermen such as Theodore Dreiser. Until his death, Field presided over the city as the "dean" of Chicago letters.

Field was a prolific writer. In addition to his daily columns, he wrote numerous poems and was frequently called "the poet of childhood." Before the *Chapbook: Semi-Monthly: A Miscellany of Belles Lettres* (1894–98) merged with the *Dial* (which was published in Chicago from 1880–1916 and in New York from 1916–20), Field was a frequent contributor; hence, one interested in his work should study the early issues of the *Chapbook.*

Over the years his reputation has suffered an eclipse partially because of the ephemeral nature of so many of the issues which he attacked. Earlier literary histories tended to discuss his works which continued to appear in the years after his death. Often these were issued as "privately printed" works; consequently, a complete bibliographical statement is made increasingly difficult because of the number of times a single work might appear with a slightly modified title. In recent years, however, Field has been considered only as a minor regional writer who happened to write some poems for children.

Field scholarship culminated with Thompson's two-volume psychological study in 1901 and his subsequent biography in 1927. In 1924 Dennis attempted a limited study of Field's periods of creativity. However, it was not until 1974 that another full-length study appeared, and it relies rather heavily upon previously published sources. There is a need for further study of the writer whose fame now rests upon a few children's poems.

Major Works

The Complete Tribune Primer. Denver: Privately printed 1881 and later issued by the Mutual Book Company of Boston in 1901.

Culture's Garland: Being Memoranda of the Gradual Rise of Literature, Art, Music and Society in Chicago, and Other Western Ganglia. Boston: Tichnor, 1887. [newspaper whimsy]

A Little Book of Profitable Tales. Cambridge: Wilson, 1889. [stories]

A Little Book of Western Verse. Chicago: Privately printed 1889 and later issued by Scribner in 1907.

With Trumpet and Drum. New York: Scribner, 1892. [poetry]

The Holy Cross and Other Tales. Chicago: Stone and Kimball, 1893. [stories]

Love Son of Childhood. New York: Scribner, 1894. [poetry]

An Auto-Analysis. Chicago: Privately printed, 1896. [autobiographical statements]

The House: An Episode in the Lives of Reuben Baken, Astronomer, and of His Wife, Alice. Scribner, 1896. [fiction]

The Love Affair of a Bibliomaniac. New York: Scribner, 1896. [essays]

Second Book of Tales. New York: Scribner, 1896. [stories]

Songs and Other Verse. New York: Scribner, 1896.

Florence Bardsley's Story: The Life and Death of a Remarkable Woman. Chicago: Way, 1897. [fiction]

Lullaby Land. New York: Scribner, 1897. [poetry]

Poems of Childhood. New York: Scribner, 1897.

Second Book of Verse. New York: Scribner, 1897.

The Writings in Prose and Verse of Eugene Field. 12 vols. New York: Scribner, 1898–1901.

How One Friar Met the Devil and Two Pursued Him. Chicago: Morris, 1900. [fiction]

A Little Book of Tribune Verse. Denver: Tandy, Wheeler, 1901.

Sharps and Flats. 2 vols. New York: Scribner, 1901. [essays]

Checklist of Secondary Sources

Burke; *DAB; LHUS.*

Below, Ida C. *Eugene Field in His Home.* New York: Dutton, 1898.

Conrow, Robert. *Field Days: The Life, Times, & Reputation of Eugene Field.* New York: Scribner, 1974.

Dedmon, Emmett. *Fabulous Chicago.* New York: Random House, 1953.

Dennis, Charles H. *Eugene Field's Creative Years.* New York: Doubleday, 1924.

———. *Victor Lawson: His Time and Work.* Chicago: Chicago, 1935.

Dreiser, Theodore. *A Book About Myself.* New York: Boni and Liveright, 1922.

Duffey, Bernard. *The Chicago Renaissance in American Letters.* East Lansing: Michigan State College, 1954.

Duncan, Hugh D. *Culture and Democracy: The Struggle for Form in Society and Architecture in Chicago and the Middle West During the Life and Times of Louis H. Sullivan.* Totowa, N.J.: Bedminster, 1965.

———. *The Rise of Chicago as a Literary Center from 1885 to 1920.* Totowa, N.J.: Bedminster, 1964.

Flanagan, J. T. "Eugene Field After Sixty Years." *UKR,* 13 (Winter 1945), 167–73.

French, Charles Newton. *Story of Little Boy Blue.* Chicago: Privately Printed, 1944.

Hart, James D. *The Popular Book: A History of America's Literary Taste.* Berkeley: U. California, 1961.

Hoffman, F. S. "Eugene Field as I Knew Him at Knox." *Knox Alumnus* (Spring 1924), 89–92.

Knight, Grant C. *The Critical Period in American Literature.* Chapel Hill: U. North Carolina, 1951.

Larned, W. T. "The Mantle of Eugene Field." *Bookman,* 41 (Jan. 1915), 44–57.

Masters, Edgar Lee. *The Tale of Chicago.* New York: Putnam, 1933.

Meeker, Arthur. *Chicago, With Love: A Polite and Personal History.* New York: Knopf, 1955.

Mott, Frank Luther. *American Journalism.* New York: Macmillan, 1941.

Nolan, Jeannette C. *The Gay Poet: The Story of Eugene Field.* New York: J. Messner, 1940.

Thompson, Slason. *Eugene Field: A Study in Heredity and Contradictions.* 2 vols. New York: Scribner, 1901.

————. *Life of Eugene Field: The Poet of Childhood.* New York: Appleton, 1927.

Williams, Kenny J. *In the City of Men: Another Story of Chicago.* Nashville: Townsend, 1974.

Wilson, Francis. *The Eugene Field I Knew.* New York: Scribner, 1898.

Ziff, Larzer. *The American 1890's: Life and Times of a Lost Generation.* New York: Viking, 1966.

Kenny J. Williams
Duke University
Durham, North Carolina

F. SCOTT FITZGERALD (1896–1940)

The works of F. Scott Fitzgerald have been as thoroughly catalogued, evaluated, and annotated as those of any modern American writer. His early reputation was based primarily on his portrayal of the Jazz Age era in American life; this perspective on his fiction began with the reviews of his first novel, *This Side of Paradise* (1920), and continued through the publication of *The Great Gatsby* (1925). It was suspended briefly in the thirties when his own favorite among his novels, *Tender Is the Night* (1934), was seen as irrelevant by a new generation of critics and reviewers. And, at his death, Fitzgerald's reputation was probably at its lowest point. But, beginning with the posthumous publication in 1941 of his unfinished novel, *The Last Tycoon,* an astonishing—and often excessive—interest in his life and writings has persisted to the present day.

This "Fitzgerald Revival," while it has spawned much spurious commentary, has had in recent years the salutary effect of at least partially shifting the emphasis of Fitzgerald scholarship and criticism from the details of his life to the fiction itself. He is now being increasingly viewed as the dedicated and skillful writer that he was. *The Great Gatsby* still receives far too great a share of this critical attention; and the short stories are the most-overlooked area of his canon; but highly readable biographies by Mizener, Turnbull, Piper, and Milford, and incisive critical studies by Miller, Lehan, Perosa, Stern, Bruccoli, and Eble present a variety of approaches to and interpretations of the life and works.

The portions of his life which Fitzgerald spent in the Midwest have always received some attention. Two of his earliest boosters were Thomas Boyd of the St. Paul *Daily News* and James Gray of the St. Paul *Dispatch.* In more recent years, novelist Powers has stressed Fitzgerald's relation to St. Paul; Gross has commented on the thematic importance of the Midwest in *The Great Gatsby*; Irish has stressed the importance of Fitzgerald's midwestern boyhood; and all of the biographers—most especially Piper—have examined the Midwest years in detail. In addition, recent publication in book form of Fitzgerald's Basil and Josephine stories, heavily drawn from his own childhood, have also focused attention on his midwestern experience.

MAJOR WORKS

This Side of Paradise. New York: Scribner, 1920. [novel]
Flappers and Philosophers. New York: Scribner, 1920. [stories]
The Beautiful and Damned. New York: Scribner, 1922. [novel]
Tales of the Jazz Age. New York: Scribner, 1922. [stories]
The Vegetable. New York: Scribner, 1923. [play]
The Great Gatsby. New York: Scribner, 1925. [novel]
All the Sad Young Men. New York: Scribner, 1926. [stories]
Tender is the Night. New York: Scribner, 1934. [novel]
Taps at Reveille. New York: Scribner, 1935. [stories]
The Last Tycoon. New York: Scribner, 1941. [novel]
The Crack-Up. Ed. by Edmund Wilson. New York: New Directions, 1945. [stories, essays, letters]
The Stories of F. Scott Fitzgerald. New York: Scribner, 1951.
Afternoon of an Author—A Selection of Uncollected Stories and Essays. New York: Scribner, 1958.
The Pat Hobby Stories. New York: Scribner, 1962.
The Letters of F. Scott Fitzgerald. Ed. by Andrew Turnbull. New York: Scribner, 1963.
The Apprentice Fiction of F. Scott Fitzgerald—1909–1917. Ed. by John Kuehl. New Brunswick, N.J.: Rutgers U., 1965. [stories, plays]
F. Scott Fitzgerald in His Own Time: A Miscellany. Ed. by Matthew J. Bruccoli and Jackson R. Bryer. Kent, Ohio: Kent State U., 1971. [poems, essays, reviews]
Dear Scott/Dear Max—The Fitzgerald–Perkins Correspondence. Ed. by John Kuehl and Jackson R. Bryer. New York: Scribner, 1971.
As Ever, Scott Fitz—: Letters Between F. Scott Fitzgerald and His Literary Agent Harold Ober 1919–1940. Ed. by Matthew J. Bruccoli, with the assistance of Jennifer M. Atkinson. Philadelphia: Lippincott, 1972.
The Basil and Josephine Stories. Ed. by John Kuehl and Jackson R. Bryer. New York: Scribner, 1973.
Bits of Paradise: 21 Uncollected Stories By F. Scott and Zelda Fitzgerald. Ed. by Scottie Fitzgerald Smith and Matthew J. Bruccoli. New York: Scribner, 1974.

CHECKLIST OF SECONDARY SOURCES

Adams, J. Donald. "F. Scott Fitzgerald." *AmMerc*, 61 (1945), 373–77. [rev.]
Barbour, Brian M. "*The Great Gatsby* and the American Past." *SouR*, n.s. 9 (1973), 288–99.
Berryman, John. "F. Scott Fitzgerald." *KR*, 8 (1946), 103–12.
Bewley, Marius. "Great Scott." *NYRB*, Sept. 16, 1965, pp. 22–24. [rev.]
Bruccoli, Matthew J. *Apparatus for F. Scott Fitzgerald's "The Great Gatsby"* [*Under the Red, White, and Blue*]. Columbia: U. South Carolina, 1974.
_____. *The Composition of "Tender is the Night"—A Study of the Manuscripts*. Pittsburgh: U. Pittsburgh, 1963.
_____. *F. Scott Fitzgerald—Collector's Handlist*. Columbus, Ohio: Fitzgerald Newsletter, 1964.
_____. *F. Scott Fitzgerald—A Descriptive Bibliography*. Pittsburgh: U. Pittsburgh, 1972.
_____. " 'A Might Collation'—Animadversions on the Text of F. Scott Fitzgerald." In *Editing Twentieth Century Texts*. Ed. by Francess G. Malpenny. Toronto: U. Toronto, 1972. Pp. 28–50.
_____, comp. *Profile of F. Scott Fitzgerald*. Columbus, Ohio: Merrill, 1971.
_____, ed. *F. Scott Fitzgerald. "The Great Gatsby"—A Facsimile of the Manuscript*. Washington, D.C.: Microcard Editions Books, 1973.
Bryer, Jackson R. *The Critical Reputation of F. Scott Fitzgerald—A Bibliographical Study*. Hamden, Conn.: Archon, 1967.

————. "F. Scott Fitzgerald," *Sixteen Modern American Authors—A Survey of Research and Criticism.* Ed. by Jackson R. Bryer. Durham, N.C.: Duke U., 1974. Pp. 277–321. [bibliographical essay]

Buntain, Lucy M. "A Note on the Editions of *Tender Is the Night.*" *SAF,* 1 (1973), 208–13.

Burhans, Clinton S., Jr. " 'Magnificently Attune to Life': The Value of 'Winter Dreams.' " *SSF,* 6 (1969), 401–12.

————. "Structure and Theme in *This Side of Paradise.*" *JEGP,* 68 (1969), 605–24.

Burton, Mary E. "The Counter-Transference of Dr. Diver." *ELH,* 38 (1971), 459–71.

Buttitta, Tony. *After the Good Gay Times—Asheville–Summer of '35—A Season With F. Scott Fitzgerald.* New York: Viking, 1974. [biography]

Callaghan, Morley. *That Summer in Paris.* New York: Coward-McCann, 1963. Pp. 149–255. [biography]

Callahan, John F. *The Illusions of a Nation—Myth and History in the Novels of F. Scott Fitzgerald.* Urbana: U. Illinois, 1972.

Casty, Alan. " 'I and It' in the Stories of F. Scott Fitzgerald." *SSF,* 9 (1972), 47–58.

Cowley, Malcolm. "F. Scott Fitzgerald: The Romance of Money." *WR,* 17 (1953), 245–55.

————. "Of Clocks and Calendars." *NR,* 104 (1941), 376–77.

Cowley, Malcolm and Robert Cowley, eds. *Fitzgerald and the Jazz Age.* Scribner Research Anthology. New York: Scribner, 1966. [anthology]

Crosland, Andrew T., comp. *A Concordance to F. Scott Fitzgerald's "The Great Gatsby."* Detroit: Gale, 1975.

Cross, K. G. W. *F. Scott Fitzgerald.* Edinburgh: Oliver and Boyd; New York: Grove, 1964.

Dahlberg, Edward. "The Fitzgerald Revival: A Dissent." *Freeman,* 2 (Nov. 1951), 90–92.

Dos Passos, John. *The Best Times.* New York: New American Library, 1966. Pp. 127–60.

Doyno, Victor A. "Patterns in *The Great Gatsby.*" *MFS,* 12 (1966), 415–26.

Eble, Kenneth. *F. Scott Fitzgerald.* New York: Twayne, 1963.

————, ed. *F. Scott Fitzgerald—A Collection of Criticism.* New York: McGraw-Hill, 1973.

Fiedler, Leslie. *An End to Innocence.* Boston: Beacon, 1955. Pp. 174–82.

Fitzgerald/Hemingway Annual, 1969. Ed. by Matthew J. Bruccoli and C. E. Frazer Clark, Jr. Washington, D.C.: NCR Microcard Editions, 1969.

Fitzgerald Newsletter (1958–1968). Ed. by Matthew J. Bruccoli. Washington, D.C.: NCR Microcard Editions, 1969.

Foster, Richard. "The Way to Read *Gatsby.*" *Sense and Sensibility in Twentieth-Century Writing: A Gathering in Memory of William Van O'Connor.* Ed. by Brom Weber. Carbondale: Southern Illinois U., 1970. Pp. 94–108.

Friedman, Norman. "Versions of Form in Fiction—'Great Expectations' and 'The Great Gatsby.' " *Accent,* 14 (1954), 246–64.

Frohock, W. M. *Strangers to This Ground—Cultural Diversity in Contemporary American Writing.* Dallas: Southern Methodist U., 1961. Pp. 36–62.

Geismar, Maxwell. *The Last of the Provincials.* Boston: Houghton Mifflin, 1943. Pp. 287–352.

Gindin, James. "Gods and Fathers in F. Scott Fitzgerald's Novels." *MLQ,* 30 (1969), 64–85.

Goldhurst, William. *F. Scott Fitzgerald and His Contemporaries.* Cleveland: World, 1963.

Graham, Sheilah. *The Real F. Scott Fitzgerald: Thirty-Five Years Later.* New York: Grosset, 1976.

————. *College of One.* New York: Viking, 1967. [biography]

————. *The Rest of the Story.* New York: Coward-McCann, 1964. [biography]

Graham, Sheilah and Gerold Frank. *Beloved Infidel—The Education of a Woman.* New York: Henry Holt, 1958. [biography]

Gross, Barry. "Back West: Time and Place in *The Great Gatsby.*" *WAL,* 8 (1973), 3–13.

————. "The Dark Side of Twenty-five: Fitzgerald and *The Beautiful and Damned.*" *BuR,* 16 (Winter 1968), 40–52.

————. "Scott Fitzgerald's *The Last Tycoon:* The Great American Novel?" *ArQ,* 26 (1970), 197–216.

————. "*This Side of Paradise*: The Dominating Intention." *SNNTS,* 1 (Spring 1969), 51–59.

Gurko, Leo and Miriam Gurko. "The Essence of F. Scott Fitzgerald." *CE,* 5 (1944), 372–76.

Harvey, W. J. "Theme and Texture in *The Great Gatsby.*" *ES,* 38 (1957), 12–20.

Hemingway, Ernest. *A Moveable Feast.* New York: Scribner, 1964. Pp. 147–86.

Higgins, John A. *F. Scott Fitzgerald: A Study of the Stories*. Jamaica, N.Y.: St. John's U., 1971.

Hindus, Milton. *F. Scott Fitzgerald: An Introduction and Interpretation*. New York: Holt, 1968.

Hoffman, Frederick J. "Points of Moral Reference: A Comparative Study of Edith Wharton and F. Scott Fitzgerald." In *English Institute Essays: 1949*. Ed. by Alan S. Downer. New York: Columbia U., 1950. Pp. 147–76.

———. *The Twenties*. New York: Viking, 1955. Pp. 91–92, 98–100, 100–18, 371–75.

———, ed. *"The Great Gatsby": A Study*. New York: Scribner, 1962.

Hyman, Stanley Edgar. "The Great Fitzgerald." *NewL* (Dec. 9, 1963), 19–20. [rev.]

Irish, Carol. "The Myth of Success in Fitzgerald's Boyhood." *SAF*, 1 (1973), 176–87.

Jacobson, Dan. "F. Scott Fitzgerald." *Encounter*, 14 (June 1960), 71–77. [rev.]

Kazin, Alfred, ed. *F. Scott Fitzgerald—The Man and His Work*. Cleveland: World, 1951.

Kopf, Josephine Z. "Meyer Wolfsheim and Robert Cohn: A Study of a Jewish Type and Stereotype." *Tradition*, 10 (1969), 93–104.

Krutch, Joseph Wood. "From the Decade This Side of Paradise." *NYTBR*, Aug. 12, 1945, pp. 1–2. [rev.]

Kuehl, John R. "Scott Fitzgerald: Romantic and Realist." *TSLL*, 1 (1959), 412–26.

———. "Scott Fitzgerald's Reading." *PULC*, 22 (1961), 58–89.

LaHood, Marvin J., ed. *"Tender Is the Night"—Essays in Criticism*. Bloomington: Indiana U., 1969.

Latham, Aaron. *Crazy Sundays—F. Scott Fitzgerald in Hollywood*. New York: Viking, 1971.

Lehan, Richard D. *F. Scott Fitzgerald and the Craft of Fiction*. Crosscurrents Modern Critiques. Preface by Harry T. Moore. Carbondale: Southern Illinois U., 1966.

Lockridge, Ernest, ed. *Twentieth Century Interpretations of "The Great Gatsby."* Englewood Cliffs, N.J.: Prentice-Hall, 1968.

Long, Robert E. "*The Great Gatsby* and the Tradition of Joseph Conrad." *TSLL*, 8 (1966), 257–76, 407–22.

McCall, Dan. " 'The Self-Same Song That Found a Path': Keats and *The Great Gatsby*." *AL*, 42 (1971), 521–30.

McNally, John J. "Boats and Automobiles in *The Great Gatsby*: Symbols of Drift and Death." *HUSSR*, 5 (1971), 11–17.

MacPhee, Laurence E. "*The Great Gatsby*'s 'Romance of Motoring': Nick Carraway and Jordan Baker." *MFS*, 18 (1972), 207–12.

Margolies, Alan. "F. Scott Fitzgerald's Work in the Film Studios." *PULC*, 32 (1971), 81–110.

Marquand, John P. "Looking Backwards—1. Fitzgerald: 'This Side of Paradise.' " *SRL*, 22 (Aug. 6, 1949), 30–31.

Mayfield, Sara. *Exiles From Paradise—Zelda and Scott Fitzgerald*. New York: Delacorte, 1971. [biography]

Milford, Nancy. *Zelda—A Biography*. New York: Harper, 1970.

Miller, James E., Jr. *F. Scott Fitzgerald—His Art and His Technique*. New York: New York U., 1964.

Mizener, Arthur. *The Far Side of Paradise*. Boston: Houghton Mifflin, 1951. Rev. ed., 1965. [critical biography]

———. *Scott Fitzgerald and His World*. New York: Putnam, 1972. [biography]

———, ed. *F. Scott Fitzgerald: A Collection of Critical Essays*. Twentieth Century Views. Englewood Cliffs, N.J.: Prentice-Hall, 1963.

Moers, Ellen. "F. Scott Fitzgerald: Reveille at Taps." *Commentary*, 34 (1962), 526–30. [rev.]

Moseley, Edwin M. *F. Scott Fitzgerald—A Critical Essay*. Contemporary Writers in Christian Perspective. Grand Rapids, Mich.: Eerdmans, 1967.

O'Hara, John. "Scott Fitzgerald—Odds and Ends." *NYTBR*, July 8, 1945, p. 3. [rev.]

Perosa, Sergio. *The Art of F. Scott Fitzgerald*. Tr. by Charles Matz and the author. Ann Arbor: U. Michigan, 1965.

Piper, Henry D. "Fitzgerald's Cult of Disillusion." *AQ*, 3 (1951), 69–80.

———. *F. Scott Fitzgerald—A Critical Portrait*. New York: Holt, 1965.

———. "F. Scott Fitzgerald and the Image of His Father." *PULC*, 12 (1951), 181–86.

———, ed. *Fitzgerald's "The Great Gatsby": The Novel, The Critics, The Background*. Scribner Research Anthology. New York: Scribner, 1970.

Powers, J. F. "Cross-Country—St. Paul, Home of the Saints." *PR*, 16 (1949), 714–21.

Schneider, Isidor. "A Pattern of Failure." *NM*, 57 (Dec. 4, 1945), 23–24. [rev.]

Shain, Charles. *F. Scott Fitzgerald.* University of Minneasota Pamphlets on American Writers, No. 15. Minneapolis: U. Minnesota, 1961.

Sklar, Robert. *F. Scott Fitzgerald—The Last Laocoön.* New York: Oxford U., 1967.

Stern, Milton R. *The Golden Moment—The Novels of F. Scott Fitzgerald.* Urbana: U. Illinois, 1970.

Stouck, David. "White Sheep on Fifth Avenue: *The Great Gatsby* as Pastoral." *Genre,* 4 (1971), 335–47.

Tomkins, Calvin. *Living Well Is the Best Revenge.* New York: Viking, 1971. [biography]

Trachtenberg, Alan. "The Journey Back: Myth and History in *Tender Is the Night,*" *Experience in the Novel—Selected Papers From the English Institute.* Ed. by Roy Harvey Pearce. New York: Columbia U., 1968. Pp. 133–62.

Turnbull, Andrew. *Scott Fitzgerald.* New York: Scribner, 1962. [biography]

Tuttleton, James W. *The Novel of Manners in America.* Chapel Hill: U. North Carolina, 1972. Pp. 162–83.

Wells, Walter. *Tycoons and Locusts—A Regional Look at Hollywood Fiction of the 1930s.* Crosscurrents, Modern Critiques. Preface by Harry T. Moore. Carbondale: Southern Illinois U., 1973. Pp. 103–21.

Jackson R. Bryer
University of Maryland
College Park, Maryland

TIMOTHY FLINT (1780–1840)

Nowhere is twentieth century lack of concern for the literary achievement of Timothy Flint better indicated than through the scarcity of bibliographical information about him. There are no systematic collections of his works, and no significant library collections of manuscript materials. Indeed, manuscript sources have almost entirely disappeared. Although many have doubtless been destroyed in the years since Flint's death, patient digging might well bring to light hitherto unknown or overlooked manuscript materials.

Critical studies of Flint have primarily been biographical and historical in emphasis, and with relatively few exceptions have not concerned themselves with Flint's literary significance. The best bibliography of early studies of Flint is to be found in Kirkpatrick's *Timothy Flint* (1911); of later studies, in Folsom's *Timothy Flint* (1965). The former work is primarily historical in focus, the latter critical. The two taken together are useful as indicators of the present strengths and weaknesses in Flint scholarship.

MAJOR WORKS

Francis Berrian, or the Mexican Patriot. 2 vols. Boston: Cummings, Hilliard, 1826. [novel]

Recollections of the Last Ten Years . . . . Boston: Cummings, Hilliard, 1826. [travel reminiscences]

Western Monthly Review. Cincinnati, 1827–30. [monthly journal, edited and mostly written by Flint]

A Condensed Geography and History of the Western States, or the Mississippi Valley. 2 vols. Cincinnati: E. H. Flint, 1828. [geography, history]

The Life and Adventures of Arthur Clenning. 2 vols. Philadelphia: Towar & Hogan, 1828. [novel]
George Mason, the Young Backwoodsman; or "Don't Give Up the Ship." A Story of the Mississippi. Boston: Hilliard, 1829. [novel]
The Lost Child. Boston: Carter & Hendee, 1830. [novel]
The Shoshonee Valley; a Romance. 2 vols. Cincinnati: E. H. Flint, 1830. [novel]
The Personal Narrative of James O. Pattie, of Kentucky. Cincinnati: J. H. Wood, 1831. [edition of pioneer narrative]
The Art of Being Happy: From the French of Droz, 'Sur L'Art D'Etre Heureux' . . . . Boston: Carter and Hendee, 1832. [translation and paraphrase]
The History and Geography of the Mississippi Valley . . . . 2 vols. Cincinnati: E. H. Flint, 1832.
Biographical Memoir of Daniel Boone, the First Settler of Kentucky . . . . Cincinnati: N. & G. Guilford, 1833. [biography]
Indian Wars of the West . . . . Cincinnati: E. H. Flint, 1833. [history, biography]
Lectures Upon Natural History, Geology, Chemistry, the Application of Steam, and Interesting Discoveries in the Arts. Cincinnati: E. H. Flint, 1833. [science]
The Bachelor Reclaimed or Celibacy Vanquished, from the French. Philadelphia: Key & Biddle, 1834. [translation and paraphrase]

CHECKLIST OF SECONDARY SOURCES

BDAL; Blanck; Burke; *CHAL; DAB;* Duyckinck; Herzberg; *OCAL.*

Folsom, James K. *Timothy Flint.* New York: Twayne, 1965.
Hamilton, John A. "Timothy Flint's 'Lost Novel' [*The Lost Child*]." *AL,* 22 (Mar. 1950), 54–56.
Kirkpatrick, John Ervin. *Timothy Flint: Pioneer, Missionary, Author, Editor. 1780–1840.* Cleveland: Clark, 1911.
Lombard, C. A. "Timothy Flint: Early American Disciple of French Romanticism." *RLC,* 36 (Avril-Juin, 1962), 276–82.
Morris, Robert L. "Three Arkansas Travelers." *AHQ,* 4 (Autumn 1945), 215–30. [Flint, Washington Irving, Friedrich Gerstaecker]
Seelye, John D. "Timothy Flint's 'Wicked River' and *The Confidence-Man.*" *PMLA,* 78 (Mar. 1963), 75–79.
Sheehan, Sister Mary Agatha. "A Study of the First Four Novels of Texas." M.A. thesis, Catholic U. of America, Washington, D.C., 1939. Pp. 62–89. [*Francis Berrian*]
Stimson, Frederick S. " 'Francis Berrian': Hispanic Influence on American Romanticism." *Hispanica,* 42 (Dec. 1959), 511–16.
Turner, Arlin. "James Kirke Paulding and Timothy Flint." *MVHR,* 34 (June 1947), 105–11.
Venable, William H. *Beginnings of Literary Culture in the Ohio Valley. Historical and Biographical Sketches.* Cincinnati: Clarke, 1891. Pp. 323–60.
Vorpahl, Ben Merchant. "The Eden Theme and Three Novels by Timothy Flint." *SRom,* 10 (Spring 1971), 105–29. [*Francis Berrian, Arthur Clenning, The Shoshonee Valley*]

James K. Folsom
University of Colorado
Boulder, Colorado

ALICE FRENCH [OCTAVE THANET]
(1850–1934)

The definitive study of the Iowan who used the pen name of Octave Thanet has been prepared by McMichael in his eminently readable biography. In addition to biographical and bibliographical detail, the work furnishes perceptive literary criticism and places French in her milieu. McMichael's bibliography lists unpublished and unlocated manuscripts and manuscript repositories. The principal repository is that in the Newberry Library, Chicago. McMichael also lists *all* of French's publications, and he should be consulted for titles less than book-length, and for the contents of collections. The influence of French on Susan Glaspell is a subject especially deserving of investigation.

MAJOR WORKS

Knitters in the Sun. New York: Houghton Mifflin, 1887. [stories]
Expiation. New York: Scribner, 1890. [novel]
Otto the Knight and other Trans-Mississippi Stories. New York: Houghton Mifflin, 1891.
Stories of a Western Town. New York: Scribner, 1893. [on Davenport, Ia.]
The Missionary Sheriff: Being Incidents in the Life of a Plain Man Who Tried to do His Duty. New York: Harper, 1897. [stories]
A Book of True Lovers. Chicago: Way & Williams, 1897. [stories]
A Slave to Duty and Other Women. New York: Stone, 1898. [stories]
The Heart of Toil. New York: Scribner, 1898. [stories]
The Captured Dream and Other Stories. New York: Harper, 1899.
The Man of the Hour. Indianapolis: Bobbs-Merrill, 1905. [novel]
The Lion's Share. Indianapolis: Bobbs-Merrill, 1907. [novel]
By Inheritance. Indianapolis: Bobbs-Merrill, 1910. [novel]
Stories That End Well. Indianapolis: Bobbs-Merrill, 1911.
A Step on the Stair. Indianapolis: Bobbs-Merrill, 1913. [novel]
And the Captain Answered. Indianapolis: Bobbs-Merrill, 1917. [novel]

CHECKLIST OF SECONDARY SOURCES

BDAL; Burke; Herzberg; *OCAL*.

Barrette, Lydia M. "Alice French (Octave Thanet)." *MS*, 41 (Nov. 1926) 83–85.
Bentzon, Th. [Marie Therese Blanc]. "Dans l'Arkansas: A Propos des Romans d' Octave Thanet." *Revue des Deux*, 133 (Feb. 1, 1896), 542–72. Tr. by Evelyn S. Schaeefer, "In Arkansas Apropos of Octave Thanet's Romances." *MM*, 6 (July and Aug. 1896), 37–47, 136–45.
Frederick, John T. "The Writer's Iowa." *Palimpsest*, 11 (Feb. 1930), 57–60.
———. "Town and City in Iowa Fiction." *Palimpsest*, 35 (Feb. 1954), 53–57.
Harper, Clio. "Alice French." *Library of Southern Literature*. Ed. by E. A. Alderman. Vol. 4. New Orleans, 1909.
James, W. P. "On the Theory and Practice of Local Color." *LA*, 213 (June 12, 1897), 743–48.
Laurence, Elwood P. "The Immigrant in American Fiction, 1890–1920." Ph.D. diss., Western Reserve U., 1943.
Lieberman, Elias. *The American Short Story: A Study of the Influence of Locality in its Development.* Ridgewood, N. J.: Editor, 1912.
Martin, Theodore K. "The Social Philosophy of Alice French." Master's thesis, Louisiana State U., Baton Rouge, 1941.
McMichael, George. *Journey to Obscurity: The Life of Octave Thanet.* Lincoln: U. Nebraska, 1965.
McQuin, Susan C. "Alice French's View of Women." *BIowa*, 20, 26, pp. 34–42.
Mayberry, George. "Industrialism and the Industrial Worker in the American Novel, 1814–1890." Ph.D. diss., Harvard U., 1942.
Morse, James Herbert. "The Native Elements in American Fiction, Since the War." *CM*, 26 (July 1883), 362–75.
Moss, Mary. "Representative American Story Tellers." *Bookman*, 24 (Sept. 1906), 21–29.
Newberry Library Bulletin, 6 (Nov. 1962), 24ff.
Portor, Laura S. "In Search of Local Color." *HM*, 145 (Aug.-Sept. 1922), 281–94, 451–66.

Reid, Mary J. "The Theories of Octave Thanet and Other Western Realists." *MM*, 9 (Feb. 1898), 99–108.

Rhode, Robert. "The Functions of Setting in the American Short Story of Local-Color, 1865–1900." Ph.D. diss., U. Texas, 1940.

Schmalenbeck, Hildegarde. "A Study of the Literary Reputation of Alice French." Master's thesis, U. Texas, 1946.

Sewell, Rebecca. "Alice French: The Octave Thanet of Literature." Master's thesis, Southern Methodist U., 1934.

Wilson, Winifred. "Octave Thanet as a Writer of Short Stories." Bachelor's thesis, U. Illinois, 1918.

Clarence A. Andrews
University of Iowa
Iowa City, Iowa

HENRY BLAKE FULLER (1857–1929)

In the midst of the bustling nineteenth-century Chicago there developed a writer who was destined to give voice to the essential characteristics of urban fiction. Henry Blake Fuller was an accomplished writer whose early exercises in romanticism gave no indication that he would one day be considered in the forefront of the realistic movement.

His most creative period was at the end of the nineteenth century; however, his period of productivity extended well into the twentieth century. His short stories, essays, plays, and verse appeared in such diverse journals as *Scribner's, New Republic, Life, Current Opinion, Harper's Monthly, Bookman, Century, Chicago Tribune Sunday Magazine, Atlantic Monthly, Everybody's, The Chapbook, Poetry, Cosmopolitan,* and *Saturday Evening Post* from 1884 to 1925. During the period from 1902 to 1903 he wrote numerous essays for the *Chicago Evening Post.* Some are literary criticism but many are social analyses dealing primarily with Chicago. In the 1920s he wrote more than 150 book reviews, many of which appeared in New York papers. Thus, by the end of his life, he had established himself not only as a critic of the city but also as a perceptive reviewer.

The attempts to assess Fuller's contributions to American letters have been sporadic. Howells thought he might become the new leader of the realistic movement; however, Wagenknecht felt that Fuller's art was hampered by his "hatred" for his environment. It was not until 1939 that a detailed critical biography appeared. In recent years there has been a resurgence of interest in the work of Fuller.

MAJOR WORKS

The Chevalier of Pensieri-Vani. Boston: Cupples, 1890. [novel]
The Chatelaine of La Trinite. New York: Century, 1892. [novel]
The Cliff-Dwellers. New York: Harper, 1893. [novel]

With the Procession. New York: Harper, 1895. [novel]
The Puppet Booth. New York: Century, 1896. [stories]
From the Other Side. Boston: Houghton Mifflin, 1898. [stories]
The New Flag. Privately printed, 1899. [novel]
The Last Refuge. Boston: Houghton Mifflin, 1900. [novel]
Under the Skylights. New York: Appleton, 1901. [stories]
Waldo Trench and Others. New York: Scribner, 1908. [stories]
Lines Long and Short. Boston: Houghton Mifflin, 1917. [poetry]
On the Stairs. Boston. Houghton Mifflin, 1918. [novel]
Bertram Cope's Year. Chicago: Seymour, 1919. [novel]
The Coffee House, by Carlo Goldoni. New York: Knopf, 1925. [translation]
The Fan, by Carlo Goldoni. New York: Knopf, 1925. [translation]
Gardens of This World. New York: Knopf, 1929. [novel]
Not on the Screen. New York: Knopf, 1930. [novel]

CHECKLIST OF SECONDARY SOURCES

DAB; LHUS; TCA.

Abel, Darrel. "Expatriation and Realism in American Fiction in the 1880's: Henry Blake Fuller." *AmLitR,* 3 (Summer 1970), 245–57.

Anderson, Sherwood. *Memoirs.* New York: Harcourt, 1942.

Banks, Nancy Houston. "Henry Blake Fuller." *Bookman,* 2 (Aug.–Sept. 1895), 15–17.

Berthoff, Warner. *The Ferment of Realism.* New York: Free Press, 1965.

Bowron, Bernard. *Henry Blake Fuller of Chicago: The Ordeal of a Genteel Realist in Ungen-. teel America.* Westport, Conn.: Greenwood, 1974.

Boyesen, Hjalmer. Review of *The Cliff-Dwellers. CosmopMag,* 16 (Jan. 1894), 373–74.

Chatfield-Taylor, Hobart C. *Cities of Many Men.* Boston: Houghton Mifflin, 1925.

Dedmon, Emmett. *Fabulous Chicago.* New York: Random House, 1953.

Dell, Floyd. "Chicago in Fiction." *Bookman,* 38 (Nov. 1913), 275–77.

Dondore, Dorothy A. *The Prairie and the Making of Middle America.* Cedar Rapids, Iowa: Torch Press, 1926.

Duffey, Bernard. *The Chicago Renaissance in American Letters.* East Lansing: Michigan State College, 1954.

Duncan, Hugh D. *Culture and Democracy: The Struggle for Form in Society and Architecture in Chicago and the Middle West During the Life and Times of Louis H. Sullivan.* Totowa, N.J.: Bedminster, 1965.

———. *The Rise of Chicago as a Literary Center from 1885 to 1920.* Totowa, N.J.: Bedminster, 1964.

Farrar, John. "The Literary Spotlight: Henry Blake Fuller." *Bookman,* 57 (Feb. 1924), 645–49.

Gant-Winn, Georgia. *The Works of Henry Blake Fuller.* Ph.D. diss., U. Pittsburgh, 1938.

Garland, Hamlin. *Afternoon Neighbors.* New York: Macmillan, 1934.

———. *Companions on the Trail.* New York: Macmillan, 1931.

———. *My Friendly Contemporaries.* New York: Macmillan, 1932.

———. *Roadside Meetings.* New York: Macmillan, 1930.

Grey, Lennox B. "Chicago and 'The Great American Novel' ": A Critical Approach to the American Epic. Ph.D. diss., U. Chicago, 1935.

Griffin, Constance. *Henry Blake Fuller: A Critical Biography.* Philadelphia: U. Pennsylvania, 1939.

Hansen, Harry. *Midwest Portraits.* New York: Harcourt, 1923.

Howells, William Dean. "Certain of the Chicago School of Fiction." *NAR,* 176 (May 1903), 739–46.

———. *Heroines of Fiction.* Vol. 2. New York: Harper, 1901.

Huneker, James. *Unicorns.* New York: Scribner, 1917.

Jones, Llewellyn. "Chicago—Our Literary Center." *Bookman,* 60 (Jan. 1925), 565–67.

Kramer, Dale. *Chicago Renaissance: The Literary Life in the Midwest, 1900–1930.* New York: Appleton, 1966.

Lawrence, Elwood P. "Fuller of Chicago: A Study in Frustration." *AQ,* 6 (Summer 1954), 137–46.

Lovett, Robert Morss. "Fuller of Chicago." *NR,* 60 (Aug. 21, 1929), 16–18.

Martin, Jay. *Harvest of Change: American Literature 1865–1914.* Englewood Cliffs, N.J.: Prentice-Hall, 1967.

Monroe, Harriet. *A Poet's Life: Seventy Years in a Changing World.* New York: Macmillan, 1938.

———. "A Tribute to Henry B. Fuller." *Poetry,* 35 (Oct. 1929), 34–41.

Morgan, Anna. *My Chicago.* Chicago: Seymour, 1918.

———, ed. *henry b. fuller.* Chicago: Seymour, 1929.

Payne, William Morton. Review of *The Cliff-Dwellers. Dial,* 15 (Oct. 16, 1893), 227–28.

Pearce, R. A. *Chicago in the Fiction of the 1890's as Illustrated in the Novels of Henry B. Fuller and Robert Herrick.* Ph.D. diss., U. Michigan, 1963.

Pilkington, John, Jr. *Henry Blake Fuller.* New York: Twayne, 1970.

Redd, Penelope. "Henry B. Fuller." *Scholastic,* 6 (Apr. 18, 1925), 5.

Reid, Mary J. "Henry B. Fuller." *Book Buyer,* 12 (Jan. 1896), 821–22.

Repplier, Agnes. "A By-Way in Fiction." In *Essays in Miniature.* Boston: Houghton Mifflin, 1899.

Riordan, Roger. "Henry Blake Fuller." *Critic,* 30 (Mar. 27, 1897), 211–12.

Rosenblatt, Paul. "The Image of Civilization in the Novels of Henry Blake Fuller." Ph.D. diss., Columbia U., 1960.

Schultz, Victor. "Henry Blake Fuller: Civilized Chicagoan." *Bookman,* 70 (Sept. 1930), 34–38.

Van Vechten, Carl. *Excavations.* New York: Macmillan, 1926.

Wagenknecht, Edward. *Cavalcade of the American Novel.* New York: Holt, 1952.

Williams, Kenny J. "Henry Blake Fuller (1857–1929)." *AmLitR,* 3 (Summer 1968), 9–13.

———. *In the City of Men: Another Story of Chicago.* Nashville: Townsend, 1974.

Ziff, Larzer. *The American 1890's: Life and Times of a Lost Generation.* New York: Viking, 1966.

Kenny J. Williams
Duke University
Durham, North Carolina

ZONA GALE (1874–1938)

To date only two full-length studies of Zona Gale's life and work have been written. The first is Derleth's, which is more anecdotal than critical. Simonson reviews her fiction, drama, poetry, and criticism, and assesses her literary position among her twentieth-century contemporaries, especially those who also wrote from the Middle West experience. For a historical survey of published criticism on Zona Gale the student should consult Simonson's piece in *American Literary Realism.* The most recent scholarly work is the dissertation by Quantic. Of the many close friends who wrote reminiscences about Zona Gale, the most notable were Garland, Sumner, and Towne. The main repositories of primary material are the Ridgely Torrence Collection in the Princeton University Library and the much more extensive Zona Gale Papers at the State Historical Society of Wisconsin, Madison.

MAJOR WORKS

Romance Island. Indianapolis: Bobbs-Merrill, 1906. [novel]
The Loves of Pelleas and Etarre. New York: Macmillan, 1907. [novel]

Friendship Village. New York: Macmillan, 1908. [stories]
Friendship Village Love Stories. New York: Macmillan, 1909. [stories]
Mothers to Men. New York: Macmillan, 1911. [novel]
Christmas. New York: Macmillan, 1912. [novella]
When I Was a Little Girl. New York: Macmillan, 1913. [stories]
Neighborhood Stories. New York: Macmillan, 1914. [stories]
The Neighbors. In *Wisconsin Plays.* Ed. by T. H. Dickinson. New York: Huebsch, 1914. [play]
Heart's Kindred. New York: Macmillan, 1915. [novel]
A Daughter of the Morning. Indianapolis: Bobbs-Merrill, 1917. [novel]
Birth. New York: Macmillan, 1918. [novel]
Peace in Friendship Village. New York: Macmillan, 1919. [stories]
Miss Lulu Bett. New York: Appleton, 1920. [novel]
Miss Lulu Bett. New York: Appleton, 1921. [play]
The Secret Way. New York: Macmillan, 1921. [poetry]
Uncle Jimmy. Boston: Walter H. Baker, 1922. [play]
Faint Perfume. New York: Appleton, 1923. [novel]
Mister Pitt. New York: Appleton, 1925. [play]
Preface to a Life. New York: Appleton, 1926. [novel]
Yellow Gentians and Blue. New York: Appleton, 1927. [stories]
Portage, Wisconsin and Other Essays. New York: Knopf, 1928. [critical essays]
Borgia. New York: Knopf, 1929. [novel]
Bridal Pond. New York: Knopf, 1930. [stories]
The Clouds. New York: French, 1932. [play]
Evening Clothes. Boston: Baker, 1932. [play]
Papa LaFleur. New York: Appleton, 1933. [novella]
Old Fashioned Tales. New York: Appleton, 1933. [stories]
Faint Perfume. New York: French, 1934. [play]
Light Woman. New York: Appleton, 1937. [novel]
Frank Miller of Mission Inn. New York: Appleton, 1938. [biography]
Magna. New York: Appleton, 1939. [novel]

CHECKLIST OF SECONDARY SOURCES

Burke; *CAA; DAB;* Herzberg; *LHUS; OCAL; TCA & Supp.*

Cooper, Frederick Tabor. "Friendship Village Love Stories." *Bookman,* 30 (Mar. 1910), 79.
Davidson, Donald. "A Worker of Ill." *SatR,* 4 (Nov. 23, 1929), 440.
Derleth, August. *Still Small Voice.* New York: Appleton-Century, 1940.
Forman, Henry. "Zona Gale: A Touch of Greatness." *WMH,* 46 (Autumn 1962), 32–37.
Gard, Robert. *Grassroots Theater: A Search for Regional Arts in America.* Madison: U. Wisconsin, 1955.
Garland, Hamlin. *My Friendly Contemporaries.* New York: Macmillan, 1932.
_____. *Afternoon Neighbors.* New York: Macmillan, 1934.
Herron, Ima H. *The Small Town in American Literature.* New York: Pageant, 1959.
Hoffman, Frederick J. *The Twenties: American Writing in the Postwar Decade.* New York: Viking, 1955.
Krutch, Joseph Wood. "Zona Gale's New Manner." *Nation,* 129 (Dec. 11, 1929), 725.
Lake, I. C. "Zona Gale's Home Becomes Library." *LJ,* 70 (Dec. 15, 1945), 1201–2.
Lewisohn, Ludwig. "Native Plays." *Nation,* 112 (Feb. 2, 1921), 189.
Loizeaux, M. D. "Talking Shop." *WLB,* 20 (Nov. 1946), 243.
Michaud, Régis. *The American Novel To-Day.* Boston: Little, Brown, 1928.
Overton, Grant. *American Nights Entertainment.* New York: Appleton, 1923.
_____. *The Women Who Make Our Novels.* New York: Dodd, Mead, 1928.
Pattee, Fred Lewis. *The Development of the American Short Story.* New York: Harper, 1923.
Quantic, Diana D. "Anticipations of the Revolt from the Village in Nineteenth Century Middle Western Fiction." Ph.D. diss., Kansas State U., 1971.
Quinn, Arthur H. *American Fiction: An Historical and Critical Survey.* New York: Appleton-Century, 1936.
Rourke, Constance. "Transitions." *NR,* 28 (Aug. 11, 1920), 315–16.
Simonson, Harold P. *Zona Gale.* New York: Twayne, 1962.

———. "Zona Gale (1874–1938)." *AmLitR*, 3 (Summer 1968), 14–17.

Sumner, Keene. "The Everlasting Persistence of This Western Girl." *AmM*, 91 (June 1921), 34–35, 137–41.

Towne, Charles Hanson. *Adventures in Editing*. New York: Appleton, 1926.

Van Doren, Carl. *Contemporary American Novelists*. New York: Macmillan, 1931.

———. *The American Novel, 1789–1939*. New York: Macmillan, 1940.

Harold P. Simonson
University of Washington
Seattle, Washington

HAMLIN GARLAND (1860–1940)

Although, during much of his long life, Hamlin Garland was regarded as a major American writer, in recent years his critical reputation has been largely as a regionalist. Most of the quite numerous obituary editorials which paid tribute to him in 1940 did so in terms similar to those expressed by the Minneapolis *Star-Journal:* Garland "was among the first to bring the middlewest into literature, and to make us see the color and drama in the settlement of an area considered poor literary material compared to the 'wild' West."

Garland's long and prolific writing career can conveniently be divided into three periods: the first, extending from *Main-Travelled Roads* (1891) through the essays in *Crumbling Idols* (1894), can be called his regional realism stage; the second, beginning with *Rose of Dutcher's Coolly* (1895) and ending with *They of the High Trails* (1916), can be seen as his romantic fiction era; and the third, from *A Son of the Middle Border* (1917) through *Afternoon Neighbors* (1934), encompasses his regional reminiscences and autobiographical volumes. Because of this variety, critics have had a difficult time deciding exactly how to describe Garland's achievement. Parrington saw him in 1930 as more of a "thwarted Romantic" than a realist; earlier, in 1928, Ruth M. Raw had seen him as a realist in technique but as a romanticist in his "attitude towards life"; and, as noted above, later post-1940 critics have viewed him mostly as a regionalist, agreeing with Bernard Duffey, who observed in 1954 that the realistic method had for Garland "the inestimable advantage of being the only literary technique by which he could hope to use his knowledge of western life" and still retain his connections with the city.

Aside from Holloway's competent 1960 biography and Pizer's excellent study of Garland's early work in the same year, there has been a dearth of worthwhile original comment in the last two decades. The realism-romanticism question has been discussed and debated and rehashed, albeit often by very astute scholars such as Pizer, Walcutt, Duffey, Ahnebrink, and Stronks. There are a series of essays on Garland's associations with and writings about various midwestern states—Iowa, Wisconsin, Minnesota, South Dakota, and Colorado. And there have been a few scholarly examinations of Garland's associations with such fellow writers as James, Markham, Herne, Crane, Eggleston, Howells, and Kirkland. But the amount of critical and scholarly territory which has been covered is relatively small; some may argue that this is due to the quality of Garland's works. It is surely true that few of these works are in print and fewer still are commonly taught in American literature courses.

MAJOR WORKS

Main-Travelled Roads. Boston: Arena, 1891. [short stories]
Jason Edwards, An Average Man. Boston: Arena, 1892. [novel]
A Member of the Third House: A Dramatic Story. Chicago: Schulte, 1892. [novel]
A Little Norsk. New York: Appleton, 1892. [novel]
A Spoil of Office: A Story of the Modern West. Boston: Arena, 1892. [novel]
Prairie Folks. Chicago: Schulte, 1893. [short stories]
Prairie Songs. Chicago: Stone and Kimball, 1893. [poems]
*Crumbling Idols: Twelve Essays on Art Dealing Chiefly With Literature, Painting and the.
    Drama.* Chicago: Stone and Kimball, 1894. [essays]
Rose of Dutcher's Coolly. Chicago: Stone and Kimball, 1895. [novel]
Wayside Courtships. New York: Appleton, 1897. [short stories]
Ulysses S. Grant: His Life and Character. New York: Doubleday and McClure, 1898.
    [biography]
The Trail of the Goldseekers. New York: Macmillan, 1899. [essays and poems]
Boy Life on the Prairie. New York: Macmillan, 1899. [autobiography]
The Eagle's Heart. New York: Appleton, 1900. [novel]
Her Mountain Lover. New York: Century, 1901. [novel]
The Captain of the Gray-Horse Troop. New York: Harper, 1902. [novel]
Hesper. New York: Harper, 1903. [novel]
The Light of the Star. New York: Harper, 1904. [novel]
The Tyranny of the Dark. New York: Harper, 1905. [novel]
Witch's Gold. New York: Doubleday, 1906. [novel]
Money Magic. New York: Harper, 1907. [novel]
The Shadow World. New York: Harper, 1908. [novel]
Moccasin Ranch: A Story of Dakota. New York: Harper, 1909. [novel]
Cavanagh: Forest Ranger. New York: Harper, 1910. [novel]
Victor Ollnee's Discipline. New York: Harper, 1911. [novel]
The Forester's Daughter. New York: Harper, 1914. [novel]
They of the High Trails. New York: Harper, 1916. [short stories]
A Son of the Middle Border. New York: Macmillan, 1917. [autobiography]
A Daughter of the Middle Border. New York: Macmillan, 1921. [autobiography]
The Book of the American Indian. New York: Harper, 1923. [short stories]
Trail-Makers of the Middle Border. New York: Macmillan, 1926. [historical novel]
Back-Trailers From the Middle Border. New York: Macmillan, 1928. [reminiscence and
    fiction]
Roadside Meetings. New York: Macmillan, 1930. [autobiography]
Companions on the Trail. New York: Macmillan, 1931. [autobiography]
My Friendly Contemporaries. New York: Macmillan, 1932. [autobiography]
Afternoon Neighbors. New York: Macmillan, 1934. [autobiography]
Forty Years of Psychic Research. New York: Macmillan, 1936. [reminiscence on psychic
    research]
The Mystery of the Buried Crosses. New York: Dutton, 1939.

Checklist of Secondary Sources

Burke; *CB; CHAL;* Herzberg; *LHUS; OCAL;* Quinn; *TCA.*

Ahnebrink, Lars. *The Beginnings of Naturalism in American Fiction: A Study of the Works of Hamlin Garland, Stephen Crane, and Frank Norris With Special Reference to Some European Influences—1891–1903.* Cambridge: Harvard U., 1950.

Arvidson, Lloyd A. *Hamlin Garland—Centennial Tributes and A Checklist of the Hamlin Garland Papers in The University of Southern California Library.* USC Library Bulletin, no. 9. Los Angeles: U. Southern California, 1962.

Bentzon, Th. "Un Radical de la Prairie." *Revue des Deux Mondes,* 157 (1900), 139–80. [interview]

Bledsoe, Thomas A. "Introduction." *Main-Travelled Roads—Six Mississippi Valley Stories.* New York: Rinehart, 1954. Pp. ix–xl.

Brigham, Johnson. "Hamlin Garland, Pioneer, Reformer and Teller of Tales." *A Book of Iowa Authors By Iowa Authors.* Ed. Johnson Brigham. Des Moines: Iowa State Teachers Assn., 1930. Pp. 95–108.

Brooks, Van Wyck. *The Confident Years—1885–1915.* New York: Dutton, 1952. Pp. 63–84, 163–84.

Browne, Ray B. " 'Popular' and Folk Songs: Unifying Force in Garland's Autobiographical Works." *SFQ,* 25 (1961), 153–66.

Bryer, Jackson R. and Eugene Harding, with the assistance of Robert A. Rees. *Hamlin Garland and the Critics—An Annotated Bibliography.* Troy, N.Y.: Whitston, 1973.

Carter, Joseph L. "Hamlin Garland and the Western Myth." Ph.D. diss., Kent State U., 1974.

Culmsee, Carlton. "A Pioneer in Modern Pessimism." *WHR,* 4 (1950), 241–50.

Dondore, Dorothy A. *The Prairie and the Making of Middle America—Four Centuries of Description.* Cedar Rapids, Iowa: Torch Press, 1926. Pp. 316–24.

Duffey, Bernard. *The Chicago Renaissance in American Letters—A Critical History.* East Lansing: Michigan State College, 1954. Pp. 75–89.

————. "Hamlin Garland's Decline From Realism." *AL,* 25 (1953), 69–74; James D. Koerner. "Comment on 'Hamlin Garland's Decline From Realism.' " *AL,* 26 (1954), 437–32; Bernard I. Duffey. "Mr. Koerner's Reply Considered." *AL,* 26 (1954), 432–35.

Earley, Jane. "An Edition of Hamlin Garland's 'Miller of Boscobel.' " Ph.D. diss., Northwestern U., 1969.

Fitch, George H. "Is the West in Literary Bondage?" *CIM,* 5 (1894), 235–44.

Flanagan, John T. "Hamlin Garland, Occasional Minnesotan." *MH,* 22 (1941), 157–68.

Flower, B. O. "A Vivid Picture of the Lights and Shadows of Western Farm Light." *Arena,* 4 (Aug. 1891), xvii–xxiii. [rev.]

Folsom, James K. *The American Western Novel.* New Haven, Conn.: College and University Press, 1966. Pp. 149–60, 180–84.

French, Warren. "What Shall We Do About Hamlin Garland?" *AmLitR,* 3 (1970), 283–89.

Fujii, Gertrude. "The Veritism of Hamlin Garland." Ph.D. diss., U. Southern California, 1970.

Gale, Zona. "National Epics of the Border." *YR,* n.s. 11 (1922), 852–56. [rev.]

Goldstein, Jesse. "Two Literary Radicals: Garland and Markham in Chicago, 1893." *AL,* 17 (1945), 152–60.

Harris, Elbert L. "Hamlin Garland's Use of the American Scene in His Fiction." Ph.D. diss., U. Pennsylvania, 1959.

Harrison, Stanley R. "Hamlin Garland and the Double Vision of Naturalism." *SSF,* 6 (1969), 548–56.

Harte, Walter B. "Hamlin Garland—A Virile New Force in Our Literature." Chicago *Sunday Inter Ocean,* Feb. 18, 1894, p. 31. [interview]

Henson, Clyde E. "Joseph Kirkland's Influence on Hamlin Garland." *AL,* 23 (1952), 458–63.

Higgins, John E. "A Man From the Middle Border: Hamlin Garland's Diaries." *WMH,* 46 (1963), 294–302.

Hilfer, Anthony. *The Revolt From the Village—1915–1930.* Chapel Hill: U. North Carolina, 1969. Pp. 18–19, 42–48.

Holloway, Jean. *Hamlin Garland—A Biography.* Austin: U. Texas, 1960.

Holsinger, Paul M. "Hamlin Garland's Colorado." *ColM,* 44 (Winter 1967), 1–10.

[Howells, William Dean.] "Editor's Study." *Harper,* 83 (1891), 638–42. [rev.]

———. "Mr. Garland's Books." *NAR*, 196 (1912), 523–28.

———. *"A Son of the Middle Border* by Hamlin Garland—An Appreciation." *NYTRB*, Aug. 26, 1917, p. 309. [rev.]

Lovett, Robert Morss. "The Two Frontiers." *NR*, 32 (Sept. 27, 1922), 14. [rev.]

McElderry, Bruce R., Jr. "Hamlin Garland and Henry James." *AL*, 23 (1952), 433–46.

———. "Introduction." *Boy Life on the Prairie.* Lincoln: U. Nebraska, 1961. Pp. v–xvi.

———. "Introduction." *Main-Travelled Roads.* New York: Harper, 1956. Pp. ix–xix.

Mane, Robert. *Hamlin Garland—L'Homme et L'Oeuvre (1860–1940).* Paris: Didier, 1968.

Martinec, Barbara. "Hamlin Garland's Revisions of *Main-Travelled Roads." ALR*, 5 (1972), 167–72.

Meyer, Roy W. "Hamlin Garland and the American Indian." *WAL*, 2 (1967), 109–25.

———. *The Middle Western Farm Novel in the 20th Century.* Lincoln: U. Nebraska, 1965. Pp. 26–27, 30–38.

Miller, Charles T. "Hamlin Garland's Retreat From Realism." *WAL*, 1 (1966), 119–29.

Morgan, H. W. *American Writers in Rebellion—From Mark Twain to Dreiser.* New York: Hill and Wang, 1965. Pp. 76–103.

Mott, Frank Luther. "Exponents of the Pioneers." *Palimpsest*, 11 (1930), 61–66.

Nevins, Allan. "Garland and the Prairies." *Literary Review of the New York Evening Post*, Aug. 19, 1922, pp. 881–82. [rev.]

Parrington, Vernon L. *Main Currents in American Thought.* New York: Harcourt, 1930. Vol. 3, pp. 288–300.

Pizer, Donald. "Hamlin Garland (1860–1940)." *ALR*, 1 (1967), 45–51. [bibliographical essay]

———. "Hamlin Garland's *A Son of the Middle Border:* An Appreciation." *SAQ*, 65 (1966), 448–59.

———. *Hamlin Garland's Early Work and Career.* Berkeley: U. California, 1960.

———. " 'John Boyle's Conclusion': An Unpublished Middle Border Story." *AL*, 31 (1959), 59–75.

———, ed. " 'The Rise of Boomtown'—An Unpublished Dakota Novel By Hamlin Garland." *SDHC*, 28 (1956), 345–89.

Raw, Ruth M. "Hamlin Garland, the Romanticist." *SR*, 36 (1928), 202–10.

Reamer, Owen J. "Garland and the Indians." *NMQ*, 34 (1964), 257–80.

Schorer, C. E. "Hamlin Garland, of Wisconsin." *WMH*, 37 (1954), 147–50.

Simpson, Claude M., Jr. "Hamlin Garland's Decline." *SWR*, 26 (1941), 223–34.

Stronks, James B. "A Realist Experiments With Impressionism: Hamlin Garland's 'Chicago Studies.' " *AL*, 36 (1964), 38–52.

Taylor, Walter F. *The Economic Novel in America.* Chapel Hill: U. North Carolina, 1942. Pp. 148–83.

Walcutt, Charles. *American Literary Naturalism, a Divided Stream.* Minneapolis: U. Minnesota, 1956. Pp. 45–65.

Whitford, Kathryn. "Crusader Without a Cause: An Examination of Hamlin Garland's Middle Border." *MASJ*, 6 (Spring 1965), 61–72.

———. "Patterns of Observation: A Study of Hamlin Garland's Middle Border Landscape." *TWASAL*, 50 (1961), 331–38.

Ziff, Larzer. *The American 1890's—Life and Times of a Lost Generation.* New York: Viking, 1966. Pp. 93–119.

Jackson R. Bryer
University of Maryland
College Park, Maryland

WILLIAM GASS (1924–   )

Though each of the works of William H. Gass has received critical acclaim at the time of publication, little serious analysis of his writing has appeared. Certainly he has not been categorized as belonging to any particular school or movement. Perhaps, indeed, this will prove impossible to determine, since Gass admits to being influenced by artists as disparate as James Joyce and Gertrude Stein. In any case, almost everyone who has approached Gass's fiction has concluded that his style is brilliant and compelling. Gilman, while speaking only of *Omensetter's Luck,* nevertheless seems to sum up the general feelings in this regard when he says that Gass creates in "language of amazing range and resiliency, full of the most exact wit, learning, and contemporary emblems, yet also full of lyric urgency and sensuous body." That Gass is not merely a stylist is recognized as well. Most critics would seem to agree with Shaun O'Connell in crediting Gass with a "dramatic evocation of the most essential human questions" in his work. A profound exploration of Gass's handling of those questions has yet to be written.

Although Gass grew up in Ohio, has spent most all of his life in the Midwest and frequently writes evocatively of place, he disavows any regionalist label. If his work were to be viewed in terms of traditional strains of fiction, it might exist most comfortably within that humanistic and aesthetic conception of the art one associates with Mann, Joyce, and Bellow.

Major Works

Omensetter's Luck. New York: New American Library, 1966. [novel]
In the Heart of the Heart of the Country and Other Stories. New York: Harper & Row, 1968.
Fiction and the Figures of Life. New York: Knopf, 1970. [essays]
Willie Master's Lonesome Wife. New York: Knopf, 1971. [novella]
On Being Blue: A Philosophical Inquiry. Boston: Godine, 1976. [extended essay]

Checklist of Secondary Sources

Burke; *CA; CN.*

Allen, Carolyn J. "Fiction and Figures of Life in *Omensetter's Luck.*" *PCP,* 9 (1974), 5–11.
Bassoff, Bruce. "The Sacrificial World of William Gass: *In the Heart of the Heart of the Country.*" *Critique,* 18 (1976), 36–58.
Bellamy, Joe, ed. *The New Fiction: Interviews with Innovative American Writers.* Urbana: U. Illinois, 1974.
Blau, Marion M. " 'How I Would Brood Upon You': The Lonesome Wife of William Gass." *GLR,* 2 (Summer 1975), 40–50.
Busch, Frederick. "But This Is What It Is Like to Live in Hell: William H. Gass's 'In the Heart of the Heart of the Country.' " *MFS,* 19 (Spring 1973), 97–108.
Gardner, John. "An Invective Against Mere Fiction." *SouR,* 3 (Spring 1967), 444–67.
Gilman, Richard. *The Confusion of Realms.* New York: Random House, 1969. Pp. 69–79.
Fogel, Stanley. "And All the Little Typtopies: Notes on Language Theory in the Contemporary Experimental Novel." *MFS,* 20 (Autumn 1974), 328–36.
French, Ned. "Against the Grain: Theory and Practice in the Work of William H. Gass." *IR,* 7 (1976), 96–107.
Haas, Joseph. "In the Heart of William H. Gass." Chicago Daily News *Panorama,* Feb. 1, 1969, pp. 4–5, 22. [interview]
Hoekzema, Loren. "Two Readings of Lyrical Space: William H. Gass's *In the Heart of the Heart of the Country* and Donald Barthelme's *City Life.*" *DAI,* 37:3612A–13A.
Kane, Patricia. "A Point of Law in William Gass's 'Icicles.' " *NCL,* 1 (Mar. 1971), 7–8.

————. "The Sun Burned on the Snow: Gass's 'The Pedersen Kid.' " *Critique*, 14 (1972), 89–96.

McCaffrey, Larry. "Donald Barthelme, Robert Coover, William H. Gass: Three Checklists." *BB*, 31 (July-Sept. 1974), 101–6.

————. "A William H. Gass Bibliography." *Critique*, 18 (1976), 59–66.

————. "The Art of Metafiction: William Gass's *Willie Master's Lonesome Wife*." *Critique*, 18 (1976), 21–35.

McCauley, Carole S. "Fiction Needn't Say Things—It Should *Make* Them Out of Words: An Interview with William H. Gass." *Falcon*, 5 (Winter 1972), 35–45.

McCormack, Thos., ed. *Afterwords: Novelists on Their Novels*. New York: Harper, 1968. Pp. 88–105.

Molyneux, Thomas W. "Signs of the Times." *ASch*, 42 (Autumn 1973), 663–70.

Mullinax, Gary. "An Interview with William Gass." *DLR*, 1 (1972), 81–87.

Schneeman, Peter. "3 Fingers/Figures Of/For Gass." *MinnR*, 4 (Spring 1973), 138–44.

Schneider, Richard. "The Fortunate Fall in William Gass's *Omensetter's Luck*." *Critique*, 18 (1976), 5–20.

Shorris, Earl. "The Well-Spoken Passions of William H. Gass." *Harper*, 244 (May 1972), 96–100.

Marion M. Blau
Northeastern Illinois University
Chicago, Illinois

SUSAN GLASPELL (1876–1948)

Critics have evaluated Susan Glaspell's fiction as belonging to the conservative, nineteenth-century regional tradition. Quinn sees her as a novelist concerned with feminist conflicts; Snell as a woman writer in the Jamesian mode; and Waterman emphasizes her midwestern qualities. Her plays, on the other hand, have generally been associated with the Provincetown Players and viewed as part of that experimental theater. Goldberg compares her to O'Neill; Lewisohn stresses the radical nature of her drama; and the emphasis in the reviews of the productions of her plays was on their *avant-garde* aspects. In their over-all assessments of her plays, both Quinn and Waterman relate the plays to the novels: Quinn calls her a realist with some experimental overtones; Waterman suggests that all her work presents the conflict between the more stable values associated with the Midwest and the chaotic conditions of modern living.

Although her plays were recognized in the 1920s as an important step toward the acceptance of modern drama in this country, and although her novels published during the 1930s and 1940s were given careful and widespread reviews, her art has been given limited critical attention in recent years. Aside from reminiscences about the Provincetown years and brief mention in histories of American drama, where she is recognized as an important experimental playwright, the major bulk of available scholarship for Susan Glaspell consists of Waterman's full-length study in 1966, his bibliographical essay in 1971, the chapter in Gould, and Bach's dissertation. None of her novels is in print, but several of the plays, especially the early one-acts, are still being produced, mostly by little-theater groups.

MAJOR WORKS

The Glory of the Conquered. New York: Stokes, 1909. [novel]
The Visioning. New York: Stokes, 1911. [novel]
Lifted Masks. New York: Stokes, 1912. [short stories]
Fidelity. Boston: Small, Maynard, 1915. [novel]
Plays. Boston: Small, Maynard, 1920.
Inheritors. Boston: Small, Maynard, 1921. [play]
The Verge. Boston: Small, Maynard, 1922. [play]
The Road to the Temple. New York: Stokes, 1927. [biography]
Brook Evans. New York: Stokes, 1928. [novel]
Fugitive's Return. New York: Stokes, 1929. [novel]
Allison's House. New York: French, 1930. [play]
Ambrose Holt and Family. New York: Stokes, 1931. [novel]
The Morning Is Near Us. New York: Stokes, 1939. [novel]
Norma Ashe. New York: Lippincott, 1942. [novel]
Judd Rankin's Daughter. New York: Lippincott, 1945. [novel]

CHECKLIST OF SECONDARY SOURCES

CA; CAA; LHUS; OCAL; TCA.

Bach, Gerhard P. "Susan Glaspell and the Provincetown Players: A Study of the Early Phase of Modern American Drama and Theatre." Ph.D. diss., U. Marburg, 1971.
Bullock, Florence Haxton. "Conflict in a Modern Midwest Family." *Chicago Sun Bookweek,* Oct. 28, 1945, p. 1. [rev.]
Chamberlain, John. "A Tragi-Comedy of Idealism." *NYTBR,* Apr. 12, 1931, p. 4. [rev.]
Crawford, Bartholow V. "Susan Glaspell." *Palimpsest,* 11 (1930), 517–21.
Dell, Floyd. *Homecoming.* New York: Farrar, 1933.
Deutsch, Helen and Stella Hanau. *The Provincetown: A Story of the Theatre.* New York: Farrar, 1931.
Dickinson, Thomas H. *Playwrights of the New American Theater.* New York: Macmillan, 1925. Pp. 208–12.
Goldberg, Isaac. *The Drama of Transition.* Cincinnati: Kidd, 1922. Pp. 471–81.
Gould, Jean. *Modern American Playwrights.* New York: Dodd, Mead, 1966. Pp. 26–49.
Hapgood, Hutchins. *A Victorian in the Modern World.* New York: Harcourt, 1939.
Hutchinson, Percy. "George Cram Cook was a Modern Lycidas." *NYTBR,* Mar. 13, 1927, p. 2. [rev.]
Lewisohn Ludwig. *Expression in America.* New York: Harper, 1932. Pp. 391–99.
Malone, Andrew E. "Susan Glaspell." *DM,* 2 (Sept. 1924), 107–11. [rev.]
Noe, Marcia. "A Critical Biography of Susan Glaspell." Ph.D. diss., U. Iowa, 1976.
Quinn, Arthur Hobson. *A History of the American Drama From the Civil War to the Present Day.* Vol. 2. New York: Harper, 1927. Pp. 209–12.
———. *American Fiction.* New York: Appleton, 1936. Pp. 714–18.
Siever, David W. *Freud on Broadway.* New York: Hermitage, 1955. Pp. 69–72.
Snell, George. *The Shapers of American Fiction.* New York: Dutton, 1947. Pp. 140–50.
Stegner, Wallace. "The Trail of the Hawkeye." *SatR,* 18 (July 30, 1938), 3–4, 16, 17.
Vorse, Mary Heaton. *Time and the Town.* New York: Dial, 1942.
Waterman, Arthur E. *Susan Glaspell.* New York: Twayne, 1966.
———. "Susan Glaspell." *AmLitR,* 4 (1971), 183–91. [bibliographical essay]
———. "Susan Glaspell." *Notable American Women.* Vol. 2. Ed. by Edward T. James. Cambridge, Mass: Belknap Press, 1971. Pp. 49–51.

Arthur E. Waterman
Georgia State University
Atlanta, Georgia

HERBERT GOLD (1924–   )

At present the only full length appraisal of Gold's work is Kuhn's unpublished doctoral dissertation. Born in Cleveland, Gold has received attention from numerous critics. Hicks writes, "In less than ten years he [Gold] has produced a body of work that establishes him as a central figure in today's literature." Swados in 1951 wrote that "If we are really at the beginning of a new era of conservatism, one can only hope that the writers who will choose to celebrate the heroic virtues of the middle-aged and the comfortably placed will be able to do so with at least a portion of Mr. Gold's benevolent wit, radical perception, and intellectual vigor." Kelley wrote of Gold's work, "It's a cerebral performance with a tangle of long, long thoughts, most of them entertainingly presented in colorful, runaway language. A fidelity ear and eye are at work here."

Boroff claims that "Gold, like very few of our major writers, has tried to stretch language to meet the new requirements of our time. He has used an idiom that is highly permutable, strained perhaps, too shifty; but it reaches out to encompass new states of mind that writers in an easier time did not have to cope with." It is perhaps the quality which Boroff identified that earlier had led Foster to assert, "Mr. Gold has an extraordinary talent for style, but also a weakness for it; he is in danger of becoming a *stylist.*"

Harry T. Moore, surveying the author's work in *Contemporary Novelists,* finds less fault with Gold's style than some critics have. Writing of *The Man Who Was Not With It,* Moore contends, "Gold makes full use of his own ability to handle colorful idiom. It crackles. But the language isn't flashed just for its own sake; it is organic. . . . Herbert Gold's tendency toward the bizarre in style exactly matches the subject matter in this book." Writing of Gold, Bergonzi argues, "As a novelist he combines the Whitman-style hipster and the Jewish immigrant."

MAJOR WORKS

Birth of a Hero. New York: Viking, 1951. [novel]
The Prospect Before Us. Cleveland: World, 1954. Also published as *Room Clerk.* New York: New American Library, 1956. [novel]
The Man Who Was Not With It. Boston: Little, Brown, 1956. Also published as *The Wild Life.* New York: Permabooks, 1957. [novel]
15 x 3 (with R. V. Cassill and James B. Hall). New York: New Directions, 1957. [stories]
The Optimist. Boston: Little, Brown, 1959. [novel]
Love & Like. New York: Dial, 1960. [stories]
Therefore Be Bold. New York: Dial, 1960. [novel]
The Age of Happy Problems. New York: Dial, 1962. [essays]
Salt. New York: Dial, 1963. [novel]
The Fathers: A Novel in the Form of a Memoir. New York: Random House, 1967. [novel]
The Great American Jackpot. New York: Random House, 1970. [novel]

The Magic Will: Stories and Essays of a Decade. New York: Random House, 1971.
My Last Two Thousand Years. New York: Random House, 1972. [novel]

CHECKLIST OF SECONDARY SOURCES

Burke; *CA; CN; LHUS; LLC; OCAL.*

Beja, Morris. *Epiphany in the Modern Novel.* Seattle: U. Washington, 1971. P. 232.
Bergonzi, Bernard. "Eat! Eat!" *NYRB,* June 1, 1967, pp. 29–31.
Boroff, David. "The Spice Without the Savor." *SatR,* 46 (Apr. 20, 1963), 45–46.
Delpeche, Jeanine. "Herbert Gold, ou l'Amérique romantique." *NLit,* 7 (June 1971), 7.
Foster, Richard. "What Is Fiction For?" *HudR,* 14 (Spring 1961), 142–49.
Gray, Rockwell. "Three Midwestern Writers." *GLR,* 3 (Summer 1976), 74–93.
Hicks, Granville. "Generations of the Fifties: Malamud, Gold, and Updike." In *The Creative
    Present,* Nona Balakian and Charles Simmons, eds. Garden City, N.Y.: Doubleday, 1963.
    Pp. 217–37.
———. "Report on Herbert Gold." *SatR,* 42 (Apr. 25, 1959), 12.
Kelley, James. "Fat Harry's Defiance." *New York Times,* Feb. 14, 1954, pp. 5, 25.
Kuhn, Howard F. "A Critical Analysis of the Novels of Herbert Gold." Ph.D. diss., U. Oregon,
    1970.
Nemerov, Howard. *Poetry and Fiction: Essays.* New Brunswick: Rutgers U., 1963. Pp. 277–87.
Seaton, A. G., ed. *The Writers Directory.* Chicago: St. James, 1971. P. 151.
Seiden, Melvin. "Characters and Ideas: The Modern Novel." *Nation,* 188 (Apr. 25, 1959),
    387–92.
Swados, Harvey. "A New Kind of Hero." *Nation,* 173 (Oct. 6, 1951), 283–84.

*R. Baird Shuman
University of Illinois
Champaign, Illinois*

JAMES HALL (1793–1868)

Variously termed a spokesman of the West and a literary pioneer of the
Ohio Valley, James Hall devoted many years to the recording of western
culture and to the imaginative interpretation of the lives of frontier citizens.
An extremely versatile man, he was prominent as a lawyer, judge, and periodical editor in Illinois, and as a banker and writer in Ohio. During his
twelve years in Illinois he edited a newspaper, a literary annual, and the
Illinois Monthly Magazine (subsequently the *Western Monthly Magazine*).
In Cincinnati, his home for three decades, he published editorials, articles,
history, verse, and fiction. His range of interest was extraordinarily wide
since he incorporated folklore, geological and archaeological material, history, and economic data into his books.

To a modern literary critic, Hall's work seems flawed by sentimentalism,
a somewhat rhetorical style, and perhaps excessive chauvinism. His one
novel is undistinguished, although it presents authentic details about early
desperadoes and highwaymen. Characterization in his tales is often stiff
and his plots seem conventional. But he knew the Ohio Valley thoroughly
and he had a sensitive ear for frontier speech and dialect. His best work is

found in his short stories, especially those which reflect life in the early French villages of Illinois and those which preserve details of the transformation of the wilderness into farms and hamlets in the early nineteenth century. According to Rusk, Hall not only edited "the most important magazine on the frontier" but was "himself the most distinguished writer of Western fiction."

Today Hall's books are generally unavailable, but a few of his tales have been preserved in anthologies of regional material or short fiction.

Major Works

Trial and Defence of First Lieutenant James Hall, of the Ordnance Department, United States' Army. Pittsburgh: [James Hall] Eichbaum and Johnson, 1820. [autobiographical pamphlet]
Letters from the West. London: Henry Colburn, 1828. [travel vignettes]
The Western Souvenir, A Christmas and New Year's Gift for 1829. Cincinnati: N. and G. Guilford [1828]. [an annual]
Legends of the West. Philadelphia: Harrison Hall, 1832. [tales]
The Soldier's Bride and Other Tales. Philadelphia: Key and Biddle, 1833. [stories]
The Harpe's Head; a Legend of Kentucky. Philadelphia: Key and Biddle, 1833. [novel]
Sketches of History, Life, and Manners in the West. Cincinnati: Hubbard and Edmands, 1832. [history—only one volume appeared]
Sketches of History, Life, and Manners in the West. Philadelphia: Harrison Hall, 1835. [history—in two volumes]
Tales of the Border. Philadelphia: Harrison Hall, 1835. [stories]
A Memoir of the Public Services of William Henry Harrison, of Ohio. Philadelphia: Edward C. Biddle, 1836. [biography]
Statistics of the West, at the Close of the Year 1836. Cincinnati: J. A. James, 1836. [historical and economic tabulations]
Notes on the Western States. Philadelphia: Harrison Hall, 1838. [rev. ed. of preceding item]
[With Thomas L. McKenney] *History of the Indian Tribes of North America.* Philadelphia: vol. 1, Edward C. Biddle, 1836; vol. 2, Frederick W. Greenough, 1838; vol. 3, Daniel Rice and James G. Clark, 1844. [history, biography, and 120 portraits of Indians]
The Wilderness and the Warpath. New York: Wiley and Putnam, 1846. [stories]
The West: Its Commerce and Navigation. Cincinnati: H. W. Derby, 1848. [economic data]
The Romance of Western History. Cincinnati: Applegate, 1857. [rev. and rearrangement of *Sketches*]

Checklist of Secondary Sources

Blanck; *DAB.*

Bay, J. C. *The Fortune of Books.* Chicago: Hill, 1941. Pp. 342–43.
Buley, R. Carlyle. *The Old Northwest, Pioneer Period 1815–1840.* Indianapolis: Indiana Historical Society, 1950. Vol. 2, pp. 527–539.
Burtschi, Mary, ed. *Seven Stories by James Hall.* Vandalia, Ill.: Fayette Co. Bicentennial of the American Revolution Commission, 1975. Pp. 114. Editor's Introduction. Pp. 9–19.
Coggeshall, William T. *The Poets and Poetry of the West.* Columbus: Follett, Foster, 1860. Pp. 71–73.
Coyle, William, ed. *Ohio Authors and Their Books.* Cleveland: World, 1962. Pp. 265–67.
Eckert, R. P., Jr. "The Path of the Pioneer." *Colophon,* n.s. 3 (Winter 1936), 404–21.
Flanagan, John T. *James Hall, Literary Pioneer of the Ohio Valley.* Minneapolis: U. Minnesota, 1941. [first book-length study of Hall]
———. "James Hall and the Antiquarian and Historical Society of Illinois." *JISHS,* 34 (Dec. 1941), 439–52.
———. "James Hall, Pioneer Vandalia Editor and Publicist." *JISHS,* 48 (Summer 1955), 119–36.
———. "Folklore in the Stories of James Hall." *MF,* 5 (Fall 1955), 159–168.

Fussell, Edwin. *Frontier: American Literature and the American West*. Princeton: Princeton U., 1965. Pp. 320–24.

James, Davis L. "Judge James Hall: A Literary Pioneer in the Middle West." *OAHSP*, Columbus: F. J. Herr, 1909. Vol. 18. Pp. 468–83.

Lee, Robert Edson. *From West to East: Studies in the Literature of the American West*. Urbana: U. Illinois, 1966. Pp. 54–57.

Meline, J. F. "Biography of the Late Judge Hall, of Cincinnati." *Cincinnati Commercial*, October 16, 1868.

Randall, Randolph C. "Authors of the *Port Folio* Revealed by the Hall Files." *AL*, 11 (Jan. 1940), 379–416.   •

――――. *James Hall, Spokesman of the New West*. Columbus: Ohio State U., 1964.

Rusk, Ralph L. *The Literature of the Middle Western Frontier*. New York: Columbia U., 1926. Vol. 1, pp. 170–75, 272–82.

Shultz, Esther. "James Hall in Shawneetown." *JISHS*, 22 (Oct. 1929), 388–400.

――――. "James Hall in Vandalia." *JISHS*, 23 (Apr. 1930), 92–112.

Thomson, Peter G. *A Bibliography of the State of Ohio*. Cincinnati: Author, 1880. Pp. 140–45.

Todd, E. W. "James Hall and the Hugh Glass Legend." *AQ*, 7 (Winter 1955), 362–70.

Venable, W. H. *Beginnings of Literary Culture in the Ohio Valley*. Cincinnati: Clarke, 1891. Pp. 361–85.

Wright, Lyle H. *American Fiction, 1774–1850*. San Marino: Huntington Library, 1939. Pp. 80–81.

John T. Flanagan
University of Illinois
Urbana, Illinois

ALBERT HALPER (1904–   )

Reviewers during the 1930s recognized Chicagoan Albert Halper's novels and stories for their sympathy to workers, for their keen social criticism, and for a dynamic and sensitive use of language. Left-wing reviewers tended to reject his work as too objective; Gold accused him of writing stale bohemianism. Lewis, on the other hand, linked him with Dickens for his solid, human portraits, brilliantly executed. Hicks praised the vitality of his realism, his ability to observe facts and to present them cogently. Farrell denounced the careless and slipshod manner of writing, but acknowledged the simplicity and feeling of the stories. Many reviewers linked him to the proletarian school, and brief mention of him in surveys continues to do so.

From the mid-1940s critics have mostly overlooked his work. Among these later critics, Klein finds Halper's main concern is for the artist's sensibility; Eisinger concludes that he neglects man as individual; Luccock focuses on his skillful portrayals of labor and of moral values; Champney praises the novels as a neglected but major achievement. Hart shows that both Halper's emphasis on the individual and his use of symbols reveal the intellectual life of a decade. *Atlantic Avenue* and *Good-bye, Union Square* are in print. A critical study (Hart) for the Twayne series is in preparation.

MAJOR WORKS

Union Square. New York: Viking, 1933. [novel]
The Foundry. New York: Viking, 1934. [novel]
On the Shore, Young Writer Remembering Chicago. New York: Viking, 1934. [stories]
The Chute. New York: Viking, 1937. [novel]
Sons of the Fathers. New York: Harper, 1940. [novel]
The Little People. New York: Harper, 1942. [novel]
Only an Inch from Glory. New York: Harper, 1943. [novel]
Ed. *This is Chicago: An Anthology*. New York: Henry Holt, 1952. [anthology]
The Golden Watch. New York: Henry Holt, 1953. [stories]
Atlantic Avenue. New York: Dell, 1956. [novel]
The Fourth Horseman of Miami Beach. New York: Norton, 1966. [novel]
Ed. *The Chicago Crime Book*. Cleveland: World, 1967. [anthology]
Good-bye, Union Square, A Writer's Memoir of the Thirties. Chicago: Quadrangle, 1970.
[autobiography]

CHECKLIST OF SECONDARY SOURCES

Burke; *CA; CAA;* Herzberg; *OCAL; TCA.*

Appel, Benjamin. "Albert Halper's New Approach." *SatR*, 26 (Oct. 9, 1943), 18. [rev.]
Berg, Louis. "Personal Memoir." *Commentary*, 51 (Apr. 1971), 98–102. [rev.]
Champney, Freeman. "Albert Halper and His Little People." *AR*, 2 (Dec. 1942), 628–34.
[rev.-essay]
Eisinger, Chester E. "Character and Self in Fiction on the Left." *Proletarian Writers of the Thirties*. Ed. David Madden. Carbondale: Southern Illinois U. 1968. Pp. 162–65.
Farrell, James T. "Saul Bergman's Sons." *SatR*, 23 (Nov. 2, 1940), 12. [rev.]
Gold, Michael. "Stale Bohemianism." *NM*, 8 (Apr. 1933), 29–30. [rev.]
Gilkes, Lillian. "Unsung History." *NM*, 45 (Nov. 24, 1942), 24–26. [rev.]
Hart, John E. "Albert Halper's World of the Thirties." *TCL*, 9 (Jan. 1964), 185–95.
_____. *Albert Halper*. Boston: Twayne, 1980.
Hicks, Granville. "Review and Comment . . . Halper Humanizes the Mail-order Company . . . ." *NM*, 25 (Nov. 23, 1927), 20–21. [rev.]
Klein, Marcus. "The Roots of Radicals: Experience in the Thirties." In *Proletarian Writers of the Thirties*. Ed. David Madden. Carbondale: Southern Illinois U., 1968. Pp. 145–48.
Lewis, Sinclair. "Blowing Loud Bugles for Albert Halper." *NYHTBR*, Sept. 9, 1934, p. 1.
[rev.]
Luccock, Halford E. *American Mirror—Social, Ethical and Religious Aspects of American Literature 1930–1940*. New York: Macmillan, 1940.
Rosenfeld, Isaac. "The Power and the Boredom." *NR*, 107 (Nov. 23, 1942), 687–88. [rev.]
Terkel, Studs. "The Hoods Among Us." *Book World, Chicago Tribune*, Dec. 3, 1967, p. 22.
[rev.]

John Hart
Albion College
Albion, Michigan

LORRAINE HANSBERRY (1930–65)

When *Raisin in the Sun* first appeared on Broadway in 1959 critics generally hailed the drama's universality and reality of characterization. Its theme revolves around the problems of a black family as it attempts to move into a previously all-white section of Chicago. The literary and social significance of the play is evidenced by the fact that its movie version is still widely viewed and the drama itself is required reading for a variety of high school and college literature courses.

Recent critics, especially Blacks, regard it as reflective of the bourgeois and assimilationist attitude of its author rather than an expression of the mass black experience. Harold Cruse points out that the play arrived on Broadway in the midst of the black middle-class social revolution and that its racial integration theme added timeliness to an otherwise old-fashioned genre (the pursuit of upward mobility). Yet Hansberry's admirers feel that the play transcends black and white social issues and concerns itself with genuine human conflicts. Some note the precision with which she develops characteristics that distinguish various members of the same family and social class.

Commentators on *The Sign in Sidney Brustein's Window* (1964) generally feel the playwright tried to integrate too many themes and burdensome details in relating the plight of an intellectual in a corrupt society. Many critics felt that Hansberry's unfinished play *Les Blancs*, first staged in 1969, presented more ideas than theatre and that its African revolutionary theme was somewhat dated. An unproduced play, "Drinking Gourd," reveals her interest in the Afro-American slave heritage.

Yet Hansberry always sought to rise above race. She believed that the award winning *Raisin in the Sun* was not a drama about the Negro question. Rather she noted it was a play "about an American family's conflict with certain mercenary values of its society, and its characters were Negroes." In *The Sign in Sidney Brustein's Window*, only one of the characters was black. Had her life not been cut short by cancer, many feel she would have moved beyond her apparent concern with middle-class problems to explore the "nobility and complexity of mankind" which long fascinated her.

Although she is regarded as America's most gifted black playwright, surprisingly little material on Lorraine Hansberry is available in collected form. The most extensive biographical material appears in *Current Biography Yearbook* for 1959. *Contemporary Black Drama* presents some interesting facts about her life, as does Harold Cruse's *Crisis of the Negro Intellectual*.

MAJOR WORKS

A Raisin in the Sun. New York: Random House, 1959. [play]
The Movement: Documentary of a Struggle for Equality. New York: Simon and Schuster, 1964. Republished as *A Matter of Colour*. Harmondsworth, Eng.: Penguin, 1965. [history]
The Sign in Sidney Brustein's Window. New York: Random House, 1965. [play]
To Be Young, Gifted and Black, Lorraine Hansberry in Her Own Words. Ed. Robert Nemiroff. New York: Signet, 1970. [autobiography]
Les Blancs: The Collected Last Plays of Lorraine Hansberry. New York: Random House, 1972.

CHECKLIST OF SECONDARY SOURCES

Burke; *CA; CB;* Herzberg.

Abraham, Doris E. "A Study of Play by Negro Playwrights, From Appearance to A Raisin in the Sun (1925–1959)." Ph.D. diss., Columbia U., 1967.

Baldwin, James. "Sweet Lorraine." *Esquire,* 72 (Nov. 1969), 139–40.

Bigsby, C. W. E. "Lorraine Hansberry." In *Confrontation and Commitment: A Study of Contemporary American Dramas 1959–66.* Columbia: U. Missouri, 1969. Pp. 156–73.

Cruse, Harold. "Lorraine Hansberry." In *The Crisis of the Negro Intellectual.* New York: William Morrow, 1967. Pp. 267–84, 409–13.

Davis, Ossie. "The Significance of Lorraine Hansberry." *Freedomways,* 5 (Summer 1965), 396–402.

Farrison, Edward W. "Lorraine Hansberry's Last Dramas." *CLA,* 16 (Dec. 1972), 188–97.

Gill, Glenda. "Techniques of Teaching Lorraine Hansberry: Literation from Boredom." *NALF,* 8 (Summer 1974), 226–28.

Grant, L. "Les Blancs." *BW,* 2 (Apr. 1971), 46–47.

Hays, P. L. "Raisin in the Sun and Juno the Paycock." *Phylon,* 33 (Summer 1972), 175–76.

Hicklin, Fannie E.F. "The American Negro Playwright, 1920–1964." Ph.D. diss., U. Wisconsin, 1965.

Holton, Orley I. "Sidney Brustein and the Plight of the American Intellectual." *Players,* 46 (June–July 1971), 222–25.

Issaacs, Harold R. "Five Writers and Their African Ancestors." *Phylon,* 21 (Fall 1960), 243–265; Part II (Winter 1967), 317–36.

Lewis, Theophilus. "Social Protest in 'A Raisin in the Sun.' " *CathW,* 140 (Oct. 1959), 31–35. [rev.]

Miller, Jordan Y. "Lorraine Hansberry." In *The Black American Writer Vol. II.* Ed. C.W.E. Bigsby. Baltimore: Penguin, 1971. Pp. 158–70.

Oliver, Clifton F. and Stephanie Sills, eds. *Contemporary Black Drama.* New York: Scribner, 1971. Pp. 29–32.

Ness, D. E. "The Sign in Sidney Brustein's Window." *Freedomways,* 11 (Nov. 1971), 359–66.

"Raisin in the Sun." *NYCTR,* 20 (Mar. 16, 1959), 344–47.

"The Sign in Sidney Brustein's Window." *NYCTR,* 25 (Oct. 26, 1964), 190–93.

"Les Blancs." *NYCTR,* 31 (Nov. 16, 1970), 154–56.

Turner, Darwin. "The Negro Dramatists Image of His Universe, 1920–1960." *CLA,* 5 (Dec. 1961), 117–20.

———. "Negro Playwrights and the Urban Negro." *CLA,* 12 (Sept. 1968), 19–25.

Turpin, Walters E. "The Contemporary American Negro Playwright." *CLA,* 9 (Sept. 1965), 12–24.

Weales, Gerald. "Thoughts on 'A Raisin in the Sun': A Critical Review." *Commentary,* 28 (June 1959), 527–30. [rev.]

———. "Losing the Playwright." *Commonweal,* 90 (Sept. 5, 1969), 542–43.

Martha H. Brown
Central Michigan University
Mt. Pleasant, Michigan

WALTER HAVIGHURST (1901–   )

Walter Havighurst has been referred to by several reviewers of his work as "the outstanding interpreter of the American Midwest." His many novels and nonfictional historical studies of midwestern personages and places stand as convincing evidence of his regional commitment. When the *Saturday Review* did its special issue (Jan. 6, 1945), "The Ohio Valley, A Regional Inventory," Havighurst served as the guest editor. One of his earlier important works, *The Long Ships Passing: The Story of the Great Lakes*, was praised by Holbrook as "the best and most readable book on the five Lakes." Twenty years later, in reviewing *The Heartland: Ohio, Indiana, Illinois*, Engle reaffirmed the praise of others by citing Havighurst as "the area's finest interpreter." Frederick, in surveying Havighurst's work up to 1950, cited his "rich sense of the regional past," his "unquestionable integrity" in using history, the "vitality of style," and the "unfailing human quality" of his writing. Frederick calls *Signature of Time* "one of the finest and most satisfying regional novels of the last quarter-century." Jones makes the same sort of claim for *The Winds of Spring*, the novel of pioneer Wisconsin which Redman praises for its "thoughtful strength" and "a beauty that promises to be enduring." Because of his ability as a narrative historian, Havighurst was selected to write the official Bicentennial history of Ohio under the auspices of the NEH and the American Association for State and Local History. Jones finds Havighurst's particular strength, in both fiction and nonfiction, to be his capacity for "fusing a fine sense of history with a finer sense of human beings."

Major Works

Pier 17. New York: Macmillan, 1935. [novel]
The Quiet Shore. New York: Macmillan, 1937. [novel]
Upper Mississippi: A Wilderness Saga. New York: Farrar, 1937 (rev. ed., 1944). [history]
The Winds of Spring. New York: Macmillan, 1940. [novel]
No Homeward Course. New York: Doubleday, 1941. [novel]
The Long Ships Passing: The Story of the Great Lakes. New York: Macmillan, 1942. Revised 1976. [history]
Land of Promise. New York: Macmillan, 1946. [history]
Signature of Time. New York: Macmillan, 1949. [novel]
George Rogers Clark: Soldier in the West. New York: McGraw-Hill, 1952. [history]
Annie Oakley of the Wild West. New York: Macmillan, 1954. [history]
Wilderness for Sale: The Story of the First Western Land Rush. New York: Hastings, 1956. [history]
Vein of Iron: The Pickands Mather Story. Cleveland: World, 1958. [history]
The Miami Years. New York: Putnam, 1958 (rev. ed. 1969). [history]
Land of the Long Horizons. New York: Coward-McCann, 1960. [literary-historical anthology]
The Heartland: Ohio, Indiana, Illinois. New York: Harper, 1962. [history]
Proud Prisoner. New York: Holt, 1964. [history]
Voices on the River: The Story of the Mississippi Waterways. New York: Macmillan, 1964. [history]
The Great Lakes Reader. New York: Macmillan, 1966. [historical anthology]
Three Flags at the Straits: The Forts of Mackinac. Englewood Cliffs, N.J.: Prentice-Hall, 1966. [history]
Alexander Spotswood: Portrait of a Governor. New York: Holt, 1967. [history]
River to the West: Three Centuries of the Ohio. New York: Putnam, 1970. [history]
Men of Old Miami, 1809–1873: A Book of Portraits. New York: Putnam, 1974. [history]
Ohio: A Bicentennial History. New York: Norton, 1976.

Written with Marion Boyd Havighurst:
  High Prairie. New York: Farrar, 1944. [novel]
  Song of the Pines. New York: Holt, 1949. [novel]
  Climb a Lofty Ladder. Philadelphia: Winston, 1952. [novel]

CHECKLIST OF SECONDARY SOURCES

CA; Herzberg; *TCA & Supp.*

Alsterlund, B. "Walter Havighurst." *WLB*, 17 (June 1943), 788.
Engle, Paul. "The Heartland." *NYTBR*, Dec. 2, 1962, p. 36. [rev.]
Fuller, Edmund. "Withdrawal and Return." *SatR*, 32 (Sept. 17, 1949), 14. [rev.]
Frederick, John T. "Walter Havighurst." *Ohio Authors and Their Books*. Ed. William Coyle. Cleveland: World, 1962.
Holbrook, Stewart. Review of *Long Ships Passing. Books* (July 19, 1942), 1.
Jones, Joel M. "To Feel the Heartland's Pulse: The Writing of Walter Havighurst." *KQ*, 2 (Spring 1970), 88–96.
Kingsland, Dorothea. "The Old Homestead." *NYTBR*, Mar. 14, 1937, p. 6. [rev.]
Redman, Ben Ray. "The Story of 'Woodpecker Jan.' " *SatR*, 21 (Apr. 13, 1940), 16. [rev.]
Sherman, Beatrice. Review of *The Winds of Spring. NYTBR*, Apr. 7, 1940, p. 6.

Joel M. Jones
University of New Mexico
Albuquerque, New Mexico

JOHN HAY (1838–1905)

Although Hay attempted every literary form practiced in post-Civil War America, and received favorable reviews and national attention for his first efforts in each field, his career as an author was pre-empted by his interest in government. Mixing irony, pathos, melodrama, realism, and local color, Hay's writings have attracted a discerning body of critics—Dennett's biography won a Pulitzer Prize in 1934. Jaher offers a judicious discussion of the dichotomy between midwestern egalitarianism and cultural elitism which makes Hay so representative of the culture of the 1870s and 1880s and has caused *The Bread-Winners* to be included in two recent scholarly reprint series.

Commentary on the *Pike County Ballads* is frequently preoccupied with the primacy of Harte or Hay in dialect ballads; however Pattee and the standard histories offer cogent evaluations of Pike literature. The furious controversy aroused by *The Bread-Winners* as an anonymous antilabor novel is thoroughly discussed by Vandersee and Sloane, with attention to the position of women and the problems of literary realism in popular novels. Montiero makes valuable contributions to the present knowledge of Hay's short stories and reportage.

Major Works

Pike County Ballads and Other Pieces. Boston: Osgood, 1871. [poems]
Castilian Days. Boston: Osgood, 1871. [travel narrative]
The Bread-Winners: A Social Study. New York: Harper, 1884. [novel]
Abraham Lincoln. A History. With John G. Nicolay. 10 vols. New York: Century, 1890. [biography]
Addresses of John Hay. New York: Century, 1906. [speeches]

Checklist of Secondary Sources

Blanck; *CHAL;* Herzberg; *LHUS.*

Chapman, A. S. "The Boyhood of John Hay." *CM,* 78 (June 1909), 444–54.
Clymer, Kenton J. *John Hay: The Gentleman as Diplomat.* Ann Arbor: U. Michigan, 1974.
Dennett, Tyler. *John Hay: From Poetry to Politics.* New York: Dodd, Mead, 1933.
Jaher, Frederic C. "Industrialism and the American Aristocrat: A Social Study of John Hay and His Novel, 'The Bread-Winners.' " *JISHS,* 65 (Spring 1972), 69–93.
[King, Clarence]. "John Hay." *SM,* 7 (April 1874), 736–39.
The Life and Works of John Hay, 1838–1905. Providence: Brown U. Library, 1961. [catalog]
Montiero, George. *Henry James and John Hay: The Record of a Friendship.* Providence: Brown U., 1965.
_____. "John Hay as Reporter: Special Correspondence on the Great Chicago Fire." *BBr,* 22 (1968), 81–94.
_____. "John Hay's Short Fiction." *SSF,* 7 (Fall 1971), 543–52.
Pattee, Fred L. *A History of American Literature Since 1870.* New York: Century, 1916. Pp. 85–91.
Sloane, David E. E. "Censoring for *The Century Magazine:* R. W. Gilder to John Hay on *The Bread-Winners,* 1882–1884." *AmLitR,* 4 (Summer 1971), 255–67.
_____. "John Hay (1838–1905)." *AmLitR,* 3 (Spring 1970), 178–88.
_____. "John Hay's *The Bread-Winners* as Literary Realism." *AmLitR,* 2 (Fall 1969), 276–79.
Thayer, William R. *The Life and Letters of John Hay.* 2 vols. Boston: Houghton Mifflin, 1916.
Thurman, Kelly. *John Hay as a Man of Letters.* Reseda, Calif.: Mojave, 1974.
Ticknor, Caroline. *A Poet in Exile: Early Letters of John Hay.* Boston: Houghton Mifflin, 1910.
Vandersee, Charles. "Introduction." *The Bread-Winners.* New Haven: College and University Press, 1973. Pp. 7–54.
_____. "The Great Literary Mystery of the Gilded Age." *AmLitR,* 7 (Summer 1974), 245–72.
Ward, Sister St. Ignatius. "The Poetry of John Hay." Ph.D. diss., Catholic University of America, 1930.

David E. E. Sloane
University of New Haven
West Haven, Connecticut

JAMES HEARST (1900–   )

There are three major sources for Hearst in Daman, Emde, and the Fall, 1974, issue of the *North American Review*. Slighter, but oft times pertinent comments are in Andrews, Engle, Frederick, Frost, Reninger, and Suckow. Paluka furnishes his standard bibliography, but the definitive one is in the

North American Review. There are manuscripts and letters at the University of Iowa and at the University of Buffalo.

MAJOR WORKS

Country Men. Muscatine, Iowa: Prairie Press, 1937. [poems]
The Sun at Noon. Muscatine, Iowa: Prairie Press, 1943. [poems]
Man and his Field: Selected Poems. Denver: Swallow, 1951. [poems]
Limited View. Iowa City: Prairie Press, 1962. [poems]
A Single Focus. Iowa City: Prairie Press, 1967. [poems]
Stranger Share Our Fire. Music by Daniel Moe. Minneapolis: Augsburg, 1968. [folk songs]

CHECKLIST OF SECONDARY SOURCES

Andrews, Clarence A. *A Literary History of Iowa*. Iowa City: U. Iowa, 1972. Pp. 148–49, *passim*.
Bluhm, Dave. "Monologue for Jim." *NAR*, 259, (Fall 1974), 14.
Daman, J. "Beyond Knowledge to Wisdom: An Introduction to James Hearst." Master's thesis, Mankato (Minn.) State College, 1968.
Emde, Jane M. "The Life and Works of James Schell Hearst." Master's thesis, U. Minnesota, 1970.
Engel, Paul. "James Hearst [poem]." *NAR*, 259, (Fall 1974), 12–13.
Frederick, John T. "I've Been Reading." *CSBW*, Sept. 5, 1943.
_____. *Out of the Midwest*. New York: McGraw-Hill, 1944. P. 301.
_____. "The Younger School." *Palimpsest*, 11 (Feb. 1930), 81.
Frost, Robert. Letter included in Lawrance Thompson, ed. *The Selected Letters of Robert Frost*. New York: Holt, 1964. Pp. 499–500.
Hearst, James. "Bibliography." *NAR*, 259 (Fall 1974), 44–49.
_____. "Reminiscences." *NAR*, 259 (Fall 1974), 39–43.
_____. "Roots of Poetry." *NAR*, 259 (Fall 1974), 15–17.
Lash, Kenneth. "James Hearst: An Introduction." *NAR*, 259 (Fall 1974), 9.
Paluka, Frank. *Iowa Authors: A Bio-Bibliography of Sixty Native Writers*. Iowa City: Friends of the University of Iowa Libraries, 1967. Pp. 165–66.
Reninger, H. Willard. "Biographical Note." In James Hearst. *Country Men*. Muscatine, Iowa: Prairie Press, 1943.
_____. "James Hearst: A Country Man as Poet." *Man and His Field* [by James Hearst]. Denver: Swallow, 1951.
_____. "Afterword." In James Hearst. *Limited View*. Denver: Swallow, 1963.
Suckow, Ruth. "Foreword." In James Hearst. *Country Men*. All editions [see *supra* and *Paluka*, p. 166].
Who's Who in Iowa, 1940.

Clarence A. Andrews
University of Iowa
Iowa City, Iowa

BEN HECHT (1893–1964)

Although Ben Hecht wrote twenty-two books, ten plays, and more than seventy screenplays, he has received little critical attention. A short bibliography can be found in Gerstenberger and Hendrick's *The American Novel 1789–1959*, and the only full length study is Roberts's dissertation.

Despite this scarcity of criticism, Ben Hecht was recognized as one of Hollywood's top screenwriters, winning his first Academy Award for an original story *Underworld* (1927), and his second for *The Scoundrel* (1935). In addition, he won the Pulitzer Prize for *The Front Page* (1928), a play based on his newspaper experience in the Chicago of the roaring twenties. He was also a good friend of other Chicago writers, including Maxwell Bodenheim, Sherwood Anderson, and Carl Sandburg. Although he may never be recognized as a great writer, he does deserve further critical evaluation.

MAJOR WORKS

Gargoyles. New York: Boni and Liveright, 1922. [novel]
A Thousand and One Afternoons in Chicago. Chicago: Covici, 1922. [stories]
The Florentine Dagger. New York: Boni and Liveright, 1923. [novel]
Humpty Dumpty. New York: Boni and Liveright, 1924. [novel]
Erik Dorn. New York: Modern Library, 1924. [novel]
Broken Necks. Chicago: Covici, 1925. [stories]
Count Bruga. New York: Boni and Liveright, 1926. [novel]
The Front Page. New York: Covici, Friede, 1928. [play]
A Jew In Love. New York: Covici, Friede, 1931. [novel]
The Champion From Far Away. New York: Covici, Friede, 1931. [stories]
The Great Magoo. New York: Covici, Friede, 1933. [play]
Actor's Blood. New York: Covici, Friede, 1936. [novel]
A Book of Miracles. New York: Viking, 1939. [novelettes]
A Guide for the Bedeviled. New York: Scribner, 1944. [novel]
I Hate Actors. New York: Crown, 1944. [novel]
A Child of the Century. New York: Simon and Schuster, 1954. [autobiography]
The Sensualists. New York: Messner, 1959. [novel]
Gaily, Gaily. New York: Doubleday, 1963. [autobiography]
Letters from Bohemia. New York: Doubleday, 1964. [letters]
In the Midst of Death. London: Mayflower, 1964. [novel]

CHECKLIST OF SECONDARY SOURCES

Burke; *CB;* Herzberg; *OCAL; TCA & Supp.*

Baldwin, Charles. *The Men Who Make Our Novels*. New York: Moffat, 1919.
"Ben Stalin." *Newsweek*, 53 (Jan. 26, 1959), 94.
Berg, L. "Brat of the Century." *Commentary*, 18 (Oct. 1954), 374. Reply by M. Geltman. *Commentary*, 18 (Dec. 1954), 272.
Cargill, Oscar. *Intellectual America*. New York: Macmillan, 1941.
Cerf, Bennett. "Trade Winds." *SatR*, 27 (June 3, 1944), 20.
"City and Summer; Tales of the City." *Newsweek*, 42 (July 6, 1953), 70.
Dawidowicz, L. S. "Ben Hecht's *Perfidy*." *Commentary*, 33 (Mar. 1962), 260–64. Reply by D. Greenberg. *Commentary*, 34 (Aug. 1962), 168.
Fincke, Gary W. "The Fiction of Ben Hecht: A Study in Polarity." *DAI*, 35:7903A–04A.
Hansen, Harry. "Lusty Looper." *SatR*, 37 (July 17, 1954), 18–19.
———. *Midwest Portraits*. New York: Harcourt, 1923.
"How to Lose Friends." *Time*, 72 (Oct. 27, 1968), 62.
"In Rusty Armor." *Time*, 63 (June 21, 1954), 108.
Karsner, David. *Sixteen Authors to One*. New York: Copeland, 1928.
"Life Had Better Be Beautiful." *Nation*, 187 (Nov. 22, 1958), 371.
McDonnell, T. P. "From Ben Hecht to Pasternak." *CathW*, 189 (Apr. 1959), 39–43.
Michaud, Regis. *The American Novel Today*. Boston: Little, Brown, 1928.
Morton, F. "Life, Loves, and Loathing of the Egregious Ben Hecht." *Reporter*, 11 (Sept. 14, 1954), 46–48.

Ravitz, Abe C. "Assault With Deadly Typewriter: The Hecht-Bodenheim Vendetta." *Cabellian*, 4 (1972), 104–11.

———. "Ballyhoo, Gargoyles and Firecrackers: Ben Hecht's Aesthetic Calliope." *JPC*, 1 (1967), 37–51.

Redman, B. R. "Theory and Practice of Ben Hecht." *SatR*, 28 (June 23, 1945), 15.

"Remember Us." *AmMerc*, 56 (Feb. 1943), 194–99.

Roberts, Ronald. "The Novels of Ben Hecht." Ph.D. diss., Baylor U., 1971.

Sherman, Stuart Pratt. *Critical Woodcuts*. New York: Scribner, 1926.

"Upper Hand." *Time*, 65 (July 20, 1953), 56.

Wain, J. "Case of Ben Hecht." *NR*, 141 (Sept. 28, 1959), 16–18.

"Wistfully Yours." *TA*, 35 (July 1951), 12–13.

Wolfert, I. "Leaping Into the Air." *Nation*, 179 (Aug. 21, 1954), 155.

Carl J. Demarkowski
University of Toledo
Toledo, Ohio

ERNEST HEMINGWAY (1899–1961)

From 1924, when Edmund Wilson and other critics responded favorably to Hemingway's *in our time* and *3 Stories & 10 Poems*, criticism of Hemingway's writing has never diminished. More is being published now than appeared in 1940, the year of the then-politically-controversial novel, *For Whom the Bell Tolls*. Despite the present critical cliché that Hemingway's reputation is in decline, few modern authors appear so frequently in literary criticism the world over. Hemingway is more than a modern American writer; he is a touchstone, a reference point.

Charting the quantity and accuracy of the criticism of Hemingway's work proves somewhat surprising. His reputation began near its zenith. Reviews of the early books, including *The Sun Also Rises* and *A Farewell To Arms*, were nearly all favorable (many critics, including Allen Tate, adopted Hemingway and wrote favorably about him on any possible occasion). But during the 1930s, when his writing was experimental so far as genre was concerned, readers grew confused, and took refuge in the personal fallacy. Freudian and Marxist criticism helped debilitate the strengths of his work, and during the 1940s little criticism of note appeared. But in 1952 were published both the fine studies by Baker and Young, the former, *The Writer as Artist*, now in its fourth edition, the latter revised in 1966 as *Ernest Hemingway: A Reconsideration*. Coupled with Hemingway's receiving the Nobel Prize for Literature in 1954, ostensibly for *The Old Man and the Sea* (1952), these books created a new depth of interest in Hemingway's work.

In the past twenty years, many excellent book-length studies of his work have appeared, both in this country and abroad. No modern American writer, except perhaps T. S. Eliot, has received such full and competent treatment. In 1967, Hanneman's bibliography of both primary and secondary materials appeared; in 1969 Baker's biography. Some idea of unpublished materials remaining can be gained from *The Hemingway Manuscripts, An Inventory*, compiled in 1969 by Young and Mann. Although Hemingway's letters are supposedly never to see print, Bruccoli and Clark have included the many interesting excerpts used in auction catalogs in their 1973 *Hemingway at Auction, 1930–1973*.

Bibliographically, in addition to Hanneman, see also the *Modern Fiction Studies* Hemingway issue of Autumn 1968; Hoffman's essay in *Sixteen Modern American Authors*; and the issues of the *Fitzgerald-Hemingway Annual* since it began publication in 1969.

Despite this wealth of critical activity, comparatively little attention has been given to Hemingway as midwestern writer. More often he is treated as an expatriate or as an aficionado of Spain, as cosmopolitan as the many figures in the various Hemingway legends. Montgomery remedies some of the lack, but much more consideration is needed. For, as Jackson J. Benson recognizes in his 1974 essay, "Hemingway in Our Time," many of his most characteristic themes came to him out of "his Midwestern, middle-class Americanism, out of the forceful Victorianism of his parents, and out of the frontier values and skills (somewhat decadently preserved in the Midwestern 'sports frontier' of Northern Michigan) passed on to him by his father."

MAJOR WORKS

3 Stories & 10 Poems. Paris: Contact Publishing Co., 1923.
in our time. Paris: three mountains press, 1924. [vignettes]
In Our Time: Stories. New York: Boni & Liveright, 1925. [vignettes and stories]
The Torrents of Spring: A Romantic Novel in Honor of the Passing of a Great Race. New York: Scribner, 1926. [parody]
The Sun Also Rises. New York: Scribner, 1926. [novel]
Men Without Women. New York: Scribner, 1927. [stories and play]
A Farewell to Arms. New York: Scribner, 1929. [novel]
Death in the Afternoon. New York: Scribner, 1932. [study of bullfighting]
Winner Take Nothing. New York: Scribner, 1933. [stories]
Green Hills of Africa. New York: Scribner, 1935. [study of big-game hunting]
To Have and Have Not. New York: Scribner, 1937. [novel]
The Spanish Earth. Cleveland: J. B. Savage, 1938. [film commentary]
The Fifth Column and the First Forty-nine Stories. New York: Scribner, 1938. [play and stories]
For Whom the Bell Tolls. New York: Scribner, 1940. [novel]
Across the River and Into the Trees. New York: Scribner, 1950. [novel]
The Old Man and the Sea. New York: Scribner, 1952. [novella]
A Moveable Feast. New York: Scribner, 1964. [reminiscence of Paris]
The Fifth Column and Four Stories of the Spanish Civil War. New York: Scribner, 1969. [play and unpublished stories]
Islands in the Stream. New York: Scribner, 1970. [novel]
The Collected Poems of Ernest Hemingway. New York: Haskell House, 1970.
The Nick Adams Stories. Ed. Philip Young. New York: Scribner, 1972.

CHECKLIST OF SECONDARY SOURCES

Aldridge, John W. "Hemingway and Europe." *Shenandoah,* 12 (Spring 1961), 11–24.

Arnold, Lloyd R. *High on the Wild with Hemingway.* Caldwell, Ida.: Caxton, 1968.

Asselineau, Roger. "Hemingway in Paris." *FHA* (1973), 11–32.

Baker, Carlos. *Ernest Hemingway: A Life Story.* New York: Scribner, 1969.

———. *Hemingway: The Writer as Artist.* Princeton, N.J.: Princeton U., 1952.

Baker, Sheridan. *Ernest Hemingway: An Introduction and Interpretation.* New York: Holt, 1967.

———. "Hemingway's Two-Hearted River." *MAQR,* 65 (Feb. 28, 1959), 142–49.

Beach, Joseph Warren. "How Do You Like It Now, Gentlemen?" *SR,* 59 (Spring 1951), 311–28.

Beebe, Maurice and John Feaster. "Criticism of Ernest Hemingway: A Selected Checklist." *MFS,* 14 (Autumn 1968), 337–69.

Benson, Jackson J. *Hemingway: The Writer's Art of Self Defense.* Minneapolis: U. Minnesota, 1969.

———. "Patterns of Connection and Their Development in Hemingway's *In Our Time.*" *Rendezvous,* 5 (Winter 1970), 37–52.

———, ed. *The Short Stories of Ernest Hemingway: Critical Essays.* Durham: Duke U., 1975.

Benson, Jackson J. and Richard Astro, eds. *Hemingway In Our Time.* Corvallis: Oregon State U., 1974.

Bishop, John Peale. "Homage to Hemingway." *NR,* 89 (Nov. 11, 1936), 39–42.

———. "The Missing All." *VQR,* 13 (Winter 1937), 106–21.

Bridgman, Richard. *The Colloquial Style in America.* New York: Oxford U., 1966. Pp. 195–230.

Bruccoli, Matthew J., ed. *Ernest Hemingway, Cub Reporter: Kansas City Star Stories.* Pittsburgh: U. Pittsburgh, 1970.

Bruccoli, Matthew J. and C. E. Frazer Clark, Jr., comps. *Hemingway at Auction, 1930–1973.* Detroit: Gale, 1973.

Burgum, Edwin B. *The Novel and the World's Dilemma.* New York: Oxford U., 1947.

Cargill, Oscar. *Intellectual America: Ideas on the March.* New York: Macmillan, 1941.

Cooke, Alistair. "Hemingway: Master of the Mid-West Vernacular." *Manchester Guardian,* Nov. 11, 1954, p. 7.

Cowley, Malcolm. *Exile's Return: A Narrative of Ideas.* New York: Norton, 1934.

———. "Hemingway: The Image and the Shadow." *Horizon,* 15 (Winter 1973), 112–17.

———. *A Second Flowering: Works and Days of the Lost Generation.* New York: Viking, 1973.

DeFalco, Joseph. *The Hero in Hemingway's Short Stories.* Pittsburgh: U. Pittsburgh, 1963.

Donaldson, Scott. "Hemingway's Morality of Compensation." *AL,* 43 (Nov. 1971), 399–420.

Doxey, William S. "The Significance of Seney, Michigan, in Hemingway's 'Big Two-Hearted River.' " *HN,* 1 (Fall 1971), 5–6.

Farrell, James T. "Ernest Hemingway's *The Sun Also Rises.*" *NYTBR,* Aug. 1, 1943.

Fenton, Charles A. *The Apprenticeship of Ernest Hemingway: The Early Years.* New York: Farrar, 1954.

Finkelstein, Sidney. "Ernest Hemingway: 1898 [sic]–1961." *Mainstream,* 14 (1961), 6–10.

Flanagan, John. "Hemingway's Debt to Sherwood Anderson." *JEGP,* 54 (Oct. 1955), 507–20.

Fuchs, Daniel. "Ernest Hemingway, Literary Critic." *AL,* 36 (Jan. 1965), 431–51.

Goldhurst, William. *F. Scott Fitzgerald and His Contemporaries.* Cleveland: World, 1963.

Gray, James. "Hemingway in Piggott." *Approach,* 48 (Summer 1963), 30–32.

Grebstein, Sheldon N. *Hemingway's Craft.* Carbondale: Southern Illinois U., 1973.

Gurko, Leo. *Ernest Hemingway and the Pursuit of Heroism.* New York: Crowell, 1968.

Gutkind, Lee Allen. Five-part series in the *Greenville News,* Greenville, Wyoming: "Wyoming People Remember Hemingway with Fondness." Sept. 28, 1970. p. 8; "Wyoming Lets a Man Be Honest With Himself." Sept. 29, p. 8; "While Writing, Hemingway 'Always Had a Bottle.' " Sept. 30, p. 8; "Hemingway Stopped Working To Hunt Bear." Oct. 1, p. 58; "Why Did Hemingway Quit Wyoming's Solitude?" Oct. 2, p. 26.

Hanneman, Audre. *Ernest Hemingway: A Comprehensive Bibliography*. Princeton, N.J.: Princeton U., 1967.

Hemingway, Gregory H. *Papa: A Personal Memoir*. Boston: Houghton, Mifflin, 1976.

Hemingway, Leicester. *My Brother, Ernest Hemingway*. Cleveland: World, 1962.

Hemingway, Mary. "Hemingway's Spain." *SR*, 50 (Mar. 11, 1967), 48–49, 102–4, 107.

———. *How It Was*. New York: Knopf, 1976.

Hoffman, Frederick J. "Ernest Hemingway." In *Fifteen Modern American Authors*. Ed. Jackson Bryer. Durham, N.C.: Duke U., 1969.

———. "The Temper of the Twenties." *MR*, 1 (Fall 1960), 36–45.

Hovey, Richard B. *Hemingway: The Inward Terrain*. Seattle: U. Washington, 1969.

Hubbel, Jay B. *Who Are the Major American Writers?* Durham, N.C.: Duke U., 1972.

Kazin, Alfred. "Ernest Hemingway as His Own Fable." *Atlantic*, 213 (June 1964), 54–57.

Lehan, Richard. *A Dangerous Crossing, French Literary Existentialism and the Modern American Novel*. Carbondale: Southern Illinois U., 1973.

Lewis, Robert W., Jr. "Hemingway's Concept of Sport and 'Soldier's Home.' " *Rendezvous*, 5 (Winter 1970), 19–27.

Lovett, Robert Morse. "Ernest Hemingway." *EJ*, 21 (1932), 609–16.

Manning, Robert. "Hemingway in Cuba." *Atlantic*, 216 (Aug. 1965), 101–8.

Marin, Dave. "Seven Hours with Papa." *SwR*, 53 (Spring 1968), 167–77.

McCormick, John. *The Middle Distance, A Comparative History of American Imaginative Literature: 1919–1932*. New York: Free Press, 1971.

Miller, Madelaine Hemingway. *Ernie: Hemingway's Sister "Sunny" Remembers*. New York: Crown, 1975.

Mizener, Arthur. "The Two Hemingways." In *The Great Experiment in American Literature: Six Lectures*. Ed. Carl Bode. New York: Praeger, 1961. Pp. 135–51.

Monteiro, George. "The Education of Ernest Hemingway." *JAmS*, 8 (Apr. 1974), 91–99.

Montgomery, Constance Cappel. *Hemingway in Michigan*. New York: Fleet, 1966.

Nash, Jay Robert. "Ernest Hemingway, The Young Years & the Chicagoans Who Knew Him." *ChiL*, 5 (Aug. 1968), 19–25.

Noble, David W. *The Eternal Adam and the New World Garden: The Central Myth in the American Novel Since 1830*. New York: Braziller, 1968.

Oldsey, Bernard. "Of Hemingway's *Arms* and the Man." *ColL*, 1 (Fall 1974), 174–89.

Paige, Whitney. "Hemingway's Michigan." *T&C*, 33 (July–Aug. 1970), 32–37.

Peterson, Richard K. *Hemingway: Direct and Oblique*. The Hague: Mouton, 1969.

Plimpton, George. "The Art of Fiction, XXI: Hemingway." *ParisR*, 18 (Spring 1958), 61–89.

Priestley, J. B. Review of *FTA*. *N&T*, 32 (Winter 1929), 11–12.

Pritchett, V. S. "Ernest Hemingway." *NSN*, 50 (July 30, 1955), 137–38.

Reardon, John. "Hemingway's Esthetic and Ethical Sportsmen." *UR*, 34 (Oct. 1967), 13–23.

Reynolds, Brad. "Afternoon with Mary Hemingway." *America*, 126 (Mar. 25, 1972), 319–20.

Reynolds, Michael S. *Hemingway's First War: The Making of A Farewell to Arms*. Princeton, N.J.: Princeton U., 1976.

Rovit, Earl. *Ernest Hemingway*. New York: Twayne, 1963.

Sanford, Marcelline Hemingway. *At the Hemingways: A Family Portrait*. Boston: Little, Brown, 1961.

Sarason, Bertram D. *Hemingway and The Sun Set*. Washington, D.C.: NCR Microcard Editions, 1972.

Scherman, David E. and Rosemarie Redlich. *Literary America: A Chronicle of American Writers with Photographs of the American Scene that Inspired Them*. New York: Dodd, Mead, 1952.

Schwartz, Delmore. "The Fiction of Ernest Hemingway." *PUSA*, 13 (Autumn 1955), 70–88.

Schorer, Mark. *The World We Imagine: Selected Essays*. New York: Farrar, 1968.

Scott, Nathan. *Ernest Hemingway, A Critical Essay*. Grand Rapids, Mich.: Eerdmans, 1966.

Shaw, Samuel. *Ernest Hemingway*. New York: Ungar, 1973.

Spender, Stephen. *Love-Hate Relations*. New York: Random House, 1974.

Spivey, Ted R. "Hemingway's Pursuit of Happiness on the Open Road." *EUQ*, 11 (Dec. 1955), 240–52.

Stein, William Bysshe. "Ritual in Hemingway's 'Big Two-Hearted River.' " *TSLL*, 1 (Winter 1960), 555–61.

Stephens, Robert O. *Hemingway's Non-fiction: The Public Voice.* Chapel Hill: U. North Carolina, 1968.

Tanner, Tony. *The Reign of Wonder: Nativity and Reality in American Literature.* Cambridge: Cambridge U., 1965.

Tate, Allen. Review of *TOS. Nation,* 123 (July 28, 1926), 89–90.

Thompson, Hunter S. "What Lured Hemingway to Ketchum?" *National Observer,* May 25, 1964, pp. 1, 13.

Torchiana, Donald T. "*TSAR:* A Reconsideration." *FHA* (1969), 77–103.

Vorpahl, Ben M. "Ernest Hemingway and Owen Wister: Finding the Lost Generation." *LCUP,* 36 (1970), 126–37.

Wagner, Linda W. "The Poem of Santiago and Manolin." *MFS,* 19 (Winter 1973), 517–30.

_____, ed. *Ernest Hemingway: Five Decades of Criticism.* East Lansing: Michigan State U., 1974.

_____. *Hemingway and Faulkner: Inventors/Masters.* Metuchen, N.J.: Scarecrow, 1975.

Walcutt, Charles C. *American Literary Naturalism, A Divided Stream.* Minneapolis: U. Minnesota, 1956.

Waldhorn, Arthur. *A Reader's Guide to Ernest Hemingway.* New York: Farrar, 1972.

Waldmeir, Joseph. "Confiteor Hominem: Ernest Hemingway's Religion of Man." *PMASAL,* 42 (1956), 277–81.

Warren, Robert Penn. "Ernest Hemingway." *Selected Essays.* New York: Random House, 1958. Pp. 80–118.

Watkins, Floyd C. *The Flesh and the Word: Eliot, Hemingway, Faulkner.* Nashville, Tenn.: Vanderbilt U., 1971.

Watts, Emily S. *Ernest Hemingway and the Arts.* Urbana: U. Illinois, 1971.

White, William, ed. *By-Line: Ernest Hemingway.* New York: Scribner, 1967.

Wickes, George. *Americans in Paris, 1909–1939.* Garden City, N.Y.: Doubleday, 1969.

Wilson, Edmund. "Hemingway: Bourdon Gauge of Morale." In *The Wound and the Bow.* Boston: Houghton Mifflin, 1941. Pp. 214–41.

_____. "The Sportsman's Tragedy." *NR,* 53 (Dec. 14, 1927), 102–3.

Wolf, Robert. Review of *IOT. NYHTB,* Feb. 14, 1926, p. 3.

Wright, Austin McG. *The American Short Story in the Twenties.* Chicago: U. Chicago, 1961.

Wylder, Delbert E. *Hemingway's Heroes.* Albuquerque, N.M.: U. New Mexico, 1969.

Yevish, Irving A. "The Sun Also Exposes: Hemingway and Jake Barnes." *MQ,* 10 (Oct. 1968), 89–97.

Young, Philip. " 'Big World Out There': *The Nick Adams Stories.*" *Novel,* 6 (1972), 5–19.

_____. *Ernest Hemingway.* New York: Rinehart, 1952. See also the revision. *Ernest Hemingway: A Reconsideration.* University Park: Pennsylvania State U., 1966.

Young, Philip and Charles Mann. *The Hemingway Manuscripts: An Inventory.* University Park: Pennsylvania State U., 1969.

Yu, Beongcheon. "The Still Center of Hemingway's World." *Phoenix* (Korea), 12 (Spring 1968), 15–44.

Linda Welshimer Wagner
Michigan State University
East Lansing, Michigan

JOSEPHINE HERBST (1897–1969)

Although Josephine Herbst was born in Iowa and educated there (for the most part), she should be thought of as a midwestern radical or proletarian novelist rather than as an Iowa regional novelist. Because of her social and political philosophies and their influence on her novels, she has tended, with other like-minded writers from the 1930s, to disappear from view.

Nevertheless, there now seems to be an upsurge of interest in her work. Pickering completed her "Biography and Check List" in 1966, and there is Gorley's 1975 dissertation. Elinor Langer is at work on a biography and Winifred Bevilacqua is writing a potential Twayne USAS book. Also in progress is Dion Kempthorne's critical introduction to Herbst's work. There are brief evaluations in Rideout and Hatcher. Two sections from a projected semi-autobiographical work appeared in *The Noble Savage*. Herbst papers in the Beineke collection at Yale include a manuscript of an early annotated version of "The Ground We Trod," an autobiography. The University of Iowa Special Collections section has a revised printer's copy of *Somewhere the Tempest Fell*. Paluka has the definitive list of editions as well as a partial list of stories and essays.

MAJOR WORKS

Nothing is Sacred. New York: Coward-McCann, 1928. [novel]
Money for Love. New York: Coward-McCann, 1929. [novel]
Pity is Not Enough. New York: Harcourt, 1933. [novel]
The Executioner Awaits. New York: Harcourt, 1934. [novel]
Rope of Gold. New York: Harcourt, 1939. [novel]
Satan's Sergeants. New York: Scribner, 1941. [novel]
Somewhere the Tempest Fell. New York: Scribner, 1947. [novel]
New Green World. New York: Hastings, 1954. [biography of John Bartram]

CHECKLIST OF SECONDARY SOURCES

CA; CAA; Herzberg; *OCAL; TCA & Supp;* Warfel.

Bevilacqua, Winifred F. "An Introduction to Josephine Herbst, Novelist." *BIowa,* 25 (1976), 3–20.
_____. "The Novels of Josephine Herbst." *DAI,* 38: 2118A–19A.
Dahlberg, Edward. *The Confessions of Edward Dahlberg.* New York: Braziller, 1971. Pp. 291–92, and *passim.*
_____. *Epitaphs of Our Times: The Letters of Edward Dahlberg.* New York: Braziller, 1967. Pp. 195–97, and *passim.*
Gourlie, John MacL. "The Evolution of Form in the Works of Josephine Herbst." Ph.D. diss., New York U., 1975.
Hatcher, Harlan. *Creating the Modern American Novel.* New York: Farrar, 1935. P. 270.
Herbst Josephine. "The Starched Blue Sky of Spain." *The Noble Savage* (vol. 1, 1960), pp. 117–177. [autobiographical]
_____. "A Year of Disgrace." *The Noble Savage,* 3 (1963), 128–60. [autobiographical]
Kempthorne, Dion. "Josephine Herbst: A Critical Introduction." Announced in *AL,* 45 (1973), 499.
Paluka, Frank. "Josephine Herbst." In *Iowa Authors: A Bio-Bibliography of Sixty Native Writers.* Iowa City: Friends of the University of Iowa Libraries, 1967. Pp. 144–45.
Pickering, Martha. "A Biography and Check List of Josephine Herbst." Ph.D. diss., U. Louisville, 1968. [Herbst cooperated on this document]
Rideout, Walter B. *The Radical Novel in the United States 1900–1954.* Cambridge: Harvard U., 1956.

Clarence A. Andrews
University of Iowa
Iowa City, Iowa

ROBERT HERRICK (1868–1938)

The works of Robert Herrick have long suffered a critical neglect undeserved by a writer so central to American literary realism, and it was not until after World War II that the first full-length work, an unpublished doctoral dissertation, was written about the author and English professor from the University of Chicago. Recently, however, scholars have shown a quickening critical interest in Herrick, for not only have there been three dissertations on his works completed during the 1970s, but there has been a new biography in the Twayne series on American authors. Garrett Press has recently undertaken the publication of photographic reprints of Herrick's works, under the able editorship of Louis J. Budd.

Without question the standard critical biography of Robert Herrick continues to be Nevius's fine work, *Robert Herrick: The Development of a Novelist*. This biography, which can be considered to be definitive unless substantial new manuscript material becomes known, views Herrick and his works from a critical perspective that was lacking in the scant earlier criticism. Early writers on Herrick generally suffered from a critical myopia that saw his works as disillusioned and vaguely Progressive tracts bent on exposing to public view the sordid machinations of business activity in the vulgar Chicago of the late nineteenth and early twentieth century. This approach was expanded by Depression critics with Marxist orientations (e.g., Hicks), for they considered Herrick's work as an incipient indictment of capitalism.

Although William Dean Howells and Björkman gave some indication of appreciating Herrick as an artist and seeker after complex realities, it was not until the relatively recent books and articles by Nevius, Taylor, Budd, and Franklin that adequate understanding and sympathy were shown for Herrick as a humanist and idealist. Recent criticism, then, considers Herrick's works to be more than exercises in social protest, and the Chicago author is at last earning his deserved place in American literature.

Major Works
Literary Love Letters and Other Stories. New York: Scribner, 1897.
The Man Who Wins. New York: Scribner, 1897. [novel]
The Gospel of Freedom. New York: Macmillan, 1898. [novel]
Love's Dilemmas. Chicago: Stone, 1898. [stories]
The Web of Life. New York: Macmillan, 1900. [novel]
The Real World. New York: Macmillan, 1901. [novel]
Their Child. New York: Macmillan, 1903. [novel]
The Common Lot. New York: Macmillan, 1904. [novel]
The Memoirs of an American Citizen. New York: Macmillan, 1905. [novel]

The Master of the Inn. New York: Scribner, 1908. [novel]
Together. New York: Macmillan, 1908. [novel]
A Life For a Life. New York: Macmillan, 1910. [novel]
The Healer. New York: Macmillan, 1911. [novel]
His Great Adventure. New York: Macmillan, 1913. [novel]
One Woman's Life. New York: Macmillan, 1913. [novel]
Clark's Field. Boston: Houghton Mifflin, 1914. [novel]
The Conscript Mother. New York: Scribner, 1916. [novel]
The World Decision. Boston: Houghton Mifflin, 1916. [essays]
Homely Lilla. New York: Harcourt, 1923. [novel]
Waste. New York: Harcourt, 1924. [novel]
Wanderings. New York: Harcourt, 1925. [stories]
Chimes. New York: Macmillan, 1926. [novel]
Little Black Dog. Chicago: Rockwell, 1931. [autobiography]
The End of Desire. New York: Farrar, 1932. [novel]
Sometime. New York: Farrar, 1933. [novel]

CHECKLIST OF SECONDARY SOURCES

Aldrich, T. B. "RH." *Century* (Mar. 1900), 678–88.
Arvin, Newton. "Homage to RH." *NR*, 82 (Mar. 6, 1935), 93–95.
Baldwin, Charles C. *The Men Who Make Our Novels*. Rev. ed. New York: Dodd, Mead, 1925. Pp. 243–50.
Berthoff, Warner. *The Ferment of Realism: American Literature, 1884–1919*. New York: Free Press, 1965. Pp. 138–41.
Björkman, Edwin. *Voices of Tomorrow*. New York: Kennerley, 1913. Pp. 260–89.
Bray, Robert. "RH: A Chicago Trio." *ON*, 1 (Mar. 1975), 63–84.
Brooks, Van Wyck. *The Confident Years 1885–1915*. New York: Dutton, 1952. Pp. 192–97.
Budd, Louis J. *RH*. New York: Twayne, 1971.
Caraher, Catherine Ann. "Thorstein Veblen and the American Novel." Ph.D. diss., U. Michigan, 1966.
Cargill, Oscar. *Intellectual America*. New York: Macmillan, 1941. Pp. 582–91.
Carlson, Douglas O. "RH: An Addendum." *AmLitR*, 3 (1968), 67–68. [bibliography]
Cooper, Frederick T. "Representative American Story-Tellers: RH." *Bookman*, 27 (Dec. 1908), 350–57. Reprinted in Cooper, F. T. *Some American Story-Tellers*. New York: Holt, 1911. Pp. 140–67.
Dell, Floyd. "Chicago In Fiction." *Bookman*, 37 (Nov. 1913), 274–75.
Dessner, Lawrence J. "RH, American Novelist." *MarkhamR*, 3 (1971), 10–14.
Duffey, Bernard. *The Chicago Renaissance in American Letters*. Lansing: Michigan State U., 1954. Pp. 113–23.
Franklin, Phyllis. "RH as Novelist and Journalist." *AmLitR*, 3 (1971), 393–95.
_____. "Time and Place in the Work of RH." Ph.D. diss., U. Miami, 1964.
_____. "A Handlist of the RH Papers at the University of Chicago." *ALR*, 8 (1975), 109–54.
Genthe, Charles V. "RH (1868–1938)." *AmLitR*, 1 (1967), 56–60. [bibliography]
Hale, Swinburne. "Mr. RH and His Realism." *HarvM*, 36 (May 1903), 105–11.
Hansen, Harry. *Midwest Portraits*. New York: Harcourt, 1923. Pp. 225–51.
Hicks, Granville. "RH, Liberal." *NR*, 67 (June 17, 1931), 129–30.
_____. *The Great Tradition*. Rev. ed. New York: Macmillan, 1935. Pp. 164–206.
Higgins, William R. "A Turn-of-the-Century Dilemma: Phillips and Herrick." Ph.D. diss., Tulane U., 1973.
Holland, Robert A. "*Together*: A Nietzschean Novel." *SatR*, 16 (Oct. 1908), 495–504.
Howells, William Dean. "The Novels of RH." *NAR*, 189 (June 1909), 812–20.
Jackson, Kenny A. "RH's Use of Chicago." *MASJ*, 5 (1964), 24–32.
Kazin, Alfred. "Three Pioneer Realists." *SatR*, 20 (July 8, 1939), 3–4. Reprinted in Kazin, Alfred. *On Native Grounds*. New York: Reynal & Hitchcock, 1942. Pp. 121–26.
Krutch, Joseph Wood. "The Longest Journey." *Nation*, 71 (Oct. 7, 1925), 388–89.
Lüdeke, Heinrich. "RH, Novelist of American Democracy." *ES*, 18 (Apr. 1936), 49–57.
Lynn, Kenneth S. *The Dream of Success*. Boston: Little, Brown, 1945. Pp. 208–40.

McIlvaine, Robert M. "RH and Thorstein Veblen." *RSWSU*, 40 (1972), 132–35.

Nevius, Blake. "The Early Novels of RH: A Critical Study." Ph.D. diss., U. Chicago, 1947.

———. "The Idealistic Novels of RH." *AL*, 21 (Mar. 1949), 56–70.

———. *RH: The Development of a Novelist.* Berkeley: U. California, 1962.

Nielsen, Harold. "The Novels of Herrick." *PL*, 19 (Sept. 1908), 337–63.

Nutley, Grace S. "The Social Criticism of RH." Ph.D. diss., New York U., 1945.

Pattee, Fred L. *The New American Literature, 1890–1930.* New York: Century, 1930. Pp. 31–34.

Pearce, Richard A. "Chicago in the Fiction of the 1890's As Illustrated in the Novels of Henry B. Fuller and RH." Ph.D. diss., Columbia U., 1966.

Seldes, Gilbert V. "The American Novel, Part II." *HarvM*, 61 (Mar. 1913), 1–11.

Simms, L. Moody, Jr. "RH and the Race Question." *NDQ*, 39 (1971), 34–38.

Spangler, George. "RH's *Waste*: Summary of a Career and an Age." *CRAS*, 2 (1971), 26–36.

———. "The Theme of Salvation in the Novels of RH." Ph.D. diss., U. California, 1965.

Stead, W. T. "Modern Wives." *RevRev*, 38 (Oct. 1908), 378–87.

Szuberla, Guy A. "Urban Vistas and the Pastoral Garden: Studies in the Literature and Architecture of Chicago (1893–1909)." Ph.D. diss., U. Minnesota, 1972.

Taylor, Walter F. "The Humanism of RH." *AL*, 28 (Nov. 1956), 287–301.

Thompson, Richard J. "Themes and Tendencies in the Social Criticism of RH." Ph.D. diss., U. Buffalo, 1964.

Towers, Tom H. "The Novels of RH." Ph.D. diss., Tulane U., 1971.

———. "Self and Society in the Novels of RH." *JPC*, 1 (1967), 141–57.

Van Doren, Carl. *American Novel, 1789–1939.* Rev. ed. New York: Macmillan, 1940. Pp. 242–44.

———. "RH." *Nation*, 113 (Aug. 31, 1921), 230–31. Reprinted in *Contemporary American Novelists 1900–1920.* New York: Macmillan, 1922. Pp. 56–65.

Wagenknecht, Edward. *Cavalcade of the American Novel.* New York: Holt, 1952. Pp. 235–44.

Weiss, Robert M. "The Shock of Experience: A Group of Chicago's Writers Face the Twentieth Century." Ph.D. diss., U. Wisconsin, 1966.

West-Furlan, Vera. "Das Problem der amerikanischen Ehe in den Romanen Robert Herricks." Ph.D. diss., U. Basel, 1935.

Charles V. Genthe   Robert Blesse
California State University   University of California
Chico, California   Los Angeles, California

EDGAR WATSON HOWE (1853–1937)

He was "a plain man who lived a plain life among plain people," said William Allen White. Take this common substance as a basic ingredient, blend with it intuitive psychological awareness and unschooled perception of the variety of social interplay, season well with a sharp iconoclastic wit and a flare for color, give the mixture a literary turn, and one comes up with the "Diogenes of Kansas," the "Sage of Potato Hill"—Edgar Watson Howe. Journalist, editor, novelist, homespun philosopher, he takes his place with early midwestern literary realists such as Joseph Kirkland and Hamlin Garland.

Perhaps best known by his contemporaries for his "paragraphs," written for his own publications (the *Golden Globe*, the *Atchison Globe*, and *E. W.*

Howe's Monthly) but widely copied in the newspapers and magazines of the world, Howe has a continuing role in the history of American journalism (see Pickett, *Ed Howe*). A larger measure of his lingering reputation, however, is based on *The Story of a Country Town* (1883), the first and best of his four novels. The endorsement of that novel by Howells and Twain helped to focus attention on the unheralded young writer from the West and aided in garnering for him serious literary consideration.

Howe's novels, even his best one, are not without serious flaws. Call him a literary pioneer, working in relative isolation and quite independently, often awkwardly, with literary tools he did not understand or could not fully control, but motivated by an intrepid desire to project a vision of life that had taken shape in the context of his own experience. The story of Edgar Watson Howe is a part of the larger story of the emergence of the realistic temper in American literature during the last part of the nineteenth century.

MAJOR WORKS

The Story of a Country Town. Atchison: Howe, 1883. [novel]
The Mystery of the Locks. Boston: Osgood, 1885. [novel]
A Moonlight Boy. Boston: Ticknor, 1886. [novel]
A Man Story. Boston: Ticknor, 1889. [novel]
An Ante-Mortem Statement. Atchison: Howe, 1891. [misc. pieces]
Ventures in Common Sense. New York: Knopf, 1919. [misc. pieces]
The Anthology of Another Town. New York: Knopf, 1920. [profiles]
Plain People. New York: Dodd, Mead, 1929. [autobiography]
E. W. Howe's Monthly. Atchison, 1911–33. [periodical]

CHECKLIST OF SECONDARY SOURCES

BDAL; Burke; CHAL; Herzberg; OCAL; TCA & Supp.

Bowman, Sylvia E. "Introduction." *The Story of a Country Town.* New York: Twayne; and New Haven: College and University Press, 1962.

Boyd, Ernest. "The Sage of Potato Hill." *Nation* (Aug. 29, 1934), 247–48.

Boynton, Percy H. "Some Expounders of the Middle Border." *EJ*, 19 (1930), 431–40.

Brune, Ruth E. "The Early Life of Edgar Watson Howe." Ph.D. diss., U. Colorado, 1949.

——. "Ed Howe in the *Golden Globe*." *WHR*, 8 (1954), 365–68.

——. "Found: Ed Howe's *Golden Globe*." *WHR*, 6 (1951–52), 99–102.

Carson, Gerald. "The Village Atheist: E. W. Howe, Purveyor of Plain Thoughts for Plain People." *Scribner*, 84 (1928), 733–39.

Eichelberger, Clayton L. and Frank L. Stallings, Jr. "Edgar Watson Howe (1853–1937): A Critical Bibliography of Secondary Comment." *AmLitR*, 2 (1969), 1–49; supplemented by Eichelberger, "Edgar Watson Howe and Joseph Kirkland: More Critical Comment." *AmLitR*, 4 (1971), 279–90.

Herron, Ima H. *The Small Town in American Literature.* Durham: Duke U., 1939. Pp. 208–16, and *passim*.

Howe, [Eu]gene A. "My Father Was the Most Wretchedly Unhappy Man I Ever Knew." *SEPost* (Oct. 25, 1941), 25.

Kathrens, Joseph R. "The Story of a Story." *Kansas City Star Magazine*, Feb. 22, 1925, p. 4; Mar. 1, 1925, pp. 8–9.

Mencken, H. L. "Introduction" to *Ventures in Common Sense.* New York: Knopf, 1919.

Mitchell, Marvin O. "Edgar Watson Howe: The Rebellion Against the Idyllic View of Provincial Life." In "A Study of the Realistic and Romantic Elements in the Fiction of Edgar

Watson Howe, Joseph Kirkland, Hamlin Garland, Harold Frederic, and Frank Norris (1882–1902)." Ph.D. diss., U. North Carolina, 1953.

Nathan, George Jean. "E. W. Howe: Unbuncombed, Unsentimental, Clear Thinking and Practical." *Haldeman-Julius Quarterly*, 1 (1927), 194–97.

Pickett, Calder M. *Ed Howe: Country Town Philosopher*. Lawrence and London: U. Kansas, 1968.

Powers, Richard G. "Tradition in Edgar Watson Howe's *Country Town*." *MASJ*, 9 (1968), 51–62.

Ropp, Phillip H. "Edgar Watson Howe." Ph.D. diss., U. Virginia, 1949.

Sackett, S. J. *E. W. Howe*. New York: Twayne, 1972.

Schorer, C. E. "Growing Up with the Country." *MJ*, 6 (1954), 12–26.

_____. "Mark Twain's Criticism of *The Story of a Country Town*." *AL*, 27 (1955), 109–12.

Schramm, Wilbur L. "Ed Howe versus Time." *SatR* (Feb. 5, 1938), 10–11.

Stronks, James B. "The Early Midwestern Realists and William Dean Howells." Ph.D. diss., U. Chicago, 1956.

_____. "William Dean Howells, Ed Howe, and *The Story oj a Country Town*." *AL*, 29 (1958), 474–78.

Van Doren, Carl. "Prudence Militant." *Century*, 106 (1923), 151–56; reprinted in *Many Minds*. New York: Knopf, 1926. Pp. 34–39.

Ward, John W. "Afterword." *The Story of a Country Town*. New York: New American Library, 1964.

Clayton L. Eichelberger
University of Texas at Arlington
Arlington, Texas

WILLIAM DEAN HOWELLS (1835–1920)

Critics and other readers of the late nineteenth and early twentieth centuries viewed W. D. Howells as a leader and storm center of the new American realists. He became the chastener of the romantic idealists, the pious guardian of realistic virtues, and the helper and encourager of all young realists on their way to more naturalistic expression in their art. When he joined the staff of the *Atlantic Monthly*, he brought to it a broader view of American literature than the editors had previously offered their readers by encouraging writers of the South, the Midwest, and the Far West. The New England writers accepted him as editor of the *Atlantic*, and he acquired some New England traits of mind as well as retaining some of his midwestern heritage. Both Henry James and Mark Twain seemed to understand the degree to which Howells transcended his native midwestern beginnings as well as the degree to which he adhered to them. They also understood his subtle humor and his ability to select the right word. Although Howells did not establish his name as a writer by exploiting the Midwest, he returned to it often in his autobiographical work as well as using midwestern characters in many of his novels.

After enjoying great popularity during the eighties and nineties, Howells found his following as a writer of fiction and his effectiveness as a critic waning in the early 1900s; by 1910 he believed that he had been replaced entirely by the younger writers whom he had encouraged to accept the example of the Spanish, French, and Russian writers. Since the battle for realism was over, scholarship about Howells dwindled in the thirties and forties; Sinclair Lewis and H. L. Mencken hooted at the old-fashioned cult of Howells. Not until World War II did scholarly interest, led by those attracted by his socialism, begin to grow again. In the late forties the Gibson-Arms Bibliography of Howells led the way, and by the 1960s James Woodress, surveying a decade of Howells criticism, foresaw the interest he would arouse among students of American Literature in the seventies. This rise in Howells interest accompanied the rise of American Studies in general. By 1974 Howells scholars were at a point of reappraisal of his work. The textual studies at Indiana University under the direction of Edwin Cady (nine volumes of the CEAA Howells Edition are in print) have made available new information to younger Howells scholars. The new editions and the wealth of information accompanying them may change approaches to his work during the next twenty years. For the casual readers of the next twenty years, Howells will be available in good texts, and many of his works may achieve a new popularity.

Major Works

Venetian Life. New York: Hurd & Houghton, 1866. [travel]
Suburban Sketches. New York: Hurd & Houghton, 1871. [essays]
Their Wedding Journey. Boston: Osgood, 1872. [novel]
A Chance Acquaintance. Boston: Osgood, 1873. [novel]
A Foregone Conclusion. Boston: Osgood, 1875. [novel]
The Undiscovered Country. Boston: Houghton Mifflin, 1880. [novel]
A Modern Instance. Boston: Osgood, 1882. [novel]
The Rise of Silas Lapham. Boston: Ticknor, 1885. [novel]
Indian Summer. Boston: Ticknor, 1885. [novel]
A Hazard of New Fortunes. New York: Harper, 1890. [novel]
A Boy's Town. New York: Harper, 1890. [autobiography]
Criticism and Fiction. New York: Harper, 1891. [criticism]
A Traveler From Altruria. New York: Harper, 1894. [romance]
The Landlord at Lion's Head. New York: Harper, 1897. [novel]
Literary Friends and Acquaintance. New York: Harper, 1900. [autobiography]
My Mark Twain. New York: Harper, 1910. [criticism]
The Leatherwood God. New York: Century, 1916. [novel]

Checklist of Secondary Sources

CHAL; DAB; LHUS; OCAL.

Anderson, Frederic, William M. Gibson, and Henry Nash Smith, eds. "Introduction." *Selected Mark Twain-Howells Letters: 1872–1910.* Cambridge, Mass.: Harvard U., 1967.
Anon. Review of *Boy's Town. Nation,* 51 (Nov. 13, 1890), 385.
Arms, George, William Gibson, and Frederic Marston, eds. "Introduction and Notes." *Prefaces to Contemporaries 1882–1920.* Gainesville, Fla.: Scholars Facsimiles and Reprints, 1957.

Beebe, Maurice. "Criticism of William Dean Howells: A Selected Checklist." *MFS*, 16 (1970), 395–419.

Bennett, George N. *William Dean Howells: The Development of A Novelist*. Norman: U. Oklahoma, 1959.

———. *The Realism of William Dean Howells, 1889–1920*. Nashville: Vanderbilt U., 1973.

Boynton, H. W. Review of *Leatherwood God*. *Bookman*, 44 (Jan. 1917), 504.

Brooks, Van Wyck. *The Ordeal of Mark Twain*. New York: Dutton, 1920.

———. *Howells His Life and His World*. New York: Dutton, 1959.

Budd, Louis J. "Howells' Blistering and Cauterizing." *OhioHQ*, 62 (July 1953), 334–47.

Cady, Edwin. *The Road to Realism: The Early Years, 1837–1885, Of William Dean Howells*. Syracuse, N.Y.: Syracuse U., 1956.

———. "Howells and Twain: The World of Midwestern Eyes." *BSUF*, 3 (Winter 1962–63), 3–8.

———. *The Realist at War: The Mature Years, 1885–1920, Of William Dean Howells*. New York: Syracuse U., 1958.

Cady, Edwin and David L. Frazier, eds. *The War of The Critics Over William Dean Howells*. Evanston: Row & Peterson, 1962.

Carrington, George C. *The Immense Complex Drama: The World and Art of The Howells Novel*. Columbus: Ohio State U., 1966.

Carrington, George C. and Ildiko de Papp Carrington. *Plots and Characters in the Fiction of William Dean Howells*. Hamden, Conn.: Archon, 1976.

Cooke, Delmar G. *William Dean Howells: A Critical Study*. New York: Dutton, 1922.

Eble, Kenneth E. "The Western Ideals of William Dean Howells." *WHR*, 11 (Autumn 1957), 331–38.

Eichelberger, Clayton L. *Published Comment on William Dean Howells through 1920: A Research Bibliography*. Boston: Hall, 1976.

Eschholz, Paul A., comp. *Critics on William Dean Howells: Readings in Literary Criticism*. Coral Gables: U. Miami, 1974.

———. "The Moral World of Silas Lapham: Howells' Romantic Vision of America in the 1880s." *RSWSU*, 40 (1972), 115–21.

Firkins, Oscar W. *William Dean Howells: A Study*. Cambridge: Harvard U., 1924.

Fischer, William C., Jr. "William Dean Howells: Reverie and the Nonsymbolic Aesthetic." *NCF*, 25 (June 1970), 1–30.

Fortenberry, George. "William Dean Howells." In *Fifteen American Authors Before 1900*. Ed. Robert A. Rees and Earl Harbert. Madison: U. Wisconsin, 1971. Pp. 229–44.

Frazier, David L. "Their Wedding Journey: Howells' Fictional Craft." *NEQ*, 42 (Sept. 1969), 323–49.

Frederic, Harold. "Novels Read in London." *New York Times*, Feb. 16, 1896, p. 17.

Fryckstedt, Olov W. *In Quest of America*. Cambridge, Mass.: Harvard U., 1958.

Girgus, Sam B. "Bartley Hubbard: The Rebel in Howells' *A Modern Instance*." *RSWSU*, 39 (1971), 315–21.

Gibson, William and George Arms. *A Bibliography of William Dean Howells*. New York: New York Public Library, 1948.

Halfmann, Ulrich. "Interviews With William Dean Howells." *AmLitR*, 6 (1973).

Halfmann, Ulrich and Don R. Smith. "William Dean Howells: A Revised and Annotated Bibliography of Secondary Comment In Periodicals and Newspapers, 1868–1919." *AmLitR*, 5 (1972), 91–121.

Hatcher, Harlan H. *Creating the Modern American Novel*. New York: Farrar, 1935. Pp. 21–33.

Hazard, Lucy L. *The Frontier in American Literature*. New York: Crowell, 1937. Pp. 230–35.

Hiatt, David F. and Edwin H. Cady. "Introduction." In *Literary Friends and Acquaintance*. Bloomington: Indiana U., 1968.

Hough, Robert L. *The Quiet Rebel: William Dean Howells As Social Commentator*. Lincoln: U. Nebraska, 1959.

Howells, Mildred. "Introduction." In *Life In Letters of William Dean Howells*. 2 vols. Garden City, N.Y.: Doubleday, 1928.

Howells, William C. *Recollections of Life in Ohio From 1813 to 1840*. Cincinnati: Clarke, 1895. Introduction by William Dean Howells. Rptd. with Intro. by Edwin C. Cady. Gainesville, Fla.: Scholars' Facsimiles and Reprints, 1963.

Hubbell, Jay B. *Who Are the Major American Writers?* Durham, N.C.: Duke U., 1972. Pp. 115–22.

Kirk, Clara M. *William Dean Howells: Traveler From Altruria.* New Brunswick, N.J.: Rutgers U., 1962.

———. *William Dean Howells and Art In His Time.* New Brunswick, N.J.: Rutgers U., 1965.

Kirk, Clara M., Rudolf Kirk, and Scott Bennett, eds. *The Altrurian Romances.* Bloomington: Indiana U. 1968.

Kirk, Clara M. and Rudolf Kirk. "Introduction." In *Criticism and Fiction and Other Essays.* New York: New York U., 1959.

Kirk, Clara M. and Rudolf Kirk. *William Dean Howells.* New York: Twayne, 1962.

Lynn, Kenneth S. *William Dean Howells: An American Life.* New York: Harcourt, 1971.

Mathews, Brander. "American Character in American Fiction." *Munsey's,* 49 (Aug. 1913), 794–97. [rev.]

McMurray, William J. *The Literary Realism of William Dean Howells.* Carbondale: Southern Illinois U., 1967.

Mews, Siegfried. "German Reception of American Writers in the Late Nineteenth Century." *SAB,* 34 (Mar. 1969), 7–9.

"Mr. Howells' 'Americanisms.' " *Critic,* n.s. 21 (Sept. 27, 1894), 193. Rptd. from the Springfield *Republican.*

Nordloh, David J. "Eating off the Same Plates: First Editions of W. D. Howells in Great Britain." *Serif,* 7 (Mar. 1970), 28–30.

———. "A Critical Edition of W. D. Howells' *Years of My Youth.*" Ph.D. diss., Indiana U., 1969.

Parker, Hershel. "The First Nine Volumes of a Selected Edition of W. D. Howells: A Review Article." *Proof 2.* Columbia, S.C.: U. South Carolina, 1972. Pp. 319–32.

Poulakis, Victoria Suzanne. "The Psychological Novels of William Dean Howells." Ph.D. diss., U. Minnesota, 1970.

Reeves, John K. "The Literary Manuscripts of William Dean Howells." *BNYPL,* 62 (June 1958), 267–68; (July 1958), 350–63.

Sinclair, Borert B. "Howells in the Ohio Valley." *SatR* (Jan. 6, 1945), 22–23.

Smith, Henry Nash and William M. Gibson, eds., with the assistance of Frederick Anderson. *Mark Twain-Howells Letters: The Correspondence of Samuel L. Clemens and William Dean Howells, 1872–1910.* 2 vols. Cambridge, Mass.: Belknap Press, 1960.

Tanselle, G. Thomas. "The Architecture of The Rise of Silas Lapham." *AL,* 37 (Jan. 1966), 430–57.

Taylor, James W. "The Swedenborgianism of W. D. Howells." Ph.D. diss., U. Illinois, 1969.

Tuttleton, James W. "Henry James: The Superstitious Valuation of Europe." In *The Novel of Manners In America.* Chapel Hill: U. North Carolina, 1972. Pp. 48–85.

Vanderbilt, Kermit. "The Undiscovered Country: Howells' Version of American Pastoral." *AQ,* 17 (Winter 1965), 643–55.

———. *The Achievement of William Dean Howells.* Princeton, N.J.: Princeton U., 1968.

———. "Howells Studies: Past, Or Passing, Or To Come." *AmLitR,* 7 (Spring 1974), 143–53.

Wagenknecht, Edward. "Longfellow and Howells." *ESQ,* 58 (1970), 52–57.

Woodress, James L. *Howells and Italy.* Durham, N.C.: Duke U., 1952.

Woodress, James L. and Stanley P. Anderson. "A Bibliography of Writing About William Dean Howells." *AmLitR,* Special Number (1969).

Woodward, James E., Jr. "Pragmatism and Pragmaticism in James and Howells." Ph.D. diss., U. New Mexico, 1969.

Wortham, Thomas. "The Indiana Edition of W. D. Howells." *NCF,* 26 (Sept. 1971), 234–39.

George Fortenberry
University of Texas at Arlington
Arlington, Texas

FRANK MCKINNEY HUBBARD (1868–1930)

"Kin" Hubbard began his career as a humorist for the *Indianapolis News* in 1901. Even though he made a considerable local reputation with the publication of his political cartoons in 1903 and 1905, it was not until the creation of Abe Martin that Hubbard's following extended beyond Indiana. For the next twenty-five years he contributed a drawing and a two-line caption to the daily edition of the *News* and in later years often a slightly longer Sunday column. In 1906 he brought out the first of the Abe Martin books, a collection of the best of the previous year's newspaper pieces. Until he died in 1930 he issued these editions each year in November in time to catch the Christmas trade. A large number of the books he published and distributed himself under the Abe Martin Publishing Company imprint. It was through these books and the increasingly wider syndication of his Abe Martin newspaper column that Kin Hubbard achieved national recognition.

The character of Abe Martin was squarely in the mainstream of American humor. Ade noted that Abe was as "quaint and droll" as Josh Billings and Artemus Ward ever dared to be. His appeal, as Blair has suggested, was to those who loved "the aphorism phrased in homely rural language." But Abe was not just a sharp-witted country bumpkin. In fact, Cordell felt that his wisdom was not that homely; it was much closer to Rochefocauld than to Will Rogers. Indeed Abe not only voiced the traditional values of industry, frugality, and common sense in which Hubbard believed, but as Norris Yates has written, his comments formed a veritable catalog of changing attitudes and fashions. Adams once remarked that Kin Hubbard's virtue was his ability to compress a whole novel into a sentence, and in a verbose nation that was a great distinction. Cracker-barrel philosopher, rural wit, or wry commentator, Abe Martin was syndicated in over 300 newspapers at the time of Hubbard's death in 1930, making him the only humorist of his time who may have rivaled Will Rogers.

All of the primary works listed below, with three noted exceptions, are collections of Hubbard's newspaper columns and were edited by him each year for book publication. Very few of these volumes have publication dates and those assigned to them represent either the copyright date or the dates listed in the Stillson and Russo checklist. Hubbard illustrated the Abe Martin column and except where noted did so for the books as well.

MAJOR WORKS

Collection of Indiana Lawmakers and Lobbyists. Indianapolis: Privately published by Hubbard, 1903. [caricatures]

Caricatures of Law Makers, Clerks and Doorkeepers of the Sixty-Fourth General Assembly of Indiana. Indianapolis: Privately published by Hubbard, 1905.

Abe Martin of Brown County, Indiana. Introd. by Meredith Nicholson. Tribute to Kin Hubbard by James Whitcomb Riley. Indianapolis: Indianapolis News, 1906.

Abe Martin of Brown County, Indiana. Indianapolis: Bobbs-Merrill, 1907.

Abe Martin's Almanack [for 1908]. Indianapolis: Bobbs-Merrill, 1907.

Abe Martin's Almanack [for 1909].With "Abe Martin of Brown County, Indiana" by James Whitcomb Riley. Indianapolis: Abe Martin, 1908.

Abe Martin's Brown County Almanack. "Rearword" by Samuel G. Blythe. Indianapolis: Abe Martin, 1909.

Brown County Folks. Indianapolis: Abe Martin, 1910.

Abe Martin's Almanack. An Appreciation of Kin Hubbard by Booth Tarkington. Drawing of Abe Martin by Gaar Williams. Garden City, N.Y.: Doubleday, 1911.

Short Furrows. Indianapolis: Bobbs-Merrill, 1911.

Short Furrows. Indianapolis: Abe Martin, 1912.

Back Country Folks. Illustrated by Francis Gallup. Indianapolis: Abe Martin, 1913.

Abe Martin's Primer. Illustrated by Francis Gallup. Indianapolis: Abe Martin, 1914.

Abe Martin's Sayings and Sketches. Indianapolis: Abe Martin, 1915.

New Sayings by Abe Martin and Velma's Vow, a Gripping Love Tale by Miss Fawn Lippincutt. Indianapolis: Abe Martin, 1916.

Abe Martin's Back Country Sayings. Indianapolis: Abe Martin, 1917.

Abe Martin on the War and Other Things. Indianapolis: Abe Martin, 1918.

Abe Martin's Home Cured Philosophy. Indianapolis: Abe Martin, 1919.

Abe Martin: The Joker on Facts. Indianapolis: Abe Martin, 1920.

Abe Martin's Almanack. Indynoplus [*sic*]: Abe Martin, 1921.

These Days. Indianapolis: Abe Martin, 1922.

Comments of Abe Martin and His Neighbors. Indianapolis: Abe Martin, 1923.

Fifty Two Weeks of Abe Martin. Indianapolis: Abe Martin, 1924.

Abe Martin on Things in General. Indianapolis: Abe Martin, 1925.

Abe Martin: Hoss Sense and Nonsense. Foreword by Franklin P. Adams. Indianapolis: Bobbs-Merrill, 1926.

Abe Martin's Wisecracks and Skunk Ridge Papers. Indianapolis: Abe Martin, 1927.

Abe Martin's Barbed Wire. Indianapolis: Bobbs-Merrill, 1928.

Abe Martin's Town Pump. Indianapolis: Bobbs-Merrill, 1929.

A Book of Indiana. Kin Hubbard, Editor-in-Chief. Indianapolis: Indiana Biographical Society, 1929. [biographies]

Abe Martin's Broadcast. Indianapolis: Bobbs-Merrill, 1930.

Abe Martin's Wisecracks. Selected by E. V. Lucus. London: Methuen, 1930.

The Hoosier Humor of Kin Hubbard. Compiled by Jack A. Stroube. Atlanta: Genesis Press, 1970.

CHECKLIST OF SECONDARY SOURCES

DAB; LHUS; OCAL.

Ade, George. "Abe Martin of Brown County." *AmM*, 70 (May 1910), 46.

Blair, Walter. *Horse Sense in American Humor: From Benjamin Franklin to Ogden Nash.* Chicago: U. Chicago, 1942. Pp. 256–73.

Chamberlin, Jo Hubbard. " 'Abe Martin'—Hoosier Sage: A Rail-Fence Philosopher and His Aphorisms." *SatR*, 27 (June 24, 1944), 19–21.

Cordell, Richard A. "Limestone, Corn, and Literature: The Indiana Scene and Its Interpreters." *SatR*, 19 (Dec. 17, 1938), 3–4, 14–15.

Kelley, Fred C. " 'Kin' Hubbard Has Won Fame by Writing Two Sentences a Day." *AmM*, 97 (Apr. 1924), 34–35. [interview]

————. *The Life and Times of Kin Hubbard: Creator of Abe Martin.* New York: Farrar, 1952.

"Kin Hubbard, Abe Martin Creator, Dies of Heart Disease at Home." *Indianapolis News*, Dec. 26, 1930, p. 1.

"Kin Hubbard Dies: Famous Humorist." *New York Times*, Dec. 27, 1930, p. 13.

Masson, Thomas L. *Our American Humorists.* New York: Dodd, Mead, 1931. Pp. 162–63.

Nichols, J. Harley. "Kin Hubbard." *IMH*, 27 (Mar. 1931), 1–9. [biographical sketch]

Noland, Stephen. "Kin Hubbard." *IMH*, 45 (June 1949), 270–72.

Shumaker, Arthur W. *A History of Indiana Literature: With an Emphasis on the Authors of Imaginative Works Who Commenced Writing Prior to World War I.* Indianapolis: Indiana Historical Bureau, 1962. Pp. 475–85.

Stillson, Blanche and Dorothy Ritter Russo. *Abe Martin—Kin Hubbard.* With an Appreciation of Kin Hubbard by John Calvin Mellett. Indianapolis: Hoosier Bookshop, 1939. [bibliography]

Tandy, Jennette. *Crackerbox Philosophers in American Humor and Satire.* New York: Columbia U., 1925. Pp. 167–70.

Who's Who in America. Vols. 6–16. Chicago: Morgan, 1910–30.

Yates, Norris W. *The American Humorist: Conscience of the Twentieth Century.* Ames: Iowa State U., 1964. Pp. 100–12.

Charles L. P. Silet
Iowa State University
Ames, Iowa

LANGSTON HUGHES (1902–67)

Little serious critical attention has been paid to Kansan Langston Hughes, although he is the most prolific of the American black writers, having published ten volumes of poetry, eight of short stories and sketches, two novels, seven children's books, a quantity of essays, translations, and a two-volume autobiography. The only full-length biography in English is the admirable and well documented work by Emanuel. A useful collection of critical essays appeared in the *CLA Journal* in June 1968, dealing with Hughes the poet, playwright, translator, etc. Subsequently, these appeared in book form as *Langston Hughes, Black Genius,* edited by O'Daniel. One of the most satisfactory of the many foreign evaluations of Hughes's work is the lengthy essay by Wagner. Aside from the aforementioned items and the reviews of his books, the best approach to the early work of Hughes appears in the three articles by Davis.

The comprehensive bibliography by Dickinson should be supplemented, especially for music and records, by O'Daniel's bibliography. A superb manuscript collection of Hughes materials is in the James Weldon Johnson Memorial Collection at Yale University Library. The collection includes drafts of stories, poems, correspondence with friends and publishers, notes, and unpublished works. Other useful collections of textual and manuscript materials are in the Schomburg Collection of the New York Public Library and in the Special Collections of the University of Kansas Library.

MAJOR WORKS

The Weary Blues. New York: Knopf, 1926. [poems]
Fine Clothes to the Jew. New York: Knopf, 1927. [poems]

Not Without Laughter. New York: Knopf, 1930. [novel]
Dear Lovely Death. Amenia, N.Y.: Troutbeck Press, 1931. [poems]
The Dream Keeper. New York: Knopf, 1932. [poems]
Scottsboro Limited. New York: Golden Stair Press, 1932. [poems]
The Ways of White Folks. New York: Knopf, 1934. [stories]
A New Song. New York: International Workers Order, 1938. [poems]
The Big Sea. New York: Knopf, 1940. [autobiography]
Shakespeare in Harlem. New York: Knopf, 1942. [poems]
Jim Crow's Last Stand. N.p.: Negro Publishing Society, 1943. [poems]
Fields of Wonder. New York: Knopf, 1947. [poems]
One Way Ticket. New York: Knopf, 1949. [poems]
Simple Speaks His Mind. New York: Simon & Schuster, 1950. [humor/essays]
Montage on a Dream Deferred. New York: Holt, 1951. [poems]
Laughing to Keep from Crying. New York: Holt, 1952. [stories]
Simple Takes a Wife. New York: Simon & Schuster, 1953. [humor & essays]
Sweet Flypaper of Life. New York: Simon & Schuster, 1955. [pictorial & narrative]
I Wonder as I Wander. New York: Rinehart, 1956. [autobiography]
Pictorial History of the Negro in America. New York: Crown, 1956. [pictorial & narrative]
Selected Poems. New York: Knopf, 1959.
Simply Heavenly. New York: Dramatists Play Service, 1959. [play]
Ask Your Mama. New York: Knopf, 1961. [poems]
The Best of Simple. New York: Hill & Wang, 1961. [humor/essays]
Fight for Freedom. New York: Norton, 1962. [history of NAACP]
Five Plays. Bloomington: Indiana U., 1963.
Something in Common, and Other Stories. New York: Hill & Wang, 1963.
Simple's Uncle Sam. New York: Hill & Wang, 1965. [humor/essays]
Black Magic. Englewood Cliffs, N.J.: Prentice-Hall, 1967. [pictorial history of the Negro in entertainment]
The Panther and the Lash. New York: Knopf, 1967. [poems]
Black Misery. New York: P. S. Eriksson, 1969. [humor/essay]
Don't You Turn Back. New York: Knopf, 1969. [poems]

CHECKLIST OF SECONDARY SOURCES

Burke, *CA; CAA; CB;* Herzberg; *LHUS; OCAL; TCA & Supp.*

Bone, Robert. *The Negro Novel in America*. New Haven: Yale U., 1958. Pp. 75–77.
Britt, D. D. "The Image of the White Man in the Fiction of Langston Hughes, Richard Wright, James Baldwin and Ralph Ellison." Ph.D. diss., Emory U., 1968.
Carey, Julian. "Jesse B. Semple Revisited and Revised." *Phylon*, 31 (Summer 1971), 158–63.
Davis, Arthur. "The Harlem of Langston Hughes' Poetry." *Phylon*, 13 (Winter 1952), 276–83.
———. "The Tragic Mulatto Theme in Six Works of Langston Hughes." *Phylon*, 14 (Winter 1955), 195–204.
Dickinson, Donald C. *A Bio-bibliography of Langston Hughes*. 2d. ed. Hamden, Conn.: Archon, 1972.
Emanuel, James. "The Short Stories of Langston Hughes." Ph.D. diss., Columbia U., 1962.
———. *Langston Hughes*. New York: Twayne, 1967.
———. "The Short Fiction of Langston Hughes." *Freedomways*, 8 (Spring 1968), 170–78.
Embree, Edwin. *Thirteen Against the Odds*. Port Washington, N.Y.: Kennikat, 1968. Pp. 117–38.
Filatova, Lydia. "Langston Hughes: American Writer." *Il*, 1 (1933), 103–5.
Gibson, Donald, ed. *Five Black Writers: Essays on Wright, Ellison, Baldwin, Hughes and LeRoi Jones*. New York: New York U., 1970. Pp. 167–89.
Gloster, Hugh. *Negro Voices in American Fiction*. Chapel Hill: U. North Carolina, 1948. Pp. 184–87, 219–22.
Haskins, James S. *Always Movin' On: The Life of Langston Hughes*. New York: Watts, 1976.
Hawthorne, Lucia. "A Rhetoric of Human Rights as Expressed in the 'Simple Columns,' by Langston Hughes." Ph.D. diss., Pennsylvania State U., 1971.
Hentoff, Nat. "Langston Hughes, He Found Poetry in the Blues." *Mayfair* (Aug. 1958), 26–27.

Jemie, Onwuchekwa. *Langston Hughes: An Introduction to the Poetry*. New York: Columbia U., 1976.

King, Woodie. "Remembering Langston Hughes." *ND*, 18 (Apr. 1969), 27–32.

Mandelik, Peter and Stanley Schatt, comps. *A Concordance to the Poetry of Langston Hughes*. Detroit: Gale, 1975.

O'Daniel, Therman. "Lincoln's Man of Letters." *LUB*, 57 (July 1964), 9–12.

————. "A Selected Classified Bibliography." *CLA*, 11 (June 1968), 349–66.

————, ed. *Langston Hughes, Black Genius*. New York: Morrow, 1971.

Ovington, Mary W. *Portraits in Color*. New York: Viking, 1927. Pp. 194–204.

Parker, John. "Tomorrow in the Writing of Langston Hughes."*CE*, 10 (May 1949) 438–41.

Patterson, Lindsay. "Locating Langston Hughes." *NewL*, 57 (Dec. 9, 1974), 17–18.

Presley, James. "The American Dream of Langston Hughes." *SwR*, 48 (Autumn 1963), 380–86.

Rogge, Heinz von. "Die Figur des Simple im Werke von Langston Hughes." *DNS*, 12 (1955), 555–66.

Spencer, T. J. and Clarence Rivers. "Langston Hughes: His Style and Optimism." *DC*, 7 (Spring 1964), 99–102.

Wagner, Jean. *Les Poetes Negres des Etats-Unis*. Paris: Istra, 1963. Pp. 423–533.

Donald C. Dickinson
University of Arizona
Tucson, Arizona

WILLIAM M. INGE (1913–73)

To date no full appraisal of the whole corpus of Inge's work exists. Shuman's *William Inge* (1965) deals with twenty-eight of his plays including four screen scenarios, one television script, and eleven one-act plays. However, no scholar has yet dealt with Inge's later work, which includes two major plays, *Where's Daddy* (1966) and *The Last Path* (1970); three one-act plays, *The Call* (1968), *The Disposal* (1968), and *A Murder* (1968); and two novels, *Good Luck, Miss Wyckoff* (1970) and *My Son Is a Splendid Driver* (1971). There presently is a pressing need on the one hand for a comprehensive critical work on Inge and on the other for a work which views his writing from a psychoanalytical viewpoint.

Writing in *Harper's* (November 1958), Brustein calls Inge "the first playwright to present the Mid-West with a degree of complexity and is the first dramatic spokesman for a matriarchal America." Shuman concurs, writing that "Inge may justifiably be called the first playwright to examine the Midwest with insight and to write seriously of it—to have concern for the sociological uniqueness of the area and for the psychological manifestations of this uniqueness as it is revealed in the reactions of its people" (pp. 17–18). Herron claims that in small-town America Inge "uncovered . . . a secret world which exists behind the screen of neighborly decorum."

Weales accuses Inge of resolving problems through "phallic romanticism."

Most of what has thus far been written about Inge, whose middle productive years were overshadowed by the fact that his first four plays—*Come Back, Little Sheba* (1949), *Picnic* (1953), *Bus Stop* (1955), and *The Dark at the Top of the Stairs* (1957)—had been huge commercial successes as well as artistic triumphs, now needs to be reassessed in the light of his last two major plays and his two novels.

MAJOR WORKS

Come Back, Little Sheba. New York: Random House, 1950. [play]
Picnic. New York: Random House, 1953. [play]
Bus Stop. New York: Random House, 1955. [play]
The Dark at the Top of the Stairs. New York: Random House, 1958. [play]
4 Plays by William Inge. New York: Random House, 1958. [first four plays]
A Loss of Roses. New York: Random House, 1960. [play]
Splendor in the Grass. New York: Bantam Books, 1961. [film scenario]
Summer Brave and Eleven Short Plays. New York: Random House, 1962. [plays]
Natural Affection. New York: Random House, 1963. [play]
Where's Daddy? New York: Dramatists Play Service, 1966. [play]
Two Short Plays. New York: Dramatists Play Service, 1968. [one-act plays]
Good Luck, Miss Wyckoff. Boston: Little, Brown, 1970. [novel]
My Son Is a Splendid Driver. Boston: Little, Brown, 1971. [novel]

CHECKLIST OF SECONDARY SOURCES

Burke; *CA;* Herzberg; *LHUS; LLC; OCAL.*

Armato, Philip. "The Bum as Scapegoat in William Inge's *Picnic.*" *WAL*, 10 (Winter 1976), 273–82.
Brustein, Robert. "The Men-Taming Women of William Inge." *Harper*, 217 (1958), 52–57.
Burgess, Charles. "An American Experience: William Inge in St. Louis, 1943–1949." *PELL*, 12 (1976), 438–68.
Clarkson, Philip B. "The Evolution from Conception to Production of the Dramas of William Inge." Ph.D. diss., Stanford U., 1963.
Epolito, Joseph. "A Study of Character in Selected Plays of William Inge." *DAI*, 35:7437A.
Gassner, John and Edward Quinn. *The Reader's Encyclopedia of World Drama*. New York: Crowell, 1969. P. 462.
Gobrecht, Eleanor A. "A Descriptive Study of the Value Commitments of the Principal Characters in Four Recent American Plays: *Picnic, Cat on a Hot Tin Roof, Long Day's Journey into Night*, and *Look Homeward, Angel.*" Ph.D. diss., U. Southern California, 1963.
Guernsey, Otis L., Jr., ed. *Directory of the American Theater, 1894–1971*. New York: Dodd, Mead, 1971. P. 75.
Hamblet, Edwin J. "The North American Outlook of Marcel Dubé and William Inge." *QQ*, 77 (1970), 374–87.
Herron, Ima H. "Our Vanishing Towns: Modern Broadway Versions." *SwR*, 51 (Summer 1966), 209–20.
———. *The Small Town in American Drama*. Dallas: Southern Methodist U., 1969. Pp. 359, 429–36.
Jones, Howard Mumford and Richard M. Ludwig. *Guide to American Literature and Its Backgrounds since 1890*. 4th ed. Cambridge: Harvard U., 1972. P. 214.
Kienzle, Siegfried. *Modern World Theater: A Guide to Productions in Europe and the United States since 1945*. New York: Ungar, 1970. Pp. 232–34.
Lewis, Allan. *American Plays and Playwrights of the Contemporary Theatre*. Rev. ed. New York: Crown, 1970. Pp. 79, 143–51, 193.
Lockwood, Patton. "The Plays of William Inge: 1948–1960." Ph.D. diss., Michigan State U., 1962.

McGraw-Hill Encyclopedia of World Drama. Vol. 2. New York: McGraw-Hill, 1972. Pp. 405–7.

Manley, Frances. "William Inge: A Bibliography." ABC, 16 (1965), 13–21.

Matlaw, Myron. Modern World Drama: An Encyclopedia. New York: Dutton, 1972. Pp. 391–92.

Miller, Jordan Y. "William Inge: Last of the Realists?" KQ, 2 (1970), 17–26.

Mitchell, Marilyn. "The Teacher as Outsider in the Works of William Inge." MQ, 17 (1976), 385–93.

Shuman, R. Baird. William Inge. New York: Twayne, 1965.

Voss, Ralph. "The Art of William Inge." DAI, 36:6692A–93A.

Weales, Gerald. American Drama Since World War II. New York: Harcourt, 1962. Pp. 41–73, 187.

Wolfson, Lester M. "Inge, O'Neill, and the Human Condition." SSJ, 22 (1957), 221–32.

R. Baird Shuman
University of Illinois
Champaign, Illinois

JAMES JONES (1921–77)

Since the publication in 1951 of his first novel, *From Here to Eternity*, James Jones has been considered a significant American author and has received some mention in most discussions of the modern novel. Much has been written about his life and works in both popular and scholarly publications. Of his eight novels, the first has consistently attracted the most attention. His second novel, *Some Came Running* (1957), is the one most clearly related to his experiences of growing up in the Midwest (Illinois), but most critics have found it disappointing. His later novels have received less attention than the first. To date, no comprehensive biography or critical study has been done. A bibliography was prepared by Hopkins in 1974. This book contains a foreword by Jones, a previously unpublished interview, and a complete listing of all materials relevant to Jones and his works, including interviews and letters. The following checklist is highly selective and represents an attempt to bring together those sources most likely to be of value to the serious student of midwestern literature.

MAJOR WORKS

From Here to Eternity. New York: Scribner, 1951. [novel]
Some Came Running. New York: Scribner, 1957. [novel]
The Pistol. New York: Scribner, 1958. [novel]
Thin Red Line. New York: Scribner, 1962. [novel]
Go to the Widow-Maker. New York: Delacorte, 1967. [novel]
The Ice Cream Headache and Other Stories. New York: Delacorte, 1968. [stories]
The Merry Month of May. New York: Delacorte, 1971. [novel]
A Touch of Danger. Garden City, N.Y.: Doubleday, 1973. [novel]
Viet Journal. New York: Delacorte, 1974. [novel]

CHECKLIST OF SECONDARY SOURCES

CA; CN; Herzberg; *LHUS; LLC; TCA & Supp.*

Aldrich, Nelson W., Jr. "The Art of Fiction XXIII: James Jones." *Paris R,* 20 (1958–59), 34–55.

Burress, Lee A., Jr. "James Jones on Folklore and Ballad." *CE,* 21 (1959), 161–65.

Carter, Steven. "James Jones, an American Master: A Study of His Mystical, Philosophical, Social, and Artistic Views." *DAI,* 36:5292A–93A.

Childs, Barney. "*Some Came Running.*" *ArQ,* 14 (1958), 86–88.

Hicks, Granville. "James Jones' '*Some Came Running*': A Study in Arrogant Primitivism." *NewL,* 41 (1958), 20–22.

_____. "The Shorter and Better Jones." *SatR,* 42 (1959), 12.

Hopkins, John R., comp. *James Jones: A Checklist.* Foreword by James Jones. Detroit: Gale, 1974.

Jones, James and William Styron. "Two Novelists Talk It Over." *Esquire,* 60 (1963), 57–59.

Kilgo, James P. "Five American Novels of World War II: A Critical Study." Ph.D. diss., Tulane U., 1972.

Mailer, Norman. "Norman Mailer *vs* Nine Writers." *Esquire,* 60 (1963), 63–69.

Ray, David. "Mrs. Handy's Writing Mill." *LM,* 5 (1958), 35–41.

Stevenson, David L. "James Jones and Jack Kerouac: Novelists of Disjunction." In *The Creative Present.* Eds. Nona Balakian and Charles Simmons. New York: Doubleday, 1963.

Viorst, M. "James Jones and the Phony Intellectuals." *Esquire,* 69 (1968), 98–101.

Edward C. Peple, Jr.
Blue Cross & Blue Shield of Virginia
Richmond, Virginia

MACKINLAY KANTOR (1904–77)

For the student interested in either the historical novel or the novel of sentiment, Kantor offers a virtually unplowed surface. The major sources of information about Kantor's life come from his books: *But Look the Morn; Author's Choice; Lobo; The Day I Met a Lion; Missouri Bittersweet;* and *I Love You, Irene.* There is much unindexed material in the *Des Moines Register and Tribune* (from his 1922 short story, "Purple," to Gordon Gammack's late 1972 column, "Conversations With MacKinlay Kantor"). Paluka has the definitive bibliography through 1967; later works are listed below.

MAJOR WORKS

Diversey. New York: Coward-McCann, 1928. [novel]
El Goes South. New York: Coward-McCann, 1930. [novel]
The Jaybird. New York: Coward-McCann, 1932. [novel]
Long Remember. New York: Coward-McCann, 1934. [novel]
Turkey in the Straw: A Book of American Ballads and Primitive Verse. New York: Coward-McCann, 1935.
The Voice of Bugle Ann. New York. Coward-McCann, 1935. [novel]
Arouse and Beware. New York: Coward-McCann, 1936. [novel]
The Romance of Rosy Ridge. New York: Coward-McCann, 1937. [novel]

The Boy in the Dark. Fiction Series, No. 1. Webster Groves, Mo.: International Mark Twain Society, 1937. [stories]
The Noise of Their Wings. New York: Coward-McCann, 1938. [novel]
Here Lies Holly Springs. New York: Pynson Printers, 1938. [novel]
Valedictory. New York: Coward-McCann, 1939. [novel]
Cuba Libre. New York: Coward-McCann, 1940. [novel]
Gentle Annie. New York: Coward-McCann, 1942. [novel]
Happy Land. New York: Coward-McCann, 1943. [novel]
Author's Choice. New York: Coward-McCann, 1944. [stories]
Glory for Me. New York: Coward-McCann, 1945. [novel in verse; filmed as *The Best Years of Our Lives*]
But Look the Morn: The Story of a Childhood. New York: Coward-McCann, 1947. [memoir]
Midnight Lace. New York: Random House, 1948. [novel]
Wicked Water: An American Primitive. New York: Random House, 1949. [novel]
The Good Family. New York: Coward-McCann, 1949. [novel]
Signal Thirty-Two. New York: Random House, 1950. [novel]
One Wild Oat. New York: Fawcett, 1950. [novel]
Don't Touch Me. New York: Random House, 1951. [novel]
Warwhoop: Two Short Novels of the Frontier. New York: Random House, 1952.
The Daughter of Bugle Ann. New York: Random House, 1953. [novel]
God and My Country. Cleveland: World, 1954. [novel]
Andersonville. Cleveland: World, 1955. [novel]
Lobo. Cleveland: World, 1957. [novel]
Silent Grow the Guns, and Other Tales of the American Civil War. New York: New American Library, 1958.
Again the Bugle. New York: American Weekly, 1958. [stories]
Frontier: Tales of the American Adventure. New York: New American Library, 1959.
It's About Crime. New York: New American Library, 1960. [stories]
If the South Had Won the Civil War. New York: Bantam, 1961. [nonfiction]
Spirit Lake. Cleveland: World, 1961. [novel]
The Guntoter, and Other Stories of the Missouri Hills. New York: New American Library, 1963.
Story Teller. New York: Doubleday. 1967. [stories]
Beauty Beast. New York: Putnam, 1968. [novel]
The Day I Met a Lion. New York: Doubleday, 1968. [selected nonfiction, including an essay on the writing of *Andersonville*]
Missouri Bittersweet. New York: Doubleday, 1969. [memoir]
Hamilton County: New York: Macmillan, 1970. [social history]
I Love You, Irene. New York: Doubleday, 1972.
The Children Sing. New York: Hawthorn, 1973. [novel]
Valley Forge. New York: M. Evans, 1975 [novel]

Checklist of Secondary Sources

CAA; CN; TCA; Warfel.

Andrews, Clarence A. *A Literary History of Iowa*. Iowa City: U. Iowa, 1972. Pp. 31–32, 222–25, *passim*.
Frederick, John T. "Town and City in Iowa Fiction." *Palimpsest*, 35 (Feb. 1954), 80–81.
Kantor, MacKinlay. "The Historical Novel." In *Three Views of the Novel*. Washington: Library of Congress, Reference Dept, 1957. Pp. 16–37.
Paluka, Frank. *Iowa Authors: A Bio-bibliography of Sixty Native Writers*. Iowa City: Friends of the University Libraries, 1967. Pp. 180–86.
Windhorn, Stan. "The Author." *SatR* (Oct. 21, 1961), 23–24.

Clarence A. Andrews
University of Iowa
Iowa City, Iowa

CAROLINE M. KIRKLAND
[MRS. MARY CLAVERS] (1801–64)

Most critics think Caroline Kirkland's major contribution to American literature rests in her midwestern books which present a realistic account, often satiric in tone, of the Michigan frontier. They cite her as an early and significant precursor of the realistic and local color movements. Twamley's thesis begins the study of the accuracy of Kirkland's depictions. Osborne, McCloskey, and Keyes, particularly, others to a lesser degree, emphasize her detailed descriptions of manners and customs, her jaundiced approach to the rhetoric and substance of republicanism, and her characterization of a desolate and disillusioning frontier life. Osborne is comprehensive, offering critiques of her major and minor works, including those not purely midwestern, setting them also in a biographical and historical context. McCloskey focuses only on *A New Home*, offering primarily plot summary and general commentary but also stressing the parallel relation between actual Michigan history and her narratives. Knudsen, likewise, stresses Michigan history but covers a broader range of works. Keyes is an important source for a thoughtful, detailed analysis of the purely midwestern material and experiences. Pattee is the only major critic who sees Kirkland as a romanticizer of the western settlements, assessing her work as propaganda for the land boom. Mabbott and Stronks provide new information about Kirkland's fictional theory and her publishing relationships, respectively. Roberts introduces letters which bear light on her relationship to her author son, Joseph Kirkland.

While Caroline Kirkland was recognized for her literary gifts during her lifetime, was received well by the reading public, and figured prominently in literary circles, her work has been given rather limited critical attention in the twentieth century. Osborne's is the only full-length study, presenting the most comprehensive primary bibliography. *A New Home—Who'll Follow?* is the only work presently in print, although several are available through the Wright microfilm series. Also her major works and several articles, reviews and letters are accessible through public and private holdings.

Major Works

A New Home—Who'll Follow? New Haven: College and University Press, 1965. [domestic and frontier sketches and narratives]
Forest Life. 2 vols. New York: C. S. Francis, 1842. [miscellany]
Western Clearings. New York: Wiley and Putnam, 1846. [miscellany]
Spenser and the Faery Queen. New York: Wiley and Putnam, 1847. [biography and criticism]

Holidays Abroad; or, Europe from the West. 2 vols. New York: Baker and Scribner, 1849.
[travel journal]
The Evening Book or, Fireside Talk on Morals and Manners, with Sketches of Western Life.
New York: Scribner, 1852. [essays]
The Book of Home Beauty. New York: Putnam, 1852. [gift book]
Garden Walks with the Poets. New York: Putnam, 1852. [verse]
*The Helping Hand, Comprising an Account of the Home for Discharged Female Convicts
and an Appeal in Behalf of That Institution.* New York: Scribner, 1853. [tract]
Autumn Hours, and Fireside Reading. New York: Scribner, 1854. [miscellany]
Personal Memoirs of George Washington. New York: Appleton, 1857. [biography]
The School-Girl's Garland. New York: Scribner, 1864. [verse]

CHECKLIST OF SECONDARY SOURCES

Blanck; Burke; *DAB*; Duyckinck; Herzberg; *LHUS*; *OCAL*; Quinn.

Boynton, Percy H. *Literature and American Life.* Boston: Ginn, 1936. P. 597.

Dondore, Dorothy A. *The Prairie and the Making of Middle America.* Cedar Rapids, Iowa:
Torch Press, 1926.

Fussell, Edwin. *Frontier: American Literature and the American West.* Princeton, N.J.:
Princeton U., 1965. Pp. 143–45.

Herron, Ima H. *The Small Town in American Literature.* New York: Pageant Books, 1959.
Pp. 147–48, *passim.*

Keyes, Langley C. "Caroline M. Kirkland: A Pioneer in Realism." Ph.D. diss., Harvard U.,
1935.

Knudsen, Louise N. "Caroline Kirkland, Pioneer." Master's thesis, Michigan State College,
1934.

Mabbott, Thomas O. "Mrs. Kirkland's 'Essay on Fiction.' " *BNYPL*, 54 (1960), 395–97.

McCloskey, John C. "Back-Country Folkways in Mrs. Kirkland's *A New Home—Who'll Follow?*" *MHM*, 40 (Sept. 1956), 297–308.

————. "Jacksonian Democracy in Mrs. Kirkland's *A New Home—Who'll Follow?*" *MHM*,
45 (Dec. 1961), 347–52.

————. "Land Speculation in Michigan in 1835–36 as Described in Mrs. Kirkland's *A New
Home—Who'll Follow?*" *MHM*, 42 (Mar. 1958), 26–34.

Osborne, William S. *Caroline M. Kirkland.* New York: Twayne, 1972.

Pattee, Fred Lewis. *The Feminine Fifties.* New York: Appleton, 1940.

————. *The First Century of American Literature, 1770–1870.* New York: Appleton, 1935. Pp.
274, 498.

Roberts, Audrey J. " 'Word-Murder': An Early Joseph Kirkland Essay Published Anony-
mously." *AmLitR*, 6 (Winter 1973), 73–79.

————. "The Letters of Caroline M. Kirkland." *DAI*, 37:3629A.

Rusk, Ralph L. *The Literature of the Middle Western Frontier.* 2 vols. New York: Columbia
U., 1926. Pp. 284–86.

Stronks, James B. "Author Rejects Publisher: Caroline Kirkland and *The Gift.*" *BNYPL*, 44
(1960), 548–50.

Twamley, Edna M. "The Western Sketches of Caroline Mathilda (Stanbury) Kirkland."
MHC, 39 (1915), 89–124.

Wendell, Barrett. *A Literary History of America.* New York: Scribner, 1901. Pp. 501–3.

Wright, Lyle H. *American Fiction 1774–1850: A Contribution Toward a Bibliography.* San
Marino, Calif.:Huntington Library, 1969. Pp. 210–11.

Rosalie Hewitt
Northern Illinois University
DeKalb, Illinois

JOSEPH KIRKLAND (1830–93)

The son of Caroline Kirkland, an American author of mid-century who concentrated on social history, Joseph Kirkland's primary profession was legal rather than literary. Eventually he gave up fiction for history, but not before he had passed on the sense of midwestern realism, in part assimilated from his mother, to Hamlin Garland.

Kirkland wrote three novels of which *Zury* (1887) is the most substantial. All of them are uneven. The truthfulness and vigor Kirkland brought to his fiction, evidence of his reliance on his own observation and experience, are offset by artistic roughness and failure to achieve coherent structure. Although he was capable of striking detail, effective dialect, and lifelike characters, his habitual authorial intrusion and his dependence on episodic plots contribute to the diffuseness and formlessness of the larger units. He was not a great artist, but most major literary histories recognize both his attempt to apply the theories of realism to his own creative endeavors and his influence on Hamlin Garland.

The assignment of Kirkland to a small group of midwestern writers including Garland, Edward Eggleston, and Edgar Watson Howe seems quite permanent. Blending in his fiction the romantic and realistic tempers and exhibiting qualities drawn from the tradition of frontier humor and from the contemporary interest in localism, he demonstrated sensitivity to the literary climate of his time; but he was supportive of emerging trends rather than innovative.

MAJOR WORKS

Zury: The Meanest Man in Spring County. Boston: Houghton Mifflin, 1887. [novel]
The McVeys. Boston: Houghton Mifflin, 1888. [novel]
The Captain of Company K. Chicago: Dibble, 1891. [novel]
The Story of Chicago. Chicago: Dibble, 1892; vol. 2 [history; completed by Kirkland's daughter Caroline], 1894.

CHECKLIST OF SECONDARY SOURCES

Ahnebrink, Lars. *The Beginnings of Naturalism in American Fiction.* Cambridge: Harvard U., 1950. Pp. 56–69, *passim.*
Barnes, Gregory A. "Joseph Kirkland's Myth of Progress." Ph.D. diss., U. Wisconsin, 1971.
Dimmock, T. B. "*Company K.*" *Figaro* (Chicago), Sept. 24, 1891, pp. 600–1. [rev.]
Dondore, Dorothy Anne. *The Prairie and the Making of Middle America: Four Centuries of Description.* Cedar Rapids, Iowa: Torch Press, 1926. Pp. 320, 325–26, 416.
Duffey, Bernard. *The Chicago Renaissance in American Letters: A Critical History.* East Lansing: Michigan State College, 1954. Pp. 32, 56, 81, 93–98.
Eichelberger, Clayton L. and Frank L. Stallings, Jr. "Joseph Kirkland (1830–1893): A Critical Bibliography of Secondary Comment." *ALR*, 2 (1969), 51–69; supplemented by Eichelberger, "Edgar Watson Howe and Joseph Kirkland: More Critical Comment." *ALR*, 4 (1971), 279–90.

Flanagan, John T. "Introduction" to *Zury: A Novel of Western Life*. Urbana: U. Illinois, 1956. [Facsimile reprint of 1887 ed.]

——. "Joseph Kirkland, Pioneer Realist." *AL*, 11 (1939), 273–84.

Garland, Hamlin. *Roadside Meetings*. New York: Macmillan, 1930. Pp. 106–8, 110–12, *passim*.

——. *A Son of the Middle Border*. New York: Macmillan, 1917. Pp. 354–55, *passim*.

——. "*Zury*." *Boston Evening Transcript*, May 16, 1887, p. 3. [rev.]

Gookin, Frederick W. *The Chicago Literary Club: A History of Its First Fifty Years*. Chicago: Printed for the Club, 1926. Pp. 120–26, 153–54, 159–60, 266–67, *passim*.

Henson, Clyde E. *Joseph Kirkland*. New York: Twayne, 1962.

——. "Joseph Kirkland (1830–1894). *AmLitR* (1967), 67–70. [biblio-essay]

——. "Joseph Kirkland's Influence on Hamlin Garland." *AL*, 23 (1952), 458–63.

——. "The Life and Work of Joseph Kirkland." Ph.D., diss., Western Reserve U., 1950.

Herron, Ima H. *The Small Town in American Literature*. Durham: Duke U., 1939; reprinted, New York: Pageant, 1959. Pp. 216–19, *passim*.

Holaday, Clayton A. "Joseph Kirkland: Biography and Criticism." Ph.D. diss., Indiana U., 1949.

——. "Joseph Kirkland's *Company K*." *JISHS*, 49 (1956), 295–307.

——. "Kirkland's *Company K*: A Twice-told Tale." *AL*, 25 (1953), 62–68.

"Home Fiction." *New York Times*, Jan. 7, 1889, p. 2. [rev. of *McVeys*]

Howells, William Dean. "Editor's Study, III." *Harper*, 77 (1888), 152–53. [rev. of *Zury*]

——. "Editor's Study, VI," *Harper*, 78 (1889), 986. [rev. of *McVeys*]

"Illinois Life in Fiction." *Atl*, 63 (1889), 276–80. [rev. of *McVeys*]

LaBudde, Kenneth J. "A Note on the Text of Joseph Kirkland's *Zury*." *AL*, 20 (1949), 452–55.

Lease, Benjamin. "Realism and Joseph Kirkland's *Zury*." *AL*, 23 (1952), 464–66.

Lewis, Lloyd. "Letters of a Pioneer Realist." *NLB*, no. 3 (1945), 3–7.

Mitchell, Marvin O. "Joseph Kirkland: The Conflict Between Realism and Sentimentality in His Fiction." In "A Study of the Realistic and Romantic Elements in the Fiction of E. W. Howe, Joseph Kirkland, Hamlin Garland, Harold Frederic, and Frank Norris (1882–1902)." Ph.D. diss., U. North Carolina, 1953.

Payne, William Morton. "Recent Fiction." *Dial*, 8 (1887), 67. [rev. of *Zury*]

——. "Recent Fiction." *Dial*, 9 (1888), 161. [rev. of *McVeys*]

"Recent Fiction—II." *OM*, 10 (1887), 214–18. [rev. of *Zury*]

Smith, Henry Nash. *Virgin Land: The American West as Symbol and Myth*. New York: Random House, 1950. Pp. 283–85, passim.

——. "The Western Farmer in Imaginative Literature, 1818–1891." *MVHR*, 36 (1949), 479–90.

Solomon, Eric. "Another Analogue for *The Red Badge of Courage*." *NCF*, 13 (1958), 63–67.

"A Strong American Romance." *New York Times*, May 22, 1887, p. 10. [rev. of *Zury*]

Weber, Harley R. "Midwestern Farm Writing in the Late Nineteenth Century: A Study in Changing Attitudes." Ph.D. diss., U. Minnesota, 1967.

Wilson, Edmund. *Patriotic Gore: Studies in the Literature of the American Civil War*. New York: Oxford U., 1962. Pp. 685, 737–39.

Clayton L. Eichelberger
University of Texas at Arlington
Arlington, Texas

HERBERT KRAUSE (1905–76)

The author of three novels, a volume of poetry, and several shorter works, chiefly in ornithology, Herbert Krause has received little critical attention apart from reviews of his books. His first novel, *Wind Without Rain,* had an enthusiastic reception. Stegner credited him with "passion, feeling as opposed to sentiment, a seeing eye, artistic integrity" and with being "clairvoyantly sensitive to the evocative power of language." *The Thresher* was received almost as favorably. Havighurst called it "an urgent, compassionate, uncompromising picture of rural life." Meyer saw the book as a culmination of the tradition of midwestern farm fiction and Krause as one of the most skilled practitioners of the form in the 1930s and 1940s.

Krause's venture into historical fiction, however, brought a more mixed critical reaction. Flanagan, who had said of the earlier books that they "combined a firm sense of place with an exciting narrative," concluded of *The Oxcart Trail* that it smelled "a little too much of the lamp to be an effective novel." Hass, however, thought it a "solid fictional performance," and Gray said that it offered "a new design for the historical novel." Krause himself spoke of it as "an unsatisfactory novel," written under pressures.

Critical comment on Krause's one volume of poetry has been restricted largely to Paul Engle's introduction to the book. His scientific writing, scattered through specialized journals, has been dealt with *in extenso* only in the Solovskoy thesis, which concludes that Krause's poetic talent, coupled with meticulous observation and scrupulous accuracy, has made for the finest type of nature writing. This thesis contains the most nearly complete bibliography of Krause's work, published and unpublished.

MAJOR WORKS

Neighbor Boy. Iowa City: Midland House, 1939. [poetry]
Wind Without Rain. Indianapolis: Bobbs-Merrill, 1939. [novel]
The Thresher. Indianapolis: Bobbs-Merrill, 1946. [novel]
The Oxcart Trail. Indianapolis: Bobbs-Merrill, 1954. [novel]

CHECKLIST OF SECONDARY SOURCES

Herzberg; Warfel; *Who's Who in America, 1960–61.*

Barry, Iris. "Told With Veracity and Power." *NYHTBR,* Feb. 12, 1939, p. 5. [rev.]
Chaikin, Nancy G. "A Man's Drive for Power." *SatR,* 30 (Feb. 8, 1947), 12. [rev.]
Fadiman, Clifton. "Books: Spain, Australia, Minnesota." *NY,* 14 (Feb. 11, 1939), 72–73. [rev.]
Flanagan, John T. "Frontier in Fiction." *MinnH,* 34 (Autumn 1954), 123–24. [rev.]
———. "The Middle Western Farm Novel." *MinnH,* 23 (June 1942), 113–47.
———. "Thirty Years of Minnesota Fiction." *MinnH,* 31 (Sept. 1950), 129–47.
Gray, James E. "Liquor, Love and Brawling on the Long Road Westward." *NYHTBR,* Apr. 4, 1954, p. 5. [rev.]
Hass, Victor P. "A Yankee in Minnesota." *NYTBR,* Apr. 11, 1954, p. 25. [rev.]
Havighurst, Walter. "Driving Force on the Prairie." *NYHTBR,* Jan. 12, 1947, p. 4. [rev.]
Meyer, Roy W. *The Middle Western Farm Novel in the Twentieth Century.* Lincoln: U. Nebraska, 1965. Pp. 160–70, 191–92, 220.
———. "The Scandinavian Immigrant in American Farm Fiction." *ASR,* 47 (Autumn 1959), 243–49.
Richards, Carmen N., ed. *Minnesota Writers.* Minneapolis: Denison, 1961. Pp. 26–33. [biographical sketch]
Solovskoy, Valborg B. "The World of Nature in the Writings of Herbert Krause." Master's thesis, Mankato State College, 1973. [contains two interviews]

Stegner, Wallace. "A Strong Novel of the Minnesota Land." *SatR*, 19 (Feb. 11, 1939), 5. [rev.]
Wallace, Margaret. " 'Wind Without Rain' and Other Recent Works of Fiction." *NYTBR*, Feb. 12, 1939, p. 6. [rev.]

Roy W. Meyer
Mankato State College
Mankato, Minnesota

RING[GOLD] LARDNER (1885–1933)

In 1924, Mencken predicted that "the professors" would come to appreciate Ring Lardner only after the changing pattern of American civilization had made his idiom and characters obsolete, with the result that they would fail to understand the true merit of his work. Mencken was wrong: Lardner suffered no critical neglect during his own day from either academic or nonacademic critics, and he has suffered none since, so that the resources which now exist for the scholarly study of his achievement are abundant. Further, nearly the only viewpoints contemporary and later critics have agreed on are that his native American (and so often, midwestern) character types are impressively—or depressingly—true to life, and that he possessed an uncanny mastery of the vernacular idiom these characters used. Because Lardner was a singularly taciturn person, cloaking personal viewpoints behind an objective mask, and because he had a dual standing as a "funny man" and as a "devastating" satirist, some of the critical commentary on him is subjective and speculative. Did he fail to recognize that he had a gift for serious literature? Was his best work, as Berryman thought, the product of a mere "accident of talent"? Did he, as Fitzgerald thought, come to lose interest in his work so that he never produced the major work of which he was capable? Was he, as Fadiman thought—and some recent critics still think—a misanthrope who hated himself and his characters? Or was he simply a puritan-minded idealist who became appalled at the discrepancy between the real and ideal worlds? These issues are the central ones in the critical commentary on Lardner, and it is not surprising that this commentary contains distortions and inaccuracies.

For its commonsense treatment of many of the foregoing issues, and for its detailed, comprehensive account of Lardner's life and career, Elder's biography is the single most valuable resource for the Lardner scholar. Caruthers's book is a work of primary value, not only because it reprints the correspondence between him and Max Perkins of Scribner's, but also because Caruthers includes a chronological checklist of the first publications of Lardner's books, stories, and magazine pieces. One of the primary problems for the Lardner scholar is that over half of the stories Lardner wrote (not to mention nonfiction works of significance) still lie buried in the pages of the mass circulation magazines in which they first appeared. Even with the helpful checklist of Caruthers, the scholar will find that the files of some of these magazines are surprisingly scarce.

MAJOR WORKS

You Know Me Al. New York: Doran, 1916. [stories]
Gullible's Travels, Etc. Indianapolis: Bobbs-Merrill, 1917. [fiction]
My Four Weeks in France. Indianapolis: Bobbs-Merrill, 1918. [humor]
Treat 'Em Rough. Indianapolis: Bobbs-Merrill, 1918. [stories]
Own Your Own Home. Indianapolis: Bobbs-Merrill, 1919. [stories]
The Real Dope. Indianapolis: Bobbs-Merrill, 1919. [stories]
The Young Immigrunts. Indianapolis: Bobbs-Merrill, 1920. [humor]
Symptoms of Being 35. Indianapolis: Bobbs-Merrill, 1921. [humor]
The Big Town. Indianapolis: Bobbs-Merrill, 1921. [fiction]
Say It with Oil. New York: Doran, 1923. [humor]
How to Write Short Stories (With Samples). New York: Scribner, 1924. [stories]
What of It? New York: Scribner, 1925. [misc. pieces]
The Love Nest and Other Stories. New York: Scribner, 1926.
The Story of a Wonder Man. New York: Scribner, 1927. [farcical autobiography]
Round Up. New York: Scribner, 1929. [stories]
June Moon. (With George S. Kaufman.) New York: Scribner, 1930. [play]
Lose with a Smile. New York: Scribner, 1933. [fiction]
First and Last. Ed. Gilbert Seldes. New York: Scribner, 1934. [anthology]
The Collected Short Stories of Ring Lardner. New York: Modern Library, 1941.
The Ring Lardner Reader. Ed. Gilbert Seldes. New York: Scribner, 1963. [anthology]

CHECKLIST OF SECONDARY SOURCES

Anderson, Sherwood. "Four American Impressions: Gertrude Stein, Paul Rosenfeld, Ring Lardner, Sinclair Lewis." *NR*, 32 (Oct. 11, 1922), 171–73. Reprinted in *Sherwood Anderson's Notebook.* New York: Boni, 1926. Pp. 47–55.
———. "Meeting Ring Lardner." *NY*, 9 (Nov. 25, 1933), 36. Reprinted in *No Swank*. Philadelphia: Centaur, 1934. Pp. 1–7.
Benchley, Robert C. "The Fate of the Funny Men." *Bookman*, 57 (June 1923), 455–57.
Berryman, John. "The Case of Ring Lardner." *Commentary*, 22 (Nov. 1956), 416–23.
Boyd, Thomas. "Lardner Tells Some New Ones." *Bookman*, 59 (July 1924), 601–2.
Bibesco, E. "Lament for Lardner." *LA*, 345 (Dec. 1933), 366–68.
Bruccoli, Matthew and Richard Layman, eds. *Ring W. Lardner: A Descriptive Bibliography.* Pittsburgh: U. Pittsburgh, 1976.
Caruthers, Clifford M., ed. *Ring Around Max: The Correspondence of Ring Lardner and Max Perkins.* DeKalb: Northern Illinois U., 1974. [Includes chronological bibliography of first publications of Lardner's books and magazine pieces—stories and nonfiction.]
Chamberlain, John. "Ring Lardner Listens in on the Life About Him." *NYTBR*, Apr. 7, 1929, p. 2.
Douglas, Donald. "Ring Lardner as Satirist." *Nation*, 122 (May 26, 1926), 584–85.
Elder, Donald. *Ring Lardner: A Biography.* Garden City, N.Y.: Doubleday, 1956.
Fadiman, Clifton. "Pitiless Satire." *Nation*, 128 (May 1, 1929), 536–37.
———. "Ring Lardner and the Triangle of Hate." *Nation*, 136 (Mar. 22, 1933), 315–17.
Farrell, James T. "Ring Lardner's Success Mad World." *NYTBR*, June, 1944, p. 3. Reprinted as "Ring Lardner's *Round Up*." In *The League of Frightened Philistines and Other Papers.* New York: Vanguard, 1945.
Fitzgerald, F. Scott. "Ring." *NR*, 75 (Oct. 11, 1933), 254–55.
Frakes, James R. "Ring Lardner: A Critical Survey." Ph.D. diss., U. Pennsylvania, 1953.
Friedrich, Otto H. *Ring Lardner.* Minneapolis: U. Minnesota, 1965. [No. 49 in The Minnesota pamphlets on American writers]

Geismar, Maxwell. "Ring Lardner: Like Something was Going to Happen." In *Writers in Crisis, The American Novel Between Two Wars*. Boston: Houghton Mifflin, 1942. Pp. 3–36.
_____. *Ring Lardner and the Portrait of Folly*. New York: Crowell, 1972.
Lardner, Ring, Jr. *The Lardners: My Family Remembered*. New York: Harper, 1976.
Latham, J. A. "The Lardners: A Writing Dynasty." *NYTMS*, Aug. 22, 1971, pp. 10–11.
Lewisohn, Ludwig. *Expression in America*. New York: Harper, 1932. Pp. 514–15.
Littell, Robert. "Ring Lardner." *NR*, 40 (Sept. 3, 1924), 25–26.
Masson, Thomas L. "Ring Lardner." In *Our American Humorists*. New York: Moffat, Yard, 1922. Pp. 25–26.
Matthews, T. S. "Lardner, Shakespeare, and Chekhov." *NR*, 59 (May 22, 1929), 35–36.
Mencken, Henry L. *The American Language: An Inquiry into the Development of English in the United States*. 2d ed., rev. and enl. New York: Knopf, 1921. Pp. 274–77, 404–05.
_____. "Lardner." In *Prejudices, Fifth Series*. New York: Knopf, 1926. Pp. 49–56.
_____. "A Humorist Shows His Teeth." *AmMerc*, 8 (June 1926), 354–55.
Nevins, Allan. "The American Moron." *SatR*, 5 (June 8, 1929), 1089–90.
Overton, Grant. "Ring W. Lardner's Belle Lettres." *Bookman*, 62 (Sept. 1925), 44–49. [based on an interview]
Patrick, Walton R. *Ring Lardner*. New York: Twayne, 1963. [contains bibliography of uncollected stories]
Salpeter, Harry. "The Boswell of New York." *Bookman*, 81 (July 1930), 384.
Schwartz, Delmore. "Ring Lardner: Highbrow in Hiding." *Reporter*, 15 (Aug. 9, 1956), 52–54.
Seldes, Gilbert. "The Singular—Although Dual—Eminence of Ring Lardner." In *American Criticism*, ed. by William A. Drake. New York: Harcourt, 1926. Pp. 222–30.
_____. "Editor's Introduction." In *The Portable Ring Lardner*. New York: Viking, 1946. Pp. 1–19.
_____. "Mr. Dooley, Meet Mr. Lardner." In *The Seven Lively Arts*. New York: Harper, 1957. Pp. 111–29.
Sherman, Stuart. "Ring Lardner: Hardboiled Americans." In *The Main Stream*. New York: Scribner, 1927. Pp. 168–75.
Stuart, Henry L. "Mr. Lardner Burlesques America." *NYTBR*, Apr. 19, 1925, p. 1.
_____. "Three Stories A Year Are Enough For A Writer." *NYTMS*, Mar. 25, 1917, p. 14. [interview]
Thurston, Jarvis A. "Ring Lardner's 'Ex Parte.' " In *Reading Modern Short Stories*. Chicago: Scott, Foresman, 1955. Pp. 42–50.
Van Doren, Carl. "Beyond Grammar: Ring W. Lardner: Philologist among the Lowbrows." *Century*, 106 (July 1923), 471–75.
Weaver, John V. "Ring Lardner—Serious Artist." *Bookman*, 54 (Feb. 1922), 586–87.
Webb, Howard W., Jr. "Ring Lardner's Conflict and Reconciliation with American Society." Ph.D. diss., U. Iowa, 1953.
_____. "The Meaning of Ring Lardner's Fiction: A Re-Evaluation." *AL*, 31 (Jan. 1960), 434–45.
_____. "Ring Lardner's Idle Common Man." *BCMVASA*, 1 (Spring 1958), 6–13.
Wheeler, John. "Unforgettable Ring Lardner." *RD*, 89 (Oct. 1966), 113–17.
Wilson, Edmund. "Mr. Lardner's American Characters." *Dial*, 78 (July 1924), pp. 69–72. Reprinted in *A Literary Chronicle: 1920–1950*. Garden City, N.Y.: Doubleday, 1956. Pp. 37–40.
Woolf, Virginia. "American Fiction." In *The Moment and Other Essays*. London: Hogarth, 1952. Pp. 94–104.

W. R. Patrick
Auburn University
Auburn, Alabama

WILLIAM ELLERY LEONARD (1876–1944)

Born in Plainfield, N.J., William Ellery Leonard migrated to Wisconsin in 1906 and spent the rest of his life, save for one year as visiting professor at New York University (1916–17), teaching at the University in Madison. His wife's tragic suicide two years after their marriage left Leonard psychologically unable to travel more than a few blocks from his home without experiencing a panic. The root causes of this situation are traced brilliantly in *The Locomotive God* (1927).

No full-length study of Leonard has yet appeared. Probably the most balanced biographical data about him are to be found in the Clough and Jorgenson assessments. Leonard is best remembered as a translator and teacher. He was concerned essentially with medieval literature and translated such epics as *Beowulf* (1923) and *Gilgamesh* (1934). Nevertheless, his far-ranging literary interests led him to write substantial quantities of poetry, much of it related to his first wife's suicide, and to write two plays, *Glory of the Morning* (1912) and *Red Bird* (1923), which were directly concerned with Wisconsin history.

Meyer, speaking of Leonard as a poet, says that "What Leonard is really doing is carrying on the traditions of great poetry before it succumbed to the cults, the isms, the ists, and the facile smart cracking jinglers who are having their day." He goes on to call Leonard "the professor as appraiser, a function he has exercised with critical acuteness in many fields. But beyond and above that he is the professor as creator, who can not only distinguish beauty from buncombe but who can fix the difference unforgettably in our minds by his contributions to the world's Literature." Leslie Fiedler in his *DAB* article credits Leonard, along with two or three others, with translating "to American soil the figure of the Romantic scholar-poet, willing to seem eccentric and to court loneliness and even social ostracism in order to live his own authentic life."

MAJOR WORKS

Sonnets and Poems. Boston: Gibson, 1906. [poems]
The Vaunt of Man and Other Poems. New York: Huebsch, 1912. [poems]
Glory of the Morning. Madison: Dramatic Society, 1912. Also printed in *Wisconsin Plays.* Ed. Thomas H. Dickinson. New York: Huebsch, 1917. [play]
Poems: 1914–1916. Privately printed, 1917. [poems]
The Lynching Bee and Other Poems. New York: Huebsch, 1920. [poems]
Red Bird. New York: Huebsch, 1923. [play]
Two Lives. New York: Huebsch, 1925. [poems]
The Locomotive God. New York: Century, 1927. [psychological autobiography]
A Son of Earth. New York: Viking, 1928. [poems]
This Midland City. Detroit: Lotus Press, 1930. [poems]

CHECKLIST OF SECONDARY SOURCES

Burke; *CA; CAA; DAB; OCAL; TCA.*

Brumbaugh, Thomas B. "Remembering William Ellery Leonard." *EUQ*, 13 (1957), 11–16.
Cason, Clarence E. "William Ellery Leonard." *VQR*, 4 (July 1928), 357–88.
Clough, Wilson O. "William Ellery Leonard, Teacher." *PrS*, 20 (Spring 1946), 23–26.
Duffy, Charles. "A Letter to Charles Bulger." *AA* (July 1948), n.p.
———. "W. E. Leonard's Annotations in a Copy of 'Poems, 1916–17.' " *MLN*, 63 (1948), 185–87.
Jones, Howard Mumford. "William Ellery Leonard." *DD*, 8 (May 1926), 332–28.
Jorgenson, Chester E. "William Ellery Leonard: An Appraisal." In A. Dayle Wallace and Woodburn O. Ross, eds. *Studies in Honor of John Wilcox.* Detroit: Wayne State U., 1958.
Kreymborg, Alfred. *Our Singing Strength.* New York: Coward, 1929. Pp. 414–48.
Leiser, Clara. "William Ellery Leonard: Some Memories and New Poems." *Tomorrow*, 8 (May 1949), 37–41.
Lewisohn, Ludwig. "Poet and Scholar." *Nation*, 116 (June 6, 1923), 660–61.
Manly, John M. and Edith Rickert, eds. *Contemporary American Literature.* New York: Harcourt, 1929. P. 216.
Meyer, Ernest L. "William Ellery Leonard." *AmMerc*, 32 (July 1934), 334–40.

R. Baird Shuman
University of Illinois
Champaign, Illinois

MEYER LEVIN (1905–   )

Critics have found Levin's writing to be at its best when dealing with collective experience and social history. Trilling has praised his representation of social emotions, Cantwell his realistic depictions of Chicago urban life, and Pritchett his "black and white reporting," which he compares favorably with Rice's *Street Scene.* Rahv places Levin in the tradition of Dreiser, Farrell, and Dos Passos, while Farrell himself called *The Old Bunch* "the most serious and ambitious novel of the current generation . . . ." However, Farrell and others (like Rahv) have remarked that Levin's very ambitiousness, the extensiveness of his social observations, results in undeveloped characters without much psychological depth. The general assessment, even in the 1930s, was that Levin was, in Kazin's words, "a novelist without spectacular talent . . . ."

There has been less consensus about the quality and the value of Levin's writing when it concerns, as it most often does, the contemporary history of the Jews and of Israel/Palestine. Lerner felt the need to argue against the charge that Levin's autobiography revealed merely a "chip-on-the-shoulder Jewishness." Syrkin calls it an eloquent analysis of the " 'shame' " of being Jewish. But Laski believes *Eva* to be a vengeful document, more like propaganda than literature. Critics have thought the kind of material Levin presents and the manner of its·presentation to be frank, candid, unblushing, or disgusting, depending on their viewpoint; however, they generally agree that his political, psychological, or philosophical insights often lack the depth of a really penetrating vision of life.

MAJOR WORKS

Reporter. New York: Day, 1929. [novel]
Frankie and Johnie. New York: Day, 1930. [novel]
Yehuda. New York: Cape and Smith, 1931. [novel]
The New Bridge. New York: Covici-Friede, 1933. [novel]
The Old Bunch. New York: Viking, 1937. [novel]
Citizens. New York: Viking, 1940. [novel]
My Father's House. New York: Viking, 1947. [novel]
In Search. New York: Horizon, 1950. [autobiography]
Compulsion. New York: Simon and Schuster, 1956. [novel]
Eva. New York: Simon and Schuster, 1959. [novel]
The Fanatic. New York: Simon and Schuster, 1964. [novel]
The Stronghold. New York: Simon and Schuster, 1965. [novel]
Gore and Igor. New York: Simon and Schuster, 1967. [novel]
The Obsession. New York: Simon and Schuster, 1973. [novel]
The Spell of Time: A Tale of Love in Jerusalem. New York: Praeger, 1974. [novel]

CHECKLIST OF SECONDARY SOURCES

Burke; *CA; CB; CN;* Herzberg; *LLC; OCAL; TCA & supp.*

Bellman, Samuel I. "The New Bunch." *SatR* (Feb. 24, 1968), 44–45. [rev.]
Cantwell, Robert. "Four Novelists of Tomorrow." *NR*, 74 (1933), 108–9. [rev.]
Deutsch, Babette. "Pity and Spirituality." *NYHTBR*, Apr. 17, 1932, p. 7. [rev.]
Farrell, James T. "Between Two Wars." *SatR* (Mar. 13, 1937), 5. [rev.]
Field, Rose. "Guilty with Mitigating Circumstances." *NYHTBR*, Oct. 28, 1956, p. 5. [rev.]
Gardner, Earle Stanley. "Killers for Kicks." *NYTBR*, Oct. 28, 1956, p. 7. [rev.]
Karp, David. "In Search of a Motive." *SatR* (Oct. 27, 1956), 16. [rev.]
Kauffmann, Stanley. "Season in Hell." *NYRB*, Feb. 20, 1964, pp. 5–6. [rev.]
Kazin, Alfred. "Before, During, After the Boom in Chicago." *NYHTBR*, Mar. 14, 1937, p. 5. [rev.]
Laski, Marghanita. "To Live in a Time of Death." *SatR* (Aug. 29, 1959), 13–14. [rev.]
Lerner, Max. "Picaresque of Faith." *NR* (July 24, 1950), 19. [rev.]
Moore, Harry T. "Anatomy of Chicago." *NR*, 90 (1937), 273–74. [rev.]
Pritchett, V. S. "New Novels." *NSN*, 5 (1933), 850–51. [rev.]
Rahv, Philip. "American Jews in Chicago." *Nation*, 144 (1937), 384–85. [rev.]
Shapiro, Charles. "The Crime of our Age." *Nation*, 183 (1956), 482–84. [rev.]
Syrkin, Marie. "An American Jew." *Nation*, 171 (1950), 151–52. [rev.]
Trilling, Lionel. "Modern Palestine in Fiction." *Nation*, 132 (1931), 684. [rev.]

Harry White
Northeastern Illinois University
Chicago, Illinois

SINCLAIR LEWIS (1885–1951)

One of the most striking and influential delineations we have of the Midwest is that drawn by Sinclair Lewis, who felt that he was engaged in mirroring and analyzing the very heart of the nation: "This is America," he wrote of the village that is the setting for *Main Street*, whose Minnesota story "would be the same in Ohio or Montana, in Kansas or Kentucky or Illinois." Fully half of Lewis's novels and dozens of his short stories are primarily midwestern. As early as *The Trail of the Hawk* and *Free Air*, he was developing his cast of characters, both the idealized and the satirized, such as housewives, farmers, doctors, salesmen, and preachers—yearners and doers and charlatans. Winnemac, his mythical midwestern state (whose chief city is Zenith), is central to four of his best books of the 1920s. Equally important is his account of the citizens of Grand Republic, Minnesota, in the 1940s (in *Cass Timberlane* and *Kingsblood Royal*). *The God-Seeker* is a historical novel of Minnesota, and the essay "Minnesota, the Norse State," gives us his version of the background and ethnography of the region. Excerpts from the "Diary" reveal his ambivalence toward it.

The study of Lewis must begin with the work of Schorer, whose fine comprehensive biography appeared in 1961 and who has contributed some dozen additional items on Lewis. Schorer has deeply influenced both our thinking about the man and our judgments of the books, especially because he compiled the "Twentieth Century Views" essays on Lewis, wrote the sketch of Lewis in the Minnesota "Pamphlets" series, selected and introduced a volume of short stories (*I'm a Stranger Here Myself*), and provided "Afterwords"—keys to interpretation—for the readily available Signet reprintings of five of the best novels from *Main Street* to *Dodsworth*. Yet one should also read the article by Davis for suggestions of biases and discrepancies that Davis finds in Schorer's work.

One can look to Grace Lewis for a nostalgic account of her first husband, to Dorothy Thompson for two perceptive sketches of the man, to Sheean for Lewis's years with Thompson, and to *From Main Street to Stockholm* for letters that reveal personal and literary relationships. Miller's memoir is vivid and sympathetic, and one can find Lewis's informal comments on life and literature in Stevens, Austin, and Manfred, conveying his human concern, which is confirmed in Howe, in Aaron ("Proud Prejudices"), and in Thomas Wolfe's fictional Lewis as Lloyd McHarg in *You Can't Go Home Again*.

There are good introductions to Lewis by Grebstein and Dooley. For Grebstein, Lewis was the "conscience of his generation," the Lynds's *Middletown* being but an "extended footnote" to the novelist's achievement. Flanagan explores the Minnesota settings of the fiction. Lundquist gives attention to Lewis's childhood there, that "stage on which Lewis saw being acted out those dramas most crucial to his conception of our eternal warfare with stupidity." Lundquist has also published a checklist which reaches to 1970 and has edited the valuable *Sinclair Lewis Newsletter*.

Geismar wrote an early negative though thorough assessment, calling Lewis the "Eternal Amateur." Cantwell had reservations about Lewis but praised his spacious and bold undertaking. There are other helpful assessments by Whipple and Kazin, and two recent revaluations by Douglas. Love finds in Lewis's image of the West a pattern of conflict between the pioneering myth and technology, and Lea provides an outline of the implied past against which Lewis measured the present. See Batchelor for Lewis's maps of Winnemac and Zenith.

For an analysis of Lewis as satirist, see Friedman, Brown, and Petrullo, and for romance motifs Holman, Robert Lewis, Moore, and Light (*The Quixotic Vision*). Several critics discuss Lewis as a writer of social fiction: Conroy, Hilfer, Tuttleton, Daniels, and Millgate, noting dissociation and remarking on his limited point of view, but acknowledging his skillful depiction of the social matrix. James S. Measell has written a useful description of early editions of the novels.

MAJOR WORKS

Our Mr. Wrenn. New York: Harper, 1914. [novel]
The Trail of the Hawk. New York: Harper, 1915. [novel]
The Job. New York: Harper, 1917. [novel]
The Innocents. New York: Harper, 1917. [novel]
Free Air. New York: Harcourt, 1919. [novel]
Main Street. New York: Harcourt, 1920. [novel]
Babbitt. New York: Harcourt, 1922. [novel]
Arrowsmith. New York: Harcourt, 1925. [novel]
Mantrap. New York: Harcourt, 1926. [novel]
Elmer Gantry. Harcourt, 1927. [novel]
The Man Who Knew Coolidge. New York: Harcourt, 1928. [novel]
Dodsworth. New York: Harcourt, 1929. [novel]
Ann Vickers. Garden City, N.Y.: Doubleday, 1933. [novel]
Work of Art. Garden City, N.Y.: Doubleday, 1934. [novel]
Jayhawker. In collaboration with Lloyd Lewis. Garden City, N.Y.: Doubleday, 1935. [play]
Selected Short Stories. Garden City, N.Y.: Doubleday, 1935.
It Can't Happen Here. Garden City, N.Y.: Doubleday, 1935. [novel]
The Prodigal Parents. Garden City, N.Y.: Doubleday, 1938. [novel]
Bethel Merriday. Garden City, N.Y.: Doubleday, 1940. [novel]
Gideon Planish. New York: Random House, 1943. [novel]
Cass Timberlane. New York: Random House, 1945. [novel]
Kingsblood Royal. New York: Random House, 1947. [novel]
The God-Seeker. New York: Random House, 1949. [novel]
World So Wide. New York: Random House, 1951. [novel]
The Man from Main Street: Selected Essays and Other Writings, 1904–1950. Ed. by Harry E. Maule and Melville H. Cane. New York: Random House, 1953.
I'm a Stranger Here Myself and Other Stories. Selected, with an Introduction, by Mark Schorer. New York: Dell, 1962.

CHECKLIST OF SECONDARY SOURCES

Burke; Herzberg; *LHUS; OCAL;* Pownall; Quinn; *TCA & Supp.*

Aaron, Daniel. "Proud Prejudices of Sinclair Lewis." *Reporter*, 9 (Aug. 4, 1953), 37–39.
———. "Sinclair Lewis, *Main Street*." In *The American Novel*. Ed. Wallace Stegner. New York: Basic Books, 1965.
Anderson, Sherwood. "Four American Impressions." *NR*, (Oct. 11, 1922), 171–73.
Ausmus, Martin R. "Sinclair Lewis, *Dodsworth*, and the Fallacy of Reputation." *BA*, 34 (Autumn 1960), 349–55.

Austin, Allen. "An Interview with Sinclair Lewis." *UR*, 24 (Mar. 1958), 199–210.

Austin, James C. "Sinclair Lewis and Western Humor. In *American Dreams and American Nightmares*. Ed. David Madden. Carbondale: Southern Illinois U., 1970.

Babcock, C. Merton. "Americanisms in the Novels of Sinclair Lewis." *AS*, 35 (May 1960), 110–16.

Barry, James D. *"Dodsworth:* Sinclair Lewis's Novel of Character." *BSUF*, 10 (Spring 1969), 8–14.

Batchelor, Helen. "A Sinclair Lewis Portfolio of Maps: Zenith to Winnemac." *MLQ*, 32 (Dec. 1971), 401–8. (20 plates.)

Beck, Warren. "How Good Is Sinclair Lewis?" *CE*, 9 (Jan. 1948), 173–80.

Benét, William Rose. "The Earlier Lewis." *SatR* (Jan. 20, 1934), 421–22.

Breasted, Charles. "The 'Sauk-Centricities' of Sinclair Lewis." *SatR* (Aug. 14, 1954), 7–8.

Brown, Daniel R. "Lewis's Satire—A Negative Emphasis." *Renascence*, 18 (Winter 1966), 63–72.

Bucco, Martin. "The Serialized Novels of Sinclair Lewis." *WAL*, 4 (Spring 1969), 29–37.

Cantwell, Robert. "Sinclair Lewis." In *After the Genteel Tradition*. Ed. Malcolm Cowley. New York: Norton, 1937.

Carpenter, Frederick I. "Sinclair Lewis and the Fortress of Reality." *CE*, 16 (Apr. 1955), 416–23.

Coard, Robert L. "Names in the Fiction of Sinclair Lewis." *GaR*, 16 (Fall 1962), 318–29.

––––––. *"Babbitt*: The Sound Track of a Satire." *SLN*, 5–6 (1973–74), 1–4.

––––––. "Sinclair Lewis's *Kingsblood Royal:* A Thesis Novel for the Forties." *SLN*, 7–8 (1975–76), 10–17.

Coleman, Arthur B. "The Genesis of Social Ideas in Sinclair Lewis." Ph.D. diss., New York U., 1954.

Conroy, Stephen S. "Sinclair Lewis's Sociological Imagination." *AL*, 42 (Nov. 1970), 348–62.

Couch, William, Jr. "The Emergence, Rise and Decline of the Reputation of Sinclair Lewis." Ph.D. diss., U. Chicago, 1955.

––––––. "Sinclair Lewis: Crisis in the American Dream." *CLAJ*, 7 (Mar. 1964), 224–34.

Daniels, Howell. "Sinclair Lewis and the Drama of Dissociation." In *The American Novel and the Nineteen Twenties*. Stratford-upon-Avon Studies, 13. Eds. Malcolm Bradbury and David Palmer. London: Arnold, 1971.

Davis, Jack L. "Mark Schorer's Sinclair Lewis." *SLN*, 3 (1971), 3–9.

Dooley, D. J. *The Art of Sinclair Lewis*. Lincoln: U. Nebraska, 1967.

Douglas, George H. *"Babbitt* at Fifty—The Truth Still Hurts." *Nation* (May 22, 1972), 661–62.

––––––. *"Main Street* After Fifty Years." *PrS*, 44 (Winter 1970), 338–48.

Fife, Jim L. "Two Views of the American West." *WAL*, 1 (1966) 34–43.

Flanagan, John T. "A Long Way to Gopher Prairie: Sinclair Lewis's Apprenticeship." *SWR*, 32 (Autumn 1947), 403–13.

––––––. "The Minnesota Backgrounds of Sinclair Lewis' Fiction." *MH*, 37 (Mar. 1960), 1–13.

Fleissner, Robert F. "L'Affaire Sinclair Lewis: 'Anti-Semitism?' and Ancillary Matters." *SLN*, 4 (1972), 14–16.

––––––. " 'Something out of Dickens' in Sinclair Lewis." *BNYPL*, 74 (Nov. 1970), 607–16.

Friedman, Philip A. "Babbitt: Satiric Realism in Form and Content." *SNL*, 4 (Fall 1966), 20–29.

Fyvel, T. R. "Martin Arrowsmith and His Habitat." *NR* (July 18, 1955), 16–18.

Geismar, Maxwell. "Diarist of the Middle Class Mind" and "A Postscript." In *American Moderns: From Rebellion to Conformity*. New York: Hill & Wang, 1958.

––––––. "Sinclair Lewis: The Cosmic Bourjoyce." In *The Last of the Provincials: The American Novel 1915–1925*. Boston: Houghton Mifflin, 1947.

Grebstein, Sheldon N. "The Education of a Rebel: Sinclair Lewis at Yale." *NEQ*, 28 (Sept. 1955), 372–82.

––––––. *Sinclair Lewis*. New York: Twayne, 1962.

––––––. "Sinclair Lewis' Minnesota Boyhood." *MH*, 34 (Autumn 1954), 85–89.

––––––. "Sinclair Lewis's Unwritten Novel." *PQ*, 37 (Oct. 1958), 400–9.

Griffin, Robert J. "Sinclair Lewis." In *American Winners of the Nobel Literary Prize*. Eds. Warren G. French and Walter E. Kidd. Norman: U. Oklahoma, 1968.

———, ed. *Twentieth Century Interpretations of "Arrowsmith."* Englewood Cliffs, N.J.: Prentice-Hall, 1968.

Gurko, Leo and Miriam Gurko. "The Two Main Streets of Sinclair Lewis." *CE*, 4 (Feb. 1943), 288–92.

Hakutani, Yoshinobu. "Sinclair Lewis and Dreiser: A Study in Continuity and Development." *Discourse*, 7 (Summer 1964), 254–76.

Helleberg, Marilyn M. "The Paper-Doll Characters of Sinclair Lewis' *Arrowsmith*." *MTJ*, 14 (1969), 17–21.

Hilfer, Anthony C. "Caricaturist of the Village Mind" and "Elmer Gantry and That Old Time Religion." In *The Revolt from the Village*. Chapel Hill: U. North Carolina, 1969.

Hoffman, Frederick J. "Sinclair Lewis's Babbitt." In *The Twenties: American Writing in the Postwar Decade*. New York: Viking, 1955.

Holman, C. Hugh. "Anodyne for the Village Virus." In *The Comic Imagination in American Literature*. Ed. Louis D. Rubin, Jr. New Brunswick, N.J.: Rutgers U., 1973.

Howe, Irving. "The World He Mimicked Was His Own." *NYTBR*, Oct. 1, 1961, p. 1.

Ianni, Lawrence A. "Sinclair Lewis's America. Ph.D. diss., Case Western Reserve U., 1962.

Kazin, Alfred. "The New Realism: Sinclair Lewis." In *On Native Grounds*. New York: Reynal and Hitchcock, 1942.

———. "Poor Old Red." *Reporter*, 25 (Nov. 9, 1961), 60–64.

Lea, James. "Sinclair Lewis and the Implied America." *Clio*, 3 (1973), 21–34.

Lewis, Grace H. *With Love from Gracie: Sinclair Lewis, 1912–1925*. New York: Harcourt, 1955.

Lewis, Robert W. "*Babbitt* and the Dream of Romance." *NDQ*, 40 (Winter 1972), 7–14.

Light, Martin. "H.G. Wells and Sinclair Lewis: Friendship, Literary Influence, and Letters." *ELT*, 5 (1962), 1–20.

———. "Lewis' Finicky Girls and Faithful Workers." *UR*, 30 (Winter 1963), 151–59.

———. *The Quixotic Vision of Sinclair Lewis*. W. Lafayette, Ind.: Purdue U., 1975.

———, ed. *Studies in "Babbitt."* Columbus, Ohio: Merrill, 1971.

Love, Glen A. "New Pioneering on the Prairies: Nature, Progress and the Individual in the Novels of Sinclair Lewis. *AQ*, 25 (Dec. 1973), 558–77.

Lundquist, James. *Checklist of Sinclair Lewis*. Columbus, Ohio: Merrill, 1970.

———. *Guide to Sinclair Lewis*. Columbus, Ohio: Merrill, 1970.

———. *Sinclair Lewis*. New York: Ungar, 1973.

Maglin, Nan B. "Women in Three Sinclair Lewis Novels." *MassR*, 14 (Autumn 1973), 783–801.

Manfred, Frederick F. "Sinclair Lewis: A Portrait" *ASch*, 23 (Spring 1954), 162–84.

Measell, James S. "A Descriptive Catalogue of Sinclair Lewis's Novels." *SLN*, 7–8 (1975–76), 2–5.

Miller, Perry. "The Incorruptible Sinclair Lewis." *Atl*, 187 (Apr. 1951), 30–34.

Millgate, Michael. "Sherwood Anderson and Sinclair Lewis." In *American Social Fiction, James to Cozzens*. Edinburgh: Oliver and Boyd, 1964.

Moodie, Clara L. "The Short Stories and Sinclair Lewis' Literary Development." *SSF*, 12 (Spring 1975), 99–107. [with checklist of stories]

Moore, Geoffrey. "Sinclair Lewis: A Lost Romantic." In *The Young Rebel in American Literature*. Ed. Carl Bode. London: Heinemann, 1959.

O'Connor, Richard. *Sinclair Lewis*. New York: McGraw-Hill, 1971.

Petrullo, Helen B. "*Babbitt* as Situational Satire." *KQ*, 1 (Summer 1969), 89–97.

———. "*Main Street, Cass Timberlane* and Determinism." *SDR*, 7 (Winter 1969–70), 30–42.

Quivey, James R. "George Babbitt's Quest for Masculinity." *BSUF*, 10 (1969), 4–7.

Richardson, Lyon N. "*Arrowsmith*: Genesis, Development, Versions." *AL*, 27 (May 1955), 225–44.

Rogal, Samuel J. "The Hymns and Gospel-Songs in *Elmer Gantry*." *SLN*, 4 (1972), 4–8.

Rosenberg, Charles E. "Martin Arrowsmith: The Scientist as Hero." *AQ*, 15 (Fall 1963), 447–58.

Schorer, Mark. "The Burdens of Biography." *To the Young Writer*. Ed. A. L. Baden. Ann Arbor: U. Michigan, 1965.

———. "The Monstrous Self-Deception of Elmer Gantry." *NR*, (Oct. 31, 1955), 13–15.

———. *Sinclair Lewis*. University of Minnesota Pamphlets on American Writers, no. 27. Minneapolis: U. Minnesota, 1963.

———. *Sinclair Lewis: An American Life*. New York: McGraw-Hill, 1961.

———. "Sinclair Lewis and the Method of Half Truths." In *Society and Self in the Novel*. English Institute Essays. Ed. Mark Schorer. New York: Columbia U., 1955.

———. "Sinclair Lewis: *Babbitt*." In *Landmarks of American Writing*. Ed. Hennig Cohen. New York: Basic Books, 1969.

———. "Two Houses, Two Ways: The Florentine Villas of Lewis and Lawrence Respectively." In *New World Writing*. Fourth Mentor Selection. New York: New American Library, 1953.

———. "The World of Sinclair Lewis." *NR*, (Apr. 6, 1953), 18–20.

Schorer, Mark, ed. "A Minnesota Diary." *Esquire*, 50 (Oct. 1958), 160–62.

———. *Sinclair Lewis: A Collection of Critical Essays*. Englewood Cliffs, N.J.: Prentice-Hall, 1962.

Sheean, Vincent. *Dorothy and Red*. Boston: Houghton Mifflin, 1963.

Sinclair Lewis Newsletter. St. Cloud, Minn.: St. Cloud State Col., 1969–

Smith, Harrison, ed. *From Main Street to Stockholm: Letters of Sinclair Lewis, 1919–1930*. New York: Harcourt, 1952.

Stevens, Betty. "A Village Radical Goes Home." *Venture*, 2 (Summer 1956), 17–26.

———. "A Village Radical: His Last American Home." *Venture*, 2 (Winter 1957), 35–48.

Stolberg, Benjamin. "Sinclair Lewis." *AmMerc*, 53 (Oct. 1941), 450–60.

Tanselle, G. Thomas. "Sinclair Lewis and Floyd Dell: Two Views of the Midwest." *TCL*, 9 (Jan. 1964), 175–84.

Thompson, Dorothy. "The Boy and Man from Sauk Centre." *Atl*, 206 (Nov. 1960) 39–48.

———. "Sinclair Lewis: A Postscript." *Atl*, 187 (June 1951), 73–74.

Tuttleton, James W. "Sinclair Lewis: The Romantic Comedian as Realist Mimic." In *The Novel of Manners in America*. Chapel Hill: U. North Carolina, 1972.

West, Rebecca. "Sinclair Lewis Introduces Elmer Gantry." In *The Strange Necessity*. New York: Doubleday, 1928.

Whipple, Thomas K. "Sinclair Lewis." In *Spokesmen*. New York: Appleton, 1928.

Yoshida, Hiroshige. *A Sinclair Lewis Lexicon with a Critical Study of His Style and Method*. Tokyo: Hoyu, 1976.

Martin Light
Purdue University
West Lafayette, Indiana

VACHEL LINDSAY (1879–1931)

When Nicholas Vachel Lindsay of Springfield, Illinois, committed suicide in 1931, he had lost most of his popularity. The audiences at his readings (the "higher vaudeville," he called them) had totalled perhaps a million people, and his first volumes of poetry had respectable sales. Considered an important poet by his contemporaries and by such eminent critics as F. O. Matthiessen, who included six Lindsay poems in *The Oxford Book of American Verse*, his reputation had sunk so low by 1965 that one major anthology of American poetry published that year neglected him entirely. Now Lindsay's reputation appears to be rising, with new interest being expressed in him both as a poet and as a fighter for progressive causes. Many critics now believe that Lindsay was a vital force in American literature between 1912 and 1925, when most of his work appeared.

Harriet Monroe's *Poetry* made him famous in 1912 when it published his first important poem, "General William Booth Enters Into Heaven," and in a few years poems like "The Congo" made him a renowned figure on the lecture circuit, although he later came to hate reciting the same popular pieces over and over again. The biographies emphasize the tragic circumstances of the poet's later life, which finally ended in suicide.

For a quick introduction to Lindsay's work, the *Collected Poems* of 1925, which contains his whimsical drawings, and the *Selected Poems*, edited by Mark Harris, are the best and most available editions. Massa's critical work is a detailed study of his philosophical development and contains a useful bibliography. The following selective bibliography includes most important primary and secondary sources. It does not include reviews, minor sources of letters, and some minor collections of other Lindsay material. Other comments on Lindsay appear in most standard histories of American literature and of the Chicago Renaissance. There is no standard, published collection of Lindsay letters, but the libraries of the University of Chicago, University of Virginia, Indiana University, Baylor University, and Dartmouth College are major repositories, as is the collection of the Lindsay home in Springfield, Illinois, which is operated as a shrine by the Vachel Lindsay Association.

MAJOR WORKS

Rhymes to be Traded for Bread. Springfield, Ill.: privately printed, 1912.
General William Booth Enters Into Heaven and Other Poems. New York: Kennerly, 1913.
The Congo and Other Poems. New York: Kennerly, 1914.
Adventures While Preaching the Gospel of Beauty. New York: Kennerly, 1914. [autobiography]
The Art of the Moving Pictures. New York: Macmillan, 1916. [criticism]
A Handy Guide for Beggars. New York: Macmillan, 1916. [autobiography, poetry]
The Chinese Nightingale and Other Poems. New York: Macmillan, 1917.
The Golden Whales of California. New York: Macmillan, 1920. [poetry]
The Golden Books of Springfield. New York: Macmillan, 1920. [poetry]
The Daniel Jazz and Other Poems. London: Bell, 1920.
Collected Poems. New York: Macmillan, 1923. [ill. ed., 1925]
The Candle in the Cabin. New York: Appleton, 1923. [poetry]
Going-to-the-Sun. New York: Appleton, 1923. [poetry]
Going-to-the-Stars. New York: Appleton, 1926. [poetry]
Johnny Appleseed and Other Poems. New York: Macmillan, 1928.
Rigmarole, Rigmarole. New York: Random House, 1929. [poetry]
The Litany of Washington Street. New York: Macmillan, 1929. [nonfiction, criticism]
Every Soul is a Circus. New York: Macmillan, 1929. [poetry]
Selected Poems of Vachel Lindsay. Ed. Hazelton Spencer. New York: Macmillan, 1931.
Selected Poems of Vachel Lindsay. Ed. Mark Harris. New York: Macmillan, 1963.
Adventures, Rhymes, and Designs. Introd. Robert F. Sayre. New York: Eakins, 1968. [poetry, short prose pieces]

CHECKLIST OF SECONDARY SOURCES

Anon. "An Evangelist in Rhyme." *Nation*, 103 (Dec. 16, 1931), 658.

———. "Mr. Vachel Lindsay Explains America." *LA*, 308 (Dec. 11, 1920), 671–73.

———. "Vachel Lindsay." *SatR*, 8 (Jan. 9. 1932), 437.

———. "Vachel Lindsay Sees a New Heaven Descending Upon the Earth." *CO*, 69 (Sept. 1920), 371–73.

———. "Why Vachel Lindsay Swears by the Log Cabin." *LD*, 88 (Feb. 20, 1926), 50.

Aiken, Conrad. "A Letter from Vachel Lindsay." *Bookman*, 74 (Mar. 1932), 598–601.

Amacher, Richard E. "Lindsay's *The Sante-Fe Trail*." *Explicator*, 5 (Mar. 1947), 33.

———. "Off 'The Sante-Fe Trail.' " *AL*, 20 (Nov. 1948), 337.

Ames, Van Meter. "Vachel Lindsay—or, My Heart is a Kicking Horse." *Midway*, 8 (1968), 63–70.

Anderson, Sherwood. "Lindsay and Masters." *NR*, 85 (Dec. 25, 1935), 194–95.

Armstrong, A. Joseph. "Letters of Vachel Lindsay to A. Joseph Armstrong." *BayB*, 43 (Sept. 1940), 1–121.

———. "Vachel Lindsay as I Knew Him." *MTQ*, 5 (Fall-Winter, 1942–43), 5–11.

Bader, A. L. "Lindsay Explains 'The Congo.' " *PQ*, 28 (Apr. 1948), 190–92.

———. "Vachel Lindsay on 'The Sante-Fe Trail.' " *AL*, 19 (Jan. 1948), 360.

Bartlett, A. H. "Voices from the Great Inland States (Sandburg and Lindsay)." *PoetryR*, 15 (Mar.–Apr., 1915), 101–10.

Benjamin, P. L. "Vachel Lindsay—A Folk Poet." *Survey*, 47 (Oct. 15, 1921), 73–74.

Bradbury, David L. "Vachel Lindsay and His Heroes." *ISUJ*, 32 (1969), 22–57.

Byrd, Cecil K. "Check List of the Melcher Lindsay Collection." *IUB*, 5 (1960), 64–106.

Cady, Edwin H. "Vachel Lindsay Across the Chasm." *IUB*, 5 (1960), 12–20.

Casmer, Carl. "Three Aprils and a Poet." *Atl*, 197 (Apr. 1955), 69–71.

Chénetier, Marc. "Knights in Disguise: Lindsay and Maiakovsky as Poets of the People." *M- 4 II* (1975), 47–62.

Davies, Charles and Llewellyn Lucas. "Two Aspects of Vachel Lindsay." *P&P*, 11 (Sept.–Nov. 1927), 294–303.

De Casseres, B. "Five Portraits on Galvanized Iron." *AmMerc*, 9 (Dec. 1926), 396–97.

Drinkwater, John. "Two American Lives." *QR* (London), 266 (Jan. 1936), 122–35.

Edwards, Davis. "The Real Source of Vachel Lindsay's Poetic Technique." *QJS*, 33 (Apr. 1947), 182–95.

Flanagan, John T. "Three Illinois Poets." *CR*, 16 (1972), 313–27.

———, ed. *Profile of Vachel Lindsay*. Columbus, Ohio: Merrill, 1970. [contains several important articles not enumerated in this checklist]

Fowler, Elizabeth T. "Annotated Edition of the Letters of Vachel Lindsay to Nellie Viera." Ph.D. diss., U. Tennessee, 1968.

Frank, Glenn. "The Rodin of American Poetry." *Century*, 102 (Aug. 1921), 638–40.

Gillilend, Marshall A. "Vachel Lindsay: Poet and Newspaper Columnist in Spokane, 1924–1929." Ph.D. diss., Washington State U., 1968.

Graham, Stephen. *Tramping with a Poet in the Rockies*. London: Macmillan, 1922.

Hallwas, John and Dennis Reader, eds. *The Vision of This Land: Studies of Vachel Lindsay, Edgar Lee Masters, and Carl Sandburg*. Macomb: Western Illinois U., 1976.

Harris, Mark. *City of Discontent*. Indianapolis: Bobbs-Merrill, 1952.

Heffernan, Miriam W. "The Ideas and Methods of Vachel Lindsay." *DA* (1949), 149.

Lee, C.P. "Adulation and the Artist." *SatR*, 22 (Aug. 19, 1940), 7.

Massa, Ann. *Vachel Lindsay: Field Worker for the American Dream*. Bloomington, Ind.: Indiana U., 1970.

———. "The Artistic Consciousness of Vachel Lindsay." *JAmS*, 2 (1968), 239–53.

Masters, Edgar Lee. "Vachel Lindsay." *Bookman*, 64 (Oct. 1926), 156–60.

———. "Vachel Lindsay and America." *SatR*, 12 (Aug. 10, 1935), 3–4.

———. *Vachel Lindsay, a Poet in America*. New York: Scribner, 1935.

Monroe, Harriet. "Notes and Queries from Mr. Lindsay." *Poetry*, 17 (Feb. 1921), 262–66.

O'Connor, N. J. "Vachel Lindsay: Poet-Prophet of the Middle West." *Landmark*, 2 (Dec. 1920), 805–8.

Orel, Harold. "Lindsay and the Blood of the Lamb." *UKCR.* 25 (Autumn 1958), 13–17.
Purkey, Raymond. *Vachel Lindsay.* Paris: Librairie A.-G. Nizet, 1968.
Rittenhouse, Jessie L. "Vachel Lindsay." *SAQ,* 32 (July 1933), 266–82.
Ruggles, Eleanor. *The West-Going Heart: A Life of Vachel Lindsay.* New York: Norton, 1959.
Scouffas, George. "Vachel Lindsay: A Student In Retreat and Repudiation." *DA* (1951), 226.
Starke, Aubrey et al. "They Knew Vachel Lindsay: A Symposium of Personal Reminiscences." *LQ,* 1 (Aug. 1934), 128–40.
Tanselle, G. Thomas. "Vachel Lindsay Writes to Floyd Dell." *JISHS,* 58 (1946), 366–79.
Tietjens, Eunice. "Bids for Premature Judgment." *Poetry,* 22 (Sept. 1923), 330–33.
Trombly, Albert E. *Vachel Lindsay, Adventurer.* Columbia, Mo.: Lucas Brothers, 1929.
Whitney, Blair. "Vachel Lindsay: The Midwest as Utopia." *M-A I* (1974), 16–21.
Wilkinson, Marguerite. "Poets of the People." *Touchstone,* 2 (Feb. 1918), 510–12.
Winberly, L. C. "Vachel Lindsay." *FM,* 14 (Mar. 1934), 212–26.
Yatron, Michael. *America's Literary Revolt.* New York: Philosophical Library, 1959.
———. "The Influence of Populism on Edgar Lee Masters, Vachel Lindsay, and Carl Sandburg." Ph.D. diss., Temple U., 1957.

Blair Whitney
Illinois Board of Higher Education
Springfield, Illinois

DAVID ROSS LOCKE
[PETROLEUM V. NASBY] (1833–88)

As a journalist, Locke wrote much that went unsigned; it would be impossible to collect it all. The most important sources for both his works and information about him are the files of the newspapers he edited: Cortland, New York, *Democrat,* 1845–50; Corning, New York, *Fountain of Temperance,* 1850; Pittsburgh *Chronicle,* 1851–53; Plymouth, Ohio, *Advertiser,* 1853–55; Mansfield, Ohio, *Herald,* 1855–56; Bucyrus, Ohio, *Journal,* 1856–61; Findlay, Ohio, *Hancock Jeffersonian,* 1861–65; Toledo, Ohio, *Blade,* 1865–88; Toledo *Weekly Blade,* 1865–88; New York *Evening Mail,* 1871–79. To this should be added *Locke's National Monthly,* 1872–76.

During his lifetime he was very famous, especially as Petroleum V. Nasby, newspaper humorist and lecturer. Furthermore, he was a leading citizen of Toledo, Ohio, and he made the Toledo *Blade* one of the most widely read newspapers in the Midwest. References to him, often unreliable, are frequent in newspapers, reminiscences, anthologies, and local histories of the latter nineteenth century. But aside from Blair's coverage there were only few and specialized scholarly studies of him before Harrison's thesis in 1961, followed up in 1969 by his biography. In the meantime came Austin's literary analysis and some noteworthy work by Jones, including his introduction to a new edition of Locke's *The Struggles of Petroleum V. Nasby* (1963). There has hardly been a great upsurge of interest in Locke, but at least we now have the scholarly groundwork. Furthermore, selections from Nasby are commonly in print in anthologies and pamphlets, and references to him, often trenchant, occur in most studies of the tradition of American humor. Critical opinion of Locke today ranges from that of Kenneth Lynn, who finds him one of those "dull phunny phellows," to that of Austin, who considers him "a political satirist rivaled only by Franklin . . . in American history."

Major Works

The Nasby Papers. Indianapolis: Perrine, 1864. [humor]
Divers Views, Opinions, and Prophecies of Yours Trooly, Petroleum V. Nasby. Cincinnati: Carrol, 1866. [humor]
Androo Johnson, His Life. New York: J. C. Haney, 1866. [humor]
Swingin' Round the Cirkle. Boston: Lee and Shepard, 1867. [humor]
Ekkoes from Kentucky. Boston: Lee and Shepard, 1868. [humor]
The Impendin Crisis uv the Democracy. Toledo: Miller, Locke, 1868. [humor]
The Struggles (Social, Financial and Political) of Petroleum V. Nasby. Boston: I. N. Richardson, 1872. [humor]
The Morals of Abou Ben Adhem. Boston: Lee and Shepard, 1875. [humor]
Inflation at the Cross Roads. New York: American News, 1875. [humor]
The President's Policy. Toledo: Blade, 1877. [humor]
A Paper City. New York: Dillingham, 1879. [novel]
The Democratic John Bunyan. Toledo: Blade, 1880. [humor]
The Diary of an Office Seeker. Toledo: Blade, 1881. [humor]
Hannah Jane. Boston: Lee and Shepard, 1882. [poem]
Nasby in Exile; or, Six Months of Travel. Toledo: Locke, 1882. [humor-travel account]
Essay on Lincoln in *Reminiscences of Abraham Lincoln by Distinguished Men of His Time*. Ed. Allen Thorndike Rice. New York: North American, 1886. Pp. 439–53. [essay]
"Prohibition." *NAR*, 143 (Oct. 1886), 382–97. [essay]
The Struggles (Social, Financial and Political) of Petroleum V. Nasby. Boston: Lee and Shepard, 1888. [same as 1872 edition plus lectures.]
The Demagogue. Boston: Lee and Shepard, 1891. [novel]
The Nasby Letters. Toledo: Blade, 1893. [humor]

Checklist of Secondary Sources

Blanck; Burke; *CA; CB*; Herzberg; *OCAL*.

Anderson, David D. "The Odyssey of Petroleum V. Nasby." *OH*, 74 (Autumn 1965), 232–46.
Anon. *Toledo Weekly Blade (Nasby's Paper), Its Rise and Progress*. Toledo: Blade, 1885. [pamphlet]
Austin, James C. "David Ross Locke." *AmLitR: 1870–1910*, 4 (Spring 1971), 192–200.
———. *Petroleum V. Nasby*. New York: Twayne, 1965.
———. "The World of Petroleum V. Nasby: Blacks, Women, and Political Corruption." *M-A III* (1976), 101–22.
Blair, Walter. *Native American Humor (1800–1900)*. New York: American Book, 1937.
Clemens, Cyril. *Petroleum Vesuvius Nasby*. Webster Groves, Mo.: International Mark Twain Society, 1936.
Harrison, John M. "David Ross Locke and the Fight on Reconstruction." *JQ*, 39 (Autumn 1962), 491–99.
———. "David Ross Locke and the Fight on Reconstruction." Master's thesis, U. Iowa, 1961.
Harrison, John M. *The Man Who Made Nasby: David Ross Locke*. Chapel Hill: U. North Carolina, 1969.
Hooper, Osman C. *History of Ohio Journalism, 1793–1933*. Columbus: Ohio State U., 1933.
Hudson, Frederic. *Journalism in the United States*. New York: Harper, 1873. [interview with "Nasby"]

Humphrey, William D. *Findlay, the Story of a Community*. Findlay, Ohio: Findlay Printing and Supply, 1961.
Jones, Joseph. Introduction to David Ross Locke. *The Struggles of Petroleum V. Nasby*. Boston: Beacon, 1963.
————. "Petroleum V. Nasby Tries the Novel: David Ross Locke's Excursions into Political and Social Fiction." *TexSE*, 30 (1951), 202–18.
Killits, John M. *Toledo and Lucas County, Ohio, 1623–1923*. Chicago: Clarke, 1923.
Landon, Melville D. *Kings of the Platform and Pulpit*. Chicago: Smedley, 1891.
Marchman, Watt P. "David Ross Locke." *ME*, 30 (May 1957), 35–38.
Minor, Dennis E. "The Many Roles of Nasby." *MarkR*, 4 (1973), 16–20.
Mott, Frank Luther. *American Journalism*. New York: Macmillan, 1950.
————. *A History of American Magazines*. Cambridge: Harvard U., 1938–
Pond, James B. *Eccentricities of Genius*. New York: G. W. Dillingham, 1900.
Ransome, Jack C. "David Ross Locke, Civil War Propagandist." *NOQ*, 20 (Jan. 1948), 5–19.
————. "David Ross Locke, The Post-War Years." *NOQ*, 20 (Summer 1948), 144–58.
Taft, William H. "David Ross Locke: Forgotten Editor." *JQ*, 34 (Spring 1957), 202–7.
Toledo *Blade*, Feb. 15–20, 1888. [several articles]
Toledo *Weekly Blade*, Feb. 23, 1888. [several articles]

James C. Austin
Southern Illinois University at Edwardsville
Edwardsville, Illinois

ROSS LOCKRIDGE, JR. (1914–48)

The primary bibliography of Ross Lockridge, Jr., consists entirely of his novel *Raintree County*, his only published work. Similarly, his secondary bibliography would be unimpressive without Leggett's short biography. Young Lockridge, formerly a disciple of his historian father and later an English instructor at Simmons College, became a natural object of conjecture when he committed suicide at age thirty-three at the beginning of what seemed a promising career. Leggett makes this drop-out his theme and examines its causes.

The secondary bibliography printed here is representative in chronology and content. Reviews of *Raintree County* by outstanding literary figures are listed, plus an anonymous review from *Newsweek*, included because it and the one by Basso strongly upset Lockridge—a bio-bibliographical fact worth noting. Lee's review was his favorite. Tindall's article is unique in praising Lockridge from a strictly artistic standpoint.

Personal letters and sources used in writing the novel remain with the family. Those interested in previous writings by Lockridge will find the long epic poem he hoped to publish, *A Dream of the Flesh of Iron*, at Lilly Library, Bloomington; his M.A. thesis on Byron's *Don Juan* at the Indiana University Library; his text for a historical pageant held at New Harmony during several consecutive years in the late 1930s at the museum library in

New Harmony, Indiana; and a "booklet," *The Harrisons,* in his file at the Indiana University Alumni Office. A copy of the last item, attached to U.S. House Doc. No. 154 in 1941 by the Benjamin Harrison Memorial Commission, is held by the British Museum and listed in their catalogue under Lockridge's name.

Major Works

Raintree County. Boston: Houghton Mifflin, 1947. An abridgement was made by Edmund Fuller for Dell Books, 1957.

Checklist of Secondary Sources

Burke; *CA; CB;* Herzberg; *LLC; OCAL; TCA Supp.*

Basso, Hamilton. "Books." *NY,* 23 (Jan. 10, 1948), 72–73.

Dessner, Lawrence J. "Value in Popular Fiction: The Case of *Raintree County.*" *Junction,* 1 (Spring 1973), 147–52.

Hilton, James. "Flashing Vision of America Lost and Found." *NYHTBR,* Jan. 4, 1948, pp. 1–2.

"Indiana Epic." *Newsweek,* 31 (Jan. 19, 1948), 93–94.

Jones, Howard Mumford. "Indiana Reflection of U.S. 1844–92." *SatR,* 31 (Jan. 3, 1948), 9–10.

Kutner, Nanette. "Ross Lockridge, Jr.—Escape from Main Street." *SatR,* 31 (June 12, 1948), 6–7. Reprinted in *Saturday Review Gallery.* New York: Simon and Schuster, 1959. Pp. 387–93.

Lee, Charles. "Encompassing the American Spirit." *NYTBR,* Jan. 4, 1948, pp. 5, 21.

Leggett, John. *Ross and Tom.* New York: Simon and Schuster, 1974.

Lutwak, Leonard. "*Raintree County* and the Epicising Poet in American Fiction." *BSUF,* 13 (Winter 1972), 14–28.

Nemanic, Gerald C. "Ross Lockridge, *Raintree County,* and the Epic of Irony." *M-A II* (1975), 35–46.

Rock, Katrine Sorensen. "Ross Lockridge, Jr." *SatR,* 31 (Oct. 16, 1948), 25. [A letter in response to Kutner's article]

Roth, Philip. "Our War of the Roses." *NR,* 137 (Nov. 11, 1957), 22. [rev. of the MGM movie, *Raintree County*]

Tindall, William York. "Many-leveled Fiction: Virginia Woolf to Ross Lockridge." *CE,* 10 (Nov. 1948), 65–71.

Williams, Jay. "The Sex Book Dr. Kinsey Didn't Sign!" *Confidential,* 2 (Mar. 1954), 32–33.

Elizabeth Steele
University of Toledo
Toledo, Ohio

DELLA LUTES (1869?–1942)

In spite of the moderate acclaim which greeted her novels as they appeared, there has been no scholarly study of Lutes or her works published to date. Considering the subject of her novels, viz., farm life in southern Michigan, it is surprising that she is completely ignored by R. W. Meyer in his *The Middle Western Farm Novel in the Twentieth Century.* Biographical information is scanty, and those sources providing any give only the broadest outline of her life, as is evidenced in Burke; however, the best sketch is her obituary notice in the *New York Times*. There exists no checklist or bibliography of her works, and all lists of her novels given in the sources below are incomplete. Lutes's importance as a chronicler of Michigan rural life of the 1880s has not been fully realized.

MAJOR WORKS

Just Away. Cooperstown, N.Y.: Crist, Scott & Parshall, 1906. [novel]
My Boy in Khaki. New York: Harper, 1918. [novel]
The Country Kitchen. Boston: Little, Brown, 1936. [novel]
Home Grown. Boston: Little, Brown, 1937. [novel]
Millbrook. Boston: Little, Brown, 1938. [novel]
Gabriel's Search. Boston: Little, Brown, 1940. [novel]
Country Schoolma'am. Boston: Little, Brown, 1941. [novel]
Cousin William. Boston: Little, Brown, 1942. [novel]

CHECKLIST OF SECONDARY SOURCES

Burke; *LHUS*.

Abbott, Harriet C. "Michigan Farm Child." *NYHTBR*, Dec. 6, 1942, p. 5. [rev.]
Becker, May L. "Memories of Rural Michigan." *NYHTBR*, Aug. 17, 1941, p. 6. [rev.]
Benet, Rosemary. "Like a Currier and Ives Print." *NYHTBR*, Sept. 1, 1940, p. 3. [rev.]
Black, Albert G. *Michigan Novels: An Annotated Bibliography*. Ann Arbor: Michigan Council of Teachers of English, 1963. P. 37.
Canfield, Dorothy. Review of *Millbrook*. *Atl*, 163 (Jan. 1939), n.p.
Field, Louise M. "Pioneer Michigan." *NYTBR*, Sept. 1, 1940, p. 14. [rev.]
―――. "The Tables Groaned." *NYTBR*, Nov. 22, 1942, p. 40. [rev.]
Flanagan, John T. "The Middle Western Historical Novel." *JISHS*, 37 (Mar. 1944), 40.
Gillard, Kathleen I. *Our Michigan Heritage*. New York: Pageant 1955. Pp. 225–26, 247.
Moffett, Anita. "A Schoolma'am of the Eighteen Eighties." *NYTBR*, Aug. 24, 1941, p. 8. [rev.]
New York Times, July 14, 1942, p. 19. [obituary]
Patton, John. "Like a Country Kitchen." *NYHTBR*, Dec. 4, 1938, p. 24. [rev.]
Wallace, Margaret. "Tales of Life in a Michigan Village in the 1880's." *NYTBR*, Dec. 11, 1938, p. 5. [rev.]

Robert Beasecker
Grand Valley State Colleges
Allendale, Michigan

FREDERICK MANFRED [FEIKE FEIKEMA] (1912–   )

Manfred's books from 1944 to 1952 were published under the name of Feike Feikema. His own explanation of his two names is in "Feikema Explains Name Change," *Publishers Weekly*, 161 (May 3, 1952), p. 1834. The definitive study of Manfred undoubtedly awaits the end of an active writing career. His early novels (*Boy Almighty, The Primitive, The Brother, The Giant*) as well as his long poem, *Winter Count*, are semiautobiographical, and, in addition, often present comments on the writer's art which may be assumed to be those of Manfred himself. Paluka is definitive through 1966 for books and editions; this checklist supplements that as well as Kellogg's *Frederick Manfred: A Bibliography*. Manfred's papers ar' at the University of Minnesota, at the University of South Dakota (which also has tapes), and at his home at Luverne, which will become a part of the Minnesota Park system.

Through 1958 the best appraisal of Manfred's work is Milton's essay in the *Western Review*. Milton continues to comment on Manfred and we may expect more from his hand. DeBoer's thesis is particularly valuable because both DeBoer and Manfred spring from the same religious roots. *Western American Literature* notes annual accretions to the Manfred bibliography, and in addition offers critics space for essays on Manfred and his work.

Major Works

The Golden Bowl. St. Paul: Webb, 1944. [novel]
Boy Almighty. St. Paul: Itasca/Webb, 1945. [novel]
This is the Year. Garden City, N.Y.: Doubleday, 1947. [novel]
The Chokecherry Tree. Garden City, N.Y.: Doubleday, 1948. [novel]
The Primitive. Garden City, N.Y.: Doubleday, 1949. [novel]
The Brother. Garden City, N.Y.: Doubleday, 1950. [novel]
The Giant. Garden City, N.Y.: Doubleday, 1951. [novel]
Lord Grizzly. New York: McGraw-Hill, 1954. [novel]
Morning Red. Denver: Swallow, 1956. [romance]
Riders of Judgment. New York: Random House, 1957. [novel]
Conquering Hero. New York: McDowell, 1959. [novel]
Arrow of Love. Denver: Swallow, 1961. [three novelettes]
Wanderlust: A Trilogy. Denver: Swallow, 1962. [rev. eds. of *The Primitive; The Brother;* and *The Giant*]
Scarlet Plume. New York: Trident Press, 1964. [novel]
The Man Who Looked Like the Prince of Wales. New York: Trident Press, 1965. Reprinted 1967 as *The Secret Place*. [novel]
Winter Count: Poems 1934–1965. Minneapolis: James D. Thueson, 1966. [novel]
Apples of Paradise and Other Stories. New York: Trident Press, 1968.
Eden Prairie. New York: Trident Press, 1968. [novel]

Checklist of Secondary Sources

CA; CB; CN; TCA; Warfel.

Austin, James C. "Legend, Myth, and Symbol in Frederick Manfred's *Lord Grizzly*." *Critique*, 6 (Winter 1963–64), 122–30.
Bebeau, Don. "A Search for Voice: A Sense of Place in *The Golden Bowl*." *SDR*, 7 (Winter 1969–1970), 79–86.
Boeveld, Bernie F. *A Study of the Depression Genre Through the Fiction of Frederick Feikema Manfred*. Master's thesis, U. Wyoming, 1971.
Burckholder, Clyde. "Frederick Manfred as a Regional Novelist." Ph. D. diss., U. Nebraska 1972.
Byrd, Forrest. "Prolegomenon to Frederick Manfred." *DAI*, 36:5276A.
DeBoer, Peter P. "Frederick Feikema Manfred: Spiritual Naturalist." *RJ*, 13 (Apr. 1963), 19–23.
_____. *Frederick Manfred: The Developing Art of the Naturalist*. Master's thesis, U. Iowa, 1961.
"Feikema Explains Name Change." *PW*, 161 (May 3, 1952), 1834–35.

Flora, Joseph M. *Frederick Manfred.* Western Writers Series. Boise, Ida.: Department of English, Boise State College, 1974.

Fridsma, Bernard. "Frederick F. Manfred." *De Strikel: Moannebled,* 4 (Dec. 1958), 168–69.

Kellogg, George. *Frederick Manfred, a Bibliography.* Swallow pamphlet no. 17. Denver: Swallow. 1965. [a less complete list in *TCL,* April 1965]

Manfred, Frederick. "Backgrounds for Western Writing." *DWMR,* 17 (Aug. 1961), 4–11.

———. "The Evolution of a Name." *Names,* 2 (1954), 106–8.

———. "Frederick Manfred Talks About Sinclair Lewis." *SLN,* 2 (Spring 1970), 1–5.

———. "In Memoriam Address (On the Occasion of the Burial of Sinclair Lewis' Ashes in Sauk Centre, Minnesota, January 28, 1951)." *MinnLR,* 44 (Feb. 15, 1951), 3. Excerpted in the *NYT.* Jan. 29, 1959, p. 19.

———. "Sinclair Lewis: A Portrait." *ASch,* 23 (Spring 1954), 162–84.

———. "Some Notes on Sinclair Lewis' Funeral." *MinnR,* 3 (Fall 1962), 87–90.

———. "The Western Novel—A Symposium: Frederick Manfred." *SDR,* 2 (Autumn 1964), 7–9.

Meyer, Roy W. *The Middle Western Farm Novel in the Twentieth Century.* Lincoln: U. Nebraska, 1965. Pp. 122–26, *passim.*

Michael, Larry A. *Literary Allusions in the Fiction of Frederick Manfred.* Master's thesis, U. South Dakota, 1965.

Milton, John R. "The American Novel: The Search for Home, Tradition, and Identity." *WHR,* 16 (Spring 1962), 169–80.

———. *Conversations with Frederick Manfred.* Salt Lake City: U. Utah, 1974. [foreword by Wallace Stegner]

———. "Frederick Feikema Manfred." *WR,* 22 (Spring 1958), 181–99.

———. "The Inception of a Saga: Frederick Manfred's 'Buckskin Man.' " *SDR,* 7 (Winter 1969–70), 87–99.

———. "Interview With Frederick Manfred." *SDR,* 7 (Winter 1969–70), 110–30.

———. "*Lord Grizzly*: Rhythm, Form and Meaning in the Western Novel." *WAL,* 1 (1966), 6–14.

———. "The Novel and the American West." *SDR,* 2 (Autumn 1964), 56–76.

——— .. "Voice From Siouxland: Frederick Feikema Manfred." *CE,* 19 (Dec. 1957), 104–11.

———. "The Western Novel: Sources and Forms." *ChiR,* 16 (Summer 1963), 74–100.

Paluka, Frank. *Iowa Authors: A Bio-Bibliography of Sixty Native Writers.* Iowa City: Friends of the University of Iowa Libraries, 1967. Pp. 226–28.

Peet, Howard. "Evolution of a Man Named Fred." Master's thesis, Moorhead State College, Minnesota. 1965.

Pruett, Jacque Suzanne. "A Critical Analysis of 'Lord Grizzly.' " Master's thesis, Colorado State University, 1968.

Roth, Russell. "Is Manfred the Midwest's Faulkner?" *Minneapolis Sunday Tribune,* Aug. 1. 1954, Feature Section, p. 1.

Schorer, Mark. *Sinclair Lewis, an American Life.* New York: McGraw-Hill, 1961. Pp. 743–45.

Snipes, David. "Frederick Manfred's Autobiographical Trilogies: *World's Wanderer* and *Wanderlust.*" Ph.D. diss., U. North Carolina, 1974.

Sorenson, Charles Somner. "A Comparison of the Views of Hamsun, Rolvaag, and Feikema on Rural Society." Master's thesis, U. Iowa, 1955.

Spies, George Henry, III. "John Steinbeck's '*The Grapes of Wrath*' and Frederick Manfred's '*The Golden Bowl*': A Comparative Study." Ed.D. diss., Ball State U., 1973.

Swallow, Alan. "The Mavericks." *Critique,* 2 (Winter 1959), 88–92. Reprinted in *An Editor's Essays of Two Decades.* Seattle and Denver: Experiment Press, 1962. Pp. 353–57.

Ter Matt, Cornelius J. "Three Novelists and a Community: A Study of American Novelists with Dutch Calvinist Origins." Ph.D. diss., U. Michigan, 1963.

Timmerman, John. "Siouxland and Suburbia." *RJ,* 9 (Oct. 1959), 9–11.

Walker, Don D. "The Mountain Man as Literary Hero." *WAL,* 1 (1966), 15–25.

"West of the Mississippi: An Interview with Frederick Manfred." *Critique,* 2 (Winter 1959), 35–56.

Williams, John. "The 'Western': Definition of the Myth." *Nation* (Nov. 18, 1961), 401–5.
Wylder, D. E. "Manfred's Indian Novel." *SDR*, 7 (Winter 1969–70), 100–9.

Clarence A. Andrews
University of Iowa
Iowa City, Iowa

EDGAR LEE MASTERS (1869–1950)

Early enthusiastic appraisal of the poetry of Masters (Boynton, Lowell, Hansen, Monroe, Untermeyer) stressed his significance as one of the Chicago Renaissance realists in the "New Poetry" movement. From the beginning he was viewed as the author of one book of verse: *Spoon River Anthology*. His extensive later writings—in poetry, fiction, biography, and political essay—have elicited only meager critical attention over the years.

Altrocchi, Derleth, and Hertz have examined the relationship of Masters to the "Revolt from the Village" group. Coffin and Yatron have identified him with Populism. Literary historians continue to record the place of *Spoon River Anthology* in the "New Poetry" movement of the second decade of this century, but the reputation of Masters has steadily declined until the bibliography in recent years has become sparse indeed. When his work is considered at all any more, it is usually within the context of discussions of regionalism (Stauffer, McElderry) or in studies of the decline of the poetic importance of the Chicago poets as a group (Waggoner). There are no published full-length biographies or critical studies, although Masters has been the subject of at least five dissertations, of which those of Hartley and Flaccus are the most comprehensive. Hartley has also published articles on Masters's work as playwright, biographer, and political essayist. Flanagan's book is a useful survey of the criticism Masters's work has elicited through the years. The primary source of details about his life continues to be his autobiography, *Across Spoon River*. Recent renewed interest in the *Spoon River Anthology*—sparked partly by a dramatized version of the book produced on the stage and on national television—has not initiated any revival in Masters scholarship.

Major Works

A Book of Verses. Chicago: Way & Williams, 1898. [poems]
Maximilian. Boston: Badger, 1902. [play]
Spoon River Anthology. New York: Macmillan, 1915. [poems]
Songs and Satires. New York: Macmillan, 1916. [poems]
The Great Valley. New York: Macmillan, 1916. [poems]
Toward the Gulf. New York: Macmillan, 1918. [poems]

Starved Rock. New York: Macmillan, 1919. [poems]
Mitch Miller. New York: Macmillan, 1920. [novel]
Domesday Book. New York: Macmillan, 1920. [poems]
The Open Sea. New York: Macmillan, 1921. [poems]
Children of the Market Place. New York: Macmillan, 1922. [novel]
Skeeters Kirby. New York: Macmillan, 1923. [novel]
The Nuptial Flight. New York: Boni & Liveright, 1923. [novel]
Mirage. New York: Boni & Liveright, 1924. [novel]
The New Spoon River. New York: Boni & Liveright, 1924. [poems]
Selected Poems. New York: Macmillan, 1925. [poems]
Lee: A Dramatic Poem. New York: Macmillan, 1926. [verse play]
Kit O'Brien. New York: Boni & Liveright, 1927. [novel]
Levy Mayer and the New Industrial Era. New Haven: Yale U., 1927. [biography]
Jack Kelso: A Dramatic Poem. New York: Appleton, 1928. [verse play]
The Fate of the Jury: An Epilogue to Domesday Book. New York: Appleton, 1929. [poems]
Lichee Nuts. New York: Liveright, 1930. [poems]
Gettysburg, Manila, Acoma. New York: Liveright, 1930. [plays]
Lincoln, the Man. New York: Dodd, Mead, 1931. [biography]
Godbey: A Dramatic Poem. New York: Dodd, Mead, 1931. [verse play]
The Tale of Chicago. New York: Putnam, 1933. [history]
Dramatic Duologues. New York: French, 1934. [plays]
Richmond: A Dramatic Poem. New York: French, 1934. [verse play]
Invisibles Landscapes. New York: Macmillan, 1935. [poems]
Vachel Lindsay: A Poet in America. New York: Scribner, 1935. [biography]
Poems of People. New York: Appleton, 1936. [poems]
Across Spoon River. New York: Farrar, 1936. [autobiography]
Walt Whitman. New York: Scribner, 1937. [biography]
The Tide of Time. New York: Farrar, 1937. [novel]
The New World. New York: Appleton 1937. [epic poem]
Mark Twain, A Portrait. New York: Scribner, 1938. [biography]
More People. New York: Appleton, 1939. [poems]
The Sangamon. New York: Farrar, 1942. [regional history]

CHECKLIST OF SECONDARY SOURCES

Burke; Herzberg; *LHUS; OCAL;* Quinn; *TCA & Supp.*

Altrocchi, Rudolph. "Edgar Lee Masters and Joinville." *MLN*, 45 (June 1930), 360–62.
Anderson, Sherwood. "Lindsay and Masters." *NR*, 85 (Dec. 25, 1935), 194–95.
Boynton, P. H. "The Voice of Chicago: Edgar Lee Masters and Carl Sandburg." *EJ*, 11 (Dec. 1922), 610–20.
Chandler, J. C. "Mr. Masters' 'Spoon River.' " *UR*, 2 (Winter 1935), 92–95.
Childs, Herbert E. "Agrarianism and Sex: Edgar Lee Masters and the Modern Spirit." *SatR*, 41 (July-Sept. 1933), 331–42.
Coffin, R. P. T. "Poets of the People." *VQR*, 13 (Jan. 1937), 126–31.
Crawford, John W. "A Defense of 'A One-Eyed View.' " *CEA*, 31 (Feb. 1969), 14–15.
_____. "Naturalistic Tendencies in *Spoon River Anthology.*" *CEA*, 30 (June 1968), 6.
Derleth, August. "Masters and the Revolt from the Village." *ColQ*, 8 (Autumn 1959), 164–67.
_____. "Three Literary Men: A Memoir of Sinclair Lewis, Sherwood Anderson, and Edgar Lee Masters." *ArtsS*, 14 (Winter 1959), 11–46.
DuBois, A. E. "Lindsay, and Especially Masters." *SatR*, 44 (July-Sept. 1936), 377–82.
Duffy, B. I. "Progressivism and Personal Revolt." *CR*, 2 (Spring 1958), 125–38.
Earnest, Ernest. "A One-Eyed View of Spoon River." *CEA*, 31 (Nov. 1968), 8–9.
_____. "Spoon River Revisited." *WHR*, 21 (Winter 1967), 59–65.
Flaccus, Kimball. "Edgar Lee Masters: A Biographical and Critical Study." Ph.D. diss., New York U., 1952.
Flanagan, John T. *Edgar Lee Masters: The Spoon River Poet and His Critics.* Metuchen, N.J.: Scarecrow, 1974.
_____. "The Spoon River Poet." *SWR*, 38 (Summer 1953), 226–37.

Fletcher, J. G. "Masters and Men." *Poetry,* 49 (Mar. 1937), 343–47.

Francoisa, M. "Dedica per Lee Masters." *Fle,* no. 11 (Mar. 12, 1950).

Galdenzi, Mirella. "Polemica e pessimismo nella Spoon River Anthology." *ALet,* 16 (1956), 52–54.

Gregory, Horace and Marya Zaturenska. *A History of American Poetry 1900–1940.* New York: Harcourt, Brace, 1946. Pp. 226–32.

Hahn, Henry. "Evolution in the Graveyard." *MQ,* 10 (Spring 1969), 275–90.

Hallwas, John and Dennis Reader, eds. *The Vision of This Land: Studies of Vachel Lindsay, Edgar Lee Masters, and Carl Sandburg.* Macomb: Western Illinois U., 1976.

Hansen, Harry. *Midwest Portraits.* New York: Harcourt, 1923. Pp. 225–51.

Hartley, Lois. "The Early Plays of Edgar Lee Masters." *BSUF,* 7 (Spring 1966), 26–38.

————. "Edgar Lee Masters—Biographer and Historian." *JISHS,* 54 (Spring 1961), 56–83.

————. "Edgar Lee Masters: A Critical Study." Ph.D. diss., U. Illinois, 1949.

————. "Edgar Lee Masters—Political Essayist." *JISHS,* 57 (Autumn 1964), 249–60.

————. "Spoon River Revisited." *BSM,* no. 1 (1963), 3–30.

Hertz, R. N. "Two Voices of the American Village: Robinson and Masters." *MinnR,* 2 (Spring 1962), 345–58.

Hilfer, Anthony C. *The Revolt from the Village, 1915–1930.* Chapel Hill: U. North Carolina, 1969. Pp. 137–48, *passim.*

Kilmer, Joyce. "Edgar Lee Masters: The Spoon River Anthologist." *Bookman,* 44 (Nov. 1916), 264–65.

Kreymborg, Alfred. *Our Singing Strength.* New York: Coward-McCann, 1929. Pp. 379–85.

Lohf, K. A. "Spoon River and After." *CLC,* 14 (Feb. 1965), 5–10.

Lowell, Amy. *Tendencies in Modern American Poetry.* New York: Macmillan, 1917. Pp. 139–232.

McElderry, B. R. et al. "The Changing Role of the Middle West." *CR,* 2 (Spring 1958), 109–50.

Monroe, Harriet. *Poets and Their Art.* New York: Macmillan, 1926. Pp. 46–55.

Narveson, Robert D. "Edgar Lee Masters' *Spoon River Anthology:* Background, Composition, and Reputation." Ph.D. diss., U. Chicago, 1962.

————. "The Two Lincolns of Edgar Lee Masters." *Discourse,* 4 (Winter 1961), 20–39.

Powys, J. C. "Edgar Lee Masters." *Bookman,* 69 (Aug. 1929), 650–55.

Puranen, Erkki. "Edgar Lee Masters ja 'Spoon River Anthology.' " *KS* (Helsingfors), 9 (1947), 88–116.

Putzel, Max. "Masters' 'Maltrauers': Ernest McGaffey." *AL,* 31 (Jan. 1960), 491–93.

Sertoli, Giuseppi. "La piccola Commedia di Spoon River." *SA,* 12 (1966), 201–29.

Sloan, M. B. "Edgar Lee Masters—A Portrait." *UR,* 1 (Summer 1935), 4–6.

Stauffer, Donald B. *A Short History of American Poetry.* New York: Dutton, 1974. Pp. 244–47.

Untermeyer, Louis. *American Poetry Since 1900.* New York: Holt, 1923. Pp. 113–32.

————. "Spoon River Critics." *Masses,* 8 (Apr. 1916), 20.

Van Gelder, Robert. "An Interview with Mr. Edgar Lee Masters." *NYTBR,* Feb. 15, 1942, p. 2.

Van Wyck, William. "Edgar Lee Masters and Twentieth Century Prosody." *Person,* 17 (Jan. 1937), 75–80.

Waggoner, Hyatt H. *American Poets: From the Puritans to the Present.* Boston: Houghton Mifflin, 1968. Pp. 448–52.

Weeg, Mary M. "The Prose of Edgar Lee Masters: Its Revelation of His Views and Its Significance in His Canon." Ph.D. diss., Indiana U., 1964.

Wood, Clement. *Poets of America.* New York: Dutton, 1925. Pp. 163–90.

Yatron, Michael. "The Influence of Populism on Edgar Lee Masters, Vachel Lindsay, and Carl Sandburg." Ph.D. diss., Temple U., 1957.

————. *America's Literary Revolt.* New York: Philosophical Library, 1969.

Warren I. Titus
George Peabody College for Teachers
Nashville, Tennessee

GEORGE BARR McCUTCHEON (1866–1928)

McCutcheon wrote chiefly in the love comedy and adventure genres popular at the turn of the century and the decade immediately following. His works of this type—*Graustark* (1901) and its sequel *Beverly of Graustark* (1904), and *Brewster's Millions* (1903)—were read widely throughout the Midwest and reflect the popular literary tastes of the region during this period. He wrote a few novels with a more realistic emphasis, some of which are set in the Midwest. *The Sherrods* (1903) and *Jane Cable* (1906) deal rather melodramatically with rural life in Indiana and with life in Chicago around the turn of the century, and two of his best later works— *Quill's Window* (1921) and *Kindling and Ashes* (1926)—also utilize an Indiana locale. *The Day of the Dog* (1904), *Sherry* (1919), and *Oliver October* (1923) are all lesser works set in the Midwest, and *Viola Gwyn* (1922) is a rather saccharine historical romance set in Indiana in the 1830s.

No book length study of McCutcheon exists at the present time. A volume on him in the Twayne U.S. Author Series is currently in progress. Banta provides a complete listing of his books. Hackett lists McCutcheon titles which became best sellers during the early years of the century. Cooper, Baldwin, and Patrick offer early assessments of his work, while more mature assessments, stressing the underlying reasons for his great popularity at the turn of the century, are found in Hart, Mott, and Wright. His own *Books Once Were Men* details his career as a book collector, and his brother's autobiography, *Drawn From Memory*, is an important source for his early years. Purdue University holds some early McCutcheon manuscripts as well as several letters by him in the George Ade papers.

MAJOR WORKS

Graustark: The Story of A Love Behind a Throne. Chicago: Stone, 1901. [novel]
Castle Craneycrow. Chicago: Stone, 1902 [novel]
Brewster's Millions. Chicago: Stone, 1903. [novel, under pseudonym "Richard Greaves"]
The Sherrods. New York: Dodd, Mead, 1903. [novel]
The Day of the Dog. New York: Dodd, Mead, 1904. [novel]
Beverly of Graustark. New York: Dodd, Mead, 1904. [novel]
The Purple Parasol. New York: Dodd, Mead, 1905. [novel]
Nedra. New York: Dodd, Mead, 1905. [novel]
Cowardice Court. New York: Dodd, Mead, 1906. [novel]
Jane Cable. New York: Dodd, Mead, 1906. [novel]
The Flyers. New York: Dodd, Mead, 1907. [novel]
The Daughter of Anderson Crow. New York: Dodd, Mead, 1907. [novel]
The Husbands of Edith. New York: Dodd, Mead, 1908. [novel]
The Man from Brodney's. New York: Dodd, Mead, 1908. [novel]
The Alternative. New York: Dodd, Mead, 1909. [novel]
Truxton King: A Story of Graustark. New York: Dodd, Mead, 1909. [novel]

The Butterfly Man. New York: Dodd, Mead, 1910. [novel]
The Rose in the Ring. New York: Dodd, Mead, 1910. [novel]
What's-His-Name. New York: Dodd, Mead, 1911. [novel]
Mary Midthorne. New York: Dodd, Mead, 1911. [novel]
Her Weight in Gold. New York: Dodd, Mead, 1912. [novel]
The Hollow of Her Hand. New York: Dodd, Mead, 1912. [novel]
A Fool and His Money. New York: Dodd, Mead, 1913. [novel]
Black Is White. New York: Dodd, Mead, 1914. [novel]
The Prince of Graustark. New York: Dodd, Mead, 1914. [novel]
Mr. Bingle. New York: Dodd, Mead, 1915. [novel]
The Light That Lies. New York: Dodd, Mead, 1916. [novel]
From The Housetops. New York: Dodd, Mead, 1916. [novel]
Green Fancy. New York: Dodd, Mead, 1917. [novel]
Shot With Crimson. New York: Dodd, Mead, 1918. [novel]
The City of Masks. New York: Dodd, Mead, 1918. [novel]
Sherry. New York: Dodd, Mead, 1919. [novel]
Anderson Crow Detective. New York: Dodd, Mead, 1920. [novel]
West Wind Drift. New York: Dodd, Mead, 1920. [novel]
Quill's Window. New York: Dodd, Mead, 1921. [novel]
Yollup. New York: Dodd, Mead, 1922. [novel]
Viola Gwyn. New York: Dodd, Mead, 1922. [novel]
Oliver October. New York: Dodd, Mead, 1923. [novel]
East of the Setting Sun: A Story of Graustark. New York: Dodd, Mead, 1924. [novel]
Romeo in Moon Village. New York: Dodd, Mead, 1925. [novel]
Kindling and Ashes Or, The Heart of Barbara Wayne. New York: Dodd, Mead, 1926. [novel]
The Inn of the Hawk and Raven: A Tale of Old Graustark. New York: Dodd, Mead, 1927.
   [novel]
Blades. New York: Dodd, Mead, 1928. [novel]
The Merivales. New York: Dodd, Mead, 1929. [novel]
Books Once Were Men: An Essay For Booklovers. New York: Dodd, Mead, 1931. [essay]

CHECKLIST OF SECONDARY SOURCES

Blanck; *DAB; TCA.*

Baldwin, Charles C. *The Men Who Make Our Novels.* New York: Dodd, Mead, 1924. Pp.
   359–66.
Banta, R. E. *Indiana Authors And Their Books; 1816–1916.* Crawfordsville, Ind.: Wabash
   College, 1949. Pp. 201–2.
Burgess, Gelett. *My Maiden Effort; Being the Personal Confessions of Well-Known American
   Authors As To Their Literary Beginnings.* Garden City, N.Y.: Doubleday, for The Authors'
   League of America, 1921. Pp. 171–74. [autobiographical]
"Buying A Ticket to Graustark." *LD,* 99 (Nov. 17, 1928), 51–52.
Cooper, Frederic T. "Some Representative American Story Tellers. XVII—George Barr
   McCutcheon." *Bookman,* 34 (Oct. 1911), 191–97.
Hackett, Alice P. *70 Years of Best Sellers; 1895–1965.* New York: Bowker, 1967. Pp. 97, 100–5.
Hart, James D. *The Popular Book; A History of America's Literary Taste.* New York: Oxford
   U., 1950. Pp. 193–94.
Kopka, James. "George Barr McCutcheon and The Graustark Legacy." *IEJ,* 6 (Winter 1972),
   3–10.
McCutcheon, George Barr. [Describes writing methods]. *Indianapolis Star Magazine,* Dec. 6,
   1908, p. 4.
McCutcheon, John T. *Drawn From Memory.* Indianapolis: Bobbs-Merrill, 1950.
Maurice, Arthur B. " 'The History of Their Books' II. Concerning George Barr McCut-
   cheon." *Bookman,* 68 (Jan. 1929), 528–29.
Mott, Frank Luther. *Golden Multitudes: The Story of Best Sellers in the United States.* New
   York: Bowker, 1947. Pp. 208–9.
Patrick, Arnold. "Getting Into Six Figures. VI: George Barr McCutcheon." *Bookman,* 61
   (May 1925), 332–35.

"Romance Out of Indiana." *New York Times,* Oct. 24, 1928, p. 28. [obituary-editorial]
Shumaker, Arthur. *A History of Indiana Literature.* Indianapolis: Indiana Historical Bureau, 1962. Pp. 394–404, 462–63, *passim.*
Wright, Scott. "Social Roles of Popular Fiction in America, 1890–1910." Ph.D. diss., U. Minnesota, 1973.

Scott Wright
College of St. Thomas
St. Paul, Minnesota

WILLIAM MAXWELL (1908–   )

Whenever a William Maxwell book has appeared in the past forty years it has received highly favorable reviews from some of the best and most famous reviewers in this country. Nevertheless, as the checklist below indicates, Maxwell has not gained the attention of the academic literary community. There are no books, no chapters in books, no articles, and no dissertations written about him. All the entries below are brief notices or reviews. Several of his works remain in print; three of his novels (slightly revised) were in paperback as recently as 1971; *The Folded Leaf* has enjoyed spurts of popularity at several American universities; Maxwell's stories continue to appear from time to time in the *New Yorker;* but he remains a neglected author. He does not write fast-paced or hard-hitting fiction; the words the reviewers most often use to describe his treatment of the Midwest include, "quiet," "evocative," "restrained," "precise," "sensitive," "subtle," "compassionate," "tragic."

MAJOR WORKS

Bright Center of Heaven. New York: Harper, 1934. [novel]
They Came Like Swallows. New York: Harper, 1937. Rev. ed., New York: Vintage, 1959. [novel]
The Folded Leaf. New York: Harper, 1945. Rev. ed., New York: Vintage, 1959. [novel]
Time Will Darken It. New York: Harper, 1948. Rev. ed., New York: Vintage, 1962. [novel]
Stories (with Jean Stafford, John Cheever, and Daniel Fuchs). New York: Farrar, 1956.
The Château. New York: Knopf, 1961. [novel]
The Old Man at the Railroad Crossing and Other Tales. New York: Knopf, 1966. [stories]
Ancestors. New York: Knopf, 1971. [autobiographical]

CHECKLIST OF SECONDARY SOURCES

Burke; *CB; CN;* Herzberg; *OCAL; TCA Supp.*

Bliven, Naomi. "Brief Encounter." *NY* (Mar. 25, 1961), 161–63. [rev. of *The Château*]
Boroff, David. "There's Mystery at Every Turn." *NYTBR,* Mar. 26, 1961, p. 4. [rev. of *The Château*]
Gill, Brendan. "A Delicate Understanding." *NY* (Sept. 4, 1948), 78. [rev. of *Time Will Darken It*]
———. "The Past Regained." *NY* (Aug. 21, 1971), 88–91. [rev. of *Ancestors*]

Hay, Sara H. "The Magnetism of the Opposites." *SatR* (Apr. 7, 1945), 9. [rev. of *The Folded Leaf*]

Jones, Ernest. "Some Recent Novels." *Nation* (Sept. 25, 1948), 353. [rev. of *Time Will Darken It*]

LaFore, Laurence. "Fables of Our Time." *NYTBR*, Mar. 13, 1966, p. 5. [rev. of *The Old Man at the Railroad Crossing*]

Loveman, Amy. "Family Life Through the Eyes of Children." *SatR* (May 1, 1937), 4. [rev. of *They Came Like Swallows*]

M. G. D. *SatR* (Nov. 9, 1946), 44–46. [rev. of *The Heavenly Tenants*]

Poore, Charles. *NYTBR*, May 2, 1937, p. 7. [rev. of *They Came Like Swallows*]

Purdy, Theodore, Jr. "American Comedy." *SatR* (Sept. 15, 1934), 109–10. [rev. of *Bright Center of Heaven*]

Sullivan, Richard. *NYTBR*, Sept. 5, 1948, p. 4. [rev. of *Time Will Darken It*]

Trilling, Diana. "Fiction in Review." *Nation* (Apr. 21, 1945), 466–67. [rev. of *The Folded Leaf*]

Watts, Harold H. "William Maxwell." *Contemporary Novelists*. Ed. James Vinson. New York: St. Martin's, 1972. Pp. 858–59.

Wilson, Edmund. "Faintness of the 'Age of Thunder' and Power of 'The Folded Leaf'." *NY* (Mar. 31, 1945), 81.

Yardley, Jonathan. *NYTBR*, Aug. 8, 1971, p. 2. [rev. of *Ancestors*]

Steven Allaback
University of California at Santa Barbara
Santa Barbara, California

HARRIET MONROE (1860–1936)

A number of literary historians have traced the origins of modern poetry to Chicagoan Harriet Monroe's founding of *Poetry: A Magazine of Verse*. Duffey recognizes the importance of *Poetry* as an outlet for midwestern poets, while Cahill points to Miss Monroe's relationship with Ezra Pound as an attempt to create international connections. As an editor, Monroe's tastes have been described as "catholic" by many critics of the magazine. Others, however, have viewed her selections as lacking in balance and foresight. The most negative critical view of *Poetry*, as a cultural influence, is espoused by Whittemore. Gregory and Zaturenska, on the other hand, assert that the "poetic renaissance" can be attributed to the birth of *Poetry*. Hansen praises Monroe's willingness to publish a variety of poets, while Aiken claims that many of her choices have perpetrated an unnatural style of poetry.

While most criticism dealing with Monroe focuses on her activities as an editor, it is important to recognize her abilities as a poet in her own right. Cahill deals at length with her poetry and suggests that the lucid language of her thoughts is marked by interesting variations of subject matter and tempo. A more critical view of Monroe's ability to integrate consistent ideas into her poetry is stressed in Feeney's dissertation.

MAJOR WORKS

Valeria and Other Poems. Chicago: De Vinne, 1891.
The Columbian Ode. Designs by Will H. Bradley. Chicago: May, 1893.
John Wellborn Root: A Study of His Life and Work. Boston: Houghton Mifflin, 1896.
The Passing Show: Five Modern Plays in Verse. Boston: Houghton Mifflin, 1903.
The Dance of Seasons. Designs by Will H. Bradley. Chicago: Seymour, 1911. [poems]
You and I. New York: Macmillan, 1914. [poems]
The New Poetry: An Anthology. Harriet Monroe and Alice Corbin Henderson, eds. New York: Macmillan, 1917. Plus later editions.
The Difference and Other Poems. Chicago: Covici-McGee, 1924.
Poets and Their Art. New York: Macmillan, 1926.
Chosen Poems: A Selection from My Books of Verse. New York: Macmillan, 1935.
A Poet's Life: Seventy Years in a Changing World. New York: Macmillan, 1938. [autobiography]

CHECKLIST OF SECONDARY SOURCES

Burke; Herzberg; *LHUS; OCAL; TCA.*

Aiken, Conrad. *Scepticism: Notes on Contemporary Poetry.* New York: Knopf, 1919.
Bogan, Louise. *The Achievement of American Poetry: 1900–1950.* Chicago: Regnery, 1951.
Cahill, Daniel J. *Harriet Monroe.* New York: Twayne, 1973.
Duffey, Bernard. *The Chicago Renaissance in American Letters: A Critical History.* East Lansing: Michigan State College, 1956.
Feeney, Joseph J. "American Anti-War Writers of World War I: A Literary Study of Randolph Bourne, Harriet Monroe, Carl Sandburg, John Dos Passos, E. E. Cummings, and Ernest Hemingway." Ph.D. diss., U. Pennsylvania, 1971.
Gregory, Horace and Marya Zaturenska. *A History of American Poetry: 1900–1940.* New York: Harcourt, 1942.
Hansen, Harry. *Midwest Portraits: A Book of Memories and Friendships.* New York: Harcourt, 1923.
Hoffman, Frederick J., Charles Allen, and Carolyn Ulrich. *The Little Magazine.* Princeton, N.J.: Princeton U., 1946.
Hough, Graham. "Reflections on a Literary Revolution." In *Image and Experience.* Lincoln: U. Nebraska, 1960. Pp. 3–83.
Johnson, Abby. "A Free Foot in the Wilderness: Harriet Monroe and *Poetry*, 1912–1936." *IQ*, 37 (1974), 28–43.
Seymour, Ralph F. *Some Went This Way.* Chicago: Seymour, 1945.
Smith, Alson. *Chicago's Left Bank.* Chicago: Regnery, 1953.
Starrett, Vincent. *Born in a Bookshop: Chapters from the Chicago Renascence.* Norman: U. Oklahoma, 1965.
Strobel, Marion. "For Harriet Monroe." *Poetry*, 49 (Dec. 1924), 143–45.
Whittemore, Reed. *Little Magazines.* University of Minnesota Pamphlets on American Writers. Minneapolis: U. Minnesota, 1963.
Williams, Ellen. *Harriet Monroe and the Poetry Renaissance: The First Ten Years of Poetry, 1912–22.* Urbana: U. Illinois, 1976.
Zabel, Morton Dauwen, ed. *Literary Opinion in America.* Rev. ed. New York: Harper, 1951.
Ziff, Larzer. *The American 1890's.* New York: Viking, 1966.

Lynn Goldman
Northeastern Illinois University
Chicago, Illinois

WILLIAM VAUGHN MOODY (1869–1910)

Resources for scholarly work on this Indiana poet and dramatist are both available and plentiful. A writer of secondary importance, but of considerable historical interest, Moody has rated an individual entry in the standard *LHUS* bibliography, and his work is discussed in almost all general treatments of his period by both cultural and intellectual historians and by critics interested in the development of American poetry and/or drama. Brown's *Estranging Dawn* presents the definitive bibliography of primary sources together with a brief essay on unpublished sources. No recent bibliography of secondary materials has been made, but listings to 1935 given in Henry and in MacKaye (see below) are extensive. Halpern includes a selective annotated bibliography, and Brown (*ALR*, 1973) reviews the criticism in some detail, adding recent items.

Moody's significant work has been published in well-edited volumes, though a major portion of his correspondence with friends—Robinson, Gates, Mason, Lovett, Herrick, Josephine Preston Peabody, and others—remains unpublished. Primary repositories of letters, manuscripts, notebooks, etc., are the Huntington Library and university libraries—Chicago, Harvard, and Princeton.

Estranging Dawn is a recent critical biography which establishes chronology and texts and makes extensive use of unpublished sources. Introductions and editorial apparatus supplied in Lovett, Manly, Mason, and MacKaye offer valuable biographical information and criticism. The published reminiscences and correspondence of Moody's friends add useful insights and data.

Moody criticism to 1935 is voluminous and varied in approach and judgment. More recent work, except for book-length treatments, is thin and marred by a lack of close scrutiny of the body of his writings. Yet most of our major critics and literary and intellectual historians have considered Moody, and a solid core of good scholarly and critical work exists. Full discussions from differing points of view are available in Henry, Halpern, and Brown. Lovett's introduction to *Selected Poems* is the best brief introduction to Moody's life and writing, and Quinn's is the best short discussion of his plays and his contribution to American drama. Moody's reputation has been in decline, but since 1940 at least a dozen doctoral dissertations have included useful reconsiderations of his work.

MAJOR WORKS

The Masque of Judgment. Boston: Small, Maynard, 1900. [play]
Poems. Boston and New York: Houghton Mifflin, 1901.

A History of English Literature. New York: Scribner, 1902. [coauthor Robert Morss Lovett]
The Fire-Bringer. Boston and New York: Houghton Mifflin, 1904. [play]
The Great Divide. New York: Macmillan, 1909. [play]
The Faith Healer. New York: Macmillan, 1910. [play]
The Poems and Plays of William Vaughn Moody. Ed. by John M. Manly. 2 vols. Boston: Houghton Mifflin, 1912.
Some Letters of William Vaughn Moody. Ed. by Daniel Gregory Mason. Boston: Houghton Mifflin, 1913.
Selected Poems of William Vaughn Moody. Ed. by Robert Morss Lovett. Boston: Houghton Mifflin, 1931.
Letters to Harriet. Ed. by Percy MacKaye. Boston: Houghton Mifflin, 1935.

Checklist of Secondary Sources

Blanck; Burke; *CHAL; DAB;* Herzberg; *LHUS; LLC; OCAL; TCA & Supp.*

Adkins, Nelson F. "Poetic Philosophy of William Vaughn Moody." *TR*, 9 (1923–24), 97.
Barr, Nash O. and Charles H. Caffin. "William Vaughn Moody: A Study." *Drama*, 1 (1911), 177–211.
Blackmur, Richard. "Moody in Retrospect." *Poetry*, 38 (1931), 331–37.
Brown, Maurice F. *Estranging Dawn: The Life and Works of William Vaughn Moody*. Carbondale: Southern Illinois U., 1973.
––––––. "Moody and Robinson." *CLQ*, 5 (1960), 185–94.
––––––. "William Vaughn Moody (1869–1910)." *AmLitR*, 6 (1973), 51–60. [rev. of the criticism]
Conner, Frederick. *Cosmic Optimism: A Study of the Interpretation of Evolution by American Poets from Emerson to Robinson*. Gainesville: U. Florida, 1949. Pp. 314–31.
Duffey, Bernard. *The Chicago Renaissance in American Letters*. East Lansing: Michigan State College, 1954. Pp. 105–9.
Eckman, Frederick. "Moody's Ode: The Collapse of the Heroic." *TexSE*, 36 (1957), 80–92.
Fussell, Edwin S. "Robinson to Moody: Ten Unpublished Letters." *AL*, 23 (1951), 173–87.
Gilde, Erna. *William Vaughn Moody als Literarische Persönlichkeit*. Hamburg: n.p., 1940.
Glasheen, Francis J. and Adaline Glasheen. "Moody's 'An Ode in Time of Hesitation.' " *CE*, 5 (1943), 121–29.
Halpern, Martin. *William Vaughn Moody*. New York: Twayne, 1964.
Henry, David D. *William Vaughn Moody: A Study*. Boston: Humphries, 1934.
Jones, Howard Mumford. *The Bright Medusa*. Urbana: U. Illinois, 1952. Pp. 57–64.
Lewis, Charleton M. "William Vaughn Moody." *YR*, n.s. 2 (1913), 688–703.
Lewis, Edwin H. *William Vaughn Moody*. Chicago: Lakeside, 1914. [pamphlet]
Lewisohn, Ludwig. *Expression in America*. New York: Harper, 1932. Pp. 302–9.
Matthiessen, F. O. *The Responsibilities of the Critic*. New York: Oxford U., 1952. Pp. 93–97.
Munson, Gorham. "The Limbo of American Literature." *Broom*, 2 (1922), 250–60.
Norton, Suzanne F. "William Vaughn Moody: Conflict and Character in the New World." *DAI*, 35:6850A.
Pickering, Jerry V. "William Vaughn Moody: The Dramatist as Social Philosopher." *MD*, 14 (1971), 93–103.
Quinn, Arthur H. *A History of the American Drama from the Civil War to the Present Day*. New York: Harper, 1927. Vol. 2, pp. 7–17.
Riggs, Thomas, Jr. "Prometheus, 1900." *AL*, 22 (1951), 399–423.
Shackford, Martha H. "Moody's *The Fire-Bringer for To-day*." *SatR*, 26 (1918), 407–16.
Shorey, Paul. "The Poetry of William Vaughn Moody." *UCR*, n.s. 13 (1927), 172–200.
Waggoner, Hyatt H. *American Poets from the Puritans to the Present*. Boston: Houghton Mifflin, 1968. Pp. 249–54.
Ziff, Larzer. *The American 1890s*. New York: Viking, 1966. Pp. 319–22.

Maurice F. Brown
Oakland University
Rochester, Michigan

JULIA A. MOORE (1847–1920)

The best collection of materials about Julia A. Moore, "The Sweet Singer of Michigan," is found in the library of Michigan State University. Assembled by Greenly for his bibliographic work on Moore, which remains definitive, it includes editions of her books, uncollected writings, contemporary reviews, notices, and news stories, and copies of correspondence. The Houghton Library at Harvard University has two manuscript letters. Moore's family, now residing in Manton, Michigan, reportedly has manuscript materials, but somewhat sensitive to the ridicule to which Moore has been subjected, they have refused to make the material available to researchers. A volume is under preparation which will include a biography of Moore by Edith Larson and Elizabeth Williamson and a complete collection of her poetry and prose edited by M. Thomas Inge.

MAJOR WORKS

Centennial, 1876: The Sentimental Song Book. Grand Rapids, Mich.: Loomis, 1876. Subsequent editions: 1877, 1893. [poems]

The Sentimental Song Book. Grand Rapids, Mich.: Loomis, 1877. Subsequent editions: 1877, 1912. [poems]

A Few Choice Words to the Public, With New and Original Poems. Grand Rapids, Mich.: Loomis, 1878. [poems and essay]

The Sweet Singer of Michigan: Later Poems. Grand Rapids, Mich.: Eaton, Lyon, 1878. [poems and reprinted reviews by others]

Original Poems. Boston: Bartlett, 1900. Cornhill Booklet, vol. 5, no. 1.

Sunshine and Shadow: Or Paul Burton's Surprise. Cadillac, Mich.: Cadillac News, 1915. [novel]

The Sweet Singer of Michigan: Poems. Edited and with an Introduction by Walter Blair. Chicago: Pascal Covici, 1928.

CHECKLIST OF SECONDARY SOURCES

Herzberg; *OCAL.*

Blair, Walter. *Mark Twain and Huck Finn.* Berkeley: U. California, 1960. Pp. 210–13.

Bradley, Sculley, Richmond Croom Beatty, and E. Hudson Long, eds. *Adventures of Huckleberry Finn.* New York: Norton, 1962. Pp. 251–54.

Brown, Curtis F. *Star-Spangled Kitsch.* New York: Universe Books, 1975. Pp. 16–23.

Clemens, Samuel L. *Following the Equator: A Journey Around the World.* New York: Doubleday, 1897. Pp. 107–8, 324–25.

Crothers, Samuel McC. "The Hundred Worst Books." *Atl,* 103 (May 1909), 577–86.

Greenly, A. H. "The Sweet Singer of Michigan Bibliographically Considered." *PBSA,* 39 (1945), 91–118.

Hill, Hamlin and Walter Blair, eds. *The Art of Huckleberry Finn.* San Francisco: Chandler, 1962. Pp. 400–1, 445–51.

Honce, Charles. *A Sherlock Holmes Birthday.* New York: Privately printed, 1938. Pp. 75–80.

Kerwin, Fred. "The World's Worst Poet: Julia Moore Revisited." *Esquire,* 52 (Dec. 1959), 164–68.

Leacock, Stephen. *Humor: Its Theory and Technique.* New York: Dodd, Mead, 1935. Pp. 127–63.

Lewis, D. B. Wyndham and Charles Lee, eds. *The Stuffed Owl: An Anthology of Bad Verse.* New York: Coward-McCann, 1930. Pp. 217–25.

Lynn, Kenneth S., ed. *Huckleberry Finn: Text, Sources, and Criticism.* New York: Harcourt, 1961. Pp. 156–62.

Michaelson, L. W. "The Worst American Novel." *NDQ,* 32 (1964), 101–3.

Mulder, Arnold. "Authors and Wolverines: The Books and Writers of Michigan." *SatR,* 19 (Mar. 4, 1939), 3–4.

Nye, Edgar. *Bill Nye and Boomerang.* Chicago: Belford, Clarke, 1881. Pp. 94–101.

Remington, Mary E. "Julia A. Moore, The Sweet Singer, Mellowed by Years." *Grand Rapids Press,* Feb. 4, 1910. [interview]

Ryder, James F. *Voigtlander and I in Pursuit of Shadow Catching.* Cleveland: Cleveland Printing, 1902. Pp. 72–73, 155–73.

Stowe, E. A. "Michigan's Nightingale." *Chicago Inter-Ocean,* Jan. 12, 1878. [interview]

Wayne, Robert J. "The Sweet Singer." *MAQR,* 45 (Feb. 18, 1939), 174–78.

Wilson, Robert. "Visit to Julia." *Cedar Springs* (Michigan) *Clipper,* Jan. 16, 1878. [interview]

Wood, Clement. *The Craft of Poetry.* New York: Dutton, 1929. Pp. 282–86.

M. Thomas Inge
Virginia Commonwealth University
Richmond, Virginia

WRIGHT MORRIS (1910–   )

Existing critical materials on the work of Wright Morris are, for the most part, general in approach; for example, such studies as Booth's on Morris's theory of fiction, Guettinger's and Trachtenberg's on the form and structure of the novels, and Waterman's on his treatment of nostalgia in his works mostly deal with Morris's entire literary output as a body. The most specific issue to receive extensive treatment is the role of the Midwest in his work; several critics have analyzed its thematic importance or its influence on his technique. Very few of his eighteen novels have received individual treatment thus far; the exceptions are *The Field of Vision, Ceremony in Lone Tree, One Day,* and *In Orbit.* Most of the criticism to date emphasizes Morris's consistent concern with the craft of fiction, but there is much room for specific, analytical study of his literary effects and how he achieves them.

The only book-length study of Morris is Madden's volume in the Twayne series; there is also a Minnesota American Authors pamphlet by Leon Howard. In addition to the bibliographies which appear in those two volumes, there is one by Linden and Madden in a special issue of *Critique* devoted to Morris (Winter, 1961–62). There have been no textual studies to date despite the availability of a number of manuscripts at the Bancroft Library, University of California, Berkeley.

Major Works

My Uncle Dudley. New York: Harcourt, 1942. [novel]
The Man Who Was There. New York: Scribner, 1945. [novel]
The Inhabitants. New York: Scribner, 1946. [photography/text]
The Home Place. New York: Scribner, 1948. [photography/text]
The World in the Attic. New York: Scribner, 1949. [novel]
Man and Boy. New York: Knopf, 1951. [novel]
The Works of Love. New York: Knopf, 1952. [novel]
The Deep Sleep. New York: Scribner, 1953. [novel]
The Huge Season. New York: Viking, 1954. [novel]
The Field of Vision. New York: Harcourt, 1956. [novel]
Love Among the Cannibals. New York: Harcourt, 1957. [novel]
The Territory Ahead: Critical Interpretations in American Literature. New York: Harcourt, 1958. [literary criticism]
Ceremony in Lone Tree. New York: Atheneum, 1960. [novel]
What a Way to Go. New York: Atheneum, 1962. [novel]
Cause for Wonder. New York: Atheneum, 1963. [novel]
One Day. New York: Atheneum, 1965. [novel]
In Orbit. New York: New American Library, 1967. [novel]
A Bill of Rites, A Bill of Wrongs, A Bill of Goods. New York: New American Library, 1968. [social commentary]
God's Country and My People. New York: Harper, 1968. [photography/text]
Green Grass, Blue Sky, White House. Los Angeles: Black Sparrow, 1970. [short stories]
Wright Morris: A Reader. Introd. Granville Hicks. New York: Harper, 1970. [anthology]
Fire Sermon. New York: Harper, 1971. [novel]
Love Affair: A Venetian Journal. New York: Harper, 1972. [photography/text]
A Life. New York: Harper, 1973. [novel]
Here is Einbaum. Los Angeles: Black Sparrow, 1973. [stories]
About Fiction. New York: Harper, 1975. [essays]
Real Losses, Imaginary Gains. New York: Harper, 1976. [stories]

Checklist of Secondary Sources

Burke; *CA; CHAL; CN;* Herzberg; *LLC; OCAL; TCA Supp.*

Baumbach, Jonathan. "Wake Before Bomb: *Ceremony in Lone Tree." Critique,* 4 (1961–62), 56–71.
Bleufarb, Sam. "Point of View: An Interview with Wright Morris." *Accent,* 19 (1959), 34–45.
Booth, Wayne. "The Shaping of Prophecy: Craft and Idea in the Novels of Wright Morris. *ASch,* 31 (1962), 608–26.
———. "The Two Worlds in the Fiction of Wright Morris. *SR,* 65 (1957), 375–99.
Carpenter, Frederic I. "Wright Morris and the Territory Ahead." *CE,* 21 (1959), 147–56.
Cohn, Jack R. "Wright Morris: The Design of the Midwestern Fiction." Ph.D. diss., U. California, Berkeley, 1970.
Garrett, George. "Morris the Magician: A Look at *In Orbit." HC,* 4 (1967), 1–12.
Guettinger, Roger J. "The Problem with Jigsaw Puzzles: Form in the Fiction of Wright Morris." *TQ,* 2 (1968), 102–19.
Harper, Robert. "Wright Morris's *Ceremony in Lone Tree*: A Picture of Life in Middle America." *WAL* (Nov. 1976), 199–213.
Howard, Leon. *Wright Morris.* Minneapolis: U. Minnesota, 1968.
Hunt, John W., Jr. "The Journey Back: The Early Novels of Wright Morris." *Critique,* 5 (1962), 41–60.
Klein, Marcus. *After Alienation: American Novels in Midcentury.* New York: World, 1965. Pp. 196–246.
Leer, Norman. "Three American Novels and Contemporary Society: A Search for Commitment." *WSCL,* 3 (1962), 67–85. [deals with *Field of Vision*]
Linden, Stanton J. and David Madden. "A Wright Morris Bibliography." *Critique,* 4 (1961–62), 77–87.

Madden, David E. "The Great Plains in the Novels of Wright Morris." *Critique*, 4 (1961–62), 5–23.

_____. "The Hero and the Witness in Wright Morris' Field of Vision." *PrS*, 34 (1960), 263–78.

_____. *Wright Morris*. New Haven, Conn.: College and University Press, 1964.

_____. "Wright Morris' *In Orbit*: An Unbroken Series of Poetic Gestures." *Critique*, 10 (1968), 102–19.

Miller, James E. "The Nebraska Encounter: Willa Cather and Wright Morris." *PrS*, 61 (1967), 165–67.

Miller, Ralph. "The Fiction of Wright Morris: The Sense of Ending." *M-A III* (1976), 56–76.

Nemanic, Gerald. "Wright Morris and the Fields of Vision." *M-A I* (1974), 120–31.

Nemanic, Gerald and Harry White. "Wright Morris." *GLR*, I (Summer 1974), 1–29. [interview]

Trachtenberg, Alan. "The Craft of Vision." *Critique*, 4 (1961–62), 41–55.

Tucker, Martin. "The Landscape of Wright Morris." *LHR*, 7 (1965), 43–51.

Waldeland, Lynne. "Wright Morris: His Theory and Practice of the Craft of Fiction." Ph.D. diss., Purdue U., 1970.

Waterman, Arthur E. "The Novels of Wright Morris: An Escape from Nostalgia." *Critique*, 4 (1961–62), 24–39.

Lynne Waldeland
Northern Illinois University
DeKalb, Illinois

WILLARD MOTLEY (1912–66)

The major scholarly resource presently available on the Chicago novelist is *The Diaries of Willard Motley*, edited and introduced by Klinkowitz and Hinton; this volume includes a history and assessment of Motley's career beyond that covered in the diaries. Motley's papers from 1957–63 are deposited at the University of Wisconsin Memorial Library, Madison. The remainder of Motley's papers were discovered in a basement on Chicago's South Side by Klinkowitz in 1971; from 1971 to 1974 they were on loan to Northern Illinois University, where Klinkowitz catalogued and cross-indexed them, preparing a full set of Xerox copies. Klinkowitz and James Giles are editing the letters; Giles and Robert Fleming are preparing the memoirs, and the originals of Motley's diaries, dated from 1926 to 1943, are copied in full in this collection. The original papers remain in the possession of the Motley family. The Wisconsin collection has been cataloged by Klinkowitz, Giles, and John O'Brien.

Through the 1960s Motley's reputation was unstable, and his work merited critical attention only because of its wide popularity. Rideout, Eisenger, and Bone all regret what they call Motley's outmoded naturalism. An investigation of Motley's unpublished manuscripts (Wood), and a consideration of how his published work was drastically censored and revised (Klinkowitz and Wood), suggests that Motley was much more of a thematic innovator and even stylist (Giles) than earlier critics might suspect. It would seem that his strongest writing was in his diaries and memoirs, which are only now being published.

MAJOR WORKS

Knock On Any Door. New York: Appleton, 1947. [novel]
We Fished All Night. New York: Appleton, 1951. [novel]
Let No Man Write My Epitaph. New York: Random House, 1958. [novel]
Let Noon Be Fair. New York: Putnam, 1966. [novel]

CHECKLIST OF SECONDARY SOURCES

Burke; Herzberg; *OCAL; TCA Supp.*; Warfel.

Bayliss, John F. "Nick Romano: Father and Son." *NALF*, 3 (Mar. 1969), 18–21.
Bone, Robert A. *The Negro Novel in America*. Rev. ed. New Haven: Yale U., 1965. Pp. 178–79.
Eisinger, Chester E. *Fiction of the Forties*. Chicago: U. Chicago, 1963. P. 70.
Ellison, Bob. "Willard Motley." *Rogue*, 8 (Dec. 1963), 21–24. [interview]
Fleming, Robert E. *Willard Motley*. New York: Twayne, 1978.
_____. "Willard Motley's Urban Novels." *Umoja: Southwestern Afro-American Journal*, 7 (Summer 1973), 15–19.
Ford, Nick A. "Four Popular Negro American Novelists." *Phylon*, 15 (1954), 29–39.
Giles, James. "Willard Motley's Concept of 'Style' and 'Material.' " *SBL*, 4 (Spring 1973), 4–6.
Hazard, Eloise P. "First Novelists of 1947." *SatR*, 31 (Feb. 14, 1948), 8.
Jarrett, Thomas D. "Sociology and Imagery in a Great American Novel." *EJ*, 38 (Nov. 1949), 518–20.
Klinkowitz, Jerome. *The Diaries of Willard Motley*. Ames: Iowa State U., 1978.
Klinkowitz, Jerome and James Giles. "The Emergence of Willard Motley in Black American Literature." *NALF*, 6 (June 1972), 31–34.
Klinkowitz, Jerome, James Giles, and John O'Brien. "The Willard Motley Papers at the University of Wisconsin." *RALS*, 2 (Autumn 1972), 218–73.
Klinkowitz, Jerome and Karen Wood. "The Making and Unmaking of *Knock On Any Door*." *Proof: Yearbook of American Bibliographical and Textual Studies*, 3 (1973), 121–37.
Major, Clarence. "Willard Motley: Vague Ghost After the Father." In *The Dark and Feeling*. New York: Third Press, 1974. Pp. 95–98.
Rideout, Walter B. *The Radical Novel in the United States*. Cambridge: Harvard U., 1956. P. 263.
Weissgarber, Alfred. "Willard Motley and the Sociological Novel." *SA* (Rome), 7 (1961), 299–309.
Weyant, Nancy J. "The Craft of Willard Motley's Fiction." *DAI*, 36:7429A.
Wood, Charles. "The 'Adventure' Manuscript: New Light on Willard Motley's Naturalism." *NALF*, 6 (June 1972), 35–38.

Jerome Klinkowitz
University of Northern Iowa
Cedar Falls, Iowa

JOHN G. NEIHARDT (1881–1973)

When John Gneisenau Neihardt, poet laureate of Nebraska, died in November 1973, he left behind the tremendous production of a seventy-five-year writing career.—hundreds of lyric poems, dozens of short stories, three novels, four verse plays, five works of history, biography, and criticism, and his lifetime labor, *A Cycle of the West*, an epic poem in more than 16,000 lines of good, often excellent blank verse. *A Cycle* begins with fur trappers on the Missouri in 1822 and ends with the Wounded Knee Massacre in 1890. While many of these works are now out of print, several have been reissued recently and appear to be enjoying new popularity, especially *Black Elk Speaks* (1932), the spiritual autobiography of an Oglala Sioux holy man, which Neihardt transformed into a work of literary art. Released in a paperback edition of 200,000, this book is now required reading in many college courses in literature, history, and anthropology. The same publisher has now also released Neihardt's best novel, *When the Tree Flowered*. Critical discussions of Neihardt's work have generally focused on his epic, but a comprehensive study by Whitney was published in 1975. The only other critical biography, by House, is now outdated.

The John G. Neihardt Papers, which include manuscripts, letters, and other related material, are a part of the Western Historical Manuscripts Collection, University of Missouri Library.

MAJOR WORKS

The Divine Enchantment. New York: White, 1900. [poetry]
A Bundle of Myrrh. New York: Outing, 1907. [poetry]
The Lonesome Trail. New York: Lane, 1907. [stories]
Man Song. New York: Kennerly, 1909. [poetry]
The River and I. New York: Putnam, 1910. [travel account]
The Dawn-Builder. New York: Kennerly, 1911. [novel]
The Stranger at the Gate. New York: Kennerly, 1912. [poetry]
Life's Lure. New York: Kennerly, 1914. [novel]
The Song of Hugh Glass. New York: Macmillan, 1915. [poetry]
The Quest. New York: Macmillan, 1916. [poetry]
The Song of Three Friends. New York: Macmillan, 1919. [poetry]
The Splendid Wayfaring. New York: Macmillan, 1920. [history]
Two Mothers. New York: Macmillan, 1921. [drama]
The Song of the Indian Wars. New York: Macmillan, 1925. [poetry]
Poetic Values: Their Reality and Our Need of Them. New York: Macmillan, 1926. [criticism]
Collected Poems. New York: Macmillan, 1926.
Indian Tales and Others. New York: Macmillan, 1926. [stories]
Black Elk Speaks. New York: Morrow, 1932. [biography]
The Song of the Messiah. New York: Macmillan, 1935. [poetry]
The Song of Jed Smith. New York: Macmillan, 1941. [poetry]
A Cycle of the West. New York: Macmillan, 1949. [poetry]
When the Tree Flowered. New York: Macmillan, 1952. [novel]
All is But a Beginning. New York: Harcourt, 1972. [autobiography]
Luminous Sanity: Literary Criticism Written by John G. Neihardt. Ed. John Thomas Richards. Cape Girardeau, Mo.: Concord, 1973.

CHECKLIST OF SECONDARY SOURCES

Burke; *CA; CAA;* Herzberg; *OCAL; TCA & Supp.*

Adkins, N. F. "A Study of John G. Neihardt's 'Song of Three Friends.' " *AmS*, 3 (Apr. 1928), 276–90.

Aly, Lucile. "The Word-Sender, John G. Neihardt and His Audiences." *QJS*, 63 (Apr. 1957), 151–54.

_____. "John G. Neihardt as Speaker and Reader." Ph.D. diss., U. Missouri, 1959.

Beach, Joseph Warren. "Fourth Dimensional." *Poetry*, 28 (Sept. 1926), 350–52.

Black, W. E. "Ethic and Metaphysic: A Study of John G. Neihardt." *WAL*, 2 (1967), 205–12.

Cuff, R. P. "Neihardt's Epic of the West." *CE*, 9 (Nov. 1947), 69–72.

DeLowry, Linda. "Dynamic Patterns: A Thematic Study of the Works of John G. Neihardt." *DAI*, 36:4484A–85A.

Flanagan, John T. "John G. Neihardt: Chronicler of the West." *ArQ*, 21 (Spring 1965), 7–20.

Grant, G. Paul. "The Poetic Development of John G. Neihardt." Ph.D. diss., U. Pittsburgh, 1958.

House, Julius T. *John G. Neihardt, Man and Poet.* Wayne, Nebraska: Jones, 1920.

Lee, Fred L. *John G. Neihardt: The Man and His Western Writings.* Kansas City, Mo.: Westerners, 1976.

McCluskey, Sally. "*Black Elk Speaks* and So Does John Neihardt." *WAL*, 6 (1972), 231–42.

Monroe, Harriet. "A Laurelled Poem." *Poetry*, 17 (Nov. 1920), 94–98.

_____. "The Nebraska Laureate." *Poetry*, 18 (July 1921), 212–23.

_____. "What of Mr. Neihardt." *Poetry*, 30 (May 1927), 99–104.

Rothwell, Kenneth S. "On Search of a Western Epic: Neihardt, Sandburg, and Joffe as Regionalists and 'Astoriadists.' " *KQ*, 2 (Spring 1970), 53–63.

Stone, Edith O. "Democratic Values in Modern Narrative Poems." Ph.D. diss., U. Michigan, 1960.

Todd, Edgeley W. "The Frontier Epic: Frank Norris and John G. Neihardt." *WHR*, 13 (Winter 1959), 40–45.

Van Slyke, Berenice. "Neihardt's Epic." *Poetry*, 27 (Mar. 1926), 328–31.

Wahlstrom, Billie. "Transforming Fact: The Poetics of History in John G. Neihardt's A Cycle of the West." *DAI*, 36:3720A.

Whitney, Blair. "John G. Neihardt: A Poet Speaks on General Education." *UCQ*, 19 (Mar. 1974), 16–19.

_____. *John G. Neihardt.* New York: Twayne, 1975.

Blair Whitney
Illinois Board of Higher Education
Springfield, Illinois

MEREDITH NICHOLSON (1866–1947)

Meredith Nicholson is most often associated with the writers of the Hoosier school: Charles Major, Gene Stratton Porter, George Barr McCutcheon, George Ade, Booth Tarkington, Lew Wallace, and Edward Eggleston. Bowman sees these writers faced with a literary predicament: "would they follow realism, lyricism or romanticism?" This conflict is evident in the work of Nicholson, for, as Shumaker notes, "it is unfortunate that he swung between romance and realism, for he was too optimistic to be a thorough realist and always spoiled his attempts at realism by tacking on a happy ending." Nicholson's writing has been both praised and condemned for its "folksiness." He preferred to consider himself an essayist rather than a novelist. However, Shumaker notes that the best-known Nicholson works today are *A Hoosier Chronicle* and *The House of a Thousand Candles.*

Nicholson was a prolific writer; eight of his books made the best seller lists between 1903–16. However, not much critical attention has centered on his work. The best information on the Hoosier school can be found in Spencer, Parrington, and Shumaker. The most complete bibliography to date is Russo and Sullivan. The Indiana Historical Society has 127 Nicholson manuscripts, and others can be found at the Lilly Library, Wabash College.

Major Works

Short Flights. Indianapolis: Bowen-Merrill, 1891. [poetry]
The Hoosiers. New York: Macmillan, 1900. [essays]
The Main Chance. Indianapolis: Bobbs-Merrill, 1903. [novel]
Zelda Dameron. Indianapolis: Bobbs-Merrill, 1904. [novel]
The House of a Thousand Candles. New York: Grosset, 1905. [novel]
Poems. Indianapolis: Bobbs-Merrill, 1906. [poetry]
The Port of Missing Man. Indianapolis: Bobbs-Merrill, 1907. [novel]
Rosalind at Red Gate. Indianapolis: Bobbs-Merrill, 1907 [novel]
The Little Brown Jug at Kildare. Indianapolis: Bobbs-Merrill, 1908. [novel]
The Lords of High Decision. New York: Doubleday, 1909. [novel]
The Siege of the Seven Suitors. New York: Houghton Mifflin, 1910. [novel]
A Hoosier Chronicle. New York: Houghton Mifflin, 1912. [semi-autobiographical novel]
The Provincial American and Other Papers. New York: Houghton Mifflin, 1912. [essays]
Otherwise Phyllis. Boston: Houghton Mifflin, 1913. [novel]
The Poet. Boston: Houghton Mifflin, 1914. [fictional biography of James Whitcomb Riley]
The Proof of the Pudding. Boston: Houghton Mifflin, 1916. [novel]
The Madness of May. New York: Scribner, 1917. [novel]
A Reversible Santa Claus. Boston: Houghton Mifflin, 1917. [novel]
The Valley of Democracy. New York: Scribner, 1918 [essays]
Lady Larkspur. New York: Scribner, 1919. [novel]
Blacksheep! Blacksheep! New York: Scribner, 1920. [novel]
The Man in the Street; Papers on American Topics. New York: Scribner, 1921. [essays]
Best Laid Schemes. New York: Scribner, 1922. [stories]
Broken Barriers. New York: Scribner, 1922. [novel]
Honor Bright: A Comedy in Three Acts. New York: French, 1923. [play, with Kenyon Nicholson]
The Hope of Happiness. New York: Scribner, 1923. [novel]
And They Lived Happily Ever After! New York: Scribner, 1925. [novel]
The Cavalier of Tennessee. Indianapolis: Bobbs-Merrill, 1928. [historical novel about Andrew Jackson]
Old Familiar Faces. Indianapolis: Bobbs-Merrill, 1929. [eight essays, some autobiographical]

Checklist of Secondary Sources

Burke: *CHAL;* Herzberg; *LHUS; OCAL; TCA.*

Baldwin, Charles C. *The Men Who Make Our Novels.* New York: Dodd, Mead, 1925. Pp. 400–4.
Banta, R. E. *Indiana Authors and Their Books 1816–1916.* Crawfordsville, Ind.: Wabash College, 1949. Pp. 237–39.
Bowman, Heath. "Those, Those Hoosiers." *SatR* (Jan. 6, 1945), 6–7.
Brooks, Van Wyck. *The Confident Years: 1885–1915.* New York: Dutton, 1952. Pp. 69, 330.
Churchill, Allen. *The Literary Decade.* Englewood Cliffs, N.J.: Prentice-Hall, 1971. P. 5.
Cordell, Richard A. "Limestone, Corn, and Literature; the Indiana Scene and its Interpreters." *SatR* (Dec. 17, 1938).

Dunn, Jacob P. *Indiana and Indianans.* Chicago: American Historical Society, 1919.
Hilfer, Anthony C. *The Revolt from the Village, 1915–1930.* Chapel Hill: U. North Carolina, 1969. Pp. 8, 17–18.
Holliday, Robert C. *Broome Street Straws.* New York: Doran, 1919. Pp. 182–94.
Knight, Grant C. *The Critical Period in American Literature.* Cos Cob, Conn.: Edwards, 1968. P. 61.
Leisy, Ernest E. *The American Historical Novel.* Norman: U. Oklahoma, 1950. P. 120.
Parrington, Vernon L. *Main Currents in American Thought: An Interpretation of American Literature from the Beginnings to 1920.* New York: Harcourt, 1958. Vol. 3, pp. xi, 364, 373.
Pattee, Fred L. *A History of American Literature Since 1870.* New York: Cooper Square, 1968. P. 410.
Russo, Dorothy R. and Thelma L. Sullivan. *Bibliographical Studies of Seven Authors of Crawfordsville, Indiana.* Crawfordsville, Ind.: Lakeside, 1952. Pp. 69–133.
Sanders, Jean. "Meredith Nicholson: Hoosier Cavalier." Master's thesis, De Pauw U., 1958.
Shumaker, Arthur W. *A History of Indiana Literature.* Indianapolis: Indiana Historical Society, 1962. Pp. 325–37, *passim.*
Smith, R. E. "Playboy of the Wabash." *Bookman* (Oct. 1920), 133–36.
Spencer, Benjamin T. "Regionalism in American Literature." In *Regionalism in America.* Ed. Merrill Jensen. Madison: U. Wisconsin, 1951. Pp. 219–60.
Sutherland, R. C. "The Kentucky Girl in Two Literary Classics." *KHSR* (Apr. 1967), 134–43.
Tanselle, G. Thomas. "The ABA Issue of Meredith Nicholson's *A Hoosier Chronicle* (1912)." *BSA*, 60 (1966), 223–24.
Tuttleton, James W. *The Novel of Manners in America.* Chapel Hill: U. North Carolina, 1972. Pp. 146, 152–59.
Van Doren, Carl. *The American Novel: 1789–1939.* New York: Macmillan, 1940. P. 214.
_____. *Contemporary American Novelists: 1900–1920.* New York: Macmillan, 1922. P. 20.
"Western Contribution to our National Spirit; Meredith Nicholson's vivid picture of *The Valley of Democracy." CO* (Dec. 1918), 385–86.
Wilson, W. E. *The Wabash.* New York: Farrar, 1940. Pp. 303–14.

Margaret Noland Mangan
Northeastern Illinois University
Chicago, Illinois

JOYCE CAROL OATES (1938–   )

In the effort to locate her on the literary landscape, critics of Joyce Carol Oates have created a bewildering assemblage: Agee, Emily Brontë, Cather, Stephen Crane, Defoe, Dreiser, Farrell, Faulkner, Ferber, Flaubert, Lawrence, Flannery O'Connor, Plath, Poe, Porter, Steinbeck, Swift, Tolstoy, and Welty. Among the recurrent descriptives resorted to by reviewers *violence* has dominated, followed variously by references to wounds and blood, to insanities and sexual obsessions of dazzling variety, to pathological states such as sado-masochism, to the more alarming emotions and the words which evoke them: *nightmare, terror, hallucination.* In defining her literary stance, critics have tended to position Oates at one extreme or another from centrist realism, and thus for some she stands foursquare in the tradition of American naturalism, while for others she is a dark flower of the gothic lately sprung into nocturnal bloom.

Essay-reviews excepted, few serious appraisals of Oates's significance have appeared, and typically, in reacting against an undiscriminating enthusiasm, these have proposed a case against Oates which asserts that the emotions of her characters are superficial, that her plots derive from a card index of stock situations, that she assumes a religious core for her works while lacking an authentic religious vision. Her diction has been called artificially supercharged; her stories have been said to hover uneasily between the literal and the symbolic. One locus of critical agreement sees Oates's finest power lying in its manner, particularly in a mesmerizing evocation of states of mind; another locates a prominent failure in matters of form and calls her structures arbitrary and even self-contradictory.

A consensus is that Oates, a writer of obvious ambition and demonstrated promise, is to be watched with immense care; and further, that to evaluate her work by anything less than the most stringent literary standards would be to do her an undeserved mischief.

Oates is a native of New York State, but has resided for several years at Windsor, Ontario, near Detroit. The social environment of that section of the Midwest has been evident in much of her recent work.

Major Works

By the North Gate. New York: Vanguard, 1963. [stories]
With Shuddering Fall. New York: Vanguard, 1964. [novel]
Upon the Sweeping Flood. New York: Vanguard, 1966. [stories]
A Garden of Earthly Delights. New York: Vanguard, 1967. [novel]
Expensive People. New York: Vanguard, 1968. [novel]
Anonymous Sins. Baton Rouge: Louisiana State U., 1969. [poems]
Them. New York: Vanguard, 1969. [novel]
The Wheel of Love. New York: Vanguard, 1970. [stories]
Love and Its Derangements. Baton Rouge: Louisiana State U., 1970. [poems]
Wonderland. New York: Vanguard, 1971. [novel]
The Edge of Impossibility. New York: Vanguard, 1972. [stories]
Marriages and Infidelities. New York: Vanguard, 1972. [stories]
Angel Fire. Baton Rouge: Louisiana State U., 1973. [poems]
Do With Me What You Will. New York: Vanguard, 1973. [novel]
The Hungry Ghosts. Los Angeles: Black Sparrow, 1974. [stories]
The Goddess and Other Women. New York: Vanguard, 1974. [stories]
Miracle Play. Los Angeles: Black Sparrow, 1974. [play]
New Heaven, New Earth: The Visionary Experience in Literature. New York: Vanguard, 1974. [essays]
The Seduction and Other Stories. Los Angeles: Black Sparrow, 1975.
The Assassins. New York: Vanguard, 1975. [novel]
The Fabulous Beasts. Baton Rouge: Louisiana State U., 1975. [poems]
The Poisoned Kiss and Other Stories . . . . New York: Vanguard, 1975.
Crossing the Border. New York: Vanguard, 1976. [stories]
Childwold. New York: Vanguard, 1976. [novel]
The Triumph of Spider Monkey. Los Angeles: Black Sparrow, 1977. [novella]
Night-Side. New York: Vanguard, 1977. [stories]

CHECKLIST OF SECONDARY SOURCES

CA; CB; CN.

Adams, Robert M. "Them." *NYTBR*, Sept. 28, 1969, pp. 4–5. [rev.]

Avant, John A. "An Interview with Joyce Carol Oates." *LJ*, 97 (Nov. 15, 1972), 3711–12.

Bedient, Calvin. "Do With Me What You Will." *NYTBR*, Oct. 14, 1973, p. 1. [rev.]

Bellamy, Joe D. "The Dark Lady of American Letters: An Interview with Joyce Carol Oates." *Atl*, 229 (Feb. 1972), 63–67.

Bower, Warren. "Bliss in the First Person." *SatR* (Oct. 26, 1968), 34–35. [interview]

Burwell, Rose Marie. "Joyce Carol Oates and an Old Master." *Critique*, 15 (1973), 48–58.

Clemens, Walter. "Joyce Carol Oates at Home." *NYTBR*, Sept. 28, 1969, pp. 4–5. [interview]

———. "Joyce Carol Oates: Love and Violence." *Newsweek*, 80 (Dec. 11, 1972), 72–77.

Dalton, Elizabeth. "Joyce Carol Oates: Violence in the Head." *Commentary*, 49 (June 1970), 75–77.

Denne, C. A. "Joyce Carol Oates' Women." *Nation*, 219 (Dec. 7, 1974), 597–99.

Gray, Paul E. "New Novels in Review." *YR*, 59 (Mar. 1970), 430–38.

Hayes, Brian P. "Wonderland." *SatR* (Oct. 9, 1971), 38. [rev.]

Hicks, Granville. "What is Reality?" *SatR*, 51 (Oct. 26, 1968), 33–34. [rev.]

Hodge, Marion. "What Moment is Not Terrible? An Introduction to the Work of Joyce Carol Oates." *DAI*, 35:5407A.

Grant, Mary. "The Tragic Vision of Joyce Carol Oates." *DAI*, 35:4520A–21A.

Kazin, Alfred. "Cassandras: Porter to Oates." In *Bright Book of Life*. Boston: Little, Brown, 1973. Pp. 165–205.

Kuehl, Linda. "An Interview with Joyce Carol Oates." *Commonweal*, 91 (Dec. 5, 1969); 307–10.

Martin, Alice. "Toward a Higher Consciousness: A Study of the Novels of Joyce Carol Oates." *DAI*, 35:5415A–16A.

McCormick, Lucienne P. "A Bibliography of Works by and about Joyce Carol Oates." *AL*, 43 (Mar. 1971), 124–32.

"Other Celebrity Voices: How Art Has Touched Our Lives." *TH*, 52 (May 1974), 31.

Pinsker, Sanford. "Isaac Bashevis Singer and Joyce Carol Oates: Some Versions of Gothic." *SouR*, 9 (Oct. 1973), 895–908.

Price, Martin. "Reason and its Alternatives: Some Recent Fiction." *YR*, 58 (Mar. 1969), 464–74. [rev.]

Sullivan, Walter. "The Artificial Demon: Joyce Carol Oates and the Dimensions of the Real." *HC*, 9 (Dec. 1972), 1–12.

"Transformations of Self: An Interview with Joyce Carol Oates." *OR*, 15 (Fall 1973), 51–61.

Walker, Carolyn. "Fear, Love, and Art in Oates' 'Plot.' " *Critique*, 15 (1973), 59–70.

Waller, G. F. "Joyce Carol Oates' Wonderland: An Introduction." *DR*, 54 (1974), 480–90.

"Writing as a Natural Reaction." *Time*, 94 (Oct. 10, 1969), 108. [portrait]

Zimmerman, Paul D. "Hunger for Dreams." *Newsweek*, 75 (Mar. 23, 1970), 108–10. [portrait]

Philip L. Gerber
State University of New York
Brockport, New York

KENNETH PATCHEN (1911–72)

With a few exceptions the work of Kenneth Patchen has been largely over-looked by academic scholarship. His supporters have been other writers,

Miller and Rexroth are outstanding examples, or other members of the literary *avant-garde* who write and/or publish books—James Laughlin of New Directions, Bern Porter, and Jonathan Williams. Patchen's experimentalism, political radicalism, and his general disregard for most aspects of the American cultural mainstream have perhaps contributed to his inaccessibility. However, two recent dissertations may be indicative of a development which will bring him within the realm of formal scholarly study.

His nearest midwestern literary relations are Vachel Lindsay and Carl Sandburg. With them he shares a restless spirit, a love of words, word-games, song, a populist feeling for the improvement of life for the common man, a dislike for the uppity and the powerful, and an innocent faith in love, humor, and the decency of Everyman.

MAJOR WORKS

Before the Brave. New York: Random House, 1936. [poetry]
The Journal of Albion Moonlight. Mt. Vernon, N.Y: Walpole, 1941. [novel]
The Dark Kingdom. New York: Ganis and Harris, 1942. [poetry]
The Teeth of the Lion. Norfolk, Conn.: New Directions, 1942. [poetry]
Cloth of the Tempest. New York: Harper, 1943. [poetry]
The Memoirs of a Shy Pornographer. New York: Laughlin, 1945. [novel]
Panels For the Walls of Heaven. Berkeley: Porter, 1946. [poetry]
Sleepers Awake. New York: Padell, 1946. [novel]
Pictures of Life and of Death. New York: Padell, 1947. [poetry]
See You in the Morning. New York: Padell, 1947. [novel]
They Keep Riding Down All the Time. New York: Padell, 1947. [poetry]
Red Wine and Yellow Hair. New York: New Directions, 1949. [poetry]
The Famous Boating Party and Other Poems in Prose. New York: New Directions, 1954.
Hurrah for Anything. Highlands, N.C.: Jonathan Williams, 1957. [poetry and drawings]
Selected Poems. New York: New Directions, 1957.
When We Were Here Together. New York: New Directions, 1957. [poetry]
Poemscapes. Highlands, N.C.: Jonathan Williams, 1958.
Love Poems. San Francisco: City Lights, 1960.
Doubleheader. New York: New Directions, 1966. [poetry]
Hallelujah Anyway. New York: New Directions, 1966. [poetry and drawings]
The Collected Poems. New York: New Directions, 1968.
Wonderings. New York: New Directions, 1971. [poetry]
In Quest of Candlelighters. New York: New Directions, 1972. [poetry]

CHECKLIST OF SECONDARY SOURCES

Burke; *CA; CN; CP;* Herzberg; *LLC; OCAL; TCA & Supp.*

Benét, William Rose. "Phoenix Nest." *SatR*, 21 (Nov. 25, 1939), 16.
Bishop, John Peale. "Midnight of Sense." In *Collected Essays*. New York: Scribner, 1948. Pp. 295–96.
Breit, Harvey. "On a Bronze Horse." *Poetry*, 60 (June 1942), 160–63.
Detro, Gene. *Patchen: The Last Interview*. Santa Barbara: Capra, 1976.
Fitzgerald, Robert. "Footnotes to These Days." *Poetry*, 54 (Sept. 1936), 340–42.
Fletcher, Ian. "Stopping the Rot." *Nine*, 2 (Jan. 1950), 50–51.
Forgotson, E. S. "Patchen's Progress." *Poetry*, 62 (Feb. 1944), 278–80.
Gould, Dennis. "Murderer of Min and Miming Poets." In *Love and War Poems*, by Kenneth Patchen. Mickelover, Derby, England: Whisper and Shout #1, 1968. Pp. 5–14.
Hogue, Herbert P. "The Anarchic Mystique of Five American Fictions." Ph.D. diss., U. Washington, 1971.
Miller, Henry. *Patchen: Man of Anger and Light*. New York: Padell, 1947.

Nelson, Raymond J. "An American Mysticism: The Example of Kenneth Patchen." Ph.D. diss., Stanford U., 1970.

Rexroth, Kenneth. "Naturalist of the Public Nightmare." In *Bird in the Bush*. New York: New Directions, 1958. Pp. 94–105.

See, Carolyn. "Kenneth Patchen, 1934–1958: A Partial Bibliography." *BB*, 23 (1961), 81–84.

———. "The Jazz Musician as Patchen's Hero." *ArQ*, 17 (1961), 136–46.

Smith, Larry R. "The World of Kenneth Patchen: Form and Function in His Experimental Art." *DAI*, 35:6161A.

Taylor, Frajain. "Puck in the Garden of the Sun." *Poetry*, 70 (Aug. 1947), 269–74.

Untermeyer, Jean S. "Problem of Patchen." *SatR*, 30 (Mar. 22, 1947), 15–16.

Paul L. Ferlazzo
Michigan State University
East Lansing, Michigan

J. F. POWERS (1917–   )

J. F. Powers is widely recognized as the leading Catholic writer of fiction in America, though the nature and relevance of his Catholicism has always been a controversial issue. Phelps says that he "has mastered a comedy of manners within a specifically Catholic terrain . . . at once concretely sectarian and concretely American Midwest." As early as 1958 Quinn rebuked Robert Bowen for asserting that Powers is "not a Catholic writer, but a writer who happens to be Catholic." More recently Boyle celebrates the way Powers's characters are "drawn by divine as well as by human commitments"; but La Guardia laments that the parochial "nature of his work precludes the possibility of universal human response," and Vickery finds that in Powers "the traditional possibilities of salvation, redemption and grace are enunciated in a symbolism that is not so much perfunctory as strained and devoid of verisimilitude," and he questions "whether there is any meaningful sense . . . in which Powers can be regarded as a Roman Catholic writer."

Despite his modest production—two collections of short stories and two novels—Powers has established himself with critics and teachers as a major figure, even if his style and subject matter precludes best sellerdom. The stories in *Prince of Darkness* (1947) and *The Presence of Grace* (1956) have been widely anthologized and are staples of college courses; the brilliant novel *Morte D'Urban* (1963) won the National Book Award and a place on the Modern Library's shelf of permanently valuable literature. Hagopian, author of the full-length study of Powers (1968), led a special seminar on his fiction at the 1970 convention of the Modern Language Association. The *PMLA* annual bibliographies list twenty items since the publication of Hagopian's book. Critics continue to be attracted by the technical beauty of his painstaking craftmanship. As Degnan observes, "a literary perfectionist, he works with a story until it possesses an almost poetic ironic tightness . . . , [also] what accounts for Powers' achievement is that he alone of today's working satirists has discovered and developed a great satirical subject: the comedy of Roman Catholicism, especially the comedy of American Catholicism."

MAJOR WORKS

Prince of Darkness. Garden City, N.Y.: Doubleday, 1947. [stories]
The Presence of Grace. Garden City, N.Y.: Doubleday, 1956. [stories]
Morte D'Urban. Garden City, N.Y.: Doubleday, 1962. [novel]
Look How the Fish Live. New York: Knopf, 1975. [novel]

CHECKLIST OF SECONDARY SOURCES

Burke; *CA; CN;* Herzberg; *LLC; OCAL; TCA Supp.*

Boyle, Robert, S. J. "To Look Outside: The Fiction of J. F. Powers." In *The Shapeless God: Essays on Modern Fiction*. Harry J. Mooney and Tom F. Staley, eds. Pittsburgh, Penn.: U. Pittsburgh, 1968. Pp. 91–115.
Degnan, James P. "J. F. Powers: Comic Satirist." *ColQ,* 16 (1968), 325–33.
Dolan, Paul J. "God'a Crooked Line: Powers' *Morte D'Urban.*" *Renascence,* 21 (1969), 95–102.
Hagopian, John V. *J. F. Powers*. New York: Twayne, 1968.
Henault, Marie. "The Saving of Father Urban." *America,* 108 (Mar. 2, 1963), 290–92.
Hinchliffe, Arnold P. "Nightmare of Grace." *Blackfriars,* 45 (Feb. 1964), 61–69.
Hynes, Joseph. "Father Urban's Renewal: J. F. Powers' Difficult Precision." *MLQ,* 29 (1968), 450–66.
La Guardia, David M. "A Critical Dilemma: J. F. Powers and the Durability of Catholic Fiction." In *Challenges in American Culture*, Ray B. Browne, Larry N. Landrum, and William K. Bottroff, eds. Bowling Green, Ohio: Bowling Green U. Popular Press, 1970. Pp. 15–35.
Laughlin, Rosemary M. "Wanderers in the Wasteland: The Characters of J. F. Powers." *BaratR,* 6 (1971), 38–48.
Lebowitz, Naomi. "The Stories of J. F. Powers: The Sign of Contradiction." *KR,* 20 (Summer 1958), 494–99.
Malloy, Sister M. Kristin, O.S.B. "The Catholic and Creativity: J. F. Powers." *ABR,* 15 (Mar. 1964), 63–80.
Merton, Thomas. "Morte D'Urban: Two Celebrations." *Worship,* 36 (Nov. 1962), 645–50.
Padilla, [Brother] Carlos Villalobos [F.M.S.]. *The Art of Short Fiction in J. F. Powers*. U. Autonoma de Mexico, 1963.
Phelps, Donald. "Reasonable, Holy and Living." *MR,* 9 (1969), 57–62.
Quinn, Sister M. Bernetta, O.S.F. "View from a Rock: The Fiction of Flannery O'Conner and J. F. Powers." *Critique,* 2 (Fall 1958), 19–27.
Scouffas, George. "J. F. Powers: On the Vitality of Disorder." *Critique,* 2 (Fall 1958), 41–58.
Sisk, John P. "The Complex Moral Vision of J. F. Powers." *Critique,* 2 (Fall 1958), 28–40.
Steichen, Donna M. "J. F. Powers and the Noonday Devil." *ABR,* 20 (1969), 528–51.
Vickery, John B. "J. F. Powers' *Morte D'Urban*: Secularity and Grace." In *The Vision Obscured: Perceptions of some Twentieth Century Catholic Novelists*, Melvin J. Friedman, ed. New York: Fordham U., 1970. Pp. 45–65.
Wedge, George F. "J. F. Powers." *Critique,* 2 (1958), 63–70.

John V. Hagopian
State University of New York at Binghamton
Binghamton, New York

JAMES PURDY (1923–   )

As a novelist, short story writer, poet, and playwright, Ohioan James Purdy's popularity has steadily grown. His ideology has been compared to that of Kafka and his style to Salinger's. Published first in England and admired by Dame Edith Sitwell, his works have been translated into more than thirty languages. Edward Albee used Purdy's novel *Malcolm* for his play of the same name, and Purdy's volume of poems, *The Running Sun* (1972), was set to music by Robert Helps and performed in New York's Alice Tully Hall.

In addition to specific studies of Purdy and his works, there are scattered references to him in such works as Howard Mumford Jones and Richard M. Ludwig's *Guide to American Literature and Its Backgrounds since 1890* and Irving Malin's *New American Gothic*. The 1960 Lippincott edition of *Color of Darkness* has a classic essay on Purdy's works by Sitwell. David Daiches has a fine essay on Purdy in the 1959 Noonday edition of *Malcolm*, and Tony Tanner's preface to the 1974 Doubleday edition of *Malcolm* and *Color of Darkness* (in one volume) deserves attention. Purdy's own comments on the American literary scene can be found in his article "Writing from Inner Compulsion" in *International Book Year* for 1972.

MAJOR WORKS

63: Dream Palace. New York: William-Frederick, 1956. [novella]
Don't Call Me By My Right Name and Other Stories. New York: William-Frederick, 1956.
Color of Darkness: Eleven Stories and a Novella. New York: New Directions, 1957.
Malcolm. New York: Farrar, 1959. [novel]
The Nephew. New York: Farrar, 1960. [novel]
Children is All. New York: New Directions, 1961. [two plays]
Cabot Wright Begins. New York: Farrar, 1964. [novel]
Eustace Chisholm and the Works. New York: Farrar, 1967. [novel]
An Oyster Is a Wealthy Beast. Los Angeles: Black Sparrow, 1967. [story and eleven poems]
Mr. Evening: A Story and Nine Poems. Los Angeles: Black Sparrow, 1968.
I Am Elijah Thrush. New York: Bantam, 1970. [novel]
Jeremy's Vision. Garden City, N.Y.: Doubleday, 1970. [novel]
On the Rebound: A Story and Nine Poems. Los Angeles: Black Sparrow, 1970. [contains drawings by the author]
The Running Sun. [poems published privately in 1971]
Sunshine Is an Only Child. New York: Aloe, 1973. [poems]
"Q&A: drama." *Esquire*, 79 (1973), 134–232. [short play]
The House of the Solitary Maggot. Garden City, N.Y.: Doubleday, 1974. [novel]
In A Shallow Grave. New York: Arbor, 1976. [novel]

CHECKLIST OF SECONDARY SOURCES

CA; CN; Herzberg; *LHUS; OCAL.*

Adams, Stephen. *James Purdy*. New York: Barnes, 1976.
Baldanza, Frank. "Playing House for Keeps with James Purdy." *ConL*, 11 (1970), 488–510.

Barron, Fred. "James Purdy." *Penthouse*, 5 (1974), 89–93. [interview]

Burris, Shirley W. "The Emergency in Purdy's 'Daddy Wolf.' " *Renascence*, 20 (1968), 94–98.

Bush, George E. "James Purdy: A Checklist." *BB*, 28 (1971), 506. [primary and secondary]

"The Choler of Despair." *TLS*, June 10, 1965, p. 474. [unsigned, but by William Weatherby]

Coffey, Warren. "The Incompleat Novelist." *Commentary*, 44 (1967), 98–103.

Chupack, Henry. *James Purdy*. New York: Twayne, 1975.

Denniston, Constance. "The American Romance Parody: A Study of Purdy's *Malcolm* and Heller's *Catch-22*." In *Emporia State Research Studies*, 14 (1965), 42–59.

Fink, Guido. "James Purdy e le gaie esqeuie del romanzo americano." *Paragone*, 21 (1970), 82–98.

Herr, Paul. "The Small, Sad World of James Purdy." *ChiR* (Autumn-Winter 1960), 19–25.

Kolve, De. "James Purdy: An Assessment." *TT*, 42 (1961), 476–77.

Kostelanetz, Richard. "The New American Fiction." *Ramparts*, 3 (1965), 57–60.

McNamara, Eugene. "The Post American Novel." *QQ*, 69 (1962), 265–75.

Malin, Irving. "Melange a Trois." *Ramparts*, 3 (1965), 79–80.

Maloff, Saul. "James Purdy's Fictions: The Quality of Despair." *Critique*, 6 (1963), 106–12.

Pomeranz, Regina. "The Hell of not Loving: Purdy's Modern Tragedy." *Renascence*, 16 (1964), 149–53.

Schott, Webster. "James Purdy: American Dream." *Nation*, 198 (1964), 300–2.

Schwarzchild, Bettina. "Aunt Alma: James Purdy's *The Nephew*." *UWR*, 3 (1967), 80–87.

———. "The Forsaken: An Interpretive Essay on James Purdy's *Malcolm*." *TQ*, 10 (1967), 170–77.

———. *The Not Right House*. Columbia: U. Missouri, 1968.

Skerrett, Joseph T., Jr. "James Purdy and the Works: Love and Tragedy in Five Novels." *TCL*, 15 (1969), 25–33.

Tanner, Tony. "Birdsong." *PR*, 39 (1972), 609–14.

———. "Frames without Pictures." In *American Fiction 1950–1970*. New York: Harper, 1971. Pp. 85–103.

Varble, Stephen. "I Am James Purdy." *IM*, 3 (1972), 28–29. [interview]

Weales, Gerald. "No Face and No Exit: The Fiction of James Purdy and J. P. Donleavy." *CAN*, 187 (1964), 143–54.

Witham, W. Tasker. *The Adolescent in the American Novel 1920–1960*. New York: Ungar, 1964.

George E. Bush
St. Francis College
Brooklyn, New York

HERBERT QUICK (1860–1925)

The doctoral dissertations predicted by Kennedy in 1926 have been written by Keen (1967) and Morain (1970), and others (Reed, Bogue) continue to fan the flickering flame of interest. Paluka has contributed the definitive bibliography of major works. There is still some scholarly interest in Quick; one scholar recently discovered that *The Brown Mouse* was filmed in 1915, perhaps the first filming of an Iowa novel. One hopes for a reprinting of at least *Vandemark's Folly*, surely one of the best novels of the nineteenth-century westward trek and pioneer settlement.

Aside from brief career summaries by Andrews, the only biographical source of consequence remains Quick's autobiography, *One Man's Life*—a fascinating, informative account of the beginnings of a prairie author's life. Unfortunately, it stops at the moment when Quick discovers Henry George and before he has begun his writing career. Other information and appraisals are listed below. Quick's manuscripts and papers are in the Iowa State Department of History and Archives, Des Moines.

MAJOR WORKS

In the Fairyland of America: A Tale of the Pukwudjies. New York: Stokes, 1901.
Aladdin & Co.: A Romance of Yankee Magic. New York: Holt, 1904.
Double Trouble: Or, Every Hero His Own Villain. Indianapolis: Bobbs-Merrill, 1906. [novel]
The Broken Lance. Indianapolis: Bobbs-Merrill, 1907. [novel]
Virginia of the Air Lanes. Indianapolis: Bobbs-Merrill, 1909. [novel]
Yellowstone Nights. Indianapolis: Bobbs-Merrill, 1911. [novel]
The Brown Mouse. Indianapolis: Bobbs-Merrill, 1915. [novel]
The Fairview Idea: A Story of the New Rural Life. Indianapolis: Bobbs-Merrill, 1919. [farm life]
Vandemark's Folly. Indianapolis: Bobbs-Merrill, 1922. [novel]
The Hawkeye. Indianapolis: Bobbs-Merrill, 1923. [novel]
The Invisible Woman. Indianapolis: Bobbs-Merrill, 1925. [novel]
There Came Two Women. Indianapolis: Bobbs-Merrill, 1924. [verse play]
One Man's Life: An Autobiography. Indianapolis: Bobbs-Merrill, 1925.
Mississippi Steamboatin': A History of Steamboating on the Mississippi and Its Tributaries. [With Edward Quick.] New York: Holt, 1926.

CHECKLIST OF SECONDARY SOURCES

Burke; Herzberg; *OCAL*; *TCA*; Warfel.

Andrews, Clarence A. "Herbert Quick: The Social Life of the Prairie." In *A Literary History of Iowa*. Iowa City: U. Iowa, 1972. Pp. 67–78.
Bogue, Allan G. "Herbert Quick's Hawkeye Trilogy." *BIowa*, 16 (Apr. 1972), 3–13.
Keen, Carl L. "The Fictional Writings of Herbert Quick." Ph.D. diss., Michigan State U., 1967.
Kennedy, A. G. "Bibliographical Department." *AmS*, 2 (Dec. 1926), 153–55.
Meyer, Roy. *The Middle Western Farm Novel in the Twentieth Century*. Lincoln: U. Nebraska, 1965. Pp. 47–56, 227–29.
Morain, Frederick G. "Herbert Quick: Iowa Democrat." Ph.D. diss., Yale U., 1970.
Murphy, Donald. "Herbert Quick, Iowa Acquires a Past." In *A Book of Iowa Authors*, ed. by Johnson Brigham. Des Moines: Iowa State Teachers Assn., 1930. Pp. 163–76.
Ogilvie, W. E. *Pioneer Agricultural Journalists*. Chicago: Leonard, 1927. Pp. 95–100.
Paluka, Frank. *Iowa Authors: A Bio-Bibliography of Sixty Native Writers*. Iowa City: Friends of the University of Iowa Libraries, 1967. Pp. 12–14.
Quick, Herbert. "I Picked My Goal at Ten—Reached It at Sixty." *AmM* (Oct. 1922), 50–51.
Reed, P. L. "Herbert Quick: Art and Iowa." *IUB* (Mar. 1967), 63–75.
Rosse, James C. "Midwestern Writers: Herbert Quick." *PrS*, 2 (Summer 1928), 225–29.
Sloan, Sam. "Misrepresentative Fiction." *Palimpsest*, 12 (Feb. 1931), 42–44.
Speake, Clara. "A List of Dialect Terms From the Works of Hamlin Garland and Herbert Quick." Master's thesis, U. Iowa, 1926.

Clarence A. Andrews
University of Iowa
Iowa City, Iowa

CONRAD RICHTER (1890–1968)

With the exception of scattered and indifferent reviews, criticism avoided Conrad Richter during the first thirty years of his literary career. That was a period, nevertheless, in which he produced two book-length philosophical essays, four novels, and numerous stories, several of which were collected in two volumes. Only after the Society of Libraries of New York University had conferred its gold medal for literature upon Richter (1942) did the first serious article appear. Sutherland, in 1945, thus first brought Richter to the attention of scholars. Even then, however, scholars failed to engage immediately in a vigorous study of Richter's works that ultimately would number twenty volumes of essays, novels, and stories. The conferral of a Pulitzer Prize in 1951 and the National Book Award in 1960 finally stirred scholarly activity. All or parts of six books and monographs, several bibliographies, three doctoral dissertations, and more than a dozen articles now deal with Richter. The definitive biographical-critical study is Edwin W. Gaston, Jr.'s, *Conrad Richter*. More recently, Marvin J. LaHood's *Conrad Richter's America* examines the dominant themes of Richter's fiction and the literary affiliation of the author with Willa Cather, Elizabeth Madox Roberts, and Caroline Miller. Between those studies, Robert J. Barnes's *Conrad Richter* focuses upon the author's southwestern works; and Clifford Edwards's *Conrad Richter's Ohio Trilogy* examines the author's only completed triptych.

MAJOR WORKS

Brothers of No Kin and Other Stories. New York: Hinds, Hayden, and Eldredge, 1924. [stories]
Human Vibration. New York: Dodd, Mead, 1926. [philosophical essay]
Principles in Bio-Physics. Harrisburg: Good Books, 1927. [philosophical essay]
Early Americana. New York: Knopf, 1936. [stories]
The Sea of Grass. New York: Knopf, 1937. [novel]
The Trees. New York: Knopf, 1940. [novel]
Tacey Cromwell. New York: Knopf, 1942. [novel]
The Free Man. New York: Knopf, 1943. [novel]
The Fields. New York: Knopf, 1946. [novel]
Always Young and Fair. New York: Knopf, 1947. [novel]
The Town. New York: Knopf, 1950. [novel]
The Light in the Forest. New York: Knopf, 1953. [novel]
The Mountain on the Desert. New York: Knopf, 1955. [novelistic essay]
The Lady. New York: Knopf, 1957. [novel]
The Waters of Kronos. New York: Knopf, 1960. [novel]
A Simple Honorable Man. New York: Knopf, 1962. [novel]
The Grandfathers. New York: Knopf, 1964. [novel]
A Country of Strangers. New York: Knopf, 1966. [novel]
The Aristocrat. New York: Knopf, 1968. [novel]

Checklist of Secondary Sources

Burke; *CB;* Herzberg; *LLC; OCAL; TCA & Supp;* Warfel.

Barnard, Kenneth J. "Presentation of the West in Conrad Richter's Trilogy." *NOQ,* 29 (Autumn 1957), 224–34.

Barnes, Robert J. *Conrad Richter.* Southwest Writers Series No. 14. Austin: Steck-Vaughn, 1968.

Carpenter, Frederic I. "Conrad Richter's Pioneers: Reality and Myth." *CE,* 12 (Nov. 1950), 77–84.

Edwards, Clifford D. *Conrad Richter's Ohio Trilogy: Its Ideas, Themes, and Relationships to Literary Tradition.* Studies in American Literature No. 18. The Hague: Mouton, 1971.

Etulain, Richard W. *Western American Literature: A Bibliography of Interpretive Books and Articles.* Vermillion: U. South Dakota, 1972.

Flanagan, John T. "Folklore in the Novels of Conrad Richter." *MF,* 2 (Spring 1952), 5–14.

_____. "Conrad Richter: Romancer of the Southwest." *SwR,* 43 (Summer 1958), 189–96.

Folsom, James K. *The American Western Novel.* New Haven: College and University Press, 1966.

Gaston, Edwin W., Jr. *Conrad Richter.* New York: Twayne, 1965.

Hutchens, John K. "Conrad Richter." *NYHTBR,* Apr. 30, 1950, p. 3.

Kohler, Dayton. "Conrad Richter: Early Americana." *CE,* 8 (Feb. 1947), 221–28.

LaHood, Marvin J. "A Study of the Major Themes in the Work of Conrad Richter, and His Place in the Tradition of the American Frontier Novel." Ph.D. diss., U. Notre Dame, 1962.

_____. "Richter's Early America." *UR,* 30 (June 1964), 311–16.

_____. "*The Light in the Forest:* History as Fiction." *EJ,* 55 (Mar. 1966), 298–304.

_____. "Richter's Pennsylvania Trilogy." *SUS,* 8 (1968), 5–13.

_____. "Conrad Richter and Willa Cather: Some Similarities." *XUS,* 9 (Spring 1970), 33–44.

_____. *Conrad Richter's America.* The Hague: Mouton, 1975.

Miller, Vincent. "Unofficial Roses." *National Review,* Sept. 11, 1962, pp. 194–96.

Pearce, T. M. "Conrad Richter." *NMQ,* 20 (Autumn 1950), 371–73.

Robinson, Cecil. *With the Ears of Strangers: The Mexican in American Literature.* Tucson: U. Arizona, 1963.

Ruff, G. Elson. "An Honest Novel of the Parsonage." *Lutheran* (May 30, 1962), 14–20.

Schmaier, Maurice. "Conrad Richter's *The Light in the Forest*: An Ethnohistorical Approach to Fiction." *Ethnohistory,* 7 (Fall 1960), 327–98.

Sutherland, Bruce. "Conrad Richter's Americana." *NMQ,* 15 (Winter 1945), 413–22.

Wilson, Dawn M. "Conrad Richter: The Novelist as Philosopher." Ph.D. diss., Kent State U., 1970.

_____. "The Influence of the West on Conrad Richter's Fiction." *ON,* 1 (Dec. 1975), 375–89.

Young, David L. "The Art of Conrad Richter." Ph.D. diss., Ohio State U., 1964.

Edwin W. Gaston, Jr.
Stephen F. Austin State University
Nacogdoches, Texas

JAMES WHITCOMB RILEY (1849–1916)

The general evaluation of Riley's artistic worth is negative. Pattee says "he must be rated finally as a comedian, a sentimentalist, an entertainer." *OCAL* finds his works a blend of "quaint whimsical lowliness, a cheerful philosophy, and frequently obstrusive pathos." *LHUS* rates him "triumphantly common." Although Shumaker cites him as second only to Long-fellow in popularity, he concludes that Riley "lived in a sort of sentimental dream." In short, it is difficult to find anyone who has taken such light art seriously. The biographies of Dickey and Crowder are more concerned with the life than the works; the Phelps edition of the letters is solid; only Carmen and Revell have attempted lengthy studies of the prose and poetry.

Because only twenty volumes of the over ninety published contain material which did not appear in earlier collections, the student should use the 1913 "Biographical Edition" for both study and text. The full annotations and other material not available elsewhere make it indispensible. The Russo bibliography is best for separating editions, printings, and reprintings. What Riley lacked in art he made up for in merchandising. The major manuscript collections are at Indiana University, the Indiana State Library, Indianapolis Public Library, Bobbs-Merrill Archives, Library of Congress, Emory, Huntington Library, Stanford, University of Chicago, Harvard, New York Public Library, and Princeton.

MAJOR WORKS

The Complete Works of James Whitcomb Riley. Ed. by Edmund H. Eitel. 6 vols. Indianapolis: Bobbs-Merrill, 1913. [biographical ed.]

CHECKLIST OF SECONDARY SOURCES

BDAL; Burke; *CHAL; DAB;* Herzberg; *LHUS; OCAL.*

Beers, Henry A. "Singer of the Old Swimmin' Hole." *YR,* n.s. 9 (1920), 395–402. Collected in Beers's *Connecticut Wits and Other Essays*. New Haven: Yale U., 1920. Pp. 31–49.
Carmen, Bliss. *James Whitcomb Riley*. New York: Privately printed, 1918.
Cottman, George S. "Some Reminiscences of James Whitcomb Riley." *IMH,* 14 (1918), 99–107.
Crowder, Richard. *Those Innocent Years: The Legacy and Inheritance of a Hero of the Victorian Era*. Indianapolis: Bobbs-Merrill, 1957.
Dickey, Marcus. *The Maturity of James Whitcomb Riley*. Indianapolis: Bobbs-Merrill, 1922.
———. *The Youth of James Whitcomb Riley*. Indianapolis: Bobbs-Merrill, 1919.
Hitt, George C. "James Whitcomb Riley." *IMH,* 32 (1936), 189–206.
Laughlin, Clara F. *Reminiscences of James Whitcomb Riley*. New York: Fleming Revel, 1916.
Masters, Edgar Lee. "James Whitcomb Riley: A Sketch of His Life and Appraisal of His Work." *Century,* 94 (1927), 704–15.
Mitchell, Minnie Belle. *James Whitcomb Riley as I Knew Him*. Greenfield, Ind.: Old Swimmin Hole Press, 1949.
Monroe, Harriet. "James Whitcomb Riley." *Poetry,* 8 (1916), 305–7.
Nicholson, Meredith. *The Hoosiers*. New York: Macmillan, 1916. Pp. 156–76.
———. "James Whitcomb Riley." *Atl,* 98 (1916), 503–14.
Nolan, Jeanette C., Horace Gregory, and James T. Farrell. *Poet of the People: An Evaluation of James Whitcomb Riley*. Bloomington: Indiana U., 1951.
Phelps, William L., ed. *Letters of James Whitcomb Riley*. Indianapolis: Bobbs-Merrill, 1930.
Price, Robert. "James Whitcomb Riley in 1876." *IMH,* 35 (1939), 129–40.
Randall, Dale B. J. "Dialect in the Verse of The Hoosier Poet." *AS,* 35 (1960), 36–50.
Richards, Louise P. "James Whitcomb Riley in a Country Newspaper." *Bookman,* 20 (1904), 18–24; 44 (1916), 79–87.
"Riley Number." *BNM,* 35 (Mar. 1907).
Revell, Peter. *James Whitcomb Riley*. New York: Twayne, 1970.

Russo, Anthony J. and Dorothy Russo. *A Bibliography of James Whitcomb Riley*. Indianapolis: Indiana Historical Bureau, 1944.
Shumaker, Arthur W. *A History of Indiana Literature*. Indianapolis: Indiana Historical Bureau, 1962. Pp. 202–19.

E. Bruce Kirkham
Ball State University
Muncie, Indiana

EDWARD PAYSON ROE (1838–88)

"No American author has ever left behind him so wide a circle of admirers as the late Rev. Edward Payson Roe," begins the memorialist dedicating "The E. P. Roe Number" of *Lippincott's Monthly Magazine* (October 1888) to the lately departed. "Up to the year 1871," Roe himself confides in " 'A Native Author Called Roe,' " a memoir appearing in the same maga-. zine, "I had written little for publication beyond occasional contributions to the *New York Evangelist,* nor had I seriously contemplated a literary life." Overwhelmed by tidings of the Chicago fire of 1871, Roe "obeyed the impulse to be on the scene as soon as possible," and after days and nights wandering "where a city had been, and among the extemporized places of refuge harboring all classes of people," he was inspired to write his first and most successful novel, *Barriers Burned Away,* which Mott and Hart discuss as one of the most appealing moral tracts of a century that thrived on such fare. Eighteen more volumes of fiction and four books about small-scale gardening flowed from Roe's prolific pen during his remaining seventeen years. Critics have not been impressed. Cowie observes that "Roe told a good story clearly and cogently but with little imagination." Dunlap insists that "Roe writes like a historian and not a novelist." Roe argued that his only chance as a writer would come from knowing what people wanted and giving it to them. "No critic has ever been so daft as to call any of my books a classic. Better books are unread because the writer is not *en rapport* with the reader." His tales were read for years in many editions in this country and abroad, but his claim to fame remains his first in which he succeeded in establishing both a sure-fire formula for fictionally exploiting contemporary catastrophes and Chicago as a literary backdrop that could compete with New York and Boston.

Major Works

Barriers Burned Away. New York: Dodd, Mead, 1872. [novel]
What Can She Do? New York: Dodd, Mead, 1873. [novel]·
Gentle Woman Roused: A Story of the Temperance Movement in the West. New York: National Temperance Society, 1874. [novel]

Opening a Chestnut Burr. New York: Dodd, Mead, 1874. [novel]
From Jest to Earnest. New York: Dodd, Mead, 1875. [novel]
Near to Nature's Heart. New York: Dodd, Mead, 1876. [novel]
A Knight of the Nineteenth Century. New York: Dodd, Mead, 1877. [novel]
A Face Illumined. New York: Dodd, Mead, 1878. [novel]
A Day of Fate. New York: Dodd, Mead, 1880. [novel]
Without a Home. New York: Dodd, Mead, 1881. [novel]
His Sombre Rivals. New York: Dodd, Mead, 1883. [novel]
An Unexpected Result, and Other Stories. New York: Dodd, Mead, 1883.
A Young Girl's Wooing. New York: Dodd, Mead, 1884. [novel]
Nature's Serial Story. New York: Dodd, Mead, 1884. [novel]
An Original Belle. New York: Dodd, Mead, 1885. [novel]
He Fell in Love with His Wife. New York: Dodd, Mead, 1886. [novel]
The Earth Trembled. New York: Dodd, Mead, 1887. [novel]
The Hornet's Nest: A Story of Love and War. New York: Dodd, Mead, 1887. [novel]
Found, Yet Lost. New York: Dodd, Mead, 1888. [novel]
"Miss Lou." New York: Dodd, Mead, 1888. [novel]
The Home Acre. New York: Dodd, Mead, 1889. [novel]
Taken Alive, and Other Stories, with an Autobiography of Edward P. Roe. New York: Dodd, Mead, 1889.
A Brave Little Quaker, and Other Stories. New York: Dodd, Mead, 1892. [five short stories selected from preceding entry]

CHECKLIST OF SECONDARY SOURCES

BDAL; Burke; *DAB;* Herzberg; *OCAL.*

Cowie, Alexander. *The Rise of the American Novel*. New York: American, 1948. Pp. 439–41.
Dunlap, George. *The City in the American Novel*. Philadelphia: U. Pennsylvania, 1934. Pp. 152–53.
Finley, Cecil. "E. P. Roe: Successful and Sentimental Religious Novels." *GLR*, 4 (Summer 1977), 26–34.
Hart, James. *The Popular Book*. New York: Oxford, 1948.
Lippincott's Monthly Magazine, 42 (Oct. 1888), 461–500. [contains a short story, "Queen of Spades," pp. 461–78; Roe's autobiography, " 'A Native Author Called Roe,' " pp. 479–97; and "Some Words About E. P. Roe," by Wm. S. Walsh, pp. 497–500]
Mott, Frank Luther. *Golden Multitudes*. New York: Macmillan, 1947.
Roe, Mary A. *E.P. Roe: Reminiscences of His Life, by his sister*. New York: Dodd, Mead, 1899.
Van Doren, Carl. *The American Novel, 1789–1939*. New York: Macmillan, 1940. P. 114.

Warren French
Indiana-Purdue University
Indianapolis, Indiana

THEODORE ROETHKE (1908–63)

The critical consensus is that Theodore Roethke has made a distinctive contribution to American letters; however, there is disagreement as to whether his achievement is merely "important," as Malkoff suggests; "major," as Martz begrudges; or "great" as Dickey enthusiastically affirms. Many critics agree with Burke that "The Lost Son" sequence is a genuine "breakthrough" and affirm what Kunitz advocated in an early review "that he stands among the original and powerful contemporary poets."

Martz points to Wordsworth as a major literary influence on Roethke's work, while Truesdale and Waggoner underscore his connections with the American Romantic mainstream of Emerson, Thoreau, Dickinson, and Whitman. Others, such as Mills and Malkoff, point to the influences of Eliot, Blake, Yeats, Thomas, and Auden, but disagree as to how Roethke's stature fares in comparison.

Because of Roethke's bouts with mental illness throughout his career, beginning while he was an instructor at Michigan State University in 1935, there has been considerable critical interest in the applicability of psychological theories to his work. Malkoff, Rosenthal, and Harrington point to the Freudian and Jungian roots of Roethke's development theme—with Malkoff seemingly the only one suggesting the limitations of this view. Seager's useful but less than satisfactory biography is yet another attempt to understand the creative process in psychological terms; however, his misunderstanding of Dabrowski's theory of "positive disintegration" clarifies little.

Among those more concerned with philosophical and metaphysical dimensions in Roethke's work are Mills, Heyen, Waggoner, and Blessing. Mills points to Roethke's theme of "identity" and Martin Buber's influence; Heyen examines Roethke's mysticism in his *Profile;* Waggoner notes his Emersonian Transcendentalism; and Blessing documents how Roethke's dynamic psychic energy became poetry.

Besides the publication of the major writings—including *The Collected Poems* (1966), *Selected Prose* (1966), *Selected Letters* (1968), and the *Notebooks* (1972)—the major biographical and bibliographical tools are at hand: Seager's biography, *The Glass House* (1968); Lane's computerized *Concordance* (1972); and McLeod's *Manuscript Checklist* (1971) and its companion *Bibliography* (1973). In addition, four critical studies and two essay collections have appeared since Roethke's death in 1963.

Roethke's works, except for the early volumes (*Open House, The Lost Son, Praise to the End!, The Waking: Poems 1933–1953*), remain in print. In addition, Roethke's poetry has appeared in every major European language, as well as in Afrikaans, Bengali, Indonesian, Persian, and Hindu. An Italian edition, essentially a reprint of the *Collected Poems,* was published in Milan in 1966, and a Polish edition, essentially a reprint of *The Far Field,* was published in Warsaw in 1971.

MAJOR WORKS

Open House. New York: Knopf, 1941. [poems]
The Lost Son and Other Poems. Garden City, N.Y.: Doubleday, 1948.
Praise to the End! Garden City, N.Y.: Doubleday, 1951. [poems]
The Waking: Poems 1933–1953. Garden City, N.Y.: Doubleday, 1953.

Words for the Wind. Garden City, N.Y.: Doubleday, 1958. [poems]
Sequence, Sometimes Metaphysical. Iowa City: Stonewall Press, 1963. [poems]
The Far Field. New York: Doubleday, 1964. [poems]
On the Poet and His Craft: Selected Prose of Theodore Roethke. Edited by Ralph J. Mills, Jr. Seattle: U. Washington, 1965. [essays and autobiography]
The Collected Poems of Theodore Roethke. Garden City, N.Y.: Doubleday, 1968. [poems]
Straw for the Fire: From the Notebooks of Theodore Roethke 1943–63. Edited by David Wagoner. Garden City, N.Y.: Doubleday, 1972.

CHECKLIST OF SECONDARY SOURCES

Biogongiari, Pero. "Roethke: LaRicerea di Unidentita." *Letteratura*, 31–35 (Gen-Giu 1967), 259–64.

Blessing, Richard A. *Theodore Roethke's Dynamic Vision.* Bloomington: Indiana U., 1974.

Boyd, J. D. "Texture and Form in Theodore Roethke's Greenhouse Poems." *MLQ*, 32 (Dec. 1971), 409–24.

Burke, Kenneth. "Cult of the Breakthrough." *NR*, 159 (Sept. 21, 1968), 25–26. [rev.]

————. "The Vegetal Radicalism of Theodore Roethke." *SR*, 58 (Winter 1950), 68–108.

Ciardi, John, Stanley Kunitz, and Allan Seager. "An Evening with Ted Roethke." *MQR*, 6 (Fall 1967), 227–42.

Dickey, James. *Babel to Byzantium: Poets and Poetry Now.* New York: Grosset & Dunlap, 1971.

"The Greatest American Poet." *Atlantic*, 222 (Nov. 1968), 53–58.

Donoghue, Denis. "Theodore Roethke: Toward the Far Field." *Lugano Review* [Switzerland], 1 (1965), 50–72.

Fauchereau, Serge. "Lectur de Theodore Roethke." *Critique*, 231–32 (Aug.–Sept. 1966), 730–35.

Flint, Roland H. "Many Arrivals Make Us Live: A Study of the Early Poetics of Theodore Roethke, 1941–1953." Ph.D. diss., U. Minnesota, 1968.

Freer, Coburn. "Theodore Roethke's Love Poetry." *NWR*, 11 (Summer 1971), 42–66.

Fukuda, Rikutaro. "Theodore Roethke: Poets I Met in America." *SE* [Japan] 51 (Oct. 1962), 24–26. [biography]

Gangewere, R. J. "Theodore Roethke: The Future of Reputation." *CSE*, 2 (1970), 65–73.

Galvin, Brendan. "Kenneth Burke and Theodore Roethke's 'Lost Son' Poems." *NWR*, 11 (Summer 1971), 67–96.

Gloege, Randall. "Suspension of Belief in the Poetry of Theodore Roethke." Ph.D. diss., Bowling Green State U., 1969.

Gustafson, Richard. "In Roethkeland." *MQ*, 7 (Autumn 1965), 167–74.

Harrington, Michael. "No 'half-baked Bacchus' from Saginaw." *Commonweal*, 89 (Feb. 21, 1969), 656–57. [rev.]

Heilman, Robert B. "Theodore Roethke: Personal Notes." *Shenandoah*, 16 (Autumn 1964), 55–64. [biography]

Heron, Philip E. "The Vision of Meaning: Theodore Roethke's 'Frau Bauman, Frau Schmidt, and Frau Schwartze'." *WS*, 34 (Winter 1970), 29–33.

Heyen, William. "Essays on the Later Poetry of Theodore Roethke." Ph.D. diss., Ohio U., 1967.

————, comp. *Profile of Theodore Roethke.* Columbus: Merrill, 1971.

Kramer, Hilton. "The Poetry of Theodore Roethke." *WR*, 18 (Winter 1954), 131–46.

Kunitz, Stanley. "News of the Root." *Poetry*, 73 (Jan. 1949), 222–25. [rev.]

————. "Roethke: Poet of Transformation." *NR*, 152 (Jan. 23, 1965), 23–29.

LaBelle, Jenijoy. "Theodore Roethke and Tradition: 'The Pure Serene of Memory in One Man'." *NWR*, 11 (Summer 1971), 1–18.

————. *The Echoing Wood of Theodore Roethke.* Princeton: Princeton U., 1976.

Lane, Gary, ed. *A Concordance to the Poems of Theodore Roethke.* Metuchen, N.J.: Scarecrow, 1972.

Lee, Charlotte I. "The Line as a Rhythmic Unit in the Poetry of Theodore Roethke." *SpM*, 30 (Mar. 1963), 15–22.

Lombardo, Agostino. "La Poesia di Theodore Roethke." In *Theodore Roethke: Sequenza Nordamericana E Altri Poesie.* Milan: Mondadori, 1966. Pp. 9–26.

Lucas, John. "The Poetry of Theodore Roethke." *OxR*, 7 (Trinity 1968), 39–64.

McKenzie, James. "A New American Nature Poetry: Theodore Roethke, James Dickey, and James Wright." Ph.D. diss., Northwestern U., 1970.

McLeod, James R. "Bibliographic Notes on the Creative Process and Sources of Roethke's 'The Lost Son' Sequence." *NWR*, 11 (Summer 1971), 97–111. [biblio-essay]

———. *Theodore Roethke: A Manuscript Checklist*. Kent, Ohio: Kent State U., 1971.

———. *Theodore Roethke: A Bibliography*. Kent, Ohio: Kent State U., 1973.

McMichael, James. "The Poetry of Theodore Roethke." *SouR*, n.s. 5 (Winter 1969), 4–25.

———. "Roethke's North America." *NWR*, 11 (Summer 1971), 149–59.

Malkoff, Karl. *Theodore Roethke: An Introduction to the Poetry*. New York: Columbia U., 1966.

Martz, William J. *The Achievement of Theodore Roethke*. Glenview, Ill.: Scott, Foresman, 1966.

Meliado, Mariolina. "Theodore Roethke." *SA* [Rome], 9 (1964), 425–545.

Mills, Ralph J., Jr. *Theodore Roethke*. Minneapolis: U. Minnesota, 1963.

———. *Selected Letters of Theodore Roethke*. Seattle: U. Washington, 1968.

Nyren, Dorothy, ed. "Roethke, Theodore (1908–1963)." In *A Library of Literary Criticism*. New York: Ungar, 1960.

Ostroff, Anthony, ed. "The Poet and His Critics: A Symposium." *NWW*, 19 (1961), 189–219.

Reichertz, Ronald R. " 'Once More, the Round': An Introduction to the Poetry of Theodore Roethke." Ph. D. diss., U. Wisconsin, 1967.

Rosenthal, Mach L. *The Modern Poets: A Critical Introduction*. New York: Oxford, 1965.

Seager, Allan. *The Glass House: The Life of Theodore Roethke*. New York: McGraw-Hill, 1968.

Scott, Nathan A. "The Example of Roethke." In *The Wild Prayer of Longing and the Sacred*. New Haven: Yale U., 1971. Pp. 76–118.

Shapiro, Karl. ["Recent American Poetry"—title in Russian]*Amerika*, n.s., 28, *Yeha* 5 [1959], 8–11.

Southworth, James G. "The Poetry of Theodore Roethke." *CE* (Mar. 21, 1960), 326.

Staples, Hugh B. "Rose in the Sea-Wind: A Reading of Theodore Roethke's 'North American Sequence'." *AL*, 34 (May 1964), 189–203.

Stein, Arnold. "Roethke: Man and Poet." *VQR*, 45 (Spring 1969), 361–64. [bio-review]

———. "Roethke's Memory: Actions, Visions, and Revisions." *NWR*, 11 (Summer 1971), 19–31.

———, ed. *Theodore Roethke: Essays on the Poetry*. Seattle: U. Washington, 1965.

Stevens, Phillip. "A Study of Kinesthetic Imagery in Selected Poetry of Theodore Roethke." Ph.D. diss., Northwestern U., 1970.

Sullivan, Rosemary. *Theodore Roethke: The Garden Master*. Seattle: U. Washington, 1975.

Truesdale, C. W. "Theodore Roethke and the Landscape of American Poetry." *MinnR*, 8 (1968), 345–57.

Toerien, Barend J. "Theodore Roethke, Met Opmerking oor Nuwere Amerikaanse Poesie." *Tydskrif vir Letterkinde* [Johannesburg], 2 (May 1963), 34–43.

Vernon, John. "Theodore Roethke's Praise to the End! Poems." *IR*, 2 (Fall 1971), 60–79.

Waggoner, Hyatt H. *American Poets: From Puritans to the Present*. Boston: Houghton Mifflin, 1968.

Williams, Harry. *"The Edge is What I Have": Theodore Roethke and After*. Lewisburg: Bucknell U., 1976.

Wolff, George A. "The Production of Time: Themes and Images in the Poetry of Theodore Roethke." Ph.D. diss., Michigan State U., 1966.

James R. McLeod
North Idaho College
Coeur d'Alene, Idaho

O[LE] E [DVART] ROLVAAG (1876–1931)

Most of the critical commentary on Rolvaag's work has centered, predictably enough, on his contributions to the literature of the American immigrant. Parrington remarks on his profound insight into the emotional experiences of the early Norwegian settlers. Boynton sees Rolvaag's importance in terms of his honest and somber recording of pioneer culture in its successive stages. Meyer uses *Giants in the Earth,* with its excellent novelistic qualities, as a yardstick in measuring other novels which deal with the pioneering theme. Flanagan feels that *Giants* is the one midwestern novel of its time which transcends local milieu to become a valuable chapter in man's epic struggle against the elements. Critics are fairly well agreed that *Giants* is by far the best novel of Rolvaag's epic trilogy of Norwegian emigration to South Dakota (the trilogy also includes *Peder Victorious* and *Their Fathers' God*).

Jorgenson, who had access to the little diary Rolvaag kept from 1896 to 1901, emphasizes the importance of the author's personal life in his writings. Haugen notes Rolvaag's anxiety over what he considered the apathetic slowness with which his countrymen were adjusting to life in America. Olson calls Rolvaag a literary genius and notes that his important book of essays, *Omkring Faedrearven,* remains in need of English translation.

MAJOR WORKS

Omkring Faedrearven. Northfield, Minn.: St. Olaf College, 1922. [essays]
Giants in the Earth. New York: Harper, 1927. Tr. of *I de dage* (Oslo, 1924) and *Riket grundlaegges* (Oslo, 1925). [novel]
Peder Victorious. New York: Harper, 1929. Tr. of *Peder Seier* (Oslo, 1928). [novel]
Pure Gold. New York: Harper, 1930. Tr. of *To tullinger* (Minneapolis, 1920). [novel]
Their Fathers' God. New York: Harper, 1931. Tr. of of *Den signede dag* (Oslo, 1931). [novel]
The Boat of Longing. New York: Harper, 1933. Tr. of *Laengselens baat* (Minneapolis, 1921). [novel]
The Third Life of Per Smevik. Minneapolis: Dillon, 1971. Tr. of *Amerika-Breve* (Minneapolis, 1912). [novel]

CHECKLIST OF SECONDARY SOURCES

Burke; *CAA; DAB; LHUS; OCAL; TCA.*

Baker, Joseph E. "Western Man Against Nature: *Giants in the Earth.*" *CE,* 4 (1942), 19–26.
Beck, Richard. "Rolvaag, Interpreter of Immigrant Life." *NDQ,* 24 (Winter 1956), 26–30.
Boynton, Percy H. "O. E. Rolvaag and the Conquest of the Pioneer." *EJ,* 18 (Sept. 1929), 535–42.
Colcord, Lincoln. Introduction to *Giants in the Earth.* New York: Harper, 1927.
————. "Rolvaag the Fisherman Shook His Fist at Fate." *AmM,* 105 (Mar. 7, 1928), 36–37.
Flanagan, John T. "The Middle Western Farm Novel." *MH,* 23 (June 1942), 113–25.
Gvale, Gudrun H. *O. E. Rolvaag: Nordmann og Amerikanar.* Ph.D. diss. Oslo: Universitetsforlaget, 1962.

Haugen, Einar. "Bibliography." In *Peder Victorious*. New York: Harper, 1929. Pp. 327–30.
_____. "O. E. Rolvaag: Norwegian-American." *NASR*, 7 (1933), 53–73.
Jorgenson, Theodore. "The Main Factors in Rolvaag's Authorship." *NASR*, 10 (1938), 135–51.
Jorgenson, Theodore and Nora O. Solum. *Ole Edvart Rolvaag, a Biography*. New York: Harper, 1939.
Laverty, Carroll D. "Rolvaag's Creation of the Sense of Doom in *Giants in the Earth*." *SCB*, 27 (1967), 45–50.
Meyer, Roy W. *The Middle Western Farm Novel in the Twentieth Century*. Lincoln, Nebr.: U. Nebraska, 1965.
_____. "The Scandinavian Immigrant in American Farm Fiction." *ASR*, 47 (Sept. 1959), 243–49.
Moore, Douglas (music) and Arnold Sundgaard (libretto). *Giants in the Earth*. Original-version premiere, Columbia University, 1951. Revised-version premiere, University of North Dakota, Apr. 4–6, 1974. [opera based on Rolvaag's novel]
Olson, Julius E. "Rolvaag's Novels of Norwegian Pioneer Life in the Dakotas." *SSN*, 9 (Aug. 1926), 45–55.
Parrington, Vernon. "Editor's Introduction." In *Giants in the Earth*. New York: Harper, 1929. Pp. ix–xx. Reprinted as "Ole Rolvaag's *Giants in the Earth*." In *Main Currents in American Thought*. New York: Harcourt, 1930. Vol. 3, 387–96.
Reigstad, Paul. "The Art and Mind of O. E. Rolvaag." Ph.D. diss., U. New Mexico, 1955.
_____. *Rolvaag: His life and art*. Lincoln: U. Nebraska, 1972.
Skard, Sigmund, Ingrid Semmingsen, and Dorothy B. Skardal. "Gudrun Hovde Gvåle: O. E. Rolvaag, Nordmann og Amerikaner." *Edda*, 53 (1965), 361–402. [opposition at doctoral disputation, Oslo]
Solum, Nora O. "The Sources of the Rolvaag Biography." *NASR*, 11 (1940), 150–59.
Steensma, Robert. "Rölvaag and Turner's Frontier Thesis." *NDQ*, 27 (Autumn 1959), 100–4.
_____. "*The South Dakota Novel*: Thoughts After a Centennial." *NDQ*, 30 (Spring 1962), 40–41.
Stevens, Robert L. "Ole Edvart Rolvaag: A Critical Study of His Norwegian-American Novels." Ph.D. diss., U. Illinois, 1955.
Thorson, Gerald, ed. *Ole Rolvaag: Artist and Cultural Leader*. Northfield, Minn.: St. Olaf College, 1974. [essays]
White, George L. *Scandinavian Themes in American Fiction*. Philadelphia: U. Pennsylvania, 1937.

Mary Ellen Caldwell
University of North Dakota
Grand Forks, North Dakota

CARL SANDBURG (1878–1967)

Allen has written that "God created Sandburg a writer, but by his own efforts he became a poet." Realizing that Sandburg's "folksy manners and his love affair with the American people" offended the critics, most of whom were "either in or close to the academic world," Allen remarked: "Sandburg's success as the voice and conscience of his time and generation, to a degree Whitman would have envied, is sufficient justification for a critical study of his life and career."

Durnell considered him a "furious and yet gentle critic of his age and its failure to live up to the best in its tradition." Thus she felt his readers had come "to associate him with the national ideal he paints . . . ."

Of fame and acceptance he wrote his friend Archibald MacLeish, "Since we are both poets—and MAJOR poets at that—and only Posterity can dispute it—and we will be pickled and bleached so pretty before ever Posterity gets in its say—so as to whether we are MAJOR or MINOR—I'm sending you dese dem and dose . . . ." He had sent MacLeish one of his recurrent sets of "definitions of poetry hot off the pan . . . ." A typical definition: "Poetry is the opening and closing of a door, leaving those who look through to guess about what is seen during a moment." He also sent Mac-Leish his typically whimsical encouragement: "We are never down till we are out and never flabbergasted till we are kaflooberated."

Mark Van Doren was certain that "Sandburg was a poet, and everybody knew he was." When Sandburg died, Van Doren wrote: ". . . the country mourned for a beloved poet who had never seemed old, so tough his strength was, so enduring his spirit, so unconquerable his humor and his own courageous love."

Sandburg thought *The People, Yes* (1936) was his best work. It is recommended as a starting place for those who might chance to be discovering Sandburg, a vast continent of a man. Anyone doing scholarly research should be alerted to such major collections as those at the University of Illinois, Knox College, Ball State University, and The Sandburg Home Sites at Flat Rock, N.C. Many papers are in the hands of the Sandburg family in Asheville, N.C. Among other items in the latter collection is an autobiographical manuscript, "Ever the Winds of Chance."

MAJOR WORKS

In Reckless Ecstasy. Galesburg, Ill.: Asgard, 1904. [poems]
Chicago Poems. New York: Holt, 1916.
Cornhuskers. New York: Holt, 1918. [poems]
The Chicago Race Riots. New York: Harcourt, 1919. New ed., 1969, with Introduction by Ralph McGill. [race and reportage]
Smoke and Steel. New York: Harcourt, 1920. [poems]
Slabs of the Sunburnt West. New York: Harcourt, 1922. [poems]
The American Songbag. Ed. New York: Harcourt, 1928. [folk songs]
Steichen the Photographer. New York: Harcourt, 1929. [biography, art, family]
The People, Yes. New York: Harcourt, 1936. [poems]
Abraham Lincoln: The War Years. 4 vols. New York: Harcourt, 1939. [biography]
Remembrance Rock. New York: Harcourt, 1948. [novel]
Complete Poems. New York: Harcourt, 1950. Rev. & exp. ed., 1970.
Always the Young Strangers. New York: Harcourt, 1953. [autobiography]
The Sandburg Range. New York: Harcourt, 1957. [representative selections chosen by Sandburg]
Honey and Salt. New York: Harcourt, 1963. [poems]

CHECKLIST OF SECONDARY SOURCES

Alexander. William. "The Limited American, the Great Loneliness, and the Singing Fire: CS's 'Chicago Poems.' " *AL*, 45 (Mar. 1973), 67–83.

Allen, Gay Wilson. *CS*. Minneapolis: U. Minnesota, 1972.

———. "CS: Fire and Smoke." *SAQ*, 59 (Summer 1960), 315–31.

Anderson, J. B. "Frost and S: A Theological Criticism." *Renascence*, 19 (Summer 1967), 171–83.

Basler, Roy P. "Your Friend the Poet—CS." *Midway*, 10 (Autumn 1969), 3–15.

Boynton, Percy H. "The Voice of Chicago: Edgar Lee Masters and CS." *EJ* (Dec. 1922), 610–20.

Canant, Ray M. "A Catalogue of the CS Collection at the University of Texas at Austin." Ph.D. diss., U. Texas, 1973.

Callaha, North. *CS, Lincoln of Our Literature: A Biography*. New York: New York U., 1970.

Cargill, Oscar. "CS:1 Crusader and Mystic." *CE*, 11 (Apr. 1950), 365–72.

Brooks, Van Wyck. *The Confident Years: 1885–1915*. New York: Dutton, 1955. Pp. 409–15.

Compton, C. H. "Who Reads CS?" *SAQ*, 28 (Apr. 1929), 190–200.

Crowder, Richard. *CS*. New York: Twayne, 1961.

Detzer, Karl. *CS: A Study in Personality and Background*. New York: Harcourt, 1941.

Deutsch, Babette. "Poetry for the People." *EJ*, 26 (Apr. 1937), 265–74.

Dobie, J. Frank. *CS & Saint Peter at the Gate*. Austin, Tex.: Encino, 1966. [pamphlet]

Duffie, Bernard. "Progressivism and Personal Revolt." *CR*, 2 (Spring 1958), 125–38.

Durnell, Hazel B. *The America of CS*. Washington: U. Press of Washington, D.C., 1965.

Flanagan, John T. "Three Illinois Poets." *CR*, 16 (Fall 1972), 313–27.

Golden, Harry. *CS*. New York: World, 1961.

Gregory, Horace and Marya Zaturenska. *A History of American Poetry, 1900–1940*. New York: Harcourt, 1946.

Haas, Joseph and Gene Lovitz. *CS: A Pictorial Biography*. New York: Putnam, 1967.

Hallwas, John and Dennis Reader, eds. *The Vision of This Land: Studies of Vachel Lindsay,· Edgar Lee Masters, and Carl Sandburg*. Macomb: Western Illinois U., 1976.

Hansen, Harry. *Midwest Portraits*. New York: Harcourt, 1923.

The Lincoln of CS: Some Reviews of "Abraham Lincoln: the War Years." New York: Harcourt, 1940. [pamphlet; reviews by Charles Beard, Robert Sherwood, Lloyd Lewis, and others]

Hoffman, D. G. "S and 'the People': His Literary Populism Appraised." *AR*, 10 (Summer 1950), 265–78.

Illinois, University Library. *The S Range: An Exhibit of Materials from CS's Library*. Introduction by John T. Flanagan. Notes by Leslie W. Dunlap. Urbana, 1958. [pamphlet]

Jones, Howard Mumford. "Backgrounds of Sorrow." *VQR*, 3 (Jan. 1927), 111–23.

Lomax, Allen. *CS Does Cowboy Songs and Negro Spirituals*. Decca Record, n.d.

Lowell, Amy. *Tendencies in Modern American Poetry*. New York: Macmillan, 1917.

Mitgang, Herbert, ed. *The Letters of CS*. New York: Harcourt, 1968.

Monroe, Harriet. "CS." *Poetry*, 24 (Spring 1924), 320–26.

Nevins, Allan. "S as Historian." *JISHS*, 45 (Winter 1952), 261–72.

Quigley, Mike. "CS, Noted Poet, Historian, and Lincoln Scholar Tells Interviewer How He Thinks the Great Emancipator Would Have Reacted to Today's Touchy Race Problems." *Ebony*, 18 (Sept. 1963), 158–59.

Ramsdell, C. W. "CS's *Lincoln*." *SouR*, 6 (Winter 1941), 439–53.

Rogers, W.G. *CS, Yes*. New York: Harcourt, 1970.

Rosenfeld, Paul. "CS." *Bookman*, 53 (July 1921), 389–96.

Sandburg, Helga. *Sweet Music*. New York: Dial, 1963.

Steichen, Edward, ed. *S: Photographers View of CS*. New York: Harcourt, 1966.

Steichen, Paula. *My Connemara*. New York: Harcourt, 1969.

Stroud, Parry E. "CS: A Biographical and Critical Study of His Major Works." Ph.D. diss., Northwestern U., 1956.

Van Doren, Carl. "Flame and Slag. CS: Poet with Both Fists." *Century*, 106 (Spring 1923), 786–92.

Van Doren, Mark. *CS. With a Bibliography of Sandburg Materials in the Collections of the Library of Congress*. Washington: Library of Congress, 1969.

Voices. CS issue. New York, 1946.

Williams, William Carlos. Review of *Complete Poems*. *Poetry*, 7–8 (Apr. 1950), 365–72.

Yatron, Michael. *America's Literary Revolt*. New York: Philosophical Library, 1959.

———. "CS: The Poet as Nonconformist." *EJ*, 48 (Dec. 1959), 524–27.

Zabel, Morton D. "S's Testament." *Poetry*, 49 (Oct. 1936), 33–45.
Zehnpfenning, Gladys. *CS: Poet and Patriot*. Minneapolis: Denison, 1963.

William Sutton
Ball State University
Muncie, Indiana

LEW SARETT (1888–1954)

During the 1920s Lew Sarett flourished as a popular poet, praised as much for his roles of forest ranger, wilderness guide, ethnologist, and university professor as for his writing. Serious critical consideration stemmed from a review in which Harriet Monroe contrasted T. S. Eliot's indoor decadence with Sarett's outdoor faith in nature. Subsequent critics have distinguished between Sarett's own lyrics and his Amerindian translations. Henderson thinks the latter faithfully capture the Chippewa humor, music, and symbolism, while others observe that they are more authentic interpretations than translations of Indian songs; all agree that Sarett has preserved a precious national heritage. Regarding Sarett's own poems, Nathan places their simple mysticism and romantic melancholy somewhere between the sensibilities of John Muir and William Cullen Bryant. Shapiro views him as a metaphysician who organizes his poetry around a theology of nature, but suggests that the result is conventional. Sarett's successive volumes drew less and less attention, so that he is remembered chiefly in older histories of American poetry. Only the posthumously published selected edition remains in print.

MAJOR WORKS

Many Many Moons. New York: Holt, 1920. [poetry]
The Box of God. New York: Holt, 1922. [poetry]
Slow Smoke. New York: Holt, 1925. [poetry]
Wings Against the Moon. New York: Holt, 1931. [poetry]
The Collected Poems of Lew Sarett. New York: Holt, 1941. [poetry]
Covenant With Earth: A Selection From the Poetry of Lew Sarett. Gainesville: U. Florida, 1956.

CHECKLIST OF SECONDARY SOURCES

CAA; OCAL; TCA & Supp.

Braithwaite, William S. "The Romantic Lore of the Red Man." *Boston Evening Transcript*, May 8, 1920, p. 8. [rev.]
Clark, Neil M. "Lew Sarett—Victor!" *AmM*, 101 (Mar. 1926), 24–25.
————. "The Story of Lew Sarett—Tenement Waif, Forest Ranger, Poet." *AmM*, 101 (Feb. 1926), 37.
Frink, Maurice. "Out A'Fishing With Lew Sarett." *Nature*, 16 (Aug. 1930), 113–16. [interview]

Hansen, Harry. *Midwest Portraits: A Book of Memories and Friendships.* New York: Harcourt, 1923. Pp. 263–86.

Hatfield, Wilbur. "Lew Sarett Speaking." *Scholastic,* 30 (May 8, 1937), 11. [interview]

Henderson, Alice C. "Tall Timber and a Loon." *Poetry,* 17 (1920), 158–61. [rev.]

Kreymborg, Alfred. *A History of American Poetry: Our Singing Strength.* New York: Tudor, 1934. Pp. 466–79.

McCole, Camilla J. "Contemporary Writers: Lew Sarett." *Writer,* 41 (1929), 120–23.

Monroe, Harriet. "A Contrast." *Poetry,* 21 (1923), 325–30. [rev.]

_____. *Poets and Their Art.* Rev. ed. New York: Macmillan, 1932.

Nathan, Leonard. "Three American Poets." *Poetry,* 90 (1957), 325–30.

Shapiro, Leo. "Lew Sarett and Nature." *Poetry,* 59 (1941), 154–58. [rev.]

Untermeyer, Louis. *American Poetry Since 1900.* New York: Holt, 1923.

Weirick, Bruce. *From Whitman to Sandburg in American Poetry.* New York: Macmillan, 1924.

Joseph W. Slade
Long Island University
Brooklyn, New York

HENRY ROWE SCHOOLCRAFT (1793–1864)

A self-educated geologist, mineralogist, and ethnologist, Schoolcraft first came to the Midwest in 1819 to investigate the lead mines of Missouri. He published several narratives of his journeys in the region, including the account of his own successful expedition to the true source of the Mississippi. His contribution to American letters, both as an observer and explorer of the Old Northwest and as an interpreter of the character of the northern Indian tribes, has largely been ignored. His numerous publications of Indian tales influenced the American apprehension of Indian culture and Longfellow's composition of *Hiawatha.* Yet his eight volume work, *Historical and statistical information respecting . . . the Indian tribes of the United States* (1851–57), which represents the work of thirty years, remains virtually untouched as historical record.

The Schoolcraft papers, the great bulk of which are in the Library of Congress, have received no systematic attention. The only extended study, Osborn's biography and panegyric, *Schoolcraft-Longfellow-Hiawatha* (1943), is both incomplete and unreliable. Information concerning Schoolcraft also exists in the archives of the Bureau of Indian Affairs, in the Department of the Interior, in the Burton Historical Library, and in the Michigan Historical Collections.

MAJOR WORKS

A view of the lead mines of Missouri . . . . New York: Wiley, 1819.

Journal of a tour into the interior of Missouri and Arkansaw . . . performed in the years 1818 and 1819. London: Phillips, 1821. American ed.: *Scenes and adventures in the Semi-Alpine region of the Ozark mountains* . . . . Philadelphia, 1853.

Narrative journal of travels through the northwestern regions of the United States . . . . Albany: Hosford, 1821.

Travels in the central portions of the Mississippi valley . . . . New York: Collins & Hanney, 1825.

The rise of the west . . . . Detroit: Whitney, 1830. [poem]

Narrative of an expedition through the upper Mississippi to Itasca lake . . . . New York: Harper, 1834.

Algic researches, comprising inquiries respecting the mental characteristics of the North American Indians. First series. New York: Harper, 1839. Reprinted as *The Myth of Hiawatha.* Philadelphia, 1856. [Indian tales and legends]

Oneonta, or The red race of America . . . . New York: Burgess, Stringer, 1844–45.

Notes on the Iroquois . . . . Albany: Pease, 1847.

The Indian in his wigwam, or, Characteristics of the red race of America . . . . New York: Graham, 1847. [folklore]

Personal memoirs of a residence of thirty years with the Indian tribes on the American frontiers . . . . Philadelphia: Lippincott, Grambo, 1851. [autobiography]

Western scenes and reminiscenes . . . Auburn, N.Y.: Derby & Miller, 1853.

Historical and statistical information respecting the history, condition and prospects of the Indian tribes of the United States. 8 v. Philadelphia: Lippincott, Grambo, 1851–57.

CHECKLIST OF SECONDARY SOURCES

BDAL; Burke; *DAB;* Duyckinck; Herzberg; *OCAL.*

Baker, James H. "The Sources of the Mississippi." *CMHS,* 6 (1894), 3–26.

Blackburn, George. "George Johnston and the Sioux-Chippewa Boundary Survey." *MH,* 51 (1967), 313–22.

Brower, J. V. "The Mississippi River and Its Sources." *CMHS,* 7 (1893).

Fabin, W. W. "Indians of the Tri-State Area, the Potowatomies, the Removal." *NOQ,* 40 (1968), 68–84.

"Henry R. Schoolcraft." *CMHS,* 7 (1893), 142–51.

"Henry R. Schoolcraft." *Annals of Iowa,* 3 (1865), 498–505.

Heslin, J. R. "The Republic of Allegania." *NYHSQ,* 51 (1967), 24–44.

Huguenin, Charles A. "The Pompey Stone." *NYFQ,* 14 (1958), 34–43.

Keiser, Albert. *The Indian in American Literature.* London: Oxford, 1933.

Luckingham, B. F. "Note of the Lead Mines of Missouri." *MHR,* 59 (1965), 344–48.

⸺. "Schoolcraft's Promotion of Scientific Interest in the Frontier." *M-A,* 47 (1965), 129–44.

⸺. "Schoolcraft, Slavery and Emancipation." *JNH,* 50 (1965), 118–21.

Marsden, Michael T. "Henry Rowe Schoolcraft: A Reappraisal." *ON,* 2 (June 1976), 153–82.

Orians, G. Harrison. "The Souvenir of the Lakes." *NOQ,* 40 (1939), 1–24.

Osborn, Chase S. *Schoolcraft-Longfellow-Hiawatha.* Lancaster, Pa.: Cattell, 1942. [biog.]

Rankin, Ernest H. "Henry Rowe Schoolcraft Visits Lake Superior." *IS,* 20 (1964), 205–10.

Rusk, Ralph L. *The Literature of the Midwestern Frontier.* 2 vols. New York: Columbia U., 1925.

Wagner, Henry R. and Charles L. Camp. *The Plains and the Rockies.* Columbus, Ohio: Long's College, 1953.

Weaver, Richard. "Henry Rowe Schoolcraft: Lyceum Lecturer." *IS,* 26 (1970), 293–96.

JoAnn Hackos
University of Texas of the Permian Basin
Odessa, Texas

KARL SHAPIRO (1912–   )

No full-length studies of Karl Shapiro and his work exist; most of his work has been treated in reviews and short critical essays. Much of what has been said about Shapiro concentrates on either his evolving quest for identity or his concept of a Jewish consciousness. Waggoner traces the development of Shapiro's philosophy and the shift in attitude expressed in early works to that expressed in *The Bourgeois Poet*. Rubin reinforces Waggoner's appraisal. Stephanchev and Mills offer brief surveys of the major themes in Shapiro's work. Malkoff examines in some detail Shapiro's concept of a Jewish consciousness and its relationship to reality, using as a principal basis for the discussion *Poems of a Jew*. Only two bibliographies of Shapiro's work and attendant criticism exist. Both are dated, but White is more useful than Quesnel. Still to be examined extensively is Shapiro's role as midwestern poet and editor of *Poetry* and *Prairie Schooner*.

MAJOR WORKS

Poems. Baltimore: Waverly, 1935.
Person, Place and Thing. New York: Reynal and Hitchcock, 1942. [poetry]
The Place of Love. Melbourne: Crozier, 1942. [poetry]
V-Letter and Other Poems. New York: Reynal and Hitchcock, 1944.
Essay on Rime. New York: Reynal and Hitchcock, 1945. [poetry]
Trial of a Poet, and Other Poems. New York: Reynal and Hitchcock, 1947.
English Prosody and Modern Poetry. Baltimore: Johns Hopkins U., 1947. [lecture]
A Bibliography of Modern Prosody. Baltimore: Johns Hopkins U., 1948.
Poems 1940–1953. New York: Random House, 1953.
Beyond Criticism. Lincoln: U. Nebraska, 1953. [lectures]
The Tenor. New York: Westminster Recording and Merion Music Co., 1956. [libretto]
Poems of a Jew. New York: Random House, 1958.
In Defense of Ignorance. New York: Random House, 1960. [essays]
The Bourgeois Poet. New York: Random House, 1964. [poetry]
A Primer for Poets. Lincoln: U. Nebraska, 1965.
Selected Poems. New York: Random House, 1968.
To Abolish Children, and Other Essays. Chicago: Quadrangle, 1968.
White Haired Lover. New York: Random House, 1968. [poetry]
Edsel. New York: Geis, 1971. [novel]
The Poetry Wreck: Selected Essays, 1950–1970. New York: Random, 1975.
Adult Book Store. New York: Random, 1976. [poems]

CHECKLIST OF SECONDARY SOURCES

Burke; *CA; CB; CP;* Herzberg; *LLC; OCAL; TCA & Supp.*

Cowley, Malcolm. "Lively and Deadly Wit." *Poetry*, 61 (Feb. 1943), 620–22. [rev.]
Daiches, David. "The Poetry of Karl Shapiro." *Poetry*, 66 (Aug. 1945), 266–73.
Fiedler, Leslie A. "On the Road; or the Adventures of Karl Shapiro." *Poetry*, 96 (June 1960), 171–78. [rev.]
———. *Waiting for the End*. New York: Stein and Day, 1964. Pp. 89–103.

Fitts, Dudley. "Mr. Shapiro's Ars Poetica." *Poetry*, 98 (Apr. 1946), 39–44. [rev.]

Fussell, Edwin. "KS: The Paradox of Prose and Poetry." *WR*, 18 (Spring 1954), 225–44.

Glicksberg, Charles I. "Karl Shapiro and the Personal Accent." *PrS*, 22 (Spring 1948), 44–52.

Kazin, Alfred. "The Poet Against the English Department." *Reporter*, 22 (June 9, 1960), 44–47.

Kohler, Dayton. "Karl Shapiro: Poet in Uniform." *CE*, 7 (Feb. 1946), 243–49.

Malkoff, Karl. "The Self in the Modern World; Karl Shapiro's Jewish Poems." In *Contemporary American-Jewish Literature*, Irving Malin, ed. Bloomington: Indiana U., 1973. Pp. 213–28.

Matthiessen, F. O. "Essay on Rime," and "Four American Poets, 1944." In *Responsibilities of the Critic*. Ed. by John Rackliffe. New York: Oxford, 1952. Pp. 53–60, 116–128.

Mills, Ralph, Jr. *Contemporary American Poetry*. New York: Random House, 1965. Pp. 101–21.

Mizener, Arthur. "Poets as Critics." *SR*, 62 (July 1954), 504–9. [rev.]

O'Connor, William Van. "Shapiro's Southwest Pacific Poems." *Poetry*, 64 (Sept. 1944), 326–34.

————. "Karl Shapiro: The Development of a Talent." *CE*, 10 (Nov. 1948), 71–77.

Quesnel, Louise. *A Bibliography of the Work of Karl Jay Shapiro 1935–1949*. Rev. by William G. Webster. Baltimore: Enoch Pratt Free Library, 1950.

Rubin, Louis D., Jr. "The Search for Lost Innocence: Karl Shapiro's *The Bourgeois Poet*." *HC*, 1 (Dec. 1964), 1–16. [rev.]

Schwartz, Delmore. "Poet's Progress." *Nation*, 156 (Jan. 9, 1943), 63–64. [rev.]

Seif, Morton. "Poet's Journey: The Struggle in the Soul of Karl Shapiro." *MenJ*, 37 (Winter 1949), 51–58.

Slotkin, Richard. "The Contextual Symbol: Karl Shapiro's Image of 'The Jew'." *AQ*, 18 (Summer 1966), 220–26.

Solotaroff, T. "Irrational Karl Shapiro." *Commentary*, 30 (Nov. 1960), 445–48.

Southworth, James G. "The Poetry of Karl Shapiro." *EJ*, 51 (Mar. 1962), 159–66.

Spender, Stephen. "The Power and the Hazard." *Poetry*, 71 (Mar. 1948), 314–18. [rev.]

Stepanchev, Stephen. *American Poetry Since 1945*. New York: Harper, 1965. Pp. 53–68.

Waggoner, Hyatt H. *American Poets from the Puritans to the Present*. Boston: Houghton Mifflin, 1968. Pp. 585–96.

White, William. *Karl Shapiro: A Bibliography*. Detroit: Wayne State U., 1960.

Whittemore, Reed. "A Letter to KS." *Poetry*, 98 (June 1961), 170–85.

Williams, William Carlos. "Shapiro Is All Right." *KR*, 8 (Winter 1946), 123–26. [rev.]

Charles R. Duke
Plymouth State College
Plymouth, New Hampshire

MAX SHULMAN (1919–)

A popular American humorist since the 1940s, Minnesotan Max Shulman has attracted little critical notice during his thirty-year career as a writer of stories, novels, plays and scripts, columns, and occasional articles. Since 1943, for example, the *MLA International Bibliography* has included only one item on his work—the article by Nash, which is more sociological than literary in its focus. No critical or bibliographical efforts have been devoted solely to Shulman, although he is included in Warfel and mentioned sparingly in Yates. He is discussed often in Steadman's dissertation. The Evans interview details his career and his views on writing. Despite the general dearth of attention given to Shulman, serious reviews of his novels and plays at their publication are numerous, particularly in *Saturday Review* and the *New Yorker*, and often more thoroughly in *Time* and the *New York Times Book Review*.

MAJOR WORKS

Barefoot Boy with Cheek. Garden City, N.Y.: Doubleday, 1943. [novel]
The Feather Merchants. Garden City, N.Y.: Doubleday, 1944. [novel]
The Zebra Derby. Garden City, N.Y.: Doubleday, 1946. [novel]
Sleep Till Noon. Garden City, N.Y.: Doubleday, 1949. [novel]
The Many Loves of Dobie Gillis. Garden City, N.Y.: Doubleday, 1949. [stories]
The Tender Trap (with Robert Paul Smith). New York: Random House, 1955. [play]
Rally Round the Flag, Boys! Garden City, N.Y.: Doubleday, 1957. [novel]
I Was a Teenage Dwarf. New York: Geis, 1959. [novel]
Anyone Got a Match? New York: Harper, 1964. [novel]
Potatoes Are Cheaper. Garden City, N.Y.: Doubleday, 1971. [novel]

CHECKLIST OF SECONDARY SOURCES

Burke; *CB;* Warfel.

Atkinson, Brooks. "Shulman-Smith Comedy Opens at Longacre." *New York Times*, Oct. 14, 1954, p. 37. [rev.]
Balakian, Nona. "Undergraduate Days." *NYTBR*, May 23, 1943, p. 32. [rev.]
Basseches, Maurice. "G.I. Joe into John Doe." *SatR*, 29 (Feb. 23, 1946), 12. [rev.]
"Bestseller Revisited." *Time*, 70 (Dec. 30, 1957), 66. [rev.]
Crisler, Ben. "Girls Were his Life." *NYTBR*, Sept. 6, 1959, p. 13. [rev.]
Evans, Glen. "Exclusive Interview with Max Shulman." *WD*, 52 (Mar. 1972), 20–22. [interview]
"Fallen Arch." *Time*, 55 (Apr. 10, 1950), 99. [rev.]
Nash, Russell W. "Max Shulman and the Changing Image of Suburbia." *MASJ*, 4 (Spring 1963), 27–38.
Nathan, George Jean. *The Theatre Book of the Year, 1946–1947*. New York: Knopf, 1947.
Steadman, Mark S. "American Humor: 1920–1955." Ph.D. diss., Florida State U., 1963.
Yates, Norris W. *The American Humorist: Conscience of the Twentieth Century*. Ames, Iowa: Iowa State U., 1964.

Albert B. Somers
Furman University
Greenville, South Carolina

WILLIAM STAFFORD (1914–   )

Although Stafford published widely in periodicals before his first collection of poems appeared in 1960, it was not until his 1962 volume received the National Book Award that his poetry began to receive a wide audience and critical attention. Even so, criticism is still limited mostly to reviews of his books. Extended assessments are few, and close explications of individual poems and of Stafford's poetic technique are only now beginning to appear. Critical reception has, however, been exceptionally favorable. Adams states that "many of Stafford's best poems are full of nostalgia . . . ." Because of Stafford's Midwest boyhood, the nostalgic elements often reflect his life in Kansas and Iowa. His poetry, Miller believes, "is pervaded by a love of the land and its life, a love for people as they move through experience by which . . . they become exemplars of the way human beings live among other human beings." "If ever this country is to have a sense of itself," claims Simpson, "it will be through work like Stafford's." Stafford's long residence in the West also manifests itself in his poems, to the extent that he is regarded by some critics principally as a western poet whose work is concerned with western themes and settings. Articles about Stafford are included in the annual bibliographies in *WAL*, and a monograph on him has been announced for the Boise State University Western Writers Series. The *Northwest Review* has recently (1973) published a special issue devoted to Stafford's work.

MAJOR WORKS

Down in My Heart. Elgin, Ill.: Brethren Publishing House, 1947. [autobiographical nonfiction]
Winterward. Ann Arbor: University Microfilms, 1954. Thesis, State U. Iowa. [poems]
West of Your City. Los Gatos, Calif.: Talisman, 1960. [poems]
Traveling Through the Dark. New York: Harper, 1962. [poems]
The Rescued Year. New York: Harper, 1966. [poems]
The Achievement of Brother Antoninus: A Comprehensive Selection of His Poems with a Critical Introduction. Glenview, Ill.: Scott, Foresman, 1967. [criticism]
Allegiances. New York: Harper, 1970. [poems]
Someday, Maybe. New York: Harper, 1973. [poems]
Going Places. Reno, Nevada: West Coast Poetry Review, 1975. [poems]

CHECKLIST OF SECONDARY SOURCES

CA; CP; OCAL.

Adams, Hazard. "Place and Movement." *Poetry*, 110 (Apr. 1967), 42–44. [rev.]
Carruth, Hayden. "In Spite of Artifice." *HudR*, 19 (Winter 1966–67), 696–97. [rev.]
Cavitch, David. "Lonely Poet, Mellow Poet." *NYTBR*, Dec. 9, 1973, p. 45. [rev.]
"A Conversation Between William Stafford and Primus St. John." *Voyages*, 3 (Spring 1970), 70–79.
Creeley, Robert. " 'Think What's Got Away . . . .' " *Poetry*, 102 (Apr. 1963), 44. [rev.]
Davison, Peter. "The New Poetry." *Atl*, 102 (Nov. 1962), 88. [rev.]
Dickinson-Brown, Roger. "The Wise, the Dull, the Bewildered: What Happens in William Stafford." *MPS*, 6 (1975), 30–38.
Engel, Bernard. "From Here We Speak." *ON*, 2 (March 1976), 37–44.
Fitts, Dudley. "A Varied Quintet." *NYTBR*, Feb. 26, 1961, p. 12. [rev.]
Galler, David. "Description as Poetry." *KR*, 29 (Jan. 1967), 144–45. [rev.]
Greiner, Charles F. "Stafford's *'Traveling through the Dark'*: A Discussion of Style." *EJ*, 15 (1966), 1015–18.
Holden, Jonathan. *The Mark to Turn: A Reading of William Stafford's Poetry.* Lawrence: U. Kansas, 1976.
Hugo, Richard. "Problems with Landscapes in Early Stafford Poems." *KQ*, 2 (1970), 33–38.
Kelley, Patrick. "Legend and Ritual." *KQ*, 2 (1970), 28–31.

Kyle, Carol A. "Point of View in 'Returned to Say' and the Wilderness of William Stafford." *WAL*, 7 (1972), 191–201.

Lensing, George and Ronald Moran. *Four Poets and the Emotive Imagination: Robert Bly, James Wright, Louis Simpson, and William Stafford*. Baton Rouge: Louisiana State U., 1976.

Lieberman, Laurence. "The Expansional Poet: A Return to Personality." *YR*, 57 (Winter 1968), 258–60. [rev.]

Lofsness, Cynthia. "An Interview with William Stafford." *IR*, 3 (Summer 1972), 92–106.

Miller, Tom P. " 'In Dear Detail, by Ideal Light': The Poetry of William Stafford." *SwR*, 56 (Autumn 1971), 341–45.

Moss, Stanley. "Country Boy." *NR*, 155 (Nov. 19, 1966), 23–24. [rev.]

Northwest Review. 13 (1973). [special issue on Stafford]

"Notes on Current Books." *VQR*, 39 (Summer 1963), xcv–xcvi. [rev.]

Pinsler, Sanford. "Finding What the World Is Trying to Be: A Conversation with William Stafford." *APR*, 4 (July 1975), 28–30.

Quinn, Sister Bernetta, O.S.F. "Symbolic Landscapes." *Poetry*, 118 (Aug. 1971), 288–89. [rev.]

Simpson, Louis. "New Books of Poems." *Harper*, 235 (Aug. 1967), 91. [rev.]

Slater, Joseph. "Immortal Bard and Others." *SR*, 49 (Dec. 31, 1966), 25. [rev.]

Smith, William J. "The New Poetry." *Harper*, 227 (Sept. 1963), 113–14. [rev.]

Spector, Robert D. "Betwixt Tradition and Innovation." *SR*, 53 (Dec. 26, 1970), 24. [rev.]

Sumner, D. Nathan. "The Poetry of William Stafford: Nature, Time, and Father." *RSWSU*, 36 (1969), 187–95.

Wagner, Linda. "William Stafford's Plain Style." *MPS*, 6 (1976), 19–30.

Womack, Judy. "Daniel Boone—'Over the Velvet Falls.' " *KFR*, 18 (1972), 21–22.

Robert H. Woodward
San Jose State University
San Jose, California

WALLACE STEGNER (1909–   )

Although a full scale study of Stegner's work has yet to appear, there is extended criticism of his work in studies by Hairston, Jensen, and the Lewises. A Twayne USAS volume on Stegner, by Forrest Robinson, is due for publication shortly. Eisenger's essays involved a review of Stegner's career to about 1960.

There are manuscripts at the University of Iowa (where Stegner was one of the first graduates of the fledgling writing program that began in the 1930s), and at Stanford (where Stegner taught for many years). The Marriott Library at the University of Utah has Stegner papers in its Western American Division. Bibliographies are in Paluka (to 1967) and in *Contemporary Novelists*, which lists some items not in Paluka.

MAJOR WORKS

Remembering Laughter. Boston: Little, Brown, 1937. [novel]
The Potter's House. Muscatine, Ia.: Prairie Press, 1938. [novelette]
On a Darkling Plain. New York: Harcourt, 1940. [novel]
Fire and Ice. New York: Duell, 1941. [novel]

Mormon Country. New York: Duell, 1942. [history]
The Big Rock Candy Mountain. New York: Duell, 1943. [novel]
Second Growth. Boston: Houghton Mifflin, 1947. [novel]
The Preacher and the Slave. Boston: Houghton Mifflin, 1950. Reissued as *Joe Hill: A Bio-
    graphical Novel.* New York: Doubleday, 1969. [novel; incl. a valuable foreword by Stegner]
The Writer in America. Kanda, Japan: Hokuseido, 1952. [criticism]
Beyond the Hundredth Meridian: John Wesley Powell and the Second Opening of the West.
    Boston: Houghton Mifflin, 1954. [biography]
The City of the Living, and other Stories. Boston: Houghton Mifflin, 1957.
A Shooting Star. New York: Viking, 1961. [novel]
Wolf Willow: A History, a Story, and a Memory of the Last Plains Frontier. New York: Vik-
    ing, 1962.
The Gathering of Zion: The Story of the Mormon Trail. New York: McGraw-Hill, 1964.
    [history]
All the Little Live Things. New York: Viking, 1967. [novel]
The Sound of Mountain Water. New York: Doubleday, 1969. [essays]
Angle of Repose. New York: Doubleday, 1971. [novel]
The Uneasy Chair: A Biography of Bernard DeVoto. New York: Doubleday, 1974.
The Spectator Bird. New York: Doubleday, 1976. [novel]

CHECKLIST OF SECONDARY SOURCES

CA; CN; Herzberg; *LLC; TCA & Supp;* Warfel.

Ahearn, Kerry. *"The Big Rock Candy Mountain* and *Angle of Repose." WAL,* 10 (May 1975),
    11–27.
Canzoneri, Robert. "Wallace Stegner: Trial by Existence." *SouR* (Autumn 1973), 796–827.
Eisenger, Chester E. *Fiction of the Forties.* Chicago: U. Chicago, 1963. Pp. 324–28.
———. Twenty Years of Wallace Stegner." *CE,* 20 (Dec. 1958), 110–16.
Flora, Joseph M. "Vardis Fisher and Wallace Stegner: Teacher and Student." *WAL,* 5
    (Summer 1970), 122–28.
Hairston, Joe B. *Wallace Stegner.* Master's thesis, U. Texas, 1966.
Hudson, Lois P. "The Big Rock Candy Mountain: No Roots—and No Frontier." *SDR,* 9
    (Spring 1971), 3–13.
Jensen, Sidney L. *The Middle Road. A Study of Wallace Stegner's Use of History in Fiction.*
    Ph.D. diss., U. Utah, 1973.
Kunitz, Stanley J. "The Compassionate Seer: Wallace Stegner's Literary Artistry." *BYU Stud-
    ies,* 14 (Winter 1974), 248–62.
Lewis, Merrill and Lorene Lewis. *Wallace Stegner.* Western Writers Series. Boise, Ida.: De-
    partment of English, Boise State College, 1972.
———. *The Works of Wallace Stegner.* Cassette tape in the Western Writers Series. Deland,
    Florida: Everett/Edwards, 1974.
Milton, John. "Conversation with Wallace Stegner." *SDR,* 10 (Spring 1971), 45–57.
Moseley, Richard. "First-Person Narrator in Wallace Stegner's *All the Little Live Things."
    NCL,* 3 (Mar. 1973), 12–13.
Nemanic, Gerald C. "Interview: Wallace Stegner." *GLR,* 2 (Summer 1975), 1–25.
Paluka, Frank. *Iowa Authors: A Bio-Bibliography of Sixty Native Writers.* Iowa City: Friends
    of the University of Iowa Libraries, 1967. Pp. 217–20.
Stegner, Wallace. "The Trail of the Hawkeye." *SatR,* 18 (July 30, 1938), 3–4.
———. "Truth and Faking in Fiction." *Writer,* 53 (Feb. 1940), 40–43.
Tyler, Robert L. "The I.W.W. and the West." *AQ,* 12 (Summer 1960), 175–87.

Clarence A. Andrews
University of Iowa
Iowa City, Iowa

PHIL[IP DUFFIELD] STONG (1899–1957)

There are three lengthy studies of Stong, of which he is the author of two. *If School Keeps* is an account of his education (and his life in a small midwestern village), and the beginning of his writing career. *Hawkeyes*, while ostensibly a "biography of the state of Iowa," is equally a revelation of Stong's mind. The December 1957 issue of the *Palimpsest*, published just after Stong's death, has essays by Stong, Frederick, and Petersen. Frederick published Stong's first short story in a 1921 issue of *Midland*, and Petersen was a close friend.

Stong's papers are in the Drake University Library in Des Moines. The definitive bibliography is in Paluka. Some manuscripts are at the University of Iowa; the present disposition of the manuscript of *Horses and Americans* (once at the now-defunct Parsons College) is unknown. Any serious student of Stong's life would find it obligatory to search the files of the Des Moines *Register* and *Tribune* from 1932 to at least 1974 (see Mills, below).

MAJOR WORKS

State Fair. New York: Century, 1932. [novel]
Stranger's Return. New York: Harcourt, 1933. [novel]
Village Tale. New York: Harcourt, 1934. [novel]
Week-End. New York: Harcourt, 1935. [novel]
The Farmer in the Dell. New York: Harcourt, 1935. [novel]
Career. New York: Harcourt, 1936. [novel]
Buckskin Breeches. New York: Farrar, 1937. [novel]
The Rebellion of Lennie Barlow. New York: Farrar, 1937. [novel]
County Fair. New York: Stackpole, 1938. [illustrations and text]
Ivanhoe Keeler. New York: Farrar, 1939. [novel]
Horses and Americans. New York: Stokes, 1939. [illustrations and text]
The Long Lane. New York: Farrar, 1939. [novel]
If School Keeps. New York: Stokes, 1940. [memoir]
Hawkeyes: A Biography of the State of Iowa. New York: Dodd, Mead, 1940.
The Princess. New York: Farrar, 1941. [novel]
One Destiny. New York: Reynal & Hitchcock, 1942. [novel]
The Iron Mountain. New York: Farrar, 1942. [novel]
Marta of Muscovy: The Fabulous Life of Russia's First Empress. Garden City, N.Y.: Doubleday, 1945.
Jessamy John. Garden City, N.Y.: Doubleday, 1947. [novel]
Forty Pounds of Gold. Garden City, N.Y.: Doubleday, 1951. [novel]
Return in August. Garden City, N.Y.: Doubleday, 1953. [novel]
Blizzard. Garden City, N.Y.: Doubleday, 1955. [novel]
Gold in Them Hills: Being An Irreverent History of the Great 1849 Gold Rush. New York: Doubleday, 1957.

CHECKLIST OF SECONDARY SOURCES

CAA; TCA; Warfel.

Andrews, Clarence. *A Literary History of Iowa*. Iowa City: U. Iowa, 1972. Pp. 14–16, 103–13.
Cao, Myra. "Some Children's Books by Iowa Writers." *Books at Iowa*, 9 (Nov. 1968), 3–21.

338 A BIBLIOGRAPHICAL GUIDE

Duffield, George C. "Coming Into Iowa in 1837." *AnIowa*, 3 (Apr. 1903), 1–8. See succeeding
    issues of *AnIowa* through 1906 for further Duffield "Memoirs of Frontier Iowa." Duffield
    was Stong's grandfather; Stong mined this material for some of his books.
Frederick, John T. "Early Iowa in Fiction." *Palimpsest*, 36 (Oct. 1955), 411ff.
——. "The Farm in Iowa Fiction." *Palimpsest*, 32 (Mar. 1951), 131–35.
——. "Iowa's Phil Stong." *Palimpsest*, 38 (Dec. 1957), 520–24.
——. "Town and City in Iowa Fiction." *Palimpsest*, 35 (Feb. 1954), 75ff.
Meyer, Roy. *The Middle Western Farm Novel in the Twentieth Century*. Lincoln: U. Nebras-
    ka, 1965. Pp. 234–35.
Mills, George. "Phil Stong's Legacy." Des Moines *Sunday Register*, Aug. 11, 1974, sec. C, p. 1.
Palimpsest, 38 (Dec. 1957), 501–30. Subject index to Stong's book-length works following p.
    530, and a "Bibliography of Periodical Literature by and about Phil Stong." Photographs.
Paluka, Frank. "Phil Stong." In *Iowa Authors: A Bio-Bibliography of Sixty Native Writers*.
    Iowa City: Friends of the University of Iowa Libraries, 1967. Pp. 146–50.
Petersen, William J. "Phil Stong in Retrospect." *Palimpsest*, 38 (Dec. 1957), 525–30.
Stong, Phil. "Christmas in Iowa." *Palimpsest*, 38 (Dec. 1957), 501–19. First appeared in *Holi-
    day*, Dec. 1952.
——. "Writer in Hollywood." *SatR*, 15 (Apr. 10, 1937), 3–4.
Zwart, Elizabeth Clarkson. "The Front Row." Des Moines *Sunday Register Picture Magazine*,
    Sept. 22, 1974, p. 2.

Clarence A. Andrews
University of Iowa
Iowa City, Iowa

RUTH SUCKOW (1892–1960)

There are two book-length studies of Iowa's Ruth Suckow, but neither approaches the value of George McMichael's study of Alice French, *Journey
to Obscurity*, in placing its subject in her midwestern milieu. Kissane's is
the typical Twayne treatment with some biography, critical assessments of
the work, and detailed bibliography. Omrcanin's work is, in Leo Gurko's
words, "placidly conventional" and "void of critical ideas . . . antiquarian."

McAlpine's recent dissertation attempts to place Suckow in the company
of two other American women writers, Jewett and Cather. Martin Mohr's
M.A. thesis (Iowa, 1955) is, by his own admission, no longer useful. The
definitive bibliography of primary works and editions is in Paluka. Kissane
and Omrcanin list reviews, stories, and essays; they also describe unpublished materials.

MAJOR WORKS

Country People. New York: Knopf, 1924. [novel]
The Odyssey of a Nice Girl. New York: Knopf, 1925. [novel]
Iowa Interiors. New York: Knopf, 1926. [stories]
The Bonney Family. New York: Knopf, 1928. [novel]
Cora. New York: Knopf, 1929. [novel]
The Kramer Girls. New York: Knopf, 1930. [novel]

The Folk Idea of American Life. New York: Scribner, 1930. [essay]
Children and Older People. New York: Knopf, 1931. [stories]
Carry-Over. New York: Farrar, 1936. [anthology containing *Country People; The Bonney Family;* and sixteen stories]
The Folks. New York: Farrar, 1942. [novel]
New Hope. New York: Farrar, 1942. [novel]
Some Others and Myself: Seven Stories and a Memoir. New York: Rinehart, 1952.
The John Wood Case. New York: Viking, 1959. [novel]
"A Cycle of the Seasons in Iowa: The Unpublished Diary of Ruth Suckow." *The Iowan* (Shenandoah, Ia.). Part I: Oct.–Nov., 1960, pp. 30–35. Part II: Dec.–Jan., 1960–61, pp. 20–29. Part III: Feb.–Mar., 1961, pp. 20–27. Part IV: Apr.–May, 1961, pp. 8–15.

CHECKLIST OF SECONDARY SOURCES

CAA; TCA & Supp; Warfel.

Baker, Joseph E. "Regionalism in the Middle West." *AR,* 4 (Mar. 1935), 603–14.

Beach, Joseph Warren. *American Fiction: 1920–1940.* New York: Macmillan, 1942. Pp. 7–8.

Davidson, Donald. *The Attack on Leviathan: Regionalism and Nationalism in the United States.* Gloucester, Mass.: Peter Smith, 1962.

Flanagan, John T. "The Middle Western Farm Novel." *MH,* 23 (June 1942), 119–21.

Frederick, John T. "The Farm in Iowa Fiction." *Palimpsest,* 32 (Mar. 1951), 121–52.

———. "Literary Evening, Iowa Style." In *Borzoi, 1925.* New York: Knopf, 1925.

———. "Ruth Suckow and the Middle Western Literary Movement." *EJ,* 20 (Jan. 1931), 1–8.

———. "Town and City in Iowa Fiction." *Palimpsest,* 35 (Feb. 1954), 49–96.

———. "The Writer's Iowa." *Palimpsest,* 11 (Feb. 1930), 57–60.

———. "The Younger School." *Palimpsest,* 11 (Feb. 1930), 78–86.

Hamblen, Abigail Ann. "The Poetry of Place." (Mount Vernon, Iowa) Cornell College *Husk,* 40 (Mar. 1961), 75–79.

Hatcher, Harlan. *Creating the Modern American Novel.* New York: Farrar, 1935. Pp. 102–6.

Herron, Ima H. *The Small Town in American Literature.* Durham, N.C.: Duke U., 1930. Pp. 409–17.

Kissane, Leedice McA. *Ruth Suckow.* New York: Twayne, 1969.

Luccock, Halford E. *American Mirror.* New York: Cooper Square, 1971. Pp. 61–63.

McDowell, Tremaine. "Regionalism in American Literature." *MH,* 20 (June 1939), 105–18.

Meyer, Roy W. *The Middle Western Farm Novel in the Twentieth Century.* Lincoln: U. Nebraska, 1965. Pp. 137–42.

Meyers, Walter L. "The Novel and the Simple Soul." *VQR,* 13 (Aug. 1937), 507.

Mott, Frank Luther. "Ruth Suckow." *A Book of Iowa Authors,* ed. by Johnson Brigham. Des Moines: Iowa State Teachers Association, 1930. Pp. 215–24.

Muehl, Lois B. "Ruth Suckow's Art of Fiction." *BIowa* (Nov. 1970), 3–12.

Nuhn, Ferner. "The Orchard Apiary: Ruth Suckow in Earlville." *Iowan* (Summer 1972), 21–24.

Omrcanin, Margaret S. *Ruth Suckow: A Critical Study of Her Fiction.* Philadelphia: Dorrance, 1972.

Paluka, Frank. *Iowa Authors: A Bio-Bibliography of Sixty Native Writers.* Iowa City: Friends of the University of Iowa Libraries, 1967. Pp. 129–31.

———. "Ruth Suckow, A Calendar of Letters." *BIowa,* (Oct. 1964), 34–40; and (Apr. 1965), 31–40.

Reninger, H. W. "Remarks at the memorial services for Ruth Suckow Nuhn. *Midwest,* 2 (Spring 1960), 13–14.

Stegner, Wallace. "The Trail of the Hawkeye." *SatR,* 18 (July 30, 1938), 2–4.

Stewart, Margaret. "A Critical Study of Ruth Suckow's Fiction." Ph.D. diss., U. Illinois, 1960.

Stong, Phil. *Hawkeyes: A Biography of the State of Iowa.* New York: Dodd, Mead, 1940. Pp. 38–57.

Clarence A. Andrews
University of Iowa
Iowa City, Iowa

BOOTH TARKINGTON (1869–1946)

It is worth noting that although Tarkington is discussed in *LHUS*—the longest of four passages is under Humor—no bibliography was included in the first edition. As all critics have agreed, Tarkington has never quite been thought respectable. Brooks said that it is a pity that Tarkington was always seated below the salt, for he had a "brilliant satirical gift that rivalled Sinclair Lewis's and a feeling like Scott Fitzgerald's for the glamour of youth." Quinn in *American Fiction* calls him a romancer and a realist whose sense of humor saved him from satire and idealism. Cowie defends Tarkington as having "five or six times as much talent as any novelist really needs" but being unable to rise above a "sensible, clean, kindly, somewhat humorous attitude" toward human experience. As Van Doren said, he "brought his wandering heroes home alike at the end and tucked them away in the Hoosier fold."

Solid ground work has been laid for any study; only the letters remain uncollected. Woodress's biography is standard. Russo and Sullivan's bibliography is complete. Dissertations by Fennimore and Bennett, and Fennimore's Twayne Series book cover all the bases; Van Nostrand's dissertation examines the fiction and drama. Van Nostrand's article and Quinn's section in *American Drama* deal with the plays. The bulk of the letters are at Princeton (200 boxes), but sizable collections are housed at Cornell, Indiana, Harvard, Stanford, New York Public, Purdue, and the Bobbs-Merrill Archives. The principal subject of most of the scholarship has been the "Growth" trilogy, but the subject is not exhausted. To date, Tarkington has not been taken seriously by many, and he should be.

MAJOR WORKS

The Gentleman from Indiana. New York: Doubleday & McClure, 1899. [novel]
Monsieur Beaucaire. New York: McClure, Phillips, 1900. [novel]
The Conquest of Canaan. New York: Harper, 1905. [novel]
In the Arena. New York: McClure, Phillips, 1905. [short stories]
His Own People. New York: Doubleday, 1907. [novel]
The Man From Home. New York: Harper, 1908. [play, with Harry L. Wilson]
Penrod. Garden City, N.Y.: Doubleday, 1914. [juvenile]
The Turmoil. New York: Harper, 1915. [novel]
Seventeen. New York: Harper, 1916. [novel]
The Magnificent Ambersons. Garden City, N.Y.: Doubleday, 1918. [novel]
Alice Adams. Garden City, N.Y.: Doubleday, 1921. [novel]
Clarence. New York: French, 1921. [play]
The Country Cousin. New York: French, 1921. [play]
Intimate Strangers. New York: French, 1922. [play]
The Midlander. Garden City, N.Y.: Doubleday, 1924. [novel]
The Plutocrat. Garden City, N.Y.: Doubleday, 1927. [novel]
Mirthful Haven. Garden City, N.Y.: Doubleday, 1930. [novel]

Presenting Lily Mars. Garden City, N.Y.: Doubleday, 1933. [novel]
The Heritage of Hatcher Ide. Garden City, N.Y.: Doubleday, 1941. [novel]
Image of Josephine. Garden City, N.Y.: Doubleday, 1945. [novel]

CHECKLIST OF SECONDARY SOURCES

Burke; *CAA; CHAL;* Herzberg; *LHUS; LLC; OCAL; TCA & Supp.*

Bennett, Carl. D. "The Literary Development of Booth Tarkington." Ph.D. diss., Emory U., 1944.
Brooks, Van Wyck. *The Confident Years: 1885–1915.* New York: Dutton, 1952. Pp. 328–36.
Cary, Richard. "Jewitt, Tarkington & the Maine Line." *CLQ,* series 4 (Feb. 1956), 89–95.
Currie, Barton. "An Editor in Pursuit of Booth Tarkington." *PULC,* 16 (Winter 1955), 80–88.
Dickinson, Asa D. *Booth Tarkington.* Garden City, N.Y.: Doubleday, 1914.
Fennimore, Keith. "A Case Study of Booth Tarkington as a Novelist." Ph.D. diss., Michigan State U., 1956.
_____. *Booth Tarkington.* New York: Twayne, 1974.
Hamblen, Abigail A. "Booth Tarkington's Classic of Adolescence." *SHR,* 3 (1969), 225–31.
Holliday, Robert C. *Booth Tarkington.* Garden City, N.Y.: Doubleday, 1919.
Nicholson, Meredith. *The Hoosiers.* New York: Macmillan, 1916. Pp. 217–21.
Quinn, Arthur H. *American Fiction: An Historical and Critical Survey.* New York: Appleton, 1936. Pp. 596–606.
_____. *A History of the American Drama from the Civil War to the Present Day.* New York: Appleton, 1936. Vol. 2, pp. 126–29.
Roberts, Kenneth. "A Gentleman from Maine and Indiana." *SEPost,* 204 (Aug. 8, 1931), 14–15.
Russo, Dorothy R. and Thelma L. Sullivan. *A Bibliography of Booth Tarkington 1869–1946.* Indianapolis: Indiana Historical Bureau, 1949.
_____. "Additions to the Tarkington Bibliography." *PULC,* 16 (Winter 1955), 89–94.
Scott, John D. "Tarkington and the 1920's." *ASch,* 26 (Spring 1957), 181–94.
Shumaker, Arthur W. *A History of Indiana Literature.* Indianapolis: Indiana Historical Bureau, 1962. Pp. 350–85.
Torrents, John E. "Booth Tarkington: A Man of the Theatre." *DAI* 35:6851A–52A.
Van Doren, Carl. *The American Novel: 1789–1939.* New York: Macmillan, 1949. Pp. 261–64.
Van Nostrand, Albert D. "The Novels and Plays of Booth Tarkington: A Critical Appraisal." Ph.D. diss., Harvard U., 1951.
_____. "The Plays of BT." *PULC,* 17 (1955), 13–39.
Wagenknecht, Edward. *Cavalcade of the American Novel.* New York: Holt, 1952. Pp. 244–51.
Woodress, James. *Booth Tarkington: Gentleman from Indiana.* Philadelphia: Lippincott, 1954.
_____. "Popular Taste in 1899: BT's First Novel." In *Essays in American and English Literature,* ed. Max F. Schultz et al. Athens, Ohio: U. Ohio, 1968. Pp. 108–21.
_____. "Tarkington's New York Literary Debut: Letters Written to His Family in 1899." *PULC,* 16 (Winter 1955), 54–79.
_____. "The Tarkington Papers." *PULC,* 16 (Winter 1955), 45–53.

E. Bruce Kirkham
Ball State University
Muncie, Indiana

AUGUSTUS THOMAS (1857–1934)

Missourian Augustus Thomas was the acknowledged dean of American playwriting for a number of years and contributed to the development of the modern stage by his consistent use of native materials and realism. Although the author of a large number of plays, his name is associated with an even greater number of plays to which he lent his prestige. As a popular public figure, Thomas was interviewed and commented on in many magazines and journals. His autobiography is the only book-length source and Nathan's caustic article coupled with the entry in the *Enciclopedia* provide the best over-all assessment of a long career that reflects the strength and weakness of the American theatre at the beginning of the twentieth century.

MAJOR WORKS

Arizona. New York: Russell, 1899. [play]
Alabama. Chicago: Dramatic Publishing, 1905. [play]
The Witching Hour. New York: Harper, 1908. [play]
As A Man Thinks. New York: Duffield, 1911. [play]
Indian Summer. New York: Rosenfield, 1913. [play]
In Mizzoura. New York: French, 1916. [play]
Mrs. Leffingwell's Boots. New York: French, 1916. [play]
Oliver Goldsmith. New York: French, 1916. [play]
The Earl of Pawtucket. New York: French, 1917. [play]
The Other Girl. New York: French, 1917. [play]
The Man Upstairs. Washington, D.C.: Commission on Training Camp Activities, 1918. [one-act play]
The Cooperhead. New York: French, 1922. [play]
The Harvest Moon. New York: French, 1922. [play]
The Print of My Remembrance. New York: Scribner, 1922. [autobiography]
Still Waters. New York: French, 1926. [play]
The Cricket of Palmy Days. New York: French, 1929. [play]
Colonel George of Mount Vernon. New York: French, 1931. [play]
A Constitutional Point. New York: French, 1932. [one-act play]
A Proper Impropriety. New York: French, 1932. [one-act play]
Editha's Burglar. New York: French, 1932. [one-act play]

CHECKLIST OF SECONDARY SOURCES

DAB; LLC; OCAL.

Brooks, Van Wyck. "Augustus Thomas' Methods of Work." *WW*, 18 (Aug. 5, 1909), 11882–5.
Cranmer, Catherine. "Interview with Augustus Thomas." *MHR*, 20 (Apr. 1926), 399–405.
Current Opinion, 75 (July 1923), 31–33. [interview]
Davenport, W.A. "Appreciation of Augustus Thomas." *WW*, 46 (May 1923), 78–83.
Davis, Ronald. "Augustus Thomas and Psychic Phenomena." *DAI* 36:6681A–82A.
Enciclopedia Dello Spettacolo. Rome: Casa Editrice Le Maschere, 1962.
Hamilton, Charles. "Estimates of Augustus Thomas." *Bookman*, 33 (June 1911), 354.
Hartt, R. "Interview with Augustus Thomas." *Outlook*, 131 (Aug. 23, 1922), 672–73.
Lewisohn, Ludwig. *Drama on the Stage.* New York: Harcourt, 1922. Pp. 89–93.
Nathan, George Jean. "In Memoriam." *AmMerc*, 8 (May 1926), 117–20.
National Cyclopedia of American Biography. New York: White, 1910. Vol. 14, p. 127.
New York Dramatic News, 64 (Mar. 3, 1917), 3. [retirement]
New York Times, Aug. 13, 1934, sec. 1, p. 5. [obit.]
Oxford Companion to the Theatre. Ed. by Phyllis Hartnoll. 3d ed. London: Oxford, 1967.
Twentieth Century Biographical Dictionary of Notable Americans. Boston: Biographical Society, 1904.
Who's Who in the Theatre. Ed. John Parker. London: Pitman, 1930.
Williams, J. D. *New York Times*, Aug. 19, 1934, 9, sec. 1, p. 4. [article]

Woollcott, Alexander. Review of *Print of My Remembrance. Bookman,* 56 (Nov. 1922), 345–46.

R. Donald Grose
University of Missouri
Columbia, Missouri

MAURICE THOMPSON (1844–1901)

Thompson, an essayist, novelist, editor, and advocate of the sport of archery, is a midwestern writer by birth, but he can be classed as both a midwestern and southern writer by residence and subject of his works. His fiction is universally judged as romantic. The only satisfactory primary bibliography is in Russo and Sullivan. His papers are at New York Public, Harvard, the Wisconsin Historical Society, and the Bobbs-Merrill Archives in Indianapolis. Wheeler has done the best biography to date, but generally Thompson has received little critical attention.

Major Works

Hoosier Mosaics. New York: Hale, 1875. [stories]
The Witchery of Archery. New York: Scribner, 1878. [essays]
Songs of Fair Weather. Boston: Osgood, 1883. [poetry]
By-Ways and Bird Notes. New York: Alden, 1885. [essays]
A Banker of Bankersville. New York: Cassell, 1886. [novel]
Sylvan Secrets. New York: Alden, 1887. [essays on bird life]
Poems. Boston: Houghton Mifflin, 1892.
Stories of Indiana. Chicago: American, 1898.
Alice of Old Vincennes. Indianapolis: Bowen-Merrill, 1900. [novel]
Rosalynde's Lovers. Indianapolis: Bowen-Merrill, 1901.

Checklist of Secondary Sources

BDAL; Burke; *DAB;* Herzberger; *LHUS; OCAL.*

Fertig, Walter L. "MT's Primitive Baptist Heritage." *IMH,* 64 (1968), 1–12.
———. "Maurice Thompson at War with the Realists." *Old Northwest,* 1 (September 1975), 239–51.
Kraut, M. K. "Maurice Thompson at Home." *Independent,* 53 (Feb. 21, 1901), 416–18.
Nicholson, Meredith. *The Hoosiers.* New York: Macmillan, 1915. Pp. 199–211.
Russo, Dorothy R. and Thelma L. Sullivan. *Bibliographical Studies of Seven Authors of Crawfordsville Indiana.* Indianapolis: Indiana Historical Bureau, 1952. Pp. 173–303.
Shumaker, Arthur H. *A History of Indiana Literature.* Indianapolis: Indiana Historical Bureau, 1962. Pp. 310–20.
Wheeler, Otis B. M. *The Literary Career of Maurice Thompson.* Baton Rouge: Louisiana State U., 1965.

E. Bruce Kirkham
Ball State University
Muncie, Indiana

JAMES THURBER (1894–1961)

Altľ ugh born and reared in Ohio, James Grover Thurber became the quintessential New Yorker and a mainstay of the *New Yorker* magazine in its first thirty years. Thurber is generally acknowledged to be the greatest American humorist since Mark Twain. He has been called a comic Prufrock in dramatizing the dilemma of modern malaise. By writing in humorous reminiscence about confusions, maladjustments, and humiliations, Thurber provided a comic catharsis. A sensitive surveyor of the literary scene and an unsystematic philosopher of the absurd, he used humor for sanity and survival.

Thurber's humor is in the romantic tradition. Though his male protagonists are usually repressed anti-heroes, henpecked and hypochondriac, they compensate in the free flight of the imagination and find refuge in escapist fantasy. Basically serious beneath his humor, Thurber presented the complexity of human nature from the age of innocence in Columbus, Ohio, to the age of anxiety in mid-century America. His world balances paradoxically the muddled campaigns of the war between timorous men and aggressive women, the innocence of animals, the wonder of words, craftsman's prose and casual cartoons, political liberalism and nostalgic conservatism. A versatile artist, he excelled at stories, fables, drama, essays, fantasies, brief biographies, cartoons, and drawings.

Aside from book reviews and journalistic articles in popular magazines, there was little scholarship on Thurber before the 1960s. The first book-length assessment is Morsberger's (1964). Since then, Black and Tobias have published critical studies, and Holmes and Bernstein have done biographies. The definitive bibliography is Bowden's. One problem for scholars is the fact that hundreds of Thurber essays, stories, and cartoons are uncollected; Bowden lists them and their location. There are collections of Thurberiana at the Ohio State University Library and the Martha Kinney Cooper Ohioana Library in Columbus. The correspondence between Thurber and E. B. White is in the Cornell University Library.

MAJOR WORKS

Is Sex Necessary? Or Why You Feel the Way You Do (with E. B. White). New York: Harper, 1929. [satiric parody]
The Owl in the Attic and Other Perplexities. New York: Harper, 1931.
The Seal in the Bedroom and Other Predicaments. New York: Harper, 1932. [cartoons]
My Life and Hard Times. New York: Harper, 1933. [mock autobiography]
The Middle-Aged Man on the Flying Trapeze: A Collection of Short Pieces, with Drawings by the Author. New York: Harper, 1935. [stories and essays]

Let Your Mind Alone! and Other More or Less Inspirational Pieces. New York: Harper, 1937.
  [stories and essays]
Cream of Thurber. London: Hamilton, 1939.
The Last Flower, A Parable in Pictures. New York: Harper, 1939.
The Male Animal (with Elliott Nugent). New York: Random House, 1940. [play]
Fables for Our Time and Famous Poems Illustrated. New York: Harper, 1940.
My World—And Welcome To It. New York: Harcourt, 1942. [stories and essays]
Men, Women and Dogs, A Book of Drawings. New York: Harcourt, 1943. [cartoons]
The Thurber Carnival. New York: Harper, 1945. [stories, essays, fables, cartoons]
The White Deer. New York: Harcourt, 1945. [fantasy]
The Beast in Me and Other Animals. New York: Harcourt, 1948. [stories, essays, cartoons]
The 13 Clocks. New York: Simon and Schuster, 1950. [fantasy]
The Thurber Album, A New Collection of Pieces about People. New York: Simon and Schuster, 1952. [biographical sketches]
Thurber Country, A New Collection of Pieces About Males and Females, Mainly of Our Own Species. New York: Simon and Schuster, 1953. [stories and essays]
Thurber's Dogs, A Collection of the Master's Dogs, Written and Drawn, Real and Imaginary, Living and Long Ago. New York: Simon and Schuster, 1955.
Further Fables for Our Time. New York: Simon and Schuster, 1956.
The Wonderful O. New York: Simon and Schuster, 1957. [fantasy]
Alarms and Diversions. New York: Harper, 1957. [stories, essays, cartoons]
The Years with Ross. Boston: Little, Brown, 1959. [biography]
Lanterns and Lances. New York: Harper, 1961. [stories and essays]
Credos and Curios. New York: Harper, 1962. [stories and essays]
A Thurber Carnival. New York: French, 1962. [revue]
Vintage Thurber. 2 vols. London: Hamilton, 1963. [stories, essays, cartoons]
Thurber & Company. New York: Harper, 1966. [cartoons and drawings]

CHECKLIST OF SECONDARY SOURCES

CB; CHAL; Herzberg; *LLC; TCA & Supp.*

Baldwin, Alice. "Congruous Laughter; The Linguistic Form of Humor in James Thurber's Casual Essays." Ph.D. diss., U. Massachusetts, 1970.
Bernstein, Burton. *Thurber: A Biography.* New York: Dodd, Mead, 1975.
Blair, Walter. *Horse Sense in American Humor.* Chicago: U. Chicago, 1943.
Black, Stephen A. *James Thurber: His Masquerades.* The Hague: Mouton, 1970.
Bowden, Edwin T. *James Thurber: A Bibliography.* Columbus: Ohio State U., 1968.
Brady, Charles. "What Thurber Saw." *Commonweal,* 75 (Dec. 8, 1961), 274–76.
Brandon, Henry. *As We Are.* Garden City, N.Y.: Doubleday, 1961. [interview]
Breit, Harvey. *The Writer Observed.* Cleveland: World, 1956. [interview]
Coates, Robert M. "Thurber, Inc." *SatR,* 21 (Dec. 2, 1939), 10–11.
Cooke, Alistair. "James Thurber in Conversation with Alistair Cooke." *Atl,* 198 (Aug. 1956), 36–40. [interview]
DeVries, Peter. "James Thurber: The Comic Prufrock." *Poetry,* 63 (Dec. 1943), 150–59.
Elias, Robert H. "James Thurber: The Primitive, the Innocent, and the Individual." *ASch,* 27 (Summer 1958), 355–63.
Holmes, Charles S. *The Clocks of Columbus: The Literary Career of James Thurber.* New York: Atheneum, 1972.
————, ed. *Thurber: A Collection of Critical Essays.* Englewood Cliffs, N.J.: Prentice-Hall, 1974.
Kramer, Dale. *Ross and The New Yorker.* Garden City, N.Y.: Doubleday, 1952.
Morsberger, Robert E. *James Thurber.* New York: Twayne, 1964.
Murrell, William. *A History of American Graphic Humor (1865–1938).* New York: Macmillan, 1938.
Petrullo, Helen B. "Satire and Freedom: Sinclair Lewis, Nathanael West, and James Thurber." Ph.D. diss., Syracuse U., 1967.
Plimpton, George and Max Steele. "The Art of Fiction." *ParisR,* 10 (Fall 1955), 35–49. [interview]

Pollard, James E. "James Thurber." *Ohio Authors and Their Books, 1796–1950*. Ed. by William Coyle. Cleveland: World, 1962.

"Priceless Gift of Laughter." *Time*, 58 (July 9, 1951), 88–90.

"Salute to Thurber." *SatR*, 44 (Nov. 25, 1961), 14–18.

Tobias, Richard C. *The Art of James Thurber*. Athens: Ohio U., 1969.

Van Doren, Mark. *The Autobiography of Mark Van Doren*. New York: Harcourt, 1958.

Walker, C. L. "The Legendary Mr. Thurber." *LadiesHJ*, 53 (July 1946), 26–27.

Yates, Norris W. *The American Humorist: Conscience of the Twentieth Century*. Ames: Iowa State U., 1964.

Robert E. Morsberger
California State Polytechnic University
Pomona, California

MARK VAN DOREN (1894–1972)

A midwesterner by birth, Mark Van Doren migrated from his native Illinois to New York in 1915 after taking his A.B. and A.M. degrees at the University of Illinois. He completed his Ph.D. in English at Columbia University and remained there as a member of the English Department for thirty-nine years. He is best known as a teacher, anthologist, critic, and poet.

Lindeman writes that Van Doren, as a poet, "continues to navigate outside the main current of the twentieth-century stream. Actually his success is based on elements emanating from an entirely different source than that which gives rise to his prosodic conservatism. He is a poet who has a certain uniqueness through his sheer ability to make honesty and sincerity count in the most ordinary sense for many people beyond, as well as within, the pale of poetry." Glimpsing this quality, Carruth speculates that Van Doren's "best poems have a level, grainy firmness about them that is quite distinct from the peculiar intermittent *bizarrerie* of other New England poetry; and in this he perhaps betrays, after all, his middle-western origin." In classifying Van Doren's poetry, Carruth writes, "His poetry falls clearly into the tradition which combines Emersonianism with modern metaphysical and humanist concerns, a synthesis that is never far from the center of American life." *Contemporary Authors* classifies Van Doren as "an Illinois metaphysician transplanted to Connecticut" and regards his work as "a studied application of his theories of knowledge, poetry, and teaching."

No full-length scholarly study of Van Doren exists; however, his wife's two biographical works, *Country Wife* (1950) and *The Professor and I* (1959), are useful resources. Van Doren's most notable midwestern work is his play, *The Last Days of Lincoln* (1959).

MAJOR WORKS

[Van Doren has published 22 volumes of poetry and has been extensively anthologized. Therefore, only a representative sampling of his books of poetry are listed below.]

Spring Thunder. New York: Seltzer, 1924. [poems]
Jonathan Gentry. New York: Boni, 1926. [poem]
A Winter Diary. New York: Macmillan, 1935. [poems]
The Transients. New York: Morrow, 1935. [novel]
Collected Poems. New York: Holt, 1939.
Windless Cabins. New York: Holt, 1940. [novel]
The Mayfield Deer. New York: Holt, 1941 [poem]
Tilda. New York: Holt, 1943. [novel]
The Country Year. New York: Sloane, 1946. [poems]
The Careless Clock. New York: Sloane, 1947. [poems]
New Poems. New York: Sloane, 1948.
The Short Stories. New York: Abelard-Schuman, 1950.
The Witch of Ramoth and Other Tales. York, Pa.: Maple Press, 1950.
In That Far Land. Iowa City: Prairie Press, 1951. [poems]
Mortal Summer. Iowa City: Prairie Press, 1953. [poems]
Spring Birth. New York: Holt, 1953. [poems]
Nobody Say a Word. New York: Holt, 1953. [stories]
Selected Poems. New York: Holt, 1954.
Home with Hazel. New York: Harcourt, 1957. [stories]
The Autobiography of Mark Van Doren. New York: Harcourt, 1958.
The Last Days of Lincoln. New York: Hill and Wang, 1959. [play]
Collected Stories. 3 vols. New York: Hill and Wang, 1962–68.
Collected and New Poems, 1924–1963. New York: Hill and Wang, 1963.
The Narrative Poems. New York: Hill and Wang, 1963.
Three Plays. New York: Hill and Wang, 1966.
100 Poems. New York: Hill and Wang, 1967.

CHECKLIST OF SECONDARY SOURCES

Burke; *CA; CAA; CN; CP; LHUS; LLC; OCAL; TCA & Supp.*

Bush, Warren V., ed. *The Dialogues of Archibald MacLeish and Mark Van Doren*. New York: Dutton, 1964.
Everett, Charles W. "Mark Van Doren at Work." *CLC*, 9 (1960), 18–21.
Kreymborg, Alfred. *Our Singing Strength*. New York: Coward, 1929. Pp. 582, 599–602.
Krutch, Joseph Wood. "The Autobiography of My Friend Mark Van Doren." *CUF*, 2 (1959), 13–16.
Libaire, Beatrice B. "New Books Appraised." *LJ*, 83 (Oct. 15, 1958), 2839.
Lindeman, Jack. "Three Poets." *Poetry*, 97 (Nov. 1960), 109–13.
Newquist, Roy. *Counterpoint*. Chicago: Rand McNally, 1964. Pp. 7, 613–24.
"One Man's Hour." *Newsweek*, 53 (Feb. 23, 1959), 67.
Seaton, A. G., ed. *The Writers Directory, 1971–73*. Chicago: St. James Press, 1971. P. 464.
Van Doren, Dorothy Graffe. *The Country Wife*. New York: Sloane, 1950.
———. *The Professor and I*. New York: Appleton, 1959.
Ward, A. C., ed. *Longman Companion to Twentieth Century Literature*. London: Longman Group, 1970. P. 546.
Young, Marguerite. "Mark Van Doren: A Poet in an Age of Defoliation." *Voyages*, 3 (n.d.), 60–62.

R. Baird Shuman
University of Illinois
Champaign, Illinois

GLENWAY WESCOTT (1901–   )

The three major studies of Wescott's work are Kahn's critical and biographical dissertation and the book by Ruekert and Johnson. The first of these studies is ground-breaking and seminal; the latter two more elaborately investigate critical and technical problems special to Wescott's fiction, particularly those of form, voice, and point of view. The most comprehensive bibliography by and about Wescott is Kahn's in the *Bulletin of Bibliography*, which is exhaustive through 1957 and acknowledged as indispensable for any study of Wescott.

During the 1920s Wescott established a substantial literary reputation and was considered, along with Fitzgerald and Hemingway, as one of America's most promising young writers. All major critics of Wescott's work agree that, with one notable exception, he never fulfilled this early promise. Critics speculate that various problems hampered his work in subsequent decades: his failure to solve aesthetic and technical problems in making fiction a way of telling the truth; his personal psychological problems; his eight years of expatriation in France, symptomatic and an exacerbation of his sense of social and spiritual alienation; his insistence on literary perfection; and his finding his talents uncongenial to shifts in social milieu.

With rural Wisconsin as metaphor, his early fiction provides insight into our Middle West, but the implications of his work extend beyond individual experience and regional boundaries to suggest a fable for America. His prose, distinguished by a precise diction and lyrical style, is a perfected instrument for creating states of mind and nostalgic recollection, ultimately dramatizing America's aspirations, failures, and quest for identity. *The Grandmothers*, Harper prize novel in 1927, is generally acknowledged as the work which most satisfactorily chronicles and orchestrates personal, family, regional, and national history.

Critics unanimously agree that his novelette *The Pilgrim Hawk* (1940), growing out of Wescott's deepened experience of the expatriate years, is his finest work. It was felt at the time it might be a harbinger of a long overdue new cycle of writing. However, his only published subsequent novel *Apartment in Athens* (1945), though briefly popular, is generally judged inferior to the previous work.

Although his work of the 1920s received critical enthusiasm, with the exception of *The Pilgrim Hawk* his subsequent work received scant critical attention. In the following decades his publication of a ballet scenario, a facetious hagiography, a rendering of Aesop's fables, various essays on personal, literary, and artistic subjects, though skillful, seemed to later critics symptomatic of Wescott's failure to solve formal problems and a trivialization of his talent. However, the three major studies agree that his literary reputation rests largely upon the gifted work of his youth, particularly *The Grandmothers* and *The Pilgrim Hawk*, both still studied as impressive examples of their genres.

MAJOR WORKS

The Bitterns: A Book of Twelve Poems. Illinois: Wheeler, 1920.
The Apple of the Eye. New York: Dial, 1924. [novel]
Natives of Rock: XX Poems: 1921–22. New York: Bianco, 1925.
The Grandmothers: A Family Portrait. New York: Harper, 1927. [novel]
Good-Bye Wisconsin. New York: Harper, 1928. [stories]
The Babe's Bed. Paris: Harrison of Paris, 1930. [story]
Fear and Trembling. New York: Harper, 1932. [essays]
A Calendar of Saints for Unbelievers. Paris: Harrison of Paris, 1932. [hagiography]
The Pilgrim Hawk: A Love Story. New York: Harper, 1940. [novelette]
"The Dream of Audubon, Libretto of a Ballet in Three Scenes." *The Best One-Act Plays of 1940*. New York: Dodd, Mead, 1941. [ballet]
Apartment in Athens. New York: Harper, 1945. [novel]
Twelve Fables of Aesop. New York: Museum of Modern Art, 1954. [newly translated vignettes]
Images of Truth: Remembrances and Criticism. New York: Harper, 1962. [essays]

CHECKLIST OF SECONDARY SOURCES

CA; CAA; CN; Herzberg; *LLC; OCAL; TCA & Supp;* Warfel.

Beach, Joseph Warren. *The Twentieth Century Novel*. New York: Appleton, 1932.
Boynton, Percy H. *Literature and American Life*. Boston: Ginn, 1936.
Brace, Marjorie. "Thematic Problems of the American Novelist." *Accent*, 6 (Autumn 1945), 44–53.
Burke, Kenneth. "A Decade of American Fiction." *Bookman*, 49 (Aug. 1929), 561–67.
Butts, Mary. "Mr. Wescott's Third Book." *Dial*, 86 (May 1929), 424–27. [rev.]
Cowley, Malcolm. *Exile's Return*. New York: Viking, 1951.
Dupee, F. W. "Return of Glenway Wescott." *NR*, 103 (Dec. 9, 1940), 807–8. [rev.]
Geismer, Maxwell. *Writers in Crisis*. Boston: Houghton Mifflin, 1942.
Hatcher, Harlan. *Creating The Modern American Novel*. New York: Farrar, 1935.
Hicks, Granville. *The Great Tradition: An Interpretation of American Literature Since The Civil War*. New York: Macmillan, 1933.
Hoffman, Frederick J. *The Twenties*. New York: Viking, 1951.
Johnson, Ira D. *Glenway Wescott: The Paradox of Voice*. Port Washington, N.Y.: Kennikat, 1971.
Kahn, Sy M. "Glenway Wescott: A Critical and Biographical Study." Ph.D. diss., U. Wisconsin, 1957.
———. "Glenway Wescott: A Bibliography." *BB*, 22 (Sept.–Dec. 1958), 156–60.
———. "Glenway Wescott: The Artist at Work." *PELL*, 1 (1965), 35–45.
Kohler, Dayton. "Glenway Wescott, Legend Maker." *Bookman*, 73 (1931), 142–45.
Langdon, Mabel. "Midwestern Writers: Glenway Wescott." *PrS*, 4 (Spring 1930), 117–23.
Miller, Fred. "Introduction." *The Grandmothers*. Modern Classics Edition. New York: Harper, 1950.
Quinn, Patrick F. "The Case History of Glenway Wescott." *FM*, 19 (Autumn 1939), 11–16.
Ruekert, William H. *Glenway Wescott*. New York: Twayne, 1965.
Schorer, C. E. "The Maturing of Glenway Wescott." *CE*, 18 (Mar. 1957), 320–26.
Suckow, Ruth. "Middle Western Literature." *EJ*, 21 (1932), 175–82.

Wilson, Edmund. "Glenway Wescott's War Work." In *Classics and Commercials*. New York: Farrar, 1950.
Zabel, Morton D. "The Whisper of The Devil." In *Craft and Character in Modern Fiction*. New York: Viking, 1957.

Sy M. Kahn
University of the Pacific
Stockton, California

JESSAMYN WEST (1902–   )

Probably the three largest collections of West materials are in the possession of the author, Whittier College Library, and Alfred S. Shivers. In addition, the library at Stephen F. Austin State University owns photocopies of some West letters to Shivers. Over a period of many years, the Indiana novelist has recorded story ideas and research information in a series of writing notebooks; she has also kept a set of journals. A few years ago she donated to Whittier College a great quantity of literary paraphernalia of which no published index or description has yet appeared. Shivers has accumulated a copy of one of the writing notebooks; close to sixty West letters and postal cards, some of which contain information on her writing aims and methods; a goodly variety of correspondence relating to her schoolmates, teachers, relatives, editors, and other acquaintances; letters to her from admirers; galleys of books; autographed books; speeches; school records; foreign reviews; maps; etc. For more information, see "Letters and Miscellaneous," in Shivers's *Jessamyn West*.

MAJOR WORKS

The Friendly Persuasion. New York: Harcourt, 1945. [stories]
A Mirror for the Sky: An Opera based on an Original Conception of Raoul Péne duBois for Portraying the Life of Audubon in a Musical Drama. Costume sketches by Raoul Péne duBois. New York: Harcourt, 1948. [operetta]
The Witch Diggers. New York: Harcourt, 1951. [novel]
The Reading Public. New York: Harcourt, 1952. Privately printed. [literary criticism]
Cress Delahanty. New York: Harcourt, 1953. [stories]
Little Men. In *Star Short Novels*. Ed. by Frederick Pohl. New York: Ballantine, 1954. Reprinted as *The Chilekings*. 1967. [novel]
Love, Death and the Ladies' Drill Team. New York: Harcourt, 1955. [stories]
To See the Dream. New York: Harcourt, 1957. [autobiographical coverage of filming of *Friendly Persuasion*]
Love is Not What You Think. New York: Harcourt, 1959. [philosophical study]
South of the Angels. New York: Harcourt, 1960. [novel]
The Quaker Reader. Selected and introduced by Jessamyn West. New York: Viking, 1962. [scholarly editing of Quaker writings]
A Matter of Time. New York: Harcourt, 1966. [novel]
Leafy Rivers. New York: Harcourt, 1967. [novel]

Except for Me and Thee. New York: Harcourt, 1967. [stories]
Crimson Ramblers of the World, Farewell. New York: Harcourt, 1970. [stories]
Hide and Seek. New York: Harcourt, 1973. [autobiography, philosophical, travelogue]
The Secret Look. New York: Harcourt, 1974. [poems]
Massacre at Fall Creek. New York: Harcourt, 1975. [novel]
The Woman Said Yes: Encounters with Life and Death. New York: Harcourt, 1976. [memoirs]

CHECKLIST OF SECONDARY SOURCES

CN; Herzberg; *OCAL; TCA.*

Bergler, Edmund. "Writers of Half Talent." *AI,* 14 (Summer 1957), 155–64.
Carpenter, Frederic. "The Adolescent in American Fiction." *EJ,* 46 (Sept. 1957), 313–19.
Dempsey, D. "Talk with Jesamyn West." *NYTBR,* Jan. 3, 1954, p. 12.
Flanagan, John T. "Folklore in Five Middle-Western Novelists." *GLR,* 1 (Winter 1975), 43–57.
———. "The Fiction of Jessamyn West." *IMH,* 67 (Dec. 1971), 299–316.
Graham, Lee. "An Interview with Jessamyn West." *WD,* 47 (May 1967), 24–27. [transcript of radio interview]
Havighurst, Walter. "Mr. Cornelius I Love You." Instructors Manual for *Masters of the Modern Short Story.* New ed. New York: Harcourt, 1953. Pp. 34–35. [comment]
Heilman, Robert B. "Shivaree Before Breakfast." In *Modern Short Short Stories: A Critical Anthology.* New York: Harcourt, 1950. Pp. 107–8.
Hutchens, John K. "On an Author." *NYHTBR,* Feb. 18, 1951, p. 2.
"Jessamyn West Discusses Readers' Demands on Writer." Eugene, Ore., *Register-Guard,* May 23, 1958.
Kempton, Kenneth. "Love, Death and the Ladies' Drill Team." *Short Stories for Study.* Cambridge, Mass.: Harvard U., 1953. Pp. 35–40. [comment]
Katope, Christopher G. "West's 'Love, Death and the Ladies' Drill Team.' " *Explicator,* 23 (Dec. 1964), item 27.
King, Brenda. "Jessamyn West." *SatR,* 40 (Sept. 21, 1957), 14.
Mast, Ray. " 'Friendly' Persuasion Author Recalled." Fullerton, Calif., *News Tribune,* Dec. 22, 1965, p. A–2. [biographical]
Shivers, Alfred S. "Jessamyn West." *BB,* 28 (Jan.–Mar. 1971), 1–3.
"Some of the Authors of 1951, Speaking for Themselves." *NYHTBR,* Oct. 7, 1951, p. 18.
West, Jessamyn. Letter in "The Mailbag" correcting the Mast article. Fullerton, Calif., *News Tribune,* Jan. 17, 1966, p. A–7.
Witham, W. Tasker. *The Adolescent in the American Novel, 1920–1960.* New York: Ungar, 1964.

Alfred S. Shivers
Stephen F. Austin State University
Nacogdoches, Texas

WILLIAM ALLEN WHITE (1868–1944)

Through his prodigious literary output, White's three separate careers (novelist and poet; editor of the Emporia, Kansas, *Gazette;* political figure) attracted wide national attention early in the twentieth century. His earlier works embodied the Midwest; his perception of the indigenous growth of the region's rural and urban cultures, coupled with contemporary man's ambitious grasp at opportunity, helped create a genuine realism in these writings. Hinshaw's biography includes an analysis of White's fiction in terms of its remarkable effect on the American reading public. The later journalistic writing was more important in generating White's reputation and influence in political affairs, yet even then he retained the early strength and clarity of his prose as he continued to write on social, moral, and economic questions.

Major collections of his work are located in the W. A. White Journalism Library in Topeka and at the Emporia State College Library.

Major Works

Sunflowers. Ed. by Thomas F. Doran and White. Lawrence, Kan.: Journal Publishing Co., 1888. [poetry]
Rhymes by Two Friends [by Albert Bigelow Paine and White]. Fort Scott, Kan.: M. L. Izor, 1893. [poetry]
The Real Issue. Chicago: Way & Williams, 1896. [novel]
The Court of Boyville. New York: Doubleday, 1899. [autobiographical novel]
Stratagems and Spoils: Stories of Love and Politics. New York: Scribner, 1901. [stories]
In Our Town. New York: McClure, Phillips, 1906. [novel]
A Certain Rich Man. New York: Macmillan, 1909. [novel]
The Old Order Changeth: A View of American Democracy. New York: Macmillan, 1910. [essays]
God's Puppets. New York: Macmillan, 1916. [stories]
The Martial Adventures of Henry and Me. New York: Macmillan, 1918. [travel sketches, novel]
In the Heart of a Fool. New York: Macmillan, 1918. [novel]
The Autobiography of William Allen White. New York: Macmillan, 1946.

Checklist of Secondary Sources

CB; DAB; Herzberg; *LHUS; OCAL; TCA.*

" 'Bill' White's Start." *LD*, 48 (Mar. 21, 1914), 642.
Blankenship, Russell. *American Literature as an Expression of the National Mind*. New York: Holt, 1931.
Clough, Frank C. *WAW of Emporia*. New York: Whittlesey House, 1941.
Clugston, W. G. "Sage of Emporia." *Midwest*, 1 (Jan. 1973), 6.
Dubbert, Joe L. "WAW's American Adam." *WAL*, 7 (Winter 1973), 271–78.
————. "WAW: Reflections on an American Life." *MarkhamR*, 4 (May 1974), 41–47.
Elkin, William. "William Allen White's Early Fiction." *HK*, 8 (Winter 1975), 5–17.
Emporia (Kan.) State College. *Bibliography of WAW, Prepared from the WAW Collection, WAW Library*. 2 vols. Emporia: State College Press, 1969.
Ferber, Edna. "Kansas, Too, Has Its 'White House.' " *LD*, 86 (July 25, 1925), 45–47.
Fisher, Dorothy Canfield. *American Portraits*. New York: Holt, 1946.
Fox, Maynard. "Book-Length Fiction by Kansas Writers, 1915–1938." *Fort Hays (Kan.) State College Studies (Language and Literature Series No. 2)*. Fort Hays, 1943.
Glaspell, Susan. *Judd Rankin's Daughter*. New York: Lippincott, 1945.
Hinshaw, David. *A Man from Kansas: The Story of WAW*. New York: Putnam, 1945.
Howe, Edgar W. *Plain People*. New York: Dodd, Mead, 1929.
Howells, William Dean. "Psychological Counter-Current in Recent Fiction." *NAR*, 173 (Dec. 1901), 876–78.
Irwin, W. "One Man in His Time." *SatR*, 29 (Mar. 16, 1946), 7–8.
Johnson, Walter. *WAW's America*. New York: Holt, 1947.
————, ed. *Selected Letters of WAW, 1899–1943*. New York: Holt, 1947.
Johnson, Walter and Alberta Paine. "Bibliography of the Published Works of WAW." *KHQ*, 15 (Feb. 1947), 22–41.

Kunitz, Stanley J., ed. *Authors Today and Yesterday*. New York: Wilson, 1933.
McKee, John D . *WAW: Maverick on Main Street*. Westport, Conn.: Greenwood, 1975.
Marble, Annie R. *A Study of the Modern Novel*. New York: Appleton, 1928.
Mencken, H. L. "The Last of the Victorians." *SS*, 29 (Oct. 1909), 153–55.
Pady, Donald S. "A Bibliography of the Poems of WAW." *BB*, 25 (Jan.–Apr. 1967), 44–46.
Paine, Albert B. "Rhymes by Two Friends." *KM*, 2 (Sept. 1909), 65–66.
Parrington, Vernon L. *Main Currents of American Thought*. 3 vols. New York: Harcourt, 1930.
Pattee, Fred L. *The New American Literature, 1890–1930*. New York: Century, 1930.
Quinn, Arthur H. *American Fiction: An Historical and Critical Survey*. New York: Appleton, 1936.
Rich, Everett. *WAW: The Man from Emporia*. New York: Farrar, 1941.
Sergeant, Elizabeth S. "The Citizen from Emporia." *Century*, 113 (Jan. 1927), 308–16.
Van Doren, Carl. *Contemporary American Novelists, 1900–1920*. New York: Macmillan, 1922.
Wilson, Gilbert B., ed. *Letters of WAW and a Young Man*. New York: Day, 1948.

Donald S. Pady
Iowa State University
Ames, Iowa

BRAND WHITLOCK (1869–1934)

Reform mayor of Toledo for eight years (1906–14) and ambassador to Belgium (1914–21), Whitlock was also a serious realistic novelist and writer of short stories. A realist in the tradition of James and Howells, Whitlock served his literary apprenticeship as a conscious craftsman, producing in the years before becoming mayor a first-rate novel of grassroots politics, *The Thirteenth District*, and just after his election a nearly naturalistic study of social forces and contrasts, *The Turn of the Balance*. As a progressive and a realist, Whitlock contributed a great deal to both movements. His shortcomings as a literary artist preclude his inclusion in any list of first-rate writers, but he wrote perceptively and well, and he deserves much more than the literary obscurity into which he has passed. The recent full-length studies by Anderson, Crunden, and Tager have helped to focus the various elements in Whitlock's career and to stir renewed interest in his life and work.

MAJOR WORKS

The Thirteenth District. Indianapolis: Bobbs-Merrill, 1902 [novel]
The Happy Average. Indianapolis: Bobbs-Merrill, 1904. [novel]
Her Infinite Variety. Indianapolis: Bobbs-Merrill, 1904. [novel]
The Turn of the Balance. Indianapolis: Bobbs-Merrill, 1907. [novel]
Abraham Lincoln. Boston: Small, 1909. [biography]
The Gold Brick. Indianapolis: Bobbs-Merrill, 1910. [stories]
The Fall Guy. Indianapolis: Bobbs-Merrill, 1912. [stories]
On the Enforcement of Law in Cities. Indianapolis: Bobbs-Merrill, 1913. [essay]
Forty Years of It. New York: Appleton, 1914. [autobiography]

Belgium: A Personal Narrative. 2 vols. New York: Appleton, 1919. [autobiography]
J. Hardin & Son. New York: Appleton, 1923. [novel]
Uprooted. New York: Appleton, 1926. [novel]
Transplanted. New York: Appleton, 1927. [novel]
Big Matt. New York: Appleton, 1928. [novel]
La Fayette. 2 vols. New York: Appleton, 1929. [biography]
Narcissus. New York: Appleton, 1931. [novel]
The Little Green Shutter. New York: Appleton, 1931. [political essay]
The Stranger on the Island. New York: Appleton, 1933. [novel]
The Letters and Journal of Brand Whitlock. Edited with a biographical introduction by Allan
   Nevins. New York: Appleton, 1936.

CHECKLIST OF SECONDARY SOURCES

Burke; *DAB;* Herzberg; *OCAL; TCA.*

Anderson, David D. *Brand Whitlock.* New York: Twayne, 1968.
_____. "Brand Whitlock's Search for the Jeffersonian Ideal." *PMASAL,* 51 (1966), 505–14.
_____. "On Re-Discovering Brand Whitlock." *Ohioana,* 8 (Fall 1965), 67–69.
"Brand Whitlock, American." *LD,* 51 (Nov. 27, 1915), 1240.
"Brand Whitlock on American Literature." *LD,* 51 (Dec. 11, 1915), 1352–53.
"Brand Whitlock's Belgium." *Outlook,* 122 (June 4, 1919), 185–86.
"Brand Whitlock, Mayor, Novelist, Democrat." *Arena,* 37 (June 1907), 623–27.
Brooks, Van Wyck. *The Confident Years, 1885–1915.* New York: Dutton, 1952.
Crunden, Robert M. *A Hero in Spite of Himself: Brand Whitlock.* New York: Knopf, 1969.
Filler, Louis. *Crusaders for American Liberalism.* New York: Harcourt, 1939.
Heydrick, Benjamin. *Americans All.* New York: Harcourt, 1921.
Howells, William Dean. "Political Novelist and More." *NAR,* 192 (July 1910), 93–100.
_____. "Typical Americans: Brand Whitlock, T. W. Higginson." *Harper,* 129 (July 1914),
   310–13.
Jones, Samuel M., III. "Brand Whitlock, the Early Years, 1896–1904." *NOQ,* 31 (Winter
   1958–59), 7–37.
_____. "Brand Whitlock's *Forty Years of It:* A Summation of American Politics in 1913."
   NOQ, 32 (Winter 1959–60), 7–14.
_____. "Brand Whitlock and the Independent Party." *NOQ,* 31 (Spring 1959), 94–112.
_____. "Brand Whitlock: Literature, 1923–1934." *NOQ,* 33 (Spring, 1961), 91–104.
_____. "Brand Whitlock: Novelist, Muckraker and Progressive." *NOQ,* 31 (Fall 1959),
   156–69.
_____. "Brand Whitlock: Transition from America to Europe." *NOQ,* 31 (Summer 1960),
   117–31.
_____. "Brand Whitlock: Years of Expatriation, 1922–1934. *NOQ,* 32 (Autumn 1960),
   173–88.
_____. "Mayor Whitlock, 1906–1913." *NOQ,* 31 (Summer 1959), 126–37.
_____. "Whitlock and World War I: 'The Old Order Changeth.' " *NOQ,* 32 (Spring 1960),
   61–78.
"Mr. Whitlock's Retirement." *Outlook,* 130 (Jan. 18, 1922), 89.
Nye, Russel B. "Populists, Progressives, and Literature: A Record of Failure." *PMASAL,* 47
   (1961).
Tager, Jack. *The Intellectual as Reformer: Brand Whitlock and the Progressive Movement.*
   Cleveland: Case Western Reserve U., 1968.

David D. Anderson
Michigan State University
East Lansing, Michigan

SOPHUS WINTHER (1893–   )

Sophus Keith Winther is best known for his Grimsen trilogy, portraying Danish immigrant life in Nebraska. His trilogy has been translated into Danish and Swedish, and he was awarded the Liberation Medal by King Christian X of Denmark. Early reviews praised his realism and presentation of midwestern immigrant experience; his novels were recognized as better than the usual farm fiction, especially in their recognition of economic forces. However, Ransom criticized the novels as "too real," and others pointed out reliance on melodrama and coincidence. The first critical essays came only after his last published novel, when Whicher compared him favorably with Sinclair Lewis and Powell asserted that Winther's scientific determinism promoted artistic unity in his fiction. Quinn echoed Whicher, and Meyer credited Winther with significant achievements in farm fiction and portrayal of immigrant experience. Recent criticism by Meldrum has provided the only critical analysis of *Beyond the Garden Gate* and has expanded on Winther's handling of the immigrant theme. Skårdal uses his fiction as source material for an analysis of Scandinavian immigrant experience. As literary critic, Winther is best known for writing the first book-length study of Eugene O'Neill. Winther is still writing, and many unpublished manuscripts (including novels, short stories, and literary criticism) are available at the Lilly Library, Indiana University; extensive correspondence to Read Bain (1923–68) is deposited in the Michigan Historical Collections, University of Michigan.

Major Works

The Realistic War Novel. Chapbook No. 35. Seattle: U. Washington Book Store, 1930. [lit. crit.]

Eugene O'Neill: A Critical Study. New York: Random House, 1934. Rev. ed., New York: Russell & Russell, 1961.

Take All to Nebraska. New York: Macmillan, 1936. [novel]

Mortgage Your Heart. New York: Macmillan, 1937. [novel]

This Passion Never Dies. New York: Macmillan, 1938. [novel; 3 novels constitute Grimsen trilogy]

Beyond the Garden Gate. New York: Macmillan, 1946. [novel]

Checklist of Secondary Sources

CA; Burke; Warfel.

Gelhorn, Martha. *SatR,* 15 (Feb. 20, 1937), 6. [rev.]

Kazin, Alfred. "Out in the Green Corn Country." *NYHTBR,* Mar. 22, 1936, p. 2.

_____. *NYHTBR,* May 8, 1938, p. 6. [rev.]

Kennedy, Sister Patricia. "The Pioneer Woman in Middle Western Fiction." Ph.D. diss. U. Illinois, 1968.

Luebke, Frederick C. "The Immigrant Novel in America." Nebraska Educational Television
    Council for Higher Education, 1969. [videotape interview]
Meldrum, Barbara. "Duality and the Dream in S. K. Winther's Grimsen Trilogy." *PrS*, 49
    (1975), 311–19.
———. "Structure and Meaning in S. K. Winther's *Beyond the Garden Gate*." *WAL*, 6 (Fall
    1971), 191–202.
Meyer, Roy W. *The Middle Western Farm Novel in the Twentieth Century*. Lincoln: U. Ne-
    braska, 1965. Pp. 72–74, 196, 240–41.
Powell, Desmond. "Sophus Winther: The Grimsen Trilogy." *ASR*, 36 (June 1948), 144–47.
Ransom, John Crowe. "Fiction Harvest." *SouR*, 2 (Autumn 1936), 417–18. [rev.]
Sandoz, Mari. "Danes on the Prairies." *SatR*, 13 (Mar. 28, 1936), 21. [rev.]
Skårdal, Dorothy B. *The Divided Heart: Scandinavian Immigrant Experience Through Lit-
    erary Sources*. Lincoln: U. Nebraska, 1974.
Tilden, David. "Adolescence in the Middle West." *NYHTBR*, Feb. 7, 1937, p. 2. [rev.]
Wallace, Margaret. "A Vigorous Tale of Nebraska Life." *NYTBR*, Mar. 22, 1936, p. 6. [rev.]
Ware, Doris Ann. "The Best Friend Eugene O'Neill Ever Had." Omaha *World-Herald, Sun-
    day Magazine of the Midlands*, Sept. 17, 1972, pp. 8, 10. [interview]
Whicher, George F. "Dane in America." *Forum*, 106 (Nov. 1946), 450–54.
Wimberly, May B. *PrS*, 10 (Summer 1936), 167–68. [rev.]

Barbara Meldrum
University of Idaho
Moscow, Idaho

CONSTANCE FENIMORE WOOLSON
(1840–1894)

Woolson has been characterized as a local colorist, a realist, and a writer of
fiction in the Jamesian manner. Pattee, Kern, Quinn, Hubbell, and Simpson view her chiefly as a local colorist (Kern in particular has dealt with her
use of midwestern materials); Woolson and some of her contemporaries
thought of her primarily as a realist; and many critics subsequently have
commented on her debt to James and Howells. Richardson, Brooks, and
Cowie have touched on this debt, but have also acknowledged her contribution to the novel of analysis and international-episode fiction. Edel has
stressed her obligation to James and noted the artistic limitations of her
work. Besides responding to Edel's criticism, Moore has considered all aspects of Woolson's fictional production and concluded that she was a gifted
minor writer whose subject matter and technique, in the light of develop-
ments in the twentieth century, may appear dated and restricted in range
but whose better work—especially in *For the Major* and *East Angels* and in
tales like "Rodman the Keeper"—manifests an integrity and overall quality worthy of mention not only for its literary value but also for its historical
significance.

Recent interest in Woolson stems mostly from Edel's treatment of her
friendship with James, an account which seeks to establish a relationship

between the two artists that led to frustration and eventual suicide. Moore has pointed out that Edel's interpretation is grounded on inference and supposition and is lacking in hard evidence. He has concluded, with Benedict and Kern, that Woolson and James were indeed "intimate friends" but that there is insufficient data to prove either that she took her life as a result of unfulfilled passion or that she actually committed suicide at all.

MAJOR WORKS

Castle Nowhere: Lake-Country Sketches. Boston: Osgood, 1875. [stories]
Two Women, 1862. New York: Appleton, 1877. [poem]
Rodman the Keeper: Southern Sketches. New York: Appleton, 1880. [stories]
Anne. New York: Harper, 1882. [novel]
For the Major. New York: Harper, 1883. [novelette]
East Angels. New York: Harper, 1886. [novel]
Jupiter Lights. New York: Harper, 1889. [novel]
Horace Chase. New York: Harper, 1894. [novel]
The Front Yard and Other Italian Stories. New York: Harper, 1895.
Dorothy and Other Italian Stories. New York: Harper, 1896.
Mentone, Cairo, and Corfu. New York: Harper, 1896. [travel sketches]
For the Major and Selected Short Stories. Ed. Rayburn S. Moore. New Haven, Conn.: College and University Press, 1967.

CHECKLIST OF SECONDARY SOURCES

BDAL; CHAL; DAB; LHUS; OCAL.

Alden, Henry M. "Constance Fenimore Woolson." *Harper*, 38 (Feb. 3, 1894), 113–14.
Benedict, Clare, ed. *Five Generations (1785–1923)*. 3 vols. London: Ellis, 1929–30. See especially 2, *Constance Fenimore Woolson*, and 3, *The Benedicts Abroad*.
Brooks, Van Wyck. *The Dream of Arcadia: American Writers and Artists in Italy, 1760–1915*. New York: Dutton, 1958. Pp. 189–96.
————. *The Times of Melville and Whitman*. New York: Dutton, 1947. Pp. 341–50.
Cowie, Alexander. *The Rise of the American Novel*. New York: American, 1948. Pp. 568–78.
Edel, Leon. *Henry James*. 5 vols. Philadelphia: Lippincott, 1953–72. See especially 2, *The Conquest of London, 1870–1881* (1962), and 3, *The Middle Years: 1882–1895* (1962). Other references appear in 4, *The Treacherous Years: 1895–1901* (1969), and 5, *The Master: 1901–1916* (1972).
Gray, Stella C. "Constance Fenimore Woolson." In *Notable American Women*. Vol. 3. Ed. by Edward T. James. Cambridge, Mass.: Belknap, 1971. Pp. 670–72.
————. "The Literary Achievement of Constance Fenimore Woolson." Ph.D. diss., U. Wisconsin, 1957.
Hubbell, Jay B. *The South in American Literature, 1607–1900*. Durham, N.C.: Duke U., 1954. Pp. 733–37.
————, ed. "Some New Letters of Constance Fenimore Woolson." *NEQ*, 14 (Dec. 1941), 715–35.
James, Henry. "Miss Constance Fenimore Woolson." *Harper*, 31 (Feb. 12, 1887), 114–15. Reprinted with changes in *Partial Portraits* (1888).
Kern, John D. *Constance Fenimore Woolson: Literary Pioneer*. Philadelphia: U. Pennsylvania, 1934.
Milledge, Luetta U. "Theme and Characterization in the Fiction of Constance Fenimore Woolson." Ph.D. diss., U. Georgia, 1971.
Moore, Rayburn S. *Constance Fenimore Woolson*. New York: Twayne, 1963.
————. "Constance Fenimore Woolson (1840–1894)." *ALR* (Summer 1968), 36–38. [bibliography]
————. "The Full Light of a Higher Criticism: Edel's Biography and Other Recent Studies of Henry James." *SAQ*, 63 (Winter 1964), 104–14. [rev. essay]

_____. "Henry James, Ltd. and the Chairman of the Board: Leon Edel's Biography." *SAQ*, 73 (Spring 1974), 261–69: [rev.]

_____. Introduction, *For the Major and Selected Short Stories of Constance Fenimore Woolson*. New Haven, Conn.: College and University Press, 1967. Pp. 7–25.

Pattee, Fred L. "Constance Fenimore Woolson and the South." *SAQ*, 38 (April 1939), 130–41.

_____. *The Development of the American Short Story: An Historical Survey*. New York: Harper, 1923. Pp. 250–55, 264.

Quinn, Arthur Hobson. *American Fiction*. New York: Appleton, 1936. Pp. 332–42.

Richardson, Lyon N. "Constance Fenimore Woolson, 'Novelist Laureate' of America." *SAQ*, 39 (Jan. 1940), 18–36.

Simpson, Claude M., ed. *The Local Colorists: American Short Stories, 1857–1900*. New York: Harper, 1960. Pp. 129–30.

Wagenknecht, Edward. *Cavalcade of the American Novel*. New York: Holt, 1952. Pp. 173–77, 526–27.

White, Robert L. "Cultural Ambivalence in Constance Fenimore Woolson's Italian Tales." *TSL*, 12 (1967), 121–29.

Rayburn S. Moore
University of Georgia
Athens, Georgia

JAMES A. WRIGHT (1927–80)

The greatest quantity of criticism of native Ohioan James Wright's work consists of reviews of his books and of essays in books of criticism of contemporary American poetry. Of the critical essays, those by Mills, Malkoff, and Howard are perhaps the most comprehensive treatments of Wright's work; other extensive discussions are those by Butscher, Crunk, Janssens, and Seay. The essays by Butscher and Seay present interesting contrasting views of Wright's poetic abilities.

Malkoff associates Wright with a group of contemporary poets who have a penchant for startling metaphors and "deep" or "subjective" images. Seay states that Wright's earlier work contained fairly conventional metrical patterns and rhyme schemes, but that he later abandoned traditional forms. Recently, however, according to Seay, he has returned to more subtle formal patterns. His dominant themes are sympathy for social outcasts, loneliness, and a desire for closer union with the natural world. Butscher feels that Wright's earlier work demonstrated modest talent but that his later collections suffer from a lapse into sentimentality.

MAJOR WORKS

The Green Wall. New Haven: Yale U., 1957. [poetry]
Saint Judas. Middletown, Conn.: Wesleyan U., 1959. [poetry]
The Branch Will Not Break. Middletown, Conn.: Wesleyan U., 1963. [poetry]
Shall We Gather At the River. Middletown, Conn.: Wesleyan U., 1968. [poetry]

Collected Poems. Middletown, Conn.: Wesleyan U. 1971.
Two Citizens. New York: Farrar, 1973. [poetry]
I See the Wind. Boston: Branden, 1974. [poetry]

CHECKLIST OF SECONDARY SOURCES

Burke; *CA; CP; LLC.*

Booth, Philip. "World Redeemed." *SatR*, 40 (July 20, 1957), 18. [rev.]
Butscher, Edward. "The Rise and Fall of James Wright." *GaR*, 28 (Summer 1974), 257–68.
Carroll, Paul. *The Poem in Its Skin.* Chicago: Follett, 1968. Pp. 189–202.
Crunk [Robert Bly?]. "The Work of James Wright." *Sixties*, 8 (Spring 1966), 52–78.
Davidson, Peter. "Three Visionary Poets." *Atl*, 229 (Feb. 1972), 106–7. [rev.]
DeFrees, Madeline. "James Wright's Early Poems: A Study in 'Convulsive' Form." *MPS*, 2 (1972), 241–52.
Deutsch, Babette. "A Fashionable Poet?" *NR*, 165 (July 17, 1971), 27. [rev.]
———. Review of *Two Citizens. NR*, 168 (Apr. 28, 1973), 25.
Dougherty, David. "James Wright: The Murderer's Grave in the New Northwest." *ON*, 2 (March 1976), 45–54.
Galler, David. "Three Poets." *Poetry*, 96 (July 1960), 185–87. [rev.]
Howard, Richard. *Alone with America: Essays on the Art of Poetry in the United States since 1950.* New York: Atheneum, 1969. Pp. 575–86.
Ignatow, David. Review of *Shall We Gather at the River. NYTBR*, Mar. 9, 1969, p. 31.
Janssens, G. A. N. "The Present State of American Poetry: Robert Bly and James Wright." *ES*, 51 (Apr. 1970), 112–37.
Kessler, Jascha. "The Caged Sybil." *SatR*, 51 (Dec. 14, 1968), 35–36. [rev.]
Lensing, George and Ronald Moran. *Four Poets and the Emotive Imagination: Robert Bly, James Wright, Louis Simpson, and William Stafford.* Baton Rouge: Louisiana State U., 1976.
McMaster, Belle M. "James A. Wright: A Checklist." *BB*, 31 (Apr.–June 1974), 71–82.
Malkoff, Karl. *Crowell's Handbook of Contemporary American Poetry.* New York: Crowell, 1973. Pp. 331–38.
Mills, Ralph J., Jr. "James Wright's Poetry: Introductory Notes." *ChiR*, 17 (1964), 128–43.
———. *Contemporary American Poetry.* New York: Random House, 1965. Pp. 197–217.
Moran, Ronald and George Lensing. "The Emotive Imagination: A New Departure in American Poetry." *SouR*, 3 (Jan. 1967), 51–67.
Robinett, Emma, " 'No Place to Go But Home': The Poetry of James A. Wright." *DAI*, 37:1553A.
Seay, James. "A World Immeasurable Alive and Good: A Look at James Wright's *Collected Poems.*" *GaR*, 27 (Spring 1973), 71–81.
Stauffer, Donald B. *A Short History of American Poetry.* New York: Dutton, 1974.
Stepanchev, Stephen. *American Poetry Since 1945.* New York: Harper, 1965. Pp. 180–85.
Stern, Richard, ed. "American Poets of the Fifties." *WR*, 21 (Spring 1957), 3.
Stitt, Peter A. "The Poetry of James Wright." *MR*, 2 (Spring 1972), 122–33.
Taylor, Richard. "Roots and Wings: The Poetry of James Wright." *DAI*, 36:1512A.
Toole, W. B. " 'At the Slackening of the Tide.' " *Explicator*, 22 (1963), 29.
Weeks, R. L. "The Nature of 'Academin.' " *ChiR*, 16 (1963), 138–44. [rev.]

G. Melvin Hipps
Furman University
Greenville, South Carolina

RICHARD WRIGHT (1908–60)

Richard Wright's fiction and essays have both benefited from and been victimized by the emergence of Afro-American literature as a separate subject of academic study. On the one hand, within the last several years his work has received long overdue scrutiny; but, on the other, much of that attention has been focused on Wright as an emblematic black writer, rather than as the careful literary craftsman and perceptive critic that he was. But there have been encouraging signs in very recent years that study of Wright may be progressing. The Chicago novel, *Native Son*, which for so many years was the only one of his works which received anything like careful scholarly examination, is no longer the sole subject of Wright research. His other novels, his early poetry, and his later travel essays have all been studied, in book-length works by Brignano, Margolies, and Bakish, and in essays by such leading critics as Jackson, Turner, and Leary. An excellent full-length biography by Fabre and a competent shorter one by Webb have presented the fascinating story of Wright's life in great detail. Finally, two of Wright's leading contemporaries, Ellison and Baldwin, have written eloquently and even movingly of his influence on their careers and writings. There is need still for further work on the travel literature and the poetry; but most of the other important areas are not only covered, but, in most cases, covered well.

MAJOR WORKS
Uncle Tom's Children: Four Novellas. New York: Harper, 1938.
Native Son. New York: Harper, 1940. [novel]
Uncle Tom's Children: Five Long Stories. New York: Harper, 1940.
Native Son, the Biography of a Young American: A Play in Ten Scenes. New York: Harper, 1941.
Twelve Million Black Voices: A Folk History of the Negro in the United States. New York: Viking, 1941.
Black Boy: A Record of Childhood and Youth. New York: Harper, 1945. [autobiography]
The Outsider. New York: Harper, 1953. [novel]
Black Power: A Record of Reactions in a Land of Pathos. New York: Harper, 1954. [essays]
Savage Holiday. New York: Avon, 1954. [novel]
The Color Curtain. Cleveland: World, 1956. [essays]
Pagan Spain. New York: Harper, 1956. [essay]
White Man, Listen! New York: Doubleday, 1957. [essays]
The Long Dream. New York: Doubleday, 1958. [novel]
Eight Men. Cleveland: World, 1961. [short stories]
Lawd Today. New York: Walker, 1963. [novel]

CHECKLIST OF SECONDARY SOURCES
Burke; *CB*; Herzberg; *LHUS*; *OCAL*; *TCA & Supp.*

Abcarian, Richard, ed. *Richard Wright's* Native Son: *A Critical Handbook.* Belmont, Calif.: Wadsworth, 1970.

Algren, Nelson. "Remembering Richard Wright." *Nation*, 192 (Jan. 28, 1961), 85.

Anon. "Return of the Native Son." *Ebony*, 7 (Dec. 1951), 100.

Bakish, David. *Richard Wright*. New York: Ungar, 1973.

Baldwin, James. *Nobody Knows My Name*. New York: Dell, 1963. Pp. 146–70.

_____. *Notes of a Native Son*. Boston: Beacon, 1955. Pp. 24–45.

Bone, Robert A. *The Negro Novel in America*. New Haven, Conn.: Yale U., 1958. Pp. 140–52.

_____. *Richard Wright*. Minneapolis: U. Minnesota, 1969.

Brignano, Russell C. "Richard Wright: A Bibliography of Secondary Sources." *SBL*, 2 (Summer 1971), 19–25.

_____. *Richard Wright—An Introduction to the Man and His Works*. Pittsburgh: U. Pittsburgh, 1970.

Brivic, Sheldon. "Conflict of Values: Richard Wright's *Native Son*." *Novel*, 7 (1974), 231–45.

Bryer, Jackson R. "Richard Wright (1908–1960): A Selected Checklist of Criticism." *WSCL*, 1 (Fall 1960), 22–33.

Burgum, Edwin Berry. *The Novel and the World's Dilemma*. New York: Oxford U., 1947. Pp. 223–59.

Davis, Arthur P. *From the Dark Tower—Afro-American Writers 1900 to 1960*. Washington, D.C.: Howard U., 1974. Pp. 147–57.

Eisinger, Chester E. *Fiction of the Forties*. Chicago: U. Chicago, 1963. Pp. 68–71.

Ellison, Ralph. *Shadow and Act*. New York: Random House, 1964. Pp. 77–94.

Embree, Edwin R. *13 Against the Odds*. New York: Viking, 1944. Pp. 25–46.

Everette, Mildred W. "The Death of Richard Wright's American Dream: 'The Man Who Lived Underground.' " *CLAJ*, 17 (1974), 318–26.

Fabre, Michel. *The Unfinished Quest of Richard Wright*. Tr. by Isabel Barzun. New York: Morrow, 1973. [biography]

Ford, Nick Aaron. "The Ordeal of Richard Wright." *CE*, 15 (1953), 87–94.

French, Warren. *The Social Novel at the End of an Era*. Carbondale: Southern Illinois U., 1966. Pp. 171–80.

Giles, James R. "Richard Wright's Successful Failure: A New Look at *Uncle Tom's Children*." *Phylon*, 34 (1973), 256–66.

Glicksberg, Charles I. "Existentialism in *The Outsider*." *FQ*, 7 (Jan. 1958), 17–26.

Gloster, Hugh Morris. *Negro Voices in American Fiction*. Chapel Hill: U. North Carolina, 1948. Pp. 222–34.

Gysin, Fritz. *The Grotesque in American Negro Fiction: Jean Toomer, Richard Wright, and Ralph Ellison*. Bern, Switzerland: Francke, 1975.

Hand, Clifford. "The Struggle to Create Life in the Fiction of Richard Wright." *The Thirties: Fiction, Poetry, Drama*. Ed. by Warren French. Deland, Fla.: Everett/Edwards, 1967. Pp. 81–87.

Harrington, Ollie. "The Last Days of Richard Wright." *Ebony*, 17 (Feb. 1961), 83–94.

Hill, Herbert, ed. *Anger and Beyond: The Negro Writer in the United States*. New York: Harper & Row, 1966. Pp. 196–212.

Howe, Irving. "Black Boys and Native Sons." *Dissent*, 10 (1963), 353–68.

Hughes, Carl Milton [pseud. of John Milton Charles Hughes]. *The Negro Novelist*. New York: Citadel, 1953. Pp. 41–68, 197–206.

Hyman, Stanley Edgar. "Richard Wright Reappraised." *Atl*, 225 (Mar. 1970), 127–32.

Jackson, Blyden. "Richard Wright: Black Boy From America's Black Belt and Urban Ghettos." *CLAJ*, 12 (1969), 287–309.

_____. "Richard Wright in a Moment of Truth." *SLJ*, 3 (Spring 1971), 3–17.

Kent, George E. "On the Future Study of Richard Wright." *CLAJ*, 12 (1969), 366–70.

Kinnamon, Keneth. *The Emergence of Richard Wright: A Study in Literature and Society*. Urbana: U. Illinois, 1972.

Lawson, Lewis A. "Cross Damon: Kierkegaardian Man of Dread." *CLAJ*, 14 (1971), 298–316.

Leary, Lewis. "*Lawd Today:* Notes on Richard Wright's First/Last Novel." *CLAJ*, 15 (1972), 411–20.

McCall, Dan. *The Example of Richard Wright*. New York: Harcourt, 1969.

Margolies, Edward. *The Art of Richard Wright*. Carbondale: Southern Illinois U., 1969.

Ray, David and Robert M. Farnsworth, eds. *Richard Wright: Impressions and Perspectives*. Introd. by Charles T. Davis. Ann Arbor: U. Michigan, 1973.

Reilly, John M. "Richard Wright: An Essay in Bibliography." *RALS*, 1 (1971), 131–80.

Rickels, Milton and Patricia Rickels. *Richard Wright*. Austin, Tex.: Steck-Vaughan, 1970.

Riesman, David. "Marginality, Conformity, and Insight." *Phylon*, 14 (1953), 245–53.

Scott, Nathan A., Jr. "Search for Beliefs: Fiction of Richard Wright." *UKCR*, 23 (1956), 19–24.

Siegel, Paul N. "The Conclusion of Richard Wright's *Native Son*." *PMLA*, 89 (1974), 517–23.

Smith, Sidonie. "Richard Wright's *Black Boy:* The Creative Impulse as Rebellion." *SLJ*, 5 (Fall 1972), 123–36.

Turner, Darwin T. *"The Outsider*: Revision of an Idea." *CLAJ*, 12 (1969), 310–21.

Webb, Constance. *Richard Wright: A Biography*. New York: Putnam, 1968.

Widmer, Kingsley. "The Existential Darkness: Richard Wright's *The Outsider*." *WSCL*, 1 (Fall 1960), 13–21.

Williams, John A. *A Biography of Richard Wright, The Most Native of Sons*. Garden City, N.Y.: Doubleday, 1970.

Jackson R. Bryer
University of Maryland
College Park, Maryland

PART 3

101 ADDITIONAL
MIDWESTERN WRITERS

BANNING, MARGARET CULKIN (1891–) Domestic novels of manners reflecting middle-class life in midwestern cities and towns. Among the better known of these sometimes cloying fictions: *Pressure* (1927); *The Clever Sisters* (1947); *Give Us Our Years* (1950); and *Mesabi* (1969).

BELLAMAN, HENRY (1882–1945) Bellaman wrote with indifferent success for years before publishing a sensational best-seller in *King's Row* (1940), a lurid tale of life in a small Missouri town. A sequel, *Parris Mitchell of King's Row* (1945) was completed by Bellaman's wife after his death.

BISSELL, RICHARD (1913–) River pilot, travel writer, and novelist, Bissell has drawn on his familiarity with the upper Mississippi in novels like *A Stretch of the River* (1950) and *High Water* (1954). Small-town life in Iowa serves as setting for *7 1/2 Cents* (1953), later recast for Broadway production as *Pajama Game*, and *Julia Harrington, Winnebago, Iowa* (1969). Conscious of the literary legacy of the Mississippi, Bissell most recently has produced *My Life on the Mississippi, or Why I am Not Mark Twain* (1973).

BOYD, THOMAS (1893–1935) Best known for three strong historical novels of the Ohio frontier: *Shadows of the Long Knives* (1925); *Samuel Drummond* (1925); and *Simon Girty, the White Savage* (1928).

CARROLL, PAUL (1927–) Irish Catholic poet from Chicago, best known as an editor (*Chicago Review, Big Table*) and promoter of young literary talents. His collected poems: *Ode of the Angels of Chicago Who Move Perpetually Towards the Dayspring of their Youth* (1968).

CASPARY, VERA (1904–) Novels of Chicago life in the 1920s, in the realistic tradition: *White Girl* (1929); *Thicker than Water* (1932); *Evvie* (1960).

CASSILL, R. V. (1919–) Notable for penetrating novels and stories containing studies of Iowa small-town life: *Eagle on the Coin* (1950); *Pretty Leslie* (1963); *The Father and Other Stories* (1965); *The Marriage and Other Stories* (1966).

COLTER, CYRUS (1910–) Chicago lawyer who began publishing fiction at the age of sixty, winning the Iowa School of Letters Award for the stories in *The Beach Umbrella* (1970). Colter has followed with two psychological novels of black ghetto life in Chicago: *The Rivers of Eros* (1972) and *The Hippodrome* (1973).

CONKLE, ELLSWORTH (1899–) A pioneer in the regional theatre movement of the 1930s whose work in the genre received considerable attention in those years. Although he has written for nearly half a century, his best remembered work is still *Crick Bottom Plays: Five Mid-western Sketches* (1928).

CONNELL, EVAN S. (1924–) Kansas City novelist who explores the lives and values of middle-class midwesterners. Best known are his studies of suburban Kansas City domesticity in *Mrs. Bridge* (1959) and *Mr. Bridge* (1969).

CORBETT, ELIZABETH (1887–) Delineates the unhurried atmosphere of small-town life in the Midwest (usually Illinois) during the nineteenth and early twentieth centuries. Her most successful character creation, "Mrs. Meigs," is brought from girlhood to old age in a series of unpretentious novels: *The Young Mrs. Meigs* (1931); *She Was Carrie Eaton* (1938); *Mr. and Mrs. Meigs* (1940); and others. Perhaps her best book is *Out at the Soldier's Home* (1941), a memoir of her early years at a national soldier's home near Milwaukee.

CROY, HOMER (1883–1965) Missouri novelist and humorist whose lambent fictions are a significant contribution to Midwest folk history. Best known are *Corn Country* (1947), reportage on regional customs and manners; *Country Cured* (1943), an autobiography; *West of the Water Tower* (1923), a realistic novel; and folksy biographies of Jesse James (1949), Cole Younger (1956), and Will Rogers (1953).

CUSCADEN, R. R. (1931–) Illinois poet [*For a Ten Pound Sailfish* (1963), *Ups and Downs of a Third Baseman* (1963)], who edited an important little magazine, *Midwest*, in the 1960s. Cuscaden has written extensively in the field of architectural criticism.

CUTLER, BRUCE (1930–) Illinois native who has become closely associated with Kansas, both as a poet and teacher. Among his quietly evocative volumes: *The Year of the Green Wave* (1960); *A West Wind Rises* (1962); *Sun City* (1964); *A Voyage to America* (1967).

DARROW, CLARENCE (1857–1938) Famous criminal lawyer associated with liberal social causes was a law partner of Edgar Lee Masters and spent most of his career in Chicago. Two important literary documents recreate his Ohio childhood in the years following the Civil War: *Farmington* (1904), a novel; and *The Story of My Life* (1932).

DAVIS, CLYDE BRION (1894–1962) Nebraska novelist, journalist, and teacher who wrote telling realistic novels of Midwest life. Among them: *The Great American Novel* (1938), newspaper life in Cleveland and Kansas City; *Nebraska Coast* (1939), pioneer life in the 1860s; *Big Pink Kite* (1960), hard times in Missouri, ca. 1907.

DERLETH, AUGUST (1909–1971) Prolific Wisconsin novelist, poet, and editor who wrote more than 100 books. A self-conscious regionalist, Derleth wrote two sets of chronicle novels (totalling sixteen volumes) set in the "Sac Prairie" region of south central Wisconsin. *Walden West* and *Return to Walden West* are journals documenting small-town life in the Midwest and represent his best work.

DE CAPITE, MICHAEL (1915–) and RAYMOND (1924–) Both have contributed insightful novels of Italian ethnic life in Cleveland. Among older brother Michael's novels: *Maria* (1943); *No Bright Banner* (1944); *The Bennet Place* (1948). Raymond has written *The Coming of Fabrizze* (1960), and *A Lost King* (1961).

DE JONG, DAVID C. (1905–1967) Native Hollander who came to Grand Rapids at thirteen and wrote a number of nostalgic characterizations of life among the Dutch in Michigan: *Belly Fulla Straw* (1934); *Light Sons and Dark* (1940); *With a Dutch Accent* (1944), an autobiography; and several others.

DORN, EDWARD (1929–) Poet best known for his most recent books, *North Atlantic Turbine* (1967), and *Gunslinger* (1968–69). Dorn's earlier poetry had a stronger regional quality, reflective of his youth in Illinois: *The Newly Fallen* (1961); *Hand Up* (1963); *Geography* (1966).

DOWNING, J. HYATT (1887–) Writer and businessman who wrote two good novels of rural South Dakota, *A Prayer for Tomorrow* (1938) and *Hope for Living* (1939), and two others focusing on the Sioux City boom during the late nineteenth century, *Sioux City* (1940) and *Anthony Trant* (1941).

DUNCAN, THOMAS (1905–   ) Iowa novelist whose robust fictions are filled with Americana of the Gilded Age and afterward. Among his novels are *O, Chautauqua* (1935); *We Pluck This Flower* (1937); *Ring Horse* (1940); *Gus the Great* (1947); *Big River, Big Man* (1959); and, most recently, *The Sky and Tomorrow* (1974).

ECKMAN, FREDERICK (1924–   ) Ohio poet, critic, and teacher whose meditative verse carries some of the fine tone of a literary mentor, Sherwood Anderson. Volumes of poetry: *Hot and Cold: Running* (1962); *The Epistemology of Loss* (1963); *Sandusky and Back* (1970); and others.

ELKIN, STANLEY (1930–   ) St. Louis novelist and satirist notable for pointed, often brilliant evocations of the grotesqueries of society in contemporary mid-America. *Boswell* (1964); *Criers and Kibbitzers* (1966), stories; *A Bad Man* (1967); *The Dick Gibson Show* (1971); *Searches and Seizures* (1973), novellas.

ENGSTRAND, STUART D. (1904–1955) Novelist with a strong sense of regional provenance. His novels usually depict rural settings in Wisconsin and Illinois: *The Invaders* (1937); *They Sought for Paradise* (1939); *Beyond the Forest* (1948); and others.

ERNO, RICHARD (1923–   ) The towns and woods of Michigan provide the setting for most of this novelist's character studies: *My Old Man* (1955); *The Hunt* (1960); *The Catwalk* (1955); *Johnny Come Jingle-O* (1967); *Billy Lightfoot* (1969). A nonfiction chronicle of a family's return to nature is *An Ultimate Retreat* (1971).

ETTER, DAVE (1928–   ) Geneva, Illinois, poet noted for images of fields, rivers, trains, minor league baseball games, and beery road side taverns. Among his books: *Go Read the River* (1966); *The Last Train to Prophetstown* (1968); *Voyages to the Inland Sea* (1971).

FAIR, RONALD (1932–   ) Stark fiction of Chicago black ghetto life: *Many Thousand Gone* (1965); *Hog Butcher* (1966); *World of Nothing* (1970); *We Can't Breathe* (1972).

FAIRBANK, JANET AYER (1878–1951) Prominent Chicago society and political figure who wrote sound historical fiction, especially in *The Smiths* (1925) about social life in Chicago, and in *The Bright Land* (1932) on pioneer days in Galena, Ill. Sister of Margaret Ayer Barnes.

FICKE, ARTHUR DAVISON (1883–1945) Another example of the businessman (Davenport, Ia., lawyer, in this case) poet so common to the Midwest, Ficke wrote of regional social ills, literary compatriots (like Floyd Dell and Alice French), and of exotic climes. He had strong connections with many of the "Chicago Renaissance" figures. Perhaps he is best known as perpetrator, with Witter Bynner, of the "Spectra" hoax, a 1917 volume of bogus experimental verse in which Ficke signed himself "Ann Knish."

FLANDRAU, GRACE (1889–1971) St. Paul local color novelist of quiet charm: *Cousin Julia* (1917); *Being Respectable* (1923); *Entranced* (1924); *Indeed This is Flesh* (1934); and others.

FREDERICK, JOHN T. (1893–1975) Long-time editor of the influential magazine *Midland* (1915–33), which gave a number of Midwest writers the encouragement of first publication. Frederick also wrote two Iowa farm novels of note: *Druida* (1923) and *Green Bush* (1925).

FRIEDMAN, ISAAC K. (1870–1931) Chicago novelist and journalist who produced several realistic pictures of turn-of-the-century urban life: *Poor People* (1900); *By Bread Alone* (1901); *Autobiography of a Beggar* (1903); *The Radical* (1907).

FULLER, IOLA (1906–   ) Michigan historical novelist. *Loon Feather* (1940), fur trading days on Mackinac Island; *The Shining Trail* (1943), Black Hawk War; *The Gilded Torch* (1957), LaSalle; *All the Golden Gifts* (1966).

GALLAGHER, W. D. (1804–94) Editor and government official on the Ohio frontier, Gallagher's nature poetry gained him reputation as a "frontier Wordsworth." Poems: *Erato I, II, III* (1835–37); *Miami Woods* (1881). Gallagher edited an important early collection of frontier literature, *Selections from the Poetical Literature of the West* (1841).

GEDDES, VIRGIL (1897–   ) Nebraska-born dramatist and poet who produced two notable plays during the years of the regional little theater movement: *The Earth Between* (1929), and *Native Ground* (1932).

GILDNER, GARY (1938–   ) Promising representative of the younger generation of Midwest poets. First three books: *First Practise* (1969); *Digging for Indians* (1971); *Nails* (1975). All draw importantly on his experience of youth and family life in Michigan and Iowa.

GRAY, JAMES (1899–1967) Minnesota novelist, critic, and journalist who produced a number of sensitive regional novels with a Minnesota background. Novels include *The Penciled Frown* (1925); *Shoulder the Sky* (1935); *Wake and Remember* (1936); *Wings of Desire* (1938); *Vagabond Path* (1941). Gray also contributed a volume in the Rivers of America series, *The Illinois* (1940), and an excellent study of cultural life in Minnesota and Wisconsin, *Pine, Stream and Prairie* (1945).

HARNACK, CURTIS (1927–   ) Iowa novelist who writes poignantly of rural and small-town life in the state. *Love and Be Silent* (1962); *The Work of an Ancient Hand* (1960); *We Have all Gone Away* (1973).

HARRISON, JIM (1937–   ) Young Michigan novelist and poet who relies a good deal on the rural backgrounds of his experience. Poetry: *Plain Song* (1965); *Locations* (1968); *Outlyer* (1971); *Letters to Yesenin* (1973). Novels: *Wolf* (1971); *A Good Day to Die* (1973); *Farmer* (1976).

HAYDEN, ROBERT (1913–   ) Detroit poet has provided a significant voice for urban Midwest Blacks. Among his volumes: *Heartshape in the Dust* (1940); *The Lion and the Archer* (1948); *A Ballad of Remembrance* (1962); *Selected Poems* (1966); *The Night-Blooming Cereus* (1972); *Angle of Ascent* (1975).

HUDSON, LOIS (1927–   ) Her first novel, *Bones of Plenty* (1962), dealt with the hard lot of the North Dakota wheat farmer during the 1930s and received high praise from critics. A volume of stories has also been published: *Reapers of the Dust: A Prairie Chronicle* (1964).

JAFFE, DAN (1933–   ) Kansas City poet, editor, and teacher. A long historical poem, *Dan Freeman* (1967), recounts the life of America's first homesteader. Jaffe is the editor of BkMk Press in Shawnee Mission, Kansas.

JOHNSON, ALVIN S. (1874–1971) Best known as a social scientist and educator who helped found the New School for Social Research. Johnson's fiction drew on his early life in northeast Nebraska. Among his novels and tales: *Spring Storm* (1936); *The Battle of the Wild Turkey and Other Tales* (1961); *A Touch of Color and Other Tales* (1964). *Pioneer's Progress* (1952) is an autobiography.

JOHNSON, FENTON (1888–1958) Chicago poet who speaks tellingly of despair among Blacks. Among his volumes: *Visions of the Dusk* (1915); *Songs of the Soil* (1916); *Tales of Darkest America* (1920), stories.

JOHNSON, JOSEPHINE (1910–   ) Her first and best novel, *Now in November* (1934), is a bleak tale of Missouri farmers, and was one of the best novels spawned by the Great Depression. Other fiction: *Winter Orchard* (1935), stories; *Jordanstown* (1937); *Wildwood* (1947);

Dark Traveler (1963); *Sorcerer's Son* (1965), stories. *Inland Island* (1969) is a personal narrative of her life on a farm in southern Ohio.

KNOEPFLE, JOHN (1923–) Poet and educator early associated with Cincinnati, later with the St. Louis literary community, and now with Sangamon State University in Springfield, Ill. The suggestive Midwest images of his poetry carry through several volumes: *Rivers into Islands* (1965); *After Grey Days and Other Poems* (1969); *Songs for Gail Guidry's Guitar* (1969); *The Intricate Land* (1970).

LANE, ROSE WILDER (1887–1968) Novels of Ozark folk in *Hill-Billy* (1926), *Cindy* (1928), and others. Pioneer life in the Dakotas is depicted in *Let the Hurricane Roar* (1933) and in *Free Land* (1938). Lane is the daughter of novelist Laura Ingalls Wilder.

LANGLAND, JOSEPH (1917–) Poet, educator, and editor whose work indicates deep roots in the rural Midwest of Minnesota and Iowa. *The Greentown* (1956) was a National Book Award nominee. Another volume is *The Wheel of Summer* (1963). Langland assisted Paul Engle in editing *Poet's Choice* (1966).

LANGLEY, DOROTHY (1904–) [pseud. Dorothy Hight Kissling] Best remembered for *Dark Medallion* (1945), a novel depicting the life of a ruined aristocratic family in southern Missouri. Among her other novels of domestic strife are *Wait for Mrs. Willard* (1944) and, *Mr. Bremble's Buttons* (1947). Recently Langley has broken a long silence to publish *Fool's Mate* (1970), a sonnet sequence, and a novel, *Tom Sawyer Comes Home* (1973).

LOGAN, JOHN (1923–) Iowa poet, editor, and educator. His verse, often regional in flavor, includes *Cycle for Mother Cabrini* (1955); *Ghosts of the Heart* (1960), and other volumes. Logan was founding editor of *Chicago Choice* and has also published a number of short stories.

LOVELACE, MAUD HART (1892–) This Minnesota novelist has written several strong historical novels, two of which are particularly notable for their depiction of her region: *The Black Angels* (1926) and *Early Candlelight* (1929).

LOWRY, ROBERT (1919–) Cincinnati novelist and journalist who has written intensely personal fiction using his home city as a backdrop. Among his novels and story collections: *Find Me in Fire* (1948); *The Big Cage* (1949); *What's Left of April* (1956); *Party of Dreamers* (1962).

MCGRATH, THOMAS (1916–) Poet whose strongly articulated images of the Plains and mid-America have dominated several collections, from *First Manifesto* (1940) to *Letter to an Imaginary Friend* (1962; 1970) and *Voices Beyond the Wall* (1974). A large selection of McGrath's poems was published in 1972 as *The Movie at the End of the World*.

MCGUANE, THOMAS (1939–) Michigan novelist, essayist, and sportsman whose earliest work, *The Sporting Club* (1969), concentrates on the author's native ground. Other novels are: *The Bushwhacked Piano* (1971); *Ninety-Two in the Shade* (1973); and *Panama* (1978).

MEEKER, ARTHUR (1902–1961) Chicago novelist of manners. Among his light-hearted portraits of Chicago social life: *The Faraway Music* (1945) on family life in the 1850s; *Prairie Avenue* (1949) on the good and declining days of a South Side residential street; and *Chicago, With Love, a Polite and Personal History* (1955).

MILTON, JOHN (1924–) Best known as editor of *South Dakota Review* and encourager of young writing talents in the northern Plains. His volumes of poetry include *The Loving Hawk* (1962); *The Tree of Bones* (1965); *This Lonely House* (1969).

MORRISON, TONI (1931–) An exceptionally talented contemporary writer whose first two novels of life among Ohio Blacks, *The Bluest Eye* (1969) and *Sula* (1974), gained strong critical acclaim.

MULDER, ARNOLD (1885–1959) Author of several scrupulously realistic novels about Michigan Hollanders: *The Dominie of Harlem* (1913); *Bram of the Five Corners* (1915); *The Outbound Road* (1919); *The Sand Doctor* (1921). An historical volume is *Americans from Holland* (1947).

NIEDECKER, LORINE (1903–70) Often praised by fellow writers, this Wisconsin poet has received much less critical attention than is warranted for her volumes of poetry: *New Goose* (1946); *My Friend Tree* (1962); *North Central* (1968); *Tenderness and Gristle: Collected Poems* (1970).

NIMS, JOHN F. (1913–   ) Scholar, translator, and poet, Nims has spent a good part of his life in Chicago. Volumes of poetry include *The Iron Pastoral* (1947); *A Fountain in Kentucky* (1950); *Knowledge of the Evening* (1960); *Of Flesh and Bone* (1967).

NORTH, STERLING (1906–75) Unpretentious novelist who writes often of small-town Wisconsin life: *Plowing on Sunday* (1934); *Night Outlasts the Whippoorwill* (1936); *Seven Against the Years* (1939). A shift to Indiana locales marks *So Dear to My Heart* (1947) and *Reunion on the Wabash* (1952). North is perhaps better known as a syndicated literary critic, first at the Chicago *Daily News* (1933–43) and later for two New York papers (1949–56).

O'MEARA, WALTER (1897–   ) Minnesotan whose historical novels, *The Grand Portage* (1951), on the fur trade, and *The Last Portage* (1961), on John Tanner's Indian captivity, are noted for solid research. Among his other fictions of the North Country: *The Trees Went Forth* (1947) on the lumber industry; *Minnesota Gothic* (1956); *The Savage Country* (1960), on Alexander Henry; *The Sioux are Coming* (1971).

OSTENSO, MARTHA (1900–63) Ostenso's realistic pictures of life on the northern prairies of Minnesota, the Dakotas, and Manitoba are unmatched. Her best known novel, *Wild Geese* (1925), is concerned with an Icelandic community in Manitoba; among her Midwest fictions: *The Mad Carews* (1927); *There's Always Another Year* (1933); *O River, Remember* (1943); *Milk Route* (1948); and *Sunset Tree* (1949).

PARKS, GORDON (1912–79) Most recently concentrated his efforts in making motion pictures after an earlier career as writer and photographer. His writings invariably are concerned with the lives of Blacks in the Midwest: *The Learning Tree* (1963), later filmed by Parks; *A Tree Full of Stars* (1965). Parks's autobiography of early years in Kansas and Minnesota is *A Choice of Weapons* (1966).

PAYNE, WILL (1865–1954) Novelist and financial editor of the Chicago *Daily News*. His realistic novels reflect the excitement and turbulence of the Chicago market place at the turn-of-the-century: *Jerry the Dreamer* (1896); *The Money Captain* (1898); *The Story of Eva* (1901); *Mr. Salt* (1908); *The Automatic Capitalist* (1909); *Overlook House* (1920).

PEATTIE, DONALD CULROSS (1898–1964) Naturalist and writer, Peattie is best known for his combination of scientific acumen and delicate prose. *A Prairie Grove* (1938) delineates a singular natural phenomenon in his home state of Illinois; *Singing in the Wilderness* (1935) is a lyric salute to Audubon; *The Road of a Naturalist* (1941) is an autobiography.

PENNELL, JOSEPH (1908–63) Kansan who wrote extensively of the familial and cultural roots of his region. *The History of Rome Hanks* (1944), a panoramic novel of America, 1860–1940, had a particularly favorable reception from critics. Lesser response accompanied two later novels, *The History of Nora Beekham* (1948), and *The History of Thomas Wagnal* (1951).

PETRAKIS, HARRY MARK (1923–   ) Noted for his sympathetic, often moving portrayals of Greek-Americans, particularly in the Chicago community. Fiction: *Lion at My Heart*

(1959); *The Odyssey of Kosta Volakis* (1963); *Pericles on 31st Street* (1965), stories; *A Dream of Kings* (1967); *Waves of Night* (1969), stories. *Stelmark* (1970) is an autobiography.

PHILLIPS, DAVID GRAHAM (1867–1911) Novelist, journalist, and social reformer whose thesis novels rarely are much concerned with sense of place. Still, his earnest, often anguished heroes and heroines frequently display a collection of mores the author attributes directly to their Midwest heritage. Among the novels reflecting this strain: *Her Serene Highness* (1902); *Golden Fleece* (1903); *Second Generation* (1907); *Light-Fingered Gentry* (1907); *Hungry Heart* (1909). *Susan Lenox* (1917) is the most midwestern of Phillips's novels, the first half describing the wayward girl's life in Cincinnati and in Indiana, the author's native state.

PIPER, EDWIN FORD (1871–1939) Nebraska-born poet and long-time professor of English (1905–39) at the University of Iowa. Elements of Midwest and Western regional folk balladry are often conspicuous in his poetry. Volumes: *Barbed Wire and Wayfarers* (1924); *Paintrock Road* (1925); *Canterbury Pilgrims* (1935), sonnets.

PORTER, GENE STRATTON (1865–1924) Prolific popular novelist whose sentimentalized portraits of rural Indiana are an accurate gauge of the nostalgic American temper in the early twentieth century. *Freckles* (1904); *A Girl of the Limberlost* (1909); *Her Laddie* (1913); many more.

POUND, ARTHUR (1884–1966) Michigan popular historian and historical novelist. *Once a Wilderness* (1934) and *Second Growth* (1935) comprise a family chronicle reflecting development in the state. *The Hawk of Detroit* (1939) is a sound historical novel on Cadillac and the founding of Detroit. Historical volumes include *Detroit, Dynamic City* (1940), and *Lake Ontario* (1945), a volume in the American Lakes series.

RANDALL, DUDLEY (1914–   ) Noted editor (*Black Poetry*, 1969) and founder of the Broadside Press in Detroit, an important outlet for contemporary black writers. His own traditional, reflective verse is manifest in *Poem, Counterpoem* (1966) written with Margaret Danner, and in *More to Remember* (1971). *Broadside Memories* (1975), is a memoir.

RILEY, HENRY H. (1813–88) Lawyer on the Michigan frontier whose accurate and humorous observations of his social environment were published in *Puddleford and Its People* (1854), and *The Puddleford Papers* (1857).

ROBERTSON, DON (1929–   ) Historical novelist and journalist who writes of social life, especially in Cleveland and Ohio. Among his novels: *The Greatest Thing Since Sliced Bread* (1965); *The Sum and Total of Now* (1966); *Paradise Falls* (1968); *The Greatest Thing that Almost Happened* (1970).

ROSELIEP, RAYMOND (1917–   ) Iowa priest, teacher, and composer of reflective verse which often draws on his rural childhood experiences. Volumes: *The Linen Bands* (1961); *The Small Rain* (1963); *Love Makes the Air Light* (1965).

SANDOZ, MARI (1901–66) Born in western Nebraska of Swiss-German immigrant parents. Sandoz's work is mostly concerned with that short grass country adjacent to the Midwest plains. Her nonfiction studies of the Plains Indians deal with tribes once dominant in the Midwest: *Crazy Horse* (1942); *Cheyenne Autumn* (1953); *The Buffalo Hunters* (1954), and others. *Love Song to the Plains* (1961) is a lyric evocation of the region. Perhaps her most popular work remains *Old Jules* (1935), the story of her father's life in the Sand Hills of western Nebraska.

SCOTT, VIRGIL (1914–   ) Novelist and educator whose early novel, *The Hickory Stick* (1948), mirrors academic life in Ohio during the Depression. *The Savage Affair* (1958) is a novel at least partly suggested by the brief life of Indiana novelist Ross Lockridge.

SEAGER, ALLAN (1906–68) This Michigan writer's novels and stories usually examine dark interior worlds of character, often within a midwestern landscape. Novels include *Equinox* (1943); *The Inheritance* (1948); *Amos Berry* (1953); *Hilda Manning* (1956); *Death of Anger* (1960). *The Old Man of the Mountain* (1950) collects shorter fiction, and *A Frieze of Girls* (1964) is an autobiography.

SEID, RUTH [pseud., JO SINCLAIR] (1913–   ) Psychological novelist who has written with incisiveness about the immigrant in urban America. Her novel of a Cleveland Jew who denied his heritage (*Wasteland*, 1946) won the Harper prize. Later novels include *Sing at My Wake* (1951); *The Changelings* (1955); and *Anna Teller* (1960).

SEIFERT, SHIRLEY (1889–   ) Missouri novelist noted for careful historical fictions: *River Out of Eden* (1940), on the founding of St. Louis; *Waters of the Wilderness* (1941), on the Americanizing of lands between the Ohio and Mississippi Rivers; *Those Who Go Against the Current* (1943), on Captain Manuel Lisa; *Captain Grant* (1946), on U. S. Grant's early career as a commander of Illinois volunteers.

SINCLAIR, HAROLD (1907–66) Sinclair is best known for his richly detailed chronicle of a small Illinois community between 1830–1914. The trilogy consists of *American Years* (1938); *The Years of Growth* (1940); and *The Years of Illusion* (1941).

STEVENS, JAMES (1892–1972) The main contribution this story-teller and conservationist made to midwestern literature is manifest in his immensely popular Paul Bunyan yarns. Reared in Iowa and later a resident of the Pacific Northwest, Stevens spent his life among the lumbermen, camps, and mills which developed as the backdrop for his writings, e.g., *Paul Bunyan* (1925), *The Saginaw Paul Bunyan* (1932), and *Paul Bunyan's Bears* (1947)— all imaginative tales centering on the mythical Northwoods lumberjack; *Big Jim Turner* (1948), a novel; and *Timber!* (1942), an evocation of life in the lumber camps.

STONE, IRVING (1903–   ) Popular biographical novelist who has turned to a number of Midwest subjects: *Immortal Wife* (1944), about Jessie Fremont; *Adversary in the House* (1947), about Eugene Debs; *The Passionate Journey* (1949), about Kansas painter John Noble; *Love is Eternal* (1954), about Mary Todd and Abraham Lincoln.

STRYCK, LUCIEN (1924–   ) Stryck has edited two collections of contemporary Midwest poetry in *Heartland* (1967) and *Heartland II* (1975). Volumes of poetry: *Taproot* (1953); *The Trespasser* (1956); *Notes for a Guidebook* (1965); *Awakening* (1973).

SULLIVAN, RICHARD (1908–   ) Small-town life in the Midwest provides the usual setting for this Wisconsin-born novelist. Among his realistic fictions: *Summer After Summer* (1942); *Dark Continent* (1943); *The World of Idella May* (1946); *First Citizen* (1948); *The Fresh and Open Sky* (1950), stories; *Congress Court* (1953).

TRAVER, ROBERT, pseud. (1903–   ) [John D. Voelker] Small-town lawyer who has written crime novels set in Upper Michigan: *Trouble Shooter* (1943); *Small Town D.A.* (1954); *Anatomy of a Murder* (1957). Traver has also written extensively about the joys of fishing in *Trout Madness* (1962); *Anatomy of a Fisherman* (1964); *Laughing Whitefish* (1965); *Trout Magic* (1974).

WALKER, MARGARET (1905–   ) The author has produced a number of steadfastly realistic novels of life in Michigan towns. *Fireweed* (1934); *Light from Arcturus* (1935); *The Brewer's Big Horses* (1940); and others.

WARD, MARY JANE (1905–   ) Evanston, Ill., novelist best known for her stark portrayal of a young schizophrenic woman in *Snake Pit* (1946). Other novels, many of which draw on her Evanston and Chicago experiences, include *The Tree Has Roots* (1937); *The Wax Apple* (1938); *The Professor's Umbrella* (1948); *A Little Night Music* (1951); *It's Different for a Woman* (1952).

WEBBER, GORDON (1912–   ) Webber's reputation rests on two excellent novels: *Years of Eden* (1951), a poetic evocation of a farm boy's life in Michigan, and *What End But Love* (1960), a larger canvas which portrays the complex history and interrelationship of the members of a single Michigan clan.

WELLMAN, PAUL (1898–1966) Kansas novelist and historian who has written extensively of local social and political conditions as well as a number of books on the Plains Indians. Novels: *The Bowl of Brass* (1944); *The Walls of Jericho* (1947); *The Chain* (1949); and others. Histories include *Death on the Prairie* (1934); *Death in the Desert* (1935); *The Trampling Herd* (1939); *Glory, God, and Gold* (1954).

WILSON, MARGARET (1882–   ) Best known for her novels of Scots pioneers in Iowa, *The Able McLaughlins* (1923) and *Law and the McLaughlins* (1935). Wilson also wrote *The Kenworthys* (1925), a genteel novel of midwestern domesticity, and a sequel, *The Painted Room* (1926).

WILSON, WILLIAM E. (1906–   ) Popular Indiana historian and historical novelist. *Crescent City* (1947) is a fictionalized history of an Ohio town from 1912–46; *Abe Lincoln at Pigeon Creek* (1949) recreates Lincoln's early years in southern Indiana; *The Raiders* (1955) is an historical novel about Morgan's Raiders. Wilson also wrote a popular history of New Harmony in the *Angel and the Serpent* (1964); *Indiana: A History* (1966); *The Wabash* (1940), in the Rivers of America series.

WOIWODE, LARRY (1941–   ) Young novelist of real promise who has thus far produced two books: *What I'm Going to Do, I Think* (1969), a psychological study of a young couple in northern Michigan wilderness, and *Beyond the Bedroom Wall* (1975), a family chronicle set in North Dakota and Illinois.

WOLFF, MARITTA (1918–   ) Writer of grimly realistic novels emphasizing the dreary life of small industrial towns in Michigan. *Whistle Stop* (1941); *Night Shift* (1942); *Buttonwood* (1962); and others.

WOODS, JOHN (1926–   ) Indiana born poet showing special affection for small-town life in the Midwest. Volumes: *The Death of Paragon, Indiana* (1955); *On the Morning of Color* (1961); *The Cutting Edge* (1966); *Keeping Out of Trouble* (1968); *Turning to Look Back: Poems 1955–1970* (1972).

WYATT, EDITH (1873–1958) Genteel novelist, poet, and critic who delineated the manners of Chicago and suburban high society in fiction such as *Every One His Own Way* (1901), stories; *True Love* (1903); *The Invisible Gods* (1923).

YAFFE, JAMES (1927–   ) Chicago-born novelist who writes often of the problems of middle-class Jews in America. *Poor Sister Evelyn* (1951), stories; *What's the Big Hurry* (1954), dealing with Jewish life in Chicago; *Nothing But the Night* (1957), based on the Leopold-Loeb case; and others.

YELLEN, SAMUEL (1906–   ) Lithuanian Jew who emigrated to the Midwest and whose novels, stories, and poems detail the cultural life of the region. *The Wedding Band* (1961) is a richly textured novel of Jews in Cleveland during the 1920s. *The Passionate Shepherd* (1957) provides a collection of stories marking the frustration of academic life in small college towns in Indiana and Ohio. Volumes of verse include *In the House* (1952); *New and Selected Poems* (1964); *The Convex Mirror: Collected Poems* (1971).

ZARA, LOUIS (1910–   ) Born of Jewish immigrant parents, Zara grew up in Chicago and has set much of his fiction in that city and in the Midwest. *Blessed is the Man* (1935) details the financial rise of a Russian-Jewish immigrant in Chicago; *Give Us This Day* (1936) and *Some for the Glory* (1937) deal respectively with the lives of ordinary Americans and politicians; *This Land is Ours* (1940) is an historical novel of the Old Northwest down to the beginnings of Chicago; and others.

101 ADDITIONAL
MIDWESTERN FICTIONAL NARRATIVES

ADAMIC, LOUIS. *Grandsons* (1935). Realistic novel of a Slovenian immigrant family in Montana and Chicago, by the inveterate political activist who was himself a native of northwestern Yugoslavia.

ALLIS, MARGUERITE. *Now We Are Free* (1952). First volume of this native Vermonter's sound historical chronicle of frontier life in Ohio and Kansas. Followed in successive years by *To Keep Us Free; Brave Pursuit; The Rising Storm;* and, in 1958, *Free Soil.*

BABCOCK, FREDERIC. *Hang Up the Fiddle* (1954). Sympathetic story of small-town Nebraska forty years ago. Charming and nostalgic.

BARR, STRINGFELLOW. *Purely Academic* (1958). Satirical view of the typical Midwest private college by the well-known American academician.

BASSO, HAMILTON. *A Touch of the Dragon* (1964). Deft portrait of an ambitious midwestern heiress (the dragon-lady). Interesting to compare with Philip Roth's *When She Was Good.*

BECK, ROBERT [pseud. Iceberg Slim]. *Pimp* (1970). Tough autobiographical novel of the Chicago black underworld which wavers between lurid sensationalism and vivid rendition of its milieu. Beck may have the distinction of being the only known procurer to compose seriously reviewed American fiction.

BOJER, JOHANN. *The Emigrants* (tr. 1925). Norwegian novel which depicts the hard life in an immigrant settlement in the Red River Valley.

BRADBURY, MALCOLM. *Stepping Westward* (1966). A mythical midwestern university (somewhat resembling Indiana University) is the setting for this novel of a British professor in conflict with American mores. Valuable for the insights of a foreigner into Midwest academic life.

BRADBURY, RAY. *Dandelion Wine* (1957). Sensitive short stories of an Illinois youth awakening to the possibilities of life. Bradbury, a native of Waukegan, Ill., has generally restricted his writing to the genre of science fiction and fantasy.

BRENNAN, LOUIS. *These Items of Desire* (1953). Strong psychological study of an Ohio girl who struggles to deal with the broken lives of her parents.

BROWN, FRANK L. *Trumbull Park* (1959). Sociological novel examining the attempts of Chicago ghetto Blacks to establish themselves in a new housing development in the suburbs.

BUCK, PEARL [pseud. John Sedges]. *The Townsman* (1945). Character study of immigrants on the Plains. A pseudonym was used because the novel drew on the author's family history. Good background detail and sensitive character portrayal.

CAPOTE, TRUMAN. *In Cold Blood* (1966). Heavily publicized "non-fictional novel" which forcefully depicts the gruesome murder of a Kansas farmer and his family.

CARRUTH, HAYDEN. *Appendix A* (1964). Partly autobiographical first novel by the New England poet and one-time editor of *Poetry* magazine. This fragmented story of the narrator's mental breakdown amidst the vagaries of a Chicago intellectual milieu has its brilliant moments, especially in an extended description of a high society cocktail party at the Blackstone Hotel.

CARSON, JOSEPHINE. *Drives My Green Age* (1957). Lyrical novel of adolescence in a small Kansas town which follows in a strong Midwest tradition going back to Dell's *Moon-Calf*, Anderson's *Windy McPherson's Son*, and Garland's *Son of the Middle Border*.

CHESNUTT, CHARLES W. *The Wife of His Youth* (1899). Artfully realistic stories of "Blue Vein" (light) black society in Cleveland at the turn of the century. Most of Chesnutt's novels and stories are set among North Carolina black communities, some of whose members eventually emigrated north to Cleveland.

COOPER, JAMES FENIMORE. *The Prairie* (1827). Novel of Leatherstocking in his ad-. vanced age amid the settlers and Sioux of the trans-Mississippi prairies.

———. *Oak Openings* (1848). Romantic novel of frontier life in Michigan, ca. 1812.

CRAWFORD, NELSON ANTRIM. *Unhappy Wind* (1930). Classic novel of a Kansas boy growing up at odds with his environment.

DANIELS, GUY. *Progress, U.S.A.* (1968). Light-hearted satire of small-town Iowa in the 1930s. A decent contribution to the long line of lyrical fictions centering on Midwest adolescence. First volume of a projected trilogy.

DAVIS, KENNETH. *Morning in Kansas* (1952). Detailed chronicle of a family in a small Kansas town.

DEVOTO, BERNARD. *We Accept with Pleasure* (1934). Satirical picture of intellectual circles in Chicago and Boston after the First World War.

DEVRIES, PETER. *The Blood of the Lamb* (1961). Poignant story of the death of a child and a man's loss of faith. Partly autobiographical novel by a Chicago native.

DICKENS, CHARLES. *Martin Chuzzlewit* (1843–44). Roughly half of this novel is set in America, mostly in Illinois. Martin's woeful experiences are a reflection of Dickens's own disagreeable impressions of the prairie frontier.

DONEGHY, DAGMAR. *The Border: A Missouri Saga* (1931). Solid historical novel of the Kansas-Missouri border war.

DOS PASSOS, JOHN. *Chosen Country* (1951). This novel of post-war Chicago is the midwestern-born author's only novel set in the region.

EHRLICH, LEONARD. *God's Angry Man* (1932). Excellent historical novel of John Brown, Kansas fanatic and martyr.

ELLIS, WILLIAM D. *The Bounty Lands* (1952). First volume of a scrupulously researched historical trilogy of frontier Ohio. Followed by *Jonathan Blair* (1954), and *The Brooks Legend* (1958).

EUSTIS, HELEN. *The Fool Killer* (1954). Lyrical novel of post-Civil War midwestern runaway in search of a better home. First-person narration begs comparison with *Huckleberry Finn* and *Catcher in the Rye*.

FAST, HOWARD. *The American* (1964). Historical novel centering on the dramatic life of Illinois governor John Altgeld, who pardoned the convicted Haymarket bombers.

_____. *Power* (1962). Novel depicting the rise of one man to important positions in the Midwest labor movement and in the auto industry. Emphasizes the corruptions engendered by power.

FINE, WARREN. *The Artificial Traveler* (1968). Surrealistic tale of carnival life in the Midwest. An impressive first novel.

FISHER, DOROTHY CANFIELD. *The Bent Twig* (1915). Autobiographical novel focusing on the author's youth in Kansas and Ohio, where she grew up in an academic family.

FISHER, VARDIS. *Children of God* (1939). Perhaps the best historical novel dealing with the trials of the early Mormon settlers in the Midwest.

FLAVIN, MARTIN. *Journey in the Dark* (1943). Minor classic dealing with the life of a small-town midwestern businessman.

FOSTER, MICHAEL. *American Dream* (1937). Chronicle of three generations of a Midwest pioneer family, told through diaries and letters.

FRANK, ARMIN. *Flesh of Kings* (1959). Grotesque tale of insanity, drunkenness, and misanthropy centering on a feud between two families of the Ohio River country.

GIBSON, WILLIAM. *The Cobweb* (1954). Probing story of a Nebraska psychiatrist and his relationships with four women. Gibson is best known as a playwright and author of *A Mass for the Dead*, a memoir of his New York childhood.

GREEN, HANNAH. *The Dead of the House* (1972). Semi-autobiographical family chronicle set in southern Ohio and Michigan. A finely-wrought and remarkable first novel.

HALDEMAN-JULIUS, EMMANUEL and MARCET. *Dust* (1921). Realistic moral tale of a Kansas pioneer whose greed finally turns all his material success to "dust."

HALL, JAMES B. *Not by the Door* (1954). Well-drawn picture of religious life in the small-town Midwest. Plot deals with a young Ohio minister's experiences with his first parish.

HANSEN, HARRY. *Your Life Lies Before You* (1935). Davenport, Ia., life at the turn of the century. The large influx of German '48ers had made the city an important intellectual center in the years prior to World War I.

HARRIS, FRANK. *The Bomb* (1909). Fictional study of a young German immigrant who throws the bomb precipitating the Haymarket Riot in Chicago. The author emphasizes the corruption of Chicago labor, police, and political forces.

HAYES, CHARLES E. *The Four Winds* (1942). Grim, naturalistic story of the decline of a Catholic farm family in Kansas during the Depression.

HINDE, THOMAS. [pseud. for Sir Thomas Willes Chitty, Baronet]. *High* (1969). Novel concerned with the imaginative and sexual life of a British novelist in residence at a midwestern university (modeled on the University of Illinois).

HINE, AL. *Lord Love a Duck* (1961). Grotesque satirical novel which examines the lives of a group of cretinous adolescents in an Iowa town.

HOUGH, EMERSON. *Mississippi Bubble* (1902). Romantic historical fiction about John Law and the great Mississippi Valley land swindle of the eighteenth century.

HAZEL, ROBERT. *Field Full of People* (1954). Poetic and tragic story of an Ohio farmer whose life is shattered by character flaws he is unable to master.

JOHNSON, CURTIS. *Hobbledehoy's Hero* (1959). Lyrical novel of an adolescent's disillusionment, set in a small Iowa town in the 1940s.

JONAS, CARL. *Jefferson Selleck* (1952). Poignant portrait of a midwestern Willy Loman, or, as James Hilton put it: "Babbitt . . . presented with real compassion."

KENNEDY, MARK. *Pecking Order* (1953). Violent life of young Blacks in the Chicago ghetto provides both setting and theme in this stark novel.

KUBLY, HERBERT. *The Whistling Zone* (1963). Academic novel focusing on the personal struggles of a young professor on a predictably dreary Midwest campus.

LEWIS, JANET. *The Invasion* (1932). Superb historical novel of the Johnston family in St. Marys, Michigan. Beginning with the marriage of Irish gentleman John Johnston to an Ojibwa woman around 1800, the author carries the family story into the twentieth-century. Details of Indian life in northern Michigan are especially well integrated into the novel.

LEWISOHN, LUDWIG. *Trumpet of Jubilee* (1937). Anxious novel of a Jewish couple who flee Nazi Germany for midwestern America only to find life among relatives and townspeople hardly more inspiring.

LINKLETTER, MONTE. *Cricket Smith* (1959). Coon Hill, Ia., provides the setting for this lyric novel of a maturing young boy who is being reared by his clergyman uncle.

LITWAK, LEO. *Waiting for the News* (1970). Tough, realistic novel of union violence in Detroit during the 1930s.

LORD, EDA. *Childsplay* (1961). Story of a girl reared in Evanston, Ill., who is torn between the influence of her conventionally prim grandmother and the freer model of her insouciant father.

LONGFELLOW, HENRY W. *Song of Hiawatha* (1855). Extended narrative poem based on Schoolcraft's researches into the customs and history of Ojibwa Indians in the northern forests.

MCCAGUE, JAMES. *Great Gold Mountain* (1958). Sensitive and reminiscent novel of small-town life in the Midwest.

MCNALLY, WILLIAM. *The Roofs on Elm Street* (1936). Chronicle of three Minnesota families during the period 1870–1920.

MAJOR, CHARLES. *The Bears of Blue River* (1900). One of the Indiana novelist's (*When Knighthood Was in Flower*) few attempts at local-color writing.

MARQUIS, DON. *Sons of the Puritans* (1939). Popular humorist (*archy and mehitabel*) born in Illinois but not later associated with the region. One may gain a clue to the reasoning behind his removal from this novel, which emphasizes the grimly repressive social environment of a small Illinois town in the late nineteenth century.

MELVILLE, HERMAN. *The Confidence Man* (1857). Complex metaphysical fiction set aboard a Mississippi riverboat. Melville visited the Galena, Ill., lead mines (and the nearby Mississippi) in 1840, but was never otherwise in the Midwest.

MICHAELSON, JOHN. *Morning, Winter and Night* (1952). Old man returns to the Ohio town of his youth and reminisces about his early development. A quietly evocative novel.

MILBURN, GEORGE. *No More Trumpets* (1933). Strong collection of short stories which explore urban life in Chicago.

MOBERG, VILHELM. *Unto a Good Land* (tr. 1954). Excellent documentary novel of Swedish immigrants in Minnesota around the middle of the nineteenth century. The author's previous novel, *The Emigrants* (tr. 1951) detailed the family's life in Sweden and the trip across the Atlantic in 1850.

MORRIS, IRA. *The Chicago Story* (1952). Chronicle novel centering on a German immigrant family involved with the meat packing industry in the twentieth century.

NORRIS, FRANK. *The Pit* (1903). Powerful naturalistic novel of the Chicago wheat market at the turn of the century.

NORRIS, FRANK CALLAN. *The Tower in the West* (1957). Harper Prize novel about a St. Louis architect and his work.

O'BRIEN, TIM. *Northern Lights* (1975). Early, evocative novel about the Minnesota north woods by the National Book Award winning war novelist for *Going After Cacciato* (1978).

O'CONNOR, WILLIAM VAN. *Campus on the River* (1959). Stories of academic life at a campus resembling the University of Minnesota, where O'Connor, scholar and literary critic, was a professor of English.

PAUL, LOUIS. *The Man Who Came Home* (1953). Amusing yarn of a midwesterner who returns home after twenty-five years abroad, with predictable results.

PROKOSCH, FREDERICK. *The Night of the Poor* (1939). Born at Madison, Wisc., Prokosch is best known as an adventurer, itinerant scholar, and novelist of the exotic. His one Midwest novel deals with a young man's hitchhiking trip along the Mississippi, during which he makes some important discoveries about his native land.

REES, GILBERT. *Respectable Women* (1954). Novel dealing with the puritanical restraints dominating a family of Kansas women in the 1890s.

REEVE, F. D. *The Red Machines* (1968). Vivid, realistic novel of itinerant wheat harvesters which follows their movement from Texas through the plains north to Saskatchewan.

ROBB, JOHN S. *Streaks of Squatter Life and Far-West Scenes* (1847). Local-color stories of the frontier Midwest which appeared originally in the St. Louis *Weekly Reveille*.

ROBERTS, KENNETH. *Northwest Passage* (1937). Fine historical novel of Robert Rogers and his Rangers in Canada and in the Great Lakes region.

ROTH, PHILIP. *Letting Go* (1962). Rich, probing novel of a young couple at the University of Chicago in the 1950s.

_____. *When She Was Good* (1967). Zesty portrait of a ferocious, man-hating woman alive and loose in the great Midwest.

RYAN, DON. *The Warrior's Path* (1937). Detailed historical novel of Ohio Valley Indians of the frontier period. Plot involves the capture of a white boy by the Delaware.

SCHLYTTER, LESLIE. *The Tall Brothers* (1941). Particularly valuable for its sound picture of a Wisconsin lumber town in the first quarter of the twentieth century.

SCHORER, MARK. *A House Too Old* (1935). Chronicle novel of a Wisconsin town between 1835–1935. The author is best known for his literary scholarship, which includes a biography of Sinclair Lewis.

SHEEAN, VINCENT. *Bird of the Wilderness* (1941). Partly tongue-in-cheek novel set in "Morbidia," Illinois, in the World War I period. Plot centers on the conflict between a patriotic young hero and his German uncle.

SHELDON, CHARLES M. *In His Steps* (1896). Early best seller about a Kansas minister who tries to follow the example of Jesus. Sentimental and moralizing work valuable mainly as a document of popular culture.

SINCLAIR, UPTON. *The Jungle* (1906). Sociological novel exposing horrible conditions among Chicago packing house workers at the turn of the century.

SMITH, LARRY. *The Original* (1972). Excellent first novel of rural tragedy set in Michigan between 1890–1920.

SMITTER, WESSEL. *F.O.B. Detroit* (1938). Exposé of conditions on the Detroit auto assembly line and the resultant tendency toward mechanization in the lives of the workers.

STEUBER, WILLIAM. *The Landlooker* (1957). Historical novel of Chicago and the Wisconsin frontier at the time of the Great Chicago Fire.

THOMAS, DOROTHY. *The Home Place* (1936). Quietly realistic novel of a Nebraska farm family in the 1930s; emphasizes the plight of both farm and city dwellers during the Depression.

THOMAS, NEWTON. *The Long Winter Ends* (1941). Interesting ethnic novel depicting the Cornish "Cousin Jack" of northern Michigan. Good use of dialect and folklore.

TOBENKIN, ELIAS. *Witte Arrives* (1916). Immigrant fiction of a Russian Jew at the University of Illinois, in Chicago, and in New York. Tobenkin later wrote a similar study in race conflict, *God of Might* (1925), which details the life of a Jewish merchant in Lincoln, Nebraska.

TUCK, CLYDE E. *The Bald Knobbers* (1910). Includes a scrupulously realized picture of folkways in the Missouri Ozarks.

VONNEGUT, KURT. *God Bless You, Mr. Rosewater* (1965). Indiana novelist's attempt to delineate the social life of his home state. Satirical portrait of middle-class America.

WATERS, FRANK. *River Lady* (1942). Historical novel of lumber shipping on the upper Mississippi during the Civil War. Written in collaboration with Houston Branch.

WELLARD, JAMES. *Affair in Arcady* (1960). Strongly flavored novel, verging on melodrama, which involves the story of an unsuccessful novelist who becomes entangled in the lives of an Arcady, Ill., family while he is writing their family history.

WHITE, STEWART EDWARD. *The Blazed Trail* (1902). Realistic novel of lumbering activities in Michigan at the turn of the century.

WILDER, THORNTON. *Heaven's My Destination* (1934). Struggles of an Illinois book salesman to live up to his ideals, which are in conflict with the ethics of the business world.

_____. *The Eighth Day* (1967). Philosophical novel which examines the effects of murder on two families; set in South America, Chicago, and Coaltown, Ill.

WILSON, HARRY LEON. *The Boss of Little Arcady* (1905). Folksy, light-hearted novel of youth in a small Illinois village, by the native Illinois humorist best known for his *Ruggles of Red Gap.*

WYCKOFF, NICHOLAS. *The Corinthians* (1950). Sound historical novel of the Mormons in Illinois and of a local man who maintains marriages with a Mormon woman in Missouri and with another, barren woman across the river in Illinois.

YOUNG, MARGUERITE. *Miss MacIntosh, My Darling* (1965). Long and complicated narrative, at times brillantly realized, dealing with the inner life of an Indiana girl.